D1502221

CITIES OF THE UNITED STATES

ISSN 0899-6075

CITIES OF THE UNITED STATES

FIFTH EDITION

A Compilation of Current Information on
Economic, Cultural, Geographic, and Social Conditions

In Four Volumes

Volume 4:
The Northeast

Connecticut
Maine
Massachusetts
New Hampshire
New Jersey
New York
Pennsylvania
Rhode Island
Vermont

THOMSON

GALE

Detroit • New York • San Francisco • San Diego • New Haven, Conn. • Waterville, Maine • London • Munich

THOMSON

GALE

Cities of the United States, Fifth Edition

Project Editors
Lisa C. DeShantz-Cook, Jacqueline K. Mueckenheim, Kristy Swartout

Editorial Support Services
Luann Brennan, Grant Eldridge, Wayne D. Fong

Imaging and Multimedia
Leitha Etheridge-Sims, Lezlie Light, Jillean McCommons, Dan Newell, Christine O'Bryan

Rights and Acquisitions
Edna M. Hedblad, Shalice Shah-Caldwell, Kim Smilay

Product Design
Jennifer Wahi

Composition and Electronic Prepress
Evi Seoud

Manufacturing
Rita Wimberley

LIBRARY OF CONGRESS CATALOGING-IN-PUBLICATION DATA

ISBN 0-7876-7369-2 (set)
ISBN 0-7876-7370-6 (v.1)
ISBN 0-7876-7371-4 (v.2)
ISBN 0-7876-7372-2 (v.3)
ISBN 0-7876-7373-0 (v.4)
ISSN 0899-6075

This title is also available as an e-book.
ISBN 1-4144-0600-2 (set)
Contact your Thomson Gale sales representative for ordering information.

Printed in the United States of America
10 9 8 7 6 5 4 3 2 1

Volume 4—The Northeast

Contents

Volume 1—The South

Contents

Volume 2—The West

Contents

Volume 3—The Midwest

Contents

INTRODUCTION

Cities of the United States (CUS) provides a one-stop source for all the vital information you need on 189 of America's top cities—those fastest-growing, as well as those with a particular historical, political, industrial, and/or commercial significance. Spanning the entire country, from Anaheim to Virginia Beach, each geographically-arranged volume of *CUS* brings together a wide range of comprehensive data. The volumes include: *The South; The West; The Midwest;* and *The Northeast.*

Within each volume, the city-specific profiles organize pertinent facts, data, and figures related to demographic, economic, cultural, geographic, social, and recreational conditions. Assembling a myriad of sources, *CUS* offers researchers, travelers, students, and media professionals a convenient resource for discovering each city's past, present, and future.

For this completely updated fifth edition, eleven new cities have been added, providing even greater access to the country's growing urban centers. The new city profiles include:

- Akron, OH
- Aurora, IL
- Casper, WY
- El Paso, TX
- Fort Smith, AR
- Henderson, NV
- Huntington, WV
- Mesa, AZ
- Nampa, ID
- Overland Park, KS
- Warwick, RI

Key Features Unlock Vital Information

Cities of the United States offers a range of key features, allowing easy access to targeted information. Features include:

- Section headings—Comprehensive categories, which include **History, Geography and Climate, Population Profile, Municipal Government, Economy, Education, Research, Health Care, Recreation, Convention Facilities, Transportation,** and **Communications** (including city web sites), make it easy for you to locate answers to your specific questions.

- Combined facts and analysis—Fact-packed charts and detailed descriptions bring you the statistics and the rest of the story.

- "In Brief" fact sheets—One-page "at a glance" overviews provide the essential facts for each state and each city profiled.

- Economic information—Detailed updates about such topics as incentive programs, development projects, and largest employers help you rate the business climate using criteria that matter to you.

- Directory information—Contact information at the end of many entry sections provides addresses, phone numbers, and email addresses for organizations, agencies, and institutions you may need to contact.

- Detailed maps—City landmarks, mileage scales, and regional insets allow you to locate many of the points of interest described in main city entries, as well as provide a greater perspective on the city in which you are interested.

- Selected bibliography listings—Historical accounts, biographical works, and other print resources suggest titles to read if you wish to learn more about a particular city.

- Web sites for vital city resources—Access points to URLs for information-rich sources, such as city government, visitors and convention bureaus, economic development agencies, libraries, schools, and newspapers provide researchers an opportunity to explore cities in more detail.

- Enlightening illustrations—Numerous photographs highlight points of interest to you.

- Handy indexing—A referencing guide not only to main city entries, but also to the hundreds of people and place names that fall within those main entries, leading you directly to the information you seek.

Designed For a Variety of Users

Whether you are a researcher, traveler, or executive on the move, *CUS* serves your needs. This is the reference long sought by a variety of users:

- Business people, market researchers, and other decision-makers will find the current data that helps them stay informed.

- People vacationing, conventioneering, or relocating will consult this source for questions they have about what's new, unique, or significant about where they are going.

- Students, media professionals, and researchers will discover their background work already completed.

Hurricanes of 2005 and Their Impact on the United States

The powerful hurricanes of 2005—Hurricane Katrina on August 29 followed by Hurricane Rita on September 24—devastated the Gulf Coast region of the United States. From Alabama to the shores of Texas, these two hurricanes had profound impact—from the loss of lives to the loss of infrastructure (utilities, roads, commerce), industry, and manufacturing. Cities directly hit by these hurricanes, such as New Orleans, Louisiana and Biloxi, Mississippi, will undergo recovery efforts for years to come, and it is unknown at the time of publication of *Cities of the United States,* 5th edition just how long and how far-reaching that recovery will be.

It is also important to note that not only are the cities hit directly by these hurricanes affected; cities that have offered refuge to evacuees and contributed greatly to the relief efforts will continue to be affected as they work to aid the recovery efforts, putting their own development initiatives on hold. Cities such as Mobile, Alabama; Baton Rouge, Louisiana; and Jackson, Mississippi will also continue to experience the effects of these unprecedented natural disasters.

The essays profiled herein for the states of Alabama, Louisiana, Mississippi, and Texas were updated prior to August 2005 and reflect information that was then current.

Definitions of Key Statistical Resources

Following are explanations of key resources used for statistical data:

ACCRA (The Council for Community Economic Research; formerly the American Chamber of Commerce Researchers Association): The Cost of Living Index, produced quarterly, provides a useful and reasonably accurate measure of living cost differences among urban areas. Items on which the Index is based have been carefully chosen to reflect the different categories of consumer expenditures, such as groceries, housing, utilities, transportation, health care, and miscellaneous goods and services; taxes are excluded. Weights assigned to relative costs are based on government survey data on expenditure patterns for midmanagement households (typically the average professional worker's home, new construction with 2,400 square feet of living space). All items are priced in each place at a specified time and according to standardized specifications. Information regarding ACCRA and the Cost of Living Index can be found at www.accra.org. Please note that the ACCRA Cost of Living Index and ACCRA housing price information are reprinted by permission of ACCRA.

Metropolitan Statistical Area (MSA): The U.S. Office of Management and Budget (OMB) provides that each Metropolitan Statistical Area must include (a) at least one city with 50,000 or more inhabitants, or (b) a U.S. Census Bureau-defined urbanized area (of at least 50,000 inhabitants) and a total metropolitan population of at least 100,000 (75,000 in New England). The term was adopted in 1983. The term "metropolitan area" (MA) became effective in 1990. During the 2000 Census, the MSA standards were revised, establishing Core Based Statistical Areas (CBSAs). CBSAs may be either Metropolitan Statistical Areas or Micropolitan Statistical Areas. It is important to note that standards, and therefore content of 1990 Census MSAs, are not identical to 2000 Census MSA standards. Additional information regarding MSAs can be found at http://census.state.nc.us/glossary/msa.html.

FBI Crime Index Total: The total number of index offenses reported to the FBI during the year through its Uniform Crime Reporting Program. The FBI receives monthly and annual reports from law enforcement agencies throughout the country. City police, sheriffs, and state police file reports on the number of index offenses that become known to them. The FBI Crime Index offenses are: murder and non-negligent manslaughter; forcible rape; robbery; aggravated assault; burglary; larceny; motor vehicle theft; and arson.

Estimates of population: Between decennial censuses, the U.S. Bureau of the Census publishes estimates of the population using the decennial census data as benchmarks and data available from various agencies, both state and federal, including births and deaths, and school statistics, among other data.

Method of Compilation

The editors of *Cities of the United States* consulted numerous sources to secure the kinds of data most valuable to you. Each entry gathers together economic information culled in part from the U.S. Department of Labor/Bureau of Labor Statistics and state departments of labor and commerce, population figures derived from the U.S. Department of Commerce/Bureau of the Census and from city and state agencies, educational and municipal government data supplied by local authorities and historical narrative based on a variety of accounts. Along with material supplied by chambers of commerce, convention and visitors bureaus, and other local sources, background information was drawn from periodicals and books chosen for their timeliness and accuracy. Through print resources, web sites, email contact, and/or phone calls with agency representatives, the information reflects current conditions.

Acknowledgments

The editors are grateful for the assistance provided by dozens of helpful chambers of commerce and convention and visitors bureau professionals, as well as municipal, library, and school employees for their invaluable generosity and expertise.

Comments and Suggestions Welcome

If you have questions, concerns, or comments about *Cities of the United States*, please contact the Project Editors:

Cities of the United States
Thomson Gale
27500 Drake Road
Farmington Hills, MI 48331
Phone: (248)699-4253
Toll-free: (800)347-GALE
Fax: (248)699-8075
URL: http://www.gale.com

Map Credits

Regional and city maps for *Cities of the United States,* 5th edition, were created by Teresa San Clementi and XNR Productions Inc.

✳ ✳ ✳ ✳

Photo Credits—Volume 4

Photographs appearing in *Cities of the United States,* 5th edition, Volume 4—*The Northeast* were received from the following sources:

CONNECTICUT:
Bridgeport—photograph by Robert A. Raslavsky. Reproduced by permission: p. 5
Danbury—photograph. © Bob Krist/Corbis: p. 17; showing John and Mary Rider house, photograph. © Lee Snider/Corbis: p. 24
Hartford—photograph. © Phil Schermeister/Corbis: p. 27; showing Mark Twain's house, photograph. © Lee Snider/Corbis: p. 36
New Haven—showing Long Island Sound, photograph. Greater New Haven Convention & Visitors Bureau. Reproduced by permission: p. 41; showing Yale University, photograph. © Robert Holmes/Corbis: p. 50
Stamford—photograph by James Blank. © James Blank. Reproduced by permission: p. 55; showing First Presbyterian Church, photograph by Francis G. Mayer. Corbis: p. 63
Waterbury—photograph. Waterbury Development Agency. Reproduced by permission: p. 67; showing the Chase Building, photograph. Waterbury Development Agency. Reproduced by permission: p. 74

MAINE:
Augusta—showing Blaine House, February 16, 2005, photograph by Pat Wellenbach. AP/Wide World Photos. Reproduced by permission: p. 81; showing Front Street on the Kennebec River, photograph. City of Augusta. Reproduced by permission: p. 88
Bangor—photograph by John R. Berube. Greater Bangor Convention & Visitors Bureau. Reproduced by permission: p. 91
Lewiston—photograph by Robert A. Raslavsky. Reproduced by permission: p. 101
Portland—photograph by James Blank. © James Blank. Reproduced by permission: p. 111; showing Head Lighthouse, photograph by James Blank. © James Blank. Reproduced by permission: p. 119

MASSACHUSETTS
Boston—photograph. FAYFOTO/Boston. Reproduced by permission: p. 127; showing Old State House, now the Museum of Boston History, 1713, photograph. FAYFOTO/Boston. Reproduced by permission: p. 137
Lowell—showing the beginning of "Mile of Mills" along the Merrimack River, photograph by Kevin Harkins. The Lowell Plan. Reproduced by permission of Harkins Photography: p. 143; showing "The Worker," bronze sculpture by Ivan and Elliott Schwartz, photograph by Kevin Harkins. The Lowell Plan. Reproduced by permission of Harkins Photography: p. 151
Springfield—photograph. City of Springfield. Reproduced by permission: p. 155; showing Springfield Armory, photograph. © Phil Schermeister/Corbis: p. 162
Worcester—photograph by Robert A. Raslavsky. Reproduced by permission: p. 167

NEW HAMPSHIRE:
Concord—showing State Capitol, 1992, photograph by Leslie O'Shaughnessy. Reproduced by permission: p. 181; showing The Pierce Manse, photograph. © Lee Snider/Photo Images/Corbis: p. 188
Manchester—photograph. Studio One. Reproduced by permission: p. 193
Nashua—photograph by Leslie O'Shaughnessy. Reproduced by permission: p. 203
Portsmouth—photograph by Leslie O'Shaughnessy. Reproduced by permission: p. 213; photograph. © David G. House/Corbis: p. 221

NEW JERSEY:
Atlantic City—photograph by James Blank. © James Blank. Reproduced by permission: p. 229; showing casinos along Boardwalk, photograph by James Blank. © James Blank. Reproduced by permission: p. 237
Jersey City—photograph. AP/Wide World Photos. Reproduced by permission: p. 241; showing Ellis Island national monument, photograph. © Gail Mooney and Thomas A. Kelly/Corbis: p. 252
Newark—photograph. New Jersey Newsphotos. Reproduced by permission: p. 255; showing Ballantine House, part of the Newark Museum, photograph by Ronald F. Moffat. New Jersey Newsphotos. Reproduced by permission: p. 265
New Brunswick—photograph. Skyviews Survey. Reproduced by permission: p. 269; showing Rutgers University, photograph. © Robert Holmes/Corbis: p. 277
Paterson—photograph. © Joseph Sohm/Corbis: p. 281; showing Statue of Alexander Hamilton, photograph. © Joseph Sohm/Corbis: p. 291
Trenton—showing State Capitol, photograph by Kathleen Marcaccio. Reproduced by permission: p. 295; showing Old Barracks Museum, photograph. © Gail Mooney and Thomas A. Kelly/Corbis: p. 302

NEW YORK:
Albany—photograph by James Blank. © James Blank. Reproduced by permission: p. 309; showing Empire State Plaza, photograph by James Blank. © James Blank. Reproduced by permission: p. 317
Buffalo—photograph by James Blank. © James Blank. Reproduced by permission: p. 321; showing Naval and Servicemen's Park, photograph by James Blank. © James Blank. Reproduced by permission: p. 332
Ithaca—photograph. Ithaca/Tompkins County Convention and Visitors Bureau. Reproduced by permission: p. 337
New York—photograph by Teresa La Forgia/Bob Romaniuk. Courtesy of Bob Romaniuk. Reproduced by permission: p. 347; showing Times Square, photograph. New York Convention & Visitors Bureau. Reproduced by permission: p. 359
Rochester—showing Genesee River skyline, photograph by James Blank. © James Blank. Reproduced by permission: p. 367; showing George Eastman House, photograph by James Blank. © James Blank. Reproduced by permission: p. 375
Syracuse—photograph by James Blank. © James Blank. Reproduced by permission: p. 379; showing Onondaga Park, photograph by Charles Wainwright. Wainwright Photo. Reproduced by permission: p. 386

PENNSYLVANIA:
Allentown—showing Trout Hall Mansion, photograph. © Lee Snider/Photo Images/Corbis: p. 393
Erie—photograph. Erie Area Convention & Visitors Bureau. Reproduced by permission: p. 403
Harrisburg—photograph by Raymond K. Gehman. National Geographic/Getty Images. Reproduced by permission: p. 413; showing Hershey Park, photograph. Hershey-Capital Region Visitors Bureau. Reproduced by permission: p. 421
Lancaster—photograph by Richard Hertzler. Reproduced by permission: p. 425; showing Amish farm, photograph by James Blank. © James Blank. Reproduced by permission: p. 433
Philadelphia—photograph. © Richard Berenholtz/Corbis: p. 437; showing Independence Hall, photograph by James Blank. © James Blank. Reproduced by permission: p. 446
Pittsburgh—showing Mount Washington, photograph by James Blank. © James Blank. Reproduced by permission: p. 451; showing Cathedral of Learning, University of Pittsburgh, photograph. Greater Pittsburgh Convention & Visitors Bureau. Reproduced by permission: p. 463
Scranton—photograph. Guy Cali Associates. Reproduced by permission: p. 469; showing coal miners with donkey, photograph by James Hosie. Lackawanna Coal Mine Tour. Reproduced by permission: p. 477

RHODE ISLAND:
Newport—showing "The Cliff Walk," photograph by John T. Hopf. Newport County Chamber of Commerce. Reproduced by permission: p. 483; showing Historic Trinity Church, built 1724: p. 492
Providence—photograph. The Providence Warwick Convention and Visitors Bureau. Reproduced by permission: p. 497
Warwick—photograph. The Providence Warwick Convention and Visitors Bureau. Reproduced by permission: p. 507

VERMONT:
Burlington—showing Malletts Bay, photograph by James Blank. © James Blank. Reproduced by permission: p. 523; showing University of Vermont campus, photograph by James Blank. © James Blank. Reproduced by permission: p. 531
Montpelier—showing State Capitol, photograph by James Blank. © James Blank. Reproduced by permission: p. 535
Rutland—photograph. Skyviews Survey. Reproduced by permission: p. 545

CITIES OF THE UNITED STATES

CONNECTICUT

The State in Brief

Nickname: Constitution State, Nutmeg State
Motto: *Qui Transtulit Sustinet* (He who transplanted still sustains)

Flower: Mountain laurel
Bird: American Robin

Area: 5,543 square miles (2000, U.S. rank: 48th)
Elevation: Ranges from sea level to 2,380 feet
Climate: Moderate with winters averaging slightly below freezing and warm, humid summers

Admitted to Union: January 9, 1788
Capital: Hartford
Head Official: Governor M. Jodi Rell (R) (until 2007)

Population
  1980: 3,108,000
  1990: 3,287,116
  2000: 3,405,565
  2004 estimate: 3,503,604
  Percent change, 1990–2000: 3.6%
  U.S. rank in 2004: 29th
  Percent of residents born in state: 57% (2000)
  Density: 702.9 people per square mile (2000)
  2002 FBI Crime Index Total: 103,719

Racial and Ethnic Characteristics (2000)
  White: 2,780,355
  Black or African American: 309,843
  American Indian and Alaska Native: 9,639
  Asian: 82,313
  Native Hawaiian and Pacific Islander: 1,366
  Hispanic or Latino (may be of any race): 320,323
  Other: 147,201

Age Characteristics (2000)
  Population under 5 years old: 223,344
  Population 5 to 19 years old: 702,358
  Percent of population 65 years and over: 13.8%
  Median age: 37.4 years (2000)

Vital Statistics
  Total number of births (2003): 43,236
  Total number of deaths (2003): 29,329 (infant deaths, 222)
  AIDS cases reported through 2003: 6,989

Economy
  Major industries: Services, agriculture, manufacturing, trade, government
  Unemployment rate: 4.9% (April 2005)
  Per capita income: $43,292 (2003; U.S. rank: 2nd)
  Median household income: $55,004 (3-year average, 2001-2003)
  Percentage of persons below poverty level: 7.9% (3-year average, 2001-2003)
  Income tax rate: Ranges from 3.0% to 5.0% tax on adjusted gross income (2000)
  Sales tax rate: 6.0% on most items

Bridgeport

The City in Brief

Founded: 1639 (incorporated, 1836)

Head Official: Mayor John Michael Fabrizi (D) (since 2003)

City Population
1980: 142,546
1990: 141,686
2000: 139,529
2003 estimate: 139,664
Percent change, 1990–2000: −1.5%
U.S. rank in 1980: 110th
U.S. rank in 1990: 123rd
U.S. rank in 2000: 172nd (State rank: 1st)

Metropolitan Area Population (PMSA)
1990: 441,952
2000: 459,479

Percent change, 1990–2000: 3.5%
U.S. rank in 1990: 1st (CMSA)
U.S. rank in 2000: 1st (CMSA)

Area: 19.4 square miles (2000)
Elevation: 25 feet above sea level
Average Annual Temperature: 51.7° F
Average Annual Precipitation: 15.5 inches of rain; 26.2 inches of snow

Major Economic Sectors: Manufacturing, trade, government, services
Unemployment Rate: 4.7% (February 2005)
Per Capita Income: $16,306 (1999)

2002 FBI Crime Index Total: 8,551

Major Colleges and Universities: University of Bridgeport; Sacred Heart University; Fairfield University; Bridgeport Engineering Institute

Daily Newspaper: *The Connecticut Post*

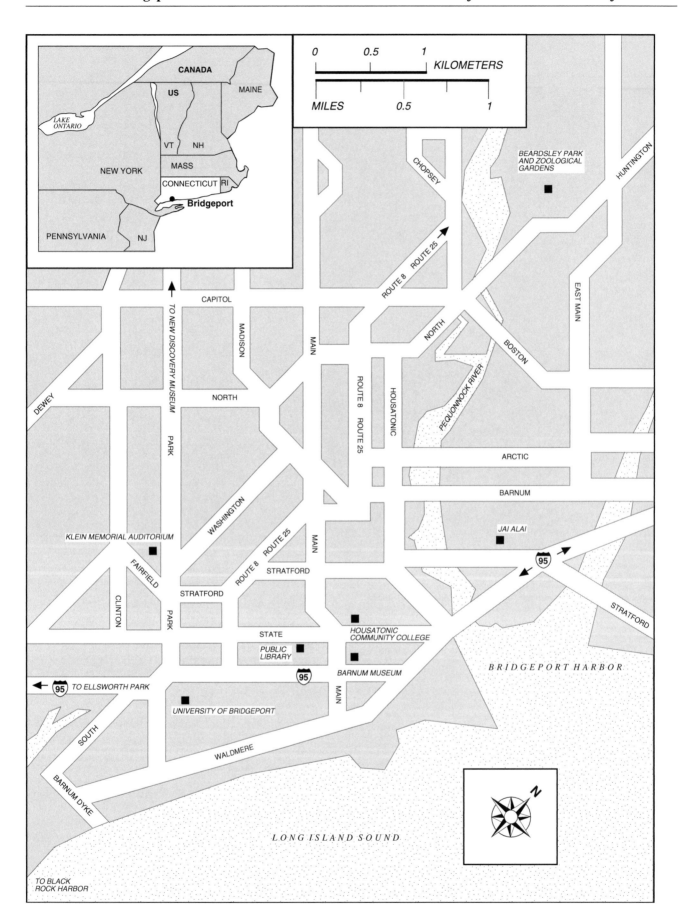

Introduction

A smokestack city known for its defense-related manufacturing activities and port facilities, Bridgeport, the largest city in Connecticut, was devastated in the early 1990s by the loss of its manufacturing base as a result of the end of the Cold War between the United States and the former Soviet Union, and actually declared itself bankrupt. Further degradation was handed to residents at the hands of their once-successful mayor, Joseph P. Ganim, who was removed from office in 2003 and convicted of municipal corruption. But at the turn of the twenty-first century, the city's bond rating was upgraded, the population was beginning to grow, jobs were slowly on the increase, a new baseball stadium and hockey arena stood along with other renovations on the city's waterfront which were beginning to draw tourists, and a feeling of optimism could be felt among the citizenry.

Geography and Climate

Bridgeport, in the southwest portion of Connecticut, sprawls for two and one-half miles along Long Island Sound at the mouth of the Pequonnock River. Located in Fairfield County, the city is situated on low-lying land that comprises two harbors, the main Bridgeport Harbor and the Black Rock Harbor two miles away. The city lies 150 miles south of Boston and 70 miles north of New York City.

Proximity to Long Island Sound keeps Bridgeport's summers warm and humid and its winters mild and relatively snow-free. Sea breezes can keep Bridgeport's mean monthly temperatures during the summer months three to five degrees lower than the temperatures posted inland.

Area: 19.4 square miles (2000)

Elevation: 25 feet above sea level

Average Temperatures: January, 28.9° F; July, 73.7° F; annual average, 51.7° F

Average Annual Precipitation: 15.5 inches of rain; 26.2 inches of snow

History

English Settlers Establish New Community

Pequonnock River Mouth Site of Village Bridgeport, situated on a commodious harbor and river estuary, was the site of at least five Native American villages and in 1659 became the site of Connecticut's first Indian reservation. The trading port of Black Rock was settled by the English in 1644, and farming communities at Stratfield and Pembroke by 1660. The city's present territory was then part of the adjoining towns of Fairfield and Stratford.

In 1765, white settlers paid the Pequonnocks to leave, and at the start of the Revolutionary War, some dozen families lived in the town. The townsfolk subsisted by farming, seaborne trading, and whaling and sealing. When Connecticut achieved statehood in 1788, about 100 settlers lived in Bridgeport.

Around 1760, commercial wharves were built on Bridgeport Harbor on the site of the present downtown. Farmers from inland towns brought their farm products to trade for imported goods, and packet boats ran to New York, Boston, and southern ports. One of the earliest merchants was Captain Stephen Burroughs, who was to invent America's decimal monetary system as a replacement for British pounds and shillings.

By the dawn of the new century, the port was thriving, and in 1800 the Borough of Bridgeport was incorporated as the first government of its kind in the state. In 1802 urban expansion caused the removal of the Golden Hill Indians from the last of their downtown reservation lands. Bridgeport became an independent town in 1821 and was soon home to major woolen mill complex and the center for saddle-making on the American continent. The year of its incorporation as a city, 1836, saw the building of one of the country's first railroads north to Albany to intercept trade goods coming east on the Erie Canal.

In 1847 the city became the home of Phineas Taylor (P.T.) Barnum, museum owner, circus founder, and promotional genius. Barnum toured Europe with Bridgeport native ''General Tom Thumb'' and brought ''Swedish Nightingale'' Jenny Lind, to see the splendor of his Oriental-styled mansion. He extended his talents to the development of his adopted city. In 1849 Mountain Grove Cemetery was laid out as a monumental sculpture garden based on an English precedent. In 1851 East Bridgeport was developed as a planned residential and manufacturing suburb radiating out from a five-acre central square. Seaside Park, known as the nation's first marine ''rural'' park, was completed in 1865 by a design team led by Frederick Law Olmsted, one of the men responsible for New York's Central Park.

Industry Shapes Bridgeport's Future

Bridgeport was the home of America's sewing machine industry in the years following the Civil War, and manufacturing continued to be a mainstay of the local economy. The greatest population surge came between 1896 and 1910 when the city swelled from under 50,000 people to more than 100,000. The influx of immigrants seeking factory jobs grew to include some 60 different ethnic groups. Later arrivals included Puerto Ricans, the largest concentration of whom settled on the city's east side.

During the late 1800s, the city was a leader in the production of rifles, corsets, typewriters, organs and pianos, and brass goods. At the beginning of the twentieth century, automobile and submarine manufacture became important. But the most pivotal industry of the city's history—armaments—took off with the commencement of World War I in 1914. Estimates are that during that terrible conflict, Bridgeport made more than two-thirds of the ordinance utilized by both sides in the conflict. The "Russian Rifle" Plant of the Union Metallic Cartridge Company, built to produce 37,500 guns for the troops of Czar Nicholas II, was the largest factory every built in America up to that time.

During the 1920s, the city became a major force in the newly developing aircraft industry. Immigrants who poured into Bridgeport included Igor Sikorsky, who produced flying boats and invented and flew the first helicopter locally. Bridgeporters coped with the Great Depression by electing Socialist Jasper McLevy as mayor during the 1930s, and he retained the office for 24 years. World War II and the ensuring Cold War saw the nation's dependency on the defense industry escalate. During the last two decades of the twentieth century, the city lost many of its one-time industrial giants to out-of-state and foreign competition.

Entering a New Century with New Goals

Today's Bridgeport is a city of diverse ethnic neighborhoods and significant historic architecture. The city has more than 3,000 structures listed on the National Register of Historic Places, more than any other Connecticut municipality. In the late 1990s, the Bridgeport Housing Authority (BHA) implemented several programs to revitalize many of the city's decaying neighborhoods. During the time when the city was a thriving manufacturing center, many housing units were built for its factory workers. The houses, including those in housing developments, began to deteriorate when jobs began disappearing in the 1960s. By 2000, the BHA had redeveloped abandoned housing all over Bridgeport, including a number of single-family homes in three different parts of the city, with federal financial assistance. In 2005, 600 units of downtown housing are in the planning phase and 800 more are being forecast for the future.

In 2003 the city was rocked by the corruption scandal of longtime mayor Joseph P. Ganim who left office at a time of the city's initial stages of resurgence. He was convicted of racketeering, extortion, and bribery and sentenced to imprisonment for nine years. The city rebounded under the guidance of new mayor, John M. Fabrizi, who has worked with city council members to stabilize the fiscal status of the community while aggressively pursuing new economic development highlighted by a mammoth $2 billion in public and private investments.

While Bridgeport has witnessed dramatic population decreases since the 1980s, the numbers are projected to steadily increase from 2005 through 2020 by the Connecticut Office of Policy & Management. And although *Connecticut Magazine* scored Bridgeport in 2003 as the lowest of 17 major cities within the state in terms of education, crime, and economic condition, the positive growth and active economic planning have infused the community with hopes for prosperous times ahead.

Historical Information: Bridgeport Public Library, Historical Collections, 925 Broad St., Bridgeport, CT 06604; telephone (203)576-7417; fax (203)576-8255

Population Profile

Metropolitan Area Residents
1990: 441,952
2000: 459,479
Percent change, 1990–2000: 3.5%
U.S. rank in 1990: 1st (CMSA)
U.S. rank in 2000: 1st (CMSA)

City Residents
1980: 142,546
1990: 141,686
2000: 139,529
2003 estimate: 139,664
Percent change, 1990–2000: −1.5%
U.S. rank in 1980: 110th
U.S. rank in 1990: 123rd
U.S. rank in 2000: 172nd (State rank: 1st)

Density: 8,720.9 people per square mile (2000)

Racial and ethnic characteristics (2000)
  White: 62,822
    Black or African American: 42,925
    American Indian and Alaska Native: 664

Asian: 4,536
Native Hawaiian and Pacific Islander: 148
Hispanic or Latino (may be of any race): 44,478
Other: 20,659

Percent of residents born in state: 50.4% (2000)

Age characteristics (2000)
Population under 5 years old: 11,397
Population 5 to 9 years old: 11,489
Population 10 to 15 years old: 10,696
Population 15 to 19 years old: 10,445
Population 20 to 24 years old: 11,207
Population 25 to 34 years old: 22,147
Population 35 to 44 years old: 20,463
Population 45 to 54 years old: 15,466
Population 55 to 59 years old: 5,576
Population 60 to 64 years old: 4,621
Population 65 to 74 years old: 7,743
Population 75 to 84 years old: 6,071
Population 85 years and over: 2,198
Median age: 31.4 years (2000)

Births (2001)
Total number: 2,268

Deaths (2001)
Total number: 1,260 (of which, 23 were infants under the age of 1 year)

Money income (1999)
Per capita income: $16,306
Median household income: $34,658
Total households: 50,305

Number of households with income of . . .
less than $10,000: 7,643
$10,000 to $14,999: 3,865
$15,000 to $24,999: 7,202
$25,000 to $34,999: 6,621
$35,000 to $49,999: 8,573
$50,000 to $74,999: 8,764
$75,000 to $99,999: 3,955
$100,000 to $149,999: 2,698
$150,000 to $199,999: 555
$200,000 or more: 429

Percent of families below poverty level: 16.2% (40.5% of which were female householder families with related children under 5 years)

2002 FBI Crime Index Total: 8,551

Municipal Government

Bridgeport, in Fairfield County, operates under a mayor-council form of government. The mayor and 20 council members are elected to two-year terms of office.

Head Official: Mayor John Michael Fabrizi (D) (since 2003; current term expires 2005)

Total Number of City Employees: 1,493 (2004)

City Information: Mayor's Office, City of Bridgeport, 45 Lyon Terrace, Bridgeport, CT 06604; telephone (203)576-7201; email mayoroffice@ci.bridgeport.ct.us

Economy

Major Industries and Commercial Activity

Manufacturing and trade, long mainstays in the Bridgeport economy, are being increasingly supplemented by the service-producing industries, particularly personal, business, and health services, as Bridgeport seeks to diversify. The defense industry, for many years a vital part of the city's economy, was hard hit by layoffs in the early 1990s. But wholesale and retail trade thrive thanks to the city's strategic location as a deep-sea port, a crossroads of interstate highways, and a hub of railroad lines, and the city is now the one of largest financial centers in New England. While not within Bridgeport itself there are a dozen *Fortune* 500 companies in Fairfield County, including General Electric, Pitney Bowes Inc., and Xerox Corporation.

Creating new employment opportunities for local workers has been a focal point for community leaders. In particular, the Bridgeport Economic Resource Center (BERC) has secured about 1,260 jobs since 2000, many in small start-up businesses like restaurants and shops. Law enforcement monies have held steady to contribute to a consistent reduction in the crime rate; meanwhile, dangerous housing projects continue to be identified and torn down in order to be replaced by better facilities. An amenity such as the new hockey arena, the Arena at Harbor Yard, draws visitors to town with college basketball, minor-league hockey, and concert events. The renovation of the waterfront and other local developments have helped to lure homebuyers wanting to escape the expensive housing market in lower Fairfield County, where median prices are substantially higher than in Bridgeport.

Items and goods produced: transportation equipment, women's underwear, electrical supplies, machinery and machine tools, fabricated metals

Incentive Programs—New and Existing Companies

Local programs—The Bridgeport Office of Planning and Economic Development offers a tax incentive development program involving real estate property tax incentives for development projects of $3 million or more. The Bridgeport Economic Resource Center (BERC) helps businesses to identify and access a wide array of business development programs. A partial listing of available incentives includes: Corporate Income & Property Tax exemptions, Corporate Sales Tax exemptions, State and Federal Enterprise Zone Benefits, Utility Benefits, and Brownfields Tax Credits.

Local banks in partnership with a variety of federal, state, and local government programs provide funds for a loan pool geared toward small and mid-sized businesses. Typical loan amounts are $500,000 or less. The Bridgeport Regional Business Council is the designated Small Business Development Center (SBDC) for Bridgeport, serving start-up and small businesses. SBDCs offer technical and management assistance, counseling, education, training programs, and loan packaging.

State programs—The Connecticut Development Authority works to expand Connecticut's business base. Among its many services are: partnering with private-sector organizations to guarantee or participate in loans for businesses that may be unable to meet credit underwriting standards; providing access to lower-cost fixed asset financing through Small Business Administration 504 Debentures and tax-exempt Industrial Revenue Bonds; offering financial incentives to companies that enhance the skills of their employees; and encouraging investment in the state's urban commercial infrastructure.

Bridgeport is part of the U.S. government's Environmental Protection Agency (EPA) program for redevelopment of abandoned industrial sites, commonly referred to as ''brownfields,'' as part of the overall agenda to attract private investors. Operated by Connecticut Brownfields Redevelopment Authority (CBRA), bonds are sold that provide businesses and developers incentive funds for investment in the designated property. Tax increment financing is available for Brownfields redevelopment.

Connecticut's financial and tax incentives also include grants and tax abatements for firms locating in State Enterprise Zones (for which Bridgeport qualifies; it is also a Foreign Trade Zone as operated by the Bridgeport Port Authority).

Job training programs—Employment training grants, both on- and off-site, and on-the-job training assistance are available through the Connecticut Department of Labor. Community and technical colleges across the state offer job and specialized skill training. The Bridgeport Economic Re- source Center (BERC) works with companies to implement Workforce Development Programs and has assisted 43 businesses and trained 275 employees since the initiative's inception.

Development Projects

A virtual plethora of development within Bridgeport is either in progress or on the way with the backing of the Bridgeport Economic Development Corporation (BEDCO). Among these improvements are the $7.4 million Seaview Avenue Industrial Park expansion, $40 million to shift businesses to the Steel Point location, and $9 million for updating historic Seaside Park. In 2002 the Derecktor Shipyards, a repair facility, was constructed at a cost of $2.5 million; the facility occupies 45,000-square-feet and created about 90 new jobs. Downtown is bustling with the City Trust Building's conversion into 120 condo units; the redevelopment of 16 vacant structures into 150,000 square feet of commercial land and 250 residential housing units; and 60,000 square feet of modernized space for a combination of retail, residential, and commercial availability. The 1998 opening of the $19 million Harbor Yard ballpark was enhanced by the 2001 debut of the 10,000-seat hockey/basketball home, the Arena of Harbor Yard. Still under consideration is a proposal for a new state-of-the-art $50 million intermodal transit center to handle assembly of trains, buses, ferries, and highway access in one downtown location.

Economic Development Information: Office of Planning and Economic Development, City Hall Annex, 999 Broad St., Bridgeport, CT 06604; telephone (203)576-7221; fax (203)332-5611; email nidohm0@ci.bridgeport.ct.us. Bridgeport Economic Resource Center, 10 Middle St., Bridgeport, CT 06604-4223; telephone (203)335-1108; fax (203)335-1297; email mdallas@berc-ct.com

Commercial Shipping

Bridgeport Harbor is one of three deep-water ports in the state. Its Cilco Terminal is one of New England's busiest deep draft ports; facilities include COMEX, bonded warehousing, and wet and dry storage. Most of the imports processed are perishable goods, and Bridgeport's is the second largest banana port on the East Coast, enabled by its 80,000-square-foot modern refrigerated warehouse. In 2002 the Bridgeport Port Authority used a $2.5 million grant from the Connecticut Department of Environmental Protection to build a 45,000-square-foot assembly facility, the Derecktor Shipyards, a major repair facility and critical to the port's users. Conrail operates a major freight yard nearby. Greater Bridgeport is on the main travel corridor from New York to New England.

Labor Force and Employment Outlook

Bridgeport boasts a skilled labor force with a relatively high education level; approximately 41 percent of the labor force are college graduates. While population began its decline in the 1980s and continued through 2005, population figures are projected to increase by the year 2020 (to more than 151,000 residents). In 2005 more than 227,000 workers were part of the metropolitan community's workforce. With the town's proximity to larger cities like New York and Boston, more than 25 million people reside and work within a 100-mile radius of Bridgeport.

The city is focusing its efforts on expanding its manufacturing base into the international marketplace, relying on its excellent port facilities and transportation network. Growth in this area is projected primarily for small businesses.

The following is a summary of data regarding the Bridgeport metropolitan area labor force, 2004 annual averages.

Size of nonagricultural labor force: 409,700

Number of workers employed in . . .
   construction and mining: 14,400
   manufacturing: 41,800
   trade, transportation, and utilities: 74,900
   information: 12,100
   financial activities: 41,700
   professional and business services: 69,600
   educational and health services: 59,500
   leisure and hospitality: 32,500
   other services: 16,800
   government: 46,400

Average hourly earnings of production workers employed in manufacturing: $20.77

Unemployment rate: 4.7% (February 2005)

Largest employers	*Number of employees*
Peoples Bank	3,443
St. Vincent Medical Center	1,800
Bridgeport Hospital	1,700
City of Bridgeport	1,493
Lacey Manufacturing Company, Inc.	400
University of Bridgeport	200
Derecktor Shipyard	150

Cost of Living

In the 1980s, property taxes in Bridgeport rose rapidly and budget deficits were commonplace. But by the late 1990s, the city administration of Mayor Ganim was receiving national acclaim for balancing budgets and cutting taxes, including instituting the first back-to-back tax cut in the city's modern history, worth $2.6 million to taxpayers. Housing prices were significantly lower than in the southern part of Fairfield County.

The following is a summary of data regarding several key cost of living factors for the Bridgeport area.

2004 (3rd Quarter) ACCRA Average House Price: $614,691

2004 (3rd Quarter) ACCRA Cost of Living Index: 153.2 (U.S. average = 100.0)

State income tax rate: 3.0% to 5.0%

State sales tax rate: 6.0% (some items are exempt)

Local income tax rate: None

Local sales tax rate: None

Property tax rate: 38.99 mills per $1,000 of actual value (2004)

Economic Information: State of Connecticut, Labor Department, 200 Folly Brook Blvd., Wethersfield, CT 06109-1114; telephone (860)263-6000

Education and Research

Elementary and Secondary Schools

Although in the late 1990s, the city announced investments of $250 million for modern buildings, classes for universal preschool, smaller classroom sizes, and broader access to computers and the Internet; by 2005 these initiatives had yet to materialize. The school district has suffered as a result with six buildings that are over a century old and 14 others at more than 50 years old. Further, the Board of Education was forced to trim its annual budget by 10 percent, or about $4.5 million, in the 2004–2005 fiscal year.

Bridgeport's public school system offers special education and handicapped services, as well as an adult education program in the evening. A magnet school program offers special opportunities for above-average students. The system includes two alternative schools and one special education facility.

The following is a summary of data regarding the Bridgeport public school system as of the 2003–2004 school year.

Total enrollment: 22,730

Number of facilities
   elementary/middle schools: 30
   senior high schools: 3
   other: 3

Student/teacher ratio: 14.7 (2003–2004)

Teacher salaries (2003–2004)
  minimum: $38,604
  maximum: $72,440

Funding per pupil: $5,909 (2004–2005)

Many parochial elementary schools and one parochial high school supplement the public school system. Private nursery schools, technical schools, and the college-preparatory University (High) School round out the city's education offerings for children.

Public Schools Information: Bridgeport Public Schools, 45 Lyon Terrace, Rm. 203, Bridgeport, CT 06604; telephone (203)576-7301; fax (203)576-8488

Colleges and Universities

Founded in 1927, the University of Bridgeport—with about 3,200 undergraduate and around 1,500 graduate students—offers bachelor's, master's, and doctoral degrees in liberal arts and professional fields and includes the only program in chiropractic and naturopathic medicine in the state. Sacred Heart University, a Catholic liberal arts college in Fairfield, enrolls 4,300 undergraduate and 1,800 graduate students and represents New England's second largest Catholic university. Fairfield University, a Jesuit institution, provides its 5,000 students with bachelor's and master's degrees with a concentration on liberal arts, education, and nursing. Bridgeport Engineering Institute in Stamford employs a work-study approach in awarding engineering degrees. Housatonic Community College trains many of the area's semiprofessional and technical workers. St. Vincent's College, a two-year co-ed facility, offers degrees in health care fields and initiated an online distance education program in the fall of 2005.

Libraries and Research Centers

With nearly 450,000 volumes and four locations, Bridgeport's is one of the largest library systems in the state. The library also has about 880 audiotapes, around 16,500 video materials, and 1,000 periodical subscriptions. Special collections include an extensive business and technology section and a collection of local history, with a focus on P.T. Barnum and circus memorabilia. The library's special interests also include art and architecture, and literature. It is a federal depository for U.S. Government publications.

Other local library facilities include the law library of the State of Connecticut (Bridgeport Branch), and two medical libraries. The Magnus Wahlstrom Library at the University of Bridgeport houses approximately 270,000 volumes along with one million microforms, 1,200 serials, and access to about 7,400 electronic books via online subscriptions. Other research and library facilities in Bridgeport include the Center for the Study of Aging at the University of Bridgeport, and the Connecticut Department of Children and Families' Library. The Connecticut Information Technology Institute, also at the university, is a joint venture between industry and education to help inventors and entrepreneurs in high-tech operations.

Public Library Information: Bridgeport Public Library, 925 Broad St., Bridgeport, CT 06604-4871; telephone (203)576-7403

Health Care

With two major hospitals and a mental health center within the city limits, Bridgeport is the health care center of Fairfield County. Bridgeport Hospital is a full-service community hospital and teaching institution serving the greater Bridgeport area and Fairfield County. The hospital is a tertiary-level hospital (highest level) with the staff and facilities to treat the most critically ill patients who are often referred from other hospitals, and is also designated a Level I Trauma Center (highest level), one of four in the state of Connecticut. The 425-bed facility is known as a leader in health care and for its specialties and innovative services. Special programs include a regional open heart center; a cancer center, which offers comprehensive diagnostic, treatment, education and support services for cancer patients; a regional center for low and high-risk births; the region's most comprehensive newborn intensive care unit, the P.T. Barnum Pediatric Center; the only burn center with dedicated beds between Boston and New York; a joint reconstruction center; comprehensive inpatient and outpatient rehabilitative care for multiple trauma, stroke, multiple sclerosis, Parkinson's disease, arthritis and other disorders; and a community wellness and health education program.

St. Vincent's Medical Center is a modern, 397-bed acute care hospital offering more than 50 specialty and sub-specialty medical and surgical disciplines. Centers of excellence comprise cardiovascular disease including angioplasty and coronary artery bypass surgery; cancer prevention, diagnosis, treatment and support; joint replacement including total knee, hip and shoulder; and women's services including a contemporary maternity center along with a Women's Imaging Center (opened June 2004) for mammograms, ultrasounds, and bone density services. St. Vincent's also is a designated Level II Trauma Center and has a landing pad for medical helicopters. It is affiliated with two medical schools—Columbia University College of Physicians and Surgeons and New York Medical College, and participates in international research programs. The Greater Bridgeport

Community Mental Health Center has 62 licensed beds and provides a 24-hour crisis service along with a variety of additional recovery programs.

Recreation

Sightseeing

Visitors can experience Bridgeport's colonial past on a narrated boat tour of historic Black Rock Harbor and Long Island Sound. Captain's Cove Seaport, an amusement and maritime center along the harbor, is home to the HMS *Rose,* a replica of a Revolutionary War era 24-gun frigate. Captain's Cove also offers shopping along a seaside boardwalk and a 350-slip marina. Connecticut's Beardsley Zoo, the state's only zoo, is open year-round and features to its quarter-million annual visitors more than 300 animals including some that are rare or endangered species from North and South America.

Arts and Culture

Much of Bridgeport's performing arts activity takes place at the 1,400-seat Klein Memorial Auditorium, including performances by the Greater Bridgeport Symphony, a regionally acclaimed professional orchestra, as well as performances by touring troupes and artists. Formed in 1961, the Greater Bridgeport Youth Symphony is made up of four performing ensembles, the Principal, the Symphony, the Concert, and the String Orchestra. As part of these groups, young musicians from the area, led by three conductors and six coaches, present concerts throughout the year. The Arena at Harbor Yard, constructed in 2001, provides a 10,000-seat venue for larger-scale musical concerts, children's shows, and other performances.

The Cabaret Theatre features the resident musical Downtown Cabaret Theatre group and the Cabaret Children's Company since 1983. The Playhouse on the Green (formerly Polka Dot Playhouse) is Bridgeport's oldest theatrical treasure, offering year-round professional theater in a 228-seat state-of-the-art theater located in the heart of Bridgeport's revitalized downtown.

Opened in 1893, the Barnum Museum displays artifacts relating to P.T. Barnum, "General Tom Thumb," Lavinia Warren, Jenny Lind, and a host of clowns. Displays concerning Bridgeport's industrial era, as well as a 2,500-year-old Egyptian mummy, a two-headed calf, and a hand-carved miniature circus complete with 5,000 figures are also featured. The Discovery Museum and Planetarium, an interactive and educational museum of art and physical science, features the duPont Planetarium, the Challenger Learning Center (dedicated to the astronauts who perished in the space shuttle tragedy in 1986) and interactive exhibits that teach the principles of physical science. A gallery of changing art exhibits, films, and children's programs rounds out the offerings, which are visited by 68,000 guests annually.

The Housatonic Museum of Art specializes in nineteenth- and twentieth-century European and American art, as well as contemporary and African and Asian ethnographic art.

Festivals and Holidays

A major regional attraction is the annual Barnum Festival and the Great Street Parade, which is held each summer. The 10-day celebration draws thousands of people for the Grucci Fireworks show "Skyblast," Champions on Parade and other events. The summer also offers water enthusiasts the St. Vincent's "Swim Across the Sound," a multi-event swimming marathon, a sailing regatta, and the WICC Bluefish Tournament, which draws fishermen from across the United States in search of the heaviest Bluefish. The University of Bridgeport's International Festival, held in April, highlights the cuisines and entertainment of more than 30 cultures. Meanwhile, Christmas time is aglow with the "Park City Lights" in Beardsley Park.

Sports for the Spectator

The Shoreline Star Greyhound Park Entertainment Complex features live parimutuel greyhound racing from mid-May through Mid-October, and year-round simulcast wagering on thoroughbred, harness, and greyhound tracks from around the country. The Bridgeport Bluefish Baseball club is an independent minor league team that plays at the Ballpark at Harbor Yard, constructed in 1998, where the games provide area residents with affordable family entertainment. The Arena at Harbor Yard was built in 2001 and seats about 10,000 for the American Hockey League's (AHL) Bridgeport Sound Tigers, who began playing in 2001 as the top affiliate of the National Hockey League's (NHL) New York Islanders. The arena also plays host to the National Collegiate Athletic Association's (NCAA) Fairfield University Stags' men's basketball team.

Sports for the Participant

Bridgeport, known as the "Park City" for maintaining nearly an acre of park land per 1,000 residents (more than 1,360 acres total), features the historic Seaside Park located on three miles of shoreline and offering fishing, baseball and softball, picnicking, and tennis. The city features 32 public parks, two dozen playgrounds, 40 tennis courts, and an 18-hole golf course. Pleasure Beach, formerly a huge draw in the area, has remained inaccessible since a devastating fire in 1996 destroyed the connecting bridge; city planners have actively been pursuing funding to restore it. The Ocean

View Skate Park offers a variety of ramps highlighted by a spectacular coastal view; the Wonderland of Ice offers public skating and hockey leagues and instruction. The Berkshire Rail Spur Trail is a 1.6 mile bicycling trail that follows a defunct rail line.

Shopping and Dining

Unique items are available at Bridgeport's Barnum Museum and Discovery Museum and Planetarium. There are many large malls within 40 miles of the city including Trumbull Shopping Park, Hawley Lane Mall, and the Dock, all located in the greater Bridgeport area. Nearby Fairfield offers a classic shopping area around its green, and antiquing can be enjoyed at the nearby Stratford Antiques Center, and throughout all of picturesque Fairfield County.

The Bridgeport area offers a wide variety of dining experiences, ranging from Bridgeport's "Little Italy," to seafood restaurants both in Bridgeport and in nearby Stratford; many overlook Long Island Sound. The downtown area boasts some excellent lunch spots, and fine cuisine is available throughout the area.

Visitor Information: Coastal Fairfield County Convention & Visitor Bureau, 297 West Ave., Norwalk, CT 06850; telephone (203)853-7770; toll-free (800)866-7925; fax (203)853-7775; email info@coastalct.com. Connecticut Office of Tourism, 505 Hudson St., Hartford, CT 06106-7106; toll-free (800)CTBOUND.

Convention Facilities

Within the greater Bridgeport area about 1,000 hotel rooms are available for a variety of functions. Small conventions can be handled by the new Arena at Harbor Yard with capacity seating of 10,000 guests and 6,000 theater-style along with room for 150 standard-size trade show booths. The Holiday Inn Bridgeport Hotel & Conference Center offers 8,500 square feet of function space, including a 5,000-square-foot ballroom, five breakout rooms, and an executive board room. The Inn, which has 234 sleeping rooms, can accommodate meetings of 16 to 500. The Stratford Ramada Inn has 6,500 square feet of exhibit space, 7 meeting rooms, and 145 sleeping rooms.

Convention Information: Coastal Fairfield County Convention & Visitor Bureau, 297 West Ave., Norwalk, CT 06850; telephone (203)853-7770; toll-free (800)866-7925; fax (203)853-7775; email info@coastalct.com

Transportation

Approaching the City

Bridgeport's city-owned Sikorsky Memorial Airport is 10 minutes from downtown (in Stratford). The airport serves the corporate and general aviation communities. The Tweed New Haven Regional Airport is about 25 miles northeast of Bridgeport and offers daily flights from two major airlines, Delta and U.S. Airways. Extensive domestic and international service is available from the New York City airports, about 60 miles away.

Both Amtrak, with at least 14 daily stops, and Metro-North, with 63 daily stops, offer rail service into Bridgeport, as do major bus lines such as Greyhound and Peter Pan. An automobile ferry runs between Bridgeport and Port Jefferson outside of New York City and carries nearly 900,000 passengers annually.

Major east-west routes include Connecticut 15 (the Merritt Parkway) and I-95 (the Connecticut Turnpike, that carries about 200,000 vehicles per day). North-south arteries include Connecticut Route 8 to the northeast and Connecticut Route 25 to the northwest.

Traveling in the City

Bridgeport's streets fan out to the north from the waterfront. The Greater Bridgeport Transit Authority (GBTA) operates 16 fixed routes in the city and environs on weekdays and includes paratransit services; reduced services are offered on weekends.

Communications

Newspapers and Magazines

Bridgeport's daily, *The Connecticut Post,* is published every morning. Other newspapers in the city include the monthly *Fairfield County Catholic,* published by the Diocese of Bridgeport, and the *Bridgeport News,* which publishes weekly.

Television and Radio

Bridgeport has one public television station, and one cable franchise. However, the city receives New York City stations as well. Two AM and two FM radio stations broadcast from Bridgeport. Connecticut Radio Information Service, headquartered in Wethersfield, broadcasts readings from daily newspapers and magazines for the benefit of state residents who are blind or cannot hold or turn pages.

Media Information: Connecticut Post, 410 State St., Bridgeport, CT 06604; telephone (203)333-0161 or 800-423-8058; fax (203)367-8158

Bridgeport Online

Bridgeport Economic Resource Center. Available www .bridgeport-econ.org

Bridgeport Hospital. Available www.bridgeporthospital.org

Bridgeport Public Library. Available www.bridgeportpublic library.org

Bridgeport Public Schools. Available www.bridgeportedu .com

City of Bridgeport Home Page. Available ci.bridgeport.ct.us

Coastal Fairfield County Convention & Visitors Bureau. Available www.coastalct.com

Connecticut Development Authority. Available www.ctcda .com

Connecticut Office of Tourism. Available www.tourism .state.ct.us

The Connecticut Post. Available www.connpost.com

St. Vincent's Medical Center. Available www.stvincents .org

State of Connecticut Labor Department. Available www .ctdol.state.ct.us

University of Bridgeport. Available www.bridgeport.edu

Selected Bibliography

Grimaldi, Lennie, *Only in Bridgeport 2000: An Illustrated History of the Park City* (Bridgeport: Harbor Publishing, 2000)

Howard, Maureen, *Natural History* (New York: Norton) Bridgeport Economic Resource Center

Waldo, George Curtis, Jr., ed., *History of Bridgeport and Vicinity* (New York, Chicago: S. J. Clarke, 1917)

Danbury

The City in Brief

Founded: 1685 (incorporated, 1889)

Head Official: Mayor Mark D. Boughton (R) (since 2001)

City Population
  1980: 60,470
  1990: 65,585
  2000: 74,848
  2003 estimate: 77,353
  Percent change, 1990–2000: 14.1%
  U.S. rank in 1980: 324th
  U.S. rank in 1990: 355th
  U.S. rank in 2000: 406th (State rank: 7th)

Metropolitan Area Population (PMSA)
  1980: 175,000
  1990: 193,597
  2000: 217,980

Percent change, 1990–2000: 12.6%
U.S. rank in 1980: 1st (CMSA)
U.S. rank in 1990: 1st (CMSA)
U.S. rank in 2000: 1st (CMSA)

Area: 44.3 square miles (2000)
Elevation: Ranges from 378 feet to 1,050 feet
Average Annual Temperature: 49.7° F
Average Annual Precipitation: 25.8 inches of rain; 26 inches of snow

Major Economic Sectors: Trade, manufacturing, services
Unemployment Rate: 3.7% (April 2005)
Per Capita Income: $24,500 (1999)
2004 ACCRA Average House Price: Not reported
2004 ACCRA Cost of Living Index: Not reported

2002 FBI Crime Index Total: 2,198

Major Colleges and Universities: Western Connecticut State University

Daily Newspaper: *News-Times*

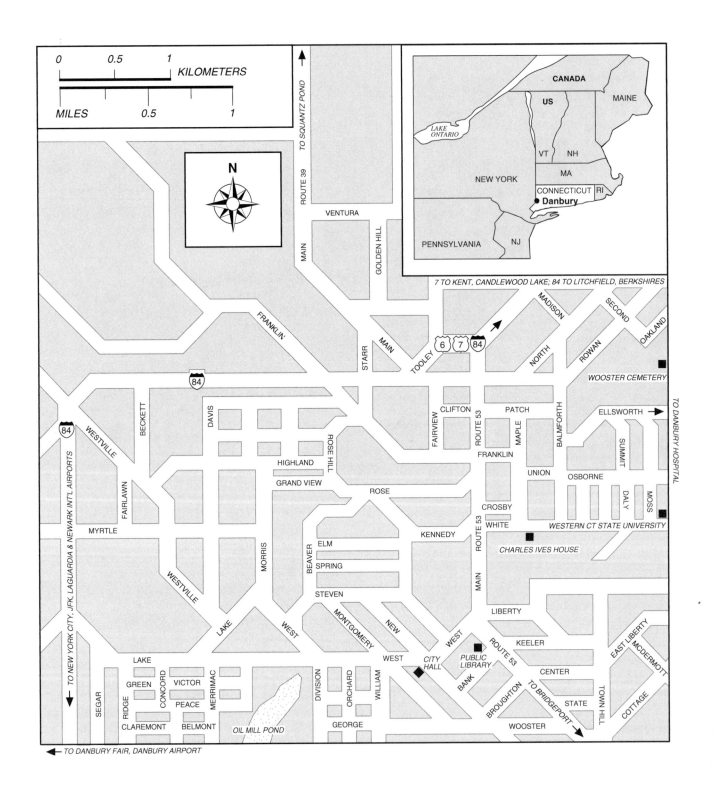

0   0.5   1

KILOMETERS

MILES   0.5   1

N

TO SQUANTZ POND

ROUTE 39

VENTURA

MAIN

GOLDEN HILL

FRANKLIN

7 TO KENT, CANDLEWOOD LAKE; 84 TO LITCHFIELD, BERKSHIRES

CANADA

US   MAINE

LAKE ONTARIO

VT   NH

MA

NEW YORK

CONNECTICUT   RI

• Danbury

PENNSYLVANIA   NJ

MADISON

SECOND

OAKLAND

STARR

MAIN

TOOLEY

6 7 84

NORTH

ROWAN

WOOSTER CEMETERY

84

FAIRVIEW

CLIFTON

PATCH

ROUTE 53

MAPLE

BALMFORTH

ELLSWORTH

SUMMIT

TO DANBURY HOSPITAL

84

WESTVILLE

BECKETT

DAVIS

ROSE HILL

FRANKLIN

UNION

OSBORNE

DALY

MOSS

TO NEW YORK CITY, JFK, LAGUARDIA & NEWARK INT'L AIRPORTS

FAIRLAWN

HIGHLAND

GRAND VIEW

ROSE

CROSBY

WHITE

ROUTE 53

WESTERN CT STATE UNIVERSITY

MYRTLE

KENNEDY

CHARLES IVES HOUSE

MORRIS

BEAVER

ELM

SPRING

STEVEN

MAIN

WESTVILLE

LAKE

WEST

MONTGOMERY

NEW

LIBERTY

EAST LIBERTY

MCDERMOTT

LAKE

DIVISION

ORCHARD

WILLIAM

WEST

WEST

CITY HALL

PUBLIC LIBRARY

ROUTE 53

KEELER

CENTER

SEGAR

RIDGE

GREEN

CONCORD

VICTOR

PEACE

MERRIMAC

BELMONT

CLAREMONT

OIL MILL POND

GEORGE

BANK

BROUGHTON

TO BRIDGEPORT

WOOSTER

STATE

TOWN HILL

COTTAGE

← TO DANBURY FAIR, DANBURY AIRPORT

Introduction

Danbury, formerly known as the Hat Capital of the World and official supplier of silk top hats to presidents, is perhaps best known today as the headquarters of Union Carbide and other industries that have moved out of metropolitan areas. Danbury is located near the beautiful rural area of Connecticut known as Litchfield Hills, an affluent region where per capita income is among the highest in the country. The creation of the city's historic downtown district in 1988 has helped to bring about an upswing in downtown development. The resurgence can be witnessed by continued population growth fueled by a high quality of living that residents enjoy.

Geography and Climate

Danbury is located in southwestern Connecticut in Fairfield County, 25 miles northwest of Bridgeport, in the foothills of the Berkshire Mountains. The city is situated on low-lying land just south of Lake Candlewood, the largest manmade lake in the state, and east of the Housatonic River. The surrounding terrain consists of rolling hills and not-very-tall mountains to the west and northwest (the western highland). Danbury's is a four-season climate; the extremes of temperature experienced throughout New England are somewhat tempered there by proximity to hills, but winters can be very cold.

Area: 44.3 square miles (2000)

Elevation: ranges from 378 feet to 1,050 feet

Average Temperatures: January, 26.5° F; July, 72.5° F; annual average, 49.7° F

Average Annual Precipitation: 25.8 inches of rain; 26 inches of snow

History

From Beans to Revolution to Hats

English settlers moving north from Norwalk took root in Danbury in 1685 and called it Swampfield though this was short-lived. Renamed Danbury in 1687 after a town in England, it was nicknamed Beantown for the beans and other vegetables that grew prolifically there, which were carted over a primitive road to be traded in Norwalk.

Danbury functioned during the American Revolution as a storage and warehouse point for patriot arms and supplies. In April 1777, British General Tryon was dispatched there to attack the city, which had received advance word of the raid but was able to round up only about 250 militia to defend itself against a British force of some 2,000 men. General Tryon captured the town and set his men to destroying patriot homes. The troops came upon stores of rum and began consuming it. Fearful that the American militia was gathering to block his way to his ships to the south of the city, Tryon ordered his drunken men out of Danbury, where they were attacked by troops led by Benedict Arnold and General David Wooster. British troops did manage to reach their ships but suffered many casualties.

The first hatmaker of record in Danbury was Zadoc Benedict, who founded a firm in 1780 that turned out three hats a day. By 1800 Danbury had emerged as a U.S. center for the manufacture of hats, part of a Connecticut pattern of factories being established in small villages rather than large industrial cities. By 1887 the city's 30 factories were turning out about five million hats a year, and Hat City became its nickname. Danbury continued to be a national center for the production of hats until the beginning of the twentieth century, when the fashion for the stiff fur derby hats produced there changed to a demand for softer hats. It is speculated that the automobile was the reason for this change in fashion—the stiff derbies would blow off in the wind. Following World War II men began to go hatless, and the industry went into a further decline from which it never recovered.

Danbury also became famous for the Danbury Fair, which originated in 1821 and by 1869 had become an annual event. The fair brought farm folk with a week's supply of food in their wagons together with city slickers for livestock and agricultural displays and competitions. Discontinued in 1981, a shopping mall now occupies the former fairgrounds.

The coming of the railroad in the 1830s (running by 1852) brought whole crews of Irish workers to Danbury, where a Roman Catholic church was built and distinctly Irish neighborhoods grew up.

From Hats to Diversified Industry, Corporate Headquarters

Although hatmaking has almost disappeared in Danbury, industry has grown rapidly there to the extent that the area is more heavily industrialized than any other labor market in Connecticut, the reverse of a trend being experienced elsewhere in the country. Beginning in the 1970s corporate headquarters leaving New York City caused explosive growth in Danbury's population, which expanded by more than 19 percent between 1970 and 1980. The I-84 corridor east of Danbury to Southbury saw an 80.3 percent increase in population. A slow yet steady shift in population to these rural areas of the state continues.

Forecasts foresee no end in Danbury's population growth. The economic development of the area has been a critical goal of the city leaders and their efforts can be witnessed in organizations such as CityCenter Danbury, which focuses on the prosperity of the downtown area. In 2004, CityCenter Danbury oversaw $18 million in public and private investments. Mayor Mark D. Boughton stated in his 2005–2006 annual budget that Danbury is ''on the rise'' with its success anchored by a high quality of life, a solid educational system, and vast recreational and cultural opportunities. The city's strengths are recognized by its sixth place ranking among Connecticut's 17 major cities by *Connecticut Magazine* in 2004 in terms of education, crime, and economic condition.

Historical Information: Danbury Museum & Historical Society, 43 Main St., Danbury, CT 06810; telephone (203)743-5200

Population Profile

Metropolitan Area Residents (PMSA)
1980: 175,000
1990: 193,597
2000: 217,980
Percent change, 1990–2000: 12.6%
U.S. rank in 1980: 1st (CMSA)
U.S. rank in 1990: 1st (CMSA)
U.S. rank in 2000: 1st (CMSA)

City Residents
1980: 60,470
1990: 65,585
2000: 74,848
2003 estimate: 77,353
Percent change, 1990–2000: 14.1%
U.S. rank in 1980: 324th
U.S. rank in 1990: 355th (State rank: 8th)
U.S. rank in 2000: 406th

Density: 1,777.4 people per square mile (2000)

Racial and ethnic characteristics (2000)
   White: 56,853
   Black or African American: 5,060
   American Indian and Alaska Native: 214
   Asian: 4,082
   Native Hawaiian and Pacific Islander: 26
   Hispanic or Latino (may be of any race): 11,791
   Other: 5,653

Percent of residents born in state: 39.8% (2000)

Age characteristics (2000)
   Population under 5 years old: 4,900
   Population 5 to 9 years old: 4,540
   Population 10 to 14 years old: 4,281
   Population 15 to 19 years old: 4,561
   Population 20 to 24 years old: 5,587
   Population 25 to 34 years old: 13,332
   Population 35 to 44 years old: 13,161
   Population 45 to 54 years old: 10,011
   Population 55 to 59 years old: 3,595
   Population 60 to 64 years old: 2,644
   Population 65 to 74 years old: 4,158
   Population 75 to 84 years old: 2,946
   Population 85 years and over: 1,132
   Median age: 35.2 years (2000)

Births (2001)
   Total number: 1,086

Deaths (2001)
   Total number: 527 (of which, 6 were infants under the age of 1 year)

Money income (1999)
   Per capita income: $24,500
   Median household income: $53,664
   Total households: 27,198

Number of households with income of . . .
   less than $10,000: 1,692
   $10,000 to $14,999: 1,335
   $15,000 to $24,999: 2,329
   $25,000 to $34,999: 2,950
   $35,000 to $49,999: 4,348
   $50,000 to $74,999: 5,836
   $75,000 to $99,999: 3,892
   $100,000 to $149,999: 3,095
   $150,000 to $199,999: 1,025
   $200,000 or more: 696

Percent of families below poverty level: 5.9% (27.9% of which were female householder families with related children under 5 years)

2002 FBI Crime Index Total: 2,198

Municipal Government

Danbury operates under the mayor-council form of government. The mayor and council members are elected to two-year terms.

Head Official: Mayor Mark D. Boughton (R) (since 2001; current term expires November 2005)

Total Number of City Employees: 554 (2005)

City Information: City Hall, 155 Deer Hill Ave., Danbury, CT 06810; telephone (203)797-4500

Economy

Major Industries and Commercial Activity

Danbury's local economy is diverse, with services, manufacturing, retail, and trade as the leading components. Major non-manufacturing sectors are services; wholesale and retail trade; and finance, insurance, and real estate. Retail trade is an integral contributor to the local economy, centered on the 1.3-million-square-foot Danbury Fair Mall. The central downtown business district continues to prosper under the guidance of CityCenter Danbury, an organization designed for the revitalization of the area. Within the district, industries such as banking, law, government, and insurance employ about 5,500 workers.

Items and goods produced: surgical instruments and supplies, electronic and railroad testing equipment, silverware, aluminum foil, aircraft parts, rubber tile, air conditioning equipment, steam generators, plastics, glue, textiles, and ball and roller bearings

Incentive Programs—New and Existing Companies

Local programs—Site selection, technology, and local development assistance is available through the Greater Danbury Chamber of Commerce, which functions as the designated Small Business Development Center (SBDC) for Danbury, serving start-up and small businesses. SBDCs offer technical and management assistance, counseling, education, training programs, and loan packaging. The Housatonic Valley Economic Development Partnership (HVEDP) assists new business owners by providing information, forms, and training. Since 2000, Danbury has administered a program that provides personal property tax relief for local businesses, their computer equipment, and peripherals. The city also offers deferral of assessments on improvements to real property for up to seven years, free sewer and water use for one year, as well as a tax abatement program that affords relief of up to $1,250 of real property tax per quarter for properties that are cleared of environmental contamination. The Greater Danbury Chapter of SCORE (Service Corps of Retired Executives), supported by the Small Business Association (SBA) assists small businesses

by giving free advice on writing business plans and obtaining financing.

State programs—The Connecticut Development Authority works to expand Connecticut's business base by providing loans and revenue bond financing for manufacturing, research and development, and other facilities. Among its many services are: partnering with private-sector organizations to guarantee or participate in loans for businesses that may be unable to meet credit underwriting standards; providing access to lower-cost fixed asset financing through Small Business Administration 504 Debentures and tax-exempt Industrial Revenue Bonds; offering financial incentives to companies that enhance the skills of their employees; and encouraging investment in the state's urban commercial infrastructure.

Connecticut Innovations (CI) provides capital and grants to assist in the development and marketing of new products and processes. Established in 1989 it has fed more than $133 million into high-technology companies within the state since 1995. Initially funded by state bonds, it now operates on investment profits.

Job training programs—Employment training grants, both on- and off-site, and on-the-job training assistance is available through the Connecticut Department of Labor. Community and technical colleges across the state offer job and specialized skill training. Several organizations in the immediate region help prepare a well-trained workforce by providing on-site training. Municipal libraries in the region provide free Internet training to businesses while the Housatonic Valley Economic Development Partnership (HVEDP) offers free resources and referrals. Partnering with the state's Department of Labor (DOL), the Danbury Connecticut Works program extends services such as workshops, career counseling, and employment referrals.

Development Projects

In 2001 the construction of the Danbury Ice Arena sparked much activity such as a new minor league hockey team, local hockey leagues, and public skating. The city's largest employer, Danbury Hospital, is scheduled in 2006 to open an outpatient diagnostic building occupying about 60,000 square feet. Western Connecticut State University has several projects either in process or recently completed, highlighted by the $5.2 million athletic complex on more than 18,000 square feet of land (built in 2004), the $48 million high-tech science building on about 122,000 square feet (finished in 2005), and a performance arts center slated for development in 2007 on 140,000 square feet.

On the industry side, Boehringer-Ingelheim Pharmaceuticals, Inc. (BIPI) announced in December 2004 their $500-

million expansion with an anticipated job growth of 500 to 700 positions.

Economic Development Information: Greater Danbury Chamber of Commerce, 39 West St., Danbury, CT 06810; telephone (203)743-5565; fax (203)794-1439; email info @danburychamber.com. Housatonic Valley Economic Development Partnership, Old Town Hall, Rte. 25, Brookfield, CT 05804; telephone (203)775-6256; fax (203)740-9167; email hvedp@wcsu.ctstateu.edu

Commercial Shipping

Danbury is located on major highways I-84 and U.S. Route 7. Metro-North, connecting the city with the New Haven line at East Norwalk, provides rail freight service. Freight movement from the region throughout the east coast is excellent. One-day service by motor freight is possible from the populous Portland, Maine to Washington, D.C. markets.

Labor Force

Danbury's workers are skilled and versatile, and area students demonstrate a high level of computer literacy. Its citizens are highly educated with about 27 percent having a bachelor's degree or higher.

The following is a summary of data regarding the Danbury area labor force, 2004 annual averages.

Size of nonagricultural labor force: 68,600

Number of workers employed in . . .
   trade, transportation, and utilities: 15,800
   information: 12,100
   professional and business services: 69,600
   wholesale and retail trade: 8,300
   leisure and hospitality: 5,200
   government: 7,800

Average hourly earnings of production workers employed in manufacturing: $16.04

Unemployment rate: 3.7% (April 2005)

Largest employers	Number of employees
Danbury Hospital	3,000
Cendant Mobility	2,200
Union Carbide	1,500
Boehringer-Ingelheim	950
Western Connecticut State University	848
Danbury Public Schools	678
G.E. Capital	not reported
Scholastic Library Publishing	not reported

Cost of Living

The following is a summary of data regarding several key cost of living factors for the Danbury metropolitan area.

2004 ACCRA Cost of Living Index: Not reported

2004 ACCRA Average House Price: Not reported

State income tax rate: graduated 3% to 5% on adjusted gross income

State sales tax rate: 6% (some items are exempt)

Local income tax rate: None

Local sales tax rate: None

Property tax rate: 24.86 mills per $1,000 of actual value (2004–2005)

Economic Information: Greater Danbury Chamber of Commerce, 39 West St., Danbury, CT 06810; telephone (203)743-5565; fax (203)794-1439; email info@danbury chamber.com. State of Connecticut, Department of Economic & Community Development, 505 Hudson St., Hartford, CT 06106-7107; telephone (860)270-8000; email DECD@po.state.ct.us

Education and Research

Elementary and Secondary Schools

The Danbury Board of Education, comprised of 11 elected representatives serving unpaid two- or four-year terms, is the district's policy-making body. The school system supports an Alternative Center for Education, before and after school programs, the "Summit" programs for gifted and talented students, the Elementary Technology Program, and special education classes. The Danbury School and Business Collaborative (DSABC) offers special programs such as mentors/tutors from the business community, job shadowing, scholarships, opportunities for high school students to earn high school and college credits simultaneously, and bilingual studies. The city also has 10 nonpublic schools.

The following is a summary of data regarding the Danbury public school system as of the 2003–2004 school year.

Total enrollment: 9,505

Number of facilities
   elementary schools: 13
   junior high/middle schools: 2
   senior high schools: 1
   other: 1

Student/teacher ratio: 14:1

Teacher salaries (2004–2005)
   minimum: $37,087
   maximum: $80,354

Funding per pupil: $5,921 (2004–2005)

Public Schools Information: Danbury Public Schools, Administrative Center, 63 Beaver Brook Rd., Danbury, CT 06810; telephone (203)797-4701

Colleges and Universities

Western Connecticut State University has consistently been rated as "Competitive plus" by Barron's *Profiles of American Colleges,* based on the ratio of full-time PhD professors to part-time faculty. The university, with two campuses and nearly 5,900 students enrolled in full- and part-time graduate and undergraduate programs, grants bachelor's degrees in business, arts and sciences, and professional studies. It also maintains a planetarium and operates a radio station.

Libraries and Research Centers

Danbury Public Library, founded in 1879, holds about 92,085 books, 311 periodicals, about 1,500 CDs, over 5,000 videos, and nearly 250 CD-ROMs. Western Connecticut State University's Ruth A. Haas Library holds nearly 174,000 volumes as well as about 5,400 periodicals, music scores, and tapes. Special collections focus on county and state history, music education, and teacher education. The University also operates the Robert S. Young Business Library with 5,800 volumes and 320 periodicals and is a U.S. government documents depository. Danbury Museum and Historical Society's research library specializes in American antiques and genealogy. Law and related topics are the focus at the Law Library at Danbury Courthouse, Department of Justice Centralized Library of the Federal Correctional Institution, and Union Carbide's Law Department Library; a library is also maintained by Danbury Hospital. The NeuroCommunication Research Laboratories, Inc. specializes in neurological diseases, psychology, and dermatology and also includes a library while the Clinical Research Center of CT/NY performs clinical trials involving rheumatology.

Public Library Information: Danbury Public Library, 170 Main St., Danbury, CT 06810; telephone (203)797-4505; fax (203)796-1677

Health Care

The health care needs of residents in the Greater Danbury area are attended to at Danbury Hospital, a 371-bed non-profit teaching hospital and regional health resource. In 2004 Solucient LLC, a national organization that examines health care quality statistics, included Danbury Hospital in its "Top 100 Hospitals: National Benchmarks for Success" report. Among its vast services the hospital houses a Level II trauma center, a cancer center, and physical rehabilitation. Other hospitals in the area include New Milford Hospital; Pope John Paul II Center for Health Care; and a number of private-sector health complexes.

Recreation

Sightseeing

Danbury's most famous sight is the Danbury Museum and Historical Society which includes two historic buildings, 1785 Rider House and 1790 John Dodd Hat Shop. Rider House, former home of a carpenter and cabinetmaker, displays tools and period furnishings. Dodd Hat Shop recreates the early and modern hatting history of the city. Danbury is the birthplace of composer Charles Ives, whose house has been fully restored and is open to the public. The Tarrywile Park and Mansion offers 21 miles of hiking, nature workshops, and special events on its 654-acre historic building and land preserve. The Military Museum of Southern New England, opened in 1985, displays an extensive collection of anti-tank weapons and World War II military vehicles. Artifacts of railroad history can be viewed at the Danbury Railway Museum, located in the restored Danbury Union Station. Vintage railroad equipment is on view in the adjacent rail yard and railroad excursions are available. Stew Leonard's unique dairy-grocery store is listed in the Guinness Book of Records and was once dubbed by the *New York Times* as "the Disneyland of dairy stores."

An immense monument at Wooster Cemetery commemorates the contributions of General David Wooster, whose hero's death in the American Revolution battle to remove the British from Danbury is said to have been the highlight of his military career. The composer Charles Ives is also buried there.

Arts and Culture

Visitors to Danbury are entertained by a variety of musical concerts performed at the Charles Ives Center for the Arts at Western Connecticut State University, most commonly during the summer months. The center presents a seasonal schedule of world-renowned artists, pop, jazz, and folk stars. Concerts are presented at the Danbury Music Centre (DMC) in Marian Anderson Recital Hall. It is the home to Danbury's symphony, string, and community orchestras along with a concert chorus. The Wooster Community Art Center

The John and Mary Rider House displays carpentry tools and period furnishings.

(WCAC) provides visual art classes and monthly fine art exhibits year-round.

The Danbury Theatre Company performs in the St. James Church Auditorium while the Berkshire Theatre is located on the Western Connecticut State University campus. Musicals at Richter (MAR) holds the title of the state's longest-running outdoor theater and presents three shows during the summer at Richter Art Center.

Festivals and Holidays

Danbury celebrates the Fourth of July with music and fireworks at the Charles Ives Center for the Arts at Western Connecticut State University. CityCenter Danbury has its annual ''Summertime Festival'' for six weeks from mid-July to the end of August featuring orchestra performances, theatrical productions, family shows, and a eclectic set of musical concerts. Food is the focus during ''Taste of Greater Danbury,'' held on CityCenter Green in September. For Halloween at the Danbury Railway Museum visitors can ride a vintage train to select a pumpkin from their special pumpkin patch; CityCenter also hosts a celebration with music and children's games. Christmastime kicks off with a downtown holiday tree lighting ceremony and the traditional Nutcracker Ballet performance at the Danbury Music Centre (DMC) along with a Santa train ride at the Danbury Railway Museum. Rounding out the year is First Night Danbury, a non-alcoholic family celebration held on New Year's Eve.

Sports for the Spectator

The minor league hockey team, the Danbury Trashers, began play in fall 2004 for the United Hockey League (UHL) and plays from October through May at the new Danbury Ice Arena, constructed in 2001. The athletics department at Western Connecticut State University brings the area a wide variety of sports to view. Among the 14 intercollegiate programs are football and men's and women's basketball, soccer, and volleyball. All are part of the National Collegiate Athletic Association's (NCAA) Division III and the Eastern College Athletic Conference (ECAC) while the football team belongs to the New Jersey Athletic Conference.

Sports for the Participant

The Housatonic River, located near Danbury, is noted for the scenic beauty to be seen along its shores, and fishing for trout and salmon on the river is a popular pastime. Fishing is also done at Lake Kenosia. While much of the 5,420-acre Candlewood Lake's shore property (60 miles) is privately owned, public beaches and marinas are located lake. Created in 1929, it is one of the country's largest manmade lakes and represents the state's largest body of water. Squantz Pond recreation area, located about 10 miles north of Danbury, offers facilities for picnickers, anglers, boaters, hikers,

swimmers, bicyclists, and winter sports enthusiasts. Wooster Mountain State Park offers part of its site to skeet shooters; the remainder of the undeveloped area is open for wilderness walks.

Richter Park offers an 18-hole golf course along with hiking while the 58-acre Rogers Park has baseball and softball fields, tennis courts, and children's playgrounds. Ice skating is available at the Danbury Ice Arena for adult and children's hockey leagues, public skating, and classes.

Shopping and Dining

Danbury's largest shopping center is also New England's largest, a mall known as Danbury Fair, and offers more than 240 shops and many restaurants on the 200-acre site of the former Danbury Fairgrounds. The mall presents an Antiques and Collectibles Show in May; other such shows are scheduled in the city throughout the year. Meeker's Hardware store in Danbury is the only hardware store on the National Register of Historic Places.

The small towns and rural areas surrounding Danbury are famous for antiques and art galleries selling the works of local artists. Crafts and casual clothing may also be found.

Danbury's restaurants cover a wide range from casual bistros, steakhouses, and seafood restaurants, to a variety of ethnic establishments serving Italian, Thai, Lebanese, Chinese, Greek, Hungarian, Dominican, and Columbian cuisine with about 20 establishments in the downtown area.

Visitor Information: The Northwest CT Convention & Visitors Bureau, PO Box 968, Litchfield, CT 06813; telephone (860)567-4506; fax (860)567-5214; email info@litchfieldhills.com

Convention Facilities

Danbury offers meeting space for small groups in a number of modern hotels, including the Holiday Inn Danbury with space for 10 to 300 people in 7 different rooms and the Ethan Allen Hotel with 15,000 square feet of meeting space with accommodations for groups up to 500 guests. The surrounding area is famous for its country inns located in renovated Victorian mansions, colonial homes, and other historic structures.

Convention Information: The Northwest CT Convention & Visitors Bureau, PO Box 968, Litchfield, CT 06813; telephone (860)567-4506; fax (860)567-5214; email info@litchfieldhills.com

Transportation

Approaching the City

The Danbury Municipal Airport, the second busiest in the state, offers general aviation services on its two runways and includes charter services, plane rentals, and hangar space. The closest major commercial airports are John F. Kennedy International and LaGuardia (both in New York City, about 65 miles away), and Newark Liberty International Airport (Newark, New Jersey). The state's largest airport is Bradley International (Windsor Locks) that saw 6.7 million passengers in 2004. Stewart International Airport in Newburgh, NY is also nearby and accessible via westbound I-84. Metro-North carries rail passengers and commuters.

Traveling in the City

The Housatonic Area Regional Transit (HART) system operates a growing network of buses. Established in 1972, it provides 15 fixed routes, paratransit services for 5 municipalities, dial-a-ride, commuter shuttle services, and a downtown trolley.

Communications

Newspapers and Magazines

Danbury's daily newspaper, the *News-Times,* is published in the morning. Scholastic Library Publishing, parent of imprints Grolier, Children's Press, Franklin Watts, and Grolier Online, publishes *The Encyclopedia Americana,* (Grolier) and maintains its international headquarters in Danbury.

Television and Radio

The formats of the three FM radio stations that broadcast from Danbury include religious, adult contemporary, and new music programming. Connecticut Radio Information Service (CRIS), with a studio in Danbury along with other locations across the state, broadcasts readings from daily newspapers and magazines for the benefit of state residents who are blind or cannot hold or turn pages.

Media Information: News-Times, 333 Main St., Danbury, CT 06810-5818; telephone (203)744-5100; fax (203)798-0209; email editor@newstimes.com

Danbury Online

City of Danbury home page. Available www.ci.danbury.ct .us

Connecticut Development Authority. Available www.ctcda .com

Danbury Community Network. Available www.danbury.org

Danbury Museum and Historical Society. Available www .danburyhistorical.org

Danbury Public Library. Available www.danburylibrary.org

Danbury Public Schools. Available www.danbury.k12.ct.us

Housatonic Valley Economic Development Partnership. Available www.newtown.k12.ct.us/~hvedp

News-Times, home page. Available www.newstimeslive .com

Selected Bibliography

Brown, Drollone P., *Sybil Rides for Independence* (Niles, Ill.: A. Whitman, 1985)

Hill, Susan B., History of Danbury, Connecticut (Heritage Books: 1998)

Hartford

The City in Brief

Founded: 1637 (incorporated,1784)

Head Official: Mayor Eddie A. Perez (since 2001)

City Population
   1980: 136,392
   1990: 139,739
   2000: 121,578
   2003 estimate: 124,387
   Percent change, 1990–2000: −13%
   U.S. rank in 1980: 117th
   U.S. rank in 1990: 127th
   U.S. rank in 2000: 200th (State rank: 2nd)

Metropolitan Area Population (PMSA)
   1990: 1,157,585
   2000: 1,183,110
   Percent change, 1990–2000: 2.2%
   U.S. rank in 1980: 35th (NECMA)

U.S. rank in 1990: 35th (NECMA)
U.S. rank in 2000: 41st (NECMA)

Area: 18 square miles (2000)
Elevation: Ranges from sea level to 294 feet above sea level
Average Annual Temperature: 49.8° F
Average Annual Precipitation: 44.1 inches of rain; 49 inches of snow

Major Economic Sectors: Services, trade, government, manufacturing, and finance, insurance, and real estate
Unemployment Rate: 5.5% (March 2005)
Per Capita Income: $13,528 (1999)
2004 ACCRA Average House Price: $372,383
2004 ACCRA Cost of Living Index: 122.1

2002 FBI Crime Index Total: 10,870

Major Colleges and Universities: Trinity College; Hartford Seminary; University of Hartford; University of Connecticut Law School

Daily Newspaper: *The Hartford Courant*

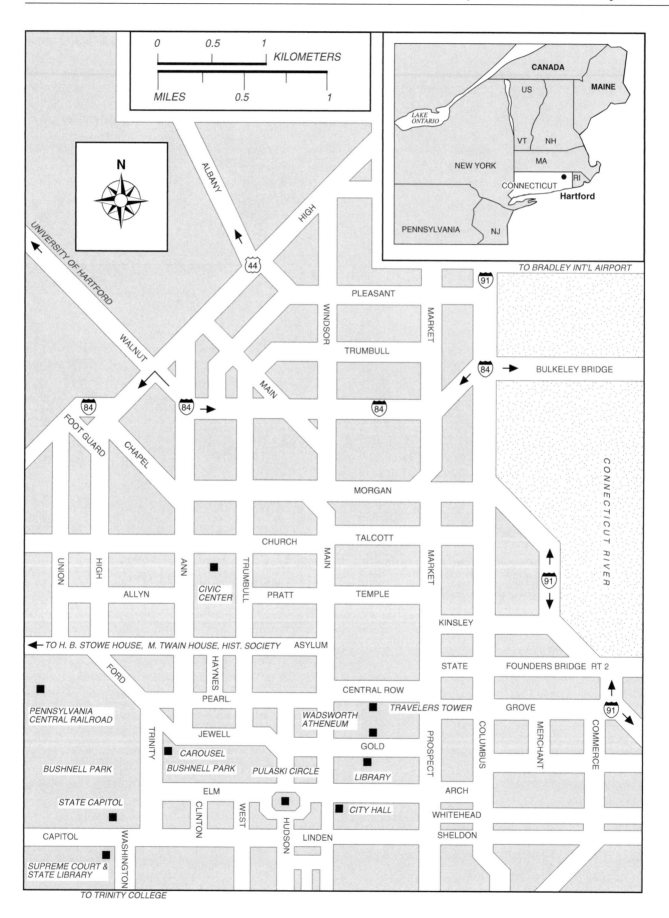

Introduction

Hartford, Connecticut's state capital and second largest city, is known as "the insurance capital of the world." Hartford's early citizens drafted the nation's first state constitution, and later inhabitants added to the city's manufacturing prestige with many innovative products and processes. Currently, Hartford is enjoying an influx of development projects and has been recognized nationally as an attractive site for businesses. With its historic architecture and traditional cultivation of arts and culture, combined with its focus on education and economic development, Hartford has become a balanced and diverse modern city.

Geography and Climate

Hartford, located in Hartford County in the center of Connecticut, is midway between New York City to the south and Boston, Massachusetts, to the north. The entire city is contained within the fertile Connecticut River Valley. Poised on a rise above the west side of the Connecticut River, the city of Hartford is set among a gently rolling landscape with extensive level areas. Hartford, at the head of the navigable portion of the river, has been a major inland port of entry.

Hartford's mild climate is typical of New England, neither very hot in the summer nor extremely cold in the winter. Storm activity building up in and moving eastward from the Berkshire Mountains, a northern branch of the Appalachian chain, accounts for the city's many summer thunderstorms. The Atlantic Ocean to the south contributes the famous wind and rain storms known locally as northeasters.

Area: 18 square miles (2000)

Elevation: Ranges from sea level to 294 feet above sea level; mean elevation is 147 feet

Average Temperatures: January, 25.1° F; July, 73.7° F; annual average, 49.8° F

Average Annual Precipitation: 44.1 inches of rain; 49 inches of snow

History

Connecticut Valley Draws New Settlers

Before settlers of European descent sailed to North America, the tribes of the Algonquin Federation had exploited the Connecticut River Valley's rich black soil to grow food crops. They called the area "Suckiaug," or black earth. The Algonquins also traveled the Connecticut River, establishing it early as an important trade route. When Adrien Block, a Dutchman working for the Dutch West Indies Company, became the first white man to explore the region in 1614, he found many prosperous Native American communities. In 1633, following a European epidemic that destroyed a majority of the native population, the Dutch colonists from New Amsterdam established a trading post on the river and built a fort on the site of modern-day Hartford. A few years later, English colonists seeking relief from the religiously oppressive Massachusetts Bay Colony drove the Dutch from their fort and renamed the settlement Hartford, after Hertford, England. It was the Dutch who inadvertently coined the term "Yankee," which has become synonymous with people and things native to New England. The Dutch called the invading English "Jankes" or "Johns," a term meaning robber or pirate. The Dutch pronunciation was quickly Anglicized and adopted into common usage.

The English colonists' leader, the Reverend Thomas Hooker, commissioned the writing of a document called the Fundamental Orders in 1639. The document was colonial North America's first constitution drawn up with the consent of the people it governed and served as a model for the U.S. Constitution. Hartford Colony then absorbed the town of New Haven and they shared the title of state capital until Hartford became the sole capital in 1873.

In 1662, Connecticut Governor John Winthrop traveled to England to request a royal charter from England's King Charles II. The charter, which superseded the Fundamental Orders, was so generous that James II, upon his succession to the British throne, wanted to revoke it. James sent Sir Edmond Adros to seize the charter but, according to legend, the document disappeared under mysterious circumstances and was hidden by patriots in the Charter Oak.

Industry, Innovation, Culture Shape Hartford

In the years prior to the American Revolution, Hartford changed from an agrarian to a mercantile society. Its shops bustled while its port throbbed with activity as ships laden with treasures from the Orient and Indies docked. It was this wealth of commercial activity that prompted the growth of Hartford as an insurance capital. Prosperous merchants, fearing the loss of the cargoes stored in warehouses along the river, subscribed to The Hartford Fire Insurance Company. Hartford's preeminence as a whaling town grew simultaneously.

When colonists eventually took up arms to win independence from England, Revolutionary General George Washington chose Jeremiah Wadsworth, a Hartford munitions merchant, as his chief of supplies. Following the war, the first woolen mill in New England was established in Hartford in 1788 and wove the cloth for President George Washington's inaugural suit. Hartford soon entered the publishing industry, producing the first American juvenile publication in 1789 and the first cookbook in 1796. The first dental gold was used in Hartford in 1812. In 1817, the first American School for the Deaf was founded. Other Hartford "firsts" included the invention and manufacture of the revolver in 1836, of oil cloth in 1837, and of machine-made watches in 1838. The first use of nitrous oxide as an anesthetic took place in Hartford in 1844, the year the city's Wadsworth Atheneum opened as the nation's first public art museum.

A Hartford native, Harriet Beecher Stowe, wrote *Uncle Tom's Cabin,* an anti-slavery novel published in 1852; the book helped speed the eruption of the Civil War. Prior to the war, Hartford was an important abolitionist site and a stop on the Underground Railroad, the route for escaping slaves. During the war, Hartford supplied arms to the Union Army. The city's largest industrial operation, Samuel Colt's Colt Patent Firearms Manufacturing Company, was a pioneer in the use of interchangeable parts for mass production. Colt's theories helped lay the foundation of the modern assembly line. In 1863 the first American accident life insurance policy was issued and Hartford furthered its progress toward becoming the world's insurance capital. Author Mark Twain settled in Hartford about this time, taking advantage of the city's flourishing publishing industry. Some six million books yearly were published in Hartford before New York took over as the East Coast publishing capital in the 1890s.

Citizenry Grows, Faces New Challenges

Hartford's population in the late nineteenth century swelled with the arrival of European and Canadian immigrants and southern African Americans eager to work in its mills and factories. The country's first bicycle plant was built in Hartford in 1877. The friction clutch was invented in Hartford in 1885, followed by the first standard measuring machine, accurate to .00001 inch, developed by Hartford's Pratt and Whitney company. Other innovations conceived in Hartford brought the city and nation into the modern age: the pay telephone in 1895, the first automobile insurance policy in 1897, and the first legislation to regulate motor traffic speed in 1901. More manufacturing innovations came from the Hartford enterprises in the first decades of the twentieth century. During World War II, Hartford industry developed a production-model radar set; the city was a major military production center throughout the war.

In the 1950s and 1960s, Hartford experienced a substantial loss of population as the middle class followed the expressways to the suburbs. Hartford's population peaked in 1950 at 177,397. As agriculture declined in the area, former farm workers, including Puerto Ricans and southern African Americans, were left in urban poverty. Ghettos developed along Hartford's old East Side. In 1968, following the assassination of Dr. Martin Luther King, Jr., the city's predominantly African American north end erupted in riots.

Hartford's city leaders responded quickly, launching massive urban renewal efforts. Constitutional Plaza, completed in 1964, includes office buildings, a hotel, a shopping mall, and research facilities. Bushnell Plaza followed, with the Hartford Civic Center opening in 1975. Older deteriorating neighborhoods began receiving attention in the 1970s and 1980s, helping attract residents back into the city. In 1981, Thirman L. Milner became the first African American mayor of Hartford and the first in any New England city. In 1987 Hartford's Carrie Saxon Perry became the first African American woman to be elected mayor of a New England city. Current Hartford mayor Eddie Perez, born in Puerto Rico, continues Hartford's tradition of diversity among government officials.

In the 1990's, Hartford experienced massive population loss and suffered from problems with crime and gangs. Since the end of that decade, however, Hartford has seen its population stabilize. Mayor Perez has dedicated himself to the continued revitalization of the Hartford area. Under his leadership, the city has developed a Neighborhood Policing Plan to augment the safety of Hartford neighborhoods. Hartford has also committed itself to improving the city's educational structure by investing $800 million into city schools during the first decade of the 2000's. Hartford's educated workforce and abundance of opportunities for development have made it an increasingly attractive setting for business, an attraction city leaders hope will help Hartford thrive in the decades to come.

Historical Information: Connecticut Historical Society, 1 Elizabeth Street, Hartford, CT 06105; telephone (860)236-5621

Population Profile

Metropolitan Area Residents (NECMA)
1990: 1,157,585
2000: 1,183,110
Percent change, 1990–2000: 2.2%
U.S. rank in 1980: 35th (CMSA)
U.S. rank in 1990: 35th (NECMA)
U.S. rank in 2000: 41st (NECMA)

City Residents
1980: 136,392
1990: 139,739
2000: 121,578

2003 estimate: 124,387

Percent change, 1990–2000: − 13%

U.S. rank in 1980: 117th

U.S. rank in 1990: 127th

U.S. rank in 2000: 200th (State rank: 2nd)

Density: 7,025.5 people per square mile (2000)

Racial and ethnic characteristics (2000)
 White: 33,705
 Black or African American: 46,264
 American Indian and Alaska Native: 659
 Asian: 1,971
 Native Hawaiian and Pacific Islander: 135
 Hispanic or Latino (may be of any race): 49,260
 Other: 32,230

Percent of residents born in state: 44.3% (2000)

Age characteristics (2000)
 Population under 5 years old: 10,116
 Population 5 to 9 years old: 10,764
 Population 10 to 14 years old: 9,959
 Population 15 to 19 years old: 10,341
 Population 20 to 24 years old: 10,689
 Population 25 to 34 years old: 18,801
 Population 35 to 44 years old: 17,398
 Population 45 to 54 years old: 13,342
 Population 55 to 59 years old: 4,723
 Population 60 to 64 years old: 3,875
 Population 65 to 74 years old: 5,935
 Population 75 to 84 years old: 4,015
 Population 85 years and over: 1,638
 Median age: 29.7 years

Births (2001)
 Total number: 2,224

Deaths (2001)
 Total number: 1,063 (of which, 30 were infants under
  the age of 1 year)

Money income (1999
 Per capita income: $13,428
 Median household income: $24,820
 Total households: 45,036

Number of households with income of . . .
 less than $10,000: 10,524
 $10,000 to $14,999: 4,560
 $15,000 to $24,999: 7,549
 $25,000 to $34,999: 6,246
 $35,000 to $49,999: 6,559
 $50,000 to $74,999: 5,567
 $75,000 to $99,999: 2,210
 $100,000 to $149,999: 1,112
 $150,000 to $199,999: 284
 $200,000 or more: 425

Percent of families below poverty level: 28.2% (49.2% of
 which were female householder families with related
 children under 5 years)

2002 FBI Crime Index Total: 10,870

Municipal Government

Hartford operates with a council-manager form of government. The nine council members and mayor are elected every two years in partisan elections. The day-to-day running of the city is left to the city manager; the council sets policy. The city, which is also the state capital, houses the state government buildings and legislature.

Head Official: Mayor Eddie A. Perez (since 2001; current term expires 2005)

Total Number of City Employees: Not reported

City Information: Mayor's Office, City of Hartford, 550 Main Street, Hartford, CT 06103; telephone (860)522-4888; fax (860)722-6606

Economy

Major Industries and Commercial Activity

Metropolitan Hartford's strong economy is based on a diverse business and industrial community. The area ranks number one in the world in gross domestic product per capita and number two in the world in labor productivity. Long a powerful insurance and financial center, it also boasts an extensive list of major high-tech manufacturing firms producing such complex products as aircraft engines, nuclear reactors, space suits, and missile components. The city is also a major data processing and telecommunications center. Other industries thriving in the area include health care and retail. With employees working in the state capitol building, the legislature, libraries, and the Supreme Court, government is another major economic sector. Hartford's physical location is a prime asset, as the city is located within 100 miles of both New York and Boston and offers access to 100 million consumers within an 8-hour drive. Additionally, Hartford is gaining a reputation as one of the nation's most wired cities, which has been an important factor in the attraction of information-oriented businesses.

Long known as the Insurance Capital of the World, MetroHartford is home to seven major insurance firms:

Aetna Inc., Travelers Property Casualty Corp., MassMutual, The Hartford Financial Services Group, CIGNA, The Phoenix Companies, and The United Health Care Company.

The area's manufacturing sector includes many *Fortune* 500 corporations and large multinational organizations. Among the best known are the Barnes Group and United Technologies Corporation, its divisions Hamilton Sundstrand and Pratt & Whitney, along with its subsidiary Otis Elevator. Henkel Loctite Corporation has its world headquarters in MetroHartford. Stanley tools and hardware are produced in the region, as are the famed Colt firearms. Still, the region's backbone are the small- to mid-size businesses, which enjoy an excellent outlook for success in the early years of the century. Recently ranked number 17 nationally in the top 40 markets for business expansion, Hartford provides a fertile environment for small-business growth.

Items and goods produced: jet engines and aerospace products; fiber optics; chemicals; biomedical pharmaceutical products

Incentive Programs—New and Existing Companies

Future success for Hartford's new and expanding businesses is boosted by an aggressive program of business incubators, and by economic incentive and financial assistance packages made available through federal, state and local government and area educational facilities. Connecticut's financial and tax incentives include grants and tax abatements for firms locating in State Enterprise Zones and the Urban Jobs Program, which provides benefits for eligible projects in Targeted Investment Communities, as well as low-cost loans and development bond financing, and funding for new product development.

The MetroHartford Alliance seeks to provide leadership in order to enable the region to fulfill opportunities related to economic growth. The Alliance pursues this goal through financing and consulting services for export-minded small businesses, through services offered to international companies seeking to locate in the area, and through working cooperatively with all parts of the region on issues vital to their common economic health. The Chamber cites as Hartford's advantages its comparatively low business costs, strategic location, availability of business services, good transportation network, and an educated work force. In recent years, Alliance projects have included efforts to retain graduates of Hartford-area colleges to the region, implementation of a marketing and communications strategy, and expanding the Small Business Task Force.

Local programs—A variety of incentives for new and existing businesses are offered through the new Hartford Economic Development Commission. Among them are employment tax credits, tax credits for co-op employees and

apprentices, assessment fixing, manufacturing personal property tax exemptions, and various other tax credits. A range of incentives are offered to businesses who locate or expand in the city's Enterprise Zone. The Growth Fund provides below-market-rate loans to help area companies add jobs. Financing is tied to the number of jobs created, and helps cover the difference between the bank loan and the actual project costs. Eligible projects include site acquisition, road work, remediation, and machinery.

State programs—The Connecticut Development Authority works to expand Connecticut's business base by working with private-sector partners to guarantee or participate in loans for businesses that may be unable to meet credit underwriting standards; providing access to lower-cost fixed asset financing through Small Business Administration 504 Debentures and tax-exempt Industrial Revenue Bonds; working to provide financial incentives to companies that enhance the skills of their employees; encouraging investment in the state's urban commercial infrastructure; providing grants and financing for businesses willing to develop areas plagued by environmental scourge; and by providing funding for companies interested in pursuing advances in information technology.

Job training programs—Capital Workforce Partners, established under the Workforce Investment Act, provides programs to assist in the development of a skilled and educated workforce. Regional CEOs oversee CWP. CWP operates six career centers through the region, each of which provides a full range of employment services, including job referral, career workshops, training, and financial aid opportunities. Employers also benefit from CWP's services, as they can receive assistance in areas such as recruitment, screening, and information on tax credit programs. The University of Connecticut Greater Hartford Campus is the designated Small Business Development Center (SBDC) for Hartford, serving start-up and small businesses. SBDCs offer technical and management assistance, counseling, education, and training programs.

Development Projects

One of Hartford's most important development projects is the 30-acre Adriaen's Landing site on the Connecticut River. The centerpiece of the project is the 540,000 square foot Connecticut Convention Center, the largest between New York and Boston. Attached to the convention center is a 22-story Marriott Hotel. Boardwalks connect the convention center with Constitution Plaza and with Riverfront Recapture, another recent Hartford development project which has reclaimed riverfront properties for parks and recreational spaces. Future developments at the site include the Connecticut Center for Science and Exploration and a residential and retail district.

The Hartford 21 project, another major development in the city, has begun a rejuvenation of the downtown neighborhoods near the Hartford Civic Center complex. One of the features of Hartford 21 is New England's largest residential tower. The project, when completed, will eliminate decaying infrastructure near the Civic Center and replace it with a 24-hour neighborhood with integrated retail, residential, and entertainment facilities.

In 2003, Rentschler field opened in East Hartford. Located on a former airfield donated by the Pratt & Whitney Corporation, the facility serves as a home field for University of Connecticut football as well as other entertainment and sporting events. Capital Community College has expanded into new space made available by the renovation of the historic G. Fox building, and has seen enrollment increase in this new 304,000 square foot space. Expansions are also in the works for the University of Hartford, where a new Performing Arts Center, Integrated Science, Engineering, and Technology complex, and new athletic fields are planned. The Blue Back Square project in West Hartford, scheduled for completion in 2006, promises 550,000 square feet of offices, luxury condominiums, and retail space. In the city of Hartford, work is underway on restoration of all buildings on the 110-acre Colt Gateway site. Commercial, residential, and light industrial space will be available when the project is completed. The Wadsworth Atheneum Museum of Art has raised $43 million for intended renovations and developments, including expansion to increase exhibit space and amenities.

Economic Development Information: MetroHartford Alliance, 31 Pratt Street, 5th Floor, Hartford, CT 06103; telephone (860)525-4451; fax (860)293-2592. Hartford Economic Development Commission, 11 Asylum St., Suite 501, Hartford, CT 06103; telephone (860)524-0725

Commercial Shipping

Hartford, New England's second busiest retail market, benefits from its location on the Connecticut River and at the apex of several major interstate highways. The Connecticut River can accommodate barge and coastal tanker traffic; the river and two major interstate highways give Greater Hartford quick and direct access to commercial ports in New Haven, Bridgeport, and New London, with a convenient sea link to the Port of New York. Greater Hartford has benefitted from the state's $6.5 billion highway improvement program, which took place throughout the 1990s. Freight rail service is provided by Boston and Maine Corp. and Consolidated Rail Corp. Bradley International Airport, 15 miles north of the city, handles 140,000 tons of air cargo each year. The airport offers a new terminal and concourse, as well as roadway and viaduct improvements in the vicinity of the airport. Facilities are available for corporate and

private aircraft, as is warehouse space for cargo processing. The Hartford-Brainard Airport provides freight service. Hartford Despatch International, based in East Hartford, is considered one of the country's foremost movers of commodities.

Labor Force and Employment Outlook

Despite mergers, consolidations, and downsizing towards the end of the 1990's, one in ten jobs in Hartford is still provided by businesses in the insurance and financial services industry. As the region's economy has diversified, members of Hartford's well-educated workforce have found employment in the many companies capitalizing on technological advancement. Precision instruments, computers, and electrical equipment are all produced in the Hartford area. Aerospace, information technology, and healthcare all look to be promising sectors for Hartford's future.

The following is a summary of data regarding the Hartford area labor force, 2004 annual averages.

Size of nonagricultural labor force: 537,600

Number of workers employed in . . .
   construction and mining: 21,100
   manufacturing: 64,100
   trade, transportation, and utilities: 88,700
   information: 11,300
   financial activities: 68,000
   professional and business services: 57,100
   educational and health services: 83,800
   leisure and hospitality: 37,800
   other services: 20,700
   government: 85,000

Average hourly earnings of production workers employed in manufacturing: $20.08

Unemployment rate: 5.5% (March 2005)

Largest employers (2004)	*Number of employees*
State of Connecticut	(no employee
Aetna Life & Casualty Company	figures available)
The Hartford	
Travelers Insurance Company	
Hartford Hospital	

Cost of Living

The following is a summary of data regarding key cost of living factors for the Hartford area.

2004 (3rd Quarter) ACCRA Average House Price: $372,383

2004 (3rd Quarter) ACCRA Cost of Living Index: 122.1 (U.S. average = 100.0)

State income tax rate: 3% to 5%

State sales tax rate: 6% for most items

Local income tax rate: None

Local sales tax rate: None

Property tax rate: 48 mills per thousand (due to state legislative relief, residential properties consisting of 1-3 units are taxed substantially lower)

Economic Information: MetroHartford Alliance, 31 Pratt Street, 5th Floor, Hartford, CT 06103; telephone (860)525-4451

Education and Research

Elementary and Secondary Schools

The Hartford Public School District is the second largest district in New England behind Boston, and the largest in Connecticut. A recent partnership of local business, the community, and the schools has brought about curriculum changes that include the addition of apprenticeship programs, a magnet school, advanced courses in science and math technology and a strong emphasis on creative problem solving to encourage career readiness. Hartford's expenditures on its schools have increased exponentially in recent years, and local government seems dedicated to continuing the upward trend. Still, test scores lag below state and national averages, although some improvement has been demonstrated.

The following is a summary of data regarding the Hartford Public Schools District as of the 2002–2003 school year.

Total enrollment: 22,734

Number of facilities
  elementary schools: 29
  junior high/middle schools: 4
  senior high schools: 4
  other: 1

Student/teacher ratio: 12.4:1

Teacher salaries
  median: $49,968

Funding per pupil: $15,635

The array of private and parochial schools in the region includes Miss Porter's School in Farmington (where actor Katharine Hepburn matriculated), the Watkinson School and Kingswood-Oxford in West Hartford, and the American School for the Deaf, also in West Hartford.

Public Schools Information: Superintendent, Hartford Public Schools, 8th Floor, 153 Market St., Hartford, CT 06103; telephone (860)527-0742

Colleges and Universities

Greater Hartford is home to a number of liberal arts and technical two- and four-year schools, including the University of Hartford, offering 86 undergraduate majors and 32 graduate programs in seven schools; Trinity College, founded in 1823, the second-oldest college in the state after Yale; Capital Community-Technical College; the six-unit complex of St. Joseph College, which includes the state's only four-year women's college; Tunxis Community College; Rensselaer at Hartford, a graduate study institute offering Master's degrees and graduate certificates; Hartford Seminary (interdenominational); and The University of Connecticut's schools of law, social work, medicine, and dentistry are also located there. The university's main branch in Storrs is 35 miles east of Hartford.

Libraries and Research Centers

The Hartford Public Library, founded in 1774, contains 573,000 volumes; its main library building straddles a below-ground-level expressway. This facility houses the Hartford Collection, consisting of works published in Hartford, by Hartford authors, or about the city. The Caroline M. Hewins Early Children's Book Collection is also found at the main library. The library system consists of the main library, nine branch libraries, and one bookmobile. A major renovation and expansion project was recently completed at the Central Library, adding 44,000 square feet of new space, a glass bridge on the pre-existing ground floor spanning the highway, and an entirely new wing.

The Connecticut State Library, housed with the State Supreme Court near the Capitol, provides extensive local historical and genealogical information. Among other artifacts, the 1662 Charter of the Colony of Connecticut is displayed at the State Library. Noted for its collection of 170,000 books and nearly 3 million manuscripts on Connecticut history and genealogy is the Connecticut Historical Society Library, which also features collections of prints and photographs, furniture, costumes and textiles, toys, and tools. Trinity College Library is known for its collection of classics and scholarly journals. The Historical Museum of Medicine and Dentistry maintains a library as well as manuscripts pertaining to the history of anesthesia.

Other Hartford research centers are the Duncan Black Macdonald Center for the Study of Islam and Christian/Muslim Relations at the Hartford Seminary, which is engaged in collecting data about mosques in the United States and Christian centers in developing Muslim nations, and the Hartford Center for Social and Religious Research. Research at the University of Connecticut in Storrs covers such topics as the environment, materials science, and computer applications.

Public Library Information: Hartford Public Library, 500 Main Street, Hartford, CT 06103; telephone (860)695-6300; fax (860)722-6900; email webmaster@hartfordpl.lib.ct.us

Health Care

A major health care provider for the Hartford region is Hartford Hospital, which has satellite health centers in addition to its main Hartford campus. The Hartford campus has 867 beds and 972 active staff physicians. The Institute of Living, a private psychiatric facility which was one of the first mental health facilities in the United States, is now associated with Hartford Hospital. The hospital is affiliated with the University of Connecticut School of Medicine. St. Francis Care is a 617-bed regional health care provider also affiliated with the University of Connecticut. Other area facilities include the John Dempsey Hospital/University of Connecticut Health Center, Connecticut Children's Medical Center (the only independent hospital in Connecticut exclusively serving children), and the Institute of Living, a private psychiatric facility.

Health Care Information: Hartford County Medical Association; telephone (203)699-2400. Connecticut State Dental Association; telephone (860)278-5550

Recreation

Sightseeing

Downtown Hartford combines Yankee colonialism with a modern business atmosphere. Historic Hartford attractions include the State Capitol atop Capital Hill. With its gold dome, gray Connecticut marble walls, and soaring arches, the capitol, which opened in 1879, is considered an architectural gem. The state legislature continues to meet in the building's chambers. Inside, memorabilia of Connecticut history include Revolutionary War hero the Marquis de Lafayette's camp bed, Civil War battle flags, ships' figureheads, and tombstones. The Old State House, the oldest in the nation, was designed by noted architect Charles Bulfinch and has been completely restored. The homes of authors Mark Twain and

Harriet Beecher Stowe have been restored and contain many original furnishings. The Butler-McCook Homestead offers a view of Victoriana, complete with paintings, silver, toys, and a backyard garden. The Isham Terry house, built in 1854 for a Hartford businessman, was designed in the Italian Vila style; its fixtures and decor have been carefully preserved. The bell in the steeple at First Church of Christ (1807) contains portions of the bell brought to Hartford by English colonists fleeing Massachusetts in 1636. Adjacent to the church is the Ancient Burying Ground, where lie the city's early leaders near Carl Andre's controversial 36-boulder "Stone Field" sculpture. Self-guided walking tours of Hartford's historic sites are available.

The home of a Hartford insurance company, The Travelers Tower, is New England's oldest skyscraper. A landmark since 1936, the tower offers a panoramic view of the Connecticut River Valley. The observation deck is open to visitors on weekdays. Aetna Insurance's headquarters on Farmington Avenue is the largest colonial brick structure in the United States. St. Joseph's Cathedral, with its huge stained-glass windows, is an example of contemporary ecclesiastical architecture. The Phoenix is housed in a boat-shaped structure thought to be the world's only two-sided building. The glass and steel structure is now connected to downtown's Riverfront Plaza. The Menczer Museum of Medicine & Dentistry displays instruments and medications used for the past two centuries. Pictures and artifacts pertaining to the 134-year history of the Police Department are on exhibit at the Hartford Police Museum.

Bushnell Park, adjacent to the state capitol, boasts a 1914 carousel with a Wurlitzer organ and 48 intricately carved and painted wooden horses. The park, designed by Frederick Law Olmstead, is reputed to be America's oldest public park. Within the park is the Pump House Gallery, site of many summer concerts; Veterans' Memorial Arch; Corning Fountain, celebrating the Native-American heritage; and a number of sculptural pieces. "Stegosaurus," a statute by Alexander Calder, is located between the Wadsworth Atheneum and City Hall. Elizabeth Park Rose Gardens contains thousands of common and rare plants, some in carefully landscaped beds and others in greenhouses. Another popular tourist attraction is the Connecticut River cruise aboard a restored steam-powered yacht.

Arts and Culture

For years, perhaps because of its corporate financial support, Hartford has enjoyed a number of nationally renowned musical and performing arts groups. The Greater Hartford Symphony Orchestra, founded in 1934 as part of the Great Depression's Works Progress Administration, is considered one of the top 20 orchestras in the country. The symphony's repertoire includes at least one modern composition at each

Author Mark Twain's home in Hartford has been restored and is open to visitors.

concert at Bushnell Memorial Hall in downtown Hartford, and during summer concerts at Bushnell Park. Musical performances are also presented by the Hartford Pops and Hartford Jazz Society which offer summertime performances in Bushnell Park.

The Connecticut Opera Association, based in Hartford, puts on four annual productions at Bushnell Memorial Hall and features some of the finest voices in the world. Major popular music concerts ranging from rock to country are held at the Hartford Civic Center Coliseum. In addition, Bushnell Memorial Hall hosts visiting opera troupes and symphonies, off-Broadway productions, jazz, blues, and comedy performances. The Meadows Music Theatre, which provides a venue for concerts of various genres, is New England's only indoor and outdoor performing arts center.

Professional theater in Hartford revived with the advent of the Hartford Stage Company, the city's resident company and considered one of the nation's leading regional troupes. The Hartford Stage Company often premieres contemporary works by American and international playwrights during an October-June season. The Hartford Stage Company also puts on Summerstage, a series of three summer stock performances. Other theater groups include the Producing Guild and TheaterWorks.

The Wadsworth Atheneum, the country's oldest public art museum and highly ranked nationally, features exhibits ranging from pre-history to the present. Some of its 45,000 works are displayed in a special exhibit for the sight-impaired while others appear in changing exhibits of contemporary art. Major collections include Baroque art, Hudson River School landscapes, Meissen and Sevres porcelain, and early American decorative arts. The Atheneum presents more than 15 special shows each year. The Museum of Connecticut History in the State Library and Supreme Court Building focuses on the manufacture of firearms, while the Connecticut Historical Society Museum features changing exhibitions on the state's history in a beautiful old building on Elizabeth Street. The Historical Museum of Medicine and Dentistry includes an old-time dentist's office, along with exhibits of instruments and medicines.

Hartford's major art gallery, the Pump House Gallery, is maintained in a refurbished Victorian pump house in Bushnell Park. Works displayed include sculpture, pottery, paintings, photographs, and fabric creations. The Matrix Gallery at the Wadsworth Atheneum features revolving exhibits of contemporary art. Real Art Ways, a multi-disciplinary arts organization, promotes and supports contemporary artists. The gallery's home, a refurbished typewriter factory on Arbor Street, provides a venue for exhibitions, lectures, concerts, readings, and workshops, as well as housing a movie theater and lounge. Artworks Gallery, located on Pearl Street, is a nonprofit artists' cooperative that has repeatedly received the Hartford Courant's label of "Best Art Gallery." CRT Craftery Gallery is the most famous African American art gallery in the United States, while the Very Special Arts CT Gallery highlights the work of artists with disabilities.

Arts and Culture Information: Greater Hartford Arts Council, 48 Pratt Street, Hartford, CT 06103; telephone (860)525-8629

Festivals and Holidays

Bushnell Park is the site of the New England Fiddle Contest, held each May, circumstances permitting. The one-day event features old-time music and prizes. Rose Weekend occurs each year in mid-June, when the roses of the Elizabeth Park Rose Garden are in full bloom. The festival includes poetry readings, music, and activities for children. The Hartford Festival of Jazz plays each July in Bushnell Park. Along with three days of music by internationally renowned artists, the Festival includes foods and crafts. August's Mark Twain Days honor Twain's legacy and the city's cultural heritage through concerts, frog jumping contests, riverboat rides, storytelling and other events. Hartford's large West Indian population celebrates its culture in a colorful West Indian/Jamaican Festival in August. The Festa Italiana, an annual two-day neighborhood party with food, crafts, music, dancing, and entertainment, is held in September, as is the African American Freedom Trail Parade. The two-day Connecticut Antiques Show comes to Hartford in mid-March. Held in the Connecticut Expo Center, the show features eighteenth- and nineteenth-century furniture and accessories.

Special annual events in downtown Hartford include First Night Hartford, a family-oriented New Year's Eve celebration; A Taste of Hartford, featuring food prepared by local restaurateurs, in June; a Fourth of July RiverFest (involving activities on both sides of the Connecticut River); Kid'riffic, a festival for children held in September; and Hartford Holidays, beginning with the Festival of Light on the day after Thanksgiving.

Sports for the Spectator

Appearing at the Civic Center are the University of Connecticut's NCAA men's and women's basketball teams, both of which have recently won national titles. The University of Connecticut's varsity football team plays home games at Hartford's Rentschler Field. Other Hartford area colleges field athletic teams in many varsity and club sports.

The Hartford Wolfpack represent Hartford in the American Hockey League. The Wolfpack play at the Hartford Civic Center and are a player development team for the New York

Rangers. Minor league baseball is represented by the class AA New Britain Rock Cats. The Hartford Wanderers Rugby Football Team plays its matches at the Glastonbury Irish-American Home Society. Cromwell is the scene of the PGA's Buick Championship tournament, a nationally televised professional golf event held in late August. Hartford also has professional and amateur boxing, a cricket team, and an annual marathon. Hartford jai alai's season is year-round and parimutuel betting is permitted.

Sports for the Participant

Hartford's riverfront supports a thriving fish population. The city's fifty public parks and squares cover more than 27,000 acres, nearly one-fourth of the city's area, allowing many outdoor sports and recreation programs. More than a million people annually picnic, jog, attend rallies, and socialize at Hartford's restored Bushnell Park. Bushnell Park also offers summer Art in the Park walking tours, tours of the historic Memorial Arch, and carousel rides. Elizabeth Park features a 2.5-acre garden of more than 15,000 rose bushes. The park as a whole encompasses over 100 acres and has picnic areas, a pond, and recreation areas. Golf is played on two public courses in Hartford, one of which, in Keney Park, was recently named one of the best in the region. Its proximity to both mountain ski resorts and ocean beaches makes Hartford a year-round athletic attraction. Nearby state parks provide facilities for camping, hiking, picnicking, fishing, snowmobiling, and cross-country skiing. The Riverfront Recapture program has revitalized a number of recreational sites along the Connecticut River. Activities such as boating, fishing, mountain biking, and orienteering are available at the riverfront parks. Riverfront Recapture also hosts a summer youth program.

Shopping and Dining

Several retail centers in downtown Hartford are easily reached on foot. Currently, Hartford's Civic Center Mall is undergoing renovations and will be transformed into a more up-to-date home for retail, dining, and entertainment establishments. The completed mall will link up with the renovated Pratt Street neighborhood. Union Station, a refurbished landmark, features stores and restaurants. Other well-known downtown shopping areas are the Pavilion at State House Square; Pearl and Asylum streets; and Richardson Mall, housed in a building listed in the National Register of Historical Landmarks. The shopping and dining area is enhanced by the popular outdoor Main Street Markets, featuring farmers' market produce, imports, handcrafted items, baked goods and entertainment. Several large shopping malls are within a few minutes' drive from Hartford.

Dining opportunities in Hartford reflect the city's multiethnic make-up. Restaurant-goers can choose from European offerings ranging from French continental to Scandinavian, German, Polish, and Italian. Asian cuisine is also found, along with the native foods of Puerto Rico. Recent years have seen an influx of West Indians, who have opened bakeries and restaurants specializing in fare such as curried chicken, ackee, codfish, and sweet potato pie. Fresh fish from the Atlantic and traditional New England favorites such as chowder and baked beans are standard menu items in many restaurants.

Visitor Information: Greater Hartford Convention & Visitors Bureau, 31 Pratt Street, 4th Floor, Hartford, CT 06103; telephone (860)728-6789; toll-free (800)446-7811

Convention Facilities

The Connecticut Expo Center is located six-tenths of a mile from downtown Hartford. Its 138,000 square feet of exhibition space allows for multiple events with on-premise show management offices, and offers more than 425 10-foot by 10-foot booths.

The Hartford Civic Center, one of New England's largest convention complexes, includes the 16,500-seat Coliseum, along with 70,000 square feet of exhibit space and nine meeting rooms. The complex also features an enclosed shopping mall, restaurants, and underground parking. It is located about 11 miles from Bradley International Airport. The Civic Center has hosted events such as the Big East Conference Women's basketball tournament, rock concerts, and family shows.

Convention Information: Greater Hartford Convention and Visitors Bureau, 31 Pratt Street, 4th Floor, Hartford, CT 06103-1592; telephone (860)728-6789; toll-free (800)446-7811

Transportation

Approaching the City

Bradley International Airport, a medium-sized hub and regional facility, is located 12 miles north of downtown Hartford in Windsor Locks. The airport is the second busiest in New England and served over six million passengers in 2004. Twelve airlines serve the airport out of two terminals, one of which was recently completed. Bradley is currently in the process of completing further renovations, including the modernization of the older terminal, the addition of restaurant and retail space, and a revamped baggage system. Brainard-Hartford Airport, built in 1921 and located in the southeast corner of the city, was the nation's first municipally-owned airport. Now state-owned, the airport is used for charter, instruction, and private aircraft.

Two interstate highways serve Hartford. I-91 runs north-south (alongside the Connecticut River in Hartford) while I-84 runs northeast-southwest. Passenger train service is provided by Amtrak, which operates passenger service to major points throughout the country, and several interstate bus companies provide long-distance passenger service. The Union Station Transportation Center, a century-old brownstone structure restored to its original beauty, serves as the region's central rail and bus station.

Traveling in the City

Connecticut Transit operates more than thirty routes in and around the city and will take tourists to many Hartford area tourist attractions outside the downtown area. The Downtown Council and Business for Downtown Hartford sponsors a Park, Shop and Dine program providing the first hour of parking free at lots and garages with a minimum purchase. The Scooter Bus system reaches many major employers downtown and throughout the city. It operates every 10 to 30 minutes from early morning to early evening. Riverfront Recapture and other downtown Hartford revitalization projects have created walkways and open areas that are conducive to pedestrian traffic in the city.

Communications

Newspapers and Magazines

Hartford's daily newspaper, *The Hartford Courant,* established in 1764, is one of the nation's oldest continuously operating newspapers. Three other daily newspapers are printed in the region: *The New Britain Herald, The Journal Inquirer,* which covers the eastern suburbs, and *The Valley Press,* which covers the western suburbs. Special interest publications include the *Inquirer,* the region's largest African American community newspaper; and other publications covering management, motor transport, neurology, psychiatry, law enforcement, and Jewish affairs in Connecticut.

Television and Radio

Two independent television stations, four stations representing the major network affiliates, a public television station, and cable service provide television viewing in the area. The Hartford area is served by more than 15 radio stations. Connecticut Radio Information Service, headquartered in Wethersfield, broadcasts readings from daily newspapers and magazines for the benefit of state residents who are blind or cannot hold or turn pages.

Media Information: *The Hartford Courant,* 285 Broad Street, Hartford, CT 06115; telephone (860)241-6200. *New Britain Herald,* 1 Herald Square, New Britain, CT 06050; telephone (860)225-4601

Hartford Online

Connecticut Development Authority. Available www.ctcda.com

Hartford Convention and Visitor's Bureau. Available www.enjoyhartford.com

The Hartford Courant. Available www.ctnow.com

Hartford Historical Society. Available www.chs.org

Hartford Public Library. Available www.hartfordpl.lib.ct.us

Hartford Public Schools. Available www.hartfordschools.org

Mayor's Office, City of Hartford. Available www.hartford.gov

MetroHartford Chamber of Commerce. Available www.metrohartford.com

Selected Bibliography

Andrews, Kenneth Richmond, *Nook Farm, Mark Twain's Hartford Circle* (Cambridge: Harvard University Press, 1950)

Antonucci, Thomas and Michael Antonucci (Eds.), *Hartford, CT (Historical Briefs, Inc., 1992)*

Barbour, Lucius Barnes, *Families of Early Hartford, Connecticut* (Baltimore: Genealogical Pub., 1977)

Clemens, Samuel, *A Connecticut Yankee in King Arthur's Court* (New York: Harper & Row, 1917)

Love, William DeLoss, *The Colonial History of Hartford, Gathered from Original Sources by William DeLoss Love* (U Chester, Conn. U: Centinel Hill Press, 1974)

Pearson, Ridley, *Chain of Evidence,* (Hyperion, 1997)

New Haven

The City in Brief

Founded: 1638 (chartered, 1784)

Head Official: Mayor John DeStefano, Jr. (D) (since 1994)

City Population
  1980: 126,089
  1990: 130,474
  2000: 123,626
  2003 estimate: 124,512
  Percent change, 1990–2000: −5.2%
  U.S. rank in 1980: 125th
  U.S. rank in 1990: 138th
  U.S. rank in 2000: 196th

Metropolitan Area Population (New Haven-Meriden, CT PMSA)
  1980: 500,474
  1990: 530,180
  2000: 542,149
  Percent change, 1990–2000: 2.2%
  U.S. rank in 1990: 1st (New York CMSA)
  U.S. rank in 2000: 1st (New York CMSA)

Area: 18.85 square miles (2000)
Elevation: 33 feet above sea level
Average Annual Temperature: 52.0° F
Average Annual Precipitation: 46.02 inches

Major Economic Sectors: Services, manufacturing, trade
Unemployment Rate: 4.9% (April 2005)
Per Capita Income: $16,393 (1999)

2002 FBI Crime Index Total: 16,044 (Bridgeport, CT MSA)

Major Colleges and Universities: Yale University; University of New Haven; Albertus Magnus College; Southern Connecticut State University; Quinnipiac College; Greater New Haven State Technical College; Gateway Community-Technical College

Daily Newspaper: *New Haven Register*

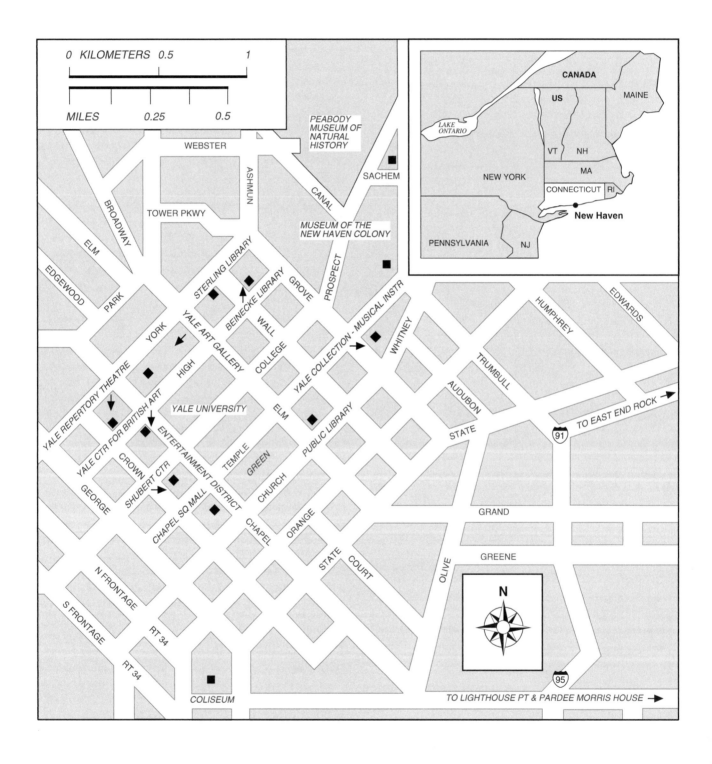

Introduction

Known variously as the home of Yale University, the city of elms, and the gateway to New England, New Haven has contributed to American life items ranging from frisbees to hamburgers to the Winchester repeating rifle to vulcanized rubber. In New Haven originated the clinical use of penicillin and mass production of manufactured goods. Modern New Haven remains a major New England seaport and distribution center with strengths in research and biotechnology. In 1998 and again in 2003, New Haven received the nation's oldest and most highly regarded civic recognition award when the National Civic League named New Haven an ''All-America City.''

Geography and Climate

New Haven, located in south-central Connecticut, is situated at the head of New Haven Bay, on Long Island Sound, and at the mouth of the Quinnipiac, Mill, and West rivers. A major port city, New Haven is bounded by the New Haven Harbor on its southeast side and by the Merritt Parkway (Connecticut Route 15) on its northwest side. The downtown area near the harbor is flat land that rises gradually to rolling hills in the outlying areas of the city.

New Haven's climate is tempered by its location on Long Island Sound. Winters are milder, with less snow accumulation, than inland winters. Typically, summers are moderately warm and humid. Precipitation is evenly spread throughout the year, and heavy snow is unusual in the immediate coastal area.

Area: 18.85 square miles (2000)

Elevation: 33 feet above sea level

Average Temperatures: January, 29.5° F; July, 74.0° F; annual average, 52.0° F

Average Annual Precipitation: 46.02 inches

History

Religious Colony Becomes Important Port

New Haven, its name declaring a new haven from religious oppression, was settled by a company of English Puritans in 1638. The group, led by the charismatic Reverend John Davenport, had originally called their settlement Quinnipiac, after the local Native American tribe of that name, but changed the town's name to New Haven in 1640. The settlement soon outgrew its confines and several neighboring towns grew up to form New Haven Colony. New Haven, however, made a poor political choice in sheltering Britain's fleeing regicidal judges who had condemned King Charles I to death in England. In 1664, as a punishment for its treachery, New Haven lost its status as an independent colony and was absorbed into the Hartford-ruled Connecticut Colony. Hartford and New Haven were co-capitals of the state from 1701 to 1873, when Hartford became the sole capital.

Colonial New Haven initially thrived on trade with the West Indies and with other towns along the Atlantic seaboard. Later, New Haven ships traveled to the Orient to import tea, porcelain, and silk. By the Revolution, New Haven was renowned not only for its flourishing sea trade but for its educational resources. Yale University had moved to New Haven in 1716 and a newspaper soon began publishing. Long Wharf was built and the first elm trees were planted on the Green in the center of the city. During the Revolutionary War, New Haven was looted and burned by invading British troops but the violence did not dull New Haven's thirst for independence from England. Roger Sherman of New Haven was the only patriot to sign all four major documents upon which the present-day U.S. government is based: the Articles of Association, the Declaration of Independence, the Articles of Confederation, and the U.S. Constitution.

In 1784, New Haven was incorporated as a city and its industrial star went into ascent. Goods manufactured in the city included Winchester repeating rifles, carriages, hardware, pianos, watches, corsets, bicycles, and cigars. Eli Whitney, a New Haven local and the inventor of the cotton gin, devised a system of manufacturing with interchangeable parts, setting the stage for mass production of goods. Also in New Haven Charles Goodyear developed vulcanized rubber, later essential to the bicycle and automotive industries. Rail travel entered the city in 1839, providing a way to transport these goods to other parts of the young nation.

Industrial Diversity Precedes Renewal

Before and during the Civil War, New Haven was an important center of Abolitionist sentiment. The war itself served to undermine one of the city's industries. With the fall of the South, the demand for New Haven-built carriages waned. Other industries took up the slack, however, notably the Winchester Repeating Arms Company, makers of the rifle that helped open the American West for settlement.

New Haven in 1957 became one of the first eastern U.S. cities to begin large-scale urban renewal of older downtown areas. The result of these first efforts was the Chapel Square Center, which restored housing and other community facilities and attracted commercial development. In 1967, racial tension exploded into serious rioting when minority groups protested that they had been left out of the development planning process. Further urban renewal included the erection of the New Haven Veterans Memorial Coliseum, as well as a market development near New Haven Harbor, a facility that houses the Long Wharf Theatre. In addition, Wooster Square, which in the 1950's was a slum, is now home to new commercial and industrial buildings and an established historic district, and in 1994 the Audubon Arts Center Complex was completed.

As of 2000, revitalization had also begun in Science Park, the East Shore community, the harbor front, Upper State Street, and many other areas of the city. The Livable City Initiative, a historic new approach to housing and neighborhood revitalization, is making a tangible difference in the city's neighborhoods, reducing vacant structures in the city by 70 percent. The Elm City—Green and Clean initiative, the revitalization of Ninth Square and the redevelopment of downtown are restoring a sense of hope and future to the fabric of the community. In 2004 the city announced plans for a $230 million development project, including $180 million in state bond funding, to relocate Gateway Community College and Long Wharf Theater to brand new facilities downtown as the first step in an ambitious development effort to transform a long vacant downtown. The city has taken steps to shore up its public school system as well. New Haven's $1.1 billion school construction program has received national and statewide attention for effectively leveraging the state's matching funds to create new and improved schools with smaller classroom sizes for New Haven's children.

Spurred by the city's resurgence, Mayor John DeStefano, Jr. referred to New Haven as "a reborn American city." In an article in the journal *Government Finance Review* Stefano further summed up the keys to the city's turnaround: "City officials have returned the jurisdiction back to a sound fiscal footing and are recreating a place where children learn in good schools, residents live in safe neighborhoods, and everyone has the opportunity to make the most of his or her talents. The city has accomplished this by following a path that avoids temporary, quick fixes in favor of creating a climate for sustainable economic growth and social well-being. New Haven has regenerated itself through competition and compassion."

Historical Information: New Haven Colony Historical Society, 14 Whitney Ave., New Haven, CT 06510; telephone (203)562-4183

Population Profile

Metropolitan Area Residents (New Haven-Meriden, CT PMSA)
1980: 500,474
1990: 530,180
2000: 542,149
Percent change, 1990–2000: 2.2%
U.S. rank in 1990: 1st (New York CMSA)
U.S. rank in 2000: 1st

City Residents
1980: 126,089
1990: 130,474
2000: 123,626
2003 estimate: 124,512
Percent change, 1990–2000: −5.2%
U.S. rank in 1980: 125th
U.S. rank in 1990: 138th
U.S. rank in 2000: 196th

Density: 6,558 people per square mile (2000)

Racial and ethnic characteristics (2000)
    White: 53,723
    Black or African American: 46,181
    American Indian and Alaska Native: 535
    Asian: 4,819
    Native Hawaiian and Pacific Islander: 79
    Hispanic or Latino (may be of any race): 26,443
    Other: 13,460

Percent of residents born in state: 50.7% (2000)

Age characteristics (2000)
    Population under 5 years old: 8,749
    Population 5 to 9 years old: 9,051
    Population 10 to 14 years old: 8,792
    Population 15 to 19 years old: 10,910
    Population 20 to 24 years old: 14,183
    Population 25 to 34 years old: 22,028
    Population 35 to 44 years old: 16,578
    Population 45 to 54 years old: 12,564
    Population 55 to 59 years old: 4,539
    Population 60 to 64 years old: 3,561
    Population 65 to 74 years old: 5,986
    Population 75 to 84 years old: 4,701
    Population 85 years and over: 1,984
    Median age: 29.3 years (2000)

Births (2001, New Haven County)
    Total number: 10,990

Deaths (2001, New Haven County)
   Total number: 8,124 (of which, 82 were infants under
      the age of 1 year)

Money income (1999)
   Per capita income: $16,393
   Median household income: $29,604
   Total number of households: 47,193

Number of households with income of . . .
   less than $10,000: 9,447
   $10,000 to $14,999: 4,335
   $15,000 to $24,999: 7,041
   $25,000 to $34,999: 5,895
   $35,000 to $49,999: 6,999
   $50,000 to $74,999: 6,924
   $75,000 to $99,999: 3,314
   $100,000 to $149,999: 2,052
   $150,000 to $199,999: 561
   $200,000 or more: 625

Percent of families below poverty level: 20.5% (51.2% of
   which were female householder families with related
   children under 5 years

2002 FBI Crime Index Total: 16,044 (Bridgeport, CT
   MSA)

Municipal Government

New Haven operates under a mayor-board of aldermen form
of government. The mayor is elected to a two-year term as
are the thirty members who make up the Board of Aldermen.

Head Official: Mayor John DeStefano, Jr. (D) (since 1994;
current term expires 2006)

Total Number of City Employees: Not reported

City Information: Mayor's Office, City of New Haven,
165 Church St., New Haven, CT 06510; telephone
(203)946-8200

Economy

Major Industries and Commercial Activity

In the 1950's, New Haven's economy was based on the
manufacturing industry. Today, while manufacturing continues to be an important component of the regional econ-

omy, the base of that economy has shifted to health,
business, and financial services, as well as retail trade. In all,
the services sector constitutes 56 percent of the local economy, with transportation and utilities (13 percent), trade (11
percent), and manufacturing (9 percent) also playing major
roles. Both government and financial services comprise
about 4 percent of the local industry base. The city benefits
from its close proximity to two major bioscience centers,
New York and Boston. Local healthcare and pharmaceutical
firms, along with Yale Medical School, constitute one of the
major concentrations of bio-medical research in the nation.
The increasingly significant and growing cluster of the biotechnology industry in Greater New Haven is one of the
results of this concentration. There are already several well-
established bio-tech firms in the region with more likely to
come. These companies alone added some 1,000 jobs to the
regional economy in the late 1990s, and continue to fuel the
economy into the 2000s. Another important element in the
Greater New Haven economy is higher education, particularly the presence of Yale University and its worldwide
reputation as a research center and its highly-skilled and
educated graduate base. Yale and other local colleges together maintain a student base of nearly 50,000 and employ
thousands of others.

Items and goods produced: pharmaceutical products, computer software, firearms, ammunition, tools, clocks and
   watches, lamps, silverware, airplane parts, oil filters,
   telephones, cutlery, chocolate

Incentive Programs—New and Existing Companies

Local programs—The city of New Haven has several business incentive programs, including programs that offer information and loans in the Aerospace, BioScience, and
Information Technology industries. General business loans
of up to $5 million and special loans for child care busi-
nesses, start-ups, and manufacturing businesses are also
available. The City of New Haven Small Business Revolving Loan Fund provides capital for start-up or expansion
of small, minority and/or disadvantaged businesses located
within and providing goods and services to New Haven's
low to moderate income neighborhoods. The Urban Jobs
and Enterprise Zone Program provides property tax abatements for manufacturers, state corporation income tax credits, and other assistance.

State programs—The Connecticut Development Authority
works to expand Connecticut's business base. Among its
many services, the Connecticut Development Authority
works with private-sector partners to guarantee or participate in loans for businesses that may be unable to meet credit
underwriting standards; provides access to lower-cost fixed
asset financing through Small Business Administration 504
Debentures and tax-exempt Industrial Revenue Bonds; provides financial incentives to companies that enhance the

skills of their employees; and encourages investment in the state's urban commercial infrastructure.

The Connecticut Development Authority offers business assistance including direct and guaranteed loans to small businesses, businesses involved in brownfield development or information technology, and businesses that are relocating or expanding. Connecticut's financial and tax incentives include grants and tax abatements for firms locating in State Enterprise Zones and Urban Jobs Program (New Haven qualifies for both), low-cost loans and development bond financing, and funding for new product development.

Job training programs—The city of New Haven, the state of Connecticut, and various local for-profit and non-profit organizations have programs that benefit workers and employers, especially in the areas of placement, recruitment and referral, technology and manufacturing job placement, apprenticeships, and on-the-job training and career development.

Development Projects

By 2005, after a decades-long decline followed by years of intelligent planning, New Haven was in the midst of a notable transformation designed to bring the city into the new millennium poised for sustained growth. Major projects include a massive $1.5 billion agenda designed to grow New Haven's downtown, where nearly half of the city's jobs are centered, and a renewed dedication to developing the New Haven waterfront. Among other considerations, the agenda includes renewal of the city's historic waterfront and initiatives creating a 269-slip marina and a permanent berth for the replica slave ship Amistad; expansion and renovation of shoreline commuter rail stations and expansion of I-95, a major artery connecting New Haven to New York City and Boston; a $2.7 million Small Business Initiative to provide small-business owners with capital resources—in the form of a revolving loan fund—as well as technical assistance in such areas as accounting, marketing and inventory control; and the creation of a federal Empowerment Zone (EZ), which gives the city access to $100 million in grants, $130 million in tax credits, and new programs aimed at implementing a strategic plan.

In the few years prior to 2005, numerous other projects aimed at improving New Haven's infrastructure have either been completed or are under way. Among them are $3.15 million in construction projects to improve Tweed-New Haven Airport and an updated master plan to map out the facility's future and improve the level of utilization; a doubling of the city's investment in parks and public works maintenance efforts and a Citywide Beautification Initiative to improve public spaces and support more than 400 community gardens and green spaces; and a Livable City Initiative that has so far rehabilitated 500 housing units, trained

500 residents in homeownership, and established the most aggressive housing code enforcement program in the state. The Ninth Square project has revamped an old industrial and shopping area into a modern shopping, business and residential center. The site of Science Park, New Haven's former Winchester Arms Company complex established in 1866 and open for more than a century, now provides a research-oriented business incubator facilitating more than 70 manufacturing companies and laboratories and over 1,400 potential job opportunities. Others include the IKEA project, in which a 2 story retail distribution of furniture owned and operated by IKEA provides 400-450 jobs with full time benefits for full and part time employees (the project also has a $50,000 commitment to the Hill Development Corporation and a $100,000 commitment to Gateway Community College for job recruitment and training for New Haven residents); and the Pfizer project, which offers a 3 story clinical research unit owned and operated by Pfizer and contributes to the sophistication of medical imaging research at Yale University.

Economic Development Information: Greater New Haven Chamber of Commerce, 195 Church St., New Haven, CT 06510; telephone (203)787-6735

Commercial Shipping

New Haven, Connecticut's largest wholesale distributing city, makes use of a major port of entry, many railroad lines, and major interstate highways. New Haven features a deep-water seaport with three berths capable of hosting vessels and barges and facilities for handling any type of break-bulk cargo. The Port of New Haven has a capacity for loading 200 trucks a day from the ground or via loading docks. The Port is serviced by the Providence and Worcester railroad connecting with CONRAIL, New England Railroad, and the Canadian National and Canadian Pacific railroads. A private switch engine for yard movements and private siding for loading and unloading of boxcars, gondolas, flatcars, and others is located at the site. The Port of New Haven has approximately 400,000 square feet of inside storage and 50 acres of outside storage available at the site. Five shore cranes with a 250-ton capacity and 26 forklifts, each with a 26-ton capacity, are also available. The Greater New Haven Chamber of Commerce contracts with Logistec Connecticut to operate New Haven's Foreign Trade Zone, providing additional tax incentives to international shipping operations into and out of New Haven's harbor area. Interstate common carriers include about 12 trucking lines.

Labor Force and Employment Outlook

The city of New Haven draws from a highly skilled labor force. More than 5,000 college graduates enter the job market from New Haven's colleges each year. Proximity to New York City and relatively lower wages make Greater New

Haven a desirable home for commuters and an attractive business site. Yale University, Yale Medical School, and projects like Science Park draw pharmaceutical and biotechnology companies as well as high-technology manufacturing firms and research and development organizations, providing and attracting a supply of highly educated workers. Employers may also draw from the pool of workers who commute to Stamford and New York from New Haven and surrounding communities.

Because New Haven's major employers are utilities, hospitals, and educational institutions, long-term prospects for economic stability are good. Tourism's impact, bolstered by New Haven's new status as a sports destination, is expected to increase its benefits to the city.

The following is a summary of data regarding the New Haven metropolitan area labor force, 2004 annual averages.

Size of nonagricultural labor force: 271,300

Number of workers employed in . . .
  mining and construction: 11,500
  manufacturing: 34,000
  trade, transportation, and utilities: 50,300
  information: 8,700
  financial activities: 14,100
  professional and business services: 25,900
  educational and health services: 61,700
  leisure and hospitality: 20,500
  other services: 10,500
  government: 34,200

Average hourly earnings of production workers employed in manufacturing: $16.19 (April 2005)

Unemployment rate: 4.9% (April 2005)

Largest employers — *Number of employees (listed from largest to smallest—no figures available)*
  Yale University
  Yale New Haven Hospital
  Hospital of St. Raphael
  Southern New England Telephone Company (SNET)
  The United Illuminating Company
  Southern Connecticut State University
  ASSA-ABLOY Sargent
  New Haven Register
  Pritchard Industries
  Knights of Columbus

Cost of Living

The cost of living in New Haven is the same or lower than most East Coast and West Coast cities but higher than cities in the Midwest. Of the 100 largest metropolitan areas in the country, New Haven is in the bottom third for overall crime,

sandwiched between Indianapolis and San Francisco. Based on the most commonly accepted methodology used to determine the most and least stressful places to live in the United States, New Haven falls within the 15 percent least stressful areas in which to live.

The following is a summary of data regarding several key cost of living factors for the New Haven-Meriden PMSA.

2004 (3rd Quarter) ACCRA Average House Price: $400,880

2004 (3rd Quarter) ACCRA Cost of Living Index: 123.9 (U.S. average = 100.0)

State income tax rate: 3% to 5%

State sales tax rate: 6% on most items

Local income tax rate: None

Local sales tax rate: None

Property tax rate: $39.53 mills (2003)

Economic Information: Greater New Haven Chamber of Commerce, 910 Chapel St., New Haven, CT 06510; telephone (203)787-6735

Education and Research

Elementary and Secondary Schools

New Haven's school system, rated among the nation's best, offers a program for talented and gifted students beginning in kindergarten, as well as special education classes and an adult education program. The district's 27 magnet schools are very popular and require a lottery system to determine placement. Magnet schools offer specialized curricula in areas such as the arts, languages, science, mathematics, and communications. In 2005 the district set ambitious goals, aiming for 95 percent of the students to be ready to succeed by the end of kindergarten; to achieve math and literacy standards; and to be ready for college, post-secondary education, the military, or the workforce by the time they had reached the 9th grade.

The following is a summary of data regarding the New Haven Public School District as of the 2004–2005 school year.

Total enrollment: 20,759

Number of facilities
  elementary schools: 29
  junior high/middle schools: 9
  senior high schools: 7
  other: 4 (transitional schools)

Student/teacher ratio: 14.4:1 (2003)

Teacher salaries
  average: $51,770 (2005)

Funding per pupil: $16,820 (2003)

Supplementing the public school system are a number of private preparatory schools, as well as parochial and nursery schools.

Public Schools Information: Public Information Office, Gateway Center, New Haven Board of Education, 54 Meadow St., New Haven, CT 06519; telephone (203)946-8450

Colleges and Universities

While the New Haven area is home to 8 colleges and universities, its most famous is Yale University, which in 2005 had approximately 11,275 graduate and undergraduate students enrolled. Founded in 1701 in Branford and moved to New Haven in 1716, Yale is a charter member of the Ivy League and rated among the top five universities in the country. The school began with the donation of books and money from Elihu Yale, a merchant who made his fortune in East India imports. Today, Yale University is noted for its schools of law, medicine, business, divinity, and computer science. Yale's libraries, museums, and other facilities are among the largest and finest in the country. Yale's cultural influence on the city is pervasive. The school's drama productions, adult lecture series, tutorial programs at local high schools, art galleries, and sports events all enhance life in New Haven. The oldest scientific publication in the United States, the *American Journal of Science,* began publishing at Yale in 1818. Other Yale ''firsts'' were the doctoral degree granted in 1861, establishment of the School of Fine Arts in 1870, and opening of the School of Forestry in 1900.

Other institutions of higher learning in New Haven include Albertus Magnus College, a Roman Catholic four-year liberal arts college of about 2,400 students (in 2005). Southern Connecticut State University, a four-year public institution with more than 12,000 students on its 168-acre New Haven campus, focuses on liberal arts and business. Gateway Community College, formerly the South Central Community College, maintains two campuses, one in North Haven and the other in Long Wharf. Nearby are New Haven University (in West Haven) and Quinnipiac University (in Hamden).

Libraries and Research Centers

The New Haven Free Public Library system consists of the main facility, Ives Memorial Library, and three branch libraries (Fair Haven, Mitchell, and Stetson), as well as a bookmobile. The system numbers some 600,000 books in its collection, which also includes large print books, a children's collection, and computer resources. Materials on local history and a wide range of audio-visual equipment and rentals are available.

Yale University Library is the fourth largest library in the country. Among its many libraries, Yale maintains the Sterling Memorial Library, housing the Yale Archives, with more than 4 million volumes, and Babylonian tablets on display. Other Yale facilities are the Beinecke Rare Book Library, displaying the Gutenberg Bible, and the school's libraries of law, medicine, drama, business, and forestry.

Another local facility is the Connecticut Judicial Branch Law Library at New Haven. The New Haven Colony Historical Society's Whitney Library maintains books, maps, and photographs, along with Chinese porcelain displays and an original cotton gin. Special interest libraries include the Albertus Magnus College Library and the Connecticut Agricultural Experiment Station's Osborne Library.

Studies of clinical cultures for the AIDS virus are performed at the Veterans' Administration (VA) Medical Center's national reference virology laboratory in West Haven. Other research programs of note include the University of Connecticut's Haskins Laboratories, which study speech production and perception in humans. Yale University's many science, economic, art, and business research programs include involvement in Science Park, an incubator for high-technology industries.

Public Library Information: Main Library, 133 Elm Street, New Haven, CT 06510; telephone (203)946-8130; fax (203)946-8140

Health Care

Health care in New Haven revolves around the Yale-New Haven Hospital (YNHH), one of the nation's top 10 medical centers and a world-renowned teaching facility. The hospital is a 944-bed tertiary care facility that includes the 201-bed Yale-New Haven Children's Hospital and the 76-bed Yale-New Haven Psychiatric Hospital. Affiliated with the Yale School of Medicine, YNHH accepts referrals from throughout the United States and the world. Relying on the skills of some 2,200 physicians working in over 100 specialties, the hospital is also overseen by nearly 450 supervised resident physicians; in all the hospital is New Haven's second leading employer with more than 6,000 on staff. In addition to being a teaching hospital, YNHH is also a community hospital featuring the state's busiest primary care center and the region's largest and most comprehensive array of maternity and pediatric services. Among the Yale-New Haven Hospital's innovations were the nation's first clinical use of penicillin, the first use of chemotherapy in cancer treatment, the first transplants of a number of organs, and New England's first in-vitro fertilization birth.

The Hospital of St. Raphael, with 511 beds, is affiliated with the Yale University School of Medicine and is a leader in cardiac, cancer and orthopedic services. The Hospital is listed as one of the 50 top hospitals in the U.S. by the American Association of Retired Persons, and lists many firsts among its accomplishments. It was the first community hospital in Connecticut to open a coronary care unit and today has the state's largest dedicated cardiothoracic intensive care unit. The hospital also was one of the first in New England to perform open-heart surgery and the first in New England with a radiation center. In 1994, Saint Raphael's became the first hospital in New England to use a robotic arm in the operating room to assist surgeons with laparoscopic surgery. The hospital initiated Project MotherCare, a mobile prenatal and primary care clinic, and Project ElderCare, a partnership with the City of New Haven to provide community-based health care to senior citizens

Health Care Information: Yale-New Haven Hospital, 20 York St., New Haven, CT 06511; telephone (203)785-4242

Recreation

Sightseeing

Yale University, whose scholarly ranks include patriot Nathan Hale; presidents Bill Clinton, George H.W. Bush, and George W. Bush; scholar Noah Webster; and statesman John C. Calhoun, is one of the nation's oldest schools. A walking tour of the campus will include a view of Connecticut Hall, built in 1717. The school's 12 colleges, the 221-foot Harkness Tower famous for its carillon concerts, and the world's largest gymnasium—the Payne Whitney Gymnasium—are highlights of the tour. Adjoining Yale University in an area known as The Green is United Church, whose congregation fervently supported the struggle against slavery. The church is regarded as an outstanding example of New England architecture. The New Haven Colony Historical Society has exhibits celebrating the exploits of several former slaves who revolted aboard the slave ship Amistad, eventually landed in New Haven, and were eventually set free by the United States Supreme Court.

One of America's first cemeteries, the Grove Street Cemetery, was founded in 1797 and contains the graves of many New Haven notables. On the eastern shore of the New Haven Harbor are Black Rock Fort, used in the Revolutionary War, and Fort Nathan Hale, a Civil War fort. The Pardee-Morris House dates from 1750 and contains many colonial Connecticut furnishings. East Rock Park offers a bird sanctuary, self-guided nature trails, picnic groves, and the Pardee Rose Garden and Greenhouse. Lighthouse Point

Park's natural history displays and its unique carousel set in an eighteenth-century pavilion on the beach are popular tourist attractions. West Rock Nature Center is a year-round 40-acre facility with displays of native wildlife. The park includes Judges' Cave, where the regicidal judges who condemned King Charles I to the block hid to escape English royal retribution. New Haven's historic Green, a national historic landmark, is ringed on one side by churches built between 1812 and 1815 in the Gothic, Federalist, and Georgian styles. Day and evening harbor cruises and educational tours of the coast are available aboard local chartered boats.

The Connecticut Afro-American Historical Society, located on the campus of Southern Connecticut State University honors the role of African-American people in New Haven and the United States. The university's Ethnic Heritage Center also highlights the cultures of Jewish-, Italian-, Irish-, and Ukranian-Americans, as well as other ethnic groups. Eli Whitney Museum, established in Whitney's restored gun factory, offers programs, lectures, and workshops about machinery and technology.

Arts and Culture

New Haven's performing arts offerings are rich. The New Haven Symphony Orchestra, the fourth oldest in the country, is nationally recognized for its performances, which are often accompanied by international guest artists. The symphony presents a summer concert series on New Haven's historic Green. Orchestra New England, a chamber ensemble, is gaining a reputation as well. Performances of touring groups and guest artists are staged at two major facilities in New Haven: the Palace and the Shubert Theater, a traditional stop for shows on their way to Broadway. Concerts include internationally renowned symphonies, concert artists, bands, and singers performing the whole musical spectrum.

Theater is popular and critically acclaimed in New Haven. The Long Wharf Theatre Company is known for its contemporary works while the Yale Repertory Theatre, home to the university's world-renowned drama schools, is heralded for its productions of the classics. Many other fine student, amateur, and professional groups enhance the cultural landscape.

Yale University has made the city of New Haven synonymous with fine museums. Yale's Peabody Museum of Natural History is New England's largest and one of its oldest science museums. The Yale Center for British Art is considered one of the foremost collections of its kind in the world. American, European, and classical works form part of the Yale University Art Gallery's collection. Artspace and the Arts Council of Greater New Haven are local arts organizations that offer support, performance and exhibition space, education, and classes for student and professional artists. The Yale Collection of Musical Instruments numbers more than 800 sixteenth- to twentieth-century instruments. A Gu-

A walking tour of Yale University takes visitors across the campus of one of the nation's oldest schools.

tenberg Bible and Audubon bird prints are on display at the Bienecke Rare Book and Manuscript Library.

The New Haven Colony Historical Society houses a museum and library of local memorabilia, including industrial and toy exhibits. The Connecticut Children's Museum stimulates the imaginations of children under eight years of age. Private galleries in New Haven include the John Slade Ely House, the Museum of American Theatre, the Munson Gallery, the Mona Berman Gallery, and the galleries of the Creative Arts Workshop and City Spirit Artists, both of which offer instruction in the arts.

Arts and Culture Information: Arts Council of Greater New Haven, 70 Audubon Street, New Haven, CT 06510; telephone (203)772-2788

Festivals and Holidays

Its location in the center of the former colonies makes New Haven a treasure-trove of Americana. The New Haven Antiques Show, held at the New Haven Coliseum, schedules a spring and fall exhibition while the Connecticut Antiques Showcase is held in November. Powder House Day, commemorating Benedict Arnold's seizure of the New Haven powder stores in the name of the Revolution, is celebrated each spring with a drill and costumed parade on the Green. In March, the Annual International Competition of Women in the Arts take place.

April's Film Festival New Haven screens features, shorts, and documentaries at three local venues. April also brings the Cherry Blossom Festival at Wooster Square. New Haven's maritime past is celebrated with East Shore Day in the harbor area in June. A week-long Summertime Street Festival runs concurrently with the Pilot Pen International Tennis Tournament. The Annual International Festival of Arts & Ideas, which is fashioned after the Spoletto and Edinburgh Festivals, takes place in June and centers around the New Haven Green. Each June on Wooster Square, the St. Anthony Italian Feast takes place, as it has for the past 105 years. The Celebrate New Haven 4th takes place each July 4 weekend and includes fireworks, entertainment, and sails on the schooner Quinnipiack. There is an annual lobster bake each July in nearby Milford. The best in contemporary crafts produced by 400 craftspeople from around the country is on display for most of November and December at the Celebration of American Crafts Creative Arts Workshop. December's UI Fantasy of Lights at Lighthouse Park on New Haven harbor allows visitors to drive through an enchanting land of more than 200,000 lights.

The city's love of music is apparent in the large crowds drawn to the summer weekend New Haven Jazz Festival held on the Green. Religious and ethnic celebrations include St. Andre's Feast in June, Santa Maria Magdelina Feast in

July, and the Greek Festival at Lighthouse Park in September. Connecticut's oldest fair, the Durham Fair, will celebrate its 86th year in September 2005.

Sports for the Spectator

The New Haven Cutters play minor league baseball at Yale Field as part of the 8-team Canadian American Association of Professional Baseball, an independent baseball league. The Sports Haven in New Haven provides horse-racing fans with simulcasts of some of the major races on four large screens and permits betting. Visitors can dine at the on-site sports bar or the Shark Bar. Several local colleges and universities field sports teams, including the Albertus Magnus Falcons, the Quinnipiac Bobcats, the Southern Connecticut State University Owls, and the New Haven University Chargers, whose contests are eagerly attended throughout the year. The Yale Bulldogs compete in one of the oldest collegiate sporting leagues in America, the tradition-rich Ivy League, with such fierce rivals as Harvard, Princeton, and Brown. Although its team can no longer compete with the top Division 1 collegiate programs, the Yale Bulldogs football team is a hugely popular local favorite that has drawn up to 70,000 fans to big home games. The Yale Bowl hosts world-class soccer tournaments during the summer. Tennis is represented by the Pilot Pen International Tennis Tournament, held each August at the new Connecticut Tennis Center. The Milton Jai Alai fronton in nearby Milford is the only remaining fronton in Connecticut.

Sports for the Participant

Water sports predominate in New Haven. Boating, swimming, and aquatic sports of all types can be enjoyed at the city's many beaches. Golf is played at the Alling Memorial Golf Course, where the 18 holes carry a par of 70. Fully 17 percent of New Haven's land is dedicated to parks. City parks include East Rock Park, the city's largest, which maintains hiking trails and an array of recreational facilities. Lighthouse Point Park features swimming and recreational facilities. Edgewood Park has a skate park, and the Walker Ice Rink has ice skating and hockey. The city has dozens of sports leagues for kids and adults, as well as swim instruction. Each fall New Haven hosts a Road Race, which draws amateur athletes from throughout the Northeast. In Ledyard, east of New Haven, the Mashantucket Pequot Indians opened a casino in 1992.

Shopping and Dining

The downtown area's bilevel shopping complex, the Chapel Square Mall, was renovated and reopened in 2004, giving the beleaguered mall a facelift that many hoped would return it to its glory days. Ann Taylor Loft, which began in New Haven 50 years prior, returned to anchor the newly restored complex. Small, family-owned shops can be found throughout New Haven, along with a variety of bookstores that serve the university community. Many unique shops can be found in the historic Wooster Square, the Arts District near Audubon, and around the Green.

A diner's paradise with a growing national reputation for its sophisticated cuisine, New Haven is home to more than 100 restaurants, many within an easy walking distance of downtown and the Green, including the Union League Café, which serves fine French cuisine in an elegant setting, and Scoozi's, New Haven's only wine bar, which offers contemporary Italian fare. Other cuisines from which to choose include American, Caribbean, Chinese, Continental, Ethiopian, Greek, Indian, Irish, Japanese, Korean, Latin American, Malaysian, Mexican, Middle Eastern, soul food, Spanish, Thai, Turkish, and vegetarian.

Visitor Information: Greater New Haven Convention & Visitors Bureau, 59 Elm St., New Haven, CT 06510; telephone (203)777-8550; toll-free (800)332-STAY

Convention Facilities

Large conventions and trade shows generally are held at New Haven Coliseum, but in 2005 Mayor John DeStefano Jr. announced plans to raze the aging facility to make way for a new development that would include a new Gateway Community College campus and a hotel and convention facility. Smaller conferences center around Yale University activities and make use of the school's facilities. About 1,500 sleeping rooms are available in New Haven; New Haven Medical Hotel, a medical recuperation center, is also open to the public. The four-star Omni New Haven Hotel at Yale provides 22,000 square feet of meeting space all on one level, including a 9200-square-foot Grand Ballroom and 19 conference rooms. The Colony Hotel is an intimate European style hotel located near the Yale campus. In Spring 2005 the old Howard Johnson in Hamden closed and was replaced by the new Clarion Hotel and Suites.

Convention Information: Greater New Haven Convention and Visitors Bureau, 59 Elm St., New Haven, CT 06510; telephone (203)777-8550; toll-free (800)332-STAY

Transportation

Approaching the City

Tweed-New Haven Airport is the fastest growing satellite airport in the Northeast, and in 2005 was named Regional

Airport of the Year by the Regional Airline Association. Located less than 10 minutes from downtown New Haven, it offers service to Philadelphia through Delta Connect and Cincinnati through U.S. Airways; from these airports New Haven air travelers can go virtually anywhere in the world. As of 2005 the airport was in negotiations to bring nonstop service to Detroit via Northwest Airlines. The airport expected to board 61,000 passengers in 2005.

New Haven's Union Station is one of Amtrak's busiest terminals in the country and provides service to Boston, Washington, D.C., and beyond; Metro-North also provides commuter service for approximately 25,000 passengers traveling the New York City/Connecticut corridor each day. A $1.2 billion plan to upgrade rail service between New Haven and Boston has cut travel time to New York City to an hour and to Boston to two hours.

Ferry service to Port Jefferson, New York runs out of nearby Bridgeport, CT.

Interstates 91 and 95, major north/south and east/west corridors, intersect in New Haven. U.S. Routes 1,5, and the Merritt/Wilbur Cross Parkway and Connecticut Route 34 all have exits and entrances in New Haven. Every major city in the northeast is within one day's drive from New Haven.

Traveling in the City

New Haven was one of the first cities in the country to benefit from urban planning. Its streets are laid out in a grid pattern of nine squares with the historic Green in the center. Bus service is offered within the city and to the suburbs via CT Transit. To relieve commuter traffic on the highways, a park-and-ride service is provided to suburbanites working in the city of New Haven.

Communications

Newspapers and Magazines

The *New Haven Register* is the weekday morning paper. It is also served by the student-run *Yale Daily News* and the weekly *Yale Herald.* Among the many special interest and scholarly titles published in New Haven are the bimonthly *American Journal of Science* and *Columbia,* the publication of the Knights of Columbus and several magazines published by Yale University.

Television and Radio

Two television stations air from New Haven, which supports one cable franchise. New York stations are also picked up in the New Haven area. Three radio stations broadcast from

New Haven, which also picks up programming from New York City, Hartford, and neighboring towns. Connecticut Radio Information Service, headquartered in Wethersfield, broadcasts readings from daily newspapers and magazines for the benefit of state residents who are blind or cannot hold or turn pages.

Media Information: *New Haven Register,* 40 Sargent Drive, New Haven, CT 06519; telephone (203)789-5200

New Haven Online

City of New Haven. Available www.cityofnewhaven.com

Connecticut Development Authority. Available www.state .ct.us/cda

New Haven Chamber of Commerce. Available www .newhavenchamber.com

New Haven Convention & Visitors Bureau. Available www .newhavencvb.org

New Haven Public Library. Available www.nhfpl.lib.ct.us

New Haven Public Schools. Available www.nhps.net

Yale-New Haven Hospital. Available www.ynhh.org

Selected Bibliography

Inside New Haven's Neighborhoods (New Haven: City of New Haven and the New Haven Colony Historical Society, 1982)

Osterweis, Rollin G., *Three Centuries of New Haven, 1638–1938* (New Haven, Yale University Press, 1953)

Panico, Alfonso E., and Neil Thomas Proto (Preface) *The Italians of the New New Haven: This Collection Is a Tribute to New Haven's Most Significant Italians of the Century (1900-2000)* (Alfonso E. Panico, 1998)

Stamford

The City in Brief

Founded: 1641 (incorporated, 1949)

Head Official: Mayor Dannel P. Malloy (D) (since 1995)

City Population
  1980: 102,466
  1990: 108,056
  2000: 117,083
  2003 estimate: 120,107
  Percent change, 1990–2000: 8.3%
  U.S. rank in 1980: 161st
  U.S. rank in 1990: 177th (State rank: 5th)
  U.S. rank in 2000: 209th

Metropolitan Area Population (PMSA)
  1990: 329,935
  2000: 353,556
  Percent change, 1990–2000: 7.1%
  U.S. rank in 1990: 1st (Greater New York, NY CMSA)
  U.S. rank in 2000: 1st (CMSA)

Area: 38 square miles (2000)
Elevation: 34 feet above sea level
Average Annual Temperature: 51.9° F
Average Annual Precipitation: 49.46 inches

Major Economic Sectors: Manufacturing, trade, services
Unemployment Rate: 4.9% (March 2005)
Per Capita Income: $34,987 (1999)

2002 FBI Crime Index Total: 2,398

Major Colleges and Universities: St. Basil's College; branches of the University of Connecticut and Bridgeport Engineering Institute

Daily Newspaper: *The Advocate*

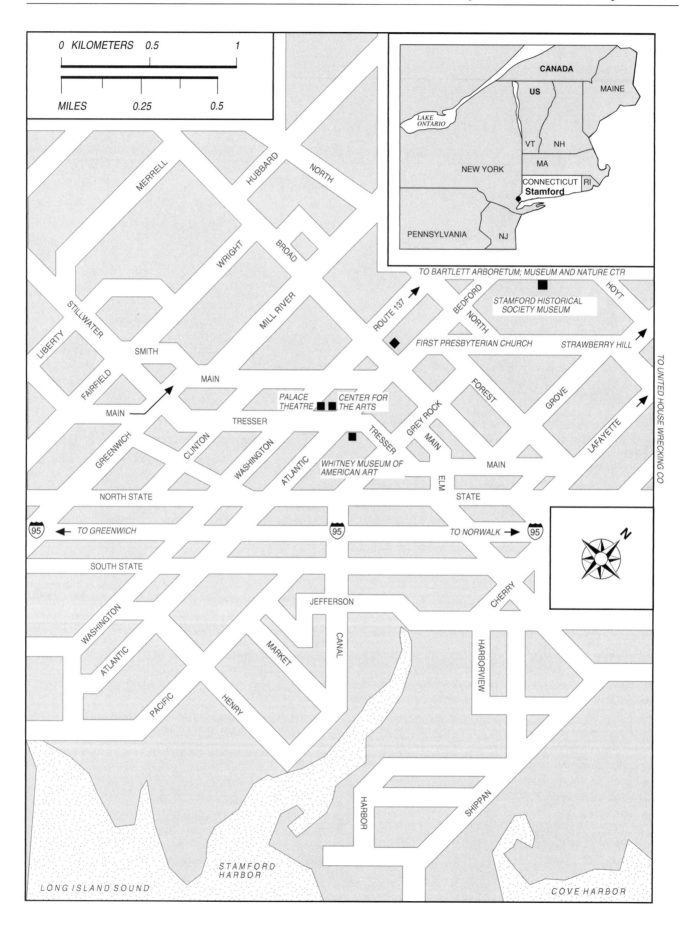

Introduction

In the twentieth century, Stamford, the fifth largest city in Connecticut, progressed from a factory hub to its current position as a research center. By the end of the twentieth century, it had also become the nation's third largest corporate headquarters community. The city enjoys both urban and suburban facets, ranging from upscale housing areas, to a handsome corporate downtown center, to areas of beautiful shoreline with parks and beaches.

Geography and Climate

Located in southwestern Connecticut, Stamford lies at the mouth of the Rippowam River on Long Island Sound. The city itself is built around a wide bay crossed by two tidal inlets. Stamford Harbor and Cove Harbor border a finger of land jutting into the bay. The city is situated on relatively flat land that is part of the Atlantic coastal plain. The serrated shoreline is connected by a series of bridges that carry automobile and rail traffic.

Stamford's New England weather is tempered by the city's proximity to Long Island Sound. Winters are milder, with less snow, than those of inland cities. Summers are warm, with moderate humidity.

Area: 38 square miles (2000)

Elevation: 34 feet above sea level

Average Temperatures: January, 29.3° F; July, 75.3° F; annual average, 51.9° F

Average Annual Precipitation: 49.46 inches

History

Religious Refuge Becomes Textile Center

In pre-colonial days, the Siwanoys, a subnation of the Wappinger tribe, lived on the land—which they called ''Rippowam''—that now constitutes the site of modern Stamford. In 1640 the Siwanoys sold the land to Nathaniel Turner, an agent for the New Haven Colony, who was looking for arable land. A year later, twenty-eight families belonging to the Congregational Church fled a church dispute in Wethersfield, Connecticut, and arrived in Rippowam to form a permanent settlement. They called their town Stam-

ford, after its English counterpart. In 1644, Stamford lost a third of its settlers when they moved to Long Island. Stamford, in turn, was absorbed into the Connecticut Colony.

Stamford, a minor port on Long Island Sound, had channels suitable only for small craft and barge traffic. The young community relied on subsistence agriculture and some crafts and only minimally on its trade with the West Indies. By the time of the Revolutionary War, Stamford, with 3,800 citizens, could boast that it was a major population center between New York City and New Haven.

Stamford continued to rely on its small industries until the founding of the Stamford Manufacturing Company in 1844. The new concern set up in the Cove Mills and began producing dyewood and licorice extracts, both crucial to the New England textile industry. In 1848, the railroad arrived, making Stamford one of the stops on the New York City-New Haven run. Soon European immigrants arrived by the trainload to work in Stamford's new mills. The Irish arrived in the 1840s, settling in the Kerrytown and Dublin sections of the city and forming Stamford's first ethnic minority.

Research and Development From Industrial Base

Aside from the arrival of the railroad, 1848 was an important year for Stamford for another reason: Linus Yale invented the first cylinder lock, revolutionizing lock design and launching an American industry. From 1868 until 1959, the Yale and Towne Company was the single largest employer in Stamford. Between 1869 and 1892 alone, the payroll grew from 30 to 31,000 employees. In the meantime, the west end of the city near the Mill River saw the opening of mills and foundries. In the business section, new banks, utilities, and factories opened. The population in 1868 stood at 9,700 people; that year a second railroad line opened, this time connecting the city with New Canaan.

By 1893, Stamford's population had swollen to almost 16,000 people; by the end of the century, the count stood at 19,000, which included a large number of Polish immigrants. Business boomed, much of it based upon the inventions of another Stamford genius, Simon Ingersoll. Ingersoll masterminded the friction clutch, the spring scale, and a steam-driven wagon, the precursor of the modern automobile.

When New York City became the East Coast industrial mecca of the late nineteenth century, Stamford developed into a residential suburb of the larger city. Following World War II, Stamford became the site of a number of research and development concerns, which added greatly to the local economy. Stamford incorporated as a city late by East Coast standards: in 1949, the city absorbed the surrounding communities to become the city of Stamford. By the 1960s, Stamford had attracted so many corporate headquarters that more commuters were traveling into Stamford each day than were commuting to New York City jobs. Much of the city's success in attracting those companies rested on its appeal as a suburb. To make way for them, most of the downtown was demolished and replaced by a boulevard of fortress-like corporate headquarters and a mall. The recession of the early 1990s saw the end of the office boom; new buildings stood empty as new businesses sought space in office parks elsewhere. Stamford found itself with a surfeit of office buildings and no downtown to go with them. But by the end of 1997, the situation had reversed, and Stamford had experienced a ''mini-boom'' with the occurrence of more than three million square feet of new, expanded or renovated construction.

By the year 2000, Stamford had increased its rental apartments by 1,000 units, and was planning for 1,000 more. In addition, the city had experienced a 27 percent decrease in the crime rate over the preceding four years. In 2005, Mayor Dannel P. Malloy said of his city: ''Stamford is a community which is economically soaring, with major economic development projects currently underway. The Stamford office market is vibrant, unemployment remains at all time lows, and our economy is well diversified. The City continues to be one of the premier business locations in the metropolitan New York market, and the residential sector in Stamford is growing with the addition of hundreds of downtown rental units. Stamford continues to be a people-oriented community with a vibrant and active arts and cultural presence.''

Historical Information: Stamford Historical Society, 1508 High Ridge Road, Stamford, CT 06903-4107; telephone (203)329-1183

Population Profile

Metropolitan Area Residents (PMSA)
1990: 329,935
2000: 353,556
Percent change, 1990–2000: 7.1%
U.S. rank in 1990: 1st (Greater New York, NY CMSA)
U.S. rank in 2000: 1st (CMSA)

City Residents
1980: 102,466
1990: 108,056
2000: 117,083
2003 estimate: 120,107
Percent change, 1990–2000: 8.3%
U.S. rank in 1980: 161st
U.S. rank in 1990: 177th (State rank: 5th)
U.S. rank in 2000: 209th

Density: 3,354 people per square mile (2000)

Racial and ethnic characteristics (2000)
   White: 81,718
   Black or African American: 18,019
   American Indian and Alaska Native: 243
   Asian: 5,856
   Native Hawaiian and Pacific Islander: 46
   Hispanic or Latino (may be of any race): 19,635
   Other: 7,608

Percent of residents born in state: 37.6%

Age characteristics (2000)
   Population under 5 years old: 8,108
   Population 5 to 14 years old: 7,452
   Population 15 to 19 years old: 6,704
   Population 20 to 24 years old: 5,669
   Population 25 to 34 years old: 20,802
   Population 35 to 44 years old: 20,202
   Population 45 to 54 years old: 15,142
   Population 55 to 59 years old: 5,665
   Population 60 to 64 years old: 4,547
   Population 65 to 74 years old: 8,271
   Population 75 to 84 years old: 5,663
   Population 85 years and over: 2,241
   Median age: 36.4 years

Births (2001, Fairfield County)
   Total number: 12,184

Deaths (2001, Fairfield County)
   Total number: 7,025 (of which 63 were infants under the age of 1 year)

Money income (1999)
   Per capita income: $34,987
   Median household income: $60,556
   Total number of households: 45,454

Number of households with income of . . .
   less than $10,000: 3,277
   $10,000 to $14,999: 2,045
   $15,000 to $24,999: 3,780
   $25,000 to $34,999: 4,010
   $35,000 to $49,999: 5,961
   $50,000 to $74,999: 8,232
   $75,000 to $99,999: 5,494
   $100,000 to $149,999: 6,216
   $150,000 to $199,999: 2,565
   $200,000 or more: 3,873

Percent of families below poverty level: 5.4% (26.8% of which were female householder families with related children under 5 years)

2002 FBI Crime Index Total: 2,398

Municipal Government

Stamford, located in Fairfield County, operates with a mayor and 40-member board of representatives system; each member is to serve a term of four years. The 40 representatives include two from each of twenty districts within the city.

Head Official: Mayor Dannel P. Malloy (D) (since 1995; current term expires 2005)

Total Number of City Employees: 2,980 (2005)

City Information: Mayor's Office, City of Stamford, 888 Washington Boulevard, Stamford, CT 06904-2152; telephone (203)977-4150; fax (203)977-5845

Economy

Major Industries and Commercial Activity

Traditionally, Stamford has been known for its corporate headquarters, manufacturing, retail and research activities. In the 1980s and 1990s, however, southwestern Connecticut blossomed, its real estate growing ever more attractive as the cost of doing business in New York City skyrocketed. By 1990, most of the city's downtown had been demolished and replaced by corporate headquarters. Like many areas of the Northeast, Stamford experienced higher vacancy rates and a slowdown in construction early in the 1990s, but by the dawn of the new century it was experiencing a tight market with low vacancy rates.

Stamford boasts an extraordinarily diverse economic base, and serves as the business center of Fairfield County. Many major U.S. companies have located their corporate headquarters in Stamford. Midway through the 2000s, Stamford remains a top-five city in the U.S. in terms of concentration of *Fortune* 500 headquarters in the country, as firms moved to the city citing lower costs of doing business and a higher quality of life. The area continues to have relatively low unemployment and continued growth was expected as more and more companies continued to grow in and relocate to the city. Among the firms located in Stamford are General Electric Capital Corporation, Pitney Bowes, Clairol, Xerox Corporation, Champion International, Gartner Group, Omega Engineering, Cadbury Beverages, Circon/ACMI, General RE Corporation, Hyperion Software, and Diaggio/United Distillers. Stamford is also home to Warburg Dillon Read, a Swiss-based international investment bank.

Stamford remains the major retail center of Fairfield County; a sizable portion of its labor force is employed in wholesale and retail trade. Research and development activities center around industrial research in chemicals, the electrical and optical fields, electronics, and pharmaceuticals. In addition, precision manufacturing maintained a significant presence in Stamford.

As of 2005, Stamford had more than 15 million square feet of office space rented, with additional space planned for the near future.

Items and goods produced: chemicals, computer software and microprocessors, electrical and electronic equipment, drugs, cosmetics, machinery, aircraft, metals, die casting, and apparel and textile products

Incentive Programs—New and Existing Companies

Local programs—The Southwestern Area Commerce and Industry Association (SACIA) is the designated Small Business Development Center (SBDC) for Stamford, serving start-up and small businesses. SBDCs offer technical and management assistance, counseling, education, and training programs. Qualified companies can take advantage of Federal Enterprise Zone benefits in Stamford. In addition to Stamford's already advantageous tax structure and rents as much as 50 percent lower than Manhattan rates, firms can qualify for significant corporate tax abatements under the Enterprise Zone and the Urban Jobs Program. Stamford was also named a Brownfields Showcase Community to demonstrate the benefits of collaborative activity on developing lands contaminated by industrial activity.

State programs—The Connecticut Department of Economic and Community Development develops and implements strategies to attract and retain businesses and jobs, revitalize neighborhoods and communities, ensure quality housing and foster appropriate development in Connecticut's towns and cities. Programs and services include loans and loan guarantees to manufacturers and job-providers, loans to women- and minority-owned businesses, planning and development services for industrial parks programs, tax credits for investments in Connecticut insurance firms, small business assistance, export assistance, and more.

Job training programs—Both on- and off-site and on-the-job training assistance is available through the Connecticut Department of Labor. Seventeen community and technical colleges across the state offer job and specialized skill training. The Connecticut Development Authority offers prime rate loans for Connecticut manufacturers to become more competitive by enhancing their employees' skills through training and development. The CDA pays 25 percent of the amount borrowed from a participating lender to invest in training, up to a maximum of $25,000. The State Department of Economic & Community Development provides counseling, job training programs, technical information and financing to help start-up and growing companies.

Development Projects

Well underway by 2005, the Mill River Corridor Project involves the creation of approximately 19 acres of new parkland along both sides of the Rippowam River and extending into downtown. The park is just the first part of a planned re-development of downtown that is expected to bring an additional $5 million in extra tax revenue annually upon completion.

The Gateway District Project was created to assemble the site for the relocation of the North American headquarters of the company now known as UBS Warburg (Swiss Bank) to Stamford. In all 12 acres of land had to be acquired and more than 20 buildings demolished to accommodate the 560,000 square-foot headquarters, which covers four city blocks in the heart of downtown and employs approximately 4,000 people.

In 2004 Stamford became one of the first major urban centers to lure a major retail store, in this case Target, to a five-story downtown location. If the store thrives the move could entice other traditionally-suburban retailers to try a downtown location, much to the surprise of industry insiders. Other downtown retail developments include a 126,000 square foot Burlington Coat Factory, and another 150,000 square feet of retail space at the Grayrock Place housing development.

Other housing projects are well underway downtown. In 2004 Stamford-based Stillwater Corp. broke ground on a 92-unit condominium project called Riverhouse with a planned occupancy date of June 2005, which was when ground was broken for another 83-unit luxury condominium development called High Grove.

Economic Development Information: Stamford Office of Economic Development, 9th Floor, Government Center, Stamford, CT; telephone (203)977-5089. Southwestern Area Commerce and Industry Association (SACIA), Ste. 230, One Landmark Square, Stamford, CT 06901-2679; telephone (203)359-3220. State Department of Economic and Community Development, 505 Hudson Street, Hartford, Connecticut 06106-7107; telephone (888)860-4628; Connecticut Development Authority, (860)258-7800

Commercial Shipping

Stamford is served by Conrail and a vast trucking fleet which makes use of the many federal and state highways that crisscross the city. Freight arrives by air at the New York City airports and is trucked into Stamford. All of the major national and international freight and shipping companies operate in the area.

Labor Force and Employment Outlook

Stamford citizens are highly educated; the city had the highest percentage of college graduates in the metropolitan area comprised of Connecticut's Fairfield County and parts of New York and New Jersey. The city's public school system turns out well-educated graduates; in fact, "Ladies Home Journal" ranked Stamford's public school system fourth among the nation's top 200 cities. Stamford's unemployment rate typically remains well below national averages. Employment gains tend to be centered in the services sector. The work force tends to be well trained and educated, which is not surprising given the technical nature of the products manufactured and the demands of the service sector. Stamford employers benefit from proximity to Yale University and other schools that provide consultation as well as education.

The following is a summary of data regarding the Bridgeport-Stamford-Norwalk NECTA metropolitan area labor force based on 2004 annual averages.

Size of nonagricultural labor force: 409,700

Number of workers employed in ...
  construction and mining: 14,400
  manufacturing: 41,800
  trade, transportation, and utilities: 74,900
  information: 12,100
  financial activities: 41,700
  business and professional services: 69,600
  educational and health services: 59,500
  leisure and hospitality: 32,500
  other services: 16,800
  government: 46,400

Average hourly earnings of production workers employed in manufacturing: $19.08 (April, 2005)

Unemployment rate: 4.9% (March 2005)

Largest private employers	Number of employees
Pitney Bowes, Inc.	3,058
UBS Warburg, Dillon, Reed	2,900
General Electric Capital Corporation	2,000
Stamford Town Center	2,000
Clairol, Inc.	1,300
Gartner Group	1,100
General Reinsurance Corp.	889

Cost of Living

Housing costs and other cost of living factors are high in Stamford and in its surrounding metropolitan area.

The following is a summary of data regarding several key cost of living factors for the Stamford area.

2004 (3rd Quarter) ACCRA Average House Price: $614,691

2004 (3rd Quarter) ACCRA Cost of Living Index: 153.2 (U.S. average = 100.0)

State income tax rate: 4.5% (corporate business tax rate: 7.5%)

State sales tax rate: 6.0%

Local income tax rate: None

Local sales tax rate: None

Property tax rate: $29.16 per $1,000 of assessed value (2005)

Economic Information: Stamford Department of Economic Development, 9th Floor, Government Center, Stamford, CT; telephone (203)977-5089

Education and Research

Elementary and Secondary Schools

Stamford's public school system offers several special programs, including bilingual and special education. Considered one of the finest systems in Connecticut, Stamford's enjoys one of the state's lowest student/teacher ratios. Teachers consistently earn national recognition for their innovative programs and are invited to share their expertise with their peers at conferences across the country. Stamford has had more Presidential Scholars than any other public schools system in Connecticut. Five schools offer magnet programs, each with a unique academic focus. Students are selected for the magnet programs via a lottery system.

The following is a summary of data regarding Stamford public schools as of the 2002–2003 school year.

Total enrollment: 15,231

Number of facilities
  elementary schools: 12
  junior high/middle schools: 4
  senior high schools: 2

Student/teacher ratio: 12.3:1

Teacher salaries (2005)
  average: $41,431

Funding per pupil: $13,337

The Stamford Catholic Regional School System and other parochial, private, and technical schools supplement Stamford's public school system.

Public Schools Information: Stamford Public Schools, PO Box 9310, Stamford, CT 06902; telephone (203)977-4105

Colleges and Universities

The University of Bridgeport's Stamford Campus offers graduate programs in Business (M.B.A.), Computer Science, Education, Counseling, Human Resource Development and Education Management and an undergraduate degree program, called IDEAL, for working adults. The University of Connecticut's Department of Plant Science maintains the 63-acre Bartlett Arboretum in Stamford. The university offers a master's of business administration program at the Stamford campus, as well as B.S. or B.A. degrees in American Studies, family studies, economics, English, history, political science, psychology, sociology, and general studies. A teacher certification program for college graduates is offered by the Neag School of Education. The J. M. Wright Regional Vocational Technical School provides programs in more than 25 trades and technical areas, and Stamford Hospital's School of Radiologic Technology has an allied medical program. The Westlawn Institute of Marine technology offers correspondence programs.

Libraries and Research Centers

Stamford's Ferguson Public Library system consists of a main library, three branches, and a bookmobile. The collection includes nearly 500,000 books and 1,200 periodicals. In 2004 there were 965,000 visitors to the library, and nearly 100,000 visitors to the library's website, which was named the top online library access in Connecticut. A $17,000 federal ''No Child Left Out'' grant helped the library's innovative Special Needs Center, which provides videos, books, and other materials to help parents of children with disabilities. Multimedia and electronic resources, art works, and Internet access are available to the public. The library is a depository for United States government and Connecticut State documents, and maintains extensive material on industries, business and management, genealogy, and local history.

Special libraries include those of the Xerox Corporation Legal Department, Clairol, Inc., CYTEC Industries, and GE Investments.

IRI Research Institute studies international agriculture and the University of Connecticut at Stamford conducts botanical research.

Public Library Information: Ferguson Library, One Public Library Plaza, Stamford, CT 06904; telephone (203)964-1000; fax (203)357-9098

Health Care

The Stamford Hospital is a not-for-profit, community teaching hospital serving Stamford and surrounding communities. It has 305 inpatient beds in medicine, surgery, obstetrics/gynecology, psychiatry, and medical and surgical intensive care units. Among its medical specialty areas are: cardiology, oncology, infectious diseases, neurology, and pulmonary medicine. The hospital also has several psychiatric services programs and is the site of a bone marrow transplant center, a Level II Trauma Center, the Jaffe MRI Center, a Day Surgery Center and Ambulatory Care Clinics; its critical care unit was recognized as one of the nation's best by the National Coalition on Healthcare. Stamford Hospital maintains an educational partnership with Columbia University College of Physicians and Surgeons for its teaching programs in internal medicine, family practice, psychiatry, obstetrics/gynecology, and surgery.

The Tulley Health Center, now affiliated with Stamford Hospital as part of the Stamford Health System, has replaced what was formerly St. Joseph Medical Center, which closed in 1998. The centrally located Tulley campus on Strawberry Hill provides convenient access to a wide range of outpatient services including the largest free-standing day surgery center in Fairfield County, the new Health & Fitness Institute, an innovative wellness facility focused on reducing health risks, their symptoms and effects; and an expanded Immediate Care Center for non-life threatening injuries and illnesses.

Health Care Information: The Stamford Hospital, PO Box 9317, Stamford, CT 06904; telephone (203)325-7000

Recreation

Sightseeing

Among Stamford's perennial premier attractions is the Bartlett Arboretum, a 63-acre nature area maintained by the University of Connecticut. Its highlights include a swamp walk, natural woodlands, cultivated gardens, ecology trails, a horticultural library, and display greenhouse. The 118-acre Stamford Museum and Nature Center, a nineteenth century park, contains a working farm, complete with farm animals and early American furniture and tools. The Center also has a planetarium, country store, nature trails, and galleries of art, natural history, and Native American items. The Champion Greenhouse presents horticulture exhibits that change with the season. The Hoyt-Barnum House, a restored blacksmith home which was built in 1699 and refurbished in 1738, represents three centuries of Stamford life. The nearby Maritime Aquarium at Norwalk attracts 525,000 visitors a year and is one of the largest attractions in Connecticut. To support the growing number of visitors and educational programs, The Maritime Aquarium recently completed its first major expansion project. Opened in April 2001, the new $9.5

million Environmental Education Center (funded through corporate, private, and state contributions) boasts new classrooms and high-tech educational equipment, plus a new main entrance, larger gift shop, and 180-seat food-service area. The move from the old gift shop also allowed for the addition of loggerhead sea turtles to the Aquarium's growing animal collection.

United House Wrecking Company's 30,000 square feet of floor space displays memorabilia such as furniture, marine salvage, antiques, musical items, and country store offerings. First Presbyterian Church, built in the shape of a fish to commemorate the early Christian symbol for Christ, was designed by Wallace K. Harrison in 1958. It features stained glass windows by Gabriel Loire of France, a Christian Memorial Walkway of flagstones, the Stamford Historical Wall tracing the city's history, and carillon concerts played by the fifty-six bells in the Maguire Memorial Tower. Many of Stamford's corporate headquarters offer tours of their facilities.

Arts and Culture

The Stamford Center for the Arts provides two homes for the performing arts in the city, and hosts more than 250 performances annually. The wonderfully restored 1927 Palace Theatre is home to the Stamford Symphony Orchestra, Chamber Orchestra, Connecticut Grand Opera, and the New England Lyric Operetta. The 1,580-seat facility also offers nationally renowned artists in live drama, music, dance, and opera performances. A recently completed multi-phase Palace Improvement Project has provided the Palace Theatre with an enlarged stage, new dressing rooms and other technical-support facilities, and improved services. The Rich Forum, with its 757-seat Truglia Theater, Mercede Promenade exhibition and gallery area, and "black box" Leonhardt Studio performing venue, brings live Broadway-quality productions to the city. Stamford Theatre Works, a resident professional theater company, offers productions at the Sacred Heart Academy Performing Arts Center. Connecticut Ballet stages several annual productions in Stamford, as does the city's resident City Ballet, often accompanied by dancers from the New York City Ballet. Canterbury Concerts is a series of baroque and classical choral and orchestral music performed at St. John's Episcopal Church, also the site of four annual programs presented by the Pro Arte Singers. Free summer concerts in Cove Island Park are performed by the National Chorale.

The Stamford Historical Society Museum presents permanent and changing exhibits of local history, and has research facilities. The Whitney Museum of American Art at Champion Plaza, a branch of the internationally-renowned New York City institution, offers five exhibitions annually (including works from Whitney's permanent collection), public education programs, special events, and docent-led gallery tours.

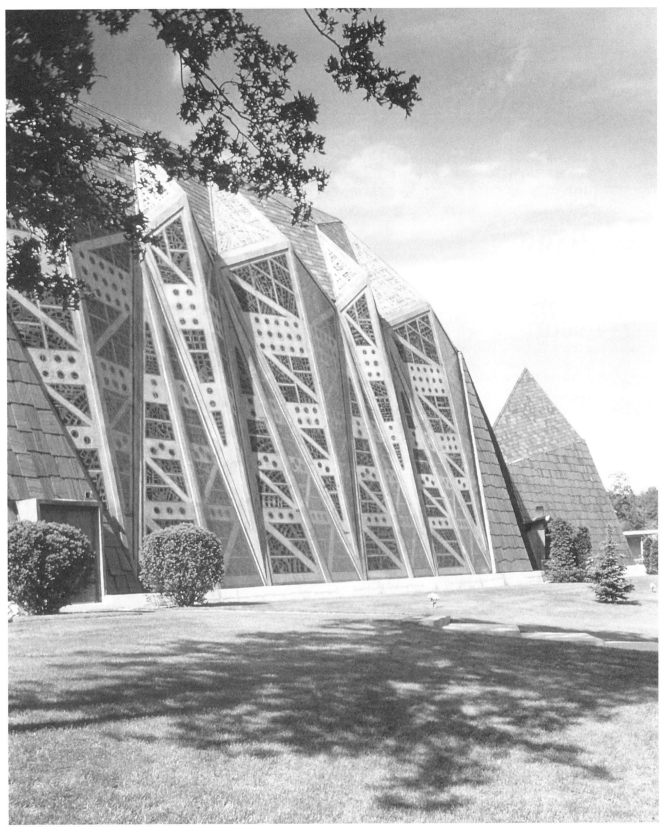

The First Presbyterian Church features the Christian Memorial Walkway, the Stamford Historical Wall, and a fifty-six bell carillon.

Festivals and Holidays

Stamford's annual festivals center around nature, and art and music. The coming of spring is heralded by the April's two-day Treetops Daffodil Festival and May's Azalea & Rhododendron Walk at Bartlett Arboretum. Spring on the Farm at the Stamford Museum and Nature Center Farm allows spectators to view plowing, sheepdog herding, and shearing. The Pink Tent Festival of the Arts is celebrated at Mill River Park in June. Music fills the July air with the sounds of the Long Island Sound Wave concerts. Ongoing mid-summer events include the annual Art in Public Places exhibition, the new French Market on Columbus Park (Tuesdays and Saturdays, July to November), and the five-concert Alive @ Five series of free outdoor performances in Columbus Park. September events include Arts, Crafts, and Blues on Bedford, the Harvest Fair at the Stamford Museum and Nature Center, Stamford Historical Society's three-day Quilt Show, and Kids' Day, which is sponsored by the Stamford Business Society. The two-day Gem and Mineral Show and Astronomy Day at Stamford Museum and Nature Center brightens November's days. Early December brings the city's Heights and Lights holiday extravaganza on Landmark Square, complete with a daredevil Santa rappelling down 22 stories from Stamford's tallest building and ending with the lighting of the city's tree. The glories of winter are celebrated at January's Winterfest at the Stamford Museum and Nature Center, and at February's Winterbloom two-day festival at Bartlett Arboretum.

Sports for the Spectator

Nearby Bridgeport has professional minor league sports with Bluefish baseball in the Atlantic League and Sound Tigers hockey, top affiliate for the New York Islanders of the National Hockey League. Local fans are also within an easy drive of several storied New York sports franchises, including the New York Yankees and Knickerbockers. The Department of Parks and Recreation annually schedules hundreds of baseball games at Cubeta Stadium, which hosts regional tournaments for league players of all ages.

Sports for the Participant

Golf and fishing are the activities of choice in Stamford, which maintains two public 18-hole courses. October's Stamford Classic Half-Marathon provides fast course loops through foliage, both downtown and at the coastline. Saltwater fishing is available aboard several charter vessels that dock in Stamford. The city's 40 parks cover more than 650 acres and include beaches, a marina, a boat basin, bridle paths, gardens, skating rinks, ball fields, basketball and tennis courts, and playgrounds. Several of the parks and yacht clubs are found along the shoreline. Cove Island Park is an 83-acre waterfront facility with a beach and the Terry Connors Rink, which has youth hockey and figure skating programs throughout the year. Scalzi Park and Cubeta Stadium has 48 acres of fields for baseball, soccer, Little League, tennis, bocce, and roller hockey. The Mianus River Park and Glen offers walking, hiking, biking and fishing in a 183-acre preserve. Indoor rock climbing classes for adults and teens are available at Go Vertical!.

Shopping and Dining

Stamford's major shopping facility is the Stamford Town Center, an enclosed mall with more than one hundred stores anchored by several noted department stores, including Macy's and Saks Fifth Avenue. Other prime shopping sites are the Bedford Street/High Ridge Fashion Plaza area, the Ridgeway Plaza, and the United House Wrecking, the state's largest antiques emporium. The nearby Norwalk Factory Outlet Center, with more than 50 stores, offers bargains on housewares, clothing, and shoes. Throughout Fairfield County, antique dealers sell furniture and house furnishings.

While seafood and New England chowders are mainstays on many menus, Stamford restaurants offer a range of culinary delights. Favorites among locals include Il Falco Ristorante (Italian), La Bretagne and Chez Jean-Pierre (French), Kujaku (Japanese and sushi), Ocean 211 (fine seafood), and Giovanni's Steak House (American).

Visitor Information: Coastal Fairfield County Convention & Visitors Bureau, 297 West Avenue, Norwalk, CT 06850; telephone (800)866-7925. State of Connecticut Tourism Division, 865 Brook St., Rocky Hill, CT 06067-3405; toll-free (800)CT-BOUND

Convention Facilities

Four downtown hotels with 1,700 rooms form the core of Stamford's meeting facilities. Meeting and banquet rooms can accommodate up to 1,100 guests. The Marriott Hotel, with 18 meeting rooms, offers 16,500 square feet of space which can be configured into additional meeting rooms or used for exhibits. The Sheraton Stamford Hotel's 26,000 square feet of exhibit space is complemented by the hotel's 15 meeting rooms. The Holiday Inn Select offers 10 meeting rooms and more than 7,000 square feet of exhibit space. The Westin Hotel's two ballrooms provide 13,000 square feet of exhibit space, supplemented by the hotel's 15 meeting rooms. The Hyatt Regency in nearby Greenwich has an additional 30,000 square feet of meeting space, a 100-seat executive amphitheater, and an outdoor pavilion.

Convention Information: Coastal Fairfield County Convention & Visitors Bureau, 297 West Avenue, Norwalk, CT 06850; toll-free (800)866-7925

Transportation

Approaching the City

For the purpose of air travel, Stamford is considered part of the New York City hub. Kennedy International Airport in Queens and LaGuardia in New York are an hour's drive from Stamford and offer full international, domestic, commuter, and freight service. Newark International Airport is a little more than an hour away.

Stamford commuters to New York City travel on the Metro-North Commuter line of the Metropolitan Transit Authority, which runs dozens of trains daily throughout the greater New York region; the MTA also operates a bus service in the region. In 2005 construction was underway on a new Downtown Transportation Center for rail, bus, and taxi service. Train service is also available to Boston, Washington, and beyond via Amtrak. Commuters can also use the Bridgeport-Port Jefferson Long Island Ferry, which runs from mid-May to the end of December. Other bus lines into Stamford include Greyhound.

Motorists can approach the city via two major north-south routes. I-95, the Connecticut Turnpike, runs along the coastline. Connecticut Route 15, the Merritt Parkway, is located further inland. I-287 runs southwest, connecting the Connecticut Turnpike with White Plains, New York. The northeast-southwest route is I-84.

Traveling in the City

Running east-west through the city and handling much of the automobile traffic are the Merritt Parkway in the northern portion of the city and the Connecticut Turnpike, closer to the harbor. Major north-south surface streets are Long Ridge Road and High Ridge Road. Stamford also maintains a bus public transportation system. Stamford Transportation Center is the hub for rail, bus, and taxi traffic.

Communications

Newspapers and Magazines

Stamford's daily, *The Advocate,* is published on Monday through Sunday. Other newspapers published locally are *Current Events* and *Know Your World Extra,* both newspapers for middle- and high-school students, and *The Sower,* a Ukranian-Catholic publication. Magazines published in Stamford include *Catalog Age, Current Science, Motorcycle Tour & Cruiser, The Sower,* and *Vegetarian Times.* Stamford is also within the circulation area of all of the major New York media providers, including the *New York Times.*

Television and Radio

No radio or television stations broadcast directly from Stamford, though many broadcasts from nearby cities are accessible to residents. Connecticut Radio Information Service, headquartered in Wethersfield, broadcasts readings from daily newspapers and magazines for the benefit of state residents who are blind or cannot hold or turn pages.

Media Information: *The Advocate,* 75 Tresser Building, Stamford, CT 06904; telephone (203)964-2200

Stamford Online

City of Stamford. Available www.ci.stamford.ct.us

Coastal Fairfield County Convention and Visitors Bureau. Available www.coastalct.com

Connecticut Development Authority. Available www.ctcda.com

Connecticut Economic Resource Center. Available www.cerc.com

Connecticut Innovations. Available www.ctinnovations.com

Ferguson Library. Available www.ferglib.org/ferg

Stamford Historical Society. Available www.stamfordhistory.org

The Stamford Hospital. Available www.stamhealth.org

Stamford Public Schools. Available www.stamford.k12.ct.us

State Department of Economic & Community Development. Available www.ct.gov/ecd

Selected Bibliography

Huntington, E. B. *History of Stamford, Connecticut: From Its Settlement in 1641, to the Present Time, Including Darien, Which Was One of its Parishes Until 1820* (Stamford: The author, 1868)

Sherwood, Herbert Francis. *The Story of Stamford* (New York: The States History Company, 1930)

Waterbury

The City in Brief

Founded: 1674 (incorporated, 1853)

Head Official: Mayor Michael J. Jarjura (since 2001)

City Population
  1980: 103,266
  1990: 108,961
  2000: 107,271
  2003 estimate: 108,130
  Percent change, 1990–2000: −0.9%
  U.S. rank in 1980: 157th
  U.S. rank in 1990: 172nd (State rank: 5th)
  U.S. rank in 2000: 238th

Metropolitan Area Population
  1980: 204,968
  1990: 221,629
  2000: 228,984
  Percent change, 1990–2000: 1.03%

U.S. rank in 1980: 1st (CMSA)
U.S. rank in 1990: 1st (CMSA)
U.S. rank in 2000: 1st (CMSA)

Area: 29 square miles (2000)
Elevation: ranges from 215 to 965 feet above sea level
Average Annual Temperature: 47.4° F
Average Annual Precipitation: 47.4 inches of rain; 35.2 inches of snow

Major Economic Sectors: Manufacturing, research, services, distribution
Unemployment Rate: 7.2% (February 2005)
Per Capita Income: $17,701 (1999)
2004 ACCRA Average House Price: Not reported
2004 ACCRA Cost of Living Index: Not reported

2002 FBI Crime Index Total: 6,524

Major Colleges and Universities: Teikyo Post; Naugatuck Valley Community Technical College; University of Connecticut (Waterbury branch)

Daily Newspaper: *The Waterbury Republican-American*

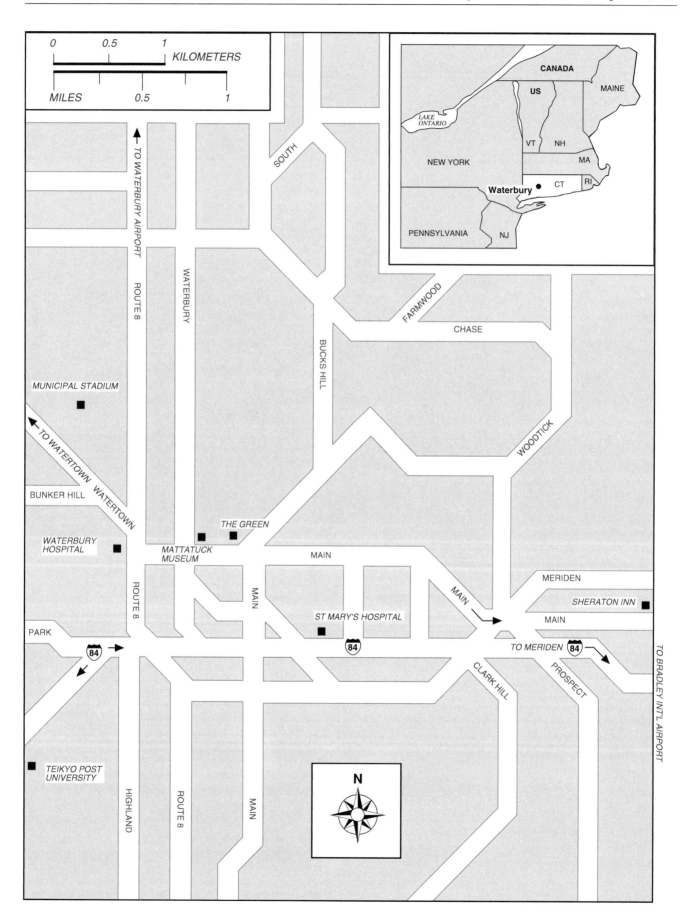

Introduction

Waterbury overcame a poor geographical setting by using Yankee ingenuity to make the city the "Brass Capital of the World." From the early 1800s until the mid-1960s, Waterbury buttons, buckles, and clocks were found in most American homes. With the decline of the brass industry after World War II, Waterbury aggressively diversified its industrial base, drawing new manufacturing and service industries to the city. Within driving distance of New York City and Boston, Waterbury offers businesses affordable housing, a skilled work force, and a revitalized downtown.

Geography and Climate

Located in west-central Connecticut, Waterbury lies in a hilly woodland portion of New Haven County. Built on a rocky plain in the Naugatuck River Valley, the city is bounded by granite hills to the east and west. The Mad River runs through the city's east side, curves to the west, and joins the Naugatuck River.

Waterbury experiences breezy spring and autumn seasons, warm, humid summers, and cold, dry winters. Snowfall averages 35 inches per year.

Area: 29 square miles (2000)

Elevation: Ranges from 215 feet to 965 feet above sea level

Average Temperatures: January, 23.8° F; July, 69.9° F; annual average, 47.4° F

Average Annual Precipitation: 47.4 inches of rain; 35.2 inches of snow

History

Industry Transforms Waterbury

The tract of land on which the Watertown/Waterbury area stands was officially purchased from the Tunxis tribe in 1677 for 38 dollars. This Native American tribe called the area "Matetcoke" or "land without trees," a name shortened to Mattatuck. The town remained Mattatuck until 1686 when it was renamed Waterbury in recognition of the abundant rivers and ponds in the area.

Growth was slow during Waterbury's first century. The lack of arable land discouraged new settlers and the residents suffered through the great flood of 1691 and the great sickness of 1712. After a century, Waterbury's population numbered just 5,000 people living in little more than 300 buildings. Waterbury hit its stride as an industrial city in the early 1800s when it began to make brass, using a technology taken from the British. Not content with exploiting the know-how, these Yankee entrepreneurs lured talented craftsmen from across the sea to set up shop in Waterbury. As the "Brass Capital of the World," the city gained a reputation for the quality and durability of its goods. Waterbury supplied brass and copper used in Boulder Dam in Colorado and safety pins made from brass wire. Waterbury's brass gears, buttons, buckles, bells, and bullets found their way into stores and homes throughout the nation. Waterbury brass also went into South American coins and minting disks for U.S. nickels. Another famous Waterbury product of the mid-1800s was Robert H. Ingersoll's one-dollar pocket watch, five million of which were sold. Other items included clocks, pewter goods, and chemicals.

The captains of industry who guided Waterbury's brass growth built their Victorian-era mansions on the Hillside close to their downtown headquarters. Not content to adorn their homes, these men of vision created beautiful office structures, including the Chase Brass headquarters and those of Anaconda American Brass. These industrialists financed the building of many of the gracious structures, which gained Waterbury its reputation for fine and varied architecture. While the brass business boomed, thousands of immigrants poured into the city seeking factory jobs, including the Irish, Italians, and Slavs.

Diversification Revives Economy

At its peak during World War II, 10,000 people worked at Scoville Brass, later renamed Century Brass. The brass manufacturing mills in the city's east end occupied more than 2 million square feet and more than 90 buildings.

In 1955, 60 hours of precipitation resulted in 19 inches of rain and caused 50-mile-per-hour flood waters. As a result of the flood, 19 Waterbury citizens died and 50 million dollars in property damage occurred.

With the closing of the last brass shop in the 1970s, this huge complex stood empty and Waterbury faced a grim future. With investment and planning, by 1983 Waterbury had successfully diversified its economy, attracting new manufacturing, research, and service firms.

Waterbury is within driving distance of both New York City and Boston, and offers workers affordable housing. In addition, Waterbury is working to revamp many of the city's unused freight yards and warehouses, and turn them into prime office space. New luxury hotels have been built, the city's south end is now home to the biggest mall in New England, and industrial parks in remodeled metal works factories are proving profitable. The city is known today for its advanced technology, historic architecture, and diverse neighborhoods.

Historical Information: Silas Bronson Library, 267 Grand Street, Waterbury, CT 06702; telephone (203)574-8222

Population Profile

Metropolitan Area Residents
1980: 204,968
1990: 221,629
2000: 228,984
Percent change, 1990–2000: 1.03%
U.S. rank in 1980: 1st (CMSA)
U.S. rank in 1990: 1st (CMSA)
U.S. rank in 2000: 1st (CMSA)

City Residents
1980: 103,266
1990: 108,961
2000: 107,271
Percent change, 1990–2000: −0.9%
U.S. rank in 1980: 157th
U.S. rank in 1990: 172nd (State rank: 4th)
U.S. rank in 2000: 238th

Density: 3,754.7 people per square mile (2000)

Racial and ethnic characteristics (2000)
White: 72,018
Black or African American: 17,500
American Indian and Alaska Native: 453
Asian: 1,615
Native Hawaiian and Pacific Islander: 61
Hispanic (may be of any race): 23,354
Other: 11,698

Percent of residents born in state: 64.1% (2000)

Age characteristics (2000)
Population under 5 years old: 8,176
Population 5 to 9 years old: 8,415
Population 10 to 14 years old: 7,681
Population 15 to 19 years old: 6,829
Population 20 to 24 years old: 6,919
Population 25 to 34 years old: 15,844
Population 35 to 44 years old: 16,183
Population 45 to 54 years old: 12,592
Population 55 to 59 years old: 4,747

Population 60 to 64 years old: 3,840
Population 65 to 74 years old: 7,223
Population 75 to 84 years old: 6,408
Population 85 years and over: 2,414
Median age: 34.9 years (2000)

Births (2001)
Total number: 2,699

Deaths (2001)
Total number: 1,556 (of which, 8 were infants under the age of 1 year)

Money income (1999)
Per capita income: $17,701
Median household income: $34,285
Total number of households: 42,655

Number of households with income of . . .
less than $10,000: 2,160
$10,000 to $14,999: 1,528
$15,000 to $24,999: 3,876
$25,000 to $34,999: 3,455
$35,000 to $49,999: 4,645
$50,000 to $74,999: 5,853
$75,000 to $99,999: 2,951
$100,000 to $149,999: 1,969
$150,000 to $199,999: 349
$200,000 or more: 219

Percent of families below poverty level: 12.7% (44.9% of which were female householder families with related children under 5 years)

2002 FBI Crime Index Total: 6,524

Municipal Government

Waterbury operates under a mayor-council form of government. The mayor is elected to two-year terms, as are the 15 aldermen.

Head Official: Mayor Michael J. Jarjura (since 2001; current term expires December 31, 2005)

Total Number of City Employees: 3,560 (2005)

City Information: Mayor's Office, City of Waterbury, 236 Grand Street, Waterbury, CT 06702; telephone (203)574-6712

Economy

Major Industries and Commercial Activity

Although manufacturing remains the mainstay of the Waterbury economy, the city is working toward diversifying its industrial base. New areas include chemical research and services such as banking. Area analysts and real estate brokers consider Waterbury a major Northeast distribution and warehouse center because of its proximity to interstate highways and affordable real estate prices. The commercial/retail segment of the city's economic base has been substantially enhanced by the development of a large regional mall, and other sizable retail projects.

Waterbury is also an attractive site for many corporations. Headquartered in Waterbury are Webster Financial Corp.; Les-Care Kitchens; Hubbard-Hall, Inc.; American Bank of Connecticut; Voltarc Technologies, Inc.; QScend Technologies, Inc.; and Waterbury Companies, Inc., among others.

Items and goods produced: fabricated brass and copper goods, plastic and paper products, automotive and screw machine products, automotive and electronic components, cold-formed fastening products, stamped metal products, women's apparel, toys, wire goods, and tool and die products for the metal fabrication industry

Incentive Programs—New and Existing Companies

The Naugatuck Valley Development Corporation (NVDC) is a nonprofit economic development corporation that services the city of Waterbury and the Naugatuck Valley Region of Connecticut. The activities carried out by NVDC range from the implementation of industrial and commercial development projects (some of which encompass more than 100 acres), to the development of Downtown Waterbury, to the administration of direct financial and development assistance for individual businesses.

Local programs—The City of Waterbury created a business incentive program that makes tax abatements and other benefits available to information technology businesses. A geographic area located within the Central Business District commonly referred to as the Information Technology Zone (ITZ) was defined to narrow the focus of economic impact. The State of Connecticut provided the funding for installing an infrastructure and wiring downtown buildings. Waterbury is classed as a labor surplus area, giving it preference in bidding on federal procurement contracts.

State programs—The Connecticut Development Authority works to expand Connecticut's business base. It offers a variety of tax, financial, and business incentives to encourage companies to locate in Connecticut. Small and large

businesses alike can take advantage of incentives such as below-market-rate loans; employee recruiting and training; reduced utility rates; and income tax, sales tax, and property tax exemptions or abatements. Information technology projects may obtain grants for a portion of the projected cost.

Job training programs—Customized job training assistance and on-the-job training are available through the Connecticut Labor Department and the local office of Workforce Connection. The Waterbury Education Department has recently teamed up with several local manufacturers to provide an apprenticeship program for the automatic screw machine industry.

Development Projects

Phase I of Waterbury's Downtown Development Plan involved the building of an arts, education, and entertainment center focusing on the Palace Theater. The focus of Phase II of the Downtown Development Project includes an area of East Main Street between the Green and Elm Street. A development is planned here that will connect the downtown area with the Brass Mills Mall and Shopping Center. The plan is to create an area that will bring people together for entertainment, cultural, and educational events. Also part of the Phase II plan is the Arts Magnet School, which opened in 2004. The school educates students in grades 6 to 12. The building, which stretches along East Main Street, consists of administrative offices, classrooms, a gymnasium, a cafeteria, as well as a media center.

The Willow/West Main Street area of Waterbury is currently in the midst of a three-phase plan for revitalization of the area. In addition to aesthetic improvements, work is underway on an off-street public parking lot, a neighborhood community center, and rehabilitation of area buildings.

In 1995, after both of Waterbury's hospitals identified the need to replace aging oncology equipment, a steering committee concluded that both Saint Mary's and Waterbury both hospitals would need to undertake extensive renovations to make the necessary improvements. It was eventually decided that the best solution was for the two hospitals to join forces by investing in new equipment and building a new off-site, state-of-the-art facility. The result of their collaboration is the Harold Leever Regional Cancer Center, opened in 2002, which utilizes the most current knowledge, skill, technology, and support services available today.

Economic Development Information: Naugatuck Valley Development Corporation, 100 Grand Street, Waterbury, CT 06702; telephone (203)756-2719; fax (203)756-9077

Commercial Shipping

Since the Naugatuck River is not navigable in the Waterbury area, railroads play a major role in the transportation of freight, especially Boston & Maine. In addition, air freight service is available out of a number of Connecticut and New York airports. Motor freight is carried by several companies based in Waterbury and by national and regional trucking firms that travel Interstate 84 and Route 8 daily.

Labor Force and Employment Outlook

Waterbury's labor force is described as available, skilled, and with a good work ethic inherited from the old-world craftsmen who built the region. Its central location enables the area to draw from a well-educated workforce. Waterbury anticipates a healthy economic future as a manufacturing, warehousing, and distribution center for the region.

The following is a summary of data regarding the Waterbury metropolitan area labor force, 2004 annual averages.

Size of nonagricultural labor force: 68,700

Number of workers employed in . . .
  construction and mining: 2,900
  manufacturing: 10,900
  trade, transportation, and utilities: 13,500
  information: 1,100
  financial activities: 2,800
  professional and business services: 5,900
  education and health services: 14,000
  leisure and hospitality: 4,700
  other services: 2,800
  government: 10,200

Average hourly earnings of production workers employed in manufacturing: $14.60

Unemployment rate: 7.2% (February 2005)

Largest employers	*Number of employees*
City of Waterbury	(the first three
St. Mary's Hospital	are identified as
Waterbury Hospital	having 1,000 or
Abbott Terrace Health Center	more employees;
Anamet, Inc.	no employee figures
Centerbank	available for the
Cedar Lane Rehabilitation	others, but they are
Center	identified as major
Connecticut Light & Power	area employers)
Company	
Sears Roebuck & Company	
Southern New England Telephone	
Stop & Shop	
Voltarc Technologies, Inc.	
U.S. Postal Service (Waterbury	
Branch)	
Waterbury Buckle Company	
Waterbury Companies, Inc.	
Waterbury Republican-American	

Cost of Living

The median sale price for houses and condominiums in Waterbury in 2000 was $94,000; in 2004 the average listing price for residential properties was $152,047.

The following is a summary of data regarding several key cost of living factors for the Waterbury area.

2004 ACCRA Average House Price: Not reported

2004 ACCRA Cost of Living Index: Not reported

State income tax rate: 3% to 5% tax on adjusted gross income

State sales tax rate: 6% on most items

Local income tax rate: None

Local sales tax rate: None

Property tax rate: $97.79 per $1,000 of assessed fair market value

Economic Information: Naugatuck Valley Development Corporation, 100 Grand Street, Waterbury, CT 06702; telephone (203)756-2719; fax (203)756-9077

Education and Research

Elementary and Secondary Schools

The Waterbury Public School District offers a number of programs for target groups such as gifted and talented students, special education students, and adult education students. The Warren F. Kaynor Regional Technical School helps to meet the special needs of high school students.

The following is a summary of data regarding the Waterbury public schools as of the 2004–2005 school year.

Total enrollment: 18,000

Number of facilities
  elementary schools: 20
  junior high/middle schools: 4
  senior high schools: 4
  other: 2

Student/teacher ratio: 22:2 (2003–2004)

Teacher salaries (2004–2005)
  minimum: $39,569
  maximum: $77,054

Funding per pupil: $10,837

Several parochial and private schools supplement the public system. St. Margaret's McTernan School is the coeducational merger of a well-known girl's school with an equally famous boy's school.

Public Schools Information: Superintendent's Office, Waterbury Public Schools, 236 Grand Street, Waterbury, CT 06702; telephone (203)574-8000

Colleges and Universities

Waterbury's four-year institutions include Teikyo Post University and an extension campus of the University of Connecticut. The U/Conn extension offers a bachelor's degree in general studies; Teikyo Post University concentrates on business, liberal arts, and equine studies.

Two-year institutions include Naugatuck Valley Community Technical College, which offers associate's degrees and certificates in dozens of liberal arts and occupational areas. Within a one-hour drive of Waterbury, students have a choice of more than 40 institutes of higher education, including Yale and Wesleyan.

Libraries and Research Centers

Waterbury's Silas Bronson Library houses a collection of 240,000 titles, 60 computer workstations, state and federal government documents depositories in its 53,000-square-foot facility The system includes a main facility on Grand Street and one branch library. Special interest libraries include those of the Mattatuck Historical Society, and the University of Connecticut, Waterbury Branch Library.

Public Library Information: Silas Bronson Library, 267 Grand Street, Waterbury, CT 06702; telephone (203)574-8222

Health Care

Health care in Waterbury is provided by the Waterbury Hospital Health Center, with 357 beds, and St. Mary's Hospital, with 347 beds. Both have cardiac rehabilitation units. Waterbury Hospital serves as a teaching hospital for area schools, while St. Mary's features industrial health services. The Harold Leever Regional Cancer Center is a joint venture partnership between Waterbury and Saint Mary's hospitals that is dedicated to outpatient cancer care. This 36,000-square-foot facility offers comprehensive cancer care using the most current knowledge, skill, technology, and support services available.

Health Care Information: Health Department, City of Waterbury, 95 Scovill St., Suite 100, Waterbury, CT 06702; telephone (203)574-6780

Recreation

Sightseeing

While other New England towns were razing their city centers in urban renewal efforts, Waterbury was preserving the architectural relics of the past. The city's 60-acre Hillside Historic District, listed on the National Register of Historic Places, includes 310 structures, many of them the carefully preserved Victorian homes of Waterbury's captains of industry. The Mattatuck Historic Society sponsors walking and bicycle tours of the area. Noted for its distinctive architecture, Waterbury maintains a set of Cass Gilbert municipal buildings, the old Union Station building with its 290-foot Italian Renaissance tower, and row upon row of carefully restored downtown storefronts.

The Railroad Museum of New England operates an excursion train between Waterbury and Thomaston. The train consists of historic, New England-related passenger and freight cars pulled by historic New Haven and Maine Central locomotives.

Arts and Culture

The city's elegant, 3,600-square-foot Palace Theatre is a major performing arts center for Waterbury. In addition to international artists and groups, the Palace is host to the Waterbury Symphony. The Symphony, a professional performing orchestra, is considered the region's best. The Waterbury Chorale, the Curtain Players, and Seven Angels Theatre Group also perform in the area. Other performing groups in the city include the Brass City Ballet, Shakesperience Productions, Siena Symphony Orchestra, Silas Bronson Library Playreaders Theater, and the various artists at the St. John's Concert Series.

The exhibits at Waterbury's Mattatuck Museum include a chronicle of the brass industry, a Connecticut Artists Collection including portraits and contemporary paintings, and industrial and local history displays. The museum, housed in a modern building facing the historic Green, is operated by the Mattatuck Historical Society. The museum also houses a 300-seat performing arts center. The new Timexpo, the Timex Museum, tells the story of Timex, dating back to the 1850s.

Festivals and Holidays

Many of Waterbury's celebrations reveal the city's rich ethnic heritage. Two festivals—the Lady of Mount Carmel Festival in July and the San Donato Festa in August—celebrate the city's Italian heritage. Outdoor parks are the sites of the Fourth of July Celebration. Several music festivals are held throughout the spring and summer.

Waterbury's City Administration Building is also known as the Chase Building.

Sports for the Spectator

The Waterbury Spirit baseball team of the Northern League East played its games at Municipal Stadium until 2001. Currently, the stadium stands dormant. Waterbury residents cheer for a variety of sports teams from other nearby cities.

Sports for the Participant

Golfers can enjoy 18-hole golf at two public courses in Waterbury: East Mountain Golf Course, with a par of 68, and Western Hills Golf Course, with a par of 72. Other facilities include numerous tennis courts, public swimming pools, and a municipal beach. Boating, water sports, and ice skating are all available on the city's many lakes and ponds.

Shopping and Dining

A large downtown shopping area featuring brick sidewalks, gas lights, old-fashioned benches, and turn-of-the-century storefronts is supplemented by several plaza malls located throughout the city. The Connecticut Store on Bank Street provides products by Connecticut manufacturers, craftsmen, artists, and authors. Malls in nearby Middlebury, New Haven, and West Hartford, and the antique shops that abound in the area, provide more extensive shopping opportunities.

New England seafood and Italian cuisine are the staples of Waterbury restaurant menus. The Westside Lobster House, with its restored Hotel Elton Ballroom, is noted for its fish dishes. Veal and pizza are mainstays of Italian eateries such as Dioro's, Bacco's, and San Marino Restaurant.

Visitor Information: Waterbury Region Convention and Visitors Bureau, 21 Church Street, Waterbury, CT 06702; telephone (203)597-9527; fax (203)597-8452

Convention Facilities

Waterbury, a growing convention and conference site, has one of the largest concentrations of rooms in the state. There are more than 900 sleeping and meeting rooms available in the area. The Connecticut Grand Hotel and Conference Center is the city's major conference center, with more than 40,000 square feet of exhibit space and meeting rooms and nearly 300 guest rooms. Smaller conferences are held at various hotels throughout the region.

Convention Information: Waterbury Region Convention and Visitors Bureau, 21 Church Street, Waterbury, CT 06702; telephone (203)597-9527; toll-free (888)588-7880

Transportation

Approaching the City

Daily bus service is provided from Waterbury to and from Bradley International Airport in Windsor Locks and the New York City airports. Several interstate bus lines and passenger trains travel into Waterbury. Connecticut Transportation Company has daily buses to and from New Haven, leaving from Waterbury's Green. Interstate I-84 East (the Yankee Expressway) connects Waterbury with Hartford and northern New England; I-84 West travels into New York and Pennsylvania. Major north-south routes include Connecticut Route 8, which connects with the Connecticut Turnpike (I-95).

Traveling in the City

Like streets in many New England towns, Waterbury's streets were planned around a central city green. Commuters experience heavy traffic on the freeways, especially during rush hours. City buses provide service in the city, running every 15 to 30 minutes with destinations including residential areas, hospitals, and downtown, as well as surrounding towns. Bonanza Bus Lines provides service to New York, Danbury, and Hartford. The Metro-North train takes commuters to New York City and all major points on the East Coast. A trolley, available for group hire, is operated by the Waterbury Convention and Visitors Commission. The Greater Waterbury Transit District provides wheelchair accessible mini-bus service.

Communications

Newspapers and Magazines

The Waterbury Republican-American, founded in 1844, is Waterbury's morning newspaper. Special interest magazines published in Waterbury include *Northeast Outdoors, Alternative Energy Retailer, Secondary Marketing Executive, Servicing Management,* and *Dry Cleaners News.*

Television and Radio

One independent television station exists in Waterbury, which also picks up New Haven and Hartford programs. A cable television franchise also operates in Waterbury. One local AM radio station broadcasts a variety of programming from Waterbury, but stations from nearby cities are available.

Media Information: Waterbury Republican-American, 389 Meadow Street, Waterbury, CT 06722; telephone (203)574-3636

Waterbury Online

City of Waterbury. Available www.waterbury-ct.gov

Connecticut Development Authority. Available www.ctcda .com

Greater Waterbury Chamber of Commerce. Available www .waterburychamber.com

Naugatuck Valley Development Corporation. Available www.nvdc.org

Silas Bronson Public Library. Available at www.bronson library.org

Waterbury Region Convention & Visitors Bureau. Available www.wrcvb.org

Waterbury *Republican-American.* Available www.rep-am .com

MAINE

The State in Brief

Nickname: Pine Tree State
Motto: *Dirigo* (I direct)

Flower: White pine cone and tassel
Bird: Chickadee

Area: 35,384 square miles (2000; U.S. rank: 39th)
Elevation: Ranges from sea level to 5,267 feet
Climate: Mild summers, long, cold winters with occasional heavy snowfall

Admitted to Union: March 15, 1820
Capital: Augusta
Head Official: Governor John Baldacci (D) (until 2007)

Population
    1980: 1,125,027
    1990: 1,227,928
    2000: 1,274,923
    2004 estimate: 1,317,253
    Percent change, 1990–2000: 3.8%
    U.S. rank in 2004: 40th
    Percent of residents born in state: 67.3% (2000)
    Density: 41.3 people per square mile (2000)
    2002 FBI Crime Index Total: 34,381

Racial and Ethnic Characteristics (2000)
    White: 1,236,014
    Black or African American: 6,760
    American Indian and Alaska Native: 7,098
    Asian: 9,111
    Native Hawaiian and Pacific Islander: 382
    Hispanic or Latino (may be of any race): 9,360
    Other: 2,911

Age Characteristics (2000)
    Population under 5 years old: 70,726
    Population 5 to 19 years old: 264,759
    Percent of population 65 years and over: 14.4%
    Median age: 38.6 years (2000)

Vital Statistics
    Total number of births (2003): 13,852
    Total number of deaths (2003): 12,429 (infant deaths, 64)
    AIDS cases reported through 2003: 518

Economy
    Major industries: Services, manufacturing, agriculture, fishing, tourism
    Unemployment rate: 4.7% (April 2005)
    Per capita income: $28,935 (2003; U.S. rank: 31st)
    Median household income: $37,619 (3-year average, 2001-2003)
    Percentage of persons below poverty level: 11.8% (3-year average, 2001-2003)
    Income tax rate: Graduated from 2.0% to 8.5% of federal adjusted gross income
    Sales tax rate: 5.0%

Augusta

The City in Brief

Founded: 1629 (incorporated, 1797)

Head Official: Mayor William E. Dowling (since 1998)

City Population
  1980: 21,819
  1990: 21,325
  2000: 18,560
  2003 estimate: 18,618
  Percent change, 1990–2000: −13.0%
  U.S. rank in 1990: 1,256th (State rank: 6th)
  U.S. rank in 2000: Not reported (State rank: 9th)

Metropolitan Area Population (Kennebec County)
  1980: 109,889
  1990: 115,904
  2000: 117,114
  Percent change, 1990–2000: 1.0%

U.S. rank in 1980: 383rd
U.S. rank in 1990: 411th
U.S. rank in 2000: 462nd

Area: 55.4 square miles (2000)
Elevation: 120 feet above sea level
Average Temperatures: January, 19.4° F; July, 70.1° F; annual average, 45° F
Average Annual Precipitation: 41.01 inches of rain; 77 inches of snow

Major Economic Sectors: Government, services, trade
Unemployment Rate: 4.8% (2004 Kennebec County)
Per Capita Income: $19,145 (1999)
2004 ACCRA Average House Price: Not reported
2004 ACCRA Cost of Living Index: Not reported

2002 FBI Crime Index Total: Not reported

Major Colleges and Universities: University of Maine at Augusta, Mid-State College

Daily Newspaper: *Kennebec Journal*

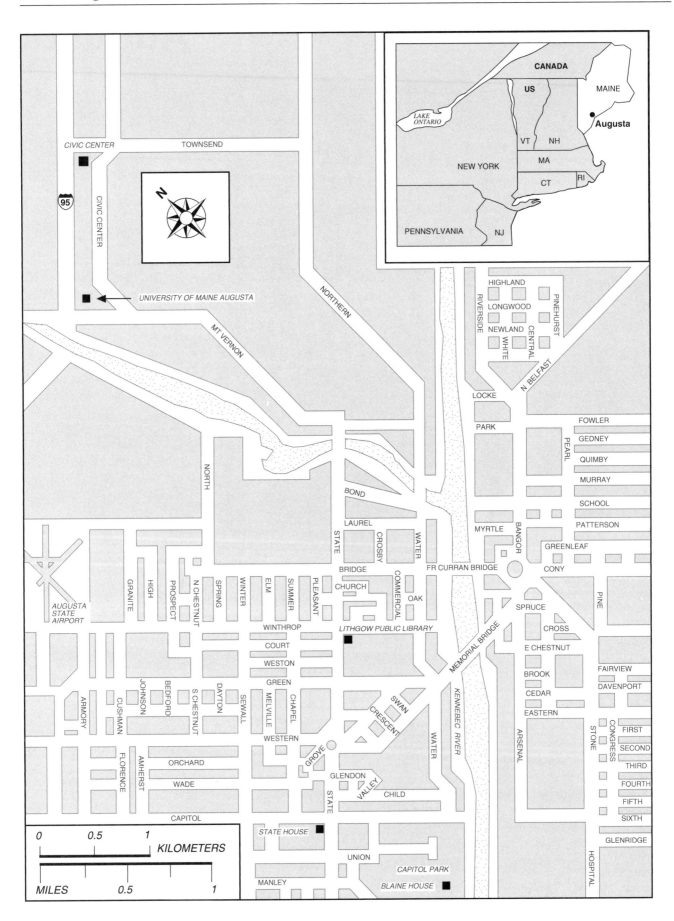

Introduction

Augusta, the capital of Maine, is the business and education center of a tourist-vacation area. The city lies in the Kennebec River Valley on both sides of the river's banks in a region noted for its fertile farmlands, rich timberlands, lakes, and scenic rolling hills. Augusta is considered one of Maine's fastest-growing cities. The presence of government lends stability to the city's economy. In the 1990s and into the early 2000s, the city has undergone a renewal with new facades on downtown storefronts, a new bus depot, a waterfront park, and a new city hall complex, the rehabilitation and reuse of landmark buildings in the city's downtown business core (including the former city hall, now an assisted living residence,) and the return of wildlife to the Kennebec River following the 1999 demolition of the Edwards Mill Dam.

Geography and Climate

Augusta rises in a series of terraces and sharp inclines east and west of the bisecting Kennebec River. Summers are pleasant; though winters have a reputation for harshness, they are not actually as severe as those experienced in places of corresponding latitude. Freezing temperatures at night are common in October and November, continuing to mid-April or early May. Precipitation is well distributed throughout the year.

Area: 55.4 square miles (2000)

Elevation: 120 feet above sea level

Average Temperatures: January, 19.4° F; July, 70.1° F; annual average, 45° F

Average Annual Precipitation: 41.01 inches of rain; 77 inches of snow

History

Native Tribes Support English, French Settlement

Thousands of years before the first English settlers arrived in the Kennebec River Valley, the region was inhabited by a tribe known as the Red Paint People, so called because their discovered graves contained a brilliant red ocher (iron oxide). Considered a highly developed people, they created implements that indicate woodworking skills, and they are known to have built small boats to explore the Kennebec Valley and beyond. The Algonquian-speaking tribes who later inhabited the region called it Cushnoc; one interpretation is that this means "the consecrated place." When the Pilgrims arrived in Massachusetts in the early 1600s, it was the Native Americans of Maine who kept them alive by sending gifts of food.

The Kennebec Valley was rich in furs, fish, and timber. Trade began in the area in 1628 when the Plymouth Colony of Massachusetts gained the Kennebec Patent. The first agent in command of the Cushnoc post was John Howland, who had been washed overboard during the *Mayflower* crossing and nearly lost. Howland shared the post with John Alden, who was immortalized in Longfellow's *The Courtship of Miles Standish.* Fur trading between the Natives and Pilgrims became highly profitable; for more than thirty years an amicable trading relationship existed until the increasing aggression of English settlers eager to exploit the land and its wealth forced the Natives to take the French side in the French and Indian Wars. English occupancy of the region was abandoned for almost one hundred years.

The next attempt to bring English settlers to the region began in 1754 with the erection of Fort Western on the Kennebec River. When the English defeated the French in 1759, settlers began moving into Fort Western and to an area south of the fort that became known as Hallowell. When Hallowell was incorporated as a town in 1771, Fort Western was included. A sawmill was built and lumber soon became an important source of wealth; in many instances pine boards took the place of currency. As the Hallowell area advanced more rapidly in wealth and population, rivalry developed between the two groups of settlers. The two communities divided; Hallowell retained its name and Fort Western became known as Harrington. In 1797 the two cities were united and renamed Augusta, possibly in honor of Pamela Augusta Dearborn, daughter of a prominent Revolutionary War soldier.

Economy Faces Change, Challenges

In 1828 a U.S. Arsenal was established in Augusta. Four years later the city became Maine's state capital. These events and the thriving river traffic that by 1840 saw a fleet of schooners traveling weekly between Augusta and Boston added to the city's prestige. A dam was constructed on the Kennebec River and cotton factories and sawmills grew up around it, attracting more settlers. By 1849 the population had grown to more than 8,000 and Augusta prospered.

The arrival of rail travel in 1851 caused a decline in river trade. The Civil War interrupted Augusta's development, and in 1865 fire devastated most of the city's business district. Still, the abundant natural resources contributed to continuing industrial and commercial prosperity. Augusta experienced mixed fortunes in the twentieth century; agriculture virtually disappeared in the area, and some industries declined. Government is the city's largest employer, providing four out of every ten jobs in the Augusta area. Employment in the service sector, especially health services, is also going strong. In the 1990s and into the early 2000s, the city has experienced rejuvenation of its waterfront and its business corridor.

Historical Information: Maine State Library, 64 State House Station, Augusta, ME 04333; telephone (207)287-5600

Population Profile

Metropolitan Area Residents
1980: 109,889
1990: 115,904
2000: 117,114
Percent change, 1990–2000: 1%
U.S. rank in 1980: 383rd
U.S. rank in 1990: 411th
U.S. rank in 2000: 462nd

City Residents:
1980: 21,819
1990: 21,325
2000: 18,560
2003 estimate: 18,618
Percent change, 1990–2000: −13%
U.S. rank in 1990: 1,256th (State rank: 6th)
U.S. rank in 2000: (State rank: 9th)

Density: 335.1 people per square mile (2000)

Racial and ethnic characteristics (2000)
  White: 17,856
  Black or African American: 93
  American Indian and Alaska Native: 89
  Asian: 250
  Native Hawaiian and Pacific Islander: 2
  Hispanic or Latino (may be of any race): 160
  Other: 270

Percent of residents born in state: 75.7%

Age characteristics (2000)
  Population under 5 years old: 928
  Population 5 to 9 years old: 1,102
  Population 10 to 14 years old: 1,096
  Population 15 to 19 years old: 1,155
  Population 20 to 24 years old: 1,142
  Population 25 to 34 years old: 2,385

Population 35 to 44 years old: 2,869
Population 45 to 54 years old: 2,714
Population 55 to 59 years old: 1,054
Population 60 to 64 years old: 831
Population 65 to 74 years old: 1,607
Population 75 to 84 years old: 1,194
Population 85 years and older: 483
Median age: 40.3 years (2000)

Births (1998)
  Total number: 222

Deaths (1998)
  Total number: 269 (of which, 0 were infants under the age of 1 year)

Money income (1999)
  Per capita income: $19,145
  Median household income: $29,921
  Total number of households: 8,591

Number of households with income of . . .
  less than $10,000: 1,312
  $10,000 to $14,999: 864
  $15,000 to $24,999: 1,446
  $25,000 to $34,999: 1,283
  $35,000 to $49,999: 1,371
  $50,000 to $74,999: 1,431
  $75,000 to $99,999: 510
  $100,000 to $149,999: 247
  $150,000 to $199,999: 37
  $200,000 or more: 90

Percent of families below poverty level: 11.4% (65.6% of which were female householder families with related children under 5 years)

2002 FBI Crime Index Total: Not reported

Municipal Government

Augusta operates under a mayor-council form of government. The mayor and eight council members are elected for three-year terms. A city manager is appointed by the council.

Head Official: Mayor William E. Dowling (since 1998; current term expires December 2006)

Total Number of City Employees: 250

City Information: City of Augusta, City Center Plaza, 16 Cony Street, Augusta, ME 04330; telephone (207)626-2300

Economy

Major Industries and Commercial Activity

As the capitol of Maine and seat of state government, Augusta is Maine's largest location for government employment; state government employs several thousand Augustans. Governmental activities are supported by financial institutions, law firms, and economic and governmental liaison consultants. Health care institutions in the region also account for a large share of service sector employment, especially MaineGeneral Medical Center, which employs 1,738 at its campuses in Augusta and nearby Waterville. Augusta is the site of a number of private sector employers with significant bases in the city, such as Central Maine Power Company, an electric utility that serves more than 560,000 customers throughout the state; and SCI Systems, which produces computer peripheral equipment. However, manufacturing employment in the area decreased during the late 1990s and into the 2000s. From 2000 through 2003, the state of Maine saw 11,430 layoffs at 163 manufacturing facilities; 1,139 of these layoffs were at Augusta-based companies. But there are new high-tech jobs emerging. Microdyne, a technology services company, has a technical support and helpdesk service center in Augusta. Augusta, like the rest of Maine, has fiber optic cable in many phone lines. This allows greater carrying capacity and is attractive to firms that demand easy linkage with other offices.

Augusta's central location has made it a major regional distribution center. Significant warehousing/distribution activity is evident within the commercial base of the community. Augusta is situated near several popular vacation areas, and tourism is another significant source of revenue.

In addition, Augusta has always been one of the state's retail hubs. In recent years, retail sales in the city have increased more than in the state as a whole during the same period. In 2001, consumer retail sales were $750,000 million, a 100 percent increase from 1991. Among all cities in Maine, Augusta is second only to Portland and Bangor in retail sales.

Items and goods produced: wood and paper products, computers, textiles, shoes, and meat processing

Incentive Programs—New and Existing Companies

Local programs—To encourage business investment in Augusta, the city offers an array of incentives, including: tax increment financing for qualified projects; loans of up to $25,000 for Augusta companies moving to another location within the city; and loans or grants of up to $400,000 to finance fixed assets, and/or up to $200,000 in gap financing for up to 40 percent of a business' development activities, for projects that benefit a percentage of low- to mid-income persons.

State programs—The Finance Authority of Maine (FAME,) assists economic development by providing capital for businesses through a wide variety of programs. FAME offers direct loans; credit enhancement through risk reduction and rate reduction programs; equity capital assistance for early-stage businesses; and cooperative programs with local agencies. Maine's Office of Business Development provides comprehensive financial, management, production, marketing, and other technical assistance to Maine businesses.

Job training programs—The Maine Quality Centers Program, coordinated by the state's technical colleges, offers customized education and training for new or expanding businesses at no cost to the businesses or to the trainees. The Capital Area Regional Vocational Center, part of the public school system, offers high school students and adults training in a variety of occupations. Special courses can be designed to meet the individual needs of employers. The Governor's Training Initiative program develops and coordinates training for companies that intend to expand or locate in Maine, reorganize to remain competitive, or upgrade worker skills.

Development Projects

In recent years considerable attention has been focused on Augusta's downtown, especially its waterfront area. A state-city partnership called the Capital Riverfront Improvement District (CRID) was established in 1999 to increase access to and use of the Kennebec River and revitalize the city's downtown. One of CRID's major current projects is the rehabilitation of the former site of Edwards Mill—a textile mill that closed in 1983 and then burned down in 1989—as an urban park. In 2004 the state granted $330,000 for the first phase of this project; CRID is currently seeking additional funds. A $500,000 restoration of the Kennebec Arsenal—a former army barracks and munitions supply house—to its original 1830 look is scheduled to begin in the summer of 2005. CRID's master plan for the city's downtown, developed by the people of Augusta and supported by state and city government, envisions a revitalized recreational waterfront, paths and parks linking the area's features and amenities, and development of the urban park. Private investment has led to revitalization of downtown's business core through the rehabilitation of landmark buildings, such as Old City Hall, the historic former home of city government, now an assisted living residence for seniors.

In 2005 an expansion of the Marketplace at Augusta shopping center began that will expand its floor space from 750,000 square feet to 960,000 square feet. A new, $55 million shopping center called Augusta Crossing is slated to open in 2006, potentially creating 850 new jobs.

Economic Development Information: Office of Economic and Community Development, City Center Plaza, 16 Cony

Street, Augusta, ME 04330; telephone (207)626-2336. Finance Authority of Maine (FAME), 5 Community Drive, PO Box 949, Augusta, ME 04332; telephone (207)623-3263

Labor Force and Employment Outlook

Because government is the major employer in Augusta, the area has a relatively stable workforce and the unemployment rate is lower than many other areas in the state. Since a significant number of low-skilled manufacturing jobs have left the area over the last two decades, Augusta citizens have had to attain more education in order to secure jobs. The number of adults with high school diplomas continues to increase in Augusta, rising from 65.6 percent in 1980, to 74.4 percent in 1990, and then 80.4 percent in 2000; the percentage of Bachelor degree holders was 15.1 percent in 1980, then 16.3 percent in 1990, jumping to 24.4 percent in 2000.

The following is a summary of data regarding the Kennebec County, Maine labor force, 2004 annual averages.

Size of nonagricultural labor force: 78,246

Number of workers employed in . . .
 construction and mining: 4,663
 manufacturing: 3,760
 trade, transportation and warehousing, and utilities: 15,818
 information: 1,005
 financial activities: 1,931
 educational and health services: 14,329
 government: 16,278

Average hourly earnings of production workers employed in manufacturing: $16.97 (statewide average)

Unemployment rate: 4.8% (2004; Kennebec County)

Largest employers	Number of employees
Central Maine Power Company	more than 1,000
MaineGeneral Medical Center	more than 1,000
SCI Systems, Inc.	500-999
Shop 'n' Save	250-499
O'Connor GMC Buick	250-499
Pine State Vending Company	250-499
Microdyne	250-499
Augusta Mental Health Institute	250-499

Cost of Living

The price of housing in Augusta is quite reasonable, and the average house sale price is usually considerably less than the average sale price in the state of Maine as a whole.

The following is a summary of data regarding cost of living factors in the Augusta area.

2004 ACCRA Average House Price: Not reported

2004 ACCRA Cost of Living Index: Not reported

State income tax rate: a graduated income tax rate from 2.0% to 8.5% of federal adjusted gross income minus all modifications, exemptions, and deductions.

State sales tax rate: 5.0%

Local income tax rate: None

Local sales tax rate: None

Property tax rate: $26.00 per $1,000 (2005)

Economic Information: Kennebec Valley Chamber of Commerce, PO Box 676, Augusta, ME 04332-0676; telephone (207)623-4559; fax (207)626-9342. Maine Dept. of Labor, Div. of Economic Analysis and Research, 20 Union St., Augusta, ME 04330-6826; telephone (207)287-2271

Education and Research

Elementary and Secondary Schools

In addition to a traditional academic program, the Augusta Public School system offers a special education program, a gifted and talented program, guidance, library media, English as a Second Language, alternative programs, and a regional vocational program. In 2003, one of the city's two middle schools—Lou Buker School—was closed and the city's seventh and eighth grades were consolidated at Hodgkins Middle School. (The closed school is now used for recreation programs.) Construction of a new, state-of-the-art Cony High School is underway as of 2005 and scheduled for completion by the end of 2006.

The following is a summary of data regarding the Augusta Public Schools District as of the 2002–2003 school year.

Total enrollment: 2,652

Number of facilities
 elementary schools: 4
 junior high/middle schools: 1
 senior high schools: 1
 other: 1 vocational/technical school

Student/teacher ratio: 10.3:1

Teacher salaries (2004-2005)
 minimum: $25,000
 maximum: $48,800

Funding per pupil: $10,073

Two parochial schools for students from kindergarten through 8th grade, and one small parochial academy for students from 1st through 12th grade, operate in Augusta, serving nearly 500 students.

Public Schools Information: Augusta School District, 40 Pierce Drive, Suite 3, Augusta, ME 04330; telephone (207)626-2468

Colleges and Universities

The University of Maine at Augusta (UMA) is one of the seven branches of the University of Maine system, which originated as an agricultural college in 1968 at Orono. UMA is comprised of three campuses, in Augusta, Bangor, and Lewiston-Auburn, with a total of nearly 6,000 students. Associate and baccalaureate programs are offered through UMA's colleges of arts and humanities; mathematics and professional studies; and natural and social sciences. The University of Maine at Augusta Senior College (UMASC), a self-governing and self-sustaining college located at UMA, is designed for persons age 50 and over. Mid-State College is a two-year institution offering programs in such areas as business, occupational education, and travel and tourism.

Libraries

Lithgow Public Library, located at Winthrop and State streets, is a Romanesque-Renaissance structure built of Maine granite in 1895. The library houses 54,000 volumes as well as 2,000 audio items, 3,000 video items, and 105 periodical subscriptions. The Maine State Library, located in the State House complex, was designed by Charles Bulfinch. The library holds 300,000 volumes on the subjects of state and local history; special collections include the Avery Collection of photographs and paintings of Mt. Katahdin and more than 100 oral history cassettes.

Special libraries are maintained by the Maine Regional Library for the Blind and Physically Handicapped, which holds 135,000 volumes; the State of Maine's Law and Legislative Reference Library, with 107,506 volumes and 480 periodical subscriptions; the University of Maine at Augusta; and Mid-State College and other area colleges.

Public Library Information: Lithgow Public Library, Winthrop Street, Augusta, ME 04330; telephone (207)626-2415

Health Care

MaineGeneral Medical Center, with campuses in Augusta and nearby Waterville, is the third-largest medical center in Maine and has 317 acute care beds. Both campuses provide emergency care, medical/surgical care, maternal and child health, and inpatient and outpatient diagnostic services. In 2002 a state-of-the-art cardiac catheterization lab opened at the Augusta campus; MaineGeneral cardiologists use it to evaluate patients' heart function and identify a variety of problems. In 2004, the center announced plans to build a $30 million cancer treatment center. The center is the clinical resource for the University of Maine at Augusta Medical Laboratory Technician Program and Associate Nursing Degree Program, and the Maine-Dartmouth Family Practice Residency Program. The center is a major eye surgery facility and also specializes in coronary care. A broad range of mental health and nursing home care is available in Augusta. Also located in the city is the Augusta Mental Health Institute.

Recreation

Sightseeing

Augusta straddles both sides of the Kennebec River. On the west side are grouped many buildings of architectural and historical interest. The State House Complex includes the State House, Maine's capitol building; Blaine House, the governor's mansion; the Maine State Museum; and the Maine State Library. The State House, a granite structure built in 1829-1832 and enlarged in 1910-1911, is surmounted by a dome topped with a gold-plated statue of the goddess Minerva; representing Augusta, she bears a pine bough torch. Blaine House, located in the capitol complex, was built in 1833 in the Federalist style; it has since been redesigned twice and now represents the semi-Colonial style. At one time the home of James G. Blaine, Speaker of the U.S. House of Representatives and 1884 presidential candidate, the mansion was presented to the state in 1919 to be used as the governor's residence. Tours of the State House and Blaine House can be arranged by contacting the Maine State Museum. Greek Revival enthusiasts can visit the Kennebec County Courthouse, built in 1830. Oblate House, designed by noted Maine architect John Calvin Stevens for Governor John Fremont Hill and his wife, a St. Louis native, is constructed of Maine granite and St. Louis brick; of the imposing estates built in the city during the late 1890s and early 1900s, only Oblate House still stands.

Capitol Park, stretching from the State House to the banks of the Kennebec River, offers pleasant vistas and native and exotic trees, shrubs, and ferns. Historically the park is of interest because of its Civil War associations. The park was the encampment for Maine regiments during the war; afterwards the site was conveyed to the city in trust for a Civil War monument. The park is the site of the Maine Vietnam War Veterans Memorial. On the other side of the river guided tours of Old Fort Western, a restored fort dating back

Front Street along the Kennebec River.

to the French and Indian War, are available from mid-June to September. The fort, designated a National Historic Landmark, is the oldest surviving wooden fort in New England. Costumed interpreters on site explain events and customs of the period.

Arts and Culture

Cultural opportunities in Augusta include a variety of theatrical and musical events. Shakespearean plays are presented at the Theater at Monmouth. The Augusta Symphony performs at various local sites throughout the year.

The natural and social history of Maine is interpreted through exhibits at the Maine State Museum, located in the State House complex. Among its exhibits are "Back to Nature," which depicts environmental habitats; "Maine Bounty" which focuses on the state's natural resources and their use; "12,000 Years in Maine," which features artifacts dating from the Ice Age through the late 1800s; and "Made in Maine" which depicts several nineteenth-century industrial scenes and displays more than 1,000 Maine-made products.

Other museums in Augusta are the Fort Western Museum at the Augusta City Center, which explains the history of the fort; and the Children's Discovery Museum, which offers "hands-on" fun for children through grade five in an interactive environment where exhibits are presented in such settings as a simulated diner, grocery store, post office, film studio, and construction site.

Festivals and Holidays

The gala event of the year in the Kennebec Valley, celebrating the clean-up of the Kennebec River, is the Whatever Family Festival. Held from mid June through early July in Augusta, Gardiner, and surrounding towns, the festival features a carnival, tournaments, music, dancing, a parade, and fireworks.

The Maine way of life is celebrated each September at the Common Ground Fair at the fairgrounds in nearby Unity. Sponsored by the Maine Organic Farmers and Gardeners Association, the fair attracts craftspeople, farmers, and chefs from throughout the state.

Sports for the Participant

The Augusta Recreation Bureau maintains many park facilities available for use by the public, including basketball and tennis courts, ball fields, swimming pools, winter skating rinks, and boat facilities on the Kennebec River. The proximity of hundreds of miles of lakes, ponds, and hills offers recreational opportunities to campers, hikers, and fishing enthusiasts. The Pine Tree State Arboretum, set on 224 acres, provides a great view of the Kennebec Valley at its

2,400-square-foot visitors center, and offers trails through woods and fields. The Kennebec River Rail Trail is a bike trail that runs along the river from Augusta toward Gardiner.

Shopping and Dining

The Marketplace at Augusta, with about 30 stores, is the largest shopping center in the area. In 2005 an expansion of the Marketplace began that will expand its floor space from 750,000 square feet to 960,000 square feet. Other major shopping centers include Turnpike Mall, Augusta Plaza, and Shaw Plaza. A new, 400,000 square-foot shopping center called Augusta Crossing is scheduled to open in 2006, near Turnpike Mall. The city also has a substantial selection of small to medium specialty shops, particularly in the downtown area. The nearby city of Hallowell, classified a National Historical District, is a favorite destination of antique buffs.

Diners in Augusta's restaurants can choose from a variety of fresh Maine seafood, including the state's famous lobster.

Visitor Information: Kennebec Valley Chamber of Commerce, PO Box 676, Augusta, ME 04332; telephone (207)623-4559

Convention Facilities

The Augusta Civic Center, described as central Maine's premier meeting place for business and entertainment, is located adjacent to Interstate 95, within minutes of Augusta State Airport and nearly 1,000 nearby hotel rooms. A prominent feature of the 32,000 square-foot center is the Paul G. Poulin Auditorium, which accommodates up to 7,000 people and can be set up as an exhibit hall. The civic center contains two ballrooms and 22 flexible capacity rooms for smaller functions.

Convention Information: Augusta Civic Center, 76 Community Drive, Augusta, ME 04330; telephone (207)626-2405; email info@augustaciviccenter.org

Transportation

Approaching the City

Augusta State Airport, located one mile from the city center, is served by US Airways Express, operated by Colgan Air. Most major state roads and highways converge in Augusta. Easy north-south access is available via the Maine Turnpike,

Interstate 95, U.S. 201, and State Road (SR) 27. East-west access is provided by U.S. 202; eastern access is via SR 3, 9, and 17.

Greyhound Bus provides daily bus service to Augusta on its Portland-Bangor run. Vermont Transit Lines, which serves northern New England, also provides public bus transportation to Augusta.

Traveling in the City

Most major attractions in Augusta are clustered near the western bank of the Kennebec River and are accessible on foot. Kennebec Valley Transit maintains bus routes.

Communications

Newspapers and Magazines

The *Kennebec Journal,* a morning newspaper, is published daily. Maine's oldest newspaper, it was founded in 1825. Magazines published in Augusta include *Maine Fish and Wildlife, Maine Motor Transport News,* and *Maine Trails.*

Television and Radio

WCBB, a public broadcasting television station, broadcasts from Augusta. Six AM and FM radio serve Augusta listeners and offer a variety of music, including oldies, adult contemporary, pop, and contemporary country.

Media Information: *Kennebec Journal,* 274 Western Ave., Augusta, ME 04332; telephone (207) 623-3811

Augusta Online

Augusta Civic Center. Available www.gwi.net/~acc

Augusta Public Schools. Available www.cony-hs.augusta .k12.me.us/default.htm

City of Augusta. Available www.ci.augusta.me.us

Finance Authority of Maine. Available www.famemaine .com

Kennebec Journal. Available www.kjonline.com

Kennecbec Valley Chamber of Commerce. Available www .augustamaine.com

Lithgow Public Library. Available www.lithgow.lib.me.us

Maine Department of Labor. Available www.state.me.us/ labor

University of Maine at Augusta. Available www.uma.maine .edu

Selected Bibliography

Grant, Gay M., *Along the Kennebec, The Herman Bryant Collection* (Arcadia:1995.)

Ulrich, Laurel, *A Midwife's Tale: The Life of Martha Ballard, Based on Her Diary* (New York: Knopf, distributed by Random House, 1990)

Bangor

The City in Brief

Founded: 1769 (incorporated 1791)

Head Official: Mayor Frank J. Farrington (since 2001)

City Population
  1980: 31,643
  1990: 33,181
  2000: 31,473
  2003 estimate: 31,550
  Percent change, 1990–2000: −9.0%
  U.S. rank in 1990: 809th (State rank: 4th)
  U.S. rank in 2000: Not reported (State rank: 3rd)

Metropolitan Area Population
  1980: 83,919
  1990: 91,629
  2000: 90,864
  Percent change, 1990–2000: −0.8%

U.S. rank in 1990: 258th
U.S. rank in 2000: 259th

Area: 34 square miles (2000)
Elevation: 158 feet above sea level
Average Annual Temperature: 43.9° F
Average Annual Precipitation: 41.7 inches of rain; 76 inches of snow

Major Economic Sectors: Services, trade, government
Unemployment Rate: 5.5% (February 2005)
Per Capita Income: $19,295 (1999)
2004 ACCRA Average House Price: Not reported
2004 ACCRA Cost of Living Index: Not reported

2002 FBI Crime Index Total: 1,630

Major Colleges and Universities: University of Maine at Orono, Husson College, Eastern Maine Community College, University College of Bangor, Beal College

Daily Newspaper: *Bangor Daily News*

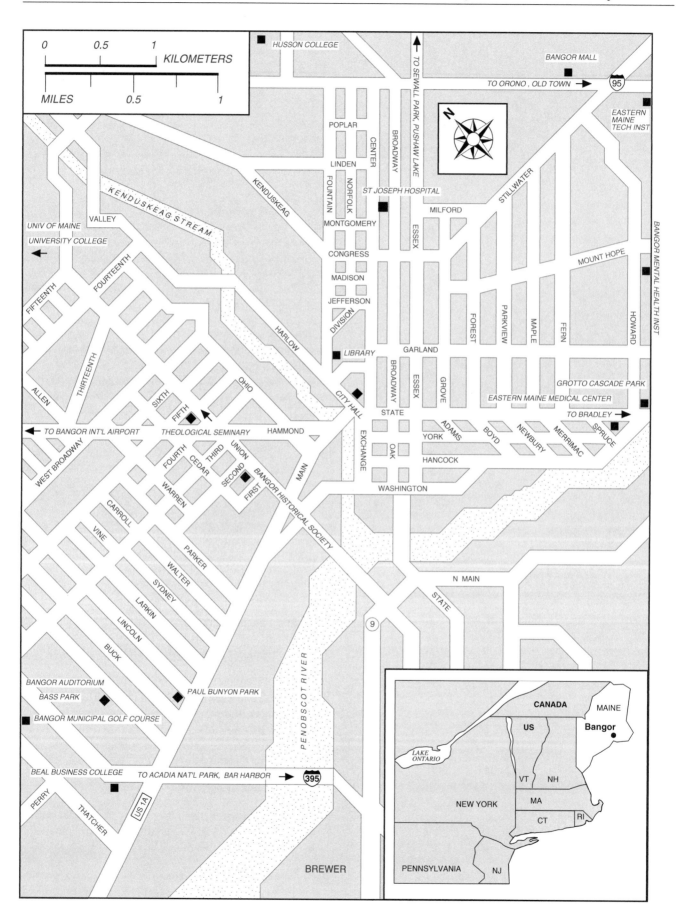

0   0.5   1

KILOMETERS

MILES   0.5   1

HUSSON COLLEGE

BANGOR MALL

TO ORONO , OLD TOWN →   95

TO SEWALL PARK, PUSHAW LAKE

EASTERN MAINE TECH INST

POPLAR

CENTER

BROADWAY

N

STILLWATER

LINDEN

FOUNTAIN

NORFOLK

ST JOSEPH HOSPITAL

MILFORD

ESSEX

KENDUSKEAG

MONTGOMERY

VALLEY

UNIV OF MAINE

UNIVERSITY COLLEGE

KENDUSKEAG STREAM

CONGRESS

MADISON

JEFFERSON

DIVISION

HARLOW

MOUNT HOPE

FOREST

PARKVIEW

MAPLE

FERN

HOWARD

BANGOR MENTAL HEALTH INST

FIFTEENTH

FOURTEENTH

THIRTEENTH

LIBRARY

GARLAND

BROADWAY

ESSEX

GROVE

OHIO

CITY HALL

ALLEN

SIXTH

FIFTH

GROTTO CASCADE PARK

EASTERN MAINE MEDICAL CENTER

TO BRADLEY →

TO BANGOR INT'L AIRPORT ←

THEOLOGICAL SEMINARY

HAMMOND

STATE

EXCHANGE

YORK

ADAMS

BOYD

NEWBURY

MERRIMAC

SPRUCE

WEST BROADWAY

FOURTH

CEDAR

THIRD

UNION

SECOND

FIRST

MAIN

OAK

HANCOCK

WARREN

BANGOR HISTORICAL SOCIETY

WASHINGTON

CARROLL

VINE

PARKER

WALTER

SYDNEY

N MAIN

STATE

LARKIN

LINCOLN

9

BUCK

PENOBSCOT RIVER

BANGOR AUDITORIUM

BASS PARK

PAUL BUNYON PARK

BANGOR MUNICIPAL GOLF COURSE

CANADA   MAINE

US   Bangor

LAKE ONTARIO

BEAL BUSINESS COLLEGE

TO ACADIA NAT'L PARK, BAR HARBOR →   395

PERRY

THATCHER

US 1A

VT   NH

NEW YORK   MA

CT   RI

BREWER

PENNSYLVANIA   NJ

Introduction

Located in the Acadia region of Maine, one of the most popular and scenic destinations in the country for summer visitors, Bangor is the third largest city in the state. Known as the Queen City of Maine, Bangor is the commercial, financial, and cultural center of the eastern and northern regions of the state. Fortunes were made in the nineteenth century in this former world capital of the timber industry, which exists today as a center for modern shopping malls, outlet centers, and industrial parks. Two of the latest editions of Macmillan's *Places Rated Almanac* rated Bangor as the best North American metropolitan area with a population of less than 100,000 people.

Geography and Climate

Bangor sprawls upon hills along the west bank of the Penobscot River, at the head of tidewater, thirty-five miles southeast of the geographic center of the state. It is located in the Acadia National Park region of Maine, which extends on the east coast from Penobscot Bay to Schoodic Point, and encompasses mountains, lakes, streams, and rocky peninsulas. Inland, the region stretches along the Penobscot River to Old Town. Kenduskeag Stream enters the city from a northerly direction. The area enjoys a four-season climate; summers are comfortable and winters are generally cold.

Area: 34 square miles (2000)

Elevation: 158 feet above sea level

Average Temperatures: January, 18.0° F; July, 68.0° F; annual average, 43.9° F

Average Annual Precipitation: 41.7 inches of rain; 76 inches of snow

History

River Powers Lumber Industry

The first settlers in the area where Bangor is now located were Abenaki Indians, residing in a peaceful village they called Kadesquit in a beautiful valley called Penobscot, "place of rocks." Their first famous visitor was the French explorer Samuel de Champlain who, in 1604, sailed up the Penobscot River. The legend was that he was searching for Norumbega, the city of gold of the poet Milton's *Paradise*

Lost. Instead Champlain found a locale near the Kenduskeag River, "most pleasant and agreeable," covered with oaks, pine, and spruce that formed the fabled forests of Maine that would later make the city's fortune in the timber trade.

Jacob Buswell was the first settler, coming from Massachusetts in 1769 to the area which would be known as Kenduskeag Plantation until 1787, when its name was changed to Sunbury. The area grew slowly, a frontier town strategically located between the forests and the opening to the sea, its revenues derived mainly from the export of fish, furs, and lumber. The American Revolution brought the British to Kenduskeag Plantation in 1779, causing most settlers there to flee. By 1791 the community, which had grown to number 576 inhabitants, had recovered enough to petition Massachusetts for incorporation as a town. Legend has it that the cleric who was sent to Boston to obtain incorporation papers was humming a religious tune known as "Bangor" while the town clerk filled out the papers; in some resulting confusion, the name "Bangor" was entered in the incorporation papers as the name of the town.

Over the next twenty years Bangor enjoyed a brisk international trade in lumber. Prosperity was interrupted by the War of 1812; in 1814 the British stormed the town, demanding its unconditional surrender. A peace treaty was signed shortly thereafter.

By 1834, Bangor's lumber and related industries made it a boom town; its population had grown from 2,808 in 1830 to 8,000 people. Millions of logs traveled down the Penobscot River to be converted in Bangor's mills, and by 1850 Bangor was the world's leading lumber port in spite of the disastrous overflow of the Penobscot River that occurred in 1846.

Lumber Industry Spawns Excesses

The mid-nineteenth century was a time of excess—sometimes riotous—for Bangor. The part of town known as the "Devil's Half-Acre" rivaled San Francisco's Barbary Coast in its heyday for drinking, debauchery, and the telling of tall tales (such as the legend of Paul Bunyan) when lumbermen and rivermen descended on Bangor during the winter months. At the same time lumber barons built stately manors, traveled widely, and encouraged the arts in Bangor, earning the city a reputation as the cultural center of the state. Bangor-built ships carried pine boards to the West Indies, where they were traded for molasses, sugar, and rum. A brisk trade grew up with the United Kingdom and Europe, while Penobscot River ice was harvested and shipped to ports on the Atlantic coast. Records of the time show that as many as 700 seafaring vessels were anchored in Bangor's harbor at one time.

By 1880 the readily accessible timber had disappeared, loggers headed west, and Bangor's glory days were over. In

1911 a large part of the city was destroyed by fire. In rebuilding, Bangor focused on an economy based on wholesale and retail trade; new industry moved into the area with the establishment of an interstate highway system and an international airport. Today Bangor is a thriving city, the commercial and cultural center of eastern Maine. The late twentieth century was marked by the passage of strict historical ordinances, downtown restoration, and an emphasis on the architectural value of the city's older neighborhoods. With a growing economy focused on the service industry, Bangor is a popular place to live as well as visit.

Historical Information: Bangor Museum and Center for History, 6 State St., Bangor, ME 04401; telephone (207)942-1900

Population Profile

Metropolitan Area Residents
1980: 83,919
1990: 91,629
2000: 90,864
Percent change, 1990–2000: −0.8%
U.S. rank in 1990: 258th
U.S. rank in 2000: 259th

City Residents
1980: 31,643
1990: 33,181
2000: 31,473
2003 estimate: 31,550
Percent change, 1990–2000: −9.0%
U.S. rank in 1990: 809th (State rank: 4th)
U.S. rank in 2000: Not reported (State rank: 3rd)

Density: 913.7 people per square mile (2000)

Racial and ethnic characteristics (2000)
White: 30,299
Black or African American: 447
American Indian and Alaska Native: 514
Asian: 463
Native Hawaiian and Pacific Islander: 36
Hispanic or Latino (may be of any race): 329
Other: 190

Percent of residents born in state: 69.6% (2000)

Age characteristics (2000)
Population under 5 years old: 1,805
Population 5 to 9 years old: 1,812
Population 10 to 14 years old: 1,857
Population 15 to 19 years old: 2,348

Population 20 to 24 years old: 2,772
Population 25 to 34 years old: 4,611
Population 35 to 44 years old: 4,921
Population 45 to 54 years old: 4,361
Population 55 to 59 years old: 1,423
Population 60 to 64 years old: 1,132
Population 65 to 74 years old: 2,103
Population 75 to 84 years old: 1,643
Population 85 years and over: 685
Median age: 36.1 years

Births (2000)
Total number: 333

Deaths (2000)
Total number: 346

Money income (1999)
Per capita income: $19,295
Median household income: $29,740
Total number of households: 13,738

Number of households with income of . . .
less than $10,000: 2,239
$10,000 to $14,999: 1,193
$15,000 to $24,999: 2,307
$25,000 to $34,999: 2,138
$35,000 to $49,999: 2,069
$50,000 to $74,999: 1,925
$75,000 to $99,999: 848
$100,000 to $149,999: 669
$150,000 to $199,999: 163
$200,000 or more: 187

Percent of families below poverty level: 11.9% (64.2% of which were female householder families with related children under 5 years)

2002 FBI Crime Index Total: 1,630

Municipal Government

The city of Bangor operates under the council-manager form of government. Nine non-partisan members of the city council are elected at large to three-year terms, with three positions on the council up for election each year in November. Immediately after election, the council selects one of its members to serve as council chair for the year. The council chair serves as mayor, and represents Bangor at ceremonial events and in interactions with state and federal government.

Head Official: Mayor Frank J. Farrington (since 2001; current term expires November 2005)

Total Number of City Employees: 787 (2004)

City Information: Bangor City Hall, 73 Harlow St., Bangor, ME 04401; telephone (207)992-4205; fax (207)945-4445

Economy

Major Industries and Commercial Activity

Bangor is the center for commercial activity in the northeastern and central regions of Maine. As such, the metropolitan area features a diversified economy. Unemployment rates are normally below state and federal levels. Over the past 10 years, total non-agricultural employment in the area has grown from 48,000 to more than 65,000. Major industries include services, wholesale/retail trade, and government, which together represent about 55 percent of the labor market. Other strong economic sectors include manufacturing, construction, finance, insurance, and real estate.

Bangor is a center for retail trade, and in recent years has generated close to a billion dollars annually in sales. Much of the sales activity was attributable to non-residents making use of the plentiful shopping facilities in the Bangor Mall and elsewhere in the city.

Healthcare is also an important segment of Bangor's economy. Providers include two major medical hospitals, Eastern Maine Medical Center and St. Joseph Hospital. Two mental health facilities are also located in the area, one state-run and one private. Together, these institutions provide the city with a large number of medical specialists who can meet almost any physical or mental need, and by extension the area supports a number of related healthcare services.

Downtown Bangor is the site of the regional headquarters for six commercial banking companies. Two of them are among the state's burgeoning community banks, those banks whose ownership remains in the communities in which they operate. According to the Bureau of Banking, in the late 1990s, the local banking and finance sector generated in excess of $1.1 billion in loan activity in the Bangor area.

Tourism is another important segment of the economy, as Bangor is a focal point for the more than four million people who annually visit Acadia National Park, the second most visited national park in the country. The area is well-known for its natural beauty, and as such thousands of tourists visit the area. Bangor's numerous restaurants, accommodations, and cultural attractions benefit from the influx of visitors.

Forest-related manufactured output, specifically paper, has long been a dominant industry in the area as well as the state. When paper is combined with lumber and wood products, forest products in total represented more than half of the manufactured output in Penobscot County in the mid-1990s. While this kind of manufacturing is still a major component to the area's economy, in the mid-2000s it is not as big of an economic player as it once was.

Items and goods produced: pulp and paper, wood products, shoes, electronics, transportation equipment

Incentive Programs—New and Existing Companies

The city of Bangor runs a variety of incentive programs, including technical, relocation, and financial assistance—both in the form of loans and tax increment financing. The city also works with the Eastern Main Development Corporation, a non-profit organization that helps businesses with marketing, manufacturing, government contracting, finance, and international trade. The state of Maine has a number of economic development programs available for Bangor businesses, including tax credits and financing.

Local programs—Community Development Block Grant Loans, administered by the Bangor Community Development Department, were made available in order to help local businesses retain and create jobs, acquire real estate for economic development purposes, and make site improvements. The loans are available up to $10,000 for each job generated or retained, and the project in question must meet the city's program goals.

State programs—Maine's Office of Business Development offers a wide variety of business assistance programs, including financing, marketing, research and development, tax reimbursement, technical assistance, and workforce training. The state's tax reimbursement program allows qualified Maine businesses to be reimbursed for local property taxes on eligible business equipment; some companies can also recover up to 80 percent of new employees' Maine income tax withholdings for up to 10 years. The Maine International Trade Center provides statewide international business assistance. The organization helps companies with technical assistance and trade counseling, import and export leads, international credit reports, workshops, and coordinated trade missions and trade shows. Their goal is to help the state's small- and medium-sized businesses succeed in international markets.

Job training programs—The Tri-County Workforce Investment Board is a local organization that helps employers and employees in Penobscot, Hancock, and Piscataquis counties; they help employees gain access to sustainable employment, training and educational opportunities, and help employers connect with a skilled workforce. Eastern Maine Community College offers short-term and specialized training and retraining courses to local businesses and other organizations.

Development Projects

The city, in cooperation with local organizations, has made extensive efforts to preserve and revitalize Bangor's downtown. Recently, the six-floor Freeses Building was acquired by the city and renovated, now serving as an elderly and assisted living facility and the home of the Maine Discovery Museum. The museum, which opened in 2001, is the largest children's museum north of Boston, with three floors of exhibits and activities. The once-vacant Bangor Furniture Buildings were turned into apartments, restaurants, and offices with the help of community development loan funds. Grant money from the city also enabled the University of Maine Museum of Art to open a new facility in downtown Bangor, occupying the first level of a former Sears department store. The museum opened in 2002 and features traveling exhibits of mainly contemporary art, along with a permanent collection of nearly 6,000 works including those by Pablo Picasso, Andrew Wyeth, and Andy Warhol. The Bangor Museum and Center for History, formerly the Bangor Historical Society, expanded by opening a second location in 2002.

In 2005, the city of Bangor and retail company L.L. Bean announced plans to open a year-round call center facility in Bangor. This will be the fourth call center L.L. Bean has in the state of Maine. The Bangor facility will be located in an unoccupied downtown building.

Economic Development Information: City of Bangor, Department of Community & Economic Development, 73 Harlow St., Bangor, ME 04401; telephone (207)992-4240; Maine Department of Economic and Community Development, telephone (207)624-9800; email biz.growth@maine.gov

Commercial Shipping

Bangor is located on I-95, the major north-south highway on the East Coast. Canada is 90 minutes away on State Route 9. Bangor & Aroostook rail lines offer freight service in central and northern Maine with connections to Canada, Maine Central and Boston & Maine railroads. A number of motor freight carriers serve Bangor, operating out of numerous trucking terminals. The deepwater port of Searsport, 20 miles from Bangor, is well suited to the import or export of bulk and break-bulk shipments. Bangor International Airport offers convenient cargo shipment services, with more than 30,000 square feet of cargo warehouse space and facilities to handle multiple major cargo operations. Bangor's Foreign Trade Zone consists of a 33-acre on-airport complex containing a central import processing building.

Labor Force and Employment Outlook

Bangor's metropolitan area labor force has experienced steady growth since 1998, at a rate of 10.9 percent over five years. The area enjoys a relatively stable labor market, with unemployment rates below both the state and federal averages. With a broad range of economic sectors, Bangor offers its residents diverse employment opportunities, with recent increases in the healthcare, retail trade, and tourism industries. Area colleges, universities, and local school systems provide a strong employment base in education. Local employees tend to have higher educations than those in other parts of the state; employees are known for high productivity, motivation, and dedication, with low absenteeism and turnover.

The following is a summary of data regarding the Bangor metropolitan area labor force, 2004 annual averages.

Size of non-agricultural labor force: 65,600

Number of workers employed in . . .
　construction and mining: 2,900
　manufacturing: 3,600
　trade, transportation, and utilities: 15,100
　information: 1,400
　financial activities: 2,300
　professional and business services: 5,600
　educational and health services: 13,100
　leisure and hospitality: 5,400
　other services: 2,000
　government: 13,900

Average hourly earnings of production workers employed in manufacturing: $16.97 (statewide average)

Unemployment rate: 5.5% (February 2005)

Largest employers	*Number of employees*
Bangor International Airport	(no employee
Bangor Mental Health Institute	figures available)
Bangor School System	
City of Bangor	
Community Health & Counseling Services	
County of Penobscot	
Dead River Company	
Eastern Maine Healthcare	
Fleet Bank of Maine	
General Electric Co.	
Maine Air National Guard	
Osram Sylvania Products, Inc.	
Shop 'N Save Supermarkets	
St. Joseph Hospital	
University of Maine	
Webber Energy Fuels	

Cost of Living

The cost of living in Bangor is moderate compared to the New England region as a whole. Housing prices, the largest single-family expenditure, are affordable, with the median single family home selling for approximately $120,000. Two bedroom apartments rent at approximately $550 to $600 per month, including heat, water, and sewer.

The following is a summary of data regarding several key cost of living factors for the Bangor metropolitan area.

2004 ACCRA Average House Price: Not reported

2004 ACCRA Cost of Living Index: Not reported

State income tax rate: ranges from 2.0% to 8.5% depending upon taxable income.

State sales tax rate: 5% (food and drugs exempt)

Local income tax rate: None

Local sales tax rate: None

Property tax rate: $22.05 per $1,000, based on 100% valuation (2004)

Economic Information: Department of Community and Economic Development, City of Bangor, 73 Harlow St., Bangor, ME 04401; telephone (207)992-4240. Maine Department of Labor, PO Box 259, Augusta, ME 04332; telephone (207)624-6400

Education and Research

Elementary and Secondary Schools

Public school education is highly prized and well supported in the Bangor metropolitan area. The Bangor school system is unique in that it is organized into schools serving four separate age levels (K-3; 4-5; 6-8; 9-12). Individual student progress is closely monitored through systematic assessments. Area students excel on achievement tests such as the Maine Educational Assessment, the Metropolitan Achievement Test, and the Scholastic Aptitude Test. More than 90 percent of graduating seniors continue their education at post-secondary institutions. Bangor's high school has been recognized by the U.S. Department of Education, which designated Bangor High as a 2001-2002 National School of Excellence—the only high school in New England to receive that designation for that year.

The following is a summary of data regarding the Bangor Public Schools as of the 2004–2005 school year.

Total enrollment: 4,022

Number of facilities
   elementary schools: 5
   intermediate schools (grades 4-5): 2
   junior high/middle schools: 2
   high schools: 1

Student/teacher ratio: 14:1

Teacher salaries
   average: $47,722

Funding per pupil: $7,652

Public Schools Information: Bangor School System, 73 Harlow St., Bangor, ME 04401; telephone (207)992-4152

Colleges and Universities

The University of Maine at Orono, the state's principal research institution, is located just north of Bangor. Its six colleges are Liberal Arts & Sciences; Business, Public Policy & Health; Education & Human Development; Natural Sciences, Forestry & Agriculture; School of Engineering Technology; and Honors College. The university offers 88 bachelor's degree programs, 64 master's degree programs, and 25 doctoral programs. Its library is ranked among the top in the country.

Eastern Maine Community College offers associate's degrees, diplomas, and certificate levels in 28 technology programs; More than 1,200 full- and part-time students are enrolled at the college, which employs more than 150 faculty members. Husson College is a four-year school that offers undergraduate and graduate degrees in a variety of disciplines. The Bangor Theological Seminary, established in 1814, awards master's and doctorate's degrees; it is the only accredited graduate school of religion in northern New England. Other post-secondary institutions in the Bangor area are University College of Bangor, Beal College, Maine Maritime Academy, the New England School of Broadcasting, Unity College, the College of the Atlantic, and Colby College.

Libraries and Research Centers

The Bangor Public Library, with more than 500,000 volumes of books, periodicals, government documents, and recordings, is one of the largest in New England and the busiest per capita in the country. The library sends more interlibrary loans each year than any other library in New England.

The University of Maine is home to the Raymond H. Fogler Library, the state's largest. Its collections include more than one million volumes, 3,400 periodical subscriptions, 1.6 million microforms, 2.25 million federal and provincial government documents, and a large number of electronic resources. The library's Ira C. Darling Marine Center houses a specialized collection focused on marine studies.

Public Library Information: Bangor Public Library, 145 Harlow St., Bangor, ME 04401; telephone (207)947-8336; fax (207)945-6694; email bplill@bpl.lib.me.us

Health Care

A number of hospitals cater to the physical and mental health care needs of Bangor area residents. The largest facility, Eastern Maine Medical Center, established in 1892, is a modern 411-bed regional hospital providing intensive care services; it is also one of three designated centers in the Maine Trauma System. St. Joseph Healthcare, operated by the Felician Sisters, offers acute care in its 100-bed hospital. One of the newest Bangor facilities is Acadia Hospital, which offers a range of inpatient and outpatient services for those in need of mental health and chemical dependency services. The state-operated Bangor Mental Health Institute is a 100-bed psychiatric hospital that serves two-thirds of the state's geographic area, providing services for people with severe mental illness.

For those in need of long-term nursing or supportive living arrangements, the metropolitan area offers a wide variety of nursing homes, assisted living facilities, and retirement village options.

Recreation

Sightseeing

Bangor's heritage has been preserved in the painstakingly restored mansions of the lumber barons in the Broadway Historic District, one of several local districts. A popular way to explore the city is by way of a historic walking tour, which takes the visitor through a number of Bangor's finest buildings representing a variety of architectural styles ranging from Colonial, Federal, Greek Revival, and Second Empire Italian.

At Fields Pond Audubon Center, visitors can take a variety of walks and canoe tours through the area's 192 acres of wetlands and forest, 1,600 feet of lakeshore, a 22-acre island, a beach, a brook, and a ravine. The recently opened

Maine Discovery Museum is the largest children's museum north of Boston, and features seven major interactive exhibit areas on three levels. Located in the historic Freeses building downtown, the museum promotes the learning and discovery of nature, geography, children's literature, music, art, science, and anatomy.

Visitors who travel farther afield into the Maine countryside will find charming villages and towns such as Old Town, where they may observe crafters constructing canoes at the Old Town Canoe Company. The Penobscot Indian Reservation at Old Town is home to members of that tribe. The town of Canaan displays Charles Lindbergh memorabilia housed in the crate that carried his plane back to America from Paris in 1927. Devotees of American domestic architecture can explore five turn-of-the century summer cottages furnished as they were by the families who lived in them at Roosevelt Campobello International Park, summer home of Franklin and Eleanor Roosevelt. The park also boasts 10 miles of walking trails, bird watching, flower gardens, a lighthouse, sea kayaking, and a number of beaches.

Arts and Culture

Bangor Symphony Orchestra, the country's oldest continuous community orchestra, has been performing since 1896. Comprised of 60 to 90 members, the orchestra performs 6 classical concerts, special events, and pops concerts during its September-May season. At the Maine Center for the Arts on the campus of the University of Maine at Orono, musical and dance events are presented throughout the year at the acoustically heralded Hutchins Concert Hall. In late spring and throughout the summer, the Bangor Band offers free weekly outdoor concerts at the Paul Bunyan Park grandstand. Other musical concert series in Bangor include the Cool Sounds of Summer concerts, held weekly at Riverfront Park, and the Arcady Music Festival, featuring international musicians.

Penobscot Theatre Company, housed in the Banger Opera House downtown, performs Broadway hits and contemporary drama during the winter months; in July and August it presents the Maine Shakespeare Festival. Recent productions include ''Dracula,'' ''The Crucible,'' and ''Long Day's Journey into Night.'' Theater students at the University of Maine present contemporary and classical works at Maine Masque Theatre from October through April.

The Bangor Museum and Center for History, exhibiting historic memorabilia from the Penobscot Valley, is housed downtown adjacent to the Maine Discovery Museum. At the Cole Land Transportation Museum visitors can learn about and view a cross section of Maine's land transportation equipment, as well as U.S. military memorabilia. The Old Town Museum commemorates the area's lumbering history, and the Penobscot Marine Museum, a 13-building complex, preserves and exhibits the history of Penobscot Bay and the maritime history of Maine. Art studios and galleries are clustered in downtown Bangor.

Anthropological exhibits relating to Native Americans are on display at the Hudson Museum on the campus of the University of Maine at Orono, which also maintains greenhouses and ornamental test gardens that can be viewed by appointment, as well as a planetarium. The university's Museum of Art, one of the country's oldest land grant university art collections, displays more than 5,700 works including an extensive collection of nineteenth- and twentieth-century European and American prints. Its collection also celebrates Maine art and artists, with works by Berenice Abbott, Winslow Homer, and Andrew Wyeth. The Maine Forest and Logging Museum in Bradley is a living history museum dedicated to the mighty Maine woods. The museum's 400-acre Leonard's Mills contains the site of a pioneer settlement, and the area comes alive every summer and fall when volunteers in period dress recreate the daily life of a logging and milling community of the 1790s.

Festivals and Holidays

Summer festivals in Bangor include a Sidewalk Arts Festival in August, and a celebration of the Fourth of July with fireworks and a parade. Bass Park is the site of a ten-day celebration of agriculture at the State Fair, held in early August. During June and July, the park is also the site for harness racing. The Music in the Park series is presented throughout the summer. October brings Octoberfest, and downtown art studios and galleries are open for touring every November. The traditional Christmas tree lighting in December is followed by a parade the next day. A winter carnival is held in February.

Sports for the Spectator

The 27-hole Bangor Municipal Golf Course presents many tournaments each year, including the Greater Bangor Open held in July. Bangor Raceway at Bass Park offers harness racing in June and July; the sport has been conducted continuously at Bass Park since 1893. The raceway hosts several legs of the Maine Breeders Stakes, the Anah Temple Shrine Trot and Parade, and the Billings Amateur Driving Series. The University of Maine's Black Bears play baseball at Mahaney Diamond; the university also fields football, basketball, and hockey teams. Husson College also has successful baseball and basketball teams.

Sports for the Participant

Recreational opportunities in and around Bangor are almost limitless. Boating and fishing on the Penobscot, golfing at several courses, camping at sites within and outside the city limits, ice skating and hockey at local arenas, and downhill and cross-country skiing are only some of the activities available. The Bangor Municipal Golf Course has been rated by the magazine *Golf Digest* as one of the top 75 public golf courses in the country. The course offers a 15-tee driving range, 2 practice greens, a complete pro shop, and restaurant. PGA professionals give group and private lessons.

Bangor Creative Playground is a specially designed park for children. Grotto Cascade Park, with its lighted water fountain and a 20-foot-high waterfall, is popular with picnickers and hikers; opposite the park, at Salmon Pool, Atlantic salmon headed upstream are a favorite catch for anglers in May and June. Sewall Park in nearby Old Town consists of 30 acres, some wooded, offering hiking, picnicking, camping, canoeing, sports facilities, fishing, and boat launching. Bangor is located not far from Acadia National Park, the second most visited national park in the country, and Baxter State Park, site of Mt. Katahdin, Maine's highest peak.

Shopping and Dining

Shopping is serious business in Bangor, a major outlet store center and home to numerous department stores, shopping centers, and malls. Downtown Bangor features specialty shops, bookstores, restaurants, and parks on the waterfront. Woven baskets and leather goods are offered at the Penobscot Indian Reservation on Indian Island, Old Town. Shoppers from a wide area are attracted to the department stores and specialty shops at Bangor Mall, the state's second-largest shopping mall. Restaurants and a 10-screen theater flank the Bangor Mall area. Airport Mall was Maine's first indoor shopping center when it opened in 1972; today it offers more than a dozen stores selling a variety of products. Antiques and collectibles are the focus at Center Mall in Brewer; within driving distance of Bangor are scores of antique shops, potteries, and gift shops.

Dining opportunities range from regional establishments specializing in lobster to ethnic restaurants specializing in Mexican, Italian, Indian, Asian, and Pakistani foods. Coffeehouses, pubs, and taverns round out Bangor's offerings.

Visitor Information: Greater Bangor Convention & Visitors Bureau, 1 Cumberland Pl., Ste. 300, Bangor, ME 04401; telephone (207)947-5205; toll-free (800)91-MOOSE

Convention Facilities

The Bangor Auditorium offers 16,000 square feet of exhibit space with a seating capacity of 6,000. The Civic Center, with 22,000 square feet of usable space, is capable of hosting 9 concurrent meetings; it has banquet seating for up to 800 people, and a 12,000-square-foot catering center. Both facilities are located at Bass Park. The entrance to the complex is graced by a statue of Paul Bunyan. Norumbega Hall, which houses the University of Maine Museum of Art, can accommodate 1,000 people in its auditorium. The Penobscot Theatre, located in the Bangor Opera House, is handicap accessible and seats 299 people.

In nearby Orono, the Best Western Black Bear Inn and Conference Center can accommodate up to 300 people for conferences and offers 68 sleeping rooms. The facilities include more than 7,900 square feet of meeting space. More than 25 hotels, motels, inns, bed and breakfasts, and camping facilities are located within the Bangor metropolitan area.

Convention Information: Greater Bangor Convention & Visitors Bureau, 1 Cumberland Pl., Ste. 300, Bangor, ME 04401; telephone (207)947-5205; toll-free (800)91-MOOSE

Transportation

Approaching the City

Bangor International Airport offers more than 50 flights per day to and from national and regional hubs as well as Florida and the Caribbean. It is served by major airlines, including Delta, American, US Airways, Continental, and Northwest, with non-stop destinations like Boston, New York, Detroit, Philadelphia, and Cincinnati. Bangor is easily reached via Interstate 95, Maine Route 2 from the north and west, Route 9 from the east, and Route 1A from the south. Rail and bus service is provided by Greyhound and Concord Trailways, providing direct connections to Amtrak in Portland or Boston.

Traveling in the City

Downtown shopping and dining sites are easily accessible on foot, and walking tours through historic areas are offered. The BAT Community Connector is a local bus service providing connections throughout the Bangor metropolitan area. Full service is available Monday through Friday, partial service on Saturday, and no service on Sunday.

Communications

Newspapers and Magazines

In operation for more than 110 years, the *Bangor Daily News* is published mornings Monday through Saturday. The paper is one of the few family-owned newspapers in the country, and has a circulation of approximately 70,000. *The Weekly* is distributed throughout the area on Fridays, and features a calendar of events, nonprofit news, and other health and welfare features.

Television and Radio

Six television stations—four major commercial stations plus PBS and Pax—have broadcast studios in Bangor. More than 15 AM and FM radio stations are broadcast in the area.

Media Information: Bangor Daily News, 491 Main St., PO Box 1329, Bangor, ME 04402; telephone (207)990-8000; toll-free (800)432-7964;

Bangor Online

Bangor Region Chamber of Commerce. Available www.bangorregion.com

Bangor School System. Available www.bangorschools.net

City of Bangor. Available www.bgrme.org

County of Penobscot. Available www.maine.gov/local/penobscot

Downtown Bangor. Available www.downtownbangor.com

Eastern Maine Healthcare System. Available www.emh.org

Greater Bangor Convention and Visitors Bureau. Available www.bangorcvb.org

Maine Department of Labor. Available www.state.me.us/labor

Selected Bibliography

Goldstein, Judith S., *Crossing Lines: Histories of Jews and Gentiles in Three Communities* (New York, NY: Morrow, 1992)

Laughead, William B., *The Marvelous Exploits of Paul Bunyan: As Told in the Camps of the White Pine Lumbermen for Generations* (Westwood, Calif: Red River Lumber Co., 1939)

Shaw, Richard R., *Bangor, Maine Volume 2: The Twentieth Century* (Arcadia, 1997)

Lewiston

The City in Brief

Founded: 1770 (incorporated, 1795)

Head Official: Mayor Lionel C. Guay Jr. (since January 2004)

City Population
    1980: 40,481
    1990: 39,757
    2000: 35,690
    2003 estimate: 35,922
    Percent change, 1990–2000: − 10.3%
    U.S. rank in 1980: 540th
    U.S. rank in 1990: 664th (State rank: 2nd)
    U.S. rank in 2000: Not reported (State rank: 2nd)

Metropolitan Area Population
    1990: 93,679
    2000: 90,830
    Percent change, 1990–2000: −3.0%

U.S. rank in 1990: 256th
U.S. rank in 2000: 268th

Area: 34 square miles (2000)
Elevation: 121 feet above sea level
Average Temperatures: 46.1° F
Average Annual Precipitation: 45.8 inches of rain, 70.1 inches of snow

Major Economic Sectors: Services, manufacturing, trade, government
Unemployment Rate: 5.5% (February 2005)
Per Capita Income: $17,905 (1999)
2004 ACCRA Average House Price: Not reported
2004 ACCRA Cost of Living Index: Not reported

2002 FBI Crime Index Total: 3,322

Major Colleges and Universities: Bates College, Lewiston-Auburn College of the University of Southern Maine

Daily Newspaper: *Sun Journal*

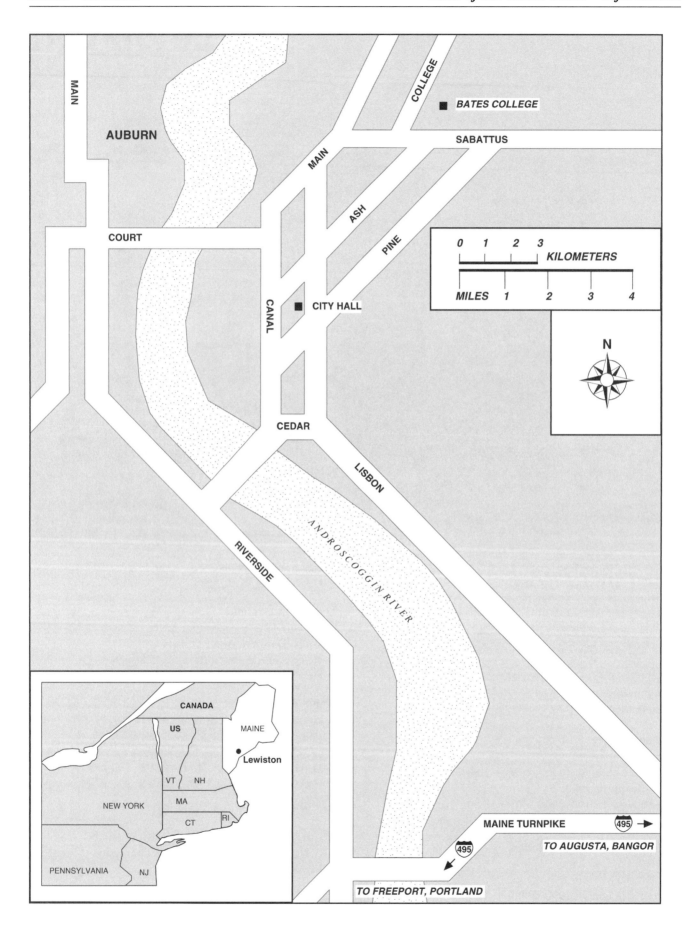

Introduction

Lewiston and Auburn, known as the Twin Cities of the Androscoggin, together form the industrial and commercial heart of Maine. Although separated by the Androscoggin River, they share nearly every city amenity and service except government. Both cities possess a diversified economy dependent on services and manufacturing. A remarkable cooperative effort between the cities brought to the region a building boom of unprecedented proportions in the late 1980s. During the decade that followed, the economy had begun shifting away from large manufacturers to entrepreneurial small companies. Lewiston continues to be one of the strongest manufacturing areas in New England.

Geography and Climate

Lewiston is located approximately 30 miles from the mouth of the Androscoggin River in the western lakes and mountains region of Maine. The city is situated on low rolling hills sloping toward the Androscoggin River. The area enjoys a four-season climate; summers are comfortable and winters are generally cold, but prolonged periods of cold weather are rare.

Area: 34 square miles (2000)

Elevation: 121 feet above sea level

Average Temperatures: January, 20.5° F; July, 71.4° F; average, 46.1° F

Average Annual Precipitation: 45.8 inches of rain, 70.1 inches of snow

History

Permission to settle the tract of land along the Androscoggin River where Lewiston and Auburn now stand was granted by the Massachusetts Bay Colony in 1768 to agents of a group referred to as the proprietors. Under the terms of the grant, fifty families in as many houses were to settle in the area, which was to be called Lewiston, by 1774. It is doubtful that these terms were complied with; the first settler, Paul Hildreth, did not build his log cabin until 1770 on the east bank of the river. Although Lewiston opened its first woolen mill in 1819 and its first cotton mill in 1844, it and neighboring Auburn grew very slowly. It is said that Auburn

took its name from Oliver Goldsmith's poem "The Deserted Village."

The growth of the Twin Cities, as they are often called, began in 1836 with the exploitation of the water power of the Androscoggin River. Lewiston grew up as a textile center, Auburn as a shoe-manufacturing center, and both cities attracted workers of French-Canadian origin to work in the factories. By the 1870s several large textile mills were operating in Lewiston, and Auburn's twenty-one factories were turning out more than two million pairs of shoes annually. Friction between the two cities broke out in 1937 during a bitter shoe strike. Many residents of one city worked in the other, and during the strike police sought to prevent strikers from crossing the bridges that connect the two cities.

By the 1960s the economy of the two cities was still dominated by the textile and shoe industries, but mills were beginning to close and shoe shops were being badly hurt by foreign competition. Into the late 1970s the cities engaged in a rivalry to attract new businesses until it was recognized that cooperation would be beneficial to the development of both. During the 1980s Lewiston and Auburn experienced a building boom; the cooperative spirit that grew up between them was marked by such factors as the sharing of economic development councils, a newly rebuilt hydroelectric facility, and the tax revenues generated by the development of industrial land. Lewiston's vitality and cultural richness were factors in its selection as the national headquarters of the forum Francophone des Affaires, an international trade group of French-speaking nations. Today Lewiston continues to be a city enriched by a strong cultural heritage, diverse economy, active artists' community, and beautiful natural resources.

Historical Information: Androscoggin Historical Society, Court Street Door, County Building, Auburn, ME 04210; telephone (207)784-0586

Population Profile

Metropolitan Area Residents
1990: 93,679
2000: 90,830
Percent change, 1990–2000: −3.0%
U.S. rank in 1990: 256th
U.S. rank in 2000: 268th

City Residents:
1980: 40,481
1990: 39,757

2000: 35,690
2003 estimate: 35,922
Percent change, 1990–2000: −10.3%
U.S. rank in 1980: 540th
U.S. rank in 1990: 664th
U.S. rank in 2000: Not reported (State rank: 2nd)

Density: 1,047.0 people per square mile (2000)

Racial and ethnic characteristics (2000)
White: 34,726
Black or African American: 561
American Indian and Alaska Native: 351
Asian: 384
Native Hawaiian and Pacific Islander: 32
Hispanic or Latino (may be of any race): 448
Other: 262

Percent of residents born in state: 75.9% (2000)

Age characteristics (2000)
Population under 5 years old: 1,983
Population 5 to 9 years old: 2,122
Population 10 to 14 years old: 2,073
Population 15 to 19 years old: 2,631
Population 20 to 24 years old: 3,090
Population 25 to 34 years old: 4,596
Population 35 to 44 years old: 5,008
Population 45 to 54 years old: 4,539
Population 55 to 59 years old: 1,718
Population 60 to 64 years old: 1,588
Population 65 to 74 years old: 2,972
Population 75 to 84 years old: 2,374
Population 85 years and over: 996
Median age: 37.6 years

Births (2001)
Total number: 1,322

Deaths (2001)
Total number: 914

Money income (1999)
Per capita income: $17,905
Median household income: $29,191
Total number of households: 15,291

Number of households with income of . . .
less than $10,000: 2,552
$10,000 to $14,999: 1,380
$15,000 to $24,999: 2,800
$25,000 to $34,999: 2,232
$35,000 to $49,999: 2,343
$50,000 to $74,999: 2,441
$75,000 to $99,999: 902
$100,000 to $149,999: 403
$150,000 to $199,999: 59
$200,000 or more: 179

Percent of families below poverty level: 10.0% (59.3% of which were female householder families with related children under 5 years)

2002 FBI Crime Index Total: 3,322

Municipal Government

Lewiston operates under a city administrator form of government, with a mayor and seven councilors elected to two-year terms. Auburn is the shire town of Androscoggin County.

Head Official: Mayor Lionel C. Guay Jr. (since January 2004; current term expires January 2006)

Total Number of City Employees: 224 (2004)

City Information: City of Lewiston, 27 Pine St., Lewiston, ME 04240; telephone (207)784-2951

Economy

Major Industries and Commercial Activity

Once known mainly for the manufacture of shoes and textiles, Lewiston and Auburn today possess a diversified economic base in both the manufacturing and non-manufacturing sectors. Androscoggin County has transformed itself to a progressive tourism and high-precision manufacturing powerhouse. Health care is the largest industry in the Lewiston-Auburn area, providing more than 6,800 healthcare-related jobs. Textile manufacturers have diversified their products to include industrial, commercial, and construction fabrics, while shoe manufacturers now produce lower volume but higher quality products.

The food and beverage industry is another growing economic sector in Androscoggin County, with major companies like Poland Spring Bottling Co., White Rock Distilleries, Lepage Bakeries, and Angostura International, Federal Distributors, Central Distributors, and Seltzer & Rydholm having facilities in the area.

Other companies in the Lewiston area include Formed Fiber Technologies, an auto parts manufacturer for companies such as General Motors and Toyota; Tambrands, a Procter & Gamble plant that makes feminine hygiene products; Panolam Industries, which makes laminated countertops and other surfaces; and Diamond Phoenix Corporation, a company that manufactures carousels, sorting/picking systems, and robotics for companies such as Boeing, Hallmark, and Lockheed Martin. In addition, retail company L.L. Bean has a telephone operations center in Lewiston, and Giger, one of the nation's largest privately owned promotional products companies, continues to print its annual Farmer's Almanac.

The Maine Department of Economic and Community Development reported that in 2002 the Lewiston-Auburn area led the state in economic development activity, and placed second in job creation. Both cities are a travel center for their section of the state and benefit from tourism.

Items and goods produced: shoes and textiles; electrical, food, metal, plastic, and printed products; ductware; dampers; high power radio frequency components

Incentive Programs—New and Existing Businesses

Both Lewiston and Auburn have track records in assisting companies with various programs and incentives, depending upon the number and quality of jobs retained. The Lewiston Economic Growth Council acts as a local liaison with local and state development agencies on behalf of interested businesses. The council also offers site search assistance by helping companies locate appropriate buildings and/or land, in conjunction with local government, real estate brokers, and private developers. Lewiston's Economic and Community Development Department also extends a variety of services to local businesses, including commercial financing, streamlined review and permitting processes, and municipally owned business park sites.

Local programs—The Lewiston Auburn Economic Growth Council offers a number of services to local businesses, including technical assistance, commercial financing, site searches, and marketing. Since the council's inception, it has leveraged almost $45 million in new local investments through financing programs. Its Economic Stimulus Loan Pool provides eligible businesses with loans up to $150,000 to be used for site purchase and development, construction, machinery and equipment, and working capital. The Micro-Enterprise Loan Program, for businesses with five or fewer employees, offers loans up to $25,000 for site purchases, construction, and equipment purchases.

State programs—The Finance Authority of Maine (FAME) assists economic development by providing capital for business, industrial, and natural resources enterprises through a wide variety of programs, including loan insurance grants, targeted lending, and taxable and tax-exempt bonds. FAME's Economic Recovery Loan Program offers subordinate financing to assist businesses in their efforts to remain viable and/or improve productivity; loans of up to $200,000 are available.

Job training programs—Through the State of Maine's Governor's Training Initiative, local businesses are eligible for partial reimbursement of training costs incurred through recruitment, assessment, workplace safety, workplace literacy, and technical training. The Maine Quality Center, in conjunction with the Maine Technical College System, provides training for workers at qualified Maine businesses. The center offers trainee recruitment, employer-specific training programs, and pre-employment screening. To participate in these programs, businesses must create at least eight new jobs which are at a high skill and wage level.

Development Projects

In recent years, Lewiston has seen a number of development projects come to fruition. With healthcare playing a vital role in the area's economy, local healthcare facilities continue to be expanded and improved. Central Maine Healthcare launched its multi-million dollar Central Maine Heart and Vascular Institute, a cardiac care center providing open-heart surgery and angioplasty procedures. Other infrastructure investments at Central Maine Medical Center include a parking garage, office expansions, and a new home for its nursing and radiology schools. St. Mary's Regional Medical Center recently built the Corinne Croteau Lepage Women's Health Pavilion; the $6 million facility is the first of its kind in Maine.

City officials are also planning for a $20 million downtown project anchored by Oxford Networks, Northeast Bank, and a campus of Andover College. The project will see the creation of two new office buildings, a new parking garage, underground utilities, new sidewalks, new streetlights, and new landscaping. The project will serve as the central hub for a state-of-the-art fiber-optic telecommunication system that will serve both Lewiston and Auburn.

Another upcoming development project in the Lewiston area is the creation of a new $45 million Wal-Mart Distribution Center, which will employ 150 to 400 people. The center will service Wal-Mart grocery stores in northern New England.

Economic Development Information: Lewiston Auburn Economic Growth Council, 95 Park St., PO Box 1188, Lewiston, ME 04243; telephone (207)784-0161. Lewiston Department of Economic and Community Development, 27 Pine St., 3rd Fl., Lewiston, ME 04240; telephone (207)784-2951. Finance Authority of Maine (FAME), 5 Community Dr., PO Box 949, Augusta, ME 04332; telephone (207)623-3263.

Commercial Shipping

Lewiston-Auburn is conveniently situated on the Maine Turnpike; exits 12 and 13 provide direct routes into the area's industrial parks. Several trucking companies operate with both interstate and intrastate authority. Rail service is available through the St. Lawrence & Atlantic Railroad, which operates a double-stack intermodal transportation facility in Auburn. In addition, Guildford Rail runs a regional rail system with daily switching service and loading dock facilities. The Auburn-Lewiston Municipal Airport provides charter service to locations in the U.S. and Canada; the area is also only 38 miles away from Portland International Jetport. Portland Harbor, 40 minutes away from Lewiston, accommodates large ships with roll-on, roll-off docks and container handling capability.

Labor Force and Employment Outlook

The local labor force boasts a strong reputation for skill and commitment with access to superior educational resources. *Industry Week* magazine once named Lewiston-Auburn the strongest manufacturing area in New England, based on productivity, specialization, and employment. Thanks to Lewiston-Auburn's central location, local employers are able to draw upon a talented workforce from the surrounding area—nearly 50 percent of the state's population is within a 30-mile radius.

The area provides many opportunities for workers to pursue education and job training—local options include six colleges, a hospital-sponsored nursing program, and an adult education program. The Maine Quality Center provides employer-specific training programs and trainee recruitment, while Auburn's Central Maine Technical College offers courses to employers at the worksite or on campus.

The following is a summary of data regarding the Lewiston-Auburn metropolitan area labor force, 2004 annual averages.

Size of nonagricultural labor force: 48,000

Number of workers employed in . . .
  construction and mining: 2,700
  manufacturing: 6,200
  trade, transportation, and utilities: 9,900
  information: 800
  financial activities: 3,000
  professional and business services: 4,900
  educational and health services: 10,000
  leisure and hospitality: 3,500
  other services: 1,300
  government: 5,800

Average hourly earnings of production workers employed in manufacturing: $16.97 (statewide average)

Unemployment rate: 5.5% (February 2005)

Largest employers (2004)	Number of employees
Sisters of Charity Health Systems	1,000 +
Central Maine Medical Center	1,000 +
Banknorth Group	500 +
Lewiston School Department	500 +
Bates College	500 +
Auburn School Department	500 +
Tambrands Inc. (paper manufacturing)	500 +
Panolam (plastics manufacturing)	500 +
L.L. Bean	300 +
City of Lewiston	300 +

Cost of Living

The average price of a single-family home in Lewiston ranges from $78,000 to $100,000.

The following is a summary of data regarding several key cost of living factors in the Lewiston-Auburn area.

2004 ACCRA Average House Price: Not reported

2004 ACCRA Cost of Living Index: Not reported

State income tax rate: a graduated income tax rate from 2.0% to 8.5% of federal adjusted gross income with modifications.

State sales tax rate: 5.0%

Local income tax rate: None

Local sales tax rate: None

Property tax rate: $27.70 per $1,000 of assessed valuation (2004)

Economic Information: Lewiston Auburn Economic Growth Council, 95 Park St., PO Box 1188, Lewiston, ME 04243; telephone (207)784-0161

Education and Research

Elementary and Secondary Schools

Lewiston takes great pride in its education system, which has gained national attention for its innovative programs that have incorporated arts into the classroom, fostered business partnerships, and started after-school programs. Lewiston students regularly score at or above national and state averages on the Iowa Test of Basic Skills and the Maine Educational Assessment. More than 70 percent of Lewiston's high school graduates continue on to postsecondary education.

The following is a summary of data regarding the Lewiston public schools as of the 2004–2005 school year.

Total enrollment: 4,600

Number of facilities
  elementary schools: 6
  junior/high middle schools: 1
  senior high schools: 1
  other: 1

Student/teacher ratio: 19:1 (elementary school)

Teacher salaries
  average: $43,749

Funding per pupil: $6,546

There are four parochial schools in Lewiston, including St. Dominic Regional High School, Holy Cross School and St. Joseph's School, and St. Peters, which together serve approximately 1,300 students. Several private Christian schools are located in the area as well.

Public Schools Information: Lewiston Public Schools, Dingley Building, 36 Oak St., Lewiston, ME 04240; telephone (207)795-4100

Colleges and Universities

Lewiston is home to historic Bates College, a highly selective liberal arts school founded by Maine abolitionists in 1855. Located on a 109-acre campus, Bates offers arts and sciences programs plus majors in anthropology, speech, and theater. The school offers a low student to faculty ratio, making close collaborations in the classroom and laboratory possible. Two-thirds of Bates's students typically study abroad, and more than two-thirds of recent graduates enroll in graduate study within 10 years after graduation. Recently, *U.S. News and World Report* recognized Bates as being among the top 25 liberal arts colleges in the country.

The University of Southern Maine's Lewiston-Auburn College is the fastest growing campus in the University system. The college's 1,700 students can choose between four-year degree programs in arts and humanities; natural, applied, social, and behavioral sciences; nursing; and leadership and organizational studies. Master's degree programs are available in leadership studies, literacy education, and occupational therapy.

Between them, St. Mary's Hospital and Central Maine Medical Center offer nursing, radiologic technology, and anesthesiology schools. The Central Maine Institute for Health Professionals offers degree programs through the Clark F. Miller School of Radiologic Technology, the School of Nuclear Medicine Technology, and the CMMC School of Nursing.

Auburn is home to Mid-State College, which offers degrees in accounting, business, medical support, computer applications, tourism and hospitality management, and early child-

hood education. The college also offers certificates in medical transcription and therapeutic massage. At Central Maine Technical College, the school offers industry-specific courses and associate's degrees in Arts General Studies or Liberal Studies. It also boasts the lowest tuition rates in the state.

Libraries and Research Centers

Lewiston maintains one central library holding 123,000 print and audio-visual volumes housed in the original granite 1902 Carnegie Library Building. The library maintains special collections on Franco-American heritage, French literature, genealogical information, and local history. It also has an active children's program and outreach program.

Among the special collections at the George and Helen Ladd Library at Bates College is the Edmund S. Muskie Archives and Special Collections Library, a collection of rare books, records, manuscript collections, and papers of the U.S. senator. Central Maine Medical Center maintains the Gerrish-True Health Sciences Library, a center for information relating to patient care, patient education, personal health, research, staff development, and wellness promotion.

Public Library Information: Lewiston Public Library, 200 Lisbon St. Lewiston, ME 04240; telephone (207)784-0135

Health Care

Lewiston and Auburn residents' health care needs are taken care of by two of Maine's finest hospitals—Central Maine Medical Center and St. Mary's Regional Medical Center. Central Maine Medical Center is a 250-bed regional referral center offering a wide range of services. It operates the largest emergency room in the region, and is one of three designated trauma centers in Maine. It is also known for its women's and children's services, including special birthing, breast care, bladder control, and osteoporosis centers. In 2003, the medical center also opened the Central Maine Heart and Vascular Institute.

St. Mary's Regional Medical Center is a regional leader in the area of women's health. Its Corinne Croteau Lepage Women's Health Pavilion houses a sophisticated birthing unit and an integrated obstetrics and gynecology practice; the Women's Imaging Center offers mammography services and bone density testing. St. Mary's neurosurgeons are also nationally recognized, having performed technologically advanced surgery not done elsewhere in the eastern U.S.

Recreation

Sightseeing

A stroll through the 109-acre campus of Bates College offers the sightseer a view of lawns, gardens, and ivy-covered buildings; one path leads to the summit of Mt. David, providing an aerial view of the Twin Cities and sometimes a glimpse of the White Mountains 50 miles to the west. Lewiston Falls and Dam are best viewed from North Bridge.

Bird fanciers visiting the area may wish to explore Thorncrag Bird Sanctuary, a 310-acre wildlife preserve for birds and small animals. The Mt. Apatite recreation area in Auburn features beautiful wooded hiking through an area once known for tourmaline mining.

Arts and Culture

With the cooperative spirit that now characterizes the relationship between Lewiston and Auburn, the two cities formed L/A Arts in 1973 in order to increase the number of cultural amenities in the area. In cooperation with local educational institutions and community organizations, the group sponsors hundreds of performances a year by artists, authors, actors, and others in the community and the schools. Nationally recognized artists regularly perform at the Olin Arts Center on the Bates College campus. Each summer, the college hosts the Bates Dance Festival, a conglomeration of showings, performances, workshops, and discussions for students, performers, educators, and choreographers. The college's Department of Theater and Rhetoric stages several theater and dance productions annually at its three campus theaters.

The Androscoggin Chorale was formed as a community chorus in 1972. In 1991, the Chorale joined with the Maine Chamber Ensemble to form the Maine Music Society. The society has since offered several successful years of performances throughout the state, including operatic performances, classical music concerts, and holiday performances. The Public Theatre, a fully professional Equity operation which has presented comedic and dramatic performances to the community for more than 10 years, was recently voted the best theatre company in Maine for the second year in a row.

The Lewiston-Auburn College/USM Atrium Gallery presents exhibitions of paintings, sculptures, and photography from artists across the state. It also hosts the annual Area Artists Exhibition and annual L/A Arts Exhibit and Auction. The Bates College Museum of Art at Olin Arts Center is home to one of the region's finest collections of masterworks on paper, including the Marsden Hartley Memorial collection. More than 40,000 square feet of space at the Creative Photographic Art Center of Maine in the historic Bates Mill Complex is dedicated to photography and other related arts. Genealogical literature, historical exhibits on the Native American culture, and Civil War artifacts are on display at the Androscoggin Historical Society Library and Museum in Auburn.

The Franco-American Heritage Collection at Lewiston-Auburn College/USM provides a significant collection of documents, photographs, artifacts, and audiovisual material relating to the area's Franco-American community. Opened in 2000, Lewiston's Franco-American Heritage Center at St. Mary's was created to preserve the area's Franco-American heritage. The center serves as a museum, performance hall, and learning center.

Since 1940, Auburn's Community Little Theatre has been producing musicals, dramas, comedies, and benefit concerts each year in the Great Falls Performing Arts Center. The Pleasant Note Coffeehouse is a combination restaurant and concert venue that presents a variety of artists ranging from up-and-coming locals to internationally known folk and jazz performers. Because of all these activities, the Lewiston-Auburn area has been designated as one of the best small arts towns in America.

Arts and Culture Information: L/A Arts, 221 Lisbon St., Lewiston, ME 04240; telephone (207)782-7228

Festivals and Holidays

Summer is festival time in Lewiston-Auburn; the season is inaugurated by the Maine State Parade, the largest such event in the state, held each May in Lewiston. In June, the Great Falls Canoe Race highlights the Androscoggin River. The Liberty Festival on July 4th draws thousands of visitors for live entertainment, food, and a fireworks display. Lewiston celebrates its French-Canadian heritage each summer with the Festival de Joie, a celebration of traditional food and music from all around the world. In mid-August the skies over Auburn and Lewiston fill with the colorful sights of the Great Falls Balloon Festival; 45 balloonists from across the Northeast take part in the event.

Sports for the Participant

A wealth of summer and winter recreational activities is available in and around Lewiston and Auburn. The proximity to mountains, forests, and lakes offers opportunities to skiers, skaters, campers, boaters, hikers, and anglers. Bicycle tours of the back roads of the region are very popular. Just north of Lewiston is the Hebron-to-Canton Rail Trail, an abandoned railroad bed turned pedestrian and bike route—a 36 mile round trip overall. For watersports enthusiasts, Lewiston plays host to the Great Falls Canoe Race each June.

The Twin Cities maintain dozens of parks and playgrounds, a supervised beach, skating rinks, and ball fields and courts.

The Ingersoll Arena in Auburn is available for public skating, skating instruction, and hockey from early October to mid-March. Sunday River Mountain Bike Park in Bethel is served by two ski lifts, and offers sixty miles of marked and patrolled trails. The Lost Valley ski area features downhill and cross-country skiing in the winter and mountain bike trails and paintball facilities in the summer. A number of golfing facilities are also located in or near Lewiston.

Shopping and Dining

The downtown areas of Lewiston and Auburn lost most of their retail trade to shopping centers in the 1980s but made a comeback as significant commercial centers in the late 1990s. Both Auburn and Lewiston have shopping malls, featuring major department stores, and Freeport—home of L.L. Bean, the outdoors outfitters—is about 30 minutes away from Lewiston. Nutcracker Sweets is an old-fashioned candy shop featuring hand-crafted chocolates, and Orphan Annie's Antiques in Auburn offers a large selection of Art Deco, Art Nouveau, Tiffany, Steuben, and other prominent French and American art glass.

Western Maine is home to many small inns where fine dining and sometimes spectacular views are available to the public. Restaurants in the Lewiston area range from inexpensive spots such as Bill Davis Luncheonette and Gipper's Sports Grill, to the international fine dining available at places like T.J.'s Restaurant and Eli's Restaurant at the Turner Highlands Country Club. Regional seafood restaurants and ethnic spots for Mexican, Chinese, and Italian cuisines are also abundant.

Visitor Information: Androscoggin County Chamber of Commerce, 179 Lisbon St., PO Box 59, Lewiston, ME 04243; telephone (207)783-2249; email info@androscoggin county.com

Convention Facilities

Lewiston's Colisee has a number of options for convention planners. Its main conference area seats up to 4,800 people. It also offers arena bowl seating, floor seating, and a hospitality suite. The Ramada Inn Conference Center offers 15,000 square feet of conference facilities that were remodeled in 2003; banquet facilities are also available. The Auburn Inn and the Coastline Inn in Auburn also offer meeting space.

Convention Information: Androscoggin County Chamber of Commerce, 179 Lisbon St., PO Box 59, Lewiston, ME 04243; telephone (207)783- 2249; email info@androscoggincounty .com

Transportation

Approaching the City

Androscoggin County is served by Auburn-Lewiston Municipal Airport, which offers charter air service to the U.S. and Canada. Portland International Airport, only 30 minutes away, has daily commercial flights. Bus service is provided by Hudson Bus Lines and Western Maine Transportation Services. The Maine Turnpike provides access by car.

Traveling in the City

Streets in Lewiston radiate from Union Square near the Androscoggin River. Local and inter-urban bus and taxi service are available. Hudson Bus Lines serves the local community.

Communications

Newspapers and Magazines

Readers in the Lewiston area are served daily by the *Lewiston Sun-Journal.* The *Maine Sunday Telegram* is also available to local readers.

Television and Radio

Lewiston and Auburn are served by nine regional television networks; cable service is also available. Thirteen AM and twenty FM radio stations serve the area.

Media Information: *Lewiston Sun Journal,* 104 Park St., Lewiston, ME 04243; telephone (207)784-5411

Lewiston Online

Androscoggin County Chamber of Commerce. Available www.androscoggincounty.com

City of Lewiston. Available www.ci.lewiston.me.us

Lewiston Auburn Economic Growth Council. Available www.economicgrowth.org

Lewiston Public Library. Available www.lplonline.org

Lewiston School Department. Available www.lewiston.k12 .me.us

Lewiston *Sun Journal.* Available www.sunjournal.com

Maine Department of Labor. Available www.state.me.us/ labor

Portland

The City in Brief

Founded: 1623 (incorporated, 1786)

Head Official: City Manager Joseph Gray, Jr. (since 2001)

City Population
  1980: 61,572
  1990: 64,157
  2000: 64,249
  2003 estimate: 63,635
  Percent change, 1990–2000: 1.8%
  U.S. rank in 1980: 327th
  U.S. rank in 1990: 361st (State rank: 1st)
  U.S. rank in 2000: 487th (State rank: 1st)

Metropolitan Area Population
  1980: 193,831
  1990: 221,095
  2000: 243,537

  Percent change, 1990–2000: 10.2%
  U.S. rank in 1990: 145th
  U.S. rank in 2000: 147th

Area: 21.2 square miles (2000)
Elevation: 34 feet above sea level
Average Annual Temperature: 45.5° F
Average Annual Precipitation: 44.3 inches rain; 71.3 inches snow

Major Economic Sectors: Services, trade, government, manufacturing
Unemployment Rate: 4.0% (February 2005)
Per Capita Income: $22,698 (1999)
2004 ACCRA Average House Price: Not reported
2004 ACCRA Cost of Living Index: Not reported

2002 FBI Crime Index Total: 3,525

Major Colleges and Universities: University of Southern Maine

Daily Newspaper: *Portland Press Herald*

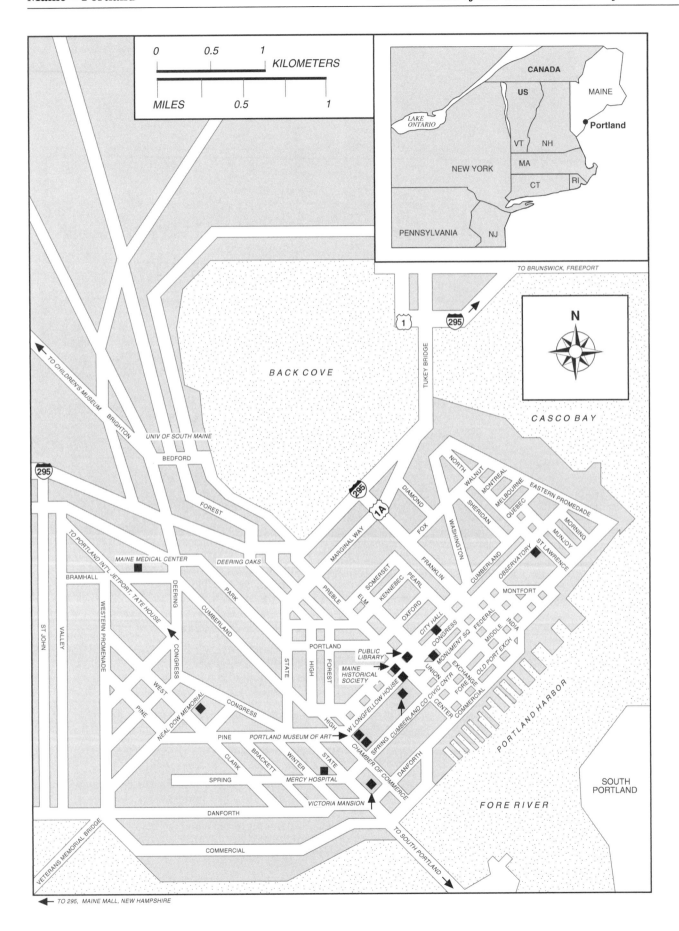

Introduction

Portland is the largest city in Maine and an important cultural, commercial, and shipping center. Called "the beautiful town that is seated by the sea" by Henry Wadsworth Longfellow, who was born there, Portland, three times destroyed by fire and rebuilt, has revived again. During the 1960s and 1970s Portland lost more than 11 percent of its population as its economy stagnated. A thoughtful urban renewal program designed to balance the process of economic growth with the preservation and restoration of what made the city unique—including its historic port district and other landmarks—has produced a culturally and economically vital city that is attracting young professionals from across America. Portland entered the new century with a deep appreciation of what makes a city livable and a commitment to ensuring that it remains so for all its citizens.

Geography and Climate

Portland lies on the southeast coast of Maine about 106 miles northeast of Boston. The city surrounds a large harbor on the southern rim of Casco Bay. Downtown Portland rests on an elevated peninsula with views of the Atlantic Ocean and the White Mountains. Summers and falls are pleasant; winters are cold with frequent thaws. Winter begins late and extends into the normal springtime. The White Mountains to the northwest keep heavy snow from reaching the Portland area and also moderate the temperature. Normal monthly precipitation tends to be uniform throughout the year.

Area: 21.2 square miles (2000)

Elevation: 34 feet above sea level

Average Temperatures: January, 22.1° F; August, 66.6° F; annual average, 45.5° F

Average Annual Precipitation: 44.3 inches rain; 71.3 inches snow

History

The first settlement on the site of Portland was built by Christopher Levett in 1623. The next year Levett returned to England, apparently to attempt to arouse interest in forming a city on the site, to be called York. He never returned, and nothing is known of the fate of the 10 men he left behind. In the ensuing years, the city was known by a succession of names and was the object of a confused flurry of land claims and counter-claims, until Massachusetts assumed control in 1652. By 1675 Falmouth, as it was then called, had achieved some prosperity, with a population of more than 400 settlers. That same year Indian wars broke out, and in 1676 the entire town was destroyed.

No permanent settlement was attempted after this until Samuel Moody was granted permission by the Massachusetts government to build a fort at Falmouth. Over the next fifty years the area grew as an important export and shipbuilding center, and by 1770 Falmouth was one of the most prosperous of the Colonial cities. At this time tensions against the British were rising and Falmouth was the scene of anti-British protests. In 1775 a British naval captain was seized by a party of Colonials and accused of spying; the captain was released on parole on condition that he return when requested. He did return a few months later, uninvited and in command of four warships. When the citizens of Falmouth refused his orders to evacuate the city or surrender their arms, the British opened fire and destroyed more than four hundred buildings. The town was not abandoned, however; during the Revolutionary War it served as an assembly ground for the military. By July 4, 1786, when the city took the name of Portland, the economy was thriving; forts and bridges were being constructed, the state's first bank and newspaper were established, and trade with the English and French was restored. Prosperity was checked by a depression from 1807 to 1809; the War of 1812 brought recovery, and Portland's industries and shipyards flourished once again. From 1820 to 1831 Portland served as the capital of Maine. Expansion continued with the development of steamboats and railroads.

City Survives War and Destruction by Fire

Portland was actively involved in the Civil War of 1861 to 1865, contributing about a fifth of its total population to the effort. Following the war the city quickly resumed its usual activity but was jolted by what was perhaps the worst in its series of disasters when, on July 4, 1866, fire destroyed most of the city. Rebuilding began immediately and many improvements were made.

Portland continued to thrive through the twentieth century's two world wars as a center of commerce, shipping, and industry. During World War II, Portland was the base for the North Atlantic Fleet of the U.S. Navy. After World War II, the city emerged as a major oil port. Following a period of decline, with the introduction of Japanese technology, the city became known once again as a major shipbuilding center.

Portland has benefitted from the spread of the Massachusetts high-technology boom and has become a national leader in technical infrastructure. During the 1980s and 1990s, Portland enjoyed increasing tourism and developed a national reputation as a highly livable city. In 2003, Portland was ranked One of America's Dozen Distinctive Destinations by the National Trust for Historic Preservation. The city has been named One of the 10 Great Adventure Towns, by *National Geographic Adventure Magazine* August 2004, and the #1 Top Market for Small Business Vitality by American City Business Journals, January 2005.

Historical Information: Center for Maine History, 485 Congress St., Portland, ME 04101; telephone (207)774-1822

Population Profile

Metropolitan Area Residents
1980: 193,831
1990: 221,095
2000: 243,537
Percent change, 1990–2000: 10.2%
U.S. rank in 1990: 145th
U.S. rank in 2000: 147th

City Residents
1980: 61,572
1990: 64,157
2000: 64,249
2003 estimate: 63,635
Percent change, 1990–2000: 1.8%
U.S. rank in 1980: 327th
U.S. rank in 1990: 361st (State rank: 1st)
U.S. rank in 2000: 487th (State rank: 1st)

Density: 3,029.2 people per square mile (2000)

Racial and ethnic characteristics (2000)
   White: 58,638
   Black or African American: 1,665
   American Indian and Alaska Native: 302
   Asian: 1,982
   Native Hawaiian and Pacific Islander: 36
   Hispanic or Latino (may be of any race): 974
   Other: 1,626

Percent of residents born in state: 67.5

Age Characteristics (2000)
Population under 5 years old: 3,305
Population 5 to 9 years old: 3,216
Population 10 to 14 years old: 3,463
Population 15 to 19 years old: 3,535
Population 20 to 24 years old: 5,413
Population 25 to 34 years old: 12,408

Population 35 to 44 years old: 10,778
Population 45 to 54 years old: 8,516
Population 55 to 59 years old: 2,641
Population 60 to 64 years old: 2,065
Population 65 to 74 years old: 4,018
Population 75 to 84 years old: 3,410
Population 85 years and older: 1,481
Median age: 35.7 years old

Births (1998)
   Total number: 759

Deaths (1998)
   Total number: 637 (of which, 1 was an infant under the age of 1 year)

Money income (1999)
   Per capita income: $22,698
   Median household income: $35,650
   Total number of households: 29,722

Number of households with income of . . .
   less than $10,000: 3,582
   $10,000 to $14,999: 2,178
   $15,000 to $24,999: 4,359
   $25,000 to $34,999: 4,473
   $35,000 to $49,999: 5,118
   $50,000 to $74,999: 5,382
   $75,000 to $99,999: 2,553
   $100,000 to $149,999: 1,258
   $150,000 to $199,999: 324
   $200,000 or more: 495

Percent of families below poverty level: 9.7% (56.6% of which were female householder families with related children under 5 years)

2002 FBI Crime Index Total: 3,525

Municipal Government

Portland, the seat of Cumberland County, operates under a council-manager form of government. The city manager is the chief executive officer, appointed by the council for an unspecified term. A nine-member council constitutes the legislative body. Five council members are selected from the five voting districts and four are elected on an at-large basis to serve staggered three-year terms. The mayor, who presides over council meetings, is selected by the council to serve a one-year term. Portland is known for its highly trained police and fire personnel.

Head Official: City Manager Joseph Gray, Jr. (since 2001; length of term unspecified)

Total Number of City Employees: 1,371 (2002)

City Information: City Hall, 389 Congress Street, Portland, ME 04101; telephone (207)879-0300

Economy

Major Industries and Commercial Activity

The Portland MSA is the strongest economic region in the state. Maine companies have a higher survival rate than the national average, as well as above-average rates of sales growth. The Portland area's concentration of population (the Portland MSA includes 25 percent of the state's population) and accessibility to other markets in New England have made the city a focal point for development. A study released by American City Business Journals in January 2005 found that the Portland metropolitan area has the strongest small-business sector (defined as companies with 100 or fewer employees) of any large metropolitan area in the United States. Portland's ratio of 3,301 such companies per 100,000 residents substantially exceeds that of all other major markets. About one third of all Portland businesses are service related, while 20 percent are retail, 10 percent government, and less than 10 percent manufacturing; the remaining few are miscellaneous businesses.

Portland is a leading wholesale distribution point for northern New England as well as an important retail center, catering mostly to pedestrian shoppers. These industries, as well as tourism, received a boost after outdoor outfitter L. L. Bean opened in nearby Freeport in 1917; since 1951, the phenomenally popular store has been open 24 hours a day. L. L. Bean's headquarters are located down the street from this flagship store, which has grown to 160,000 square feet and draws nearly three million visitors annually. Many businesses have opened stores in the area in recent decades, from independent boutiques in the Old Port and Arts District areas to the shops at South Portland's Maine Mall—the largest indoor mall in the state—to more than 125 outlet stores anchored by L. L. Bean.

Services, especially health services, play a very important part in the Portland area's economy; the Maine Medical Center, the largest hospital in the state, is one of the city's largest employers. In recent years, the city has seen growth in its service industries without significant erosion in other sectors of the economy.

The finance industry has a long tradition in Portland, and the third-largest banking and financial services company in New England—Bank North Group—is headquartered there. UnumProvident, a holding company headquartered in Tennessee, has a significant presence in Portland; its subsidiary Unum Life Insurance Company of America is based in Portland.

Portland's port is the largest in New England in terms of tonnage. Portland is one of the chief trading ports on the Atlantic coast and plays a major role in Maine's paper and pulp trade. The state's annual lobster catch is the largest in the country; Portland is a major center for this activity, having benefited from efforts begun by environmentalists in the 1960s to clean up rivers and harbors.

Items and goods produced: food and paper products, leather goods, metals and machinery, lumber and wood

Incentive Programs—New and Existing Companies

Local programs—Portland's Economic Development Center (EDC) serves as the city's one-stop shop for starting, expanding, or relocating a business. EDC serves as an information clearinghouse and offers assistance with permits and regulations; financial incentives; site selection; marketing and public relations; and business technical assistance and development. The Resource Hub is a one-stop business assistance center for entrepreneurs and small businesses. The Downtown Portland Corporation (DPC), an arm of the city's Economic Development Department, seeks to combine the resources and initiative of the public and private sectors to promote downtown growth.

State programs—The Finance Authority of Maine (FAME,) assists economic development by providing capital for businesses through a wide variety of programs. FAME offers direct loans; credit enhancement through risk reduction and rate reduction programs; equity capital assistance for early-stage businesses; and cooperative programs with local agencies. Maine's Office of Business Development provides comprehensive financial, management, production, marketing, and other technical assistance to Maine businesses.

Job training programs—The Career Center at Portland, part of the state of Maine government, assists businesses seeking employees and individuals seeking jobs. Networking and workshops are part of the center's programming. Through the Career Center, the Maine Apprenticeship Program (MAP) offers on-the-job training in a variety of occupations. Maine's community colleges partake in the Maine Career Advantage program that combines academics with internships.

Development Projects

Transportation to and within Portland has been enhanced in recent years with Amtrak's new Downeaster line, running between Boston and Portland, and the new Portland Explorer Express Bus Service, which runs between major downtown locations, the Maine Mall, the airport, and the bus-rail station.

Portland's Planning and Development Department reported in 2004, "We are excited to see renewed interest in the rehabilitation of buildings on Congress Street for both residential and office development." The Congress Street area lining a ridge above Old Port has gradually seen renewed life since the mid-1990s, when the Maine College of Art moved into the vacant Proteous department store building there; the area is now referred to as the Arts District. In 1999, the federal Environmental Protection Agency awarded a $500,000 grant to the city to help clean up the Bayside area, a once-bustling industrial area the city aims to revitalize. City officials created a number of short- and long-term strategies to kick-start development in Bayside, including acquiring land, making Portland's regulatory process more business-friendly, and building new housing. Completed developments in Bayside as of 2004 include new housing, two new office buildings, two new retail outlets, and a new natural food store, located in a formerly vacant warehouse.

In September 2004 Portland's city council voted to amend the city's historic preservation ordinance to grant additional decision-making authority to the Historic Preservation Committee, now renamed the Historic Preservation Board; following the amendment, the board now makes the final decision as to whether major projects meet preservation ordinance standards.

Economic Development Information: Downtown Portland Corporation, 389 Congress St., Portland, ME 04101; telephone (207)874-8683. Economic Development Department, City of Portland, 389 Congress St., Portland, ME 04101. Finance Authority of Maine (FAME), 5 Community Drive, PO Box 949, Augusta, ME 04332; telephone (207)623-3263

Commercial Shipping

The deepwater Port of Portland is the largest in New England based on volume of tonnage handled, with more than 21 million tons of cargo landing annually. Pulpwood, fish, and other food products are among the items routinely shipped through the port. Among all U.S. transatlantic ports, it is the closest to Europe. The port has a dredged deepwater channel and provides excellent berthing for all sizes of vessels. The city has two major marine terminals: Portland International Marine Terminal and Merrill's Marine Terminal.

Portland International Jetport, one of the largest such facilities in the Northeast, is served by Airborne Express and Federal Express. Air cargo totals at the airport in 2004 were 33,622,563 pounds. Freight rail service is provided by Spring-

field Terminal Railway and the St. Lawrence & Atlantic Railroad Company. More than 30 interstate truck carriers have local terminals and main or branch offices there.

Labor Force and Employment Outlook

Portland's labor force is young and well educated; 83 percent of registered job seekers hold secondary or post secondary degrees. The city is said to support more lawyers per capita than anywhere else in the country except Washington, D.C. Portland is the employment center for Cumberland County, with 42.1 percent of all jobs located within the city. Analysts predict that in-migration of people from large urban areas will continue. An unemployment rate tending to be below the national average reflects the city's sturdy economy. Employment projections to 2012 call for faster than average growth in Portland.

The following is a summary of data regarding the Portland metropolitan area labor force, 2004 annual averages.

Size of nonagricultural labor force: 193,900

Number of workers employed in . . .
   construction and mining: 10,600
   manufacturing: 15,800
   trade, transportation and utilities: 42,000
   information: 4,700
   financial activities: 15,900
   professional and business services: 21,600
   educational and health services: 32,900
   leisure and hospitality: 19,500
   other services: 6,000
   government: 25,000

Average hourly earnings of production workers employed in manufacturing: $13.88

Unemployment rate: 4.0% (February 2005)

Largest employers (Greater Portland area)	*Number of employees*
L.L. Bean, Inc.	5,400-5,600
Maine Medical Center	4,600-4,800
UnumProvident	3,400-3,600
Delahaize	2,300-2,500
Bank North Group	1,900-2,100
Verizon	1,600-1,800

Cost of Living

Many people have been attracted to Portland because of its relative affordability; however, overall costs, including home costs, have risen. State and local spending has tended to increase at a rate below the national average.

The following is a summary of data regarding several key cost of living factors for the Portland area.

2004 ACCRA Cost of Living Index: Not reported

2004 ACCRA Average House Price: Not reported

State income tax rate: a graduated income tax rate from 2.0% to 8.5% of federal adjusted gross income minus all modifications, exemptions, and deductions.

State sales tax rate: 5.0%

Local income tax rate: None

Local sales tax rate: None

Property tax rate: $26.53 per $1,000 of actual value (2005)

Economic Information: Portland Regional Chamber, 60 Pearl Street, Portland, ME 04101; telephone (207)772-2811

Education and Research

Elementary and Secondary Schools

The Portland Public School System (PPS) enjoys a reputation for excellence and has been ranked among the top 10 education systems in the nation. Maine's largest and most diverse school district, PPS offers a challenging academic curriculum with a wide array of educational choices, including expeditionary learning and vocational training. The district's learning facilities range from a one-room schoolhouse on Cliff Island, to the second-oldest public high school in the nation, to a state-of-the-art elementary school under construction as of 2005.

The following is a summary of data regarding the Portland Public School District as of the 2004–2005 school year.

Total enrollment: 7,500

Number of facilities
  elementary schools: 10
  junior high/middle schools: 4
  senior high schools: 3

Student/teacher ratio: 11.2:1 (2002-2003)

Teacher salaries
  median: $47,682 (elementary school); $49,719 (high school)

Funding per pupil: $10,302

Approximately 3,000 Portland area students attend the city's 19 parochial and private schools.

Public Schools Information: Portland Public Schools, 331 Veranda St., Portland, ME 04103; telephone (207)874-8111

Colleges and Universities

The University of Southern Maine (USM) is the largest campus of the University of Maine system's seven campuses. USM has three campuses, in Portland, Gorham, and Lewiston, with a total enrollment of 11,007. USM offers more than 40 academic programs in its colleges of Arts and Sciences, Education and Human Development, and Nursing and Health Professions; and its schools of Business, Public Service, Law, and Applied Sciences, Engineering, and Technology. The Maine College of Art is an independent school of art and design offering Bachelor and Master of Fine Arts degrees. The University of New England, a highly-ranked regional university, offers degree programs in health sciences, natural sciences, human services, management, education, and the liberal arts, and has the only medical school—the University of New England College of Osteopathic Medicine—in the state of Maine. The university is comprised of two campuses; the primary one is located in nearby Biddeford, while the secondary one, known as Westbrook College, is in Portland. Renowned Bowdoin College, founded in 1794, is located in Brunswick, about 25 miles northeast of Portland. Bowdoin graduated some of New England's most famous nineteenth-century writers, including Harriet Beecher Stowe, and was a home base for Arctic exploration, having graduated Robert E. Peary. Two-year institutions in the Portland area include Andover, with campuses in Portland and Lewiston; and South Portland's Southern Maine Community College. The Salt Institute for Documentary Studies offers semester-long programs in documentary studies.

Libraries and Research Centers

The Portland Public Library serves as the major resource library for the Southern Maine Library District, part of the Maine Regional Library System. It has five branches and one bookmobile. The main building, located in the heart of downtown Portland, maintains a collection of 315,603 volumes, 1,880 periodical subscriptions, 2,450 compact discs, 2,870 video cassettes, 6,990 audio cassettes, and 400 phonograph records. Special services include an Art Department, a HealthShare Program, a children's art series, and a collection of resources on Maine history, genealogy, and fine printing. The Maine Historical Society Research Library holds more than one million books, manuscripts, and maps related to Maine and New England history. Area colleges and universities also maintain libraries; among these are the Donald L. Garbrecht Law Library at the University of Southern Maine, which has 371,000 volumes and 3,328 periodical subscriptions; undergraduate libraries at the university house more than 400,000 items plus a special collection of antique maps, globes, and atlases.

Research facilities located in Portland include the Maine Medical Center Research Institute, which specializes in biology, genetics, outcomes and health services research, and clinical research; the University of Maine Marine Law Institute, the only law school-affiliated marine policy research program in the Northeast; the University of Southern Maine Center for Business and Economic Research; and its Small Business Development Center.

Public Library Information: Portland Public Library, 5 Monument Square, Portland, ME 04101; telephone (207)871-1700; fax (207)871-1715

Health Care

Portland's Maine Medical Center, a major clinical and teaching affiliate of the University of Vermont College of Medicine, is the largest hospital in the state and a major referral center for northern New England. A 606-bed facility, it is an active research center as well as a teaching hospital. Every year, the hospital cares for more than 27,000 inpatients and more than 500,000 outpatients, and performs more than 16,000 surgeries. The hospital offers a full range of medical services and is widely known for its cardiac diagnostic and open-heart surgery programs, renal dialysis and kidney transplants, oncology, nuclear medicine, and rehabilitation. As of 2005, the hospital is embarking on an expansion project that will include a new obstetrics and newborn building, a parking garage, a helipad, and a central utility plant.

Mercy Hospital, a 177-bed community hospital, offers a complete range of diagnostic services and operates The Birthplace, the Recovery Center for recovering addicts, an inpatient Eating Disorders Program, an ambulatory care center, oncology centers, and a home care and hospice service. Mercy is a leader in Maine in orthopedic surgery, joint replacement surgery, and interventional procedures. Other facilities in Portland include New England Rehabilitation Hospital of Portland, an 82-bed facility specializing in physical rehabilitation; and Westbrook Community Hospital, specializing in treatment for alcoholism, drug abuse, and eating disorders. Greater Portland also supports a variety of the latest types of elderly housing and care centers, and along with traditional health care has a thriving community of healers and alternative-therapy specialists.

Health Care Information: Public Information Office, Maine Medical Center, 22 Bramhall Street, Portland, ME 04102; telephone (207)662-0111

Recreation

Sightseeing

Portland is a rejuvenated city that combines modern and historic buildings and districts with a thoughtful sense of what makes the city unique and lends it character. Walking tour brochures, available at the convention and visitors bureau, guide the visitor to Portland landmarks, the historic sites and buildings in downtown Portland, and the Old Port Exchange, reconstructed after the fire in 1866 and given a facelift in the early 1990s. This charming Victorian-style area of shops, galleries, and restaurants features cobblestone streets and old-fashioned gas street lamps, all contained in about a twelve-block area.

Northeast of Monument Square along Congress Street, interesting sights include the Wadsworth-Longfellow House, and the Neal Dow Memorial. The Wadsworth-Longfellow House, the first brick house in Portland, was built in 1786 by General Peleg Wadsworth, grandfather of poet Henry Wadsworth Longfellow. Longfellow lived there during his childhood, and the house, which contains personal possessions of the Wadsworth and Longfellow families, has been restored to the 1850s period. The Neal Dow Memorial, a mansion built in 1829 for a prominent Maine politician, prohibitionist, and abolitionist, contains the Dow family's furniture, paintings, and china. Victoria Mansion, southeast of Monument Square, is an Italianate structure notable for its elaborate woodcarvings, trompe l'oeil walls and ceilings, stained glass, furnishings designed by noted interior designer Gustave Herter, and imported marble mantels. East of Monument Square is Portland Observatory, where flags were once flown to announce the return of ships; an excellent view of the harbor is available from its 86-foot tower. The beautifully landscaped Eastern and Western promenades at either end of the city offer views of Casco Bay's Calendar Islands and the mountains to the west. The actual number of Calendar Islands is disputed; they are so-called because an early explorer declared that the bay ''had as many islands as there are days in the year.''

Stroudwater Village, one of Portland's oldest neighborhoods, houses the remains of mills, canals, and homes dating back 250 years. In the center of the village is Tate House, built in 1755 by George Tate, ships' mast agent for the English navy and later for the Czar of Russia. The house retains many of its eighteenth-century furnishings and re-

Tours of the city's harbor, islands, and historic lighthouses such as the Portland Head Lighthouse are available.

sembles a London townhouse. Boat tours of the harbor and its islands, historic lighthouses, and forts are also available.

Arts and Culture

Portland is the state's cultural showplace. Portland Performing Arts Center showcases the Portland Stage Company, whose seven-production season extends from September through May. Considered Maine's premier professional theatre, their productions range from classic to new. Theatrical performances are also presented by the Mad Horse Theatre Company, which offers cutting-edge works at the Portland Performing Arts Center; Maine Children's Theatre; and Portland Lyric Theatre, which brings Broadway musicals to South Portland in a September to May season. Summer visitors are entertained by a variety of professional theatrical performances as well as musical and other entertainment.

Dance performances are scheduled by the Portland Ballet Company, which has a repertoire of more than 30 ballets ranging from classic to contemporary. Maine State Ballet, based in nearby Falmouth, also presents ballet in Portland.

The nationally acclaimed Portland Symphony Orchestra, under the direction of Toshiyuki Shimada, performs at Merrill Auditorium. The orchestra offers classical and pops concerts from October through April, plus ''Independence Pops'' concerts in July and ''Magic of Christmas'' concerts in December. The Portland Opera Repertory Theatre (PORT) performs grand opera in the city's Merrill Auditorium during summer and winter. The Portland Concert Association presents dance, opera, musical theater, jazz, and classical music throughout the year. The 1929 State Theatre offers a variety of music performances.

The Portland Museum of Art displays fine and decorative arts dating from the eighteenth century to the present. Featured are works by American artists such as Winslow Homer, John Singer Sargent, Rockwell Kent, Marsden Hartley, Andrew Wyeth, and Hiram Powers, and by such European artists as Auguste Renoir, Henri Toulouse-Lautrec, Edgar Degas, and Mary Cassatt. An extensive glass collection features the work of Louis Comfort Tiffany. The museum's primary building, designed by I. M. Pei and Partners, strives to capture the quality of ''portland light'' for the benefit of the art displayed there. Its neighboring buildings are the McLellan House, which dates from 1801, and the L.D.M. Sweat Galleries, a 1911 Beaux Arts structure; both of these buildings display American paintings and decorative arts.

The Museum of African Culture, formerly the Museum of African Tribal Art, is the only museum in New England devoted exclusively to Sub-Saharan African tribal arts. The art and artifacts of its permanent collection total more than 1,500 items. The Institute of Contemporary Art, located on the campus of the Maine College of Art, showcases new trends in contemporary art. The Salt Gallery exhibit features student and professional work in documentary studies/photography. The Children's Museum of Maine offers participatory exhibits for children up to 10 years of age, including a farm, a grocery store, a car repair shop, and a vet clinic. Portland's smaller museums include the Fire Museum, showcasing antique fire-fighting equipment; Maine Narrow Gauge Railroad Company & Museum, which exhibits a parlor car, coaches, and locomotives, also offers 30-minute train rides along Casco Bay; the Portland Harbor Museum (formerly the Spring Point Museum) featuring local history and views of Portland Harbor; and the exhibits of the Maine Historical Society.

Festivals and Holidays

The Portland Flower Show, a four-day event held in March offering a taste of spring, is the largest flower show in northern New England. The show features landscaping displays, lectures, floral auctions, and food. Portland's visitors and residents enjoy summer sidewalk art shows, street festivals, and outdoor performances by puppeteers, clowns, comics, and musicians. The Old Port Festival, held in June, is Maine's largest one-day event. Held throughout the Portland's waterfront district, it features performance and visual artists, concerts, food vendors, crafts, parades, and more. Other June celebrations include the Greek Heritage Festival and the L. L. Bean Paddle Sports Festival. Independence Day is celebrated during a Fourth of July Festival featuring a fireworks display. The Portland Festival of Nations, also in July, celebrates the city's ethnic diversity and features an international bazaar. Maine's largest gathering of performance and visual artists, writers, circus performers, crafts experts, and chefs occurs in mid-August during the Maine Festival in nearby Brunswick. Art on the Porch presents works by more than 30 artisans. The MS Regatta Harborfest, also held in August, is Maine's largest sailing race. A fundraiser for Multiple Sclerosis, events include a Gala Charity Auction, and a weekend of activities that include sailboat, tugboat, and powerboat parades, a sailboat regatta, and a shore-side festival at the Maine State Pier in Portland. A variety of agricultural fairs are held in the region during the fall. The Christmas season is heralded by the Light Up Your Holidays tree-lighting ceremony in late November, featuring hayrides and caroling. The year culminates with Maine's official New Year's Eve celebration. Known as New Year's Portland, festivities include theatrical and musical performances of all kinds, plus indoor fireworks and special programs for children.

Sports for the Spectator

The American Hockey League's Portland Pirates entertain hockey fans at the 8,798-seat Cumberland County Civic Center from fall to spring. Hadlock Field is home to the

Eastern League Double A baseball team, the Sea Dogs, an affiliate of the Boston Red Sox. Cruise lines and helicopter charter services in Portland offer whale watching expeditions.

Sports for the Participant

The Portland region is blessed with an abundance of coastline offering sandy beaches and opportunities for swimming, sailing, camping, whitewater rafting, fishing, and lobstering. The city boasts more than 100 miles of nature and walking trails, including a network of 10 miles of trails that line the bay. The Portland area has 11 professional golf courses and 124 tennis courts. The Portland Parks and Recreation Department maintains an extensive park system, including the Riverside Golf Course, Eastern Promenade, and Deering Oaks Park, designed by Olmsted. Many state parks and ski areas are located nearby.

Shopping and Dining

Portland and its environs offer shopping opportunities of all descriptions. The centerpiece of Portland is the Old Port Exchange, where nineteenth-century buildings and warehouses have been restored and converted to a wide variety of specialty stores. The downtown area is a colorful mix of shops and restaurants in a Victorian setting; side streets leading to the bay contain small shops offering the interesting and unusual. The Maine Mall, located in South Portland, is the largest indoor shopping center in the state, with more than 140 stores. Freeport, 12 miles north of Portland, is home to L. L. Bean, the famous outdoor outfitter. Open 24 hours a day all year round, the store has been so successful that it has attracted more than 125 outlet stores to the area. The 30,000 square-foot Portland Public Market features more than 30 locally-owned businesses selling a wide range of fresh or preserved foods grown or produced in Maine. The city's Arts District, located a few blocks from the waterfront, is home to more than 50 galleries and spotlights Maine's premier artists.

As a tourist center and the home of a sophisticated populace, Portland boasts a wide variety of dining opportunities. The city purportedly has more restaurants per capita than any other city except San Francisco. Hundreds of Portland's restaurants offer traditional ''Downeast'' fare such as the famed Maine lobster, clams, mussels, and other fresh seafood, as well as ethnic and international specialties. Sidewalk cafes, where diners may enjoy the fresh sea air in a casual setting, are very popular in the city.

Visitor Information: Convention and Visitors Bureau of Greater Portland, 245 Commercial Street, Portland, ME 04101; telephone (207)772-5800. State Visitor Information; telephone (800)533-9595

Convention Facilities

Conventioneers make use of the Cumberland County Civic Center. With 34,500 square feet of exhibition space, the Civic Center is one of Maine's largest convention facilities. It is set in the heart of downtown Portland.

Merrill Auditorium, Portland's premier performing arts venue, is available for meetings; it provides seating for 1,909. Portland Exposition Building, built in 1914, is the second-oldest arena in continuous operation in the nation; the arena hosts trade shows, conferences, special events, and civic meetings, as well as concerts and sporting events.

Downtown and area hotels offer meeting space to accommodate large and small groups. There are more than 2,000 hotel and motel rooms in and around Portland.

Convention Information: Convention and Visitors Bureau of Greater Portland, 245 Commercial Street, Portland, ME 04101; telephone (207)772-5800

Transportation

Approaching the City

Portland International Jetport, which accommodates more than 1.2 million passengers annually, is 10 minutes from the downtown area. The Jetport is served by six major carriers. Intrastate flights are available from several major cities. Airport limousine and bus service is offered to and from Portland and other major cities in Maine.

Interstate highways 95 (Maine Turnpike) and 295 provide direct and convenient access to Portland's employment and population centers. Canadian roads join the Maine Turnpike from the north. Concord Trailways buses stop at Portland enroute between Boston and Bangor; Vermont Transit offers frequent service among Portland, Boston, and Maine's coastal and inland points. Amtrak's new Downeaster route runs four daily round-trips between Portland and Boston, with stops at eight communities in between.

From April to October the *Scotia Prince* provides passenger and auto ferry service between Portland and Yarmouth, Nova Scotia, Canada. Large oceangoing vessels can dock at the Port of Portland; each year, Portland hosts an average of 40 cruise ships.

Traveling in the City

Perhaps the best way to explore Portland, a small and interesting city, is on foot. The Chamber of Commerce and Convention and Visitors Bureau provide walking tour brochures. The Metro bus service operates eight daily routes throughout the city. The new Portland Explorer Express Bus Service runs between major downtown locations, the Maine Mall, the bus-rail station, and the airport. Taxi service is available, as well as ferry service to the Casco Bay Islands.

Communications

Newspapers and Magazines

Portland Newspapers supplies newspaper readers in Portland with the *Portland Press Herald* every morning except Sunday, and the *Maine Sunday Telegram* on Sunday. *Portland,* a magazine devoted to lifestyles, business, and real estate news, and performing arts and fiction reviews, is also published in Portland, as is the quarterly *PortCity Life. Maine History,* a semiannual scholarly journal, covers local history. Locally published special interest magazines include the *Ocean Navigator, Alaska Fisherman's Journal, Seafood Business, National Fisherman, Professional Mariner, Audiofile,* which has news about the audiobook business, and *The Cafe Review,* which covers art, poetry, and literature. *The Northeast,* a tabloid published eight times yearly, was founded in 1873 and is the oldest continuous news journal of the Episcopal Church.

Television and Radio

Television viewers in Portland may choose from four network affiliates, one public broadcasting station, and cable television. Ten AM and FM radio stations broadcast a variety of musical formats.

Media Information: Portland Newspapers, 390 Congress Street, Portland, ME 04104; telephone (207)791-6650

Portland Online

City of Portland. Available www.ci.portland.me.us

Greater Portland Chamber of Commerce. Available www .portlandregion.com

Greater Portland Convention & Visitors Bureau. Available www.visitportland.com

Maine Historical Society. Available www.mainehistory.org

Maine Office of Tourism. Available www.visitmaine.com

Portland Public Library. Available www.portlandlibrary .com

Press Herald and *Maine Sunday Telegram.* Available www .pressherald.mainetoday.com

Selected Bibliography

Gold, Susan Dudley and Jill Cournoyer, *The History of Union Wharf, 1793-1998* (Custom Communications, 1998)

Portland: A Publication of Greater Portland Landmarks Incorporated (Portland, Me: Greater Portland Landmarks, 1973)

MASSACHUSETTS

The State in Brief

Nickname: Bay State, Old Colony
Motto: *Ense Petit Placidam Sub Libertate Quietem* (By the sword we seek peace, but peace only under liberty)

Flower: Mayflower
Bird: Chickadee

Area: 10,554 square miles (2000; U.S. rank: 44th)
Elevation: Ranges from sea level to 3,487 feet
Climate: Temperate, with a colder, drier climate in the western portion of the state

Admitted to Union: February 6, 1788
Capital: Boston
Head Official: Governor Mitt Romney (R) (until 2007)

Population
  1980: 5,737,000
  1990: 6,016,425
  2000: 6,349,097
  2004 estimate: 6,416,505
  Percent change, 1990–2000: 5.5%
  U.S. rank in 2004: 13th
  Percent of residents born in state: 66.1% (2000)
  Density: 809.8 people per square mile (2000)
  2002 FBI Crime Index Total: 198,890

Racial and Ethnic Characteristics (2000)
  White: 5,367,287
  Black or African American: 343,454
  American Indian and Alaska Native: 15,015
  Asian: 238,124
  Native Hawaiian and Pacific Islander: 2,489
  Hispanic or Latino (may be of any race): 428,729
  Other: 236,724

Age Characteristics (2000)
  Population under 5 years old: 397,268
  Population 5 to 19 years old: 1,277,845
  Percent of population 65 years and over: 13.5%
  Median age: 36.5 years (2000)

Vital Statistics
  Total number of births (2003): 80,345
  Total number of deaths (2003): 55,836 (infant deaths, 425)
  AIDS cases reported through 2003: 8,397

Economy
  Major industries: Services, trade, manufacturing, agriculture, tourism
  Unemployment rate: 4.7% (April 2005)
  Per capita income: $39,408 (2003; U.S. rank: 4th)
  Median household income: $52,084 (3-year average, 2001-2003)
  Percentage of persons below poverty level: 9.7% (3-year average, 2001-2003)
  Income tax rate: 5.3%
  Sales tax rate: 5% on most items (does not include food and clothing)

Boston

The City in Brief

Founded: 1630 (chartered, 1822)

Head Official: Mayor Thomas M. Menino (D) (since 1994)

City Population
   1980: 562,994
   1990: 574,283
   2000: 589,141
   2003 estimate: 581,616
   Percent change, 1990–2000: 2.6%
   U.S. rank in 1980: 20th
   U.S. rank in 1990: 20th (State rank: 1st)
   U.S. rank in 2000: 23rd (State rank: 1st)

Metropolitan Area Population (PMSA)
   1980: 2,806,000
   1990: 3,227,707
   2000: 3,406,829
   Percent change, 1990–2000: 6.2%

   U.S. rank in 1980: 7th (CMSA)
   U.S. rank in 1990: 7th (CMSA)
   U.S. rank in 2000: 7th (CMSA)

Area: 48 square miles (2000)

Elevation: Ranges from 15 to 29 feet above sea level

Average Annual Temperature: 51.6° F

Average Annual Precipitation: 42.53 inches of rain; 42.6 inches of snow

Major Economic Sectors: Services, trade, manufacturing, government

Unemployment Rate: 4.9% (March 2005)

Per Capita Income: $23,353 (1999)

2003 FBI Crime Index Total: 35,049

Major Colleges and Universities: Boston University; Tufts University Medical School; Harvard University School of Medicine; Boston College; New England Conservatory of Music; School of the Museum of Fine Arts; University of Massachusetts at Boston; Massachusetts Institute of Technology

Daily Newspapers: *The Boston Globe; Boston Herald*

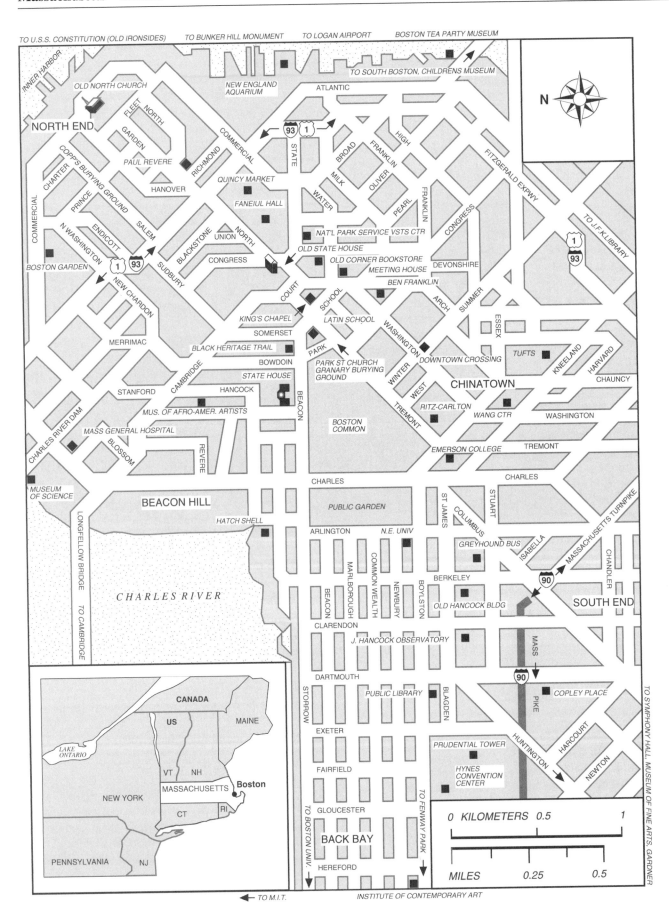

TO U.S.S. CONSTITUTION (OLD IRONSIDES)   TO BUNKER HILL MONUMENT   TO LOGAN AIRPORT   BOSTON TEA PARTY MUSEUM

INNER HARBOR

N

TO SOUTH BOSTON, CHILDRENS MUSEUM

ATLANTIC

OLD NORTH CHURCH

NEW ENGLAND AQUARIUM

NORTH END

FLEET   NORTH   GARDEN

COMMERCIAL

STATE

HIGH

BROAD   FRANKLIN   OLIVER

93   1

PAUL REVERE

RICHMOND

COPP'S BURYING GROUND   CHARTER   PRINCE   SALEM   HANOVER

QUINCY MARKET

FANEIUL HALL

MILK   WATER   PEARL   FRANKLIN   CONGRESS

FITZGERALD EXPWY

TO J.F.K.LIBRARY

1

COMMERCIAL   N WASHINGTON   ENDICOTT

BLACKSTONE   UNION   NORTH

NAT'L PARK SERVICE VSTS CTR

DEVONSHIRE

93

1   93

BOSTON GARDEN

SUDBURY

CONGRESS

OLD STATE HOUSE

OLD CORNER BOOKSTORE

MEETING HOUSE

ARCH   SUMMER

NEW CHARDON

COURT

BEN FRANKLIN

SCHOOL

KING'S CHAPEL

LATIN SCHOOL

WASHINGTON

ESSEX

MERRIMAC

SOMERSET

BLACK HERITAGE TRAIL

PARK

PARK ST CHURCH GRANARY BURYING GROUND

WINTER

DOWNTOWN CROSSING

TUFTS   KNEELAND   HARVARD

CHAUNCY

CAMBRIDGE

BOWDOIN

STATE HOUSE

STANFORD   HANCOCK

WEST

CHINATOWN

MUS. OF AFRO-AMER. ARTISTS

BEACON

TREMONT

RITZ-CARLTON

WANG CTR   WASHINGTON

CHARLES RIVER DAM

BLOSSOM

MASS GENERAL HOSPITAL

REVERE

BOSTON COMMON

EMERSON COLLEGE

TREMONT

MUSEUM OF SCIENCE

CHARLES

CHARLES

BEACON HILL

PUBLIC GARDEN

ST JAMES   COLUMBUS   STUART

MASSACHUSETTS TURNPIKE

CHANDLER

HATCH SHELL

ARLINGTON   N.E. UNIV

GREYHOUND BUS

ISABELLA

90

SOUTH END

LONGFELLOW BRIDGE

TO CAMBRIDGE

CHARLES RIVER

COMMON WEALTH   MARLBOROUGH   NEWBURY   BOYLSTON

BERKELEY

OLD HANCOCK BLDG

MASS   PIKE

BEACON

J. HANCOCK OBSERVATORY

90

CLARENDON

CANADA

US   MAINE

DARTMOUTH

STORROW

PUBLIC LIBRARY   BLAGDEN

COPLEY PLACE

PIKE

HUNTINGTON   HARCOURT   NEWTON

LAKE ONTARIO

VT   NH

EXETER

PRUDENTIAL TOWER

TO SYMPHONY HALL, MUSEUM OF FINE ARTS, GARDNER

NEW YORK

MASSACHUSETTS   • Boston

FAIRFIELD

HYNES CONVENTION CENTER

CT   RI

PENNSYLVANIA   NJ

TO BOSTON UNIV.

GLOUCESTER

TO FENWAY PARK

0   KILOMETERS   0.5   1

BACK BAY

HEREFORD

MILES   0.25   0.5

← TO M.I.T.   INSTITUTE OF CONTEMPORARY ART

Introduction

The Atlantic Ocean has played an important role throughout Boston's history. Situated on one of the world's finest natural harbors, Boston was once the maritime capital of the colonial United States. Known variously as the birthplace of the American Revolution, the site of New England's largest fleet of clipper ships, meeting place of America's literati, and home of many venerable educational and cultural institutions, Boston remains the largest city in the six New England states. During the 1980s, Boston gained fame as a high technology and defense research center, as well as a good place in which to conduct business. This was in part attributable to the vast network of research facilities connected with schools in the region. Since the economic downturn that occurred in 1988 through 1992, the city has been enjoying an economic recovery, with several large ongoing projects that will improve its infrastructure, including the famous (or to some, infamous) Big Dig. The city remains one of the country's premier tourist attractions. In recent years, various sources have ranked Boston among the best large cities in which to live in the United States.

Geography and Climate

Massachusetts's Shawmut Peninsula, upon which Boston is located, lies at the mouths of the Charles and Mystic rivers. The rivers flow into Boston's inner harbor and then into Boston Harbor itself. This harbor is part of Massachusetts Bay and leads ultimately to the North Atlantic Ocean. Boston's Harbor Islands are located in the inner harbor. Shawmut was originally a hilly peninsula that was separated almost entirely from the mainland by marshy swamps. Over the years, Boston's hills were leveled to fill in the back bay marshes; nonetheless, Boston's terrain remains rolling today.

Fog and humidity are by-products of Boston's proximity to water. Rain is frequent throughout the spring and summer, while snow falls regularly throughout the winter, making Boston one of the nation's wettest cities. Atlantic Ocean breezes keep Boston's climate relatively mild compared to other cities in the northeastern United States. Those same Atlantic breezes, however, help rank Boston among the country's windiest cities and occasionally blow into full-fledged storms called "nor'easters."

Area: 48 square miles (2000)

Elevation: 15 to 29 feet above sea level

Average Temperatures: January, 29.3° F; July, 73.9° F; annual average, 51.6° F

Average Annual Precipitation: 42.53 inches of rain; 42.6 inches of snow

History

Site on Peninsula Settled by Puritans

The point of land that juts into a natural harbor connecting with the Atlantic Ocean and forms the site of present-day Boston was once occupied by Native American tribes. They named the peninsula "Shawmut," which meant variously "land accessible by water" in reference to the harbor or "land with living fountains," a comment on the area's abundant fresh water springs. When two-thirds of the native population succumbed to a European disease against which they carried no immunity, the way was clear for trans-Atlantic settlers.

The area's first white settler from across the Atlantic arrived on the peninsula in the 1620s. William Blackstone, an English clergyman, was the leader of a small band who eventually returned to England, leaving Blackstone alone in his home atop what was later Boston's Beacon Hill. Blackstone and subsequent English settlers eventually became friendly with the local native tribes, whose democratic form of tribal governance, some historians claim, influenced the country's founding fathers in their conception of the Declaration of Independence and U.S. Constitution.

Boston was founded in 1630 by a Protestant religious sect called the Puritans. They named the new town for their former home in Lincolnshire, England. The same year, Boston was declared the capital of the Massachusetts Bay Colony. Bounded on three sides by water, Boston soon became the colonies' major New England seaport and the largest British settlement on the continent as well. When the Massachusetts Bay Colony's charter was revoked in 1684, Boston for the first time was subject to direct British authority.

Although unused to trans-Atlantic interference in their affairs, Bostonians nevertheless enjoyed a flowering of thought and culture never allowed during the years of strict Puritan dominance. As it developed into a major colonial center, Boston was the site of the calling of the nation's first Grand Jury in 1635; the opening of the nation's oldest school, the Boston Latin School, in 1635; the building of the first post office in 1639; the chartering of the colonies' first bank in 1674; the publication of the nation's oldest newspaper, *Publick Occurrences Both Forreign and Domestick,* banned after one issue in 1690; and the publishing of the nation's first long-running newspaper, the *Boston News-Letter,* in 1704. By 1750, Boston's population was 15,000 people.

Revolution Precedes Maritime Supremacy

Continued protest over the British Crown's introduction of a series of unpopular taxes (including those on stamps and tea) brought British soldiers to Boston in 1768. The colonists' rallying cry soon became "No taxation without representation!" Two years later, in 1770, British soldiers opened fire on a hostile crowd gathered in front of the Old State House. Five people were killed, including Crispus Attucks, a mulatto and the first African American to fall in America's fight for freedom from colonial status. The confrontation, dubbed the "Boston Massacre," further inflamed Bostonians and patriots throughout the thirteen colonies. In 1773, Samuel Adams and a group of followers dressed as Indians carried out the "Boston Tea Party" by emptying the holds of three British ships and dumping their shipment of taxable tea into Boston Harbor. The British Parliament responded by closing the port, effectively stifling the city's economy.

Troops of Minutemen began to drill throughout the colonies. Then, in 1775, ill feeling intensified when colonists learned that the British troops planned to seize weapons stockpiled in Concord, eighteen miles west of Boston. On the night of April 18, two lanterns were hung in the belfry of Boston's Old North Church, signaling that the British were approaching by land. Silversmith Paul Revere received the message and rode through the night to warn his colleagues at Concord. Revere was arrested along the way, but a second rider, Charles Dawes, delivered the warning. On April 19, British troops found the Minutemen armed and prepared for the confrontation that would become known as the "shot heard 'round the world." It was the first battle of the American Revolutionary War.

Following the Revolution, Boston once again resumed its maritime activity. Outgoing cargoes included ocean fish and rum from New England and tobacco from the South. Incoming goods included molasses from the West Indies, used to distill rum. With the successful resolution of the War of 1812, Boston began a lucrative trade with China. U.S. ships sailed around Cape Horn and into the Orient and India, returning to the United States with tea, silks, and spices. The design of a new and faster vessel, the clipper ship, further enhanced Boston's maritime supremacy. The invention of the water-powered loom made Boston an important textile center, and its wool industry grew to rival England's.

Boston received its city charter in 1822 and chose a mayor-council form of government. The original hilly Shawmut Peninsula upon which the city was built covered 800 acres surrounded by salt marshes, mudflats, and inlets of water. As Boston outgrew her site in the 1800s, most of the hills were leveled and used as fill to create Boston's famous Back Bay district. Boston's tax base grew when the city annexed neighboring towns such as Noddle's Island, which was re-

named East Boston. In 1821, Boston opened Boston English High School, the nation's oldest high school.

Manufacturing, Finance, Education Take Lead

Boston's population remained largely of English descent until the mid-1800s, when the first waves of European immigrants began to arrive. The Cabots and Lodges were typical of the leading Puritan families who became known as the Boston Brahmins. The city experienced an upsurge in manufacturing around the mid-1800s, aided by the invention of the railroad. Among the new industries were the making of shoes and other leather goods, until recently a mainstay of the Boston economy. Irish peasants seeking refuge from the potato famines in Ireland found work in Boston's factories and on the wharves. They settled in East Boston and Charlestown, which remain blue-collar Irish enclaves.

From the end of Puritan domination, Boston had been a religiously tolerant city. In the mid-1800s, Boston became the site of two major movements in the United States. The Unitarian Church was founded when a portion of dissatisfied Congregationalists broke away and formed a new sect. The Unitarian Church, in turn, became a progenitor of the Transcendental movement of the late nineteenth century. Boston was also the focus of the New England Anti-Slavery Society, founded in 1832. The Society's publication, *The Liberator,* helped identify North-South differences that eventually erupted into the Civil War. Boston's African American population in the mid-1800s was sizable, in part because Massachusetts had declared slavery illegal in 1783. By the time of the Civil War, Boston was the center of the Abolitionist Movement and a stop on the Underground Railroad, which aided escaping slaves.

During the Civil War, Boston supplied 26,000 soldiers and sailors to the Union and acted as an important military seaport. When the war ended, Boston's maritime importance diminished, though the city gained prominence in the world of finance. Meanwhile, intellectuals who gathered in Boston helped reunite the divided nation. Poets like James Russell Lowell, Henry Wadsworth Longfellow, and James Greenleaf Whittier, along with novelist Nathaniel Hawthorne, jurist Oliver Wendall Holmes, philosophers Ralph Waldo Emerson and Henry David Thoreau, and historians William H. Prescott and Francis Parkman wrote about the American spirit and helped define the American character. It was Holmes who, noting this concentration of influential thinkers, dubbed Boston the "hub of the solar system."

Set-Backs Countered by Redevelopment

By 1900, Boston's population had reached 561,000, partially swelled by the new wave of Italian immigrants who settled on Boston's North End. Along with the French-Canadians who arrived next, they combined with the resident Irish to make Boston the nation's second largest Roman Catholic archdiocese. An established population, Boston's Irish began to figure in municipal politics. John F. "Honey" Fitzgerald was the town's first Irish mayor. He was elected to two terms, in 1906 and again in 1910. He established a political dynasty that included U.S. President John Fitzgerald Kennedy among his descendants. Fishing, food processing, shoe making, and wool products were viable Boston industries at the turn of the century, by which time the demand for ship building had diminished. Like many of the nation's industrialized cities, Boston suffered economically between the world wars. First Prohibition, which made the manufacture and sale of alcoholic beverages illegal, destroyed the rum trade, then the Great Depression of the 1930s undermined Boston's financial market and, finally, New England's textile industry moved South in search of less expensive labor. At this time, Boston began to acquire a dual reputation for corrupt machine politics and racial segregation. The city did a great deal to end corruption when council seats were declared open in 1951. Racial tension, however, continues to be a problem in Boston. Tempers flared over court-ordered pupil busing intended to desegregate the city's schools, and some Boston neighborhoods have yet to be integrated.

Following World War II, Boston's population grew to a peak of 801,000 in 1950, then began to level off and eventually declined. Its industries were mature and its infrastructure aging. The diminishing tax base led to an increase in taxes levied and a subsequent loss of the white middle class population to the suburbs. This trend, however, was countered in 1957 with the establishment of the Boston Redevelopment Authority, formed to revitalize the city. Through the efforts of this group, the Prudential Tower, a major office complex, was built in downtown Boston, along with a public auditorium, apartments, and office-retail structures. A new government center was constructed adjacent to historic Faneuil Hall, and other projects included shopping areas, neighborhood renewal, and development of waterfront and historic districts. Boston also benefitted from the electronics research industry that emerged in the region in the 1950s.

Boston grew rapidly on the strength of its high-tech and defense-related research industries until the late 1980s. A combination of factors including high taxes, wages, office lease rates, and housing costs began to drive businesses to surrounding communities and states. Boston has, however, received high marks from analysts for its responsible handling of these and other fiscal problems. A strong economic turnaround which began around 1993 is continuing into the new century. As host to the Democratic National Convention in 2004, Boston promotes tourism (always a staple of its economy) to boost its national image.

At the beginning of the new century, Boston's Mayor Tom Menino said of his city: "The major challenge facing Boston in the twenty-first century is that of new prosperity; how to renew Boston in a way that honors the beautiful historic city left in our care. We are fortunate to be living in one of those rare times in our City's life, a time when we have a chance to reinvent Boston and preserve the best of it for many years to come." Today's Boston remains a mecca for education and culture, and is a forward-looking city steeped in tradition and history.

Historical Information: The Bostonian Society, 15 State Street, Boston, MA 02109; telephone (617)720-1713

Population Profile

Metropolitan Area Residents (PMSA)
1980: 2,806,000
1990: 3,227,707
2000: 3,406,829
Percent change, 1990–2000: 6.2%
U.S. rank in 1980: 7th (CMSA)
U.S. rank in 1990: 7th (CMSA)
U.S. rank in 2000: 7th (CMSA)

City Residents
1980: 562,994
1990: 574,283
2000: 589,141
2003 estimate: 581,616
Percent change, 1990–2000: 2.6%
U.S. rank in 1980: 20th
U.S. rank in 1990: 20th (State rank: 1st)
U.S. rank in 2000: 23rd (State rank: 1st)

Density: 12,165.8 people per square mile (2000)

Racial and ethnic characteristics (2000)
   White: 320,944
   Black or African American: 149,202
   American Indian and Alaska Native: 2,365
   Asian: 44,284
   Native Hawaiian and Pacific Islander: 366
   Hispanic or Latino (may be of any race): 85,089
   Other: 46,102

Percent of residents born in state: 47.4% (2000)

Age characteristics (2000)
   Population under 5 years old: 32,046
   Population 5 to 9 years old: 33,721
   Population 10 to 14 years old: 32,553
   Population 15 to 19 years old: 43,631

Population 20 to 24 years old: 70,084
Population 25 to 34 years old: 124,762
Population 35 to 44 years old: 86,420
Population 45 to 54 years old: 63,554
Population 55 to 59 years old: 22,746
Population 60 to 64 years old: 18,288
Population 65 to 74 years old: 31,154
Population 75 to 84 years old: 21,675
Population 85 years and older: 8,507
Median age: 31.1 years

Births (2002)
Total number: 8,005

Deaths (2002)
Total number: 4,416 (of which, 56 were infants under the age of 1 year)

Money income (1999)
Per capita income: $23,253
Median household income: $39,629
Total households: 239,603

Number of households with income of . . .
less than $10,000: 37,230
$10,000 to $14,999: 15,764
$15,000 to $24,999: 27,276
$25,000 to $34,999: 27,496
$35,000 to $49,999: 35,928
$50,000 to $74,999: 41,496
$75,000 to $99,999: 23,784
$100,000 to $149,999: 18,496
$150,000 to $199,999: 5,491
$200,000 or more: 6,642

Percent of families below poverty level: 15.3% (25.4% of which were female householder families with related children under 5 years)

2002 FBI Crime Index Total: 35,049

Municipal Government

Boston operates under a mayor-council form of government; the mayor is elected to four-year terms and the council members to two-year terms. In addition to governing the city of Boston, the mayor and council act as commissioners for the county of Suffolk. Their jurisdiction covers cities outside Boston's city limits: Chelsea, Revere, and Winthrop.

Head Official: Mayor Thomas M. Menino (D) (since 1994; current term expires January 2006)

Total Number of City Employees: 16,049, including police, fire, and school (2004)

City Information: Mayor's Office, City of Boston, One City Hall Plaza, Boston, MA 02201; telephone (617)635-4500

Economy

Major Industries and Commercial Activity

Since the 1988–1992 downturn, Boston experienced an ongoing economic recovery, with increased employment rates, improvement in the office market, strong sales, and tremendous gains in residential real estate. As in many places across the country, Boston's economy was affected by the events on September 11, 2001. Especially hit were the travel, financial services and high technology sectors, which alone lost nearly 32,000 jobs between 2001 and 2003. Loss of jobs in those areas leveled off in 2004 and began to regain some lost ground, especially in tourism.

Other sectors such as education and health care were not as hard hit. While manufacturing in Boston has lost some ground, it remains an important sector of the economy and is joined by several other traditional industries and some new ones. Boston is considered one of the top places in which to do business in the United States. Major industries include finance, high-technology research and development, tourism, medicine, education, commercial fishing, food processing, printing and publishing, and government.

Early in its history, Boston made its name as a center for the processing of wool and the manufacture of clothing, textiles, shoes, and leather goods. While the shoe and textile industries have suffered in recent decades, they remain significant contributors to Boston's economy.

In the last 20 years, city employment continued to shift from traditional labor intensive manufacturing jobs to technology and service jobs. The economy of metropolitan Boston now primarily rests on high technology, finance, professional and business services, defense, and educational and medical institutions. The city's economy is more specialized in the financial, business and professional services and educational and medical sectors than the suburban economy, which is more specialized in high technology and the defense industry.

Boston's financial district includes major banks such as Fleet Bank, purchased in 2004 by Bank of America, and investment firms like Fidelity Investments. Insurance firms such as John Hancock Financial Services are also a significant presence.

Boston is one of the country's top 10 tourist attractions, focusing on the city's 62 historic sites, its nearly 2,000 restaurants, and its hundreds of hotels. Tourism is a year-round industry in Boston, which hosted 16.3 million visitors in 2004, spending $7.9 billion.

The medical schools of both Tufts University and Harvard University are located in Boston, as is Massachusetts General Hospital, the major teaching hospital for both schools. Education is a thriving segment of Boston's economy; within the city limits are 10 colleges and universities, 6 technical schools, 4 art and music schools, and 6 junior colleges. In towns and suburbs surrounding Boston, educational institutions include many prestigious secondary and boarding schools.

More than two million pounds of fish are caught in the waters in and around Boston each year, making fishing, food processing, and food storage prime industries. Boston is one of the nation's foremost fishing port and wool market. Both large and small printing operations employ thousands of workers in the metropolitan area. Boston's print fare includes several national magazines, scholarly and technical journals, and the Christian Science publications. For years, Boston has been home to the *Atlantic Monthly,* one of the oldest literary publications in the United States.

As the capital of the Commonwealth of Massachusetts, Boston is the workplace of many state and municipal employees.

Items and goods produced: machinery, medical and navigational instruments, chemicals, metals, rubber products and clothing, computers, software, missiles and missile guidance systems, ships, shoes and boots, textiles.

Incentive Programs—New and Existing Companies

Local programs—Boston's Office of Business Development provides key resources to support small business development. The office offers a full range of services—from financial and referral services to business facade improvement to site finder services—so that each business owner receives whatever help is needed. Businesses may obtain loans through the Boston Local Development Corporation, and financing through the Boston Industrial Development Financing Authority, which issues bonds to finance the capital needs of Boston businesses. ReStore Boston provides grants and loans to renovate store fronts, and provides architectural assistance to do so. The office also has a free Commercial Space for Lease finding service.

State programs—The Massachusetts Business Resource Team, under the Executive Office of Economic Development, exists to help businesses relocate to the state, expansion of existing businesses, and creation of new businesses. For new companies, there are Small Business Development Centers in Boston and across Massachusetts, which advise and educate entrepreneurs. The Capital Access Program helps businesses secure loans from approved banks. Ex-

panding or relocating businesses can take advantage of a 3 percent investment tax credit against the corporate excise tax for the construction of manufacturing facilities, or the purchase or lease of equipment. Businesses moving to an ''economic opportunity area'' or an ''economically distressed area'' have access to special tax credits and incentive programs. For manufacturers looking for working capital, the Economic Stabilization Trust can provide funds to help get the business on the road to recovery. For businesses willing to move or expand into brownfield areas, Massachusetts provides low cost assessment and remediation programs, and alternative financing options. Technology firms can receive assistance with the Research and Development Tax Credit and the Emerging Technology fund, which provides loans for specialized equipment purchases and R & D,, and biotechnology companies can receive funds for new job creation through the Jobs Creation Incentive Payment. All businesses can take advantage of Safety Training grants for education to improve workplace safety. The Massachusetts Export Center provides counseling, education and technical assistance for businesses in global markets. For business involved in the fishing industry, Seafood Loans assist in the construction or renovations of buildings or equipment.

Job training programs—Boston's Office of Jobs and Community Service (JCS) receives funding from the U.S. Department of Labor, HUD, and the Massachusetts Departments of Education and Transitional Assistance. The state provides matching grants from the Workplace Training Fund to pay for employee training. The state's 32 One-Stop Career Centers provide job finding assistance and career counseling for potential employees; and listing services, job fairs, and recruiting assistance for employers. JCS provides planning and oversight to a large network of community-based organizations who provide residents with a rich variety of training programs. These include basic education, GED and diploma programs, English as a Second Language, job readiness, and a variety of skills training. Additionally, JCS is a partner in a one-stop career center called The Work Place, which coordinates the functions of the Boston Neighborhood Jobs Trust, oversees various human service programs, and houses Read Boston, a major literacy initiative to ensure that all children are reading-proficient by the third grade. There are incentive grants for training when hiring an unemployed worker, or someone receiving public assistance.

Development Projects

The real estate market in Boston continues to thrive with multi-million dollar projects. A special focus is development of the South Boston Waterfront area, and the Fort Point Channel Arts District. Artists for Humanity has a new ''green,'' environmentally-aware 23,500 square foot center providing studio and gallery space for teaching art to inner-city youth. In 2006, construction will begin on a 22,000 square foot addition to Boston's Children's Museum, also in South Boston. Nearby will be a 400-room Marriot Renaissance Hotel, expected to cost $140 million, which will open in 2007. Boston Harbor Residences, a high-end, two-tower rental and condominium development, opens in 2005. Breaking ground in 2005 is the massive $230 million Battery Wharf mixed-use project in the North End, which will be composed of four buildings and include high-end condos and the luxury Regent Boston hotel.

In 2004, the Onyx Hotel, a hip, pet-friendly boutique hotel, opened in North Station. The Saltonstall office building at 100 Cambridge St. was completely overhauled, and in 2004 re-opened as a 279,000 square foot mixed-use tower of condominiums, office and retail space. In the Fenway neighborhood, Trilogy, a $200-million, 651,000-square-foot mixed use development, broke ground in 2004 to bring housing, 42,000 square feet of retail space, and underground parking to Boylston St. and Brookline Ave. Construction will begin soon on a new emergency and trauma center for the UMass Memorial Medical Center, in Worcester, which is expected to cost $129 million. In the Longwood Medical Area, Beth Israel Deaconess Medical Center will start construction on a 700,000 square foot research center, the first building of which will open in 2007. Also in Longwood, the Massachusetts Mental Health Center will get a $200 million make-over in 2005, adding medical offices, research space, and housing, both market value and low-income apartments. A new Intercontinental Hotel at 500 Atlantic Avenue will feature 424 hotel rooms on the first 12 floors, with luxury condos on the floors above, in a $255 million development.

Economic Development Information: Boston Redevelopment Authority, One City Hall Square, Boston, MA 02201; telephone (617)722-4300; fax (617)248-1934. MassDevelopment, 160 Federal Street, Boston, MA 02110; toll-free (800)445-8030. Boston Business Journal, 200 High Street, Suite 4B, Boston, MA 02110; telephone (617)330-1000; fax (617)330-1016

Commercial Shipping

Boston is the oldest continuously active port in the America's. Today, Boston's exports include grains and metals and its imports are petroleum products, automobiles, and general container cargo. In 2004 the port handled 1.3 million tons of general cargo, 1.5 million tons of non-fuels bulk cargo and 12.8 million tons of bulk fuel. Boston's popularity as a port is easily understood: it accommodates even the largest ocean going freighters. One of the best natural harbors in the United States, the Fort Point Channel is 40 feet deep and 7 miles long. Nearly 40 miles of docks and wharves line the shores of Boston's inner harbor, mainly between South Boston and Charlestown. The Massachusetts Port Authority operates the docks.

Facilities include the Conley Container Terminal, the center of container handling, with 2000 feet of berthing space; Boston Autoport, processing nearly 100,000 cars a year; Commonwealth Pier, a huge dry dock in South Boston; and Fish Pier, one of the world's largest and oldest in the country. Cruiseport and Black Falcon Cruise Terminal is a stopping point for 15 cruise lines, such as Norwegian and Cunard. Boston's shipping needs are also accommodated by the network of highways running through and around the city, a large commercial trucking fleet, railroads, and delivery services.

Labor Force and Employment Outlook

As the home of world-renowned colleges and universities, Boston boasts a highly educated work force. The minority population, including the Hispanic population, is on the increase. Educational institutions are an important source of new, highly skilled professionals for the city's labor force.

Wages in the Boston area tend to be high, as are taxes and office lease rates. Entrepreneurial software and biotechnology companies attracted to the assets of the Massachusetts Institute of Technology have tended to locate in East Cambridge, just across the Charles River from Boston. Analysts have given the city high marks in recent years for improvements in management, and a strong academic and research base should continue to stand Boston in good stead.

The following is a summary of data regarding the Boston metropolitan NECTA labor force, 2004 annual averages.

Size of nonagricultural labor force: 2,398,900

Number of workers employed in . . .
  natural resources and mining: 1,200
  construction: 100,500
  manufacturing: 231,200
  trade, transportation and utilities: 424,100
  information: 72,800
  financial activities: 182,800
  professional and business services: 374,200
  educational and health services: 431,600
  leisure and hospitality: 206,900
  other services: 85,700
  government: 288,000

Average hourly earnings of production workers employed in manufacturing: $18.65

Unemployment rate: 4.9% (March 2005)

Largest private employers	*Number of employees*
Massachusetts General Hospital Corporation	14,907
Fidelity Investments	11,250
Beth Israel Deaconess Medical Center	8,568

Largest private employers	*Number of employees*
Brigham & Women's Hospital, Inc.	8,421
Boston University	8,297
Children's Hospital	5,116
New England Medical Center	5,077
John Hancock Life Insurance Co.	4,793
Boston Medical Center	4,650
Harvard (business and medical schools)	4,557

Cost of Living

When compared with the national average, living in Boston is expensive, even more so than in other New England cities. The high cost of housing contributes to the overall expense. According to the Tax Institute, in 2005 Massachusetts residents had a much lower state and local tax burden than they used to: the state now ranked 32nd in the nation, and its personal income tax ranked it 12th lowest among states who have an income tax.

The following is a summary of data about key cost of living factors for the Boston area.

2004 (3rd Quarter) ACCRA Average House Price: $466,429

2004 (3rd Quarter) ACCRA Cost of Living Index: 135.4 (U.S. average = 100.0)

State income tax rate: 5.3%; 12% on short-term capital gains.

State sales tax rate: 5.0% on most items; does not include food and clothing

Local income tax rate: None

Local sales tax rate: None

Property tax rate: $10.73 per $1,000 valuation (residential); $32.68 per $1,000 valuation (commercial and other)

Economic Information: Greater Boston Chamber of Commerce, One Beacon St., Fourth Floor, Boston, MA 02108; telephone (617)536-4100. Boston Assessor, telephone (617)635-4287. The Tax Foundation, 2001 L Street, N.W. Suite 1050,Washington, D.C. 20036, telephone (202)464-6200

Education and Research

Elementary and Secondary Schools

Boston's school district is one of the nation's 60 largest. Boston spends nearly 30 percent of its annual budget on school matters, and its system excels in special education classes. The Boston School Committee is a seven member board, whose member are appointed by Mayor Menino. In 2005 the district was a finalist for the Broad Prize for Urban Education, the fourth time in as many years.

The following is a summary of data regarding the Boston public schools as of the 2004–2005 school year.

Total enrollment: 58,310

Number of facilities
  elementary schools: 66
  elementary and middle schools: 11
  middle schools: 18
  high schools: 25
  other: 7 early learning centers, 6 special education centers

Student/teacher ratio: 13:1

Teacher salaries
  minimum: $40,707
  maximum: $76,336

Funding per pupil: $10,739 (2003-2004)

Several prestigious private secondary schools also operate in Boston, among them the Commonwealth School, known for its focus on humanities and languages. Boston University's Academy, a five-year private preparatory school on its campus, permits students to take freshman-year college classes while still in high school. Boston also has an active parochial school system.

Public Schools Information: Boston Public Schools, Central Administration Office, 26 Court St., Boston, MA 02108; telephone (617)635-9000

Colleges and Universities

In the mid-2000s, the New England Board of Higher Education reported 68 colleges and universities in the Boston metropolitan area, at which approximately 250,000 students were enrolled. Once nicknamed the "Athens of America," Boston is home to some of the most venerable institutions of learning in the country. Boston University, founded in 1839, excels in medicine, law, foreign studies, and computing. Tufts and Harvard universities maintain their medical schools in Boston to take advantage of the teaching/learning opportunities offered by city hospitals such as Massachusetts General. Among the four-year liberal arts schools in Boston are Emerson, which publishes the *Emerson Review* twice yearly, and Emmanuel, a Roman Catholic women's institution. The University of Massachusetts maintains a commuter campus in Boston. Northeastern University is a small, mostly residential school, Wheelock College focuses on early childhood education and human services, and Simmons College and Suffolk University are small co-educational schools.

Boston-area technical schools include the Franklin Institute of Boston (for engineering), Massachusetts College of Pharmacy and Allied Health Sciences, Boston Technical Center, the Northeastern Institute of Industrial Technology, the New England School of Art and Design, the Women's Technical Institute and Wentworth Institute of Technology (for engineering). Boston's fine arts schools include The Berklee College of Music, a world renown independent school of music, not only in performance, but in composition, recording engineering, and music management. Boston's other fine arts schools include the Boston Conservatory of Music (with the Boston Chamber Music Society in residence), Massachusetts College of Art, the Art Institute of Boston, New England Conservatory of Music, and the School of the Museum of Fine Arts. Among the city's two-year colleges are Bay State Junior College, Bunker Hill Community College, Fisher College, Labourne College, and Roxbury Community College.

Nearby institutions of note include Harvard University, Radcliffe College, and the Massachusetts Institute of Technology in Cambridge, along with Boston College in Chestnut Hill and Brandeis University in Waltham.

Libraries and Research Centers

Boston's public library system, established in 1854, serves patrons in the city and several suburbs and is the nation's first instance of a tax-supported system. It maintains 26 neighborhood branches that house more than 13 million books and a bookmobile, and has over 2.2 million visitors a year. The main library, an Italian Renaissance building in downtown Copley Square, contains a rare book collection and is decorated with murals by John Singer Sargent and art work by other famous American painters and sculptors. The President John F. Kennedy Memorial Library and Museum is also found in Boston, along with a number of specialized law, finance, technical, and educational libraries.

Many research institutions are grouped in and around Boston, covering topics ranging from engineering to philosophy. Boston University facilities conduct research on foreign affairs, communication, computing, medicine, polymer chemistry, and a host of other subjects. Harvard University's research efforts include business, international affairs, law, medicine, physics, computers, and more. Massachusetts Institute of Technology's research programs focus on engineering, biotechnology, ocean studies, chemistry, robotics, electronics, and others. Research institutes of colleges include the Boston Biomedical Research Institute, the Boston Sickle Cell Center, and the Alzheimer's Disease Re-

search Center, three offerings that serve to underline Boston's prominence in the medical research field.

Public Library Information: Main Library, Boston Public Library, 700 Boylston St., Boston, MA 02117-0286; telephone (617)536-5400; fax (617)236-4306

Health Care

Few places in the country have more doctors than Boston—more than 500 per 100,000 people—and health care is among the best. More than 20 inpatient hospitals are located within the city, including Massachusetts General Hospital, Brigham and Women's Hospital, Beth Israel Hospital, Children's Hospital, New England Deaconess Hospital, the New England Medical Center and Boston Medical Center. The city is also home of the medical and dental schools of Tufts, Harvard, and Boston universities.

Boston's history of medical research is a long one. Massachusetts General was the first hospital to use anesthetic and to reattach a severed human limb. It also worked with the Massachusetts Institute of Technology and the Shriners Burn Institute to pioneer the development of artificial skin. Brigham & Women's Hospital gained national recognition for its testing of the birth control pill. In addition to fine hospitals and renowned medical schools, Boston is also home to a Comprehensive Cancer Treatment Center. A number of cardiac rehabilitation centers and hospices for the critically ill also operate facilities in Boston.

Health Care Information: Massachusetts Medical Society Headquarters, 860 Winter Street, Waltham Woods Corporate Center, Waltham, MA 02451-1411; telephone: (781)893-4610 or (781)893-3800

Recreation

Sightseeing

Boston's great appeal to visitors and residents alike is its compactness; it is a very walkable city and many of its attractions are planned around that fact. Maps are available at the National Park Service Visitor Center on State Street. The Freedom Trail, a 2.5-mile walking tour, passes the sixteen major sites of colonial Boston. A red line painted on the sidewalk marks the way. The trail begins at the Boston Common, with 48 acres and the oldest public park in the United States. The next stop is the gold-domed State House, built in 1795. Designed by Charles Bulfinch, it sits atop

The Declaration of Independence was read in front of the (1713) Old State House, now home to the Museum of Boston History.

what remains of Beacon Hill. Next is Park Street Church, birthplace of the Abolitionist Movement, and farther on is the Granary Burying Ground, resting place of such notables as Mother Goose, victims of the Boston Massacre, John Hancock, Samuel Adams, Paul Revere, and Peter Faneuil. King's Chapel, formerly an Anglican Church, became the nation's first Unitarian Church. Ben Franklin's statue stands on the grounds of the country's first public school, the Boston Latin School, which was opened in 1635. The Old Corner Bookstore survived to host meetings of the Transcendentalists and other Boston literati, while the Old South Meeting House rang with the sermons of the Puritans. The Old State House, built in 1713, was the scene of the Boston Massacre and revolutionary rhetoric such as the first reading of the Declaration of Independence. Faneuil Hall is next door, and a step down the street is Paul Revere's house and Old North Church. Copp's burying ground, the *USS Constitution,* and the Bunker Hill Monument complete the Trail.

Boston's long-standing commitment to equality is highlighted in another walking tour, the Black Heritage Trail. In existence for more than 350 years, Boston's African American community predates the Civil War by 120 years. Abolitionist meeting places and Underground Railroad stops are featured on the tour. Sights of a modern nature include a view from the 740-foot-high observation deck in the John Hancock Observatory or a glimpse of the stars through a telescope at the Boston University Observatory. Boston's parks are popular regional attractions, including the famous Harbor Islands. Next to Boston Common is the 24-acre Boston Public Park featuring an ornamental lake and swan boat rides. The parks follow the Fenway, a tree-lined boulevard, south to Jamaica Plain and the Arnold Arboretum, a botanical garden. The Esplanade, which runs along the Charles River, is a popular park and home of the Hatch Shell, where the Boston Pops plays its summer concerts. The Boston Harborwalk is a public walkway along the waterfront, connecting neighborhoods, parks, restaurants and attractions along the trail from Charlestown to Dorchester.

In Cambridge, Harvard University's several gardens draw crowds, as do its Fogg Art Museum and Harvard Coop, the university bookstore. A bit north, in Charlestown, are the Charles River Dam and the Charlestown Naval Yard. Boston's varied neighborhoods prove popular with visitors year after year. Beacon Hill, in downtown Boston, was settled by prosperous Yankee ship builders and their families, known as the Boston Brahmins. The elegant townhouses, gas lamps, and lacy iron fences still line the streets of Beacon Hill. The Back Bay is home to Boston's newer developments, including Copley Place, the John Hancock Building, and the Prudential Tower. The South End and its brick bow-windowed homes are undergoing a revitalization as new residents and businesses move back into the area. Boston's Chinatown houses the country's third largest Chinese popu-

lation, along with restaurants and stores specializing in traditional Chinese fare and ware. The North End is home to Boston's Italian community, while South Boston remains a solidly Irish enclave.

Lovers of the New England countryside might consider a day trip to Concord, thirty miles west of Boston. Attractions there include Fruitlands, a collection of small museums displaying treasures from nineteenth-century transcendentalism and other mystical movements, and Shaker Village.

Arts and Culture

Boston, home to a number of major museums, a world-class symphony, several legitimate theaters, and a premier dance company, is considered one of the nation's top cultural centers. Rated outstanding by music lovers the world over, the Boston Symphony Orchestra (BSO) performs at Symphony Hall. An offshoot of the BSO, the Boston Pops, has gained fame under the batons of the late maestro Arthur Fiedler and maestro/composer John Williams, and currently maestro Keith Lockhart. Other orchestras include the New England Conservatory Symphony Orchestra, the Boston Conservatory Orchestra, and the Boston Philharmonic Orchestra. Chamber concerts are programmed by the Handel and Hayden Society, while the Boston Musica Viva plays contemporary music.

Theatergoers in Boston can enjoy everything from tragedy to comedy, all performed by well-regarded professional troupes. Major groups include the American Repertory Theatre, and the Huntington Theatre Company. Several smaller repertory companies, small theaters, university groups, and a Boston's Children's Theatre augment the professional stage offerings. Dance is popular in Boston, which is home to the Boston Ballet, the fourth largest ballet company in America, and Dance Umbrella, New England's largest presenter of contemporary and culturally diverse dance from around the world. The Boston Ballet performs at the Wang Center for the Performing Arts, an opulent former motion picture palace. Other dance groups include the Art of Black Dance and Music, Beth Soll and Company, the Boston Flamenco Ballet, Concert Dance Company of Boston, and the Ramon de los Reyes Spanish Dance Theatre. Boston supports the Boston Lyric Opera, and many nightclubs featuring musical performances from rock and roll to folk music.

The Museum of Fine Arts is world renowned for its Oriental, Egyptian, and classical collections. The Museum of Science, complete with dinosaurs, space capsules, an OmniMax Theatre, and the Charles Hayden Planetarium, sits on a finger of land jutting into the Charles River. Italian Renaissance art is the attraction at the Isabella Stewart Gardner Museum, considered one of the world's finest private art museums. The Institute of Contemporary Art offers a multimedia look at the newest in art, while the Computer Museum, the first in the United States devoted exclusively to computing, houses a venerable computer, the MIT Whirlwind. The museum has merged with, and is now housed at, the Museum of Science. The New England Aquarium, with 2,000 fish and sea animals, occupies a five-story building on Boston's waterfront. Hands-on exhibits and tours are offered, as are whale-watching cruises.

Among the attractions at the Fogg Art Museum at Harvard University are works by Rembrandt, William Blake, and the French impressionists. German art is featured at the Busch-Reisinger Collection, which is on display at the Fogg Museum. The Botanical Museum and the Gray Herbarium, both part of Harvard, exhibit two of the finest flora displays in the world. Also at Harvard, the Peabody Museum of Archaeology and Ethnology displays relics of the Mayans, Pacific Islanders, and Native Americans. Other Boston museums include the *USS Constitution* Museum, Children's Museum of Boston, the museum at the John Fitzgerald Kennedy Library, the Museum of the National Center of Afro-American Artists, the Sports Museum of New England, the DeCordova Museum and Sculpture Park, the Museum of African American History and the Boston Tea Party Museum and Shop.

Arts and Culture Information: Greater Boston Convention-Visitor's Bureau, telephone (888)SEE-BOSTON

Festivals and Holidays

Many of Boston's festivities center around historic, religious, and maritime events. The celebration by the Irish community of St. Patrick's Day on March 17, a day that is also known locally as Evacuation Day, commemorates the retaking of Boston from the British by the Colonial Army during the Revolutionary War. In early June, costumed residents march through Boston in the Ancient and Honorable Artillery Parade. The Battle of Bunker Hill Day follows on June 17, the anniversary of one of the bloodiest battles of the Revolutionary War. June 24 through June 26 is Boston's First Folk Festival. The New England Spring Flower Show, one the oldest and biggest indoor shows in the country, draws 170,000 visitors during a 9-day period.

For six days at the beginning of July, Boston's HarborFest jubilantly celebrates the nation's birthday. Events include a Chowderfest, Children's Day, the reading of the Declaration of Independence from the balcony of the Old State House, and the July Fourth rendition of the 1812 Overture, replete with cannon, and followed by a dazzling fireworks display. The Italian Feasts take place each weekend from late June through August in Boston's North End. Their major event is the Feast of St. Anthony in June. On December 15, in a reenactment of the Boston Tea Party, citizens playing the parts of disgruntled colonists disguise themselves as Native Americans and dump crates of British tea into Boston Har-

bor. The year culminates with First Night, a 10-hour jubilee of indoor and outdoor performances, a parade and fireworks, welcoming the new year.

Sports for the Spectator

Boston is home to five professional sports teams whose games annually draw hundreds of thousands of fans. The professional basketball team, the National Basketball Association's Celtics, play their home games at the city's downtown FleetCenter, as do the Boston Bruins, the National Hockey League team. The Boston Red Sox, the city's professional baseball team, compete in the American League East. They play their home games at Fenway Park, one of the country's most beloved ball parks, from April to October. The New England Patriots, part of the National Football League's East Division, and the New England Revolution of the MLS play their games at Gillette Stadium in suburban Foxboro. The Patriots, like Boston's other professional teams, are eagerly followed by scores of fans throughout New England.

A popular annual event is the Boston Marathon, run on the third Monday in April, which in Massachusetts is the holiday Patriot's Day. Boston's is the oldest marathon; thousands of runners from around the country and the world participate annually in this event.

In October, the focus shifts to the Charles River and the Head of the Charles Regatta international sculling event. Horse racing is scheduled from spring through late fall in and around Boston. Flat and harness racing are run at Suffolk Downs in East Boston. Parimutuel betting is permitted by law. Athletes at Boston-area colleges and universities compete in a wide range of collegiate sports. College hockey fans come out in February for the Beanpot, an annual tournament between Harvard, Boston University, Boston College, and Northeastern for the city championship. Polo matches are held at nearby Myopia Polo Grounds in Hamilton, MA.

Sports for the Participant

Its proximity to water makes Boston a natural attraction for sports enthusiasts. Anglers can enjoy saltwater fishing in the Atlantic Ocean or fresh water fishing in inland rivers. Boaters can sail the Atlantic coastline or canoe inland. Swimmers can choose between public beaches along the ocean or civic pools within the city. Municipal golf courses, tennis courts, baseball diamonds, playgrounds, and tot lots are maintained in the city. Since 1995, more than $120 million has been spent to rehabilitate the city's 215 parks. Ice skating outdoors is popular in the winter months at the Frog Pond on Boston Commons and throughout the year at the city's indoor municipal facilities. Boston is close to excellent ski runs, horseback riding trails, and mountain climbing areas.

Shopping and Dining

Boston's shopping areas range from carefully restored colonial shops to gleaming glass and steel towers. Quincy Market, dating from 1826, is a cobblestone square surrounded by small shops in renovated warehouses. Nearby, Faneuil Hall's ground floor contains a modern shopping mall. Downtown Crossing, Boston's original marketplace, is an outdoor pedestrian mall encompassing several streets. It is anchored by a Boston institution, Filene's Department Store, which is noted for the zeal of the shoppers hunting for bargains in its basement. Copley Place, an indoor mall connecting four office buildings and two hotels, has upscale stores such as Tiffany & Co., Louis Vuitton, and Neiman Marcus. Other popular shopping sites are Charles Street on Beacon Hill, a mecca for antique hunters, and Newbury Street, referred to by locals as the new Rodeo Drive. Across the Charles River in Cambridge is the Harvard Coop, world famous as a comprehensive supplier to the university's students and its entire academic community.

With almost two thousand restaurants, Boston offers everything from traditional seafood dishes to continental and ethnic cuisines. Fresh saltwater catches include clams, lobster, oysters, bluefish, and scrod. Boston has been called ''Beantown,'' a term that originated with the Puritans who, out of respect for the Sabbath, did not cook on Sunday. Instead, they relied on food prepared the day before, and one popular menu item was baked beans. Clam and seafood chowders, baked beans, and Indian pudding are still staples on many Boston menus.

Continental cuisine, sometimes blended with American nouvelle cuisine, is now the specialty of several respected Boston restaurants. Ethnic specialties include a small but flavorful sampling of restaurants in downtown Boston's Chinatown. At the North End, diners relish northern Italian specialties such as pasta and cappuccino. In neighborhoods such as Dorchester and Jamaica Plain, a wave of immigration has brought restaurants specializing in the cuisines of Vietnam, Ireland, Spain, and other ethnicities.

Visitor Information: Greater Boston Convention & Visitors Bureau, Two Copley Place, Suite 105, Boston, MA 02116-6501; toll-free (888)SEE-BOSTON; fax (617)424-7664

Convention Facilities

Boston is a popular meeting site for groups of all kinds and sizes. Completed in 2004, the Boston Convention and Exhi-

bition Center has 516,000 square feet of contiguous exhibit space, 82 meeting rooms, and a 40,000 square foot ballroom. Built on the South Boston waterfront, it is minutes from Logan Airport. Another major venue is the John B. Hynes Veterans Memorial Convention Center, encompassing more than 289,000 square feet of meeting, exhibition and banquet space. Five exhibit halls and 37 meeting rooms can host large conventions or several small conventions simultaneously. Thirteen major hotels are located within walking distance of the center, which is in Boston's Back Bay area, convenient to shopping and other amenities.

World Trade Center Boston offers a ground-floor Main Hall measuring 120,000 square feet; on that floor are theater seating for 5,000 participants and classroom and banquet seating for 3,000 diners. Located on Commonwealth Pier, it opened in January 1986, for the purpose of furthering international trade among and economic development of all the New England states.

Unique meeting and reception sites in Boston include the facilities of a Victorian mansion, a lounge, a ballroom-style entertainment complex, and a rock dance club among many others. The metropolitan area supports about 45,000 hotel rooms; 17,000 of them are in Boston and Cambridge. Suburban to Boston are the meeting and exhibition facilities of the Royal Plaza Trade Center, which contains 43,000 square feet of exhibit space and the Bayside Expo Center, which offers 240,000 square feet of exhibit space and 17,000 square feet of additional meeting room space.

Convention Information: Greater Boston Convention & Visitors Bureau, Two Copley Place, Suite 105, Boston, MA 02116-6501; toll-free (888)SEE-BOSTON; fax (617)424-7664. Massachusetts Convention Center Authority, 415 Summer Street, Boston, MA 02210; telephone (617)954-2000; fax (617)954-2299

Transportation

Approaching the City

Visitors arriving in Boston by air arrive at Logan International Airport, located in East Boston just two miles from downtown Boston. Its location in Massachusetts Bay puts Boston's airport 200 miles closer to Europe than New York City. In 2005, Logan was ranked the nation's 19th busiest airport; it is served by 39 airlines. Logan can be reached by car, by public transportation on the ''T'' Blue Line, and by water aboard the Airport Water Shuttle.

Boston's access routes by automobile include Interstate-90, the Massachusetts Turnpike, which is the major east-west artery. Massachusetts Service Route 9, another east-west road, accommodates suburban traffic. I-93 runs north-south through Boston where it is called the Northeast Expressway. Encircling the city is Massachusetts Service Route 128. More than seven hundred high-technology firms have established facilities along Massachusetts SR 128 and I-495, making them heavily traveled freeways.

Boston can also be reached by railroad and by bus. The city is served by three Amtrak lines: the Downeaster connects Boston with Portland, Maine; the Regional, serving cities along the coast south to Newport News, Virginia.; and the Acela Express, a 150-mph train that makes the trip from Washington, D.C. in 7 hours. South Station and North Station, the Amtrak and Massachusetts Bay Transportation Authority terminals, are on opposite sides of Boston's downtown business district. Those arriving by Greyhound/ Trailways and Peter Pan Bus Lines disembark at the Greyhound Bus Terminal downtown.

Traveling in the City

Boston is a very walkable city, and walking tours depart from a number of locations. According to local sources, driving in Boston can be a confusing experience even for natives. Heavy traffic, narrow one-way streets, limited parking, traffic rotaries, and jay-walking pedestrians combine to make driving difficult in Boston, especially in the downtown area. Most residents leave their cars at home and ride Boston's superb public transportation, known as the ''T.'' This rapid transit system includes elevated lines, subways, and surface routes. Trolleys, street cars, and buses supplement the ''T.'' Private transportation includes Amtrak commuter trains, taxis, and ferry boats.

The ''T'' is operated by the Massachusetts Bay Transportation Authority (MBTA). Boston's system is the oldest in the country, and all five lines converge downtown. Boston is one of only five U.S. cities to use trolleys and street cars as a regular part of its transportation system. Amtrak runs two commuter trains from surrounding suburbs into Boston, one of which is operated by the MBTA and is known locally as the ''Purple Line.'' Two ferry systems convey passengers on the rivers and channels around Boston.

Communications

Newspapers and Magazines

Boston's two major daily newspapers, *The Boston Globe* and the *Boston Herald,* are both published in the morning.

The Boston Globe, established in 1872, is New England's largest daily and Sunday newspaper. The respected *The Christian Science Monitor* is published in Boston on weekdays. An international edition is also available. Local business news is featured in the *Boston Business Journal.*

Boston Magazine, Boston's city magazine, is published monthly. Tourist-oriented publications include *Panorama* and *The Boston Phoenix,* an alternative weekly publication providing detailed arts and entertainment information, and *WHERE* magazine, published monthly. Magazines of national interest published in Boston include the *Harvard Business Review, Inc. Magazine, Horticulture, Animals, Health Journal,* and *The Writer.* For many years, Boston has published *The Atlantic Monthly,* one of the nation's oldest literary magazines. As might be expected with Boston's many educational and high-tech institutions, the city also publishes an array of academic and technical journals, both commercially and for professional societies.

Television and Radio

The Boston area is the sixth largest media market in the country, served by five major networks, a public broadcasting station, and a Spanish language station. Special programming includes the Christian Science Monitor Syndicate and a channel for the hearing impaired. Cable television is also available. More than 20 AM and FM radio stations in the Boston area program a variety of music, talk shows, interview programs, and religious offerings. As a special service to travelers, Tunnel Radio broadcasts travel and road conditions inside Boston's heavily traveled South Station Tunnel.

Media Information: The Boston Globe, 135 Morrissey Blvd., Boston, MA 02107; telephone (617)929-2000

Boston Online

Boston Convention & Visitors Bureau. Available www .bostonusa.com

The Boston Globe. Available www.boston.com

Boston Public Library. Available www.bpl.org

Boston Public Schools. Available www.boston.k12.ma.us

City of Boston. Available www.cityofboston.gov

City of Boston Redevelopment Authority. Available www .cityofboston.gov/bra

Greater Boston Chamber of Commerce. Available www .bostonchamber.com

Massachusetts Business Development Corporation. Available www.mass-business.com

Massachusetts Convention Center Authority. Available mccahome.com

Massachusetts Medical Society. Available www.massmed.org

Massachusetts Office of Business Development. Available www.state.ma.us/mobd

Selected Bibliography

Campbell, Robert, and Peter Vanderwarker, *Cityscapes of Boston* (Boston: A Peter Davison Book/Houghton Mifflin Company, 1992)

Kennedy, Lawrence W., *Planning the City upon a Hill: Boston Since 1630* (Boston: University of Massachusetts Press, 1992)

Uncommon Boston: A Guide to Hidden Spaces and Special Places (Boston: Addison-Wesley Publishing Company, 1990)

Lowell

The City in Brief

Founded: 1686 (incorporated 1836)

Head Official: City Manager John Cox (since 2000)

City Population
   1980: 92,418
   1990: 103,439
   2000: 105,167
   2003 estimate: 104,351
   Percent change, 1990–2000: 1.7%
   U.S. rank in 1980: 188th
   U.S. rank in 1990: 188th
   U.S. rank in 2000: 243rd

Metropolitan Area Population (PMSA)
   1990: 280,578
   2000: 301,686

Percent change, 1990–2000: 7.5%
U.S. rank in 1990: 7th (CMSA)
U.S. rank in 2000: 7th (CMSA)

Area: 14 square miles (2000)
Elevation: 110 feet above sea level
Average Annual Temperature: 51.6° F
Average Annual Precipitation: 42.8 inches of rain; 42.6 inches of snow

Major Economic Sectors: Services, trade, manufacturing
Unemployment Rate: 5% (February 2005)
Per Capita Income: $17,557 (1999)
2004 ACCRA Median House Price: Not reported
2004 ACCRA Cost of Living Index: Not reported

2002 FBI Crime Index Total: 4,258

Major Colleges and Universities: University of Massachusetts at Lowell, Middlesex Community College

Daily Newspaper: *The Lowell Sun*

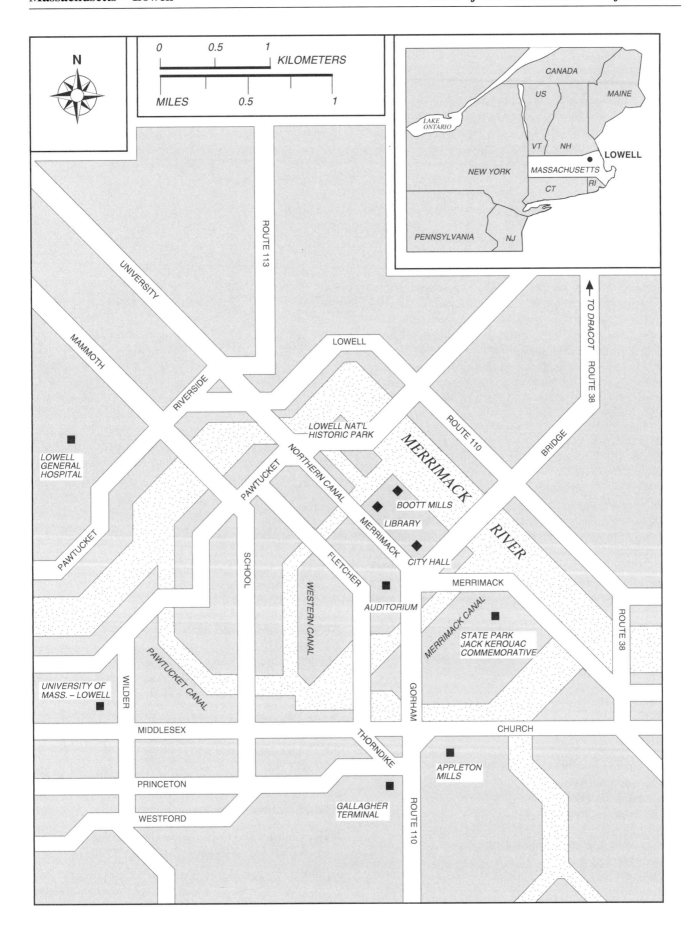

Introduction

Lowell, once the textile capital of the world, grew in the shadow of the huge mills lining the Merrimack River. Its ancient canals earned the city the nickname "Venice of America." With the southward movement of the textile industry in the 1920s, Lowell sought to diversify its economy to include a variety of manufactured products. By 1984, however, the town's economy had become as dependent on the mini-computer as it had formerly been on cotton. The early mill days are commemorated in the city's splendidly preserved industrial architecture. Lowell, whose downtown has been designated an urban national historical park, exists today as a living reminder of the processes and consequences of the Industrial Revolution.

Geography and Climate

The city of Lowell, located in Middlesex County at the confluence of the Merrimack and Concord rivers, is 25 miles northwest of Boston. The city stands on a plateau in the Merrimack Valley, surrounded by hills of 100- to 200-foot elevations. Lowell's four-season climate is typical of New England. Summers are warm with a humid period lasting several weeks; winters are cold and moderately snowy.

Area: 14 square miles (2000)

Elevation: 110 feet above sea level

Average Temperatures: January, 24.7° F; July, 72.5° F; annual, 51.6° F

Annual Average Precipitation: 42.8 inches of rain; 42.6 inches of snow

History

River Powers Textile Industry

For many years the site of present-day Lowell was an annual meeting ground for the tribes of the Pennacook Confederacy, who fished for salmon and shad in the waters of the Merrimack River. In 1686 the Confederacy sold the land to English farmers migrating from Boston. The farmers' town, named East Chelmsford, grew slowly until the Pawtucket Canal was completed in 1796. The canal bypassed the Pawtucket Falls to carry New Hampshire lumber to Newburyport, where it was used in shipbuilding. The demand for ships declined by 1815, but by then the site of East Chelmsford had attracted the attention of the Boston Manufacturing Company. It was the height of England's Industrial Revolution and U.S. President Thomas Jefferson knew that America must build factories if the young country was ever to become economically independent of Europe. Jefferson sought to avoid the squalor of England's mill towns by designating specific manufacturing sites in the United States. Jefferson's plan coincided with the Boston Manufacturing Company's search for a site with abundant water for powering its textile mills.

In 1821 mill executives Patrick Tracy Jackson and Nathan Appleton arrived in East Chelmsford, attracted by the potential of the 34-foot drop of the Pawtucket Falls and the confluence of the Concord and Merrimack Rivers. Jackson and Tracy, with their agent Kirk Boott, established a mill for cotton production and calico printing and called the new enterprise the Merrimack Manufacturing Company. In 1826 the town was renamed in honor of Francis Cabott Lowell, whose genius had revolutionized the textile industry. Lowell's power loom made it possible to transform raw cotton into finished fabric within a single factory. Lowell's liberal operating philosophy also influenced Jackson and Appleton, who set out to build a model factory with good working conditions and cash wages. The mills grew up in a mile-long stretch on the banks of the Merrimack River, and a network of canals was dug to provide transportation and to divert water power to the factories.

In 1826 Lowell boasted 2,500 residents, a number that swelled to 17,000 by 1836 when Lowell also claimed 8 large textile mills and 7,500 textile workers. The Boston & Lowell Railroad arrived in 1835, furthering the city's expansion. Many of the workers, or "operatives," arriving in Lowell were Yankee farm girls attracted by the wages and the chance for independence. They lived in company boarding houses, their lives strictly regulated by bells. Their 12-hour day and 6-day week left little time for recreation, but the women found time to support churches, lyceums, schools, banks, concerts, and libraries. From 1840 to 1845, the operatives published *The Lowell Offering,* an early women's literary magazine. Under the editorship of Sarah Bagley, they also published *The Voice of Industry,* a paper calling attention to workers' grievances.

Reform, Immigration Precede
High-Technology Growth

Technological innovations kept pace with the growth of the textile industry, but working conditions did not. By 1845, workers in the "city of spindles" were making less and working longer hours than when the mills opened. A series of strikes and walkouts finally led to the reduction of the workday from 13 to 11 hours in 1853. The first city-wide strike in 1903 was unsuccessful, but in 1912, workers did lobby successfully for a wage increase. Sarah Bagley, the Factory Girls Association, and the Lowell Female Reform Association are some of the names associated with the textile reform movement, a precursor of the major labor movements of the 1900s.

One reason early reform attempts met with little success was the influx of unskilled, uneducated immigrants eager to replace the Yankee farm girls at the looms. Irish arrived in the 1820s to help build the canals and mills. They were followed by Portuguese in the 1850s, French-Canadians in the 1860s and 1870s, southern African Americans in the 1870s, Greeks and European Jews in the 1880s, Poles in the 1890s, and Armenians in the first part of the twentieth century.

Around 1910 the South began to challenge the Northeast for the leadership of the textile industry. Lowell peaked in 1924 as a major textile center and began to investigate ways to diversify its economy. It sought new manufacturing firms and began to capitalize on its unique history as one of the American Industrial Revolution's first planned communities. In the latter half of the 20th century Lowell once again became known as a model city, this time for its economic and cultural revitalization. Wang Laboratories Inc. moved its corporate headquarters to Lowell in the early 1970s, spurring further growth of high-technology industries and, in 1978, Lowell National Historic Park was created to preserve the city's mills, canals, and workers' housing. Since 1975, more than 250 historic buildings have been restored, with 63 alone having generated $52 million in private investment.

By the early 1990s, Lowell had fallen on hard times. The Bank of New England failed (it has since been taken over by Fleet Bank), and Wang Laboratories filed for bankruptcy protection. The former Wang Laboratories building has since been transformed into a successful state-of-the-art office complex, while Wang has moved its headquarters to nearby Tewksbury. The Lowell National Historical Park has grown into a major tourist attraction. Lowell's ethnic diversity was augmented by a wave of immigrants from Southeast Asia and Latin America; many of whom boosted the local economy with small business initiatives. Famous Lowellians include painter James McNeill Whistler, actor Bette Davis, and novelist Jack Kerouac.

The City of Lowell is currently implementing a master plan for the next two decades, a vision for the future aimed at improving quality of life and capitalizing on cultural, natural and historical resources. Endorsed in 2003, the master plan will serve as a framework for future development and investment in Lowell. Major components of the plan are aimed at making Lowell a ''lifetime city'' where residents can enjoy all stages of life at various income levels, and preserving Lowell's identity as unique from Greater Boston.

Historical Information: Lowell National Historical Park, 67 Kirk Street, Lowell, MA 01852; telephone (978)970-5000

Population Profile

Metropolitan Area Population (PMSA)
1990: 280,578
2000: 301,686
Percent change, 1990–2000: 7.5%
U.S. rank in 1990: 7th (CMSA)
U.S. rank in 2000: 7th (CMSA)

City Residents
1980: 92,418
1990: 103,439
2000: 105,167
2003 estimate: 104,351
Percent change, 1990–2000: 1.7%
U.S. rank in 1980: 188th
U.S. rank in 1990: 188th (State rank: 4th)
U.S. rank in 2000: 243rd

Density: 7,635.6 people per square mile (2000)

Racial and ethnic characteristics (2000)
  White: 72,145
  Black or African American: 4,423
  American Indian and Alaska Native: 256
  Asian: 17,371
  Native Hawaiian and Pacific Islander: 38
  Hispanic or Latino (may be of any race): 14,734
  Other: 6,813

Percent of residents born in state: 62.2% (2000)

Age characteristics (2000)
  Population under 5 years old: 7,696
  Population 5 to 9 years old: 8,261
  Population 10 to 14 years old: 7,945
  Population 15 to 19 years old: 8,111
  Population 20 to 24 years old: 8,892
  Population 25 to 34 years old: 18,025
  Population 35 to 44 years old: 16,137
  Population 45 to 54 years old: 11,588
  Population 55 to 59 years old: 4,026
  Population 60 to 64 years old: 3,173

Population 65 to 74 years old: 5,683
Population 75 to 84 years old: 4,173
Population 85 years and older: 1,457
Median age: 31.4 years

Births (2003)
Total number: 1,696

Deaths (2002)
Total number: 863 (of which, 18 were infants under the age of 1 year)

Money income (1999)
Per capita income: $17,557
Median household income: $39,192
Total households: 37,992

Number of households with income of . . .
less than $10,000: 4,858
$10,000 to $14,999: 2,733
$15,000 to $24,999: 4,572
$25,000 to $34,999: 4,900
$35,000 to $49,999: 6,519
$50,000 to $74,999: 7,743
$75,000 to $99,999: 3,587
$100,000 to $149,999: 2,259
$150,000 to $199,999: 512
$200,000 or more: 309

Percent of families below poverty level: 13.6% (45.5% of which were female householder families with related children under 5 years)

2002 FBI Crime Index Total: 4,258

Municipal Government

Lowell operates with a council-manager form of government. The elected nine-person council serves a two-year term of office. The council appoints a salaried professional city manager, who serves for an unspecified term, and a ceremonial mayor.

Head Official: City Manager John Cox (since 2000)

Total Number of City Employees: 2,000 (2005)

City Information: Office of the City Manager, Lowell City Hall, 375 Merrimack Street, Lowell, MA 01852; telephone (978)970-4000

Economy

Major Industries and Commercial Activity

Lowell is a diversified industrial city. Service is a major sector of the local economy with more than a quarter of total employment. Manufacturing, trade, transportation, and government are other key sectors. Tourism is an economic mainstay, with the downtown area welcoming about 500,000 visitors annually.

Lowell is succeeding in transforming its economic base. This effort has included the renovation of many of the city's historic textile mills, many of which now contain affordable, attractive office space. Lowell boasts an impressive roster of businesses that include Coca-Cola, M/A Com, Raytheon, NYNEX, and Textron, alongside long-established firms such as Colonial Gas, Joan Fabrics Corporation, and the Lowell *Sun Publishing Company.* Small businesses abound in Lowell as well, supported by the city's business environment which includes two full-service hotels and three bed-and-breakfasts.

Current plans for Lowell suggest the downtown area may become a trendy, affordable bedroom community for daily commuters to Boston, just 25 miles away. Downtown improvements are also expected to attract Boston businesses seeking low-cost, high-quality satellite offices.

Items and goods produced: textiles, yarns and threads, textile machinery, knitwear, wire and cable, plastics, computer hardware and software, electronic publishing and printing

Incentive Programs—New and Existing Companies

Local programs—Organizations helping business in Lowell include the Lowell Plan, Inc., the Lowell Development and Financial Corporation, and the City of Lowell's Division of Planning and Development. Businesses moving to Lowell's designated Renewal Community can receive employee wage credits and tax deductions. The Lowell Small Business Assistance Center offers $5,000 grants to profitable, expanding business with income of $50,000 or less; it also provides entrepreneurial support such as planning, education and technical assistance. Preservation grants and incentives are available for projects in the Lowell Historic District and Lowell National Park. The Technical Assistance Program provides grants to retailers in the downtown area; funds may be used in a variety of areas including marketing, e-commerce, merchandising, legal, accounting, and design. The Downtown Venture Fund Program offers low-interest loans to specialty retailers and restaurants.

State programs—The Massachusetts Office of Business Development administers the Economic Development Incentive Program, which fosters business growth and job creation in specific locations. Incentives include state tax credits, an abandoned building deduction for renovating unused space, investment tax credits, and special property tax assessments. MassDevelopment provides financing for new facilities, job creation, equipment, and land purchases. Its many offerings include term working capital loans for businesses affected by adverse market conditions, below market rate financing for equipment purchases between $50,000 and $500,000, real estate loans up to $3 million, and loans for specialized equipment in the technology industry. MassDevelopment may also guarantee private loans. The Economic Stabilization Trust lends working capital to small and medium manufacturing companies when traditional financing is unavailable. The Massachusetts Business Resource Team matches businesses with specific needs to the appropriate state program.

Job training programs—The state Workforce Training Fund provides resources for Massachusetts employers to train or retrain new and existing workers. Its offerings include the Express Program, which grants up to $15,000 to small companies and labor organizations; the General Program which administers grants up to $1 million; and the Hiring Incentive Training Program which covers up to $2,000 in training costs for new employees. UMass-Lowell takes part in the city's economic development strategy by actively providing technical assistance to local start-up companies in need of engineering support. Middlesex Community College offers career training and skill upgrading during the day, evenings and weekends, and online; on-site job training is also available.

Development Projects

Projects underway as of 2005 include the Route 3 lane expansion, an ongoing urban renewal initiative in the Jackson/Middlesex/Appleton area of downtown, $7.72 million worth of improvements to the Lowell Canal, and safety upgrades at various intersections. A portion of the Boott Cotton Mills will be converted into condominium housing with 41 phase one units scheduled for completion in September 2005. Reconstruction of Moulton Square took place in 2003 and 2004, including replacement and installation of playground equipment, improved pedestrian crossings, slowed traffic, and beautification. Lowell General Hospital opened its new Endoscopy Center in 2003.

Economic Development Information: Economic Development Department, Lowell City Hall, JFK Civic Center, 50 Arcand Drive, Lowell, MA 01852; telephone (978)970-4252; fax (978)446-7014. The Lowell Plan, Inc., 11 Kearney Square, Lowell, MA 01852; telephone (978)459-9899; fax

(978)454-7637. Massachusetts Office of Business Development, 600 Suffolk St., Fourth Floor, Lowell, MA 01854; telephone (978)970-1193; fax (978)970-1570

Commercial Shipping

The Boston & Maine Railroad, with tracks throughout the U.S. Northeast and the Canadian Maritime provinces, can also ship freight elsewhere in the United States by using a series of connector routes. The Boston & Maine runs through Lowell, which is also served by several trucking fleets.

Labor Force and Employment Outlook

Lowell is considered the quintessential "working class" town. Far from its textile heritage, Lowell's workforce has diversified into education, software development, health care, research, and electronics. A rich multi-ethnic community contributes increasingly to small business growth; entrepreneurship is expected to be significant to Lowell's economy in the years to come. Employment in manufacturing continues to decline.

The following is a summary of data regarding the Lowell metropolitan area labor force, 2004 annual averages.

Size of nonagricultural labor force: 117,000

Number of workers employed in . . .
   construction and mining: 7,200
   manufacturing: 20,200
   trade, transportation and utilities: 21,700
   information: 5,800
   financial activities: 4,300
   professional and business services: 15,700
   educational and health services: 12,600
   leisure and hospitality: 9,800
   other services: 23,100
   government: 15,900

Average hourly earnings of production workers employed in manufacturing: $16.89 (statewide)

Unemployment rate: 5.0% (February 2005)

Largest employers	*Number of employees*
M/A COM, Inc.	1,650
Saints Memorial Medical Center	1,334
Lowell General Hospital	1,320
UMass-Lowell	1,055
Middlesex Community College	950
Verizon	600
Demoulas Supermarkets	500
Community Teamwork Inc.	500
Joan Fabrics	463
Lowell Sun Publishing	350

Cost of Living

The following is a summary of data regarding several key cost of living factors for the Lowell area.

2004 ACCRA Cost of Living Index: Not reported

2004 ACCRA Median House Price: Not reported

State income tax rate: 5.3% on earned income; 12% on capital gains

State sales tax rate: 5.0% on most items; exemptions include food, heating fuel and prescription drugs

Local income tax rate: None

Local sales tax rate: None

Property tax rate: $10.18 per $1,000 of 100% of assessed value, residential; $20.20 per $1,000 of 100% of assessed value, commercial

Economic Information: Division of Planning and Development, Lowell City Hall, JFK Civic Center, 50 Arcand Drive, Lowell, MA 01852; telephone (978)970-4252; fax (978)446-7014. Greater Lowell Chamber of Commerce, 144 Merrimack Street, Lowell, MA 01852; telephone (978)459-8154; fax (978)452-4145

Education and Research

Elementary and Secondary Schools

The Lowell Public School system, administered by the Lowell School Committee, offers a strong commitment to literacy, technology, and multiculturalism. Its 23 elementary and middle schools stream into Lowell High, a progressive facility organized around the concept of "small learning communities." Lowell High's eight "academies" range in focus from fine arts to engineering; qualifying students may also enroll in the prestigious Latin Lyceum which offers a four-year classical college entrance program. In 2000 Lowell Public Schools was selected for the Teacher Career Advancement Program, a pilot grant program aimed at attracting and retaining highly qualified educators. In 2003 Lowell committed more than a million dollars to professional development and updated classroom materials as part of a new mathematics initiative. Lowell also offers alternative education and adult education.

The following is a summary of data regarding the Lowell public schools as of the 2004–2005 school year.

Total enrollment: 14,708

Number of facilities
  elementary schools: 16
  junior high/middle schools: 7
  senior high schools: 1
  other: 5

Student/teacher ratio: 13.1:1

Teacher salaries
  average: $55,140 (2003)

Funding per pupil: $8,407 (2003)

An extensive choice of charter and private schools, as well as the Greater Lowell Technical High School in nearby Tyngsboro, supplements the public system.

Public Schools Information: Lowell Public Schools, 155 Merrimack Street, Lowell, MA 01852; telephone (978)937-7604

Colleges and Universities

UMass Lowell, formerly Lowell University, dates back to the 1890s. The 1975 merger of Lowell State College and Lowell Technological Institute created the current campus; in 1991 it became part of the University of Massachusetts system. UMass Lowell offers a range of undergraduate, doctoral and professional degrees to its 12,000 students. Its colleges are closely allied with the local community as part of a commitment to public service.

Middlesex Community College is the largest community college in Massachusetts, offering 78 degree and certificate programs as well as non-credit courses and career training. Bachelor's degree completion is offered in partnership with Salem State College.

Libraries and Research Centers

The Samuel S. Pollard Memorial Library, Lowell's public library, is located in historic Memorial Hall. The newly reconstructed facility boasts elaborate interior and exterior architecture and includes a series of massive murals commemorating the Civil War. The library's collection includes 236,000 volumes as well as CDs, DVDs and microfilm; special collections focus on local history, genealogy and historic newspapers. As part of the Merrimack Library Consortium the Pollard Library has access to 1.5 million books at 35 locations.

Special interest libraries include the Lowell Law Library, located at the Superior Courthouse, and the libraries of the city's hospitals. UMass Lowell supports the Center for Atmospheric Research, which uses physics and other sciences to study the phenomenon of dynamism; Centers for Industrial Competitiveness and Sustainable Production; the Toxics Use Reduction Institute; and the Institute for Visualization and Perception Research. The University's Center for Lowell History holds a collection of historical photographs and other artifacts, and its Research Foundation explores many areas of physical science, communication and economics. A Research Library at the New England Quilt Museum is open by appointment to serious researchers on that subject.

Public Library Information: Samuel S. Pollard Memorial Library, 401 Merrimack Street, Lowell, MA 01852; telephone (978)970-4120; fax (978)970-4117

Health Care

Two major acute care hospitals are located in the city. Saints Memorial Medical Center is the largest health care provider in the region; areas of specialty include comprehensive cancer care, dialysis, rehabilitative medicine, and pediatrics. Lowell General Hospital offers cancer care, a sleep lab and neurodiagnostic facility, pain management and wound healing centers, and a nationally recognized obstetric program. Both facilities also maintain 24-hour emergency departments.

Health Care Information: Lowell General Hospital, 295 Varnum Avenue, Lowell, MA 01854; telephone (978)937-6000. Saints Memorial Medical Center, 1 Hospital Drive, Lowell, MA 01852; telephone (978)458-1411

Recreation

Sightseeing

Lowell's unique status as the country's first planned industrial community has been recognized with the designation of the Lowell National Historical Park. Covering 141 acres of downtown land, the park's textile mills, canals, museum exhibits, and nineteenth century buildings are connected by trolley service. The Patrick J. Mogan Cultural Center is a restored 1836 boardinghouse for young women employed in the textile mills. It features an early nineteenth-century kitchen, bedrooms, and exhibits on labor history. The Pawtucket and Eastern Canals have been enhanced by walkways, landscaping, and public art, and boat tours are available. Other sights include the Lower Locks, the Appleton Mills, the School Street Cemetery, which dates from the 1770s, and the Homage to Women statue, which honors the American working woman.

Arts and Culture

The Lowell Memorial Auditorium is home to the award-winning Merrimack Repertory Theatre and plays host to a number of other cultural events, from touring Broadway

musicals to boxing matches. Originally built in 1922, the restored facility seats 3,000. UMass Lowell's College of Fine Arts presents jazz and other music and dance events on campus at Durgin Hall. Outdoor concerts are presented in the summertime at Boarding House Park.

Whistler House Museum of Art, birthplace of artist James McNeill Whistler, has been preserved and is operated by the Lowell Art Association. The painter's works are featured among the museum's collection of nineteenth and twentieth century art. The New England Quilt Museum and the Boott Cotton Mills Museum reflect the community's link to the textile industry. The Cotton Mills Museum also houses the Tsongas Industrial History Center, New England Folklife Center, Lowell Historical Society, and Boott Gallery. The American Textile History Museum focuses on the origins of the Industrial Age and the history of American textiles. Brush Art Gallery and Studios is a non-profit workspace where visitors have the opportunity to observe local craftspeople engaged in the creative process. University Gallery is the city's leading space for the presentation of contemporary artists. Pieces of sculpture evocative of the city's industrial past are on view throughout the downtown.

Arts and Culture Information: Lowell Office of Cultural Affairs, 66 Merrimack Street, Lowell, MA 01852; telephone (978)441-3800

Festivals and Holidays

The Lowell Folk Festival is the largest free folk festival in the country. Featuring ethnic music, dance, and entertainment on outdoor stages, this three-day event takes place in July. The Lowell Summer Music Festival takes place Friday and Saturday evenings at Boarding House Park, from July to September. This eclectic mix of concerts includes bluegrass, big band, zydeco, pop, and folk music in an open air setting. Touted as a celebration of beer, music and food, the Lowell Rib 'n' Brews Festival takes place in September. Also in September is the Lowell Irish Festival. The first weekend of October brings Jack Kerouac fans from around the world to Lowell Celebrates Kerouac, an homage to the *On the Road* writer and Lowell High alumnus. Lowell kicks off the holiday season with its City of Lights Parade in November, featuring marching bands, floats and holiday decorations. Other events include Winterfest in February, Patriots Day Celebrations in April, and Doors Open Lowell in May, a celebration of the city's historic architecture.

Sports for the Spectator

Lowell is one of just three New England cities with two professional sports teams. The 6,000-seat Tsongas Arena is home to the Lowell Lock Monsters, an American Hockey League affiliate of the Carolina Hurricanes, and UMass Lowell's top-ranked River Hawks hockey team. LeLacheur

Statue of "The Worker" by brothers Ivan and Elliott Schwartz.

Park is home to the Lowell Spinners, a Class A affiliate of the Boston Red Sox, and UMass Lowell's River Hawks baseball team. Lowell is also less than an hour's drive to Boston's major-league sporting events.

The Sun newspaper sponsors the Lowell Golden Gloves boxing tournament, held in January and February each year. This multi-match event pits youth level boxers from all of New England against one another, with winners going on to the annual tournament. The Golden Gloves matches are held in Lowell Memorial Auditorium.

Sports for the Participant

Lowell offers a full range of recreational activities. Sailing, fishing, waterskiing and other water sports are popular pursuits on the Merrimack and Concord Rivers. Lowell-Dracut-Tyngsborough State Forest is located within the city, with 6 miles of trails for hiking, skiing, horseback riding, backpacking, and cycling; a 30-acre lake there is used for skating and fishing. Lowell also maintains 34 playgrounds, 42 tennis courts and 6 golf courses. Atlantic Ocean beaches are less than an hour's drive; the White Mountains are a two-hour drive to the north in New Hampshire.

Shopping and Dining

Lowell offers downtown shopping with small department stores and other specialty shops. At the Boott Museum Store, books, prints, cloth, posters, and other historical items can be bought. Lucy Larcom Park (named after a local author and ''mill girl'') along the Merrimack Canal is the site of a Friday Farmer's Market.

Indian, French country, Italian, and Lebanese restaurants coexist happily with Lowell's oyster bars and seafood houses. The Athenian Corner Restaurant is reputed to offer New England's largest selection of Greek food.

Visitor Information: Lowell Office of Cultural Affairs, 66 Merrimack Street, Lowell, MA 01852; telephone (978)441-3800. Greater Merrimack Valley Convention and Visitors Bureau, 9 Central Street, Suite 201, Lowell, MA 01852; telephone (978)459-6150; fax (978)459-4595

Convention Facilities

The Lowell Memorial Auditorium seats up to 3,000 and can accommodate medium-sized trade shows with up to 90 exhibit booths. The auditorium also offers a variety of meeting rooms and lounges for media conferences and receptions. The nearby Doubletree Hotel Lowell has more than 15,000 square feet of meeting space, a business center and catering services. The Paul E. Tsongas Arena is a full-service convention venue with function rooms overlooking the Merrimack River; it offers seating for 8,000 and 30,000 square feet of exhibit space. The Courtyard by Marriott, about 2.5 miles from downtown Lowell, is suitable for smaller meetings. Within the Greater Lowell area, approximately 4,000 guest rooms are available in a number of hotels.

Convention Information: Greater Merrimack Valley Convention and Visitors Bureau, 9 Central Street, Suite 201, Lowell, MA 01852; telephone (978)459-6150; fax (978)459-4595

Transportation

Approaching the City

Boston's Logan International Airport, a 40-minute drive to the southeast, offers complete domestic, international, and freight air service. Manchester Airport in New Hampshire is slightly closer and offers domestic service. Vermont Transit Lines bus service and Massachusetts Bay Transit Authority rail lines both arrive at Gallagher Terminal.

Interstate-495 cuts through the city, running east and west and intersecting with Massachusetts Route 3, which runs north-south. The Lowell Connector allows highway access from these major arteries into downtown Lowell.

Traveling in the City

Lowell Regional Transit Authority (LRTA) provides local and suburban bus service out of Gallagher Terminal. LRTA also offers Road Runner services for elderly and disabled patrons.

Communications

Newspapers and Magazines

The Sun is the city's daily newspaper, published on weekday evenings on weekdays and weekend mornings. Special-interest publications originating in Lowell include *Outlet,* an independent performance magazine, and *Le Journal de Lowell,* a French-language newspaper.

Television and Radio

Lowell is serviced by a cable television franchise and receives commercial television stations originating in Boston.

One AM and one FM radio station broadcast from Lowell, including a student station at the UMass Lowell.

Media Information: *The Sun,* 15 Kearney Square, Lowell, MA 01853; telephone (978)458-7100

Lowell Online

City of Lowell. Available www.ci.lowell.ma.us

Greater Lowell Chamber of Commerce. Available www .greaterlowellchamber.org

Greater Merrimack Valley Convention & Visitors Bureau. Available www.merrimackvalley.org

Lowell National Historical Park. Available www.nps.gov/ lowe

Lowell Public Schools. Available www.lowell.k12.ma.us

Lowell Small Business Assistance Center. Available www .lowellsbac.org

Pollard Memorial Library. Available www.pollardml.org

The Sun. Available www.lowellsun.com

Selected Bibliography

Selden, Bernice, *The Mill Girls: Lucy Larcom, Harriet Hanson Robinson, Sarah G. Bagle* (New York: Atheneum, 1986)

Springfield

The City in Brief

Founded: 1636 (incorporated, 1852)

Head Official: Mayor Charles Ryan (since 2002)

City Population
    1980: 152,319
    1990: 156,983
    2000: 152,082
    2003 estimate: 152,157
    Percent change, 1990–2000: −3.1%
    U.S. rank in 1980: 103rd
    U.S. rank in 1990: 111th (State rank: 3rd)
    U.S. rank in 2000: 150th (State rank: 3rd)

Metropolitan Area Population
    1990: 587,844
    2000: 591,932
    Percent change, 1990–2000: 0.7%

U.S. rank in 1990: 68th
U.S. rank in 2000: 71st

Area: 33.2 square miles (2000)
Elevation: 101 feet above sea level
Average Annual Temperature: 50.45° F
Average Annual Precipitation: 43.9 inches of rain; 50.2 inches of snow

Major Economic Sectors: Manufacturing, trade, services
Unemployment Rate: 5.8% (February 2005)
Per Capita Income: $15,232 (1999)
2004 ACCRA Average House Cost: Not reported
2004 ACCRA Cost of Living Index: Not reported

2002 FBI Crime Index Total: 14,299

Major Colleges and Universities: American International College, Springfield College, Springfield Technical Community College, Western New England College

Daily Newspaper: *The Republican*

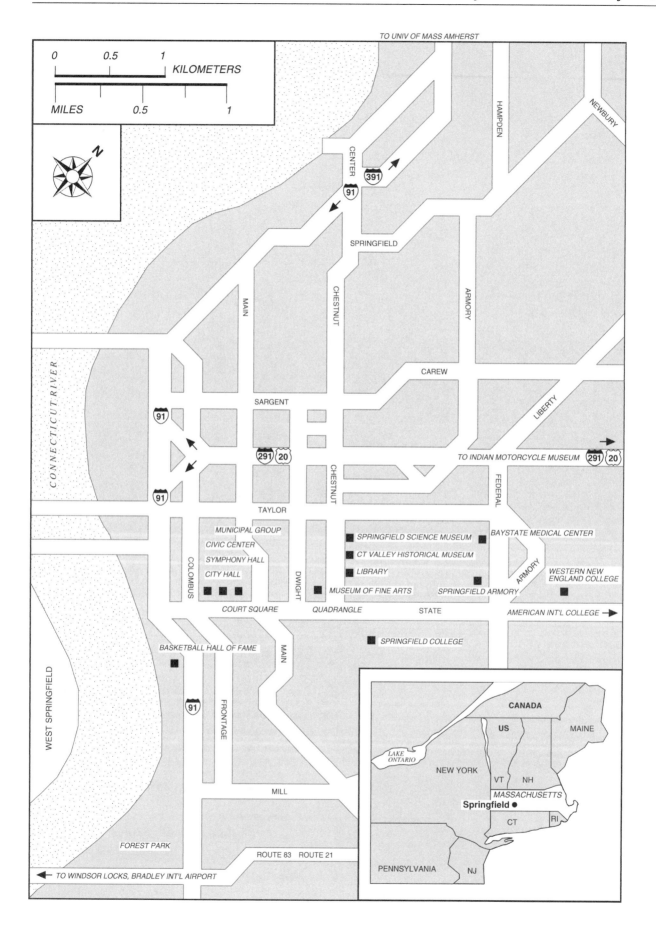

Introduction

The home of the Springfield Armory and a number of private firearms manufacturers, Springfield early attracted scores of talented artisans to its manufacturing concerns. Today Springfield, one of the oldest settlements in America and the third largest city in Massachusetts, is best known for its growing service industry, which is anchored by a major insurance firm. Its location on interstate roadways and rail lines makes the city the wholesale and retail trade center for western Massachusetts.

Geography and Climate

The city of Springfield, in Hampden County in western Massachusetts, is 80 miles west of Boston. Located on the east bank of the Connecticut River, the city lies in the Pioneer Valley, a plateau formed between the Holyoke Range of mountains (a part of the White Mountain chain) to the east and the Green Mountains to the west. Springfield enjoys a New England climate, with cold, snowy winters and warm summers.

Area: 33.2 square miles (2000)

Elevation: 101 feet above sea level

Average Temperatures: January, 26.8° F; July, 74.1° F; annual average, 50.45° F

Average Annual Precipitation: 43.9 inches of rain; 50.2 inches of snow

History

Connecticut River Supports Farming Settlement

In 1636 fur trader William Pynchon led a group of settlers westward from Boston to a site on the west bank of the Connecticut River in western Massachusetts. The fledgling community, named Agawam, soon retreated to the river's east bank to escape raids by the native Sokoki tribe, who resented the damage done to their corn by the settlers' livestock. In 1640 the town was renamed Springfield in honor of Pynchon's English birthplace. The town was burned in 1675 during King Philip's War but was soon rebuilt.

Springfield grew as a farming and mercantile site, depending upon the Connecticut River for water, transportation, and industrial power. In 1776 General George Washington selected Springfield as the site for a national arsenal, which was built in 1777. The town then became an important source of supplies for the American Continental Army during the Revolutionary War. The arsenal's first weapon was a musket. Following the war, Daniel Shays, leader of Shays's Rebellion, led an unsuccessful attempt to seize the arsenal in 1787. In 1794 the federal government established the arsenal as the Springfield Armory.

The Springfield Armory and later the arrival of the railroad did much to boost the city's economic prosperity. Skilled artisans, including metal workers and inventors, flocked to the city, attracted by work in the Armory and its suppliers. By the mid-nineteenth century, Springfield and the Pioneer Valley (named for the early English settlers) had developed a diverse industrial base. The Western Railroad began running between Springfield and Worcester, MA, in 1839. The G. & C. Merriam Company published its first *Merriam-Webster Dictionary* in Springfield in 1847. Smith & Wesson established a manufacturing facility in the city in 1857, successfully producing the first self-primed metallic ammunition. Three years later Milton Bradley, a manufacturer of games, was founded in Springfield. Other products manufactured in the city included clothing, paper, machinery, and swords.

Industry Joins Armory in Local Economy

During the Civil War era, abolitionist John Brown lived in Springfield and made it an important stop on the Underground Railroad that aided slaves fleeing the South. The Springfield Armory supplied Springfield rifles for the Union Army during the Civil War. These rifles were also used in the Franco-Prussian War. Poet Henry Wadsworth Longfellow visited the Armory on his honeymoon and described the stacks of rifles in the poem "The Arsenal at Springfield."

James Naismith, the father of basketball, set down the rules of the game in Springfield in 1891. In 1893 Charles and Frank Duryea invented what is often regarded as the first gasoline-powered automobile in the United States. The Duryeas' first car was a two-cycle, one-cylinder model. Two years later the brothers founded the first automobile company in the nation, the Duryea Motor Wagon Company. A Duryea vehicle won the country's first automobile race, held that year in Chicago. George Hendee invented the motorcycle in 1901 in Springfield. It was inventions such as these and the industries they engendered that brought about what historians call "the second colonization of New England." Huge numbers of immigrants arrived on the country's eastern shores and moved westward in search of work. In Springfield, as elsewhere, the Irish came first to build the railroads and canals. They were followed by the French-Canadians, who sought work in the textile mills. Later arrivals included the Germans, Scots, Italians, Jews, Russians, Poles, Portuguese, Greeks, African Americans, and Hispanics.

During World War I, the Springfield Armory again played an important role in the country's defense, supplying the Springfield rifles which were the infantryman's stock issue. By the Second World War, the Armory was supplying Garand semiautomatic rifles for the U.S. Army and Marine Corps. The Indian Motorcycle Company closed its doors in 1953, but its fame as the builder of the first U.S. motorcycles lives on in the Indian Motorcycle Museum. Though the Springfield Armory was deactivated in 1968, the city is still home to a number of small arms manufacturers who continue the craft, including Smith & Wesson and Dan Wesson Arms. The Armory itself has been designated a national historic site.

Springfield elected its first female mayor, Mary Hurley, in 1990. A decade later, in 2002, Charles Ryan was reelected mayor of Springfield. Having served in this capacity from 1962 to 1967, Ryan promises to improve the city's economy by capitalizing on his past experience, reestablishing friendly and efficient relations between the city government and Springfield's people and businesses, and developing the area's capacity for entrepreneurship and technology.

Historical Information: Connecticut Valley Historical Museum, 194 State St., Springfield, MA 01103; telephone (413)263-6800; toll-free (800)625-7738; email info @springfieldmuseums.org

Population Profile

Metropolitan Area Residents
1990: 587,844
2000: 591,932
Percent change, 1990–2000: 0.7%
U.S. rank in 1990: 68th
U.S. rank in 2000: 71st

City Residents
1980: 152,319
1990: 156,983
2000: 152,082
2003 estimate: 152,157
Percent change, 1990–2000: −3.1%
U.S. rank in 1980: 103rd
U.S. rank in 1990: 111th (State rank: 3rd)
U.S. rank in 2000: 150th (State rank: 3rd)

Density: 4,737.7 people per square mile (2000)

Racial and ethnic characteristics (2000)
White: 85,329
Black or African American: 31,960
American Indian and Alaska Native: 569
Asian: 2,916
Native Hawaiian and Pacific Islander: 143
Hispanic or Latino (may be of any race): 41,343
Other: 25,016

Percent of residents born in state: 59.3% (2000)

Age characteristics (2000)
Population under 5 years old: 11,606
Population 5 to 9 years old: 12,945
Population 10 to 14 years old: 12,504
Population 15 to 19 years old: 12,343
Population 20 to 24 years old: 12,023
Population 25 to 34 years old: 21,246
Population 35 to 44 years old: 21,861
Population 45 to 54 years old: 17,670
Population 55 to 59 years old: 6,237
Population 60 to 64 years old: 4,741
Population 65 to 74 years old: 9,245
Population 75 to 84 years old: 7,315
Population 85 years and older: 2,346
Median age: 31.9 years

Births (2003)
Birth rate per 1,000 residents: 15.9

Deaths (2003)
Total number: 666 (of which, the infant death rate was 4.5)

Money income (1999)
Per capita income: $15,232
Median household income: $30,417
Total households: 57,178

Number of households with income of . . .
less than $10,000: 9,677
$10,000 to $14,999: 5,359
$15,000 to $24,999: 9,224
$25,000 to $34,999: 7,594
$35,000 to $49,999: 8,652
$50,000 to $74,999: 9,727
$75,000 to $99,999: 4,105
$100,000 to $149,999: 2,130
$150,000 to $199,999: 326
$200,000 or more: 384

Percent of families below poverty level: 19.3% (62.2% of which were female householder families with related children under 5 years)

2002 FBI Crime Index Total: 14,299

Municipal Government

The city of Springfield is governed by a strong-mayor/council form of government. The mayor is elected to two-year terms while the nine-member at-large city council serves two-year concurrent terms with the mayor.

Head Official: Mayor Charles Ryan (since 2002; current term expires 2006)

Total Number of City Employees: 2,278 (2003)

City Information: Mayor's Office, City of Springfield, 36 Court Street, Springfield, MA 01103; telephone (413)787-6100

Economy

Major Industries and Commercial Activity

Historically, the Springfield Armory drew skilled metal workers to the city. This manufacturing expertise has broadened to include a number of diverse concerns. The city's service industry has been growing in importance, although manufacturing remains a mainstay of the Springfield economy. The industrial base of the city is particularly diverse, as Springfield is home to significant insurance, chemical, paper, government, and health care facilities. This diverse foundation is especially beneficial in difficult economic periods. The recession that struck the nation in the late 1990s, borne from a decline in the technology industry, had a lesser impact on Springfield due to its relatively low concentration of technological companies. Still, the local economy did struggle to some extent. In 2004 the Pioneer Valley Planning Commission updated the decade-old Pioneer Valley Plan for Progress to address economic concerns through seven plans of action that include cross-border collaboration with the Hartford, Connecticut, region; improving education and technology; and supporting existing industries like agriculture and manufacturing as well as emerging industries like knowledge creation, healthcare, and plastics. The report recognizes that small businesses are growing in importance; as testament, a study released in 2005 by the U.S. Small Business Administration's Office of Advocacy ranked Springfield third of 394 regions for entrepreneurship and innovation. The Plan for Progress also recognizes that efficiencies in production processes continue to shift the local economy away from manufacturing toward services. While the number of manufacturing jobs had decreased between 1969 and 2001, employment in the service industry jumped

from 150,000 to 200,000 over the same time period. The fastest growing service sectors are healthcare and education.

Among the companies headquartered in Springfield are Massachusetts Mutual Life Insurance Co., Merriam-Webster Inc., Smith & Wesson Corp., and the retail food company Big Y Foods Inc.

Items and goods produced: firearms, envelopes and stationery, chemicals, machinery, electrical equipment, rubber goods, printed matter, automobile accessories, forged metals, games and toys, educational equipment.

Incentive Programs—New and Existing Companies

Local programs—The city of Springfield assists in securing financing for new and expanding businesses from a variety of financing programs offered by the State of Massachusetts. The city offers property tax relief, development assistance, potential Enterprise Community benefits, and assistance with job training and workforce development.

State programs—Under the Massachusetts Economic Development Incentive Program, Springfield is designated an Economic Target Area, an area ripe to attract and retain businesses. Approved "certified projects" with this area are eligible for state investment tax credit, abandoned building tax deductions, and municipal tax benefits. Massachusetts also offers tax increment financing, emerging technology funds, tax credits for research and development, a predevelopment assistance program, a capital access program, and bond, equipment, and export financing programs.

Job training programs—The Regional Employment Board allocates and oversees worker training programs in Hampden County designed to meet the specific needs of employers. FutureWorks, Inc. is a quasi-public agency serving both as a "one-stop" career center and a fully-equipped applicant processing, screening, and training agency. The Division of Economic Development of Springfield Technical Community College promotes the development of a highly-skilled workforce through education and customized training.

Development Projects

One of the largest development projects underway in the mid-2000s was the MassMutual Center. The $71 million expansion and renovation project, scheduled for completion in late 2005, will transform the Springfield Civic Center into a new facility with more than 40,000 square feet of exhibition space, 9,000 square feet of meeting space, and an arena that can seat up to 8,000 people. The historic Court Square Park, adjacent to the center, is undergoing $500,000 in restoration and beautification efforts to accompany the center's grand opening.

Springfield College launched a fund-raising campaign in June 2005 to raise $40 million for the construction or renovation of five buildings. Proposals to build a hotel and an entertainment-oriented retail complex on the site of the former Naismith Memorial Basketball Hall of Fame, which moved to a new location in 2002, were under consideration in mid-2005.

Economic Development Information: Pioneer Valley Planning Commission, 26 Central St., West Springfield, MA 01089-2787; telephone (413)781-6045; fax (413)732-2593; email info@pvpc.org. Western Massachusetts Economic Development Council, 255 Padgette St., Ste. 1, Chicopee, MA 01022; telephone (413)593-6421; toll-free (888)593-6421; fax (413)593-5126; email feedback@westernmassedc.com

Commercial Shipping

Westover Metropolitan Airport, fifteen miles northeast of Springfield in Chicopee, serves as the region's principal air cargo handling facility. Boston & Maine Railroad and a vast fleet of commercial trucks also haul freight into Springfield.

Labor Force and Employment Outlook

Business leaders describe Springfield's labor force as skilled, with a strong work ethic. The region dubs itself the "Knowledge Corridor" due to the concentration of institutions of higher learning. The labor pool is not restricted to Springfield residents; rather, more than 26,000 workers commute daily across the state lines of Connecticut and Massachusetts.

The following is a summary of data regarding the Springfield metropolitan area labor force, 2004 annual averages.

Size of nonagricultural labor force: 294,200

Number of workers employed in . . .
  construction and mining: 10,500
  manufacturing: 39,200
  trade, transportation and utilities: 60,600
  information: 4,700
  financial activities: 16,300
  professional and business services: 23,900
  educational and health services: 53,200
  leisure and hospitality: 26,700
  other services: 11,300
  government: 47,900

Average hourly earnings of production workers employed in manufacturing: $15.43

Unemployment rate: 5.8% (February 2005)

Largest employers	*Number of employees*
Baystate Health System	6,300
Springfield Public Schools	4,600
Sisters of Providence Health System	4,039

Largest employers	*Number of employees*
MassMutual Financial Group	4,000
City of Springfield	2,278
Center for Human Development	1,069
Peter Pan Bus Lines	850
The Republican	800
U.S. Postal Service	774
Western New England College	650

Cost of Living

Springfield refers to itself as "the city of homes." The Springfield Redevelopment Authority assists prospective homeowners through the Home Ownership Opportunity Program, the Springfield Housing Finance Mortgage Pool, and a HUD Joint Venture for Affordable Housing Award.

The following is a summary of data regarding several key cost of living factors in the Springfield area.

2004 ACCRA Cost of Living Index: Not reported

2004 ACCRA Average House Cost: Not reported

State income tax rate: 5.95% on earned and business income

State sales tax rate: 5.0% on most items; does not include food and clothing, heating fuel and drugs

Local income tax rate: None

Local sales tax rate: None

Property tax rate: residential, $19.41 per $1,000 of assessed value; commercial, $34.54 per $1,000 of assessed value (2004)

Economic Information: Greater Springfield Chamber of Commerce, 1441 Main St., Springfield, MA 01103; telephone (413) 787-1555. Pioneer Valley Planning Commission, 26 Central St., West Springfield, MA 01089-2787; telephone (413)781-6045; fax (413)732-2593; email info @pvpc.org

Education and Research

Elementary and Secondary Schools

The Springfield Public School System includes pioneering programs in race relations, vocational and technical education, business education, toddler preschool, schools for gifted and talented children, and magnet schools. The Community Service Learning Program involves every child from kindergarten through high school in volunteer community work.

Specialized schools in the system include the Massachusetts Career Development Institute and SAGE, the Springfield Adolescent Graduation Experience.

The following is a summary of data regarding the Springfield public school system as of the 2003–2004 school year.

Total enrollment: 25,955

Number of facilities
  elementary schools: 31
  junior high/middle schools: 6
  senior high schools: 6
  other: 9, including one K-8 school

Student/teacher ratio: 11.6:1 (2004–2005)

Teacher salaries
  average: $47,036

Funding per pupil: $6,263

In addition to about 34 parochial schools, Springfield's private schools include two specialized secondary institutes. The MacDuffie School is a college-preparatory school for girls and boys.

Public Schools Information: Springfield Public Schools, 195 State St., Springfield, MA 01103; telephone (413)787-7100

Colleges and Universities

With four colleges within the city limits and several nationally acclaimed schools within driving distance, Springfield is near the hub of western Massachusetts's academic community. Springfield College, a private school specializing in physical education and health and fitness, offers 50 undergraduate and 13 graduate majors. Western New England College focuses on liberal arts, business, law, and engineering; this private school enrolls 4,550 students, 500 of which are pursuing law degrees. American International College, a private liberal arts school, confers more than 30 undergraduate and graduate degrees in arts, business administration, and education. Springfield Technical Community College grants associate's degrees or certificates in business, health, liberal arts, engineering, and technologies to 7,000 students; the college occupies the complex established by George Washington as the nation's first arsenal, the Springfield Armory, now a national historic site. The Springfield campus of Cambridge College enrolls approximately 390 students.

Libraries and Research Centers

The Springfield City Library, the second largest system in New England, features nearly 800,000 volumes held among 10 branches. The main branch is situated in the Quadrangle, a cultural complex it shares with Springfield's four major museums. Among its services are an employment resource center, comprehensive business collections, on-line data base searching, an African American history collection, an art and music collection that includes musical scores, 300 periodicals, 20 newspapers, a children's department, and material for special adult reading needs. The library's other special interests include New England and French genealogy, the Holocaust, local history, WWI and WWII propaganda, and American wood engravings. Additionally, the library serves as a depository for federal government documents and Massachusetts state documents.

In addition to the college and hospital libraries, special libraries in Springfield include the Massachusetts Trial Court Library, Hampden Law Library, the Springfield Armory National Historic Site Library and Archives, the Hickox Library at the Naismith Memorial Basketball Hall of Fame, and the Connecticut Valley Historical Museum Research Library. Massachusetts Mutual Life Insurance Company has a company library.

The American International College Curtis Blake Center studies learning disorders and A.I.C.'s Oral History Center studies western Massachusetts and Connecticut oral history. Springfield College does research in physiology and physical fitness.

Public Library Information: Springfield Library, 220 State St., Springfield, MA 01103; telephone (413)263-6828; fax (413)263-6817; email askalibrarian@springfieldlibrary.org

Health Care

The health care needs of Springfield residents are met by three major medical facilities in the city and more than a dozen acute care facilities in western Massachusetts. The Baystate Medical Center, one of the state's largest hospitals, is a teaching hospital affiliated with Tufts University and UMass Medical School. It features a state-of-the-art neonatal intensive care unit and is the only tertiary care referral medical center serving the western portion of the state. Baystate encompasses a Children's Hospital, the Wesson Women & Infants Unit, and the D'Amour Center for Cancer Care. The Shriners' Hospital for Children, operated by the Melha Temple, specializes in children's orthopedics, extensive outpatient services, and research into orthotics and prosthetics. The 226-bed Mercy Hospital, one of three general community hospitals operated in the Pioneer Valley by the Sisters of Providence, is a full-service healthcare facility.

Health Care Information: Baystate Health System, 280 Chestnut St., Springfield, MA 01199; telephone (413)794-0000

Housing one of the world's most extensive weapons collections, the Springfield Armory, now a national historic site, was established in 1794.

Recreation

Sightseeing

Springfield, the birthplace of basketball, is the home of the Naismith Memorial Basketball Hall of Fame, an international shrine honoring the creator of the game, its players, and its coaches. The Hall of Fame features a cinema that places the visitor in the midst of an exciting game, a chance to shoot hoops from a moving walkway, and a locker-room filled with memorabilia of the stars.

Springfield is also the site of the Springfield Armory National Historic Site, where General George Washington established the Springfield Armory in 1794. While the arsenal itself closed in 1968, a large firearms museum is now housed there, one of the most extensive collections of weapons in the world.

The Indian Motorcycle Museum and Hall of Fame celebrates the birthplace of the motorcycle and its manufacture by the Indian Company. In addition to vintage motorcycles, on display are other Indian products such as airplane engines, outboard boat motors, lawnmowers, street cleaners, and snowmobiles.

Among Springfield's historic areas are the McKnight District, whose 900 Victorian homes rank it as the largest of its type in New England; Mattoon Street, with its brick row houses and gas lamps; Sterns Square, a small park resulting from the collaboration of sculptor Augustus St. Gaudens and architect Stanford White; and Court Square, a part of the Massachusetts Heritage State Park Program. New England village life comes alive at Storrowton Village Museum in West Springfield.

Forest Park, an idyllic refuge within the city, mixes recreational offerings with a zoo, an amphitheater, paddleboats, and a miniature train ride. Riverfront Park was established in 1978 to promote recreational use of the Connecticut River. Peter Pan now runs hour-long narrated river cruises from the park from May through October.

Flanking the Court Street Square in downtown Springfield are the City Hall, boasting Corinthian columns and 27 varieties of marble, and the Campanile, a 300-foot carillon bell tower. The Campanile and City Hall are part of the Municipal Group, which also includes Symphony Hall.

Arts and Culture

Springfield's major performing arts centers are the Springfield Civic Center, Symphony Hall, and the CityStage. The Civic Center is the site of touring concert and musical performances throughout the year; it is undergoing a renovation that will transform it into the MassMutual Center. Symphony Hall, dedicated in 1913 and renowned for its acoustics and ornate architecture, is home to the Springfield Symphony Orchestra. This symphony, the city's resident professional performing and educational group, also performs at area parks in the summer; among its repertoire are classical, chamber, opera, and popular pieces. CityStage is a professional, not-for-profit theater that hosts a variety of musical and dramatic programs.

The Quadrangle is the site of the Springfield City Library and the city's four major museums. European and American graphics, sculptures, and paintings, including the works of Claude Monet and Degas, are on display at the Museum of Fine Arts. The George Walter Vincent Smith Art Museum houses the collection of the museum's namesake, which includes such pieces as Samurai arms and armor, Middle Eastern rugs, the largest collection of Chinese cloisonné outside of Asia, and Japanese glass, jades, bronzes, lacquers, porcelain, and paintings. The social and economic life of the Pioneer Valley is traced at the Connecticut Valley Historical Museum, which also features arts and crafts by local artisans. The Springfield Science Museum houses the country's first American-built planetarium, along with an observatory, a fresh-water aquarium, and dinosaur and African exhibit halls. Also located at the Quadrangle is the Dr. Seuss National Memorial Sculpture Garden, commemorating the beloved characters invented by one of Springfield's most famous residents, Theodor Geisel, better known as Dr. Seuss.

The Hatikvah Holocaust Education & Resource Center is a not-for-profit organization dedicated to educating about the past and combating prejudice in contemporary society. The Zoo in Forest Park teaches children about the animal world on a 4.5-acre site. The Avis Neigher Gallery, at the Tower Square, is a non-profit artists' collaborative and gallery for local artists. Exhibits of contemporary and traditional art are ongoing. The Zone Art Center serves as a gallery for international and local artists, as well as a showcase for music, poetry, films, and theater.

Arts and Culture Information: Springfield Library & Museums Association, 220 State St., Springfield, MA 01103; telephone (413)263-6800; toll-free (800)625-7738; email info@springfieldmuseums.org

Festivals and Holidays

Many of Springfield's holiday festivals center around basketball, beginning with the opening of the professional and college season in November. The Peachbasket Festival and Tip-Off Classic, including opening games, parades, and parties, is held in downtown Springfield. In the National Basketball Association (NBA) Hall of Fame Game, the defending NBA champions play a league opponent in an October exhibition game. The ''greats'' of the game are enshrined in the Basketball Hall of Fame Enshrinement Ceremony in October, closing out the season.

The city invites residents and visitors to bring their appetites to the World's Largest Pancake Breakfast, an event held on the Saturday closest to May 14th, the anniversary of the city's founding in 1636; about 75,850 servings of pancakes were dished out in 2002. Other Springfield events include the Peter Pan Taste of Springfield food festival in June, and Star-Spangled Springfield, the city's Fourth of July celebration that features fireworks over the Connecticut River and a concert by the Springfield Symphony Orchestra. A summer concert series is presented in the city's parks.

The Puerto Rican Cultural Festival takes place in July, and is followed by the Mattoon Street Arts Festival in September. Springfield area Greeks celebrate their culture at the September Glendi Festival, while local Italians turn out in force at the October Columbus Day Parade. To mark the beginning of the Christmas season, the Annual Parade of the Big Balloons takes place the day after Thanksgiving. It is followed by a month of holiday festivities throughout the city, including First Night, a traditional New Year's Eve extravaganza that launches the new year. Bright Nights at Forest Park starts the week before Thanksgiving and runs through the first week of January; this two-and-one-half-mile drive through lighting displays boasts 350,000 lights in a variety of seasonal displays.

West Springfield is the site of The Big E (Eastern States Exposition), a 17-day fair in September and October with entertainment and cultural competitions that is one of the largest fairs in the nation. That city also hosts the American Craft Council's Craft Fair, one of the largest and most prestigious in the country, and Boating USA, the Camping & Outdoor Show, and the Sportsmen's Show at the Eastern States Exposition facility.

Sports for the Spectator

The Springfield Falcons of the American Hockey League play home games at the Springfield Civic Center. The Civic Center also hosts basketball's annual NBA Hall of Fame Game, and the Collegiate Tip-Off Classic. Founded in 2001, the Springfield Spirit is a National Women's Basketball League team. The Springfield Junior Pics, a member of the USA Hockey Junior B Division, play at the Springfield Olympia Ice Center.

Springfield is home to numerous collegiate sporting events. Springfield College offers men's and women's basketball, cross country, gymnastics, lacrosse, soccer, swimming and diving, tennis, track and field, and volleyball; men's baseball, football, golf, and wrestling; and women's field hockey and softball. American International College offers 16 varsity sports for men and women, while Springfield Technical Community College is home to 8 intercollegiate sports teams. Western New England College offers men's and women's basketball, cross country, lacrosse, soccer, and tennis; men's baseball, football, golf, ice hockey, and wrestling; and women's field hockey, softball, swimming, and volleyball.

Elsewhere in Massachusetts, sports abound. The Western Massachusetts Pioneers, a member of the United Soccer League, play home games in Ludlow at the Lusitano Stadium, the only "soccer specific" stadium in New England. Boston is home to baseball's Red Sox, basketball's Celtics, and hockey's Bruins. The New England Patriots, an NFL team, and the New England Revolution, a Major League Soccer team, play home games at Foxborough's Gillette Stadium.

Sports for the Participant

Springfield's 42 city parks offer the full complement of team and individual sports. The 735-acre Forest Park offers skating rinks, tennis courts, and nature trails. The city boasts two golf courses, Franconia Golf Course and Veteran's Golf Course. Access to the Connecticut River is provided at Bassett's Boat Company and at Riverfront Park. Fishermen, bicyclists, downhill and cross-country skiers, campers, and hikers can all find prime facilities within a few miles of the city.

Shopping and Dining

Downtown Springfield shopping includes the specialty boutiques at Tower Square, which is anchored by three department stores and houses more than 30 specialty stores. The Eastfield Mall, located on Boston Road, offers more than 60 retail venues as well as a 16-screen movie theater. The Smith & Wesson Factory Store offers a selection of apparel, gifts, and accessories, all personalized with the legendary Smith & Wesson logo and name. Craft and art stores abound in the city; antique lovers can find items of Americana throughout the Pioneer Valley.

Springfield cuisine ranges from traditional Yankee dishes to Southeast Asian offerings, reflecting the city's ability to keep pace with the culinary offerings of its newest immigrants. Some specialties include dishes made with area produce such as apples and brown sugar, seafood from nearby lakes, "boiled dinners," and Indian pudding. Restaurants range from Gus & Paul's, a New York-style deli, to Lido Ristorante, a family-oriented Italian-American spot, to The Student Prince and Fort Restaurant, which features a wide selection of German-American food.

Visitor Information: Greater Springfield Convention & Visitors Bureau, 1441 Main St., Springfield, MA 01103;

telephone (413)787-1548; toll-free (800)723-1548; fax (413)781-4607; email info@valleyvisitor.com

Convention Facilities

The Springfield Civic Center, currently the city's largest event facility, comprises an arena seating 10,000 people, an exhibition hall with 38,500 square feet, a banquet hall, and meeting rooms. The center is undergoing a $71 million expansion and renovation that will transform it into the MassMutual Center, scheduled to open in late 2005. MassMutual will offer more than 40,000 square feet of exhibition space, 9,000 square feet of meeting space that can be divided into up to five rooms, and an arena that can seat up to 8,000 people. Additional conference space is offered by both the Springfield Symphony Hall and the not-for-profit CityStage, both of which can accommodate meetings, receptions, and presentations.

Major hotels include the Sheraton Springfield Monarch Place, with 27,000 square feet of conference space, 19 meeting rooms, and one of the largest ballrooms in western Massachusetts; and the Springfield Marriott, which features 265 guest rooms and more than 15,000 square feet of meeting and exhibit space; it is connected to Tower Square shopping.

One of New England's major multiuse sites, the 175-acre Eastern States Exposition, with three buildings and 275,000 square feet of space, is located in nearby West Springfield. The University of Massachusetts in Amherst features the University Conference Services, with 116 guest rooms and 36 meeting rooms, and Mullins Center, a state-of-the-art facility with 10,500 set arena and 40,000 square feet of exhibit space and meeting rooms.

Convention Information: Greater Springfield Convention & Visitors Bureau, 1441 Main St., Springfield, MA 01103; telephone (413)787-1548; toll-free (800)723-1548; fax (413)781-4607; email info@valleyvisitor.com

Transportation

Approaching the City

Springfield is 18 miles north of Bradley International Airport in Windsor Locks, Connecticut. Fifteen airlines at Bradley offer 232 daily flights to 75 destinations in the United States, Canada, and the Caribbean. Shuttle buses and limousines run between the airport and Springfield. Westover Metropolitan Airport and several private airports also serve Springfield.

Amtrak schedules trains between Springfield and many cities such as Boston, New York, Philadelphia, Washington, D.C., Chicago, and Montreal. In addition, Peter Pan Bus Lines connect Springfield with numerous cities throughout the Northeast.

Two major New England road arteries intersect in Springfield: the east-west running Massachusetts Turnpike (Interstate-90) and the north-south traveling Interstate-91 with its branch, Interstate-291, running through downtown.

Traveling in the City

Springfield's downtown is located on the east bank of the Connecticut River; the rest of the city spreads out to the east. Local transportation, provided by the Pioneer Valley Transit Authority, extends into 24 communities along 43 bus routes.

Communications

Newspapers and Magazines

Springfield's daily newspaper is the *The Republican.* Special interest publications include *The Catholic Observer* and *BusinessWest,* a biweekly business journal serving western Massachusetts.

Television and Radio

Springfield is served by a number of television stations: two commercial networks, one Public Broadcasting Service station, and one channel franchise. According to the 2003 *Broadcasting & Cable Yearbook,* Springfield ranks fourth among the nation's top market for cable television, as 86 percent of households have access to cable. Two AM and three FM radio stations broadcast a variety of music, news, and college-oriented programs.

Media Information: BusinessWest, 1441 Main St., 6th Fl., Springfield, MA 01103; telephone (413)781-8600; fax (413)781-3930. *The Republican,* 1860 Main St., Springfield, MA 01101; telephone (413)788-1000

Springfield Online

Baystate Health System. Available www.baystatehealth.com

BusinessWest. Available www.businesswest.com

City of Springfield. Available www.cityofspringfieldmass .com

Greater Springfield Convention & Visitors Bureau. Available www.valleyvisitor.com

Massachusetts Office of Business Development. Available www.state.ma.us/mobd

Pioneer Valley Planning Commission. Available www.pvpc.org

The Republican. Available www.repub.com

Springfield Armory National Historic Site. Available www.nps.gov/spar

Springfield Library. Available www.springfieldlibrary.org

Springfield Library & Museums Association. Available www.quadrangle.org

Springfield Public Schools. Available www.sps.springfield.ma.us

Western Massachusetts Economic Development Council. Available www.westernmassedc.com

Selected Bibliography

Clark, Rusty, *West Springfield, Massachusetts: Stories Carved in Stone* (West Springfield, MA: Dog Pond Press, 2004)

Cruikshank, Ginger, *Springfield, MA, Volume 1* (Mount Pleasant, SC: Arcadia Publishing, 1999)

Prisch, Michael H., *Town into City: Springfield, Massachusetts, and the Meaning of Community* (Cambridge, Mass: Harvard University Press, 1972)

Worcester

The City in Brief

Founded: 1673 (incorporated, 1722)

Head Official: City Manager Michael V. O'Brien (since 2004)

City Population
1980: 161,799
1990: 169,759
2000: 172,648
2003 estimate: 175,706
Percent change, 1990–2000: 1.7%
U.S. rank in 1980: 91st
U.S. rank in 1990: 101st
U.S. rank in 2000: 139th (State rank: 2nd)

Metropolitan Area Population (PMSA)
1990: 478,384
2000: 511,389

Percent change, 1990–2000: 6.9%
U.S. rank in 1990: 7th (MSA)
U.S. rank in 2000: 7th (MSA)

Area: 38 square miles (2000)
Elevation: 473 feet above sea level
Average Annual Temperature: 46.8° F
Average Annual Precipitation: 47.60 inches of rain; 67.4 inches of snow

Major Economic Sectors: Services, trade, manufacturing, government
Unemployment Rate: 5.5% (March 2005)
Per Capita Income: $18,614 (1999)

2002 FBI Crime Index Total: Not reported

Major Colleges and Universities: University of Massachusetts Medical School; Clark University; Worcester Polytechnic Institute; College of the Holy Cross; Worcester State College; Assumption College; Becker College

Daily Newspaper: *Telegram & Gazette*

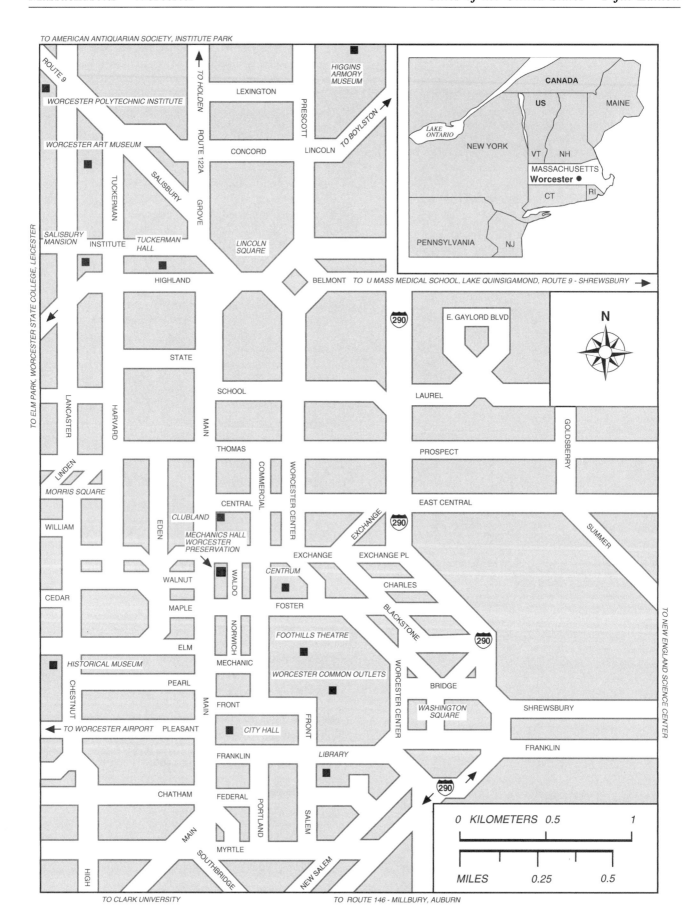

Introduction

Historically and culturally rich Worcester is emerging as a center for research and the production of a number of high-technology products. Its central location and network of roads and railways ensure that Worcester will continue to be a major New England retail and distribution center. Known for its historic attractions and natural beauty, the city has been gaining a reputation as a tourist attraction with colonial-era buildings, fine museums, and a well-developed park system. An increasing focus on services has allowed Worcester's workforce to adapt to current economic realities.

Geography and Climate

Located in the geographic center of the Commonwealth of Massachusetts, Worcester is about 40 miles west of Boston. It is the only major industrial city in the United States not located on a lake, river, or sea coast. The city is also the center of an urbanized metropolitan area that includes the towns of Auburn, Boylston, Holden, Leicester, Millbury, and Shrewsbury. Worcester, the hub of Worcester County, is situated on a series of rolling hills overlooking the Blackstone River. Lake Quinsigamond, seven miles long and one of the many lakes and ponds within the city limits, marks the eastern boundary of the city.

Its proximity to the Atlantic Ocean, Long Island Sound, and the Berkshire Mountains creates rapidly changing weather conditions in Worcester. While the mild weather is typical of New England, storms can blow in, depositing rain, snow, sleet, and fog. These storms are known locally as northeasters.

Area: 38 square miles (2000)

Elevation: 473 feet above sea level (mean elevation)

Average Temperatures: January, 23.3° F; July, 69.9° F; annual average, 46.8° F

Average Annual Precipitation: 47.60 inches of rain; 67.4 inches of snow

History

Plantation Becomes Transportation Center

The first Englishmen to visit the area surrounding present-day Worcester arranged in 1673 to purchase eight square miles of land near Lake Quinsigamond. They made the bargain with the resident Nipmucks, giving them twelve pounds sterling. The English called their settlement Quinsigamond Plantation. These first settlers and those who followed them in 1675 were eventually driven out by the Nipmucks when they learned that the newcomers did not intend to share the land. A third, successful attempt at settling the area came in 1713 when Jones Rice built his home atop Union Hill. By 1722, the settlement was large enough to incorporate as a town, renamed Worcester in honor of the English county and town.

Worcester early became a transportation center, initially as a stagecoach stop on the way west from Boston. Just prior to the American Revolution, rebel printer Isaiah Thomas printed his anti-British newspaper, *The Massachusetts Spy,* from Worcester; he later gave the first public reading of the Declaration of Independence in 1776. Following the war, Thomas built his printing business into the country's largest publishing house, printing the first dictionary in the United States in 1788. Shays's Rebellion, in 1786 and 1787, tested the country's new constitution when a company of poor men from the towns north of Worcester entered the city and seized the courthouse. Their protest against poor government ended when a volunteer army expelled them.

Worcester was one of only a few major U.S. industrial centers that was able to thrive without being located on a navigable river or coastline. The local water supply was adequate to provide steam to run its mills, which turned out wire, nails, and paper. The population stood at 58,300 people in 1800 when textile production became the next major industry in Worcester, including the weaving of the country's first corduroy at a Worcester cotton mill. In 1828 the Blackstone Canal opened, connecting Worcester with Providence, Rhode Island. A period of industrialization and expansion followed, fueled by the arrival of the railroad in 1835. Once again, Worcester flourished as a transportation hub, shipping out manufactured goods via rail to Springfield, Norwich, and Boston. In 1837 the first power loom capable of intricate designs was invented by William Chompton, whose loomworks in Worcester revolutionized the industry.

Manufacturing Precedes High-Technology

During its industrialization, Worcester relied increasingly on the labor of women and children. A women's rights movement blossomed, culminating in the First Women's Suffrage National Convention in 1851, followed by a second convention in 1852. The women then agreed to put aside their own cause and focus on the Abolitionist Movement that was then gaining followers in the North. The city subsequently became a stop on the Underground Railroad for slaves escaping North. In 1848 Worcester helped create the

Free-Soil Party, which advocated allowing Kansas to enter the Union as a free state.

After the Civil War, Worcester resumed its quick industrial pace. The first bicycle was built in Worcester, leading to a national bicycling craze. During the last half of the century, Worcester experienced an influx of immigrants eager to work in its mills and plants. Irish, Canadian, and Swedish workers arrived before 1900, followed by Poles, Italians, Lithuanians, Greeks, Armenians, Syrians, and Lebanese. By 1920 Worcester's population had grown to 179,754 people.

Worcester continued its manufacturing course, taking advantage of new technologies as they were invented, including automation, mass production, and the assembly line. During World War II, many of the city's plants were converted to the war effort and 27,000 men and women from Worcester served in the armed forces. The USS *Worcester,* a 17,000-ton light cruiser, was launched in 1948.

Worcester's population peaked in 1950 at 203,000 people. Like many industrial centers in the north, Worcester experienced difficult years in the 1960s and 1970s. Much of the textile industry moved south in search of cheaper labor, and the expressways lured a majority of the city's middle class to the suburbs. Worcester enjoyed an economic revival late in the 1970s, spurred by the building of the Centrum Civic Center and the Galleria Shopping Center downtown.

In recent years, the city has been marketing itself to business as a research and high technology center with a solid manufacturing base. Worcester is rapidly becoming known as a hub for education, research, and business. Reflecting that development, approximately one third of Worcester's population is employed by the service industry, while another third work in a professional or managerial capacity. The education and flexibility of the city's populace have allowed it to move relatively comfortably through a period of economic transition.

Historical Information: Worcester Historical Museum & Library, 30 Elm St., Worcester, MA 01609; telephone (508)753-8278

Population Profile

Metropolitan Area Residents
1990: 478,384
2000: 511,389
Percent change, 1990–2000: 6.9%
U.S. rank in 1990: 7th (MSA)
U.S. rank in 2000: 7th (MSA)

City Residents
1980: 161,799
1990: 169,759
2000: 172,648 (of which, 82,914 were males and 89,734 were females)
2003 estimate: 175,706
Percent change, 1990–2000: 1.7%
U.S. rank in 1980: 91st
U.S. rank in 1990: 101st
U.S. rank in 2000: 139th (State rank: 2nd)

Density: 4,596.5 people per square mile (2000)

Racial and ethnic characteristics (2000)
   White: 133,124
   Black or African American: 11,892
   American Indian and Alaska Native: 769
   Asian: 8,402
   Native Hawaiian and Pacific Islander: 96
   Hispanic or Latino (may be of any race): 26,155
   Other: 12,504

Percent of residents born in state: 63.5% (2000)

Age characteristics (2000)
   Population under 5 years old: 11,142
   Population 5 to 9 years old: 11,854
   Population 10 to 14 years old: 11,381
   Population 15 to 19 years old: 13,769
   Population 20 to 24 years old: 15,622
   Population 25 to 34 years old: 26,781
   Population 35 to 44 years old: 25,578
   Population 45 to 54 years old: 19,711
   Population 55 to 59 years old: 6,756
   Population 60 to 64 years old: 5,665
   Population 65 to 74 years old: 10,956
   Population 75 to 84 years old: 9,582
   Population 85 years and over: 3,851
   Median age: 33.4 years

Births (2003)
   Total number: 9,529

Deaths (2002)
   Total number: 691

Money income (1999)
   Per capita income: $18,614
   Median household income: $35,623
   Total households: 67,083

Number of households with income of . . .
   less than $10,000: 9,744
   $10,000 to $14,999: 5,126
   $15,000 to $24,999: 9,059
   $25,000 to $34,999: 9,058
   $35,000 to $49,999: 10,830

$50,000 to $74,999: 11,965
$75,000 to $99,999: 5,771
$100,000 to $149,999: 3,931
$150,000 to $199,999: 800
$200,000 or more: 799

Percent of families below poverty level: 14.1% (57.1% of which were female householder families with related children under 5 years)

2002 FBI Crime Index Total: not reported

Municipal Government

Worcester operates with a council-city manager form of government, with eleven council members elected to two-year terms. Six council members are elected at large and five are elected by district. A mayor presides over the council and is elected by a separate ballot at each biennial election. The city manager is appointed by the council and serves at its pleasure. Worcester is also the county seat for Worcester County, although the county has performed no functions of governance since 1998, when all former county activities were assumed by other governmental agencies.

Head Official: City Manager Michael V. O'Brien (since 2004; open contract evaluated yearly)

Total Number of City Employees: 1,805 (not including school department employees) (2004)

City Information: Office of the City Manager, City Hall, 455 Main Street, Worcester, MA 01608; telephone (508)799-1175; fax (508)799-1208

Economy

Major Industries and Commercial Activity

Worcester, the second largest city in the Commonwealth of Massachusetts and located at its geographic center, is a major manufacturing, distribution, service, retail, and trading center for New England. Worcester's economy is diverse, with more than 5,000 firms of all types in the metropolitan area. This diversity has served Worcester well in periods of economic downturn, as the economy is not dependant on the success of a single sector. While the national economy continues to struggle, Worcester has experienced modest growth and can boast of many positive economic indicators. Worcester is home to diverse manufac-

turing firms, retailers, service companies, and wholesale businesses. Economic incentives and assistance programs help draw businesses to Worcester and retain existing firms.

Worcester's colleges and universities comprise the second largest employer in the city. Developments in biotechnology and high tech industries, the health industry, manufacturing, and downtown development highlight Worcester's areas of greatest recent growth. Many emerging industries such as fiber optics, electronics, and advanced ceramics are flourishing. Further, the presence of so many higher education opportunities in Worcester mean that the community's workforce is highly skilled and well-trained. The educational level of Worcester's workforce has been an additional draw to businesses in the fields of health, technology, pharmaceuticals and professional services.

An important indicator of Worcester's economic health is the number of ongoing development projects and business relocations in the area. Business development in Worcester has been steady and strong since 2000, and more than 100 companies expressed interest in relocating to the Worcester area during the 2004 fiscal year.

Items and goods produced: abrasives; steel and wire goods; ball valves; sprinklers; grinding wheels; woolens and worsteds; textile, grinding, and labeling machinery; machine tools; dies; airplane and electronics parts; shoes; leather and knitted goods; looms; firearms; automotive accessories; boilers; plastics; wrenches; precision tools and gauges; chairs; carpets and rugs

Incentive Programs—New and Existing Companies

Local programs—The District Improvement Financial Program, or DIF, is a locally driven public financing alternative that allows municipalities to fund public works, infrastructure, and development projects. Projects qualifying under DIF receive advantages such as the avoidance of any new tax levies and negotiable finance terms. The Worcester Regional Chamber of Commerce also has a Business Assistance Program, which focuses on retaining existing businesses and attracting new business to the Worcester area. The Chamber of Commerce has the capabilities to assist in site searches and other technical aspects of the relocation or expansion process.

State programs—The state of Massachusetts offers a wide array of business and financial incentives, as well as assistance in coordinating business development and relocation. The Economic Development Incentive Program, or EDIP, was designed to create and retain businesses in target areas. State tax incentives are available to qualifying projects, including a five percent investment tax credit for tangible, depreciable assets as well as municipal tax incentives such as special tax assessments and Tax Increment Financing.

Job training programs—Area educational institutions work closely with local companies to design practical programs of study to prepare students for entry into the job market in such fields as electronics, machine operation, computer technology, health care, culinary arts, and clerical skills. Upgrading and retraining programs are also available.

The city's Office of Employment and Training works closely with the local employment and training network providers to offer a diverse range of programs. The Office aims to prepare residents for entry into the workforce by providing access to important occupational skills matching the needs of regional employers. The Worcester Workforce Central One Stop Career Center provides jobseekers with information regarding both training and employment opportunities, including job banks, notifications of on-site recruitment, resources pertaining to training and continuing information programs, and information on distance learning opportunities. The Massachusetts Division of Employment and Training administers the Workforce Training Fund, which provides resources to businesses to train both new and current employees. The Hiring Incentive Training Grant Program provides additional incentives for businesses hiring employees who have been out of work for over a year.

Development Projects

Development projects have been thriving in Worcester since the turn of the century. The Massachusetts Biomedical Initiatives, an independent, tax-exempt corporation dedicated to the growth of biotechnology has completed two Worcester facilities. Named the MBIdeas Innovation Center, this facility has lead to the formation of over 12 companies and the creation of 65 new jobs, as well as investment into the Worcester community. The Innovation Center also plans a new life sciences business with its own sophisticated facility.

The Union Station development project is a $32 million renovation of one of Worcester's most beautiful buildings. Abandoned in 1975 after the decline of the railroads, the historic 1911 French Renaissance building stood vacant for more than 20 years. In renovating the building, particular attention was paid to the restoration of its original stained glass ceilings, marble columns, and mahogany woodworking. Today, the station is a functional transportation center, serving as a hub for train, taxi, and bus lines. A restaurant, blues lounge, and the FDR American Heritage Center Museum and Special Collections Showcase are also housed within Union Station. Additionally, commercial rental space is available on the first and second floors of the station.

In 2003 work was completed on the initial phase of the South Worcester Industrial Park, a complex project involving the environmental remediation and rehabilitation of eleven acres of blighted and abandoned property. Projects such as the South Worcester Industrial Park are vital to the continued development of the Worcester area, as space for new and expanding business is at a premium. When completed, the Industrial Park will provide space for private businesses interested in developing new industrial facilities.

June 2004 marked the starting point of the redevelopment of a one million square foot outlet mall at the heart of Worcester in the CitySquare project. The project aims to create a mixed-use facility over the next five years, with space dedicated to uses as diverse as medical, office, residential, retail, and entertainment. CitySquare will feature an open-air street grid and will be centered around a green space. Its proximity to important downtown features and to transportation facilities mean that CitySquare will be an important step in transforming the core of downtown Worcester.

Economic Development Information: Office of Planning and Community Development, City of Worcester, 418 Main Street, Worcester, MA 01608; telephone (508)799-1400. Worcester Business Development Corporation, 33 Waldo Street, Worcester, MA 01608; telephone (508)753-2924

Commercial Shipping

Worcester's central location makes it easily accessible by multiple means of transportation. Highways I-90, Route 495, and Route 290 all provide convenient access to multiple locations within the city. Ten daily MBTA commuter rail trains provide service between Worcester and Boston's Back Bay and South stations. Amtrak service is available from Union Station, with daily trains departing for destinations such as Boston, Chicago, and New York. The Worcester Bus Terminal is serviced by both Greyhound and Peter Pan Trailways, while local bus transportation is provided by the Worcester Regional Transit Authority. The Worcester Regional Airport is convenient to downtown and is open to private and business flights. The Port of Worcester is one of the nation's largest inland container yards, and its terminals serve as railheads for export or domestic shipments of containerized freight from New England to the West Coast.

Labor Force and Employment Outlook

With its strong academic and technical education resources, research facilities, and manufacturing base, Worcester continues to prove an attractive site for new and relocating high-technology firms. Development projects announced or in the planning stages are expected to insure construction jobs in the region while also ensuring a continuing source of investment into the community.

The following is a summary of data regarding the Worcester metropolitan area labor force, 2004 annual averages.

Size of nonagricultural labor force: 243,500

Number of workers employed in . . .
    construction and mining: 10,300
    manufacturing: 29,700
    trade, transportation, and utilities: 45,300
    information: 4,000
    financial activities: 14,100
    professional and business services: 29,100
    educational and health services: 45,900
    leisure and hospitality: 21,900
    other services: 9,100
    government: 34,200

Average hourly earnings of production workers employed in manufacturing: $15.71

Unemployment rate: 5.5% (March 2005)

Largest employers (2004)	Number of employees
EMC Corporation	7,200
UMass Memorial Health Care	7,195
UMass Medical School	6,040
Bertucci's Corporation	5,000
Fallon Community Health Plan	4,636
Waters Corp.	3,600
Worcester Public Schools	3,458
Allmerica Financial/The Hanover Insurance Company	2,305

Cost of Living

The cost of groceries, health care, utilities and transportation, and miscellaneous goods and services in Worcester is slightly above the national average.

The following is a summary of data regarding several key cost of living factors in the Worcester area.

2004 (3rd Quarter) ACCRA Average House Price: $372,500

2004 (3rd Quarter) ACCRA Cost of Living Index: 114.6 (U.S. average = 100.0)

State income tax rate: 5% on earned income

State sales tax rate: 5% on most items; does not include food and clothing

Local income tax rate: None

Local sales tax rate: None

Property tax rate: $31.44 per $1,000 (2004)

Economic Information: Worcester Area Chamber of Commerce, 33 Waldo Street, Worcester, MA 01608; telephone (508)753-2924

Education and Research

Elementary and Secondary Schools

The Worcester Public School System is administered by the Worcester School Committee, which consists of seven voting members. Students have the option of attending one of seventeen magnet schools devoted to various disciplines. Children in grades three through six may attend one of many PEAK enrichment programs. Sponsored by area businesses, foundations and individuals, the nonprofit Alliance for Education operates programs providing grants for teachers, Community Reading Day, the Regional Science Fair and an extensive school-business partnership program.

The following is a summary of data regarding the Worcester Public School District as of the 2002–2003 school year.

Total enrollment: 25,689

Number of facilities
    elementary schools: 39
    junior high/middle schools: 4
    senior high schools: 6
    other: 1

Student/teacher ratio: 12:1

Teacher salaries
    minimum: $39,134
    maximum: $56,664

Funding per pupil: $11,964 (2001-2002)

A system of separate, publicly supported vocational schools supplements the public school system. Twenty-three parochial schools educate an additional 1,000 students. Many private schools of note are located in the area, including Worcester Academy, and the Bancroft School.

Public Schools Information: Superintendent of Schools, Worcester Public Schools, 20 Irving Street, Worcester, MA 01609; telephone (508)799-3116

Colleges and Universities

Worcester is home to nine highly rated coeducational colleges and universities, as well as a medical school and veterinary school. Worcester's higher education offerings include UMass Medical Center, which is one of three campuses of the Commonwealth's university. The School of Medicine was one of only 14 medical centers in the country to be awarded a Robert Wood Johnson grant, providing $2.5 million in funding to encourage training in primary care fields. The Medical Center is part of a medical complex that includes a teaching hospital, graduate schools of biomedical sciences and nursing, and a program of molecular medicine. Another publicly-funded school is Worcester State College, which awards bachelor's and master's degrees in the arts, sciences, and education, and has expanded to offer professional programs in biomedical sciences, business, and healthcare fields. Quinsigamond Community College is state-funded and offers two-year associate's degrees.

Private schools include the highly regarded Worcester Polytechnic Institute; Becker College, with two campuses; Curry College, satellite campus; Tufts University School of Veterinary Medicine in Grafton, Clark University, noted for its graduate research program, Anna Maria College, Nichols College, and Massachusetts College of Pharmacy and Health Sciences. Catholic schools include the College of the Holy Cross, an undergraduate Jesuit institution with many prestigious alumnus, and Assumption College.

Private and public institutions in the Worcester area cooperate with colleges and universities from nearby communities in the Colleges of Worcester Consortium. With 13 member institutions, the consortium provides such benefits as cross-registration for students, inter-campus bus service, and joint bid contracts on products and services.

Libraries and Research Centers

The Worcester Public Library, part of the Central/Western Massachusetts Automated Resource Sharing consortium, operates a main library and two branches. The collection includes more than 900,000 volumes, including government documents. Among the library's special features are the Talking Book Library for the Blind, and the grant resource center.

Among its special resources, Worcester boasts the library of the American Antiquarian Society, which has one of the largest collections of printed matter about the United States' first 250 years. Clark University's Guy H. Burnham Map and Aerial Photography Library is a repository for all maps of the U.S. Geological Survey. Also at Clark University, the Goddard Library carries the papers of Dr. Robert Goddard, father of U.S. rocketry. The Worcester County Horticultural Society holds one of the most complete collections of its kind in New England. The Higgins Armory Museum includes a library, and local libraries covering a number of topics are open to researchers.

Among its research centers Worcester counts the Worcester Foundation for Biomedical Research, an independent research organization that invented the birth control pill. Worcester Polytechnic Institute operates several research laboratories, focusing on such areas as automation, robotics, nuclear energy, materials testing, manufacturing engineering, ceramics, fire safety, heat treatment, metallurgy, artificial intelligence, and bioengineering. Worcester State

College administers a Community Education Development Center. Using a holistic approach, the Heinz Warner Institute at Clark University studies the ways that behavior affects psychological development. At the Massachusetts Biotechnology Research Park, more than fifteen companies and institutions have established operations promoting the biotechnology industry in the state and in the nation. Among these are the University of Massachusetts Medical Center; the Massachusetts Biotechnology Research Institute, the scientific and educational arm of the park; and BASF Bioresearch Corporation, whose state-of-the-art research and development center works on cures for cancer and disorders of the immune system.

Public Library Information: Main Library, City of Worcester, 3 Salem Square, Worcester, MA 01608; telephone (508)799-1655, fax (508)799-1652

Health Care

Ten general hospitals in the Worcester area (five within the city) minister to local health care needs, including rehabilitation, long-term and chronic care. The keystone of Worcester's health care system is the University of Massachusetts Memorial Health Care. A merger between the University of Massachusetts Medical Center and the Medical Center of Central Massachusetts, it is the largest health care network in central and western Massachusetts. It includes the university's medical school, graduate programs, and a tertiary care facility with 783 beds on three campuses. UMass Memorial Medical Center is the region's only Level I trauma center. Four community hospitals are members of the UMass Memorial system. The center's purchase of Two Biotech has allowed the campus to expand its research capabilities and provides a base for its new Cancer Center. The 264,000 square foot Lakeside expansion project will provide new facilities for emergency care, radiology, intensive care, as well as operating space. Other projects include a Cardiac Catheterization Center, a renovated Endoscopy Center, and a Pediatric Infusion Suite, all at the University Campus. A major development at the Memorial Campus is a new Women's Health Center, allowing for centralized treatment at a single location.

In 2000, the downtown Worcester Medical Center opened as a partnership between Saint Vincent Healthcare System and Fallon. The Medical Center has 299 beds in its inpatient area and offers several specialty care centers and outpatient services. Saint Vincent Hospital, a 348-bed acute care hospital located within the Medical Center, has historic roots dating back to 1893.

Health Care Information: UMass Medical Center, Medical Center Library, 55 Lake Avenue North, Worcester, MA 01655-2397; telephone (508)856-0011

Recreation

Sightseeing

Worcester's colonial past and high-technology present fuse: historic homesteads coexist with science centers and modern sculpture. The American Antiquarian Society, dating to 1812, is the third oldest historical society in the country. The Society maintains a collection of materials pertaining to American history and culture; tours are held on Wednesdays. Salisbury Mansion is another architectural artifact; this 1772 home, one of the best documented in New England, has been restored under the auspices of the Worcester Historical Museum. The home has been recreated to replicate the life of the Salisbury family during the early to mid-1800s. Old Sturbridge Village, located near Worcester in Sturbridge, is a recreated 1830s village that is open year-round. Talks, walking tours, and performances are highlights of the Sturbridge Village experience and vary throughout the year. The Ecotarium is a multi-million dollar natural science and environmental education center on the old New England Science Center 60-acre campus. Inside is the three-level hands-on exhibit hall, a multimedia planetarium, and a solar-lunar observatory. Outside are a maze of nature trails, a train ride, a 100-foot tower that uses wind to generate power, and an indoor-outdoor zoo. The American Sanitary Plumbing Museum offers a unique look at antique fixtures, tools and accoutrements of the plumbing world.

Worcester's ''Artworks in Our Parks'' program has gained national attention for its innovative combination of park preservation and outdoor sculpture. Memorials, statues, bridges, and fountains by leading artists can be found throughout Worcester's parks. Floral displays can also be enjoyed at the Worcester County Horticultural Society, located in Boylston, which also offers lectures and workshops. The Broad Meadow Brook Conservation Center and Wildlife Sanctuary, the largest urban wildlife sanctuary in New England, offers more than five miles of marked trail on over 400 acres. Broad Meadow Brook also features nature exhibits and programs appealing to visitors of all ages.

Arts and Culture

Music Worcester, Inc. presents Worcester's 140-year-old Music Festival which draws crowds each fall to Mechanics Hall, as do the international Arts Series, and the Mass Jazz Festival. The group also produces chamber ensemble, world music, jazz, and choral performances. The city's choral

tradition includes the All Saints Choir of Men and Boys, established in 1868, and the country's oldest continuous choir. Many other choral groups entertain the region's audiences, offering barbershop quartet melodies, sacred music, and Broadway hits. Perhaps the most famous is the Worcester Chorus, which performs with the Worcester Orchestra. Tuckerman Hall, designed by Josephine Wright Chapman, one of America's first female architects, is home to the Central Massachusetts Symphony Orchestra.

Grand opera and children's operas are staged by Opera Worcester and the Salisbury Lyric Opera Company. The Central Massachusetts Symphony performs many of its concerts at Tuckerman Hall and Mechanics Hall, and its summer offerings at Institute Park. College of the Holy Cross music performing ensembles include the Brass Ensemble, College Choir, Chamber Players, Crusader Band, Schola Cantorum, Jazz Ensemble, Jazz Combo, Liturgical Music Ministry, Madrigal Singers, and Opera Scenes workshop, all of which perform regularly in a variety of settings both on and off campus.

Worcester theater claimed national attention with the emergence of the Worcester Foothills Theatre Company in 1974. This residential troupe stages some seven productions annually. Other companies include the Worcester Forum Theatre Ensemble, the Clark University Theatre Program, Worcester Children's Theatre, the Peter Pan Players and Side Show Troupe children's groups, and Phoenix Players. Performances by the Pyramid Gypsy Dance Company have helped gain renown for Worcester's dance community.

The Worcester Art Museum, one of the largest and finest in the country, houses a notable collection of Dutch, English, Italian, and French masters in 36 galleries. Museum holdings span 50 centuries and include a complete room from a medieval French monastery. The Museum's collection consists of 35,000 pieces, including paintings, sculpture, photography, prints, decorative arts, and drawings. The Worcester Historical Museum, founded in 1877, maintains exhibits of American history and a library, and sponsors self-guided walking tours of the city. Changing exhibits and special programs highlight contributions of groups and individuals over the course of Worcester's history. The Higgins Armory Museum displays more than 100 suits of armor, part of the most comprehensive collection in the Western World and also hosts an annual renaissance fair.

Art galleries include Gallery 70 at the Heywood Gallery, which showcases emerging artists from the Boston area; the Fletcher/Priest Gallery, which focuses on contemporary art; and the Prince and Potter Gallery, which offers artwork and contemporary crafts. The Iris & B. Gerald Cantor Art Gallery on the campus of Holy Cross College attempts to link displays to the broad intellectual aims of the college's liberal

arts curriculum. Arts Worcester is a private, non-profit organization that hosts satellite galleries and advocates for the
arts in the Worcester region.

Arts and Culture Information: Worcester Cultural Commission, Office of Planning and Community Development,
418 Main St., Worcester, MA 01608; telephone (508)799-
1400

Festivals and Holidays

Worcester's festival season begins with the Central Massachusetts Flower Show, sponsored by the local horticultural
society in February and the Worcester Wine and Food Festival at Union Station, also in February. The show features 30
gardens and displays from 10 garden clubs. May brings a
Craft Fair at the Worcester Craft Center, and the Worcester
Spring Home Show. St. Mary's Albanian Orthodox Church
and St. Spyridon Greek Orthodox Church jointly celebrate a
festival in June. July is the time for fireworks during the
Festival at East Park; the Sunday series played by the
Central Massachusetts Symphony in Institute Park also
takes place in July. The Annual Abbott's Mime Festival and
the Worcester County Music Association Concert series
both play in Institute Park in August. The Irish Festival at
Quinsigamond College and the Boticelli Ball at Mechanics
Hall are annual August events.

The Worcester County Music Association's Annual Music
Festival in October, begun in 1858, is the oldest music
festival in the United States. Entertainment includes symphonic programs, ballet, opera, choral music, and performances by individual artists. The Horticultural Hall hosts
the Harvest Fest and Autumn Show while Mechanics Hall
hosts the Black Debutantes' Ball. December brings a Christmas Lighting Parade and the First Night Celebration on New
Year's Eve.

Sports for the Spectator

Worcester has a long sporting history, as the city was home
to one of the eight original National League (baseball) teams
and hometown of the author of *Casey at the Bat.* Today, the
Worcester Tornadoes of the CanAm Professional Baseball
Association play in Worcester at Fitton Field. The region's
universities offer mens' and womens' varsity sports.
Worcester's Centrum Centre offers events such as
motocross races and has played host to preliminary rounds
of the NCAA basketball and ice hockey tournaments. Boston, an hour's drive from Worcester, offers professional
baseball, basketball, and hockey.

Sports for the Participant

With 47 parks covering more than 1,200 acres, outdoor
athletes can always find something to do in Worcester. Elm
Park, near the city's center, was the country's first park
purchased with tax money. It was renovated thanks to a $1.5
million state grant; its charm owes much to its ornamental

bridges, under which skaters glide in winter. Other activities
there include jogging, sunbathing, picnicking, tennis, and
basketball. Both Elm Park and the Worcester Common, set
aside as open space in 1669, are on the National Registry of
Historic Places. Quinsigamond State Park is the city's largest and includes two beaches and facilities for picnicking,
boating, and fishing. Green Hill Park, Worcester's largest
public park, includes an 18-hole golf course, picnic groves, a
skating pond, a little league field, handball courts ski run,
and the Barnyard Farm and Educational Area petting zoo. A
recent addition to Worcester's sporting scene is the
"upscale" Boston Billiard Club. Worcester is conveniently
located near the northern New England mountains, state
parks, ski lodges, and bays and beaches. Golfing opportunities abound in the greater Worcester area.

Shopping and Dining

A multitude of discount stores and factory outlets bring
shoppers from miles around to Worcester and its neighboring towns. The bargain stores offer locally produced
items such as clothing, shoes, and fabric. Greendale Mall,
which boasts more than 54 shops and restaurants, features
pseudo-Victorian brick and iron decor and is filled with
plants and flowers under an atrium ceiling. Tatnuck Book-
seller & Sons' expanded operation on Chandler Street displays 10,000 square feet of books in a new location that also
features retail outlets and a cultural center. The Perkins Farm
Marketplace is a community shopping center just north of
the Massachusetts Turnpike. Worcester has many unique
shops featuring the crafts and wares of local artisans. Antique shops are also plentiful in the Worcester area.

Worcester restaurants delight palates, whether serving
sturdy New England fare in colonial settings or nouveau
American cuisine in streamlined luxury. Ethnic food can be
had as well, including Greek, Italian, Indian, and Jewish
Kosher dishes. Legal Seafood Outlet offers more than 300
varieties of seafood. Shrewsbury Street, traditionally known
for its Italian cuisine, has seen the opening of several new
upscale restaurants. To the north of Worcester, the Nashoba
Valley Winery offers a gourmet restaurant as well as a
winemaking and distillation facility and a brewery; tastings
are available throughout the week.

Visitor Information: Massachusetts Office of Travel and
Tourism, 100 Cambridge Street, Boston, MA 02202; telephone (617)727-3201

Convention Facilities

Worcester's entertainment and convention center, formerly
known as the Centrum Centre, was renamed the DCU Center
in 2004. Equally capable of hosting sporting events, shows,

and concerts, the venue is well-known as a premier entertainment facility. The DCU's convention center offers over 100,000 square feet of exhibit space and more than 20,000 square feet of meeting space, as well as a ballroom, kitchen facilities, and administrative offices. Plans for future development of the DCU complex include a convention hotel adjacent to the DCU, which will be connected to the Center by a skyway.

The Beechwood Hotel, adjacent to the UMass Medical Center, offers facilities for meetings and groups as well as for special events such as weddings. The Hotel's Grand Ballroom alone provides 4,200 square feet of space which may be subdivided as the size of groups dictates. The Holiday Inn has 11 meeting rooms and more than 20,000 square feet of space available for meetings and conventions.

Historic Mechanics Hall, renovated in the early 1990s and seating up to 1,600 people, offers 14,000 square feet of exhibit space. Most local colleges and museums act as supplemental meeting sites, offering limited exhibit space and seating for groups of 40 to 1,000 people.

Convention Information: Worcester County Convention and Visitors Bureau, 33 Waldo Street, Worcester, MA 01608; telephone (508)753-2920

Transportation

Approaching the City

Interstate-190 links Route 2, the Mohawk Trail, with the city of Worcester. Interstate 290 connects I-495 with the city and eventually links with the Massachusetts Turnpike, where I-290 becomes I-395, the main route south through Connecticut. Worcester acts as a hub for several smaller state highways; Route 9 links the city to Shrewsbury, an eastern suburb. Route 146, the Worcester-Providence Highway, acts as an alternate north-south route to I-290/I-135.

Logan International Airport near Boston is one hour to the east of Worcester. Transportation into Worcester is provided by airport limousine services, buses, and taxis.

Traveling in the City

The Worcester Regional Transit Authority operates more than 60 buses on 28 routes serving Worcester and 13 surrounding communities. Rush-hour traffic can be heavy. I-290 is the heavily traveled east-west route north of downtown, while I-190 takes the bulk of the north-south traffic.

Communications

Newspapers and Magazines

Worcester is served by one daily newspaper, the *Telegram & Gazette*. The Worcester County Newspapers group publishes weekly papers for surrounding towns. Special interest newspapers include the *Worcester Business Journal, Catholic Free Press, The Senior Advocate, Crusader, The Scarlet* (a collegiate newspaper), and the *Jewish Chronicle*. Magazines published include *Worcester Magazine, Economic Geography,* and *International Figure Skating*.

Television and Radio

Local residents can pick up the major networks from Boston and one cable television company operates in Worcester. Eight AM and FM radio stations broadcast programming, and several others are received in Worcester; formats range from jazz, eclectic, classic rock, news, and talk.

Media Information: Telegram & Gazette, 20 Franklin Street, Worcester, MA 01613; telephone (508)793-9100. *Worcester Business Journal,* 172 Shrewsbury Street, Worcester, MA 01604; telephone (508)755-8004

Worcester Online

City of Worcester. Available at www.ci.worcester.ma.us

Worcester & Central Massachusetts Tourist Council. Available www.worcester.org

Worcester Chamber of Commerce. Available www.worcesterchamber.org

Worcester Convention & Visitors Bureau. Available www.worcester.org

Worcester History Museum. Available www.worcesterhistory.org

Worcester Public Library. Available www.worc.publib.org

Worcester Public Schools. Available www.wpsweb.com/schools.htm

Worcester *Telegram & Gazette*. Available www.telegram.com

Selected Bibliography

Goyer, Jane, *So Dear to My Heart: Memories of a Gentler Time* (New York: Harper & Row, 1990)

NEW HAMPSHIRE

The State in Brief

Nickname: Granite State
Motto: Live free or die

Flower: Purple lilac
Bird: Purple finch

Area: 9,350 square miles (2000; U.S. rank: 46th)
Elevation: Ranges from sea level to 6,288 feet at Mt. Washington
Climate: Moderate, with comfortable summers and long, snowy winters; weather in general is changeable and influenced by proximity to the Atlantic Ocean and the White Mountains
Admitted to Union: June 21, 1788 **Capital:** Concord
Head Official: Governor John Lynch (D) (until 2007)

Population

1980: 921,000
1990: 1,109,252
2000: 1,235,786
2004 estimate: 1,299,500
Percent change, 1990–2000: 11.4%
U.S. rank in 2004: 41st
Percent of residents born in state: 43.3% (2000)
Density: 137.8 people per square mile (2000)
2002 FBI Crime Index Total: 28,306

Racial and Ethnic Characteristics (2000)

White: 1,186,851
Black or African American: 9,035
American Indian and Alaska Native: 2,964
Asian: 15,931
Native Hawaiian and Pacific Islander: 371
Hispanic or Latino (may be of any race): 20,489
Other: 7,420

Age Characteristics (2000)

Population under 5 years old: 75,685
Population 5 to 19 years old: 268,480
Percent of population 65 years and over: 12%
Median age: 37.1 years (2000)

Vital Statistics

Total number of births (2003): 14,398
Total number of deaths (2003): 9,756 (infant deaths, 52)
AIDS cases reported through 2003: 530

Economy

Major industries: Manufacturing, tourism, trade, mining, agriculture
Unemployment rate: 3.4% (April 2005)
Per capita income: $34,703 (2003; U.S. rank: 7th)
Median household income: $55,166 (3-year average, 2001-2003)
Percentage of persons below poverty level: 6% (3-year average, 2001-2003)
Income tax rate: None on earned income; 5% on interest and dividends (with some exceptions); 7% business profits tax
Sales tax rate: None

Concord

The City in Brief

Founded: 1725 (incorporated, 1733)

Head Official: Mayor Michael L. Donovan (since 2003)

City Population
1980: 30,400
1990: 36,006
2000: 40,687
2003 estimate: 41,823
Percent change, 1990–2000: 10.3%
U.S. rank in 1990: 738th (State rank: 3rd)
U.S. rank in 2000: Not reported

Metropolitan Area Population (Merrimack County)
1980: 98,302
1990: 120,005
2000: 136,225
Percent change, 1990–2000: 13.3%

U.S. rank in 1990: 409th
U.S. rank in 2000: 277th

Area: 64 square miles (2000)
Elevation: 288 feet above sea level at the State House
Average Annual Temperature: 45.9° F
Average Annual Precipitation: 50.3 inches of rain; 65 inches of snow

Major Economic Sectors: Manufacturing, government, distribution, transportation
Unemployment Rate: 4% (New Hampshire, March 2005)
Per Capita Income: $21,976 (1999)
2004 ACCRA Average House Price: Not reported
2004 ACCRA Cost of Living Index: Not reported

2002 FBI Crime Index Total: Not reported

Major Colleges and Universities: Franklin Pierce Law Center; New Hampshire Technical Institute

Daily Newspaper: *Concord Monitor*

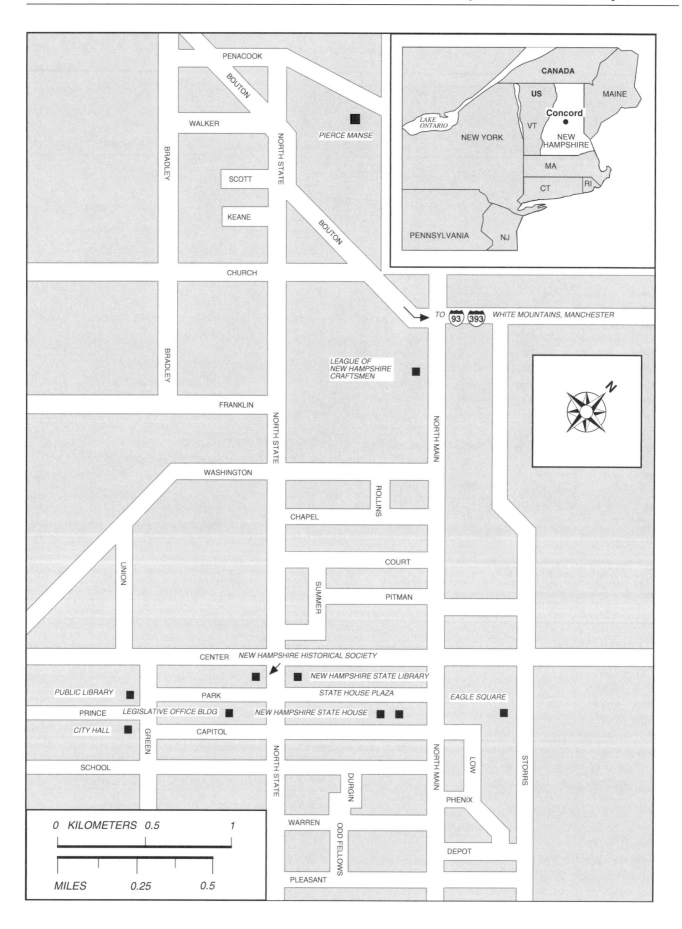

Introduction

The third largest city in New Hampshire, Concord is the state capital and a major manufacturing, distribution, and transportation center in the south-central section of the state. The home of the Concord stagecoach, U.S. President Franklin Pierce, and Christian Science founder Mary Baker Eddy, Concord is a city steeped in history. It is a modern city as well, with strong links to the finance and insurance industries. The spotlight shines on the city every four years when New Hampshire citizens vote in the first national presidential primary.

Geography and Climate

Concord, situated on the west bank of the Merrimack River, is located in south-central New Hampshire. Part of Merrimack County, Concord is 70 miles north of Boston and 18 miles north of Manchester, New Hampshire's largest city. Concord's terrain is hilly, with heavily wooded areas and many ponds and streams. Soil in the area is thin and rocky, suitable mostly for root crops such as potatoes.

Northwesterly winds are prevalent in the Concord area, providing cool dry air all year long. Temperatures are moderate in both summer and winter; average yearly snowfall is 65 inches. The short growing season calls for hardy, frost-resistant crops.

Area: 64 square miles (2000)

Elevation: 288 feet above sea level at the State House

Average Temperatures: January, 21.1° F; July, 70° F; annual average, 45.9° F

Average Annual Precipitation: 50.3 inches of rain; 65 inches of snow

History

Merrimack River Site Becomes State Capital

The site of present-day Concord was occupied as early as 1660 when a trading post operated on the west bank of the Merrimack River. The Pennacook tribe called the area "penna cook," which meant "crooked place" or "bend in the river." The Pennacooks and the area's European settlers coexisted for many years, sharing the bounty of the Merrimack River Valley. The real influx of European settlers began in 1727, when the Massachusetts Bay Colony gave permission for a settlement to be built called Pennacook Plantation. The town was incorporated by Massachusetts in 1733 and renamed Rumford. In 1741 New Hampshire challenged Massachusetts's dominion over Rumford and a series of border arguments ensued. The town was reincorporated by New Hampshire in 1765 and called Concord to mark the ending of the strife. The townspeople subsisted by farming, later supplementing their crops with a saw mill and a grist mill powered by the waters of the Merrimack River.

Partly because of its friendly relations with the neighboring Native American tribes, the town grew rapidly. By the time of the Revolutionary War, Concord could muster three companies of troops who saw service in the battles of Lexington, Concord (Massachusetts), and Bunker Hill. The town's war hero, General John Stark, is remembered with a statue in front of the State House. New Hampshire played a key role in U.S. history when it became the ninth state to ratify the Constitution in 1788. Only nine states were required and the signing is commemorated with a plaque at Walker and Boutin streets.

In 1808 Concord became the capital of New Hampshire and the site of the biennial meeting of the General Court, the largest state legislature in the country. At one time, the lower house sat more than four hundred legislators who were elected at the township level. Industry began to flourish after the War of 1812, when the newly dug Middlesex Canal facilitated water transport between Concord and Boston. This transportation-distribution link was strengthened when the rail lines began operating between the two cities in 1842.

Distribution Needs Shape Concord's Future

History of another sort was made in 1813 when wheelwright Lewis Downing opened his Concord wagon building business. After coach builder J. Stephen Abbot arrived to offer engineering improvements in 1827, the business grew rapidly. The Concord stagecoach became the vehicle of choice for the Wells Fargo Company, which hauled both freight and passengers to the American West. From 1826 until 1900, the Abbot and Downing Company built three thousand coaches in shops that occupied six acres and employed 275 people. Orders for the wagon were received from around the world, including Peru, Mexico, Australia, and South Africa. The Civil War created a further demand for Abbot and Downing's wagons, which were used as ambulances and to haul army supplies.

Two other industries that thrived in Concord in the mid-nineteenth century were granite quarrying and publishing. The granite quarries north of town yielded stone used in the facade of the State House and the Library of Congress in Washington, D.C. Printing was the forte of the Rumford

Press, at one time the third largest printer in the country. Among the prestigious magazines printed by Rumford were the *Atlantic Monthly* and *Reader's Digest.* Rumford Press grew to employ six hundred workers, whose products required the establishment of a separate branch of the U.S. Post Office to handle the extra mail.

Franklin Pierce, the only New Hampshireman elected to the Oval Office, served as the nation's fourteenth president. He lived in Concord from 1857 until his death in 1869. Mary Baker Eddy, founder of the Christian Science religion, was born five miles from Concord and later lived in the city. She built the granite First Church of Christ, Scientist in the Gothic Revival style in 1905. Concord's economy diversified as the years passed. By the mid-1900s, the city was established as a distribution point for dairy products and apples. Concord also supported growth in manufacturing, especially electrical products. Insurance and services are expected to remain important economic sectors into the twenty-first century.

Today's Concord, though by all accounts a small and still-charming city, thrives with a strong economic, educational, arts, and cultural climate. Downtown developments in the last years of the twentieth century and early in the new century, particularly in the form of tourist attractions and retail, have made Concord even more attractive to its residents and visitors.

Historical Information: New Hampshire Historical Society, 30 Park Street, Concord, NH 03301; telephone (603)228-6688

Population Profile

Metropolitan Area Residents
1980: 98,302
1990: 120,005
2000: 136,225
Percent change, 1990–2000: 13.3%
U.S. rank in 1990: 409th
U.S. rank in 2000: 277th

City Residents
1980: 30,400
1990: 36,006
2000: 40,687
2003 estimate: 41,823
Percent change, 1990–2000: 10.3%
U.S. rank in 1990: 738th (State rank: 3rd)
U.S. rank in 2000: Not reported

Density: 632.9 people per square mile (2000)

Racial and ethnic characteristics (2000)
White: 38,863
Black or African American: 421
American Indian and Alaska Native: 120
Asian: 598
Hispanic or Latino (may be of any race): 591
Other: 139

Percent of residents born in state: 54.2% (2000)

Age characteristics (2000)
Population under 5 years old: 2,373
Population 5 to 9 years old: 2,666
Population 10 to 14 years old: 2,717
Population 15 to 19 years old: 2,576
Population 20 to 24 years old: 2,420
Population 25 to 34 years old: 6,176
Population 35 to 44 years old: 7,235
Population 45 to 54 years old: 5,817
Population 55 to 59 years old: 1,854
Population 60 to 64 years old: 1,289
Population 65 to 74 years old: 2,355
Population 75 to 84 years old: 2,086
Population 85 years and older: 1,123
Median age: 37 years

Births (2003)
Total number: 445

Deaths (2001)
Total number: 400

Money income (1999)
Per capita income: $21,976
Median household income: $42,447
Total households: 16,325

Number of households with income of . . .
less than $10,000: 1,198
$10,000 to $14,999: 998
$15,000 to $24,999: 2,017
$25,000 to $34,999: 2,191
$35,000 to $49,999: 3,183
$50,000 to $74,999: 3,552
$75,000 to $99,999: 1,788
$100,000 to $149,999: 899
$150,000 to $199,999: 251
$200,000 or more: 248

Percent of families below poverty level: 6.2% (16.3% of which were female householder families with related children under 5 years)

2002 FBI Crime Index Total: Not reported

Municipal Government

Concord operates with a council-manager form of government. The mayor is elected to a two year term. Four councilors are elected at large while ten are elected by ward. The at-large councilors serve staggered four-year terms while ward councilors serve for two years. The council appoints a professional city manager who serves under a contract and is responsible to the city council. Local government is said to encourage industrial growth.

Head Official: Mayor Michael L. Donovan (since 2003; term expires November 2005)

Total Number of City Employees: 476 (2005)

City Information: City Manager, Administration Department, City Hall, 41 Green Street, Concord, NH 03301; telephone (603)225-8570

Economy

Major Industries and Commercial Activity

Concord, the capital of New Hampshire, is a major distribution, industrial, and transportation hub. As the state capital and county seat for Merrimack County, Concord is headquarters to numerous state, county, local and federal agencies. It is also the site of several major law firms and professional agencies.

While government forms a portion of its economic base, its proximity to highways and railways makes it an excellent site for distributing goods. Many of the products manufactured in Concord are known and used worldwide. The fastest growing segment of the economic base is the service industry, comprising education, finance, and medical services.

More than 5,000 people in are employed in the delivery of healthcare services in Concord, making it one of the largest concentration of healthcare providers in the state. Tourism is important to the city and the region; the New Hampshire International Speedway in nearby Loudon brings approximately $50 million in tourism dollars to Concord annually.

Items and goods produced: printed goods; mobile and modular structures; electric components; electrical instruments; non-ferrous foundry products; heat treatment equipment; architectural and structural granite; communication testing equipment; dictating supplies and equipment; belting, brass, and leather products

Incentive Programs—New and Existing Companies

Local programs—The State of New Hampshire, which levies no state sales or income tax, is considered one of the most favorable climates for doing business in the nation. Because so much is provided at the state level, few incentives are offered at the city-town level. In fact, by state law, New Hampshire cities are prohibited from offering tax breaks to private industry. However, cities such as Concord do aid businesses indirectly by helping to market industrial sites and by promoting available energy/utility savings programs.

State programs—The state's incentives include no general sales or use tax, no general personal income tax, no capital gains tax, no inventory tax, no property tax on machinery or equipment, one of the lowest unemployment insurance rates in the country, investment tax incentives, job tax credits, and research & development tax incentives. In 2004 the State of New Hampshire instituted the Community Reinvestment Opportunity Program (CROP), which offers tax credits that may be used against business profit taxes and business enterprise taxes. Qualifying CROP projects must create new jobs as well as expand the state economic base.

Job training programs—The Small Business Development Center, which is funded by the Small Business Association, the State of New Hampshire, and the University of New Hampshire, offers management counseling, training, and resource information to the state's small business community through six sub-centers. The New Hampshire Employment Program (NHEP) aids individuals in obtaining financial aid to prepare for and find employment. The NHEP On-The-Job Training Program offers employers incentives to hire and train eligible applicants.

Development Projects

The City, in conjunction with the Capital Regional Development Corporation (CRDC), the Greater Concord Chamber of Commerce, and other state and federal agencies, recently completed construction of the Corporate Center at Horseshoe Pond. Through the creation of a $5 million Tax Increment Finance (TIF) District, the city was able to acquire and develop the land, which was then sold to the CRDC, who cleaned up the land and marketed parcels to developers. With $4.4 million in private donations, the city was able to construct the Grappone Conference Center.

The cities of Concord and Penacook have partnered as part of a Neighborhood Revitalization Project with a plan that focuses on enhancing quality of life within the two communities. The Revitalization Plan utilizes input from residents and builds partnerships between the city, residents, and civic minded organizations.

Economic Development Information: Concord Economic Development Department, City Hall, 41 Green Street, Concord, NH 03301; telephone (603)225-8595; Capital Region Development Council, 91 North State Street, Concord, NH 03301-0664; telephone (603)228-1872

Commercial Shipping

Concord, located at the hub of several major New England interstate highways, is a center for motor freight activity. Ten carriers service the area. The New England Southern Railroad provides freight service. Freight is also handled at the Concord Municipal Airport, about two miles from downtown.

Labor Force and Employment Outlook

Concord's labor force is described as competent, dedicated, plentiful, skilled, available, stable, and with excellent education and training. Unemployment insurance costs remain relatively low. Recently, Concord was ranked fourth in terms of per capita income in "The New England Rating Guide to Life in America's Small Cities."

The service industry, the fastest growing segment of Concord's economy, is anchored by education, finance, medical services, and insurance. Concord is the headquarters of six insurance companies and the site of several banks. It also is one of the few communities in the state with both industrial park space and construction sites available.

The following is a summary of data regarding the area labor force, 2004 annual averages (Nashua, NH-MA MSA).

Size of nonagricultural labor force: 129,100

Number of workers employed in . . .
   construction and mining: 5,900
   manufacturing: 26,000
   trade, transportation and utilities: 30,500
   information: 2,000
   financial activities: 8,000
   professional and business services: 12,700
   educational and health services: 15,300
   leisure and hospitality: 10,300
   other services: 4,500
   government: 14,000

Average hourly earnings of workers employed in manufacturing (Nashua, NH-MA MSA): $15.97

Unemployment rate (New Hampshire): 4.0% (March 2005)

Largest employers	*Number of employees*
Concord Hospital	2,700
Steeplegate Regional Mall	1,100
Jefferson-Pilot Financial	618
Cigna Healthcare	400

Largest employers	*Number of employees*
Genesis Eldercare Network	375
St. Paul's School	315
Concord Litho	225
Riverside Millwork (RIVCO)	175
Beede Electrical Instrument Co.	107

Cost of Living

New Hampshire depends more upon real property taxes for revenue than most states as it does not have general income, sales, or use taxes. Substantial revenue is collected from taxes on gasoline, tobacco, alcohol, and parimutuel betting.

The following is a summary of data regarding several key cost of living factors in the Concord area.

2004 ACCRA Average House Price: Not reported

2004 ACCRA Cost of Living Index: Not reported

State income tax rate: none on salaries and wages of residents; limited tax upon interest and dividends received by individuals, trusts, estates and partners in excess of $2,400. There is a $10 "Resident Tax" on all persons between 18 and 60 years of age with some exceptions. Concord has passed an ordinance eliminating this tax for residents of the city.

State sales tax rate: None (business profits tax is 8.5%)

Local income tax rate: None

Local sales tax rate: None

Property tax rate: $28.07 (Union) or $31.53 (Merrimack Valley) per $1,000 (2003)

Economic Information: Concord Economic Development Department, City Hall, 41 Green Street, Concord, NH 03301; telephone (603)225-8595. New Hampshire Department of Resources and Economic Development, 172 Pembroke Road, Concord, NH 03302; telephone (603)271-2411

Education and Research

Elementary and Secondary Schools

Notable among the offerings of the Concord School District are the Artist-in-the-Schools Program, which brings professionals into the classroom to teach their crafts, and the Environmental Education Program, which is supplemented by a centrally located Science Center and the thirty-acre White Farms classroom. The Concord Regional Vocational Center is located on the premises of Concord High School. Concord High School/Area 11 Vocational Center offers training in the requirements of high-technology companies. Every classroom in the district, from Kindergarten through 12th grade, is equipped with Internet access.

The following is a summary of data regarding the Concord public schools as of the 2003–2004 school year.

Total enrollment: 5,358

Number of facilities
  elementary schools: 9
  junior high/middle schools: 1
  senior high schools: 1

Student/teacher ratio: 15.5:1

Teacher salaries (2003-2004)
  minimum: $29,757
  maximum: $52,373

Funding per pupil: $8,593

Concord's parochial facilities include two Catholic schools (one elementary/junior high school and one high school) and a Christian school. Its Episcopal school, St. Paul's Preparatory, is one of the most famous feeder schools for Harvard, Yale, and Princeton universities.

Public Schools Information: Administrative Offices, Concord School District, 16 Rumford Street, Concord, NH 03301; telephone (603)225-0811

Colleges and Universities

Concord is home to the Franklin Pierce Law Center (Franklin Pierce College's Continuing Education campus) and the New Hampshire Technical Institute. Founded in 1973, the Franklin Pierce Law Center's aim is to help students of diverse backgrounds develop as attorneys in a non-competitive atmosphere. The center promotes a strong sense of community responsibility in its graduates. The New Hampshire Technical Institute, a public two-year college, offers associate's degrees in engineering, business, health, and computer science. Manchester-based Hesser College offers courses at its Concord campus in the Gateway Office Center in South Concord. The college is best known for its criminal justice program, in which graduates go on to work in law enforcement, probation and parole or corrections. Other degree programs offered include business, early childhood education and computer sciences.

Libraries and Research Centers

The Concord Public Library system consists of the main library, the Penacook Branch Library, and a bookmobile. The system holds more than 150,000 volumes, which include an extensive periodical collection, DVDs and video recordings, and audio books. The Concord Room at the main library is a research facility with materials about local history. Framed prints, reproductions, and photographs are displayed throughout the library. The library has an extensive children's collection and a youth program promotes reading by the young. Special services for cardholders include interlibrary loans and Internet training.

Located in Concord and boasting more than 500,000 volumes are the New Hampshire State Library, the oldest in the country, and the State Supreme Court Law Library. The Franklin Pierce Law Center Library adds another 220,000 volumes to the area's overall legal holdings. Collections in the State Library cover transportation, pollution, public utilities, and statistical and historical resources. Other special interest libraries in Concord include the Governor's Office of Energy and Community Service library, the New Hampshire Historical Society Library, which specializes in genealogy and rare documents, and the Patent, Trademark and Copyright Research Foundation Library. The Ohrstrom Library on the campus of St. Paul's School is housed in a graceful building that combines Gothic influences with the style of Frank Lloyd Wright. Research centers in the city include New Hampshire Chapter of Nature Conservancy research library which focuses on rare plants and animals, and the PTC Research Foundation of Franklin Pierce Law Center which studies practical problems dealing with industrial and intellectual property.

Public Library Information: Concord Public Library, 45 Green Street, Concord, NH 03301; telephone (603)225-8670

Health Care

Concord is a leading health center for central New Hampshire, providing extensive medical and mental health facilities. Concord Hospital, a regional general hospital, is licensed for 205 beds and is a Level II Regional Trauma Center. Its staff of 360 active, honorary, and consulting doctors includes physicians, surgeons, and dentists. Services are provided in 50 specialties; special centers affiliated with the hospital are the Breast Care Center, Center for Cardiac Care, Center for Orthopaedic Care, the Payson Center for Cancer Care, The Family Place, and a walk-in urgent care center. New Hampshire Hospital, a state mental health institution, specializes in inpatient care of the mentally ill. The hospital has been a pioneer in the development of special treatment programs for mentally ill children. HealthSouth Rehabilitation Hospital provides inpatient and outpatient therapy and Riverbend Community Mental Health, Inc. serves both individuals and families.

Health Care Information: Concord Hospital, 250 Pleasant Street, Concord, NH 03301; telephone (603)225-2711

The Pierce Manse was the home of former president Franklin Pierce from 1842 to 1848.

Recreation

Sightseeing

Capitol Square contains most of Concord's public buildings, including the State Capitol, a state office building, the state library, the Concord Public Library, the New Hampshire Historical Society, City Hall, the post office, and several churches. The State Capitol, the nation's oldest, features New Hampshire granite and Vermont marble. The legislature still meets in the original chambers of this 1819 neoclassical structure, which also houses 157 portraits of famous native sons. Among the statues and historical markers in the square flanking the Capitol is the Memorial Arch, erected in 1891 to honor the state's soldiers and sailors.

The Pierce Manse, the Concord home of President Franklin Pierce, was built in 1838; it has been restored and is maintained by the "Pierce Brigade." The Conservation Center demonstrates the many uses of passive solar energy and wood-heating energy through a number of exhibits. Among its attractions are an envelope room, a wood-chip gasifier furnace, and fiberglass water tubes.

The Canterbury Shaker Village allows visitors to experience the Shaker way of life at the country's oldest Shaker community. Among its 25 original and reconstructed buildings are an eighteenth-century Meetinghouse and Dwellinghouse, both intact and on their original sites.

The Christa McAuliffe Planetarium, named for America's first teacher in space, offers expeditions through space at a 92-seat theater with a domed screen featuring the wraparound images and sound.

Arts and Culture

The Capitol Center for the Arts presents touring theatrical groups, dance companies, and musical acts. Concord City Auditorium is home to the Concord Community Concerts and the Walker Lecture Series. The New Hampshire Philharmonic Orchestra, a resident professional group, performs classical works at concerts in the Concord and Manchester area. The Community Players of Concord, a non-profit performing theater troupe, stages its offerings at Concord's City Auditorium. Danse Papillon/Petit Papillon presents holiday performances locally and throughout New England. The historic Never's Second Regiment Band, in continuous existence since 1861, plays military marches, overtures, musicals, pop tunes, and symphonic works. This semiprofessional performing band plays at parks and theaters throughout the state. Other area performing arts groups include the Youth Symphony and the Concord Chorale. The Granite State Symphony Orchestra, which plays at the Capitol Center for the Arts, is comprised of the state's finest professional musicians who play classical music at a cost accessible to people of all ages.

The Museum of New Hampshire History has exhibitions about the state's landscape, people, and traditions. From the world-famous Concord Coach—the stagecoach that won the American West—to superb nineteenth-century White Mountain paintings and rare examples of New Hampshire-made furniture, more than four centuries of Granite State history unfold in its award-winning exhibitions.

The prestigious League of New Hampshire Craftsmen makes Concord its headquarters. Founded in 1932 to encourage the preservation of dying home arts, the League now is nationally recognized, and its craft items are eagerly sought by retailers. The League maintains its own stores throughout the state to sell the items made by members, who are local artisans. Craft items range from glassware and ceramics to leather and wood products, textiles, jewelry, prints, furniture, and jams.

Arts and Culture Information: Community Development Department, 41 Green Street, Concord, NH 03301; telephone (603)225-8595

Festivals and Holidays

More than 80 regional artists and craftspeople display, demonstrate, and sell their wares at the annual Merrimack County Artisans Craft Show in April. The Summer Band Festival, which runs from June through August, features the Historic Never's Second Regiment Band in performances of military and symphonic music. The New Hampshire Folk Festival is held on the last Sunday in August in Concord. Begun in 1958, the August Antiques Show in Concord is cosponsored by the New Hampshire Historical Society and features displays and sales by 75 dealers. Other antique shows include the Tri-State Collectors' Exhibition in mid-October and the April Concord Antiques Fair. Race Fever takes over downtown Concord in early July. The annual Arts and Crafts Fair, held at Mt. Sunapee State Park in Newbury the first week in August, showcases the works of more than 300 craftspeople and artists. The annual Concord Christmas Tree Lighting Event happens at the State House Plaza in November, with a concert, petting zoo, hayrides, a visit from Santa, and other family-friendly activities. New Hampshire's New Year's Eve Celebration of the Arts is held in Concord. Performances of all kinds are held at 30 different sites throughout the city, culminating in a fireworks display.

Sports for the Spectator

Concord is the site of two excellent sports facilities, which makes it a natural choice to host statewide sports meets. Everett Arena, with its indoor ice rink, sees much high-school level hockey competition, while Memorial Field, with its series of playing fields, hosts football, baseball, and track meets. From April through October, area auto racing enthusiasts are attracted to the New Hampshire International Speedway, located in nearby Louden. The 70,000-seat speedway is the largest in New England.

Sports for the Participant

Concord, an hour's drive from the Atlantic coastline to the east and a 90-minute drive from the White Mountains to the north, is a sports enthusiast's paradise. Swimming, fishing, and water sports are popular along New Hampshire's eighteen-mile stretch of ocean coastline, as well as in neighboring Maine and Massachusetts. Premium downhill and cross-country skiing, as well as camping, hiking, and rock climbing can be enjoyed in the White Mountain resort area. More than 1,000 acres of publicly-owned land have been reserved for the future open-space and recreational needs of the community.

Within the city limits are more than 300 acres of well-equipped parks and playgrounds. One municipal and two private golf courses are located in Concord; the city maintains three public swimming pools. Hikers enjoy an extensive trail system. The city's Recreation Department offers tennis, swim, and archery lessons, as well as youth soccer and track and field teams. The Everett Arena hosts an active hockey team and sponsors summer training in the sport.

Shopping and Dining

Concord's main shopping area consists of 10 blocks along Main Street surrounding Eagle Square Park and several adjacent streets downtown. Steeplegate Mall, anchored by The Bon-Ton, Circuit City, JCPenney, and Old Navy, has more than 75 stores and specialty shops. Other shopping plazas in the city feature department, discount, and specialty stores. The most famous of Concord's stores is the Concord League Gallery, operated by the League of New Hampshire Craftsmen, which offers crafts fashioned by local artisans. The shop is housed in the five-story former Eagle Hotel and Tavern on Main Street.

New England fare is the standard offering at most of Concord's restaurants, along with fish and seafood fresh from the nearby Atlantic coast, and apple pie sweetened with New Hampshire's own maple syrup. A variety of ethnic cuisine, including Asian, Italian, and Mexican, can also be found.

Visitor Information: Greater Concord Chamber of Commerce, 40 Commercial Street, Concord, NH 03301; telephone (603)224-2508

Convention Facilities

The new Grappone Conference Center, adjacent to the Marriott Courtyard, has more than 9,400 square feet of meeting space, including seven meeting rooms and the Granite Ballroom. Other convention and meeting facilities are available at various hotels and restaurants throughout the area.

Transportation

Approaching the City

Local air carriers use facilities at the Concord Municipal Airport, located approximately two miles east of downtown. Flight training is offered at the airport, which also serves as a Federal Aviation Administration Weather Service Station. The nearby Manchester Airport offers daily passenger service on nine airlines. Full international and domestic service is available at Logan International Airport, 75 miles to the southeast in Boston, Massachusetts.

Intercity bus lines traveling through Concord include Vermont Transit, Greyhound, and Concord Trailways. Concord is located at the junction of Interstates 93, 89, 393, and New Hampshire Route 4. State highways running through the area include 3A, 9, 13, 36, 103, and 106. I-93 is the major north-south artery, while I-89 branches to the northwest, as do highways 3 and 4. Running east-west are highways 106 and 202.

Traveling in the City

Concord's main business district occupies a seven-block area between Main and State streets. The state government area dominates the business center with several buildings at Capitol and Main streets. Its compact downtown makes Concord an eminently walkable city; however, taxicabs are also available. Concord Area Transit (CAT) provides bus service through downtown Concord and surrounding areas, Monday through Friday.

Communications

Newspapers and Magazines

The *Concord Monitor* is published daily. New content is also posted daily on the paper's website, which also includes a database of archived articles and Internet-only features. Special interest publications originating in Concord include the *New Hampshire Bar Journal; Forest Notes,* a quarterly forestry magazine; and *WomenWise,* a quarterly women's health publication.

Television and Radio

In addition to tuning in one local commercial and one local educational channel, television viewers in Concord enjoy cable programming. Several commercial television channels from Boston and Manchester are also received in Concord. Six AM and FM radio stations' signals originate in Concord, including a National Public Radio affiliate.

Media Information: The *Concord Monitor,* PO Box 1177, Concord, NH 03302-1177; telephone (603)224-5301

Concord Online

Capital Regional Development Council. Available www .crdc-nh.com

The City of Concord home page. Available www.ci.concord .nh.us

Concord Chamber of Commerce. Available www.Concord nhchamber.com

Concord Hospital. Available www.concordhospital.org

Concord Monitor. Available www.concordmonitor.com

Concord Public Library. Available www.onconcord.com/ library

Concord School District. Available www.concord.k12.nh.us

New Hampshire Department of Resources and Economic Development. Available www.dred.state.nh.us

New Hampshire Historical Society. Available www .nhhistory.org

Selected Bibliography

Cary, Lorene, *Black Ice* (New York: Knopf: Distributed by Random House, 1991)

Concord, N.H. City History Commission, *History of Concord, New Hampshire, From the Original Grant in Seventeen Hundred and Twenty-Five to the Opening of the Twentieth Century* (Concord, N.H., The Rumford Press, 1903)

Wiseman, David, *Thimbles: A Novel* (Boston: Houghton Mifflin, 1982)

Manchester

The City in Brief

Founded: 1722 (incorporated, 1846)

Head Official: Mayor Robert A. Baines (since 2000)

City Population
  1980: 90,936
  1990: 99,567
  2000: 107,006
  2003 estimate: 108,871
  Percent change, 1990–2000: 7.5%
  U.S. rank in 1980: 192nd
  U.S. rank in 1990: 199th (State rank: 1st)
  U.S. rank in 2000: 239th (State rank: 1st)

Metropolitan Area Population (PMSA)
  1990: 173,783
  2000: 198,378
  Percent change, 1990–2000: 14.2%

U.S. rank in 1990: 5th (CMSA)
U.S. rank in 2000: 7th (CMSA)

Area: 33 square miles (2000)
Elevation: 346 feet above sea level
Average Annual Temperature: 45.5° F
Average Annual Precipitation: 39.87 inches of rain; 64 inches of snow

Major Economic Sectors: Manufacturing, wholesale and retail trade, services
Unemployment Rate: 4.2% (February 2005)
Per Capita Income: $21,244 (1999)
2004 ACCRA Average House Price: Not reported
2004 ACCRA Cost of Living Index: Not reported

2002 FBI Crime Index Total: 3,545

Major Colleges and Universities: St. Anselm College; University of New Hampshire at Manchester

Daily Newspaper: *New Hampshire Union Leader*

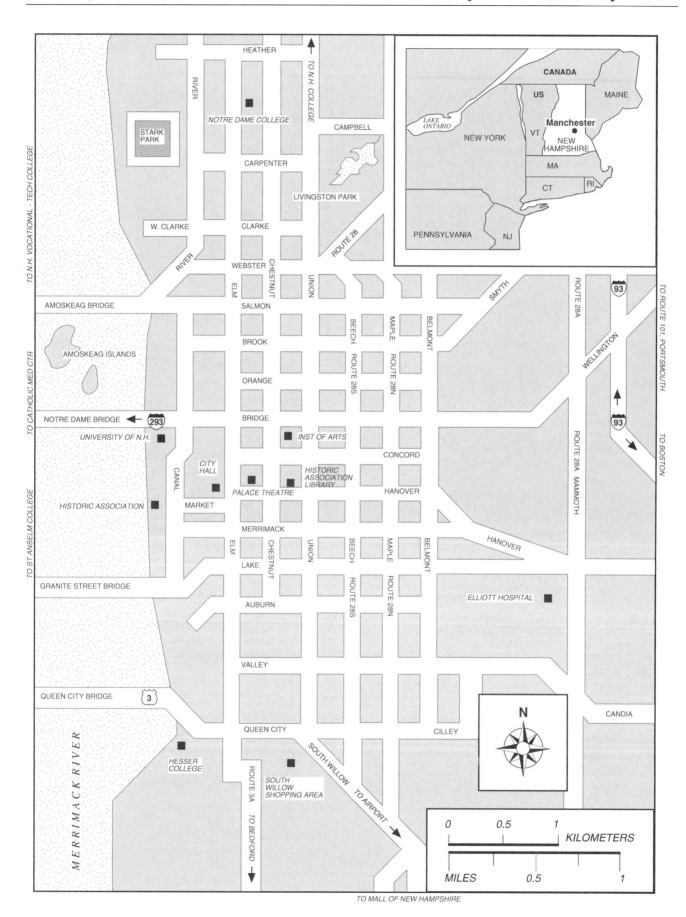

Introduction

Manchester, once the quintessential company town, has emerged from the shadow of the gigantic Amoskeag Manufacturing Company to become New England's largest city north of Boston. With a diversified economy and a growing population, Manchester is considered one of the best places to do business in the United States.

Geography and Climate

The largest city in the three northern-most New England states, Manchester straddles the Merrimack River 20 miles north of the New Hampshire-Massachusetts border and 60 miles north of Boston. Manchester is located in a valley surrounded by woods, lakes, the Amoskeag Falls, and the Presidential Chain of the White Mountains. The city, located in Hillsborough County, is the center of a developing urban corridor with Concord to the north and Nashua to the south.

Northeasterly winds contribute to Manchester's long, snowy winters (average snowfall is 64 inches) and its mild summers. Humidity is moderate all year long.

Area: 33 square miles (2000)

Elevation: Ranges from 110 to 570 feet above sea level; mean elevation, 346 feet above sea level

Average Temperatures: January, 19.7° F; July, 70° F; annual average, 45.5° F

Average Annual Precipitation: 39.87 inches of rain; 64 inches of snow

History

Amoskeag Falls Support Industry

The abundant river fish and forest game in the Merrimack River Valley attracted the attention of the Native American Pennacooks long before the European traders and trappers arrived in the valley in the early 1700s. The Pennacooks called the river falls area "Namoskeag," meaning "place of much fish." A permanent white settlement was established in 1722 by Scots-Irish Presbyterians who saw the manufacturing potential of the falls, which came to be called the Amoskeag Falls. Until their factories were built, they subsisted on fishing and logging. They later used the 85-foot drop of the Amoskeag Falls to power their textile mills. First known as Old Harry's Town, the settlement changed names when it changed hands, becoming Tyngstown in 1735 when it was absorbed by the Massachusetts Bay Colony. The town was rechristened Derryfield in 1751.

Benjamin Prichard selected the area for the construction of the new nation's first textile mills on the banks of the Merrimack River in 1805. Derryfield changed its name again in 1810, taking the name of Manchester, after England's industrial giant. The proponent of this final name change was Samuel Blodgett, who visited England and later engineered the building of a canal around the Amoskeag Falls. The canal linked Manchester with Boston, opening the way for great industrial expansion.

In 1831, a group of merchants purchased the failing Amoskeag Cotton and Woolen Factory and reopened as the Amoskeag Manufacturing Company. At its height, the company operated 700,000 spindles and 23,000 looms, shipping nearly five million yards of cloth each week. The millyard occupied more than eight million square feet of floor space and employed 17,000 people. Amoskeag's operating philosophy was one of benevolent paternalism as the company built homes, schools, and hospitals for its employees. The company also radically altered the makeup of Manchester's population when it invited thousands of French-Canadians to work in its mills. While best known for its textiles, the Amoskeag yards did produce other products, including locomotives. In the second half of the nineteenth century, Amoskeag and Manchester's other mills wove enough cloth each year to encircle the world twice.

Mills Decline, Economy Diversifies

Prosperity continued until the Great Depression of the 1930s. National financial woes, labor unrest, aging machinery, and competition from less expensive southern labor combined to bring about Amoskeag Manufacturing Company's demise. In 1935 it declared bankruptcy. However, the operation was saved. This time, a group of businessmen raised $5 million, purchased the yards, renamed the concern Amoskeag Industries, and developed a plan to diversify Manchester's economy.

By the 1980s Manchester had grown into New Hampshire's largest city. New industries led to new building, including the renovation of the millyard into smaller manufacturing units. Following an economic slowdown during the early 1990s, the rest of the decade saw Manchester's economy turn around dramatically. Recent years have seen the continued development of the downtown area, with the building of the Verizon Wireless Arena, Riverfront Stadium, and new shops and restaurants.

Historical Information: Manchester Historic Association, 129 Amherst Street, Manchester, NH 03101-1809; telephone (603) 622-7531

Population Profile

Metropolitan Area Residents (PMSA)

1990: 173,783
2000: 198,378
Percent change, 1990–2000: 14.2%
U.S. rank in 1990: 5th (CMSA)
U.S. rank in 2000: 7th (CMSA)

City Residents

1980: 90,936
1990: 99,567
2000: 107,006
2003 estimate: 108,871
Percent change, 1990–2000: 7.5%
U.S. rank in 1980: 192nd
U.S. rank in 1990: 199th (State rank: 1st)
U.S. rank in 2000: 239th (State rank: 1st)

Density: 3,270.3 people per square mile (2000)

Racial and ethnic characteristics (2000)
White: 98,178
Black or African American: 2,246
American Indian and Alaska Native: 326
Asian: 2,487
Native Hawaiian and Pacific Islander: 38
Hispanic or Latino (may be of any race): 4,944
Other: 1,880

Percent of residents born in state: 56.5% (2000)

Age characteristics (2000)
Population under 5 years old: 7,162
Population 5 to 9 years old: 7,171
Population 10 to 14 years old: 7,064
Population 15 to 19 years old: 6,693
Population 20 to 24 years old: 7,419
Population 25 to 34 years old: 18,106
Population 35 to 44 years old: 17,636
Population 45 to 54 years old: 13,832
Population 55 to 59 years old: 4,506
Population 60 to 64 years old: 3,588
Population 65 to 74 years old: 6,564
Population 75 to 84 years old: 5,415
Population 85 years and over: 1,850
Median age: 34.9 years

Births (2003)
Total number: 1,559

Deaths (2001)
Total number: 991

Money income (1999)
Per capita income: $21,244
Median household income: $40,774
Total households: 44,254

Number of households with income of . . .
less than $10,000: 3,996
$10,000 to $14,999: 2,649
$15,000 to $24,999: 5,961
$25,000 to $34,999: 5,998
$35,000 to $49,999: 8,288
$50,000 to $74,999: 9,672
$75,000 to $99,999: 4,329
$100,000 to $149,999: 2,225
$150,000 to $199,999: 521
$200,000 or more: 615

Percent of families below poverty level: 7.7% (51.3% of which were female householder families with related children under 5 years)

2002 FBI Crime Index Total: 3,545

Municipal Government

The City of Manchester is governed by a Board of Mayor and Aldermen. Each alder represents one ward, with two at-large. In non-partisan contests, the mayor is elected to a two-year term; the alders are elected to simultaneous two-year terms.

Head Official: Mayor Robert A. Baines (since 2000; current term expires 2006)

Total Number of City Employees: 1,280 (2000)

City Information: Mayor's Office, City of Manchester, One City Hall Plaza, Manchester, NH 03101; telephone (603)624-6500

Economy

Major Industries and Commercial Activity

Once a single-industry town dependent on the textile industry, Manchester has diversified its economy to include manufacturing (more than 200 manufacturing firms are located there), wholesale and retail trade, information processing, and the service industry. More than 85 percent of the workforce is involved in sales, finance, and service companies. Manchester is considered the major insurance and financial center north of Boston, housing the area's largest savings and commercial institutions. The city is also the northeastern states' principal distribution center.

The City of Manchester provides assistance to businesses interested in locating or expanding in the area through the Manchester Economic Development Office (MEDO).

Items and goods produced: knitting and textile machinery, leather goods, electrical and electronic components, automobile accessories, and plastic, lumber, metal and wood products

Incentive Programs—New and Existing Companies

Local programs—The State of New Hampshire, which levies no state sales or income tax, is considered one of the most favorable climates for doing business in the nation. Because so much is provided at the state level, few incentives are offered at the city-town level. In fact, by state law, New Hampshire cities are prohibited from offering tax breaks to private industry. However, cities such as Manchester do aid businesses indirectly by helping to market and develop industrial sites. In addition, Manchester's banks are willing to supply financing to all deserving enterprises. The non-profit Manchester Development Corporation may make loans to promote the economic development of the city. The city has designated the Economic Development Office as administrator of a revolving loan fund to provide "gap" or secondary financing for businesses locating within Manchester.

State programs— The state's incentives include no general sales or use tax, no general personal income tax, no capital gains tax, no inventory tax, no property tax on machinery or equipment, one of the lowest unemployment insurance rates in the country, investment tax incentives, job tax credits, and research & development tax incentives. In 2004, the State of New Hampshire instituted the Community Reinvestment Opportunity Program (CROP), which offers tax credits that may be used against business profit taxes and business enterprise taxes. Qualifying CROP projects must create new jobs as well as expand the state economic base.

Job training programs— The Small Business Development Center, which is funded by the Small Business Association, the State of New Hampshire, and the University of New Hampshire, offers management counseling, training, and resource information to the state's small business community through six sub-centers. The New Hampshire Employment Program (NHEP) aids individuals in obtaining financial aid to prepare for and find employment. The NHEP On-The-Job Training Program offers employers incentives to hire and train eligible applicants.

Development Projects

The Granite Street widening project is a $19 million joint effort between the City of Manchester and the New Hamp-

shire Department of Transportation. When complete in 2007, downtown Manchester will see improvements to traffic flow as well as access and safety improvements. In 2005 the city broke ground for the development of the Northwest Business Park. The development of 140 acres on Northwest Drive off of Hackett Hill Road will provide for increased business facilities, increased tax revenues, and new jobs. The estimated $20 million development is scheduled for completion in 2017. Construction is also underway on Manchester Place Apartments—a $40 million high-end residential apartment complex that will include 204 residential units, a 300-car parking facility, and 5,200 square feet of retail space. Recently completed projects include the $24.3 million Riverfront Stadium, home of the New Hampshire Fisher Cats AA baseball team; an upgraded water treatment facility; and $2.725 million worth of upgrades to the McQuade building, an historic downtown landmark.

Economic Development Information: Manchester Economic Development Office, One City Hall Plaza, Room 110, Manchester, NH 03101; telephone (603)624-6505. New Hampshire Small Business Development Center, 33 Commercial Street, Manchester, NH 03101-1796; telephone (603)624-2000

Commercial Shipping

Manchester, located on the main line of the Guilford Rail Systems, maintains excellent freight service south to Boston and north to Montreal and connecting lines. A large fleet of commercial trucks is also available for shipping goods to all parts of the country. Air freight service is offered at Manchester Airport, the state's major airport. Air freight lines and U.S. Customs service are also available; the industrial area surrounding the airport has been designated a Foreign Trade Zone. Daily delivery service includes Federal Express, United Parcel Service, and DHL. Since the Merrimack River is not navigable, Manchester is not a port city; however, the Port of New Hampshire in Portsmouth is located 45 minutes east of Manchester.

Labor Force and Employment Outlook

Manchester's computer and other high-tech industries and its financial and professional services have contributed to the growth of Manchester's economy since the late 1980s. Manchester's labor force is described as industrious and the city boasts one of the best records in the nation in terms of hours lost through strikes. In 2005, *Inc. Magazine* ranked Manchester the 21st best city (out of 274 cities ranked) in which to do business.

The following is a summary of data regarding the Manchester metropolitan area labor force, 2004 annual averages.

Size of nonagricultural labor force: 99,300

Number of workers employed in . . .
    construction and mining: 5,300
    manufacturing: 9,500
    trade, transportation and utilities: 20,800
    information: 3,300
    financial activities: 8,800
    professional and business services: 12,000
    educational and health services: 16,000
    leisure and hospitality: 8,300
    other services: 4,100
    government: 11,200

Average hourly earnings of production workers employed in manufacturing: $17.38

Unemployment rate: 4.2% (February 2005)

Largest employers (2004)	Number of employees
Elliot Hospital	3,875
Verizon Communications	1,750
Catholic Medical Center	1,700
Public Service of New Hampshire	1,250
Citizens Bank	1,225
Banknorth	1,153
Filene's	1,050
Anthem Blue Cross & Blue Shield	940
Southern NH University	700
Associated Grocers of NE, Inc.	608

Cost of Living

The cost of living is reasonable in New Hampshire. The lack of a sales tax stretches residents' purchasing dollars. Having one of the lowest crime rates in the country, as well as one of the lowest auto theft rates, keeps insurance rates affordable.

The following is a summary of data regarding several key cost of living factors in the Manchester area.

2004 ACCRA Average House Price: Not reported

2004 ACCRA Cost of Living Index: Not reported

State income tax rate: None (business profits tax is 8.5%)

State sales tax rate: None on salaries and wages of residents; limited tax upon interest and dividends received by individuals, trusts, estates and partners in excess of $2,400. There is a $10.00 ''Resident Tax'' on all persons between 18 and 60 years of age with some exceptions. Concord has passed an ordinance eliminating this tax for residents of the city.

Local income tax rate: None

Local sales tax rate: None

Property tax rate: $27.92 per $1,000 of assessed valuation (2005)

Economic Information: Greater Manchester Chamber of Commerce, 889 Elm Street, Manchester, NH 03101; telephone (603)666-6600

Education and Research

Elementary and Secondary Schools

The Manchester School District is the state of New Hampshire's oldest and largest public school system. The district's special services include a comprehensive special education program for students from pre-school through high school, as well as programs for the gifted, handicapped, and adults. An English as a Second Language program serves students with limited English proficiency. Music and arts programs, athletics, and community service opportunities are available at the middle and high school levels. Manchester also benefits from a $7 million state-funded vocational center that trains high school students from Manchester and two neighboring towns. The Manchester School of Technology provides vocational training to high school students.

The following is a summary of data regarding the city of Manchester School District as of the 2003–2004 school year.

Total enrollment: 17,655

Number of facilities
    elementary schools: 15
    junior high/middle schools: 4
    senior high schools: 3
    other: 1

Student/teacher ratio: 14.9:1

Teacher salaries
    average: $44,814

Funding per pupil: $6,943

The city's private schools include the Derryfield School, a private co-educational school that enrolls more than 350 students in grades 6 through 12. Schools with a religious affiliation include the Manchester Jewish Community School, Trinity High School, and schools affiliated with the Diocese of Manchester.

Public Schools Information: City of Manchester School District, 196 Bridge Street, Manchester, NH 03104-4985; telephone (603)624-6300

Colleges and Universities

Manchester's institutions of higher learning offer a mix of liberal arts education and technical training. Four-year liberal arts schools include Saint Anselm College and the University of New Hampshire at Manchester, which opened its downtown campus in a renovated mill building in 1986. Hesser College is a two-year technical college that offers more than 25 certificate, diploma, associate, or bachelor degree options. The New Hampshire Technical College provides associate degree programs as well as diploma and certificate programs. The New Hampshire Institute of Art offers a four-year bachelor of fine arts program.

Libraries and Research Centers

Manchester's public library numbers more than 350,000 volumes among its holdings of books, periodicals, recordings, prints, software, and state and U.S. government publications. The main library on Pine Street is supplemented by a branch on North Main Street. Attractions include a children's room, books for hearing- and sight-impaired patrons, and computers and fax machines for public use. The library's comprehensive website allows patrons access to the library's catalog, online articles and research databases, and a calendar of library events.

The Shapiro Library at New Hampshire College maintains a business and finance collection while St. Anselm's Geisel Library focuses on religious and philosophical holdings. The Manchester Historic Association Library preserves and promotes the history of the city and houses several textile design files. The Max I. Silber Scouting Library presents a wide selection of Boy Scout memorabilia, including original paintings of *Boy's Life* covers and the full collection of ''Scouts on Stamps.'' Other genealogical, college, law, and medical libraries are located throughout the city.

Public Library Information: Manchester City Library, 405 Pine Street, Manchester, NH 03104; telephone (603)624-6550

Health Care

Catholic Medical Center and Elliot Health System are the main health care providers serving the Manchester area. The 330-bed Catholic Medical Center offers a full range of medical and surgical care in 25 subspecialties, a 24-hour emergency department, inpatient and outpatient rehabilitation services, psychiatric services, and diagnostic imaging. It is home to the New England Heart Institute, which, in addition to its full range of cardiac services, is a pioneer in innovative surgical procedures and a national center for advanced clinical trials. Elliot Health System is Southern New Hampshire's largest provider of comprehensive healthcare services. The 296-bed Elliot Hospital, the city's only Level II trauma center, is the designated trauma center for the greater Manchester area. The hospital also houses the Elliot Regional Cancer Center, the Max K. Willscher Urology Center, and one of three Level 3 Neonatal Intensive Care Units in the state. The Elliot Physician Network operates offices throughout the area.

Health Care Information: Elliot Hospital, One Elliot Way, Manchester, NH 03103; telephone (603)669-5300; Catholic Medical Center, 100 McGregor Street, Manchester, NH 03102; telephone (603)668-3545 or (800)437-9666

Recreation

Sightseeing

The remnants of the Amoskeag Millyards along the Merrimack River still attract visitors. Many of the 139 red brick buildings, which once lined the river banks for more than a mile, have been remodeled into office, retail, and manufacturing space, as well as residential townhouses. Manchester's west side still echoes with the French spoken in this predominantly French-Canadian neighborhood. On Elm Street, the home of General John Stark—hero of the Battle of Bunker Hill in the Revolutionary War—has been preserved. The Amoskeag Fishways Learning and Visitors Center, located on the Merrimack River, is an environmental education center.

Arts and Culture

As the cultural hub of the state, Manchester offers an artistic calendar that incorporates everything from performances and exhibits by famous artists to student shows at coffee houses.

The jewel in Manchester's performing arts crown is the New Hampshire Symphony Orchestra, which performs a series of classical concerts yearly and features international guest artists. Opera New Hampshire, based in Manchester, stages grand opera throughout the year. The New Hampshire Symphony Orchestra, Opera New Hampshire, the New Hampshire Philharmonic, and the Granite State Orchestra perform at the Palace Theatre, a refurbished 1915 vaudeville and opera house. The Manchester Community Music School sponsors the Greater Manchester Youth Symphony Orchestra and offers classes and programs for all ages taught by some of New Hampshire's finest music educators. The Dana Center at Saint Anselm College offers classical theatre performances, contemporary dance concerts, and film showings. Stage One Productions stages dinner theater performances at the Chateau Restaurant. The New Thalian Players, produce professional community theatre productions.

Among New England's finest museums is the Currier Museum of Art in Manchester. Its permanent and revolving collections include paintings, glassware, silver, and pewter items dating from the thirteenth through the twentieth centuries. The Currier owns and offers public tours of the Zimmerman House, designed in 1950 by Frank Lloyd Wright. The Franco-American Centre terms itself the leading source of information about French culture, heritage, and history in North America. The Centre boasts a library and a museum, and offers classes, films, and Bastille Day activities. Science Enrichment Encounters (SEE) Science Center, an interactive learning center, provides hands-on exhibits to help children explore all areas of science. The Manchester Historic Association maintains displays of Native American artifacts, furniture from colonial times, and other local memorabilia. Galleries are clustered downtown and in other areas.

Festivals and Holidays

Manchester hosts a variety of ethnic and cultural festivals throughout the year, especially during the summer months. In June, the Talarico Dealerships Jazz and Blues Festival is held at the Palace Theatre, and the Strawberry Shortcake Festival is held in Valley Cemetery. Both the African-Caribbean Celebration and the Latino Festival are held in Veterans Park during the month of August. Also in August is Greekfest, a two-day festival hosted by the Assumption Greek Orthodox Church. The Mill City Festival, held in September, celebrates the local ethnicity of Manchester with live music, local food, kayak demonstrations, and a general store featuring items made in New Hampshire. Glendi, an annual celebration of Greek culture and heritage, is held at St. George Orthodox Cathedral in September. Other annual events include the Greater Manchester Horse Show at the Deerfield Fairgrounds in May, and the New Year's Eve First Night Celebration.

Sports for the Spectator

Three professional sports teams call Manchester home. The New Hampshire Fisher Cats are the AA baseball affiliate of the Toronto Blue Jays. They play their home games at the new Riverfront Stadium, located along the banks of the Merrimack River. The Manchester Wolves, an arena football team, play at the Verizon Wireless Arena. The Manchester Monarchs play professional ice hockey in the Eastern Conference of the American Hockey League. Saint Anselm College fields 10 men's and 10 women's teams in 13 different sports, including basketball, lacrosse, and football.

Sports for the Participant

Manchester's two noteworthy recreational attractions are its in-town ski area and its boat launches. The 53-acre McIntyre

Ski Area, located within the city limits and operated by the city, provides snow skiing, snowboarding, and a tubing park. The facility is equipped with snow-making equipment, two double chairlifts, a tow rope, and lighting. Within the city, boats can be launched onto the Piscataquog River on the west side and onto the Merrimack River from ramps at three eastside sites. The city's 55 parks, encompassing 900 acres, feature swimming pools, baseball diamonds, ice rinks, tracks, tennis courts, and a beach. Skateboarders gather at the Adam D. Curtis Skateboard Park. The Derryfield Country Club is an 18-hole municipal golf course. Within an hour's drive of Manchester are some of the state's best skiing, rock climbing, hiking, camping, boating, swimming, and fishing.

Shopping and Dining

Manchester's tax-free shopping draws shoppers from throughout the region. Downtown Manchester boasts more than 60 locally owned stores that feature clothing, furniture, books, antiques, and locally made products. The Mall of New Hampshire is anchored by Filene's, Best Buy, JCPenney, and Sears. The mall's offerings include more than 120 retail stores and a food court. The Tanger Outlet Center, in nearby Tilton, has more than 50 brand name and designer outlet stores.

Cuisine in Manchester reflects the city's ethnic diversity. Brazilian, French-Canadian, Irish, Spanish, Korean, Mexican, and Vietnamese cuisine are among the ethnic flavors found in Manchester's restaurants. They coexist with local favorites such as New England-style seafood, steak, and home-style cooking.

Visitor Information: Manchester Area Convention & Visitors Bureau, 889 Elm Street, 3rd Floor, Manchester, NH 03101; telephone (603)666-6600

Convention Facilities

Manchester's largest convention facility is suitable for mid-sized meetings: The Center of New Hampshire Radisson features more than 65,000 square feet of function and exhibit space. Its meeting and banquet facilities accommodate up to 2,000 people. The Center's Expo Center has 5 private meeting rooms and room for up to 210 booths. The adjoining ballroom is one of the largest in the state. Other sites that offer meeting facilities are the Comfort Inn and Conference Center, the Sheraton Four Points, and the Tara Wayfarer Inn.

Convention Information: Center of New Hampshire Radisson, 700 Elm Street, Manchester, NH 03101; telephone (603)625-1000

Transportation

Approaching the City

Competitive airfares and expanded flight schedules have positioned Manchester Airport as a viable alternative to Boston's Logan Airport. In 2004 a 74,000 square foot addition to the airport was completed. Nine airlines provide daily flights out of the airport, which is the largest commercial passenger and air cargo airport in northern New England. Non-stop flights are available to several major cities in the U.S. that offer worldwide connections.

Manchester, encircled by major highways, is the focal point of New Hampshire's interstate road system. Major north-south routes include the Frederick E. Everett Turnpike and Interstate-93, which carry traffic from Boston, through Manchester, and on to Concord. East-west arteries include U.S. Route 101, which runs east to Portsmouth on the coast, west to Keene, and southwest to Nashua. A bypass loop of I-93, named I-293, encircles the city to the west and south and handles some of the commuter traffic to the suburbs.

Several bus lines service Manchester, including Vermont Transit Lines and Concord Trailways. Shuttle and limousine service to Logan International Airport, 90 minutes away, is also available.

Traveling in the City

Manchester's main north-south streets run parallel with the Merrimack River while east-west streets run perpendicular to the river. The Manchester Transit Authority (MTA) maintains access within the metropolitan area with 14 bus routes; special services are available for those who are physically unable to use the fixed-route scheduled buses.

Communications

Newspapers and Magazines

The Union Leader Corporation publishes the *New Hampshire Union Leader* each morning, Monday through Saturday, and the *New Hampshire Sunday News*. The newspaper's Internet website publishes new content daily and maintains a searchable archive of past articles. A weekly New Hampshire edition of the *Boston Globe* is published in Manchester. *The Hippo* is a free entertainment and features newspaper published every Thursday. *The Registry Review* is a statewide real estate and financial newspaper. Magazines include the monthly *Business NH* as well as the *New Hampshire Business Review, New Hampshire Magazine,* and *The Red Brick Review,* a literary magazine.

Television and Radio

A national affiliate television station and an independent station are located in Manchester. The city receives Boston television programming as well. Cable television is provided locally. Five AM and FM commercial radio stations broadcast from Manchester.

Media Information: *Union Leader,* Union Leader Corporation, 100 William Loeb Drive, PO Box 9555, Manchester, NH 03108-9555; telephone (603)668-4321; fax (603)668-0382

Manchester Online

City of Manchester. Available www.manchesternh.gov

Greater Manchester Chamber of Commerce. Available www.manchester-chamber.org

Manchester City Library. Available www.manchester.lib.nh.us

Manchester School District. Available www.mansd.org

Manchester *Union Leader.* Available www.theunion leader.com

New Hampshire Division of Travel & Tourism Development. Available www.visitnh.gov

Selected Bibliography

Manchester Historic Association, Manchester, New Hampshire, *Centennial Celebration of Manchester, N.H., June 13, 1810–1910* (Manchester, NH: Published by authority of the city government, 1910)

Nashua

The City in Brief

Founded: 1656 (incorporated 1853)

Head Official: Mayor Bernard A. Streeter (since 2000)

City Population
　1980: 67,865
　1990: 79,662
　2000: 86,605
　2003 estimate: 87,285
　Percent change, 1990–2000: 8.7%
　U.S. rank in 1980: 289th
　U.S. rank in 1990: 270th (State rank: 2nd)
　U.S. rank in 2000: 324th (State rank: 2nd)

Metropolitan Area Population (PMSA)
　1990: 168,233
　2000: 190,949
　Percent change, 1990–2000: 13.5%

U.S. rank in 1990: 5th (CMSA)
U.S. rank in 2000: 7th (CMSA)

Area: 30.8 square miles (2000)
Elevation: 169 feet above sea level
Average Annual Temperature: 47.6° F
Average Annual Precipitation: 41.46 inches of rain; 55 inches of snow

Major Economic Sectors: Manufacturing, retail, finance, service
Unemployment Rate: 3.7% (state average, March 2005)
Per Capita Income: $25,209 (1999)
2004 ACCRA Average House Price: Not reported
2004 ACCRA Cost of Living Index: Not reported

2002 FBI Crime Index Total: Not reported

Major Colleges and Universities: Daniel Webster College; Rivier College; New Hampshire Technical College

Daily Newspaper: *The Nashua Telegraph*

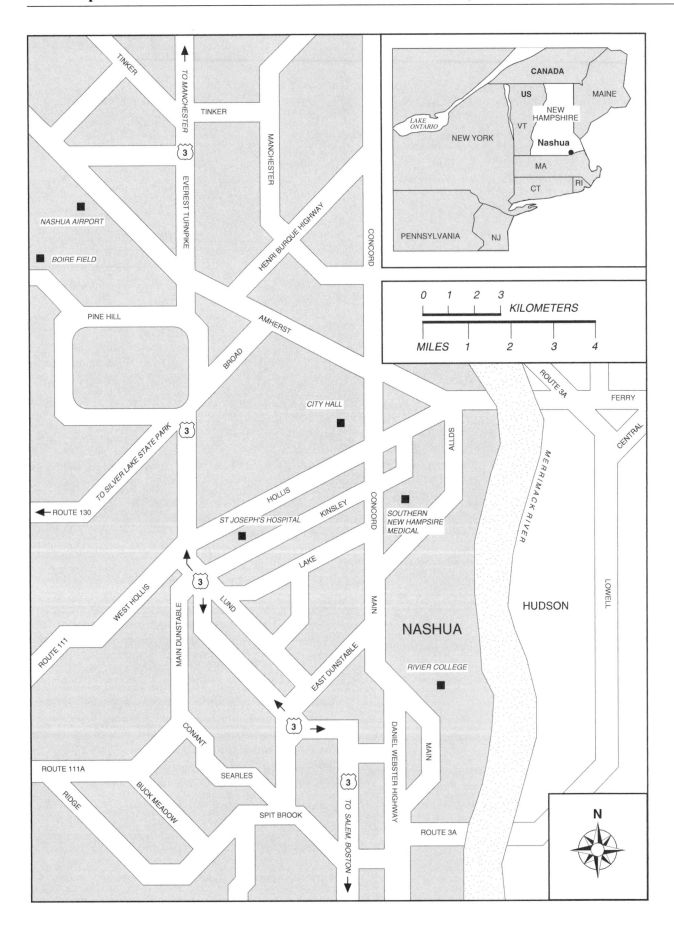

Introduction

Nashua, consistently ranked near the top among the nation's best places to live by *Money* magazine, is New Hampshire's second largest city. Having become prominent as a cotton mill town during the Industrial Revolution, Nashua has since diversified its economic base to include service, retail, and financial firms. High-technology products and research are relative newcomers to Nashua, whose location in the "Gateways Region" between New Hampshire and Massachusetts makes it a prime business and transportation site.

Geography and Climate

Located in southernmost New Hampshire, just four miles north of the Massachusetts border, Nashua perches on the east bank of the Merrimack River. Manchester lies 15 miles to the north. The Nashua River runs east-west through the city. The thin, rocky soil in the Merrimack Valley plain is better suited for sustaining forests than for producing agricultural crops. Nashua is part of a designation known as the "Golden Triangle," which includes Manchester and Salem, New Hampshire as well. The area surrounding Nashua is called the Gateways Region and takes in 14 communities.

Fall in Nashua is lovely and summers are warm and mostly free of humidity. Autumn brings crisp, clear days, and winters can be very cold with lots of snow. Dramatic and sudden weather changes can produce fog, hail, rain and snow storms and, on occasion, flooding.

Area: 30.8 square miles (2000)

Elevation: 169 feet above sea level

Average Temperatures: January, 22.8° F; July, 72.0° F; annual average, 47.6° F

Average Annual Precipitation: 41.46 inches of rain; 55 inches of snow

History

Canal, Mills Establish Nashua

Long before European settlers ventured into the Merrimack River Valley, the 14 tribes of the Algonquin Federation lived there. They fished in the rivers and streams, hunted in the heavily wooded forests, and harvested pumpkin, squash, and corn from the sandy soil of the plain. The first white men to penetrate the Merrimack's wilderness came in 1652 and were scouts from the Massachusetts Bay Colony sent in search of the colony's northern boundary. An area of 200 square miles around present-day Nashua was then declared for the colony. Trading and land grants followed, and the first permanent settlement, called Dunstable, was founded in 1673. The hostility of the Native Americans toward the encroaching settlers flared into a series of "Indian wars." The fighting was so constant and so fierce that Dunstable could count a citizenry of only 25 persons some 50 years after the town was founded.

In 1741 a boundary settlement placed Dunstable within New Hampshire. Growth was slow, hampered by difficult transportation, poor soil, and the loss of many men to the Continental Army during the Revolutionary War. Then, in 1804, the Middlesex Canal opened, making Dunstable the head of navigation on the Merrimack River and connecting the city with its most important market, Boston. The first to seize advantage of the town's location was Daniel Abbot, a lawyer. In 1823 Abbot and his partners chartered the Nashua Manufacturing Company, a mill run by water power to make textiles. At one time, the Nashua Manufacturing Company was the largest producer of blankets in the world, employing one-fifth of the city's workers. In addition to the Yankee farm girls who worked in the mills, the steady work attracted first Irish and then French-Canadian immigrants. Over time, the Nashua Manufacturing Company laid out the city's streets, built its Olive Street Church, encouraged business enterprises, and erected homes and boarding houses for its workers.

Dunstable changed its name in 1837 to Nashua, the name of one of the tribes in the Algonquin Federation. The city briefly split in 1842 over the location of a new town hall, but the factions were reunited in 1853 when the city became chartered. The Civil War followed and the Nashua mills produced thousands of suits of cotton underwear for the Union Army soldiers.

Economy Diversifies Following Mill Closings

The railroad had put Nashua on the line between Concord to the north and Boston to the southeast. Ethnic groups seeking work in the mills, including Greeks, Poles, and Lithuanians, used the trains to reach Nashua. The mills prospered and so did the mill owners, who erected their stylish mansions along Concord Street. In the twentieth century the advent of synthetics and competition from the southern mills combined to bring the New England mills to their knees, including the Nashua Manufacturing Company. In 1948, just four years after receiving a government award for service to the military during World War II, the mill shut its doors. The blow was made more severe because the area's largest employer, Textron, also shut down its Merrimack River Valley operation after the war. More than 3,500 Textron workers were left jobless and thousands of feet of mill space stood empty.

Through the efforts of an organization called the Nashua, NH, Foundation, Nashua's impending economic disaster was averted. Sanders Associates, among others, elected to occupy the mill space and helped diversify the city's economy. Heavy industry was attracted to the area in the 1950s and 1960s, followed by the service and high-technology industries in the 1970s and 1980s. While some manufacturing firms have recently left Nashua, new employers have cropped up to take their place.

In the past two decades, Nashua's evolvement into a regional commercial and industrial hub has positively impacted the city, resulting in the expansion of employment, housing, educational facilities, and medical services. In his 2004 State of the City address, Mayor Bernard Streeter called Nashua a "premiere city," one that is considered by other New England cities to be "progressive" and "citizen and business friendly."

Historical Information: Nashua Historical Society, 5 Abbott Street, Nashua, NH 03064; telephone (603)883-0015

Population Profile

Metropolitan Area Population (PMSA)
1990: 168,233
2000: 190,949
Percent change, 1990–2000: 13.5%
U.S. rank in 1990: 5th (CMSA)
U.S. rank in 2000: 7th (CMSA)

City Residents
1980: 67,865
1990: 79,662
2000: 86,605
2003 estimate: 87,285
Percent change, 1990–2000: 8.7%
U.S. rank in 1980: 289th
U.S. rank in 1990: 270th (State rank: 2nd)
U.S. rank in 2000: 324th (State rank: 2nd)

Density: 2,843.5 people per square mile (2000)

Racial and ethnic characteristics (2000)
    White: 77,291
    Black or African American: 1,740

    American Indian and Alaska Native: 275
    Asian: 3,363
    Native Hawaiian and Pacific Islander: 29
    Hispanic or Latino (may be of any race): 5,388
    Other: 2,642

Percent of residents born in state: 36.5% (2000)

Age characteristics (2000)
    Population under 5 years old: 5,644
    Population 5 to 9 years old: 6,307
    Population 10 to 14 years old: 6,147
    Population 15 to 19 years old: 5,281
    Population 20 to 24 years old: 5,001
    Population 25 to 34 years old: 13,733
    Population 35 to 44 years old: 15,242
    Population 45 to 54 years old: 11,813
    Population 55 to 59 years old: 4,185
    Population 60 to 64 years old: 3,210
    Population 65 to 74 years old: 5,296
    Population 75 to 84 years old: 3,511
    Population 85 years and over: 1,235
    Median age: 35.8 years

Births (2003)
    Total number: 1,103

Deaths (2001)
    Total number: 650

Money income (1999)
    Per capita income: $25,209 (1999)
    Median household income: $51,969
    Total households: 34,360

Number of households with income of . . .
less than $10,000: 1,982
$10,000 to $14,999: 1,692
$15,000 to $24,999: 3,698
$25,000 to $34,999: 3,586
$35,000 to $49,999: 5,389
$50,000 to $74,999: 7,889
$75,000 to $99,999: 4,887
$100,000 to $149,999: 3,802
$150,000 to $199,999: 1,060
$200,000 or more: 635

Percent of families below poverty level: 5.0% (41% of which were female householder families with related children under 5 years)

2002 FBI Crime Index Total: Not reported

Municipal Government

Nashua operates with a mayor-aldermanic form of government. While the mayor is the city's chief executive officer, the city's 15 aldermen serve as the its legislative body. The mayor and six at-large alders are elected to four-year terms (with three of the at-large members elected every two years). Nine ward alders are elected to two-year terms.

Head Official: Mayor Bernard A. Streeter (since 2000; current term expires 2007)

Total Number of City Employees: 843 (2005)

City Information: Mayor's Office, City of Nashua, 229 Main Street, Nashua, NH 03060; telephone (603)589-3260

Economy

Major Industries and Commercial Activity

Nashua is home to a number of industries, including computers, health care, and high technology. Since the 1950s, Nashua has become a virtual incubator for high technology, and a wide variety of electronic components and computer products are produced locally. Nashua ranks high for its business environment as a result of having acceptable corporate tax and wage rates, the educational level of the work force, the interstate highway system, and the absence of New Hampshire sales and income taxes. While maintaining a strong manufacturing base, Nashua is the major retail, service, and financial center for southern Hillsborough County and adjacent Massachusetts communities. The absence of a sales tax makes the city a shopping mecca.

Items and goods produced: printing and publishing, electronic equipment (especially software), fabricated metal products, machinery

Incentive Programs—New and Existing Companies

Local programs—The State of New Hampshire, which levies no state sales or income tax, is considered one of the most favorable climates for doing business in the nation. Because so much is provided at the state level, few incentives are offered at the city-town level. In fact, by state law, New Hampshire cities are prohibited from offering tax breaks to private industry. In Nashua, the Office of Economic Development is a one-stop source for resources needed to start or expand a business. The city's revolving loan fund, in partnership with private financial institutions, provides small businesses and industries with gap financing.

State programs—The state's incentives include no general sales or use tax, no general personal income tax, no capital gains tax, no inventory tax, no property tax on machinery or equipment, one of the lowest unemployment insurance rates in the country, investment tax incentives, job tax credits, and research and development tax incentives. In 2004, the State of New Hampshire instituted the Community Reinvestment Opportunity Program (CROP), which offers tax credits that may be used against business profit taxes and business enterprise taxes. Qualifying CROP projects must create new jobs as well as expand the state economic base.

Job training programs—The Small Business Development Center, which is funded by the Small Business Association, the State of New Hampshire, and the University of New Hampshire, offers management counseling, training, and resource information to the state's small business community through six sub-centers. The New Hampshire Employment Program (NHEP) aids individuals in obtaining financial aid to prepare for and find employment. The NHEP On-The-Job Training Program offers employers incentives to hire and train eligible applicants.

Development Projects

In July of 2004, Southern New Hampshire Medical Center broke ground on a $17 million construction project that will expand the hospital's cardiac care and emergency room offerings. In 2005 Nashua's other main hospital, St. Joseph Hospital, broke ground on a $25 million expansion and relocation of its Cardiovascular Center, Oncology Center, Endoscopy Surgicenter, and Phlebotomy department. The 64,000 square foot addition with adjoin the main hospital via a central atrium that will serve as the hospital's new main entrance.

Nashua plans to introduce commuter rail service to the city that will provide access to Boston via Lowell, Massachusetts. The city is developing the project in conjunction with the New Hampshire Department of Transportation and the Nashua Regional Planning Commission. The estimated cost of the project, which includes a station, parking, track improvements, train set, and an operating subsidy, is $70.1 million.

Economic Development Information: Office of Economic Development, City of Nashua, 229 Main St., Nashua, NH 03060; telephone (603)589-3070. New Hampshire Small Business Development Center, Rivier College, Sylvia Trotter Hall, 420 Main Street, Nashua, NH 03060-5086; telephone (603)897-8587

Commercial Shipping

While at one point Nashua hosted four different railroad depots, train travel declined with the advent of the automobile. Today, only the Guilford Industries rail line runs through Nashua. Several motor freight carriers service the city, which is home to a number of warehouses.

Labor Force and Employment Outlook

Nashua boasts a reliable, abundant, highly skilled and trained workforce. The expansion of high-technology companies in the region during the last decades of the twentieth century created a core of experienced workers in technology development and management. The Nashua region has a labor force of nearly 130,000 workers, with skills ranging from software and electronic engineering, to component assembly and bench work. Although recent years have seen the relocation of long-established businesses and a loss of manufacturing jobs to lower cost foreign labor markets, new businesses such as software firms and major retailers and franchises continue to establish themselves in Nashua. Other established businesses have expanded as well. Since 2003 the unemployment rate in Nashua has continued to drop and is slightly below the national average. The fastest growing economic sector is retail and services, especially services connected to travel, tourism, and recreation.

The following is a summary of data regarding the Nashua metropolitan area labor force, 2004 annual averages.

Size of nonagricultural labor force: 129,100

Number of workers employed in . . .
   construction and mining: 5,900
   manufacturing: 26,000
   trade, transportation and utilities: 30,500
   information: 2,000
   financial activities: 8,000
   professional and business services: 12,700
   educational and health services: 15,300
   leisure and hospitality: 10,300
   other services: 4,500
   government: 14,000

Average hourly earnings of production workers employed in manufacturing: $15.97

Unemployment rate: 3.7% (state average, March 2005)

Largest employers
(2004 estimates)	Number of employees
BAE Systems North America	1,000
Southern New Hampshire Medical Center	1,000
St. Joseph Hospital and Trauma Center	1,000
Teradyne Connection Systems Inc.	1,000
City of Nashua	1,000
Hewlett Packard	500
Nashua Corporation	500

Largest employers
(2004 estimates)	Number of employees
GL &V Pulp Group Inc.	250
GN Netcom/Unex Inc.	250

Cost of Living

New Hampshire has been called one of the last great tax havens in the United States. The state depends more upon real property taxes for revenue than most states as it does not have general income, sales, or use taxes. Substantial revenue is collected from taxes on gasoline, tobacco and alcohol, and parimutuel betting.

The following is a summary of data regarding several key cost of living factors in the Nashua area.

2004 ACCRA Average House Price: Not reported

2004 ACCRA Cost of Living Index: Not reported

State income tax rate: None on salaries and wages of residents; limited tax upon interest and dividends received by individuals, trusts, estates and partners in excess of $2,400. There is a $10.00 "Resident Tax" on all persons between 18 and 60 years of age with some exceptions.

State sales tax rate: None

Local income tax rate: None

Local sales tax rate: None

Property tax rate: $19.85 per $1,000 of assessed value, 2004)

Economic Information: Office of Economic Development, City of Nashua, 229 Main Street, Nashua, NH 03060; telephone (603)589-3070

Education and Research

Elementary and Secondary Schools

Among the Nashua School District's special offerings are nursery school and kindergarten, special education, English as a Second Language, an enrichment program, classes for the learning disabled and handicapped, and adult education. The district's "Credit Recovery" program offers learning additional opportunities to high school students at risk of dropping out. A number of Nashua schools have been "adopted" by local companies that provide tutoring, career guidance, field trips, minicourses, and faculty training. In the 2002–2003 school year the district opened two new schools: Nashua High School North and the Academy of Learning & Technology.

The following is a summary of data regarding the Nashua School District #42 as of the 2003–2004 school year.

Total enrollment: 13,325

Number of facilities
  elementary schools: 12
  junior high/middle schools: 4
  senior high schools: 2

Student/teacher ratio: 15:1

Teacher salaries
  average: $43,969

Funding per pupil: $7,433

Private and parochial schools in Nashua include Small World Country Day School, Bishop Guertin School, Nashua Catholic Regional Junior High School, and St. Christopher School.

Public Schools Information: Nashua School District #42, 141 Ledge St., Nashua, NH 03061-0687; telephone (603)594-4300

Colleges and Universities

Daniel Webster College, founded as a junior college in 1965, now offers bachelor's and associate's degrees in aeronautics, computer science, business, and engineering. The college abuts the Nashua Airport, where aeronautics students intern. The college's MBA program is designed specifically for working adults. New Hampshire Community Technical College, which is supported by the state, offers associate's and applied science degrees, as well as technical and business certificates. The college is one of seven in the state vocational-technical college system. Rivier College, a private Catholic institution, awards associate's, bachelor's, and master's degrees in 20 areas of study, including business, education, liberal arts, sciences, nursing, and paralegal support. Its nursing program is affiliated with St. Joseph Hospital. Satellite campuses of many larger area colleges are located in Nashua.

Libraries and Research Centers

The Nashua Public Library maintains the state's second largest collection and circulates more items than any other library in New Hampshire. Its collection comprises more than 200,000 volumes. Extensive reference, business, and periodical sections are supplemented by computerized research services, a large media collection, and an active program for children. The library also has materials in more than 24 foreign languages. Public computer terminals provide access to the Internet, research databases, and software applications. The Chandler Branch Library and a bookmobile complete the public library system.

The Anne Bridge Baddour Library at Daniel Webster College maintains a collection of print, media, and electronic resources. Specialized resources are available to supplement all of the college's academic fields. Rivier College's Regina Library includes three floors of books, meeting rooms, a reference room, and an "electronic classroom" for hands-on instruction sessions. Other special libraries include those of Nashua Corporation and Sanders—A Lockheed Martin Company.

Public Library Information: Nashua Public Library, 2 Court Street, Nashua, NH 03060-3465; telephone (603)589-4600

Health Care

St. Joseph Hospital in Nashua, with 208 beds, includes a Level 2 Trauma Center—the federally designated regional trauma center for the Greater Nashua area. St. Joseph is a full-service hospital whose facilities and services include the New England Rehabilitation Center, oncology and cardiac centers, a physician-referral service, and programs in breast health, maternity care, occupational health, and chemical dependency. Southern New Hampshire Regional Medical Center, with 188 beds, specializes in kidney dialysis, women and child care, same-day and laser surgery, and speech and hearing problems. In April 2004 the hospital opened a state-of-the-art pediatrics unit. The recently opened Nashua Center for Healthy Aging centralizes the hospital's senior services.

Health Care Information: St. Joseph Hospital, 172 Kinsley Street, Nashua, NH 03060; telephone (603)882-3000. Southern New Hampshire Medical Center, 8 Prospect Street, Nashua, NH 03061; telephone (603)577-2200

Recreation

Sightseeing

The Nashua Historical Society's collection of local history details the city's beginning as part of the Massachusetts Bay Colony and its evolution as a mill town in the 1800s. The Society also maintains a collection of Native American artifacts and a library. The Abbot-Spaulding House, which is owned by the Society, is a restored Federal-style home built in 1804 for Daniel Abbot, owner of the first cotton mill in Nashua. Among the home's many fine period pieces are glass, china, and portraits, including one of President Franklin Pierce. Nashua's North End, a residential neighborhood which includes the Nashville Historic District, features many handsome homes from the early nineteenth century to the early twentieth century, many of them in the Victorian style. Downtown Nashua's buildings of historic and architectural interest include the Hunt Memorial Building, built in the Gothic style.

Canobie Lake Park in nearby Salem combines an amusement park with a pool, small bird and animal zoo, train rides, and riverboat cruises. In nearby Merrimack is the Anheuser-Busch Brewery, which offers tours as well as performances by the brewery's 12 Clydesdale horses.

Arts and Culture

The Nashua Symphony Orchestra, a professional symphony comprised of professional musicians from southern New Hampshire and the Boston, Massachusetts area, is New Hampshire's oldest professional orchestra. The orchestra and the Nashua Symphony Choral Society, a volunteer chorus with 125 members, perform year-round (sometimes together) at the Edmund M. O'Keefe Auditorium. The Nashua Chamber Orchestra performs both classical favorites and avant garde works written for small orchestral ensembles. The 16 players of the Nashua Flute Choir use piccolos and a variety of flutes to produce their music. Dance is presented by the Granite State Ballet Company, which performs classical ballet and contemporary works throughout Northern New England. The city's Actorsingers stage two musicals each year and one children's production.

Ten miles away, in Milford, the American Stage Festival offers Broadway dramas, musicals, comedies, and a children's series. The group also offers some Nashua performances. Nashua Theatre Guild produces comedic and dramatic plays throughout the year, with some summer performances at Greeley Park. The Granite Statesmen, an all-male a capella singing chorus, preserve the All-American art of Barbershop harmony.

The Nashua Public Library offers a variety of activities for young and old, including lectures, a free outdoor film series, a weekly noon-time concert series, art shows, and exhibits. The Rivier College Art Gallery presents five exhibits annually, and offers films, lectures, and workshops. An ongoing series on multicultural events, including ethnic cooking classes and dance classes, is presented at the Chandler Memorial Library.

Arts and Culture Information: Nashua Center for the Arts, 14 Court Street, Nashua, NH 03060; telephone (603)883-1506

Festivals and Holidays

Downtown Nashua's Spring Awakening is an annual event; springtime also brings the annual art show at Greeley Park and the Taste of Nashua, in which downtown restaurants offer samples of their favorite dishes to a background of live jazz. The Summerfest Program annually sponsors a Downtown Block Party and Pancake Breakfast, a Sidewalk Art Show, and jazz and ballet concerts. A Fourth of July field day and fireworks are held at Holman Stadium. Twist The Night Away in September provides residents with a trip back in time. Antique cars line the street and people dressed in poodle skirts and leather jackets be-bop to fifties and sixties music on three stages.

Held in Downtown Nashua along the river, October's free River Harvest Festival celebrates Nashua's heritage. Highlights include live ethnic entertainment, boating exhibits and seasonal foods. Downtown is the site of November's Winter Holiday Stroll, a Victorian-style, candlelight stroll followed by a tree-lighting ceremony, musical, theatrical and dance performances, and ice sculptures. Many shops stay open and offer creative displays or goodies.

Sports for the Spectator

Nashua's Holman Stadium is home to the National Pride baseball team, a member of the independent Atlantic League of Professional Baseball. Rivier College, a member of the NCAA Division III, fields teams in basketball, volleyball, soccer, baseball, cross country, and softball.

Sports for the Participant

A federal fish hatchery is located in Nashua, whose two rivers supply some excellent fishing. Among the city's parks are the popular Mine Falls Park, located between the Nashua River and a three-mile long canal. Seven points provide access to hiking, walking, snow shoeing, and fishing. Three public swimming pools are open June through August. The Parks and Recreation Department sponsors several recreational sports leagues, including baseball, softball, lacrosse, and basketball. Golf is played at a dozen public and private courses in the region.

White-water rafting enthusiasts can enjoy weekend trips on the nearby Contoocook River. Silver Lake State Park, seven miles from Nashua, offers camping and hiking. Bicycling in the city and surrounding hillside is a popular pastime. Proximity to the White Mountains and the Atlantic Ocean guarantees fine downhill skiing, swimming, and water sports.

Shopping and Dining

Nashua lives up to its reputation as the retailing center of southern New Hampshire, offering tax-free shopping at a number of ultra-modern malls, as well as traditional downtown shopping. Pheasant Lane Mall, with one million square feet of space, is the largest shopping center in New England, boasting two stories and 150 stores. It is anchored by Filene's, JCPenney, Macy's, Target, and Sears. Royal Ridge Mall caters to the shopper in search of collectibles. Downtown Nashua features several blocks of small specialty shops, including one of the outlets of the League of New Hampshire Craftsmen. The League, founded in 1932 to encourage practitioners of the dying home industries, features art works by local artisans. Items include blown glass, leather bags, ceramics, jewelry, woven pieces, wood carvings, furniture, prints, and homemade jams. A weekly farmer's market operates downtown in the summer.

Both casual and elegant dining experiences are available in Nashua and at nearby country inns. Menus offer a variety of ethnic dishes and New England traditional cuisine, such as chowders and fish stews, seafood, baked beans, and Indian pudding. Asian, Brazilian, and Italian cuisines are among the city's ethnic offerings.

Visitor Information: New Hampshire Division of Travel and Tourism Department, 172 Pembroke Road, Concord, PO Box 1856, Concord, NH 03302-1856; telephone (603)271-2665

Convention Facilities

More than 2,000 guest rooms and suites are available in the Gateways Region, whose principal convention site is Nashua. The largest facility in Nashua is the Sheraton Nashua Hotel, with 336 guest rooms and more than 25,000 square feet of meeting rooms. The Crowne Plaza Nashua Hotel features 206 handicap-accessible guest rooms and 20 meeting rooms. Other meeting and banquet facilities are available at the Holiday Inn and the Comfort Inn.

Convention Information: Greater Nashua Chamber of Commerce, 151 Main Street, Nashua, NH 03060; telephone (603)881-8333. Crowne Plaza Nashua Hotel, 2 Somerset Parkway, Nashua, NH 03063-1969; telephone (603)886-1200. Sheraton Nashua Hotel, 11 Tara Boulevard, Nashua, NH 03062; telephone (603)888-9970

Transportation

Approaching the city

Boston's Logan International Airport, an hour's drive to the southeast, provides full commercial and freight air service.

Regularly scheduled buses travel between Nashua and Logan daily. Just outside Nashua's northwestern city limit is Nashua Airport, which is a noncommercial air field. Manchester Airport, about 25 minutes from Nashua, has daily connections to major cities.

The Nashua area is the starting point for two of the state's major four-lane highways, U.S. Route 3 and Interstate-93. Route 3, the F.E. Everett Turnpike, runs north-south through the western portion of the city. I-93 passes by the city to the east and is connected to Nashua by the east-west traveling New Hampshire Route 111.

Traveling in the City

Nashua's Main Street runs north-south through downtown, while the major east-west surface street is Hollis Street. Traffic is heavy due to unprecedented population growth. In-town bus service is provided by the Nashua Transit System (NTS). Six fixed "City Bus" routes cover the city's most populous neighborhoods and most commercial and industrial areas. Residents with special mobility needs may utilize the NTS's Citylift program. Plans call for a commuter rail service to be instituted between Nashua and Lowell, Massachusetts, and thence to Boston. A Nashua station site is planned for the end of E. Spit Brook Road.

Communications

Newspapers and Magazines

The *Nashua Telegraph* is published daily. The newspaper's Internet edition also publishes new content daily. The *1590 Broadcaster,* a local weekly newspaper, is published each Wednesday. *Gateways* is an annual guidebook to the region published by the Chamber of Commerce. *Parenting New Hampshire* is a monthly parenting magazine with an affiliated website.

Television and Radio

While no television signals originate in Nashua, the city does receive the commercial and Public Broadcasting System stations from Boston. A local firm provides cable television in Nashua. One AM and one FM radio station broadcast from Nashua.

Media Information: Nashua Telegraph, 60 Main Street, PO Box 1008, Nashua, NH 03060-2720; telephone (603)882-2741

Nashua Online

City of Nashua. Available www.ci.nashua.nh.us

Greater Nashua Chamber of Commerce. Available www
.nashuachamber.com

Nashua Public Library. Available www.nashua.lib.nh.us

Nashua School District. Available www.nashua.edu

The *Nashua Telegraph.* Available www.nashuatelegraph
.com

Southern New Hampshire Medical Center. Available www
.snhmc.org

St. Joseph Hospital. Available www.stjosephhospital.com

Portsmouth

The City in Brief

Founded: 1623 (incorporated 1849)

Head Official: Mayor Evelyn F. Sirrell (since 1998)

City Population
  1980: 26,254
  1990: 25,925
  2000: 20,784
  2003 estimate: 21,002
  Percent change, 1990–2000: −19.8%
  U.S. rank in 1980: 909th
  U.S. rank in 1990: 1,044th
  U.S. rank in 2000: Not reported (State rank: 13th)

Metropolitan Area Population (PMSA)
  1990: 223,271
  2000: 240,698
  Percent change, 1990–2000: 7.8%

U.S. rank in 1990: 5th (CMSA)
U.S. rank in 2000: 7th (CMSA)

Area: 15.7 square miles (2000)
Elevation: 20 feet above sea level
Average Annual Temperature: 44.7° F
Average Annual Precipitation: 46 inches of rain; 62 inches of snow

Major Economic Sectors: Tourism, government, retail and service industries, fishing and agriculture
Unemployment Rate: 1.4% (April 2005)
Per Capita Income: $27,540 (1999)
2004 ACCRA Average House Price: Not reported
2004 ACCRA Cost of Living Index: Not reported

2002 FBI Crime Index Total: 860

Major Colleges and Universities: Extension Campus of New Hampshire College

Daily Newspaper: *The Portsmouth Herald*

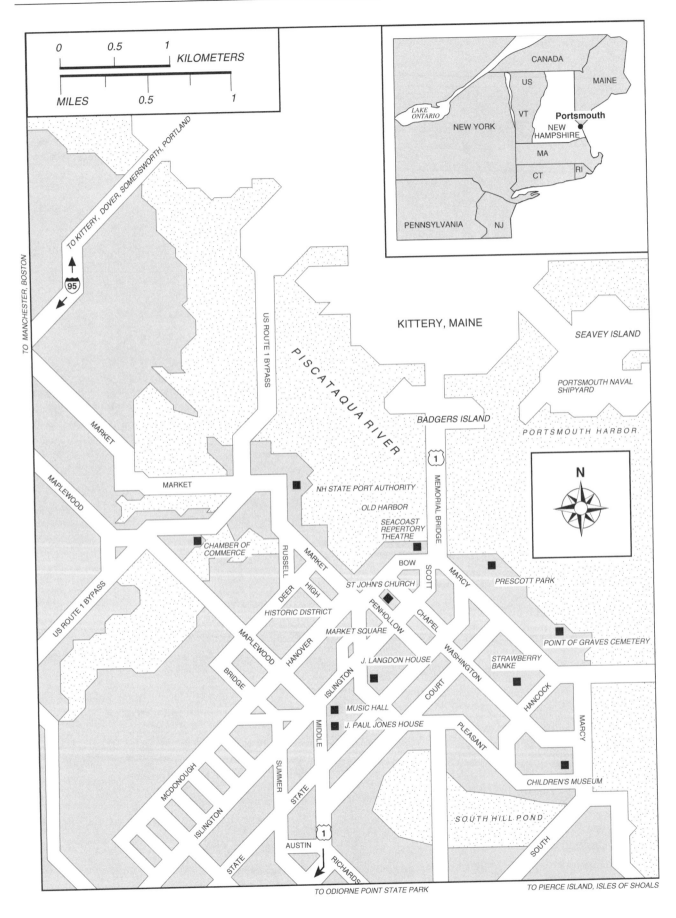

Introduction

Portsmouth has the distinction of being New Hampshire's first settlement, its second oldest city, its first capital, and its only seaport. For many years, Portsmouth's livelihood depended upon the sea; since the Revolutionary War, city life has centered around the Portsmouth Naval Shipyard. The yard, which once built clipper ships and now builds and repairs submarines, was the site of the signing of the Treaty of Portsmouth ending the Russo-Japanese War in 1905, though in 2005 it faces possible closure. Today Portsmouth enjoys a reputation as one of the finest vacation spots in New England. It also represents economic opportunity for businesses with its tax advantages and global access via its port along with community leaders' efforts to draw high-technology firms to the city.

Geography and Climate

Portsmouth, located in southeastern New Hampshire in Rockingham County, is equidistant from Portland, Maine, to the north and Boston, Massachusetts, to the south. About three miles inland from the Atlantic Ocean, Portsmouth is at the mouth of a broad tidal basin for six inland rivers. Portsmouth itself lies on the banks of the Piscataqua River. On the opposite bank of the Piscataqua is the city of Kittery, Maine site of the Portsmouth Naval Shipyard. The only seaport in the state, Portsmouth has one of the deepest harbors in the world. The land around the harbor is hilly, sloping down to Piscataqua Bay.

Portsmouth's winters are relatively mild and wet because of the mitigating influence of the Atlantic Ocean; average snowfall during the winter is 62 inches. Summer, which can be warm and humid, is sometimes lightened by ocean breezes. The traditional New England storms off the Atlantic, known locally as "northeasters," are mostly spent by the time they reach Portsmouth.

Area: 15.7 square miles (2000)

Elevation: 20 feet above sea level

Average Temperatures: January, 19.9° F; July, 69.5° F; annual average, 44.7° F

Average Annual Precipitation: 46 inches of rain; 62 inches of snow

History

Shipbuilding, Trading Establish Portsmouth

When English settlers migrating north from Massachusetts Bay Colony reached the site of modern Portsmouth, they encountered the Piscataquas, Native Americans who were part of the Algonquin Federation. The settlers adopted the name Piscataqua for their new town but soon changed the name to Strawbery Banke, a comment on the lush fruit carpeting the area. By 1633, the townsfolk had built a grist mill that used the waters of the Piscataqua River, and the Great House, a large community residence.

In 1653 the 60 families living in the town petitioned to change its name to Portsmouth. When New Hampshire was separated from Massachusetts Bay Colony by royal edict in 1679, Portsmouth became the capital of the new colony. Surrounded by forests of oak and white pine and at the edge of one of the world's deepest harbors, Portsmouth developed an economy based on shipbuilding and trading. The town thrived on its agriculture and fishing businesses and the fast growing mast-building industry. Shipbuilding boomed as the colonies moved toward the Revolutionary War. During the conflict, Portsmouth's shipyards produced three ships—the *America,* the *Raleigh,* and the *Ranger*—along with numerous privateers.

Following the war, many new wharves and shipyards were built along Portsmouth Harbor. In 1800 a government yard was added, the Portsmouth Naval Shipyard, to build and repair warships. In the meantime, commercial trade was brisk, as Portsmouth formed one of the points in the New England-West Indies-Great Britain triangle. Rum, molasses, sugar, and cocoa from the West Indies were shipped to Portsmouth and stored in its warehouses. Some of the goods were shipped on to England, along with cargoes of New Hampshire lumber. Portsmouth's merchant fleet also sailed south to the Indies, laden with lumber, oil, and livestock. Coal from England was distributed inland from Portsmouth warehouses, completing the trade triangle.

Shipbuilding Decline Diversifies Economy

The merchant class of Portsmouth lived very profitably from the trade, building large Federalist and Georgian-style manors and supporting the arts. The *New Hampshire Gazette,* originally called the *Portsmouth Gazette,* began publishing weekly in 1756. Portsmouth's fortunes declined in 1808 when Concord was named the state capital. Its fortunes suffered further with the invention of steamships and the growing popularity of the Massachusetts ports.

After the Civil War, Portsmouth became known for its breweries and shoe factories. The city was wired for electric lights in 1870 and free postal delivery began there in 1887. The construction of the Little Bay-Dover bridge in 1874 undermined the usefulness of the Piscataqua River as an avenue to inland communities. The Portsmouth Naval Shipyard continued to contribute to the country's military needs. In World War II, the yard's 20,000 employees built some 70 submarines. During 1953 the prototype submarine USS *Albacore* (a National Historic Landmark and Historic Mechanical Engineering Landmark) and the first two atomic-powered submarines were built in the yard.

Three bridges span the Piscataqua River in modern Portsmouth, one of which, the Memorial Bridge, was built to commemorate World War I. Ships continue to sail into Portsmouth, now an official port of entry and foreign trade zone. Modern cargoes consist of oil, gas, salt, limestone, and other products, with petroleum products comprising 90 percent of the cargoes. Much of the waterfront is now devoted to parks and gardens, while the once-bustling warehouses have been transformed into condominiums, shops, and offices.

Established in 1956, the Pease Air Force Base in Portsmouth was one of the first military installations in the country to close as a result of the 1989 Base Closure and Realignment Act. In March 1991, all 10,715 military and other related personnel, and their dependents, left and took with them an annual payroll of about $110 million. Their departure took a heavy toll on the region's economy, already suffering as a result of the recession that began in the late 1980s.

Although the loss of the base seemed extremely negative at the time, the closure actually provided a unique opportunity for New Hampshire and its Pease Development Authority (PDA) to initiate the development of Pease International Tradeport, which is both a commercial airport and an economic development project. Simultaneously, the Port of New Hampshire began a major expansion project, which has led to a great increase in the port's trade potential.

City's Perseverance Tested as Twenty-First Century Begins

In 2005 the area faces the possibility of a major economic challenge with the proposed closure of Portsmouth Naval Shipyard recommended by the U.S. Department of Defense. Hearings began in July 2005 to discuss whether to retain the historic yard with a final decision expected in early 2006. The impact on the region would be significant as it employs some 4,500 workers; however, it would take several years before the site could officially be closed as environmental cleanup would be intensive.

The proliferation of Internet-based companies, or ''dot-com'' companies, brought approximately 400 related firms to the area in the late 1990s, though most went out of business during the economic downturn early in the new

century. The prosperity that the financial influx brought resulted in great strides in cultural activities and dining establishments that remain.

While the population has declined significantly in recent decades—the most dramatic between 1990–2000 with a nearly 20 percent loss—the metropolitan area has steadily expanded. The business climate is advantageous as many incentive programs exist along with a lack of sales or income tax in the city and state. Rockingham County, in particular, has shown positive growth in business indicators since 2004 with a solid start in the first quarter of 2005 giving residents cause for optimism.

Historical Information: Historic District Commission, c/o Planning Department, City of Portsmouth, 1 Junkins Ave., Portsmouth, NH 03801; telephone (603)610-7216; fax (603)427-1593

Population Profile

Metropolitan Area Residents (PMSA)
1990: 223,271
2000: 240,698
Percent change, 1990–2000: 7.8%
U.S. rank in 1990: 5th (CMSA)
U.S. rank in 2000: 7th (CMSA)

City Residents
1980: 26,254
1990: 25,925
2000: 20,784
2003 estimate: 21,022
Percent change, 1990–2000: −19.8%
U.S. rank in 1980: 909th
U.S. rank in 1990: 1,044th
U.S. rank in 2000: Not reported (State rank: 13th)

Density: 1,333.4 people per square mile (2000)

Racial and ethnic characteristics (2000)
   White: 19,443
   Black or African American: 442
   American Indian and Alaska Native: 44
   Asian: 508
   Native Hawaiian and Pacific Islander: 5
   Hispanic or Latino (may be of any race): 280
   Other:

Percent of residents born in state: 37.3% (2000)

Age characteristics (2000)
   Population under 5 years old: 1,009
   Population 5 to 9 years old: 981
   Population 10 to 14 years old: 997

Population 15 to 19 years old: 886
Population 20 to 24 years old: 1,187
Population 25 to 34 years old: 4,002
Population 35 to 44 years old: 3,524
Population 45 to 54 years old: 2,952
Population 55 to 59 years old: 1,021
Population 60 to 64 years old: 841
Population 65 to 74 years old: 1,629
Population 75 to 84 years old: 1,215
Population 85 years and over: 540
Median age: 38.5 years

Births (2002)
Total number: 230

Deaths (2001)
Total number: 257

Money income (1999)
Per capita income: $27,540
Median household income: $45,195
Total households: 9,933

Number of households with income of . . .
less than $10,000: 899
$10,000 to $14,999: 574
$15,000 to $24,999: 1,105
$25,000 to $34,999: 1,140
$35,000 to $49,999: 1,629
$50,000 to $74,999: 2,174
$75,000 to $99,999: 1,177
$100,000 to $149,999: 822
$150,000 to $199,999: 256
$200,000 or more: 157

Percent of families below poverty level: 6.4% (39.2% of which were female householder families with related children under 5 years)

2002 FBI Crime Index Total: 860

Municipal Government

Portsmouth operates under a manager-council form of government. Nine council members are elected to two-year terms. The member receiving the largest number of votes becomes the mayor in any municipal election. The council retains the services of a full-time professional city manager.

Head Official: Mayor Evelyn F. Sirrell (since 1998; current term expires 2005)

Total Number of City Employees: 881 (2002)

City Information: Mayor's Office, City of Portsmouth, 1 Junkins Ave., Portsmouth, NH 03802-0628; telephone (603)610-7200

Economy

Major Industries and Commercial Activity

Portsmouth is a part of the northeast market area that serves about a third of the nation's population in addition to eastern Canada. Major economic sectors in Portsmouth include tourism, the retail and service industries, and fishing and agriculture. One of the area's major employers is the Portsmouth Naval Shipyard across the Piscataqua River from Portsmouth in Kittery, Maine. This facility, which repairs nuclear submarines, also supports attendant vendors and manufacturers, and in the early 1990s completed construction of a $34 million enclosed dry dock.

The Pease International Tradeport, an airport and economic development project on the site of the former air base, is the current location of more than 150 businesses employing some 5,000 people on about 3.6 million square feet of new or renovated space. Several regional carriers provide daily departures to a variety of destinations. Landside developments at the Tradeport include the National Passport Center and the National Visa Center. The site has also attracted several high-tech businesses including Lonza Biologics (formerly Celltech Biologics), a London-based firm, which is now one of the area's largest employers.

The Port of Portsmouth is a center for exporters and importers of road salt, scrap metal, fuel oil, building materials, and other goods; many exporters are located in Portsmouth. Overall, more than five million tons of cargo per year makes the short journey to and from the Atlantic Ocean to the port's dock.

Items and goods produced: machinery, electronic components, plastics, liquefied propane, gypsum products, shoes, microwave parts, tools and dies, drinks, buttons, reaming tools, wire and cable, computer connective hardware

Incentive Programs—New and Existing Industries

Local programs—The State of New Hampshire, which levies no state sales or income tax, is considered one of the most favorable climates for doing business in the nation. Portsmouth relies on services provided by the Small Business Development Center, Leadership Seacoast (a group of community leaders), Service Corps of Retired Executives (SCORE), Chamber of Commerce workshops and seminars, and the efforts of the Economic Development Commission in encouraging businesses and providing forums for business contacts.

The Portsmouth Economic Development Commission provides a one-stop information and referral center for business consulting for startup or expanding firms. Financing support is offered by the Portsmouth Economic Development Loan Program (PEDLP) for prospective or existing small business owners in the area. Incentives for qualified businesses are funded by PEDLP monies along with private and federal loans and can be directed toward acquiring land and buildings, buying machinery and equipment, and other approved projects.

Portsmouth's Community Development Department and Chamber of Commerce have developed the Microenterprise Assistance Program to encourage economic development within the city by providing business counseling services to small businesses that would not normally be able to afford such services. The free counseling may include marketing development, loan proposals, assistance with developing business plans, cash flow analysis and financial planning, productivity studies, contracts and agreements, and skills transfer to the small business owner.

State programs—An International Trade Resource Center at the former Pease Air Force Base in Portsmouth provides information and assistance for exporters or for those investigating an expansion into foreign markets. The state of New Hampshire's incentives include no general sales or use tax, no general personal income tax, no capital gains tax, no inventory tax, no property tax on machinery or equipment, one of the lowest unemployment insurance rates in the country, investment tax incentives, job tax credits, and research & development tax incentives. For manufacturers, business and technical support are available along with financing that is free from taxation.

Job training programs—The Small Business Development Center, which is funded by the U.S. Small Business Association (SBA), the State of New Hampshire, and the University of New Hampshire, offers free management counseling, low cost training, and resource information to the state's small business community through six sub-centers. The federally-funded New Hampshire Workforce Opportunity Council (WOC) provides business and industry with customized classroom training and on-the-job training of eligible workers.

Development Projects

Business at the Pease International Tradeport continues to expand under the Pease Development Authority (PDA) and maintains 3.6 million square feet of new or renovated space. Plans are underway to double the number of employees at the Tradeport from about 5,000 to 10,000. The Port Authority of Portsmouth is implementing a long-existing plan to add new piers that will allow for greater cargo capacity and room for vessel overflow. Another project long in the planning phase (since 1988) is a new library building that finally began construction during the summer of 2005 with occupancy anticipated for July 2006.

Economic Development Information: Greater Portsmouth Chamber of Commerce, 500 Market St., PO Box 239, Portsmouth, NH 03802-0239; telephone (603)436-3988. New Hampshire Office of Business and Economic Development, c/o NH Business Resource Center, PO Box 1856, 172 Pembroke Rd., Concord, NH 03302-1856; telephone (603)271-2341 or (603)271-2591; fax (603)271-6784; email info@nheconomy.com. New Hampshire Small Business Development Center, c/o Rochester Chamber of Commerce, 18 S Main St., Ste. 2A, Rochester, NH 03867; telephone (603)330-1929; fax (603)330-1948; email wdaniel@cisunix.unh.edu

Commercial Shipping

The only seaport in the state and the only deepwater harbor between Portland, Maine, and Boston, Massachusetts, Portsmouth remains a major New England port of entry. The port, a designated Foreign Trade Zone, includes a state-operated marine terminal. Container service to Halifax and European destinations is available weekly. The port continues to play an increasingly important role in Atlantic shipping, and, as of 2005, the Port Authority was in the process of adding new piers to facilitate the handling of more cargo and barge services. Public and private terminals along the Piscataqua River account for in excess of five million tons of cargo per year. In addition to the port facilities, Portsmouth shipping includes the Guilford Transportation Industries railroad and around 20 regular truck route carriers. Air freight service is available at three commercial airports within an hour's drive.

Labor Force and Employment Outlook

Portsmouth workers are described as young, well-educated, with a good work ethic, and attracted to the city in part because of the short commute to work. The labor pool includes workers with diversified skills while the nearby colleges offer strong academic and technical support. Nearly 42 percent of those older than 25 years have a bachelor's degree or higher while 91 percent are high school graduates.

Considered a viable alternative to Boston for both living and working, Portsmouth is ideally situated for business expansion in both national and international markets with the Port of Portsmouth offering area manufacturers direct worldwide access. The redevelopment of the former Pease Air Force Base has created numerous commercial business opportunities for companies that repair, maintain, and retrofit aircraft as well as vendors and suppliers for those types of facilities.

In 1999 the eCoast Technology Roundtable was established to recruit high-tech businesses and professionals to the area.

The following is a summary of data regarding the Portsmouth metropolitan area labor force, 2004 annual averages.

Size of nonagricultural labor force: 54,300

Number of workers employed in . . .
   construction and mining: 1,800
   manufacturing: 4,000
   trade, transportation, and utilities: 11,300
   information: 1,600
   financial activities: 4,800
   professional and business services: 8,000
   educational and health services: 5,500
   leisure and hospitality: 6,300
   other services: 1,600
   government: 9,400

Average hourly earnings of production workers employed in manufacturing: Not reported

Unemployment rate: 1.4% (April 2005)

Largest employers in the Portsmouth region	*Number of employees*
Liberty Mutual Insurance Co.	1,800
Portsmouth Regional Hospital	1,000
City of Portsmouth	881
Demoulas Market Basket	425
Lonza Biologics	390
Erie Scientific/Sybron Lab Products	310
Pan Am Airlines	300
U.S. Department of State National Passport Center	259
Shaw's Supermarkets, Inc.	226
U.S. Department of State National Visa Center	215

Cost of Living

New Hampshire historically ranks among the lowest in the nation in the percentage of residents' income collected for state taxes and fees. New Hampshire depends more upon real property taxes for revenue than most states as it does not have general income, sales, or use taxes. Substantial revenue is collected from taxes on gasoline, tobacco, alcohol, and parimutuel betting.

The following is a summary of data regarding several key cost of living factors in the Portsmouth area.

2004 ACCRA Cost of Living Index: Not reported

2004 ACCRA Average House Price: Not reported

State income tax rate: None on earned income; 5% on interest and dividends (with some exceptions); 8.5% business profit taxes; 18% inheritance and estate tax

State sales tax rate: None

Local income tax rate: None

Local sales tax rate: None

Property tax rate: $17.17 per $1,000 of valuation (2004)

Economic Information: Community Development Department, City of Portsmouth, 1 Junkins Ave., Portsmouth, NH 03801; telephone (603)610-7218

Education and Research

Elementary and Secondary Schools

Portsmouth public schools' curricula include both college, preparatory, and vocational programs, as well as programs for the physically and mentally impaired. Comprised of instructors, school officials, students, and parents, the 19-member Greater Portsmouth Education Partnership Council (GPEPC) works with the community to improve the school system and annually awards district educators and civic partners.

The following is a summary of data regarding the Portsmouth Public Schools as of the 2003–2004 school year.

Total enrollment: 2,696

Number of facilities
   elementary schools: 3
   junior high/middle schools: 1
   senior high schools: 1

Student/teacher ratio: 11.3:1

Teacher salaries
   average: $44,282

Funding per pupil: $11,583

Three private or parochial schools enroll about 525 students.

Public Schools Information: Superintendent's Office, Portsmouth School Department, 50 Clough Dr., Portsmouth, NH 03801; telephone (603)431-5080; fax (603)431-6753

Colleges and Universities

An extension of New Hampshire College operates in Portsmouth, along with the Antioch New England Graduate

School, Franklin Pierce College, and Hesser College. A number of other schools are located within driving distance, notably the University of New Hampshire in Durham, which is about 14 miles away. The University offers its nearly 12,600 undergraduates and graduate students a choice of more than 100 majors. The New Hampshire Community Technical College (NHCTC) is in nearby Stratham. Collaborative efforts by the University of New Hampshire Division of Continuing Education, the College for Lifelong Learning (part of the University System of New Hampshire), and New Hampshire Technical College resulted in the establishment of the Pease Education and Training Center, which offers course work to help those in business and industry in the greater Portsmouth region.

Libraries and Research Centers

Portsmouth Public Library maintains a collection of about 145,000 volumes and 5,000 audio materials, 6,000 video materials, and more than 750 periodicals along with city documents, tapes, and maps. Special collections include information about local history including World War II records. The library staffs a children's room and offers a variety of special children and teen programs.

Special libraries include the Portsmouth Athenaeum, a library-museum specializing in local New Hampshire, Maine, and New England history, as well as genealogy and marine, naval, and shipping interests. At Strawbery Banke, the Thayer Cumings Historical Reference Library specializes in art and architecture, decorative arts, local history, and preservation. Its holdings include photo and manuscript collections. The Portsmouth Naval Shipyard Library covers computers, electronics, engineering, and submarines. Masonic information pertaining to New Hampshire is catalogued in the James E. Whalley Museum and Library.

Portsmouth is the summer home of the Shoals Marine Laboratory (SML), a research program of Cornell University run in conjunction with the University of New Hampshire. This marine biology and coastal oceanography facility is located on 95 acres on Appledore Island, the largest of the Isles of Shoals and six miles from Portsmouth in the Gulf of Maine.

Public Library Information: Portsmouth Public Library, 8 Islington St., Portsmouth, NH 03801; telephone (603)427-1540; fax (603)433-0981; email info@lib.cityofportsmouth.com

Health Care

Portsmouth area residents are served by the Portsmouth Regional Hospital, a full service, 179 bed medical center with

staff of about 130 physicians. The hospital provides an inpatient and outpatient behavioral health center along with a 24-hour emergency department, rehabilitation services, women's care services including maternity care, and the latest medical equipment. Staffed by about 50 surgeons, the surgery department has state-of-the-art laser equipment, and extensive diagnostic resources, including CAT and MRI scanning, X-ray, cardiac stress, testing, ultrasound and mammography. The Heart & Lung Center has multidisciplinary capabilities, and the Wound Care Center treats wounds using an innovative, comprehensive approach.

The Behavioral Health Services unit treats adults and adolescents in crisis who are suffering from mental illness, substance abuse or an acute emotional or psychological problem. Services provided include full inpatient care, medically supervised detoxification, and an evening Adult Intensive Outpatient program.

Health Care Information: Portsmouth Regional Hospital, 333 Borthwick Ave., Portsmouth, NH 03801; telephone (603)436-5110

Recreation

Sightseeing

Portsmouth, a charming New England seaport, retains its colonial heritage through careful preservation of its buildings, some of which date from the 1600s. Many of these historic structures can be viewed on a walking tour along the Portsmouth Trail, which is a collection of six buildings, including the Governor John Langdon House. Langdon served five years as governor of the state and was a signer of the U.S. Constitution. The John Paul Jones House, also on the tour, was the temporary dwelling of the naval patriot during the outfitting of the ships USS *Ranger* and USS *America.* The four other homes include Federalist and Georgian mansions of early politicians and merchants. Other Portsmouth buildings of note are the Old State House, built in 1758, and Pitt Tavern, site of Loyalist meetings prior to the Revolutionary War. The Strawbery Banke Museum, a living museum, occupies 10 acres in the city's South End in the heart of the maritime community.

Thirty-five buildings built between 1695 and the 1820s have been preserved and co-exist with restored shops where craftsmen demonstrate vanishing arts such as barrel and candle making. St. John's Church, an Episcopal church built in 1807, contains an antique Bible, baptismal font, and box pews. The nearby Point of Graves Cemetery contains tombstones dating back to 1682.

Harbor cruises and whale watches are popular attractions at Portsmouth Harbor.

Other attractions in Portsmouth center around the port area. Prescott Park, on the banks of the Piscataqua River, contains the Sheafe Warehouse, where John Paul Jones outfitted the USS *Ranger*. The warehouse now houses an art gallery and hosts an annual arts festival. Harbor cruises and whale watches are popular further down the river in Portsmouth Harbor. A trip to the Isles of Shoals, a group of islands just off the coast, reveals the landing site of Captain John Smith around 1614. Across the Piscataqua River in Kittery, Maine, is the Portsmouth Naval Shipyard, a U.S. naval installation since the Revolutionary War. The base, which is actually located on Seavey's Island, has built ships ranging from frigates to submarines. Albacore Park and Memorial Garden house the USS *Albacore,* a prototype for modern submarines.

Odiorne Point State Park, near Portsmouth Harbor, contains a nature center with exhibits of sea life and displays on coastal issues. Narrated, cocktail, live music, and fall foliage cruises of the harbor and the Piscataqua River are available. Water Country water park, spread over 47 acres, offers 15 different water rides, other activities, and snack bars and restaurants.

Arts and Culture

It is remarkable that a city of Portsmouth's size can support several theater groups along with five theaters, a children's museum, a ballet company, a lively music scene, and a former button factory inhabited by artisans. Founded in 1977, the Pontine Movement Theatre is a professional performing and touring group specializing in mime. The group performs at the Market Square studio. A variety of classic and original productions are presented by the intimate, 75-seat Players' Ring Theater, while the award-winning Seacoast Repertory Theatre at the Bow Street Theatre building (circa 1892) offers a wide range of plays, workshops, and children's activities. Ballet New England performs contemporary and traditional dance; classical music is the forte of the Historic North Church Music Series. The Music Hall, built in 1878, presents a celebrity series of dance, music, theater, and other events from September through May.

Among the attractions at the Children's Museum of Portsmouth are a lobstering exhibit, a submarine that can be boarded, and nature and computer centers. Portsmouth's numerous galleries showcase paintings, collectibles, and sculpture exhibits that depict the sea as well as arts and crafts.

Festivals and Holidays

The New Year is hailed in Portsmouth by the non-alcoholic First Night celebration spotlighting live entertainment and fireworks. Warm weather brings art fairs, including the summer-long Prescott Parks Art Festival and the Ceres Street Crafts Fair held in the Old Harbor Area. The Bowstreet Artisans Fair at the Seacoast Repertory Theatre in July is the largest fine arts and crafts fair held in southern New Hampshire. The Children's Museum of Portsmouth celebrates its birthday in July with the entire community. June features the Harbor Arts Jazz Festival, which is held at the Music Hall, and the day-long Market Square Day festival with food, music, and arts and crafts booths. The Strawbery Banke Museum's ''Candlelight Stroll,'' held the first two weekends in December, rounds out the festival year.

Sports for the Participant

Its proximity to the Atlantic Coast provides Portsmouth with an abundance of sports. In summer, the city's parks offer picnicking, fishing, boating, swimming, and hiking. Albacore Park, at the Port of the Portsmouth Maritime Museum, staffs a visitor's center. The park system includes Four Tree Island Park and Pierce Island Park. Prescott Park, the site of a summer festival series, cultivates garden displays while the Urban Forestry Center maintains nature trails, an arboretum, gardens, and a historic house. Saltwater fishing is popular, with several companies offering boating services. The city maintains 16 tennis courts, two indoor and outdoor pools, and a golf course. In the winter, excellent skiing can be found in the White Mountains, a two-hour's drive to the north. Odiorne Point State Park, a 15-minute drive from downtown, offers numerous summer and fall outings, including flotsam and jetsam hikes and leaf hunts.

Shopping and Dining

Portsmouth shopping is especially appealing because there is no sales tax. Its most picturesque shopping section may be the Old Harbor Area at Bow and Ceres streets. The warehouses and customs offices of the once busy colonial seaport have been transformed into boutiques, craft shops, and restaurants. Downtown shopping is available along Congress Street. Two of the better-known outlet malls in the area are Kittery Outlet Mall in Kittery, Maine and the North Hampton Outlet on U.S. Route One. Major retailers can be found in the city of Newington at the Fox Run Mall. The Portsmouth Farmers Market sells homemade foods and arts and crafts from May to early November.

Portsmouth, the self-proclaimed ''restaurant capital of New England,'' offers mostly classic seacoast fare in its nearly 100 restaurants, about half of which are in the downtown area. Many eateries are located in refurbished warehouses, historic homes, and breweries overlooking the water. Ethnic menus include Italian, Tuscan, Chinese, Polynesian, Japanese, Mexican, and Continental cuisine. Choices can range from the trendy Portsmouth Brewery to the Parisian feel of Cafe Mirabelle to the Blue Mermaid World Grill, which features a varied menu of specialties seasoned with flavors from around the world.

Visitor Information: Greater Portsmouth Chamber of Commerce, 500 Market St., PO Box 239, Portsmouth, NH 03802-0239; telephone (603)436-3988

Convention Facilities

Facilities within the city can accommodate small- to medium-sized meetings and include more than 1,300 guest rooms and around 100 restaurants. The largest hotel is the Sheraton Harborside Hotel Portsmouth, featuring 15 meeting rooms highlighted by a ballroom that accommodates 150 to 200 guests. The city is full of picturesque inns and bed-and-breakfasts.

Convention Information: Greater Portsmouth Chamber of Commerce, 500 Market St., PO Box 239, Portsmouth, NH 03802-0239; telephone (603)436-3988

Transportation

Approaching the City

Since 1993 regional airline service has operated at the Pease International Tradeport. Pan American Airways operates to and from Sanford, Florida and Gary, Indiana. Air travelers can also use facilities at Logan International Airport, one hour to Portsmouth's south in Boston, Massachusetts; at Portland International Airport, one hour to the north in Portland, Maine; or Manchester Airport in Manchester, New Hampshire, which connects the southern part of the state to Washington, New York, Chicago, Philadelphia, and Pittsburgh. Frequent daily limousine service is available between Logan and Portsmouth.

Bus transportation to Portsmouth is available on C&J Trailways, which also serves Logan airport. C & J's Portsmouth stop is at the Park and Ride bus terminal at Pease International Tradeport. Ferries are available between Portsmouth and Kittery, Maine. Passenger rail extends from Boston to Newburyport, Massachusetts. Service is also available within the state to Dover and Durham.

Interstate 95 is a direct link connecting Portsmouth with Portland, Maine, and Boston; it extends as far north as the Canadian provinces and south to Key West, Florida. The Spaulding Turnpike (Rte. 16) connects the city to Dover, Rochester, and further north to the White Mountains. U.S. Route 101 stretches west through Manchester and eventually to Keene, New Hampshire. U.S. Route 4 leads into the city from Concord to east. All roads are passable year-round to the experienced traveler.

Traveling in the City

Portsmouth, which grew inland from the banks of the Piscataqua River, developed around a series of narrow, winding, often one-way streets in the downtown area. The main thoroughfares converge at Market Square in the center of downtown Portsmouth. Memorial Bridge connects Portsmouth with Kittery, Maine. Other traffic can use I-95 and the U.S. Route 1 Bypass, both with bridges across the river. Other bridges in the city cross South Mill Pond and provide a link with Pierce Island.

Traffic in the city blossoms during the summer tourist season when the city's population doubles. Bridge traffic is especially heavy during these months. Cooperative Alliance for Seacoast Transportation (COAST), the regional transit line since 1981, provides bus service to the combined metropolitan area of Portsmouth, Rochester, Dover, Somersworth, and Durham. Walking the brick-paved streets and taking the downtown trolley during the summer are the best ways to get to know Portsmouth, and horse-drawn carriages are available.

Communications

Newspapers and Magazines

The Portsmouth Herald, is published each weekday evening and in the mornings on weekends. Magazines published in Portsmouth include *Red Owl,* a literary magazine, and *Coastline,* a publication of the Chamber of Commerce.

Television and Radio

One television channel broadcasts from Portsmouth, and the city receives the major networks via the Boston channels. Portsmouth does have its own cable television franchise. One FM radio station and one AM station broadcast programming such as easy listening and album-oriented rock music from Portsmouth.

Media Information: The Portsmouth Herald, 111 Maplewood Ave., Portsmouth, NH 03801; telephone (800)439-0303; fax (603)427-0550; email news@seacoastonline.com

Portsmouth Online

City of Portsmouth. Available www.cityofportsmouth.com

Greater Portland Chamber of Commerce. Available www .portcity.org

Pease Development Authority. Available www.peasedev
.org

The Portsmouth Herald. Available www.seacoastonline
.com

Portsmouth Public Library. Available www.cityofports
mouth.com/Library

Portsmouth School Department. Available www.cityofports
mouth.com/school/index.htm

Strawbery Banke Museum. Available www.strawberybanke
.org

Selected Bibliography

Lenski, Lois, *Ocean-born Mary* (Stokes, 1939)

Rogers, Mary Cochrane, *Glimpses of an Old Social Capital (Portsmouth, New Hampshire) as Illustrated by the Life of the Reverend Arthur Browne and His Circle* (Boston, Printed for the subscribers, 1923)

Tanner, Virginia, *A Pageant of Portsmouth: A Pageant in Celebration of the Tercentenary of the First Settlement in New Hampshire, Spring of 1623* (Concord, N.H.: Rumford Press, 1923)

Wahl, Jan, *The Screeching Door: or, What Happened at the Elephant Hotel* (New York: Four Winds Press, 1975)

NEW JERSEY

The State in Brief

Nickname: Garden State
Motto: Liberty and Prosperity

Flower: Purple violet
Bird: Eastern goldfinch

Area: 8,721 square miles (2000; U.S. rank: 47th)
Elevation: Ranges from sea level to 1,803 feet
Climate: Moderate with marked differences between the northwest and southeast extremities

Admitted to Union: December 18, 1787
Capital: Trenton
Head Official: Governor Richard Codey (D) (until 2006)

Population
  1980: 7,365,000
  1990: 7,730,188
  2000: 8,414,350
  2004 estimate: 8,698,879
  Percent change, 1990–2000: 8.9%
  U.S. rank in 2004: 10th
  Percent of residents born in state: 53.4% (2000)
  Density: 1,134.4 people per square mile (2000)
  2002 FBI Crime Index Total: 259,789

Racial and Ethnic Characteristics (2000)
  White: 6,104,705
  Black or African American: 1,141,821
  American Indian and Alaska Native: 19,492
  Asian: 480,276
  Native Hawaiian and Pacific Islander: 3,329
  Hispanic or Latino (may be of any race): 1,117,191
  Other: 450,972

Age Characteristics (2000)
  Population under 5 years old: 563,785
  Population 5 to 19 years old: 1,720,322
  Percent of population 65 years and over: 13.2%
  Median age: 36.7 years (2000)

Vital Statistics
  Total number of births (2003): 117,127
  Total number of deaths (2003): 73,589 (infant deaths, 660)
  AIDS cases reported through 2003: 17,089

Economy
  Major industries: Manufacturing, tourism, agriculture, services, trade, mining, fishing
  Unemployment rate: 4.2% (April 2005)
  Per capita income: $40,002 (2003; U.S. rank: 3rd)
  Median household income: $55,221 (3-year average, 2001-2003)
  Percentage of persons below poverty level: 8.2% (3-year average, 2001-2003)
  Income tax rate: 1.4% on first $20,000; 1.75% on next $30,000; 2.45% on next $20,000, 3.5% on next $10,000, 5.525% on $70,000, 6.37% over $150,000
  Sales tax rate: 6%

Atlantic City

The City in Brief

Founded: 1783 (incorporated, 1854)

Head Official: Mayor Lorenzo Langford (since 2001)

City Population
   1980: 40,199
   1990: 37,986
   2000: 40,517
   2003 estimate: 40,385
   Percent change, 1990–2000: 6.7%
   U.S. rank in 1980: 547th
   U.S. rank in 1990: 700th (State rank: 17th)
   U.S. rank in 2000: 741st

Metropolitan Area Population (PMSA)
   1990: 319,416
   2000: 354,878

Percent change, 1990–2000: 10.0%
U.S. rank in 1990: 7th (CMSA)
U.S. rank in 2000: 6th (CMSA)

Area: 11.3 square miles (2000)
Elevation: 6 to 8 feet above sea level
Average Annual Temperature: 53° F
Average Annual Precipitation: 40.3 inches of rain; 15.7 inches of snow

Major Economic Sectors: Tourism and conventions, services, trade, real estate development
Unemployment Rate: 6.6% (February 2005)
Per Capita Income: $15,402 (1999)
2004 ACCRA Average House Price: Not reported
2004 ACCRA Cost of Living Index: Not reported

2002 FBI Crime Index Total: 5,346

Major Colleges and Universities: None

Daily Newspaper: *The Press of Atlantic City*

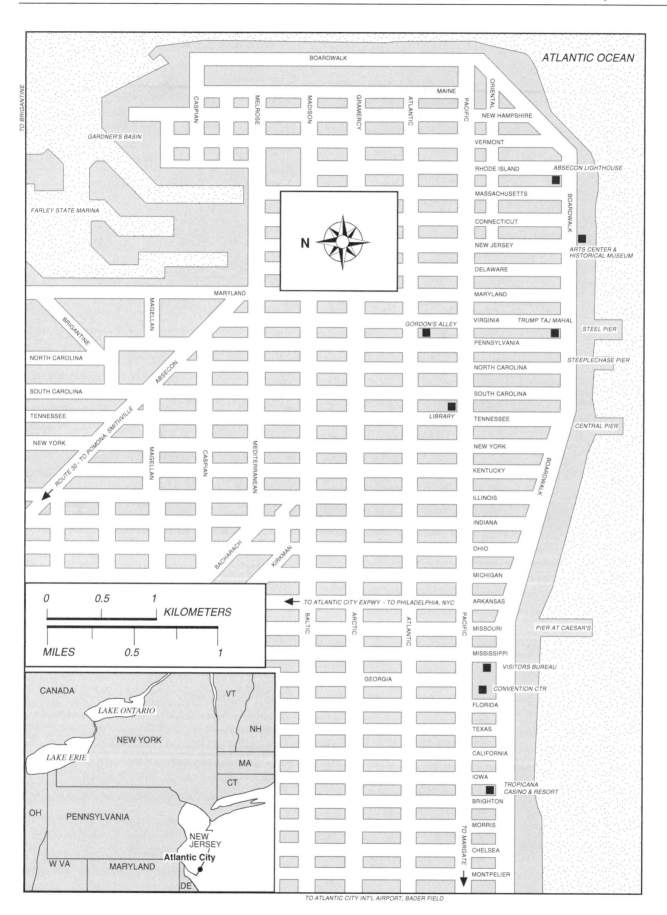

Introduction

A Victorian-era resort and the inspiration for the board game *Monopoly,* Atlantic City is now one of the nation's top tourist destinations. The city's attractions are legendary: a 5-mile-long boardwalk with entertainment piers stretching out over the Atlantic Ocean, 12 gambling casinos, luxury hotels and restaurants, luscious saltwater taffy and fudge, and sandy beaches. Much of Atlantic City's economy supports and thrives on its convention trade, which annually brings nearly 5,000 shows to the city's famous convention complex and casino/hotels.

Geography and Climate

Atlantic City, in southeast New Jersey, lies on narrow, sandy Absecon Island several miles off the mainland. The island, separated from the mainland by a series of low-lying meadows and a narrow strait, is 60 miles southeast of Philadelphia and 100 miles south of New York City.

Atlantic City's climate, while generally continental, is influenced by the proximity of the Atlantic Ocean. Summers start later and last longer than on the mainland and winters are milder. Precipitation is moderate and distributed throughout the year. The exception is the heavy rainfall attendant on the occasional hurricane which blows in off the coast.

Area: 11.3 square miles (2000)

Elevation: 6 to 8 feet above sea level

Average Temperatures: January, 30.9° F; July, 74.7° F; annual average, 53.0° F

Average Annual Precipitation: 40.3 inches of rain; 15.7 inches of snow

History

Railroad Alters Quiet Fishing Settlement

The first to enjoy the beaches and fishing off Absecon Island were members of the Lenni-Lenape tribe. They named their sandy summer home Absecon, meaning "place of swans." These Native Americans were followed in 1783 by New Jersey settlers who established a permanent site for a fishing village at the north end of the island. They called their town Absecon. For a half century, the inhabitants lived uneventful

lives on the 10-mile long sandbar. Then, in the early 1850s, Dr. Jonathan Pitney realized the island's tremendous potential as a health spa and resort. In 1852, Pitney and a group of visionary business investors obtained a railroad charter that brought the Camden & Atlantic Railroad to the island. Railroad engineer Richard Osborne planned a city on the site of the village of Absecon and in 1854 Atlantic City was incorporated.

The resort/spa succeeded beyond anyone's imagining. Wealthy businessmen and their families from Philadelphia and up and down the East Coast flocked to the new resort. To capitalize on its beaches, the townspeople laid down the first boardwalk in 1870, laying wooden planks upon the beach so that it could be enjoyed even during the hottest part of the day. With the construction of the boardwalk and its accompanying eateries and amusement stands, Atlantic City became a major tourist attraction. Vacationers and invalids coexisted happily in the Victorian-era town, living in ornate wooden boarding houses and enjoying the boardwalk in the rolling chairs invented in the city in 1884. The first of a half-dozen amusement piers was built in 1882, contributing to the city's carnival-like atmosphere. Saltwater taffy was created in 1883 when an entrepreneur's candy stand on the beach was flooded during high tide. The enterprising merchant immediately dubbed his saturated delicacies "saltwater" taffy. By 1887, heavy tourist traffic decreed the building of a second rail line into the city. In 1895 a visitor returning from Europe introduced to local merchants German-style picture postcards which instantly became popular on Atlantic City souvenir stands.

By 1915 traffic again warranted expanded services, this time in the form of the famous jitney line, which provided tourists with transportation in private automobiles. The first Miss America Pageant was held in Atlantic City in 1921; it was discontinued in 1928 and revived in 1935. The Atlantic City Auditorium/Convention Hall on the boardwalk opened in 1929. It was in 1929 that Charles Darrow introduced *Monopoly,* the board game that made Atlantic City's streets well known throughout America. During World War II, the U.S. Army used Atlantic City as a training site. A 1944 hurricane washed away nearly half the boardwalk, but it was quickly rebuilt.

Legalized Gambling Revitalizes City

Following the war, Atlantic City's tourist trade tapered off as economical airfare to the exotic Caribbean and Florida became available. Without the proceeds of the summer trade that sustained the city year-long, Atlantic City sank into disuse and widespread urban decay. In 1974, New Jersey residents voted not to approve a gambling law that was on the ballot. In 1976, the resolution appeared again but was restricted to introducing gambling into Atlantic City in the hope of reviving the resort's economy. The second resolution was approved and Atlantic City became the first city in the eastern half of the U.S. to offer legal gambling. The first casino/hotel, Resorts International, opened in May 1978, and was quickly followed by 10 others. By 1988, the casino industry employed 40,000 people and was a major draw for the city's 30 million annual visitors. Property in Atlantic City was valued at $6 billion by 1988.

Since the institution of the gambling industry, Atlantic City has been plagued by persistent rumors about organized and street crime. Many experts agree, however, that Atlantic City's casinos are free of organized crime. Street crime is being addressed directly by increased police presence, and indirectly through an energetic redevelopment plan for the city. As a result of the city's efforts, the crime rate dropped nearly 50 percent between 1988 and 2003.

The city's casino revenue reinvestment program, along with city, state, and federal dollars, is being used to revitalize decaying neighborhoods off the boardwalk and to attract additional retail and office business. With the creation of the Special Improvement District, most of the city's downtown commercial district now displays decorative fencing, pavements and lights, new trees, banners, and other aesthetic enhancements. The Casino Reinvestment Development Authority has invested $225 million in new residential construction, building 1,897 new housing units within Atlantic City's boundaries. For fiscal year 2005, the city has $2,736,159 budgeted for redevelopment and improvements.

Atlantic City offers conventioneers, vacationers, casino- and beach-goers a convenient place to network and relax, and is within a day's driving distance of one-third of the nation's population.

Historical Information: Historian, Atlantic City Free Public Library, One North Tennessee Avenue, Atlantic City, NJ 08401; telephone (609)345-2269. Atlantic City Arts Center and Historical Museum, New Jersey Avenue & Boardwalk, Atlantic City, NJ 08401; telephone (609)347-5837

Population Profile

Metropolitan Area Residents
1980: 276,000
1990: 319,416
2000: 354,878
Percent change, 1990–2000: 10.0%
U.S. rank in 1990: 7th (CMSA)
U.S. rank in 2000: 6th (CMSA)

City Residents
1980: 40,199
1990: 37,986
2000: 40,517
2003 estimate: 40,385
Percent change, 1990–2000: 6.7%
U.S. rank in 1980: 547th
U.S. rank in 1990: 700th (State rank: 17th)
U.S. rank in 2000: 741st

Density: 3,574 people per square mile (2000)

Racial and ethnic characteristics (2000)
   White: 10,809
   Black or African American: 17,892
   American Indian and Alaska Native: 193
   Asian: 4,213
   Native Hawaiian and Pacific Islander: 24
   Hispanic or Latino (may be of any race): 10,107
   Other: 5,575

Percent of residents born in state: 45.8%

Age characteristics (2000)
   Population under 5 years old: 3,041
   Population 5 to 9 years old: 3,250
   Population 10 to 14 years old: 2,690
   Population 15 to 19 years old: 2,398
   Population 20 to 24 years old: 2,650
   Population 25 to 34 years old: 6,415
   Population 35 to 44 years old: 6,151
   Population 45 to 54 years old: 4,676
   Population 55 to 59 years old: 1,836
   Population 60 to 64 years old: 1,676
   Population 65 to 74 years old: 2,971
   Population 75 to 84 years old: 2,019
   Population 85 years and over: 744
   Median age: years 34.7 (2000)

Births (2002)
   Total number: 792

Deaths (2002)
   Total number: 570 (of which 13 were infants under 1 year of age)

Money income (1999)
   Per capita income: $15,402
   Median household income: $26,969
   Total households: 15,886

Number of households with income of . . .
   less than $10,000: 3,209
   $10,000 to $14,999: 1,543
   $15,000 to $24,999: 2,639
   $25,000 to $34,999: 2,347
   $35,000 to $49,999: 2,430

$50,000 to $74,999: 1,878
$75,000 to $99,999: 1,003
$100,000 to $149,999: 488
$150,000 to $199,999: 133
$200,000 or more: 216

Percent of families below poverty level: 19.1% (42.3% of which were female householder families with related children under 5 years)

2002 FBI Crime Index Total: 5,346

Municipal Government

Atlantic City has a mayor-council form of government. The mayor and nine council members are elected to four-year terms; three council members are elected at large and six are elected by ward (district).

Head Official: Mayor Lorenzo Langford (D) (since 2001; current term expires November 2005)

Total Number of City Employees: Not reported

City Information: Atlantic City Hall, 1301 Bacharach Boulevard, Atlantic City, NJ 08401; telephone (609)347-5300

Economy

Major Industries and Commercial Activity

The convention and tourism industry rebuilt Atlantic City's economy in the late 1980s and through the 1990s. Now one of the nation's top tourist attractions, the city boasts 13 gambling casino/hotels, which attracted 33 million visitors in 2004. Coupled with its famous beaches and boardwalk, Atlantic City's superb hotel accommodations annually draw nearly 5,000 conventions, trade shows, and meetings. Since 1975, the casinos have funneled $7 billion back into the city's economy in addition to creating some 55,000 jobs. A tax on casino gross revenue provides $300 million annually for state programs for seniors and the disabled. In addition, the Atlantic City Cape Community College features a Casino Career Institute, which has trained more than 46,000 students for employment in the gaming industry.

Although much of Atlantic City's economic development centers around the casinos, the local government has been pursuing its goal to diversify the economy through the development of themed restaurants, retail shopping, night clubs, museums, theaters, minor league baseball and other recreational attractions. Non-casino industries in Atlantic City include services, retail trade, real estate development, distilling, and deep sea fishing. Many of the goods produced are by-products of the convention/tourism trade.

Items and goods produced: saltwater taffy, clothing, bottles and glassware, plastics, boats, paints, hosiery, baby carriages, reed furniture, chinaware, creamery and poultry products, fish and seafood

Incentive Programs—New and Existing Businesses

Local programs—Among the public and private agencies assisting businesses in Atlantic City are the Atlantic City Department of Planning and Development, the Casino Re-Investment Development Authority, the Atlantic County Improvement Authority, Atlantic City Housing Authority and Urban Redevelopment Agency, the Atlantic City–New Jersey Coordinating Council, and Atlantic County and its agencies. These agencies oversee casino re-investment funds, more than $100 million in city monies, and substantial luxury tax revenues.

State programs—The New Jersey Economic Development Authority (EDA) offers a wide range of financial, real estate development, and technical services to encourage business development and growth in the state. The majority of its assistance is to small and mid-sized businesses. The EDA issues bonds to provide financing at favorable interest rates for business ventures, and makes low-interest loans and guarantees loans made by private investors and lenders. It also offers a full range of real estate development services to stimulate both private and public development projects. In addition, the EDA administers a business incentive program that provides grants to expanding or relocating businesses that will create new jobs in New Jersey. Loans and grants also are available to municipalities and private property owners to encourage the clean-up and redevelopment of hazardous sites around the state. The New Jersey Urban Development Corporation provides low-interest loans to developers and businesses seeking to construct facilities in urban areas, including small business incubators.

The New Jersey Small Business Development Corporation (NJSBDC) network specializes in business planning, growth strategy, management strategy, and loan packaging, along with providing help in selling goods and services to government agencies, help to entrepreneurs in commercializing new technologies, linking up companies to local manufacturers who serve as mentors, and counseling for companies regarding overseas trade.

Job training programs—The New Jersey Business Employment Incentive Program Loan Program allows companies to receive up to an 80 percent rebate for ten years for the additional state income tax generated by creating new jobs.

The state's business Relocation Assistance Grant Program provides relocation grants to businesses that create a minimum of 25 new full time jobs in the state.

Development Projects

The $268 million Atlantic City Convention Center is the cornerstone of a $5.6 billion renaissance that has transformed Atlantic City into a major visitor and meeting destination. Contributing to the popularity of the area is the Boardwalk Hall, originally built in 1929 and listed on the National Register of Historic Places. This carefully renovated Atlantic City Convention Center has been fully refurbished to blend the ambience of Atlantic City's original heyday with the amenities and accommodations that visitors expect in the twenty-first century. In 2003 *Billboard* magazine named Boardwalk Hall, renovated in 2001, as the top-grossing midsize arena in the United States.

The $4 million Atlantic City Visitor Welcome Center, located on the Expressway, services tourists as they approach town by car. Located next to Sandcastle Stadium in Chelsea Heights is the ice skating and hockey rink, Flyers Skate Zone.

In late 2004, Borgata Hotel Casino and Spa announced a $347 million expansion that would include a 45-story hotel tower, complementing previously revealed plans for a $200 million investment in expanded casino, restaurant, and shopping space. This will expand Borgata's guest rooms from 2,000 to 2,500 and add 100 suites and 200 luxury condominiums to the complex.

Economic Development Information: Casino Re-Investment Development Authority, 1014 Atlantic Ave., Atlantic City, NJ 08401; telephone (609)347-0500. Atlantic City Department of Planning and Development, City Hall, Suite 604, 1301 Bacharach Blvd., Atlantic City, NJ 08401; telephone (609)347-5404. New Jersey Commerce, Economic Growth & Tourism Commission, 20 W. State St., PO Box 839, Trenton, NY 08625; telephone (609)777-0885

Commercial Shipping

Freight shipped via air arrives at Philadelphia International Airport, Atlantic City International Airport in Pomona, and at Bader Field (Atlantic City Municipal Airport) near downtown. The closest major container shipping ports are in New York, New Jersey, and Philadelphia. Atlantic City is adjacent to the Garden State Parkway and is serviced by the Atlantic City Expressway.

Labor Force and Employment Outlook

Between 1975, the dawn of the era of legalized gambling in Atlantic City, and 2001, the combined wages of hotel workers in Atlantic City rose from $15 million to $1.1 billion.

The service sector continues to be Atlantic City's largest employer.

Plans are well underway to make the city a world-class resort through airport modernization and expansion and revitalization of the casino industry, and to pursue economic diversity through non-casino hotels, a theme park, beach and boardwalk enhancements, a new convention center, and a revitalized central business district. State-mandated casino reinvestments are earmarked for housing construction and economic development.

The following is a summary of data regarding the Atlantic City labor force, 2004 annual averages.

Size of nonagricultural labor force: 149,500

Number of workers employed in . . .
  construction and mining: 6,600
  manufacturing: 4,500
  trade, transportation, and utilities: 21,900
  information: 1,100
  financial activities: 4,400
  professional and business services: 9,800
  educational and health services: 17,200
  leisure and hospitality: 57,400
  other services: 4,100
  government: 22,600

Average hourly earnings of production workers employed in manufacturing: $15.67 (2004 statewide average)

Unemployment rate: 6.6% (February 2005)

Largest employers	*Number of employees*
Atlantic City Hilton Casino Resort	(no employee
Bally's Atlantic City	figures available)
Borgata Casino Hotel & Spa	
Caesars	
Harrah's Atlantic City	
Resorts Atlantic City	
Sands Casino Hotel	
Showboat Casino Hotel	
Tropicana Casino & Resort	
Trump Marina Casino Resort	
Trump Plaza Hotel & Casino	
Trump's Taj Mahal Casino Resort	

Cost of Living

The following is a summary of data regarding several key cost of living factors in the Atlantic City area.

2004 ACCRA Average House Price: Not reported

2004 ACCRA Cost of Living Index: Not reported

State income tax rate: 1.4% for total income of $1 to
$20,000; 1.75% for total income of $20,001 to $35,000;
3.5% for total income of $35,001 to $40,000; 5.525% for
total income of $40,001 to $75,000; 6.37% for total
income of $75,001 to $500,000; 8.97% for total income
of $500,001 and up (2004).

State sales tax rate: 6%

Local income tax rate: None

Local sales tax rate: None (3% alcoholic beverage tax and
9% lodging and related services tax)

Property tax rate (effective): $2.96 per $100 of assessed
value (2004)

Economic Information: Atlantic City Department of Planning & Development, City Hall, Atlantic City, NJ 08401;
telephone (609)347-5404

Education and Research

Elementary and Secondary Schools

Among its many special programs, the Atlantic City public
schools offer a gifted and talented program, a preschool
program, English as a Second Language, a K & 1 Write to
Read program, and a special truancy program. The school
system has instituted a computerized managed instruction
program that provides most students access to the schools'
computer labs. Special software developed to coincide with
texts in use and standardized tests complements the hardware. The high school, Atlantic City High, opened in the
mid-1990s following an investment of some $80 million.
Atlantic City's schools saw an increase in test scores in
2004, most notably in elementary language proficiency. Just
over 60 percent of students were deemed at least proficient
in language in 2004, up from 22 percent in 2003. High
schoolers saw a combined increase of 4.5 percent in writing
and mathematics in 2004. Among the challenges that face
educators in the Atlantic City school system is the high rate
of poverty; in 2005, 81.5 percent of enrolled students were
identified as living below poverty level.

The following is a summary of data regarding the Atlantic
City Public School system as of the 2004–2005 school year.

Total enrollment: 7,159

Number of facilities
  elementary schools: 8
  junior high/middle schools: 2
  senior high schools: 1

Student/teacher ratio: 25:1

Teacher salaries
  average: $53,897 (2004)

Funding per pupil: $11,123 (2004)

Public Schools Information: Atlantic City Public Schools,
1300 Atlantic Avenue, 5th Floor, Atlantic City, NJ 08401;
telephone (609)343-7200

Colleges and Universities

The nearest institution of higher learning is Richard Stockton College of New Jersey in Pomona, an easy commute to
the west. The school offers bachelor's degrees in business,
arts, and sciences. Special programs include interdisciplinary studies in gerontology, Judaism, Africana studies, Latin
American/Caribbean studies, teacher education, and
women's studies. Together with its academic curricula,
Stockton offers students cooperative education, internships,
and study abroad. Atlantic Community College, based in
Mays Landing, holds "casino schools" in Atlantic City,
teaching tourists the skills needed to play the games of
chance in the city's casinos.

Libraries and Research Centers

The public library system consists of the Atlantic City Free
Public Library, the main facility, and the Richmond Branch
Library. In addition to its 104,000 volumes, the system
makes available magazines, videos, records, and cassettes.
The library's History of Atlantic City Collection includes
books, periodicals, pamphlets, postcards, maps, Miss Amer-
ica yearbooks, and period souvenirs. Information about New
Jersey history and genealogy is also catalogued.

Within Atlantic City are several specialized libraries, including the U.S. Federal Aviation Administration's Technical
Information Research Facility at the Atlantic City Airport;
and the Health Science Library of the Atlantic City Division
of the Atlantic City Medical Center. The William J. Hughes
Technical Center Library is a leading aviation research and
testing facility designated as an emergency space shuttle landing site. At the Marine Mammal Stranding Center, mammals
that have been rescued and deemed beyond saving are studied
for what they can reveal about mammalian illness.

Public Library Information: Atlantic City Free Public Library, One North Tennessee Avenue, Atlantic City, NJ
08401; telephone (609)345-2269; fax (609)345-5570

Health Care

Founded in 1898, the AtlantiCare Regional Medical Center
on Pacific Avenue is licensed for 540 beds. The center is a

teaching hospital affiliated with Hanneman University in Philadelphia and the University of Medicine and Dentistry of New Jersey. Specialties include cardiology, emergency care, and the Joint and Spine Institute, and the hospital has the region's only Level II trauma care center and neonatal intensive care center. Through the Ruth Newman Shapiro Regional Cancer Center the hospital offers rapid detection of malignant conditions and care including radiation and chemotherapy.

Health Care Information: Atlantic City Medical Center, 1925 Pacific Avenue, Atlantic City, NJ 08401; telephone (609)344-4000

Recreation

Sightseeing

Opened in 1999, the $4 million Atlantic City Visitor Welcome Center, located on the expressway just outside the city, provides guests with up-to-date information on hotels, restaurants, attractions, shopping, festivals, events, and regional cultural and historical sites. The Boardwalk Information Center, in the center of town, provides walk-in visitors with regional guides and information on various attractions and amenities.

Atlantic City's premier attraction is its boardwalk, a nearly five-mile-long steel, concrete, and wooden structure stretching along the Atlantic Ocean beach. The structure was described in 1909 by a travel writer for a national magazine as "overwhelming in its crudeness—barbaric, hideous and magnificent." Roughly paralleling Atlantic and Pacific avenues, the boardwalk is 60 feet wide and home to a variety of shops, amusement stands, and eateries. Its surface is a patterned design of bethaburra, a Brazilian hardwood. Along its length, and well worth a close look, is Donald Trump's $1 billion Taj Mahal, adorned with Hindu elephant gods, multicolored onion domes, minarets, and $14 million of chandeliers.

The boardwalk continues its southward stretch into neighboring communities such as Ventnor. Running perpendicular to the Boardwalk are a series of entertainment piers, many of which have been destroyed and rebuilt several times. Central Pier is known for its observation tower. Steeplechase Pier features children's amusements. Steel Pier, first opened in 1898, was a noted entertainment area. In 1990, the pier reopened as a family entertainment facility under the auspices of the Trump Taj Mahal complex. Garden Pier attracts culture lovers to the Arts Center and Historical Museum. Now a mall called Ocean One, the former Million Dollar Pier features shops and restaurants. The Tivoli Pier,

part of the Trop World resort, is a 2-acre amusement park reminiscent of Atlantic City's carnival days. Legalized gambling and the glitter of the luxurious casino/hotels lining the boardwalk are other popular tourist attractions.

Ripley's Believe It Or Not Museum has attracted the curious since 1996. The Absecon Lighthouse, which was built in 1854, was reopened to the public after a $3 million facelift. The 228-step historic structure is the tallest lighthouse in New Jersey and offers a bird's eye view of Atlantic City's dazzling skyline and the back bay area. Lucy the Margate Elephant is a six-story wood and metal structure built in the shape of an elephant. Located in nearby Margate and initially used as a bazaar site in 1881, Lucy is now a national historic site. Wheaton Village portrays life in an 1888 glass-making village; the Towne of Historic Smithville features colonial buildings and specialty shops. At the Marine Mammal Stranding Center and Museum in Brigantine, visitors can discover the wonders of the sea and learn about the care of ailing sea creatures.

Arts and Culture

Performing arts in Atlantic City take the form of top name entertainment offered at the casino/hotels' lounges and "big rooms," many of which seat more than 1,000 patrons. Innumerable singers, musicians, entertainers, dancers, and comedians, most of them Hollywood and Broadway stars, have taken the stage in Atlantic City. Recent improvements to Brighton Park along the boardwalk include a new amphitheater, which offers summertime concerts. Jazz concerts are scheduled at Historic Gardner's Basin.

Located on the boardwalk's Garden Pier is the Atlantic City Arts Center and Historical Museum. The center hosts art exhibits and shows all year long while the museum focuses on the city's 150-year history. The Circle Gallery on Park Place and the Lenox China Showroom are popular tourist stops. The Noyes Museum in Oceanville features a collection of regional duck decoys. Staff of the Ripley's Believe It Or Not Museum in Atlantic City are noted in the Ripley hierarchy for their ability to find particularly unusual exhibits. The Ocean Life Center at Gardner's Basin has 8 tanks totaling 29,800 gallons of live exhibits, including a 23,000 gallon tank featuring the fish of northern New Jersey and a 750 gallon touch tank. Interestingly, the Ocean Life Center is accessible by car, on foot, and by boat.

Arts and Culture Information: Atlantic County Office of Cultural Affairs, 40 Farragut Avenue, Mays Landing, NJ 08330; telephone (609)625-2776

Festivals and Holidays

Atlantic City's most famous annual event is the Miss America Pageant, held the second week of September. Begun in

Atlantic City's popular boardwalk offers shops, amusement stands, and entertainment piers.

1921, the pageant generates an aura of festivity, including the Miss America Ocean Powerboat Race. Other annual events include the Atlantic City Boat Show in January and the Antique Auto Show in February. The city's Easter Parade has been an eagerly awaited event for generations of Atlantic City residents and visitors alike. In late May comes the symbolic Unlocking of the Ocean. The city sponsors Boardwalk Art Shows in June and September. In early July, the annual New Jersey Fresh Seafood Festival, described as a ''sea appreciation party,'' takes place at Historic Gardner's Basin Maritime Park, a turn-of-the-century fishing village. Anglers are attracted to the Atlantic City Tuna Tournament in late July. The Wedding of the Sea in mid-August is celebrated with music, floats, a parade, sidewalk sales, and ceremonies held at Mississippi Avenue and the beach. Atlantic City's Marlin Tournament is held each August as well.

Sports for the Spectator

The Atlantic City Race Course, 14 miles west of the city, presents thoroughbred racing during the summer and simulcasts of racing events the remainder of the year. The Atlantic City Surf, a professional baseball team affiliated with the Atlantic League, plays near Bader Field in the $14.5 million Sandcastle Stadium, a 75,000-square-foot facility. The 5,900-seat stadium offers grandstand and premium deck seating, 20 luxury skyboxes, oversized concession areas, a souvenir shop, team clubhouses, administrative offices and 2,000 parking spaces. Other professional sports events, especially boxing matches, are sponsored by the city's casino/hotels. Annual events include the National Powerboat Races, State Sailing Championships, Shop Rite LPGA (women's golf) tournament (formerly the Atlantic City Classic), and professional polo matches, bowling competitions, and bicycle races.

Sports for the Participant

It is the pristine beaches along Absecon Island that draw thousands of swimmers and water sports enthusiasts every year. Surfers ride the breakers that wash the beaches, and sailors and powerboaters enjoy the ocean and inlet waters in the area. Ocean fishing is a popular sport, both from the shores of the coastal waters and from the decks of boats miles out to sea. Facilities in and around Atlantic City accommodate those wishing to play squash, tennis, racquetball, and golf. Bicycling, walking, and jogging along the boardwalk are picturesque as well as good exercise. Many of the casino/hotels offer guests complete fitness and athletic facilities.

Shopping and Dining

Atlantic City's most unusual shopping destination is Shops on Ocean One at Arkansas Avenue and the Boardwalk. Built in the shape of a luxury ocean liner, Ocean One features 150 stores, restaurants, and an amusement park, all spread over three levels and extending over the ocean. The city's major downtown shopping area occupies Atlantic Avenue and the avenues intersecting it. The Hamilton Mall in Mays Landing is the area's largest shopping center, boasting more than 150 stores and restaurants. In nearby Pleasantville, the Shore Mall offers 75 shops and eateries, plus a movie theater complex. For the bargain hunter, every Tuesday and Saturday the Cowtown Rodeo in Woodstown has a flea market. Historic Wheaton Village in Millville is a replica of a Victorian glass-making town, complete with gift and craft shops, plus there are several other uniquely themed, quaint shopping plazas throughout neighboring communities.

Delicatessen fare and fresh seafood are noteworthy Atlantic City offerings. Many of the delis along the Boardwalk feature stacked sandwiches, kosher hot dogs, and garlic dill pickles, the likes of which are seldom seen south of New York City. Fresh catches from the Atlantic include oysters, crabs, clams, and a variety of deep-sea fish. Dining is elegantly formal in many of the casino/hotel restaurants, a number of which specialize in assorted international cuisines. Traditional American fare can be had at colonial-era inns in Historic Smithville. Atlantic City is also the birthplace of salt water taffy and visitors may sample dozens of flavors along the boardwalk and in candy shops. The Historic Renault Winery and Vineyard in Egg Harbor City is renowned along the East Coast for its wines and gourmet food.

Visitor Information: The Atlantic City Convention & Visitors Authority, 2314 Pacific Ave., Atlantic City, NJ 08401; telephone (609)348-7100; toll-free (888)222-3683. State of New Jersey, Dept. of Commerce, Energy, and Economic Development, Div. of Travel and Tourism, CN-826, Trenton, NJ 08625-0826; telephone (609)777-0885; toll-free (800)847-4865

Convention Facilities

Atlantic City is home to one of the largest municipal convention complexes in the nation. Located on the boardwalk between Georgia and Mississippi avenues, the Atlantic City Convention Center occupies 7 acres. The center features 500,000 square feet of exhibition space, 45 meeting and function rooms accommodating 50 to 3,000 conventioneers, and a Grand Ballroom accommodating up to 3,600. The East Hall main auditorium offers a 137-foot high column-free ceiling and seats nearly 22,000. When not used for conventions and trade shows, the center hosts numerous sporting events, including boxing, tennis, and football matches. The city's 13 casino hotels also offer meeting facilities; for example, the Trump Taj Mahal features more than 175,000 square feet of meeting space. In addition to guest rooms, casino/hotels offer fine restaurants and lounges that seat up to 1,000 people and feature top-name entertainment. Space is also available at the new Atlantic City Rail Terminal.

Convention Information: Atlantic City Convention & Visitors Bureau, Attn: Convention Services Director, 2314 Pacific Avenue, Atlantic City, NJ 08401; telephone (609)348-7100; fax (609)345-3685

Transportation

Approaching the City

Atlantic City International Airport in Pomona is nine miles west of Atlantic City. A three-phase multimillion-dollar expansion and modernization project has doubled and modernized terminal space and plans call for further expansion. Atlantic City International Airport is serviced by Spirit Airlines and Delta Connection. Bader Field, the Atlantic City Municipal Airport near downtown Atlantic City, accommodates commuter and charter flights and private planes. The city intends the eventual closing of Bader Field to make it available for private development. Major airports handling Atlantic City traffic are Philadelphia International Airport, 60 miles to the west, and Newark International Airport, 140 miles to the north. Limousine and bus service is available to Atlantic City from both airports.

Numerous commercial and charter buses travel into Atlantic City; the public bus terminal is at Arctic and Arkansas avenues. New Jersey Transit train service is available from cities in New Jersey and from Philadelphia, Washington, D.C., and New York City. Trains arrive at the Rail Terminal, immediately adjacent to the Convention Center Complex.

The major highway into Atlantic City is the Atlantic City Expressway. U.S. 30 reaches the city via Absecon Boulevard while U.S. 40/322 parallels Albany Avenue; both are surface routes and tend to be congested. The Garden State Parkway runs north-south outside the city and is a major access route.

Traveling in the City

Atlantic City follows a rigid grid pattern. Streets running parallel to the Atlantic Ocean are known by ocean or sea names; streets running perpendicular bear states' names. The city has placed Monopoly Board style street signs along the Boardwalk, together with 1920s style light fixtures and art deco facade treatments to pavilions. The boardwalk runs

along the ocean, curving westward to follow Absecon Channel.

Atlantic City's famous jitneys still offer travel in small private cars in Atlantic City. Boardwalk trams, taxis, buses, and rental cars are available. Parking spaces are at a premium, both in garages and on the streets. The convention center has 1,400 parking spaces available to visitors. Casino/hotel guests pay to have their vehicles sheltered.

Communications

Newspapers and Magazines

Atlantic City's daily newspaper, *The Press of Atlantic City,* appears each morning. *Atlantic City Magazine,* with its listings of events, is published monthly.

Television and Radio

One television station originates in Atlantic City, NBC-10. Atlantic City also receives Philadelphia stations and is serviced by a cable television franchise. The four AM and FM radio stations in the city broadcast a variety of music, talk, and religious shows.

Media Information: *The Press of Atlantic City,* 1000 W. Washington Ave, Pleasantville, NJ 08232; telephone (609)272-7000

Atlantic City Online

Atlantic City Convention & Visitors Bureau Authority. Available www.atlanticcitynj.com

Atlantic City Free Public Library. Available library.atlantic .city.lib.nj.us/ac

Atlantic City Public Schools. Available alpha1.acboe.org

City of Atlantic City Home Page. Available www.cityof atlanticcity.org

New Jersey Commerce & Economic Growth Commission. Available www.state.nj/commerce/dcedhome.htm

New Jersey Economic Development Authority. Available www.njeda.com

Selected Bibliography

Carnesworthe, pseud., *Atlantic City. Its Early and Modern History* (Philadelphia, W.C. Harris, 1868)

Hall, John F., *The Daily Union History of Atlantic City and County, New Jersey. Containing Sketches of the Past and Present of Atlantic City and County . . .* (Atlantic City, N.J., The Daily Union Printing Co., 1900)

Levi, Vicki Gold, *Atlantic City, 125 Years of Ocean Madness: Starring Miss America, Mr. Peanut, Lucy the Elephant, the High Diving Horse, and Four Generations of Americans Cut-ting Loose* (New York: C.N. Potter: Distributed by Crown Publishers, 1979)

Wilson, Harold F., *The Jersey Shore: A Social and Economic History of the Counties of Atlantic, Cape May, Monmouth, and Ocean* (New York: Lewis Historical Publishing, 1953, 3 vols.)

Jersey City

The City in Brief

Founded: 1630, (incorporated, 1820)

Head Official: Mayor Jerramiah Healy (D) (since 2005)

City Population
1980: 223,532
1990: 228,537
2000: 240,055
2003 estimate: 239,097
Percent change, 1990–2000: 4.8%
U.S. rank in 1980: 61st
U.S. rank in 1990: 67th (State rank: 2nd)
U.S. rank in 2000: 73rd (State rank: 2nd)

Metropolitan Area Population
1990: 553,099
2000: 608,975
Percent change, 1990–2000: 9.2%

U.S. rank in 1980: 1st (CMSA)
U.S. rank in 1990: 1st (CMSA)
U.S. rank in 2000: 1st (CMSA)

Area: 14.9 square miles (2000)
Elevation: 20 feet above sea level
Average Annual Temperature: 52.6° F
Average Annual Precipitation: 47.4 inches of rain; 27.8 inches of snow

Major Economic Sectors: Trade, services, government, manufacturing
Unemployment rate: 5.4% (February 2005)
Per Capita Income: $19,410 (1999)

2002 FBI Crime Index Total: 12,182

Major Colleges and Universities: Jersey City State College, St. Peter's College, Hudson County Community College

Daily Newspaper: *Jersey Journal*

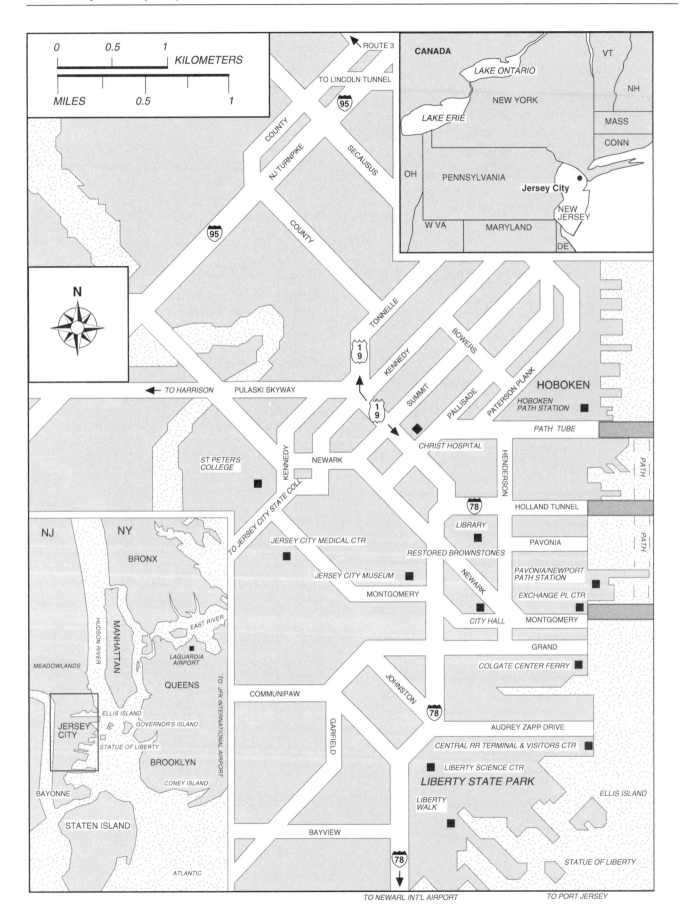

Introduction

Jersey City, once touted as "the city with everything for industry," still fulfills that promise. Its waterfront on the Hudson River, dubbed the Gold Coast, has been the focus in recent years of billions of dollars of development projects that are luring financial giants and others from Manhattan and the world. The second largest city in New Jersey, Jersey City attracts business with major air, water, rail, and highway transportation arteries, abundant utilities at reasonable rates, a growing service sector, and an established manufacturing base. Respected health care and educational facilities, along with blocks of reclaimed brownstone houses and impressive new developments, make Jersey City a desirable place to live as well.

Geography and Climate

Jersey City lies on a peninsula between the Hudson and Hackensack rivers in northeastern New Jersey. Seven miles to the west is Newark, and across the Hudson River to the east is New York City's lower Manhattan skyline. The terrain ranges from low-lying flood plains to gently rolling hills. While Jersey City's climate tends to be continental, influenced by winds from the west, it does experience temperature extremes throughout its four seasons. Summers are hot and humid and winters are moderately snowy.

Area: 14.9 square miles (2000)

Elevation: 20 feet above sea level

Average Annual Temperatures: January, 30.6° F; July, 74.6° F; annual average, 52.6° F

Average Annual Precipitation: 47.4 inches of rain; 27.8 inches of snow

History

Dutch Explore Tribal Land

Before the coming of Europeans, the indigenous Algonquian tribe who called themselves Lenape, "the People," lived in the Hudson County region. A peaceful people, they were respected by other tribes and often called to settle disputes between rivals, hence they became known as the "Grandfather tribe." White settlers renamed the Lenape Delawares, for the Delaware River they had designated for Lord de la Warr, then governor of the Jamestown Colony.

In 1609, English navigator Henry Hudson, financed by the Dutch East India Company, explored the area in his third unsuccessful attempt to find a passage to Asia by setting out north and west from Europe. Jersey City abounds with Dutch street names because it was Michael Pauw, an agent of the Dutch West India Company, who purchased and pioneered a permanent European settlement there in 1630. Pauw and his fellow trappers encountered Native Americans of the Delaware tribe and began trading with them. For the next 20 years the peninsula served as a western gateway for trade with other Native American tribes. This land of present day Jersey City and Hoboken, which the Indians had called Communipaw and Harsimus (both are spelled at least 15 different ways in historical documents) was dubbed Pavonia, by Pauw's Latinization of his own name, and Paulus Hook, after the next governor of the area, Michael Paulusen. In 1638, William Kieft was sent to Pavonia as the new director general of the colony. His swindling trade practices and brutality, culminating in 1643 in an unprovoked massacre of the Raritan tribe, (who had come to the Dutch for refuge from their warring enemies to the north, the Mohawks) resulted in an eight month war with the Indians, and sickness and poverty spread over the settlement. In 1647 Petrus Stuyvesant became the new director general of New Amsterdam and enacted a policy of conciliation that led to an uneasy peace with the Indians for a while. This peace was disturbed in 1655, when a Delaware maiden was killed for trespassing in a settler family's peach orchard in what is now lower Manhattan. The natives fled back across the Hudson River to Pavonia, then exacted revenge by driving out all white people from the Jersey Shore. Whoever did not flee was killed; livestock was slaughtered, and every building burnt down. The Dutch fled to New Amsterdam (now New York) to escape, but after five years went by, they wished to return to the fertile farmlands and hunting grounds of Pavonia. Stuyvesant re-bought the land from the Indians in a ceremony which included nine chiefs, and made sure the new settlement was built so as to be more easily defended.

The settlement shifted to English rule in 1664 when Charles II, who had always thought he owned it, gave it to his brother James, Duke of York. After a brief period of struggle with the Dutch, they asserted permanent control there in 1674, renaming the land New Jersey in honor of the largest island in the English Channel, where James' friend George Cartaret was born. Jersey City itself was known during this early English time as the Towne of Bergen. For the next century, agriculture and transportation occupied the region, where ferries traveled across the Hudson to and from New York. Jersey City was also an important stop on first the road route and then the stagecoach route from New York to Philadelphia.

Bergen, Paulus Hook, Harsimus, Communipaw Cove—all the old communities that became the core of modern Jersey City and Hoboken—played crucial parts throughout the Revolutionary War. After the earlier skirmishes at Lexington and Bunker Hill, it became obvious the British were turning their focus, and their naval strength, to the New York-New Jersey area in late June 1776. George Washington recognized the strategic importance of the region, ordered fortifications to be made quickly, and named the Bergen militia. Skirmishes and all out battles went on between the patriots and the British, along with their many Tory sympathizers in the region, but the British maintained an outpost on Paulus Hook until the night of August 18, 1779, when American Major Henry ''Light Horse Harry'' Lee led a surprise attack on the fort. Lee captured about a third of the English garrison while Americans suffered only two casualties. The humiliating loss of Paulus Hook was followed by a brutal winter of 1779-1780 wherein people could walk back and forth from New York to New Jersey on the ice to buy and sell increasingly rare and expensive firewood. The English forces began to lose their strength and resolve. In October of 1780, General Lafayette joined with the American forces to challenge the English at the place Jersey City Cemetery is now. The British retained a small hold on the area for the next couple of years but were finally driven out of America in 1783.

Modern Jersey City Emerges

In 1812, steam ferry service began with Robert Fulton's *Jersey.* Old Paulus Hook was incorporated as Jersey City in 1820, but only a small part of the size it is now, and was still considered part of the town of Bergen. Jersey City's first police force, the ''watch,'' was formed in 1829. When an 1834 treaty settled the middle of the Hudson River as the boundary between New York and New Jersey, development of Jersey City began in earnest. The Morris Canal extension to Jersey City in 1836, then two railroad lines arriving in the same year, bolstered the city's transportation and distribution capabilities. Coal from Pennsylvania could be shipped in to fuel factories, and the factories' goods readily shipped out anywhere in the United States. Resulting industry included the Colgate-Palmolive Company, makers of soaps, perfumes, and toiletries, which relocated from New York City to Jersey City in 1847. That year the *Hibernia,* was the first Cunard (luxury yacht makers of the Queen Mary II and Queen Elizabeth II) liner to dock at Port Jersey. Jersey City also became home of the Joseph Dixon Crucible Company, famous for lead pencils; the Dummer's Jersey City Glass Company, known for its flint glass; Isaac Edge's fireworks factory; and the American Pottery Company. From 1860 to 1870 Jersey City's population shot from 7,000 to 29,000, a

tribute to the economic strength of the city's factories, but also due to several municipalities in the area voting to consolidate themselves under the name Jersey City in 1869. Among the immigrants arriving through Port Jersey to work in the plants were Germans, Polish, Irish, and Italians. Prior to and during the Civil War, Jersey City was an important station on the Underground Railroad for escaping slaves, who entered the city hidden aboard Erie Canal boats. Jersey City was also a major embarkation point for Union soldiers.

Following the Civil War, activity centered around struggles between competing railroads and political infighting in municipal government. In the 1870s the first paid fire department was hired and the first public high school was opened. A railway tube between Jersey City and New York City opened in 1910.

Jersey City suffered from World War I aggressions when, on the night of July 30, 1916, German saboteurs exploded ammunition-laden railroad cars into Black Tom Island (which now comprises a south side portion of Liberty State Park, across from the Statue of Liberty and Ellis Island.) The blast was felt as far as Manhattan and Philadelphia, Connecticut and Maryland. Property losses were estimated at $22 million, $1 million of which went to replace glass in Jersey City windows.

A three decade political era began in 1917, when Frank Hague became mayor; his Democratic machine remained in power for the next 30 years. The Colgate clock, largest in the world, with a face spanning 50 feet in diameter and a 23-foot minute hand weighing over a ton, was erected in 1924, and in 1927 the Holland Tunnel opened. In 1937 Roosevelt Stadium opened and eventually became one of the fields upon which the great Jackie Robinson played when he broke major league baseball's color barrier in 1946.

Jersey City's population peaked at 299,000 in 1950. Residents and businesses, lured to suburbs accessible by new highways, began to leave the city in the 1950s. In response, older brownstone row homes were rehabilitated and massive downtown redevelopment projects were sponsored by private, municipal, state, and federal government dollars. Liberty State Park opened in 1976, and the first New Jersey Waterfront Marathon was run in 1985. By the late 1980s, Jersey City had become a ''back office'' site for businesses fleeing high rent and other exorbitant business costs in New York City. In fact, Jersey City was the only one of the state's six largest cities to gain both in population and employment during the recession of the late 1980s and early 1990s. In 1994, ten major firms relocated to the city, bringing more than 6,000 new jobs. Nearly 30 firms moved to or began operations within the city during the 1990s, and the skyline was transformed from rail yards and warehouses along the Hudson River to modern office towers and trendy artist's neighborhoods. Massive ongoing development projects into the new millenium promise continuing prosperity for Jersey City.

Historical Information: Historian, Jersey City Library, 472 Jersey Avenue, Jersey City, NJ 07302; telephone (201)547-4503

Population Profile

Metropolitan Area Residents

1980: 556,972
1990: 553,099
2000: 608,975
Percent change, 1990–2000: 9.2%
U.S. rank in 1980: 1st (CMSA)
U.S. rank in 1990: 1st (CMSA)
U.S. rank in 2000: 1st (CMSA)

City Residents

1980: 223,532
1990: 228,537
2000: 240,055
2003 estimate: 239,097
Percent change, 1990–2000: 4.8%
U.S. rank in 1980: 61st
U.S. rank in 1990: 67th (State rank: 2nd)
U.S. rank in 2000: 73rd (State rank: 2nd)

Density: 16,111 people per square mile (2000)

Racial and ethnic characteristics (2000)
   White: 81,637
   Black or African American: 67,994
   American Indian and Alaska Native: 1,071
   Asian: 38,881
   Native Hawaiian and Pacific Islander: 181
   Hispanic or Latino (may be of any race): 67,952
   Other: 36,280

Percent of residents born in state: 42.6% (2000)

Age characteristics (2000)
   Population under 5 years old: 16,631
   Population 5 to 9 years old: 17,321
   Population 10 to 14 years old: 16,383
   Population 15 to 19 years old: 15,542
   Population 20 to 24 years old: 19,094
   Population 25 to 34 years old: 46,541
   Population 35 to 44 years old: 37,799
   Population 45 to 54 years old: 28,268
   Population 55 to 59 years old: 10,463
   Population 60 to 64 years old: 8,575

Population 65 to 74 years old: 12,534
Population 75 to 84 years old: 8,099
Population 85 years and older: 2,805
Median age: 32.4 years

Births (2002, Jersey City)
   Total number: 3,743

Deaths (2002, Hudson County)
   Total number: 4,576 (of which, 64 were infants under the age of 1 year)

Money income (1999)
   Per capita income: $19,410
   Median household income: $37,862
   Total households: 88,617

Number of households with income of . . .
   less than $10,000: 13,002
   $10,000 to $14,999: 6,188
   $15,000 to $24,999: 10,567
   $25,000 to $34,999: 11,437
   $35,000 to $49,999: 13,759
   $50,000 to $74,999: 15,335
   $75,000 to $99,999: 8,174
   $100,000 to $149,999: 6,523
   $150,000 to $199,999: 1,851
   $200,000 or more: 1,781

Percent of families below poverty level: 16.4% (48.9% of which were female householder families with related children under 5 years)

2002 FBI Crime Index Total: 12,182

Municipal Government

Since a charter revision in 1960, Jersey City has operated with a mayor-council form of government. There are nine council members, six elected by wards and three at large; they and the mayor all serve four-year terms. The mayor does not vote on legislation, but may veto ordinances within ten days of passage by the Municipal Council. The Council needs six votes to override the mayor's veto. Jersey City is also the seat of Hudson County government.

Head Official: Mayor Jerramiah Healy (D) (since 2005, current term expires 2008)

Total Number of City Employees: 2,500 (2000)

City Information: Office of the Mayor, 280 Grove St., Jersey City, NJ 07302; telephone (201)547-5200

Economy

Major Industries and Commercial Activity

Jersey City, which is located in the heart of the New Jersey/New York City metropolitan area, experienced an economic renaissance in the 1990s, and the growth trend continues into the 21st century. Traditionally dependent on sectors such as transportation and distribution, the city is now focusing on what they've targeted as FIRE (Finance, Insurance, and Real Estate) businesses. There has been an incredible 500 percent growth in these types of businesses in Jersey City since 1993. High rent, taxes, and utility costs in adjacent Manhattan have prompted many New York firms to relocate partial or entire operations across the Hudson River to Jersey City, creating what is known as "back office space." Since the early 1990s, many major firms have relocated or begun new operations in Jersey City. The phenomenon is so marked that Jersey City's new state-of-the-art corporate developments are being called "the sixth borough" and "Wall Street West." Jersey City has no city income tax, no corporate or payroll tax, no commercial rent tax, 30 percent lower utilities than New York City's Con Ed, and rent on Class A office space is about a third less than in Manhattan. The Jersey City Economic Development Corporation (JCEDC), a nonprofit corporation formed in 1980 by the city council, is the main business proponent of the city and administers most of the business incentive monies and job training programs. JCEDC is dedicated to revitalization that benefits residents as well as companies through its citywide commercial reconstruction program called HUB, for Holistic Urban Building.

Items and goods produced: electronic products, steel products, soaps and toiletries, cork, cosmetics, chemical products, cans and bottles, paint and varnish, various processed foods, coke, graphite, shoes, slippers, and sandals, elevators, lamps, automobile and aircraft parts, oil refining equipment, clothing, and chocolate

Incentive Programs—New and Existing Companies

Local programs—The Jersey City Economic Development Corporation (JCEDC), administers business loans and Small Business Administration micro-loans through its subsidiary Community Lending and Investment Corporation (CLIC). CLIC has apportioned 195 loans since its beginning and created and retained 3,022 jobs in the community, and helped reinvest $55 million, resulting in more than $4 billion in capital investments. Besides CLIC, the JCEDC oversees several other main programs including the Construction Management Department, which oversees all building projects from large to small, and the Urban Enterprise Zone (UEZ) program, which promotes development in designated sections of the city. Qualifying businesses in the UEZs are eligible for tax incentives, marketing assistance, financial counseling, and reduced unemployment insurance. Certified Zone retailers get a reduced sales tax of three percent, which is reinvested in further business development in the city. Two programs under the Urban Enterprise Zone have improved quality of life in targeted neighborhoods. Special Improvement Districts (SID) is in commercial districts citywide. Neighborhood business and property owners organize under the Business Improvement Districts (BID) program; they are private nonprofit organizations which obtain for their communities things like supplemental security and street sanitation. JCEDC also maintains a Business Information Center which offers very small businesses technical assistance and financial advice.

State programs—Programs funded by the state of New Jersey are for the most part administered at the local level by the Jersey City Economic Development Corporation. The state of New Jersey's Economic Development Authority (EDA) runs two programs for expanding or relocating businesses. The Business Employment Incentive Program offers grants to those companies that create jobs in New Jersey; grants can equal up to 80 percent of what would be the state income taxes for new employees. Companies must create at least 25 new full time permanent jobs, except for new technology businesses like the biotech industry, which need to create only 10 new jobs. Bonus incentives exist for businesses that generate 500 jobs or invest more than $20 million. Businesses must maintain location in New Jersey for at least one and a half times longer than the duration of the grant, which can be up to 10 years. The Business Relocation Assistance Grant program helps businesses that move to New Jersey as well as companies that move within the state to bigger facilities. Applicants must be approved by the state Treasurer, and greater consideration is given to jobs which pay more than one and a half times higher than minimum wage. In 2004, the EDA funded 10 projects in Hudson County, including three in Jersey City proper, with total funding exceeding $46 million. EDA provides a wide range of other services as well, in the forms of tax credits, bonds, grants, and real estate development which focus on brownfield renewal and other such development where there would otherwise be none. There are 24 other financial assistance programs offered by EDA; several of these programs focus on aiding women and minorities in joining the business world.

The New Jersey Urban Development Corporation provides lower-than-market loans to developers and businesses seeking to construct facilities in urban areas, including small business incubators. The New Jersey Division of International Trade helps companies dependent on international commerce with advice and access to trade missions and foreign trade shows. The New Jersey Small Business Development Corporation network specializes in business planning and growth strategy, loan packaging, and help in selling goods and services to government agencies, help to entrepreneurs in commercializing new technologies, linking up companies to local manufacturers who serve as mentors, and counseling for companies regarding overseas trade.

Job training programs—Several job training programs are available at the state and local level. New Jersey's welfare reform program, called Work First NJ, assists people on welfare in becoming self sufficient through education and job training. Another state funded program offered by New Jersey Economic Development Authority is the Entrepreneurial Training Institute (ETI), an intensive eight-week course that teaches aspiring new business owners about basic business operations and building a financial plan; ETI also helps them get financial aid upon graduation. The New Jersey Department of Labor and Workforce Development provides several programs. Under the Department of Labor, Workforce New Jersey operates several One-Stop Career Centers throughout the state, two of which are in Jersey City. The One-Stop Career Center is a resource for both employers and job seekers which integrates job training, job placement, and unemployment services. The Urban League of Hudson County started with a job training and placement program for seniors, and now offers a wide range of job training and related social services, such as child care assistance.

Development Projects

The most recent major redevelopment projects in Jersey City are divided into the areas of Downtown and the Waterfront, Journal Square, the HUB at Martin Luther King, Jr. Drive, the Warehouse District Artist in Residence program, Saint Peter's College/McGinley Square Area Improvement project, residential development, and various commercial and industrial developments.

The Colgate Center is a waterfront development that contains nine office towers, a residential building, and a marina with ferries to Manhattan. 101 Hudson in Colgate Center is currently the tallest building in New Jersey, and Goldman Sachs has purchased other Hudson Street property with plans to erect the future tallest building in New Jersey. Notable tenants of Colgate Center include Merrill Lynch; Lehman Brothers Holdings; Hartz Mountain; Essex Waterfront, LLC; Lord, Abbett, and Co.; American Express Travel Related Services; National Discount Brokers; and Datek Online. On the drawing board to be added to Colgate Center are two more residential complexes, a helicopter pad on a pier at the marina, a 798-space parking garage, an outdoor pool and a gym.

Harborside Financial Center is another waterfront development with five million square feet of office space and approval for more commercial space as well as residential units, North Pier Apartments with a stunning view of the harbor and lower Manhattan, and the new Hyatt Regency Hotel. Major tenants of Harborside include Deutsche Bank, DLJdirect Holdings, TD Waterhouse, Exodus Communications, Morgan Stanley Dean Witter, Dow Jones, the American Institute for Certified Public Accountants, SunAmerica Asset Management, Garban Intercapital America, Forest Laboratories, and TradeWeb.

Five luxury hotels have opened in the city since 2000: the Hyatt Regency at Harborside; Candlewood Suites, just north of Harborside; the Courtyard Marriott, located by the Newport/Pavonia PATH subway station; a new $60 million Hilton; and a Doubletree Club Suites which is also near Harborside Financial Center.

Grove Street is an area under much development recently, with a 306-unit luxury apartment complex with adjoining office tower and commercial and retail space; the Christopher Columbus Towers, under construction in 2005; and the sale of the International Financial Building for more than $152 million by Mack-Cali Realty to a joint venture of German companies. Major residents of the International Financial Building are PCN Bank, NTT Data Communications, and Donaldson, Lufkin, and Jenrette. The Newport area is another spot of major development in the downtown and waterfront of Jersey City. Between the Newport Mall and the Newport Tower, (presently the second tallest building in New Jersey) there are 4.3 million square feet of office space, 7,000 residential units, 1,200 hotel rooms, and 300,000 square feet of commercial space, attracting such tenants as the FDIC, Sears and JCPenney, Brown Brothers Harriman, Sterns, Filene's, First Chicago Trust, and USA Network.

Recent renovations in Journal Square, in the heart of the city, were done at the historic Loew's Theater, 26 Journal Square, the Trust Company Building, and the PATH subway plaza. General street beautification such as specialty sidewalks, old style street lamps, specially landscaped plaza and traffic islands for pedestrians, and a fountain, have lured new businesses and residents to the neighborhood. ADP, Dreyfus, and the NY/NJ Port authority are important tenants there.

The HUB at Martin Luther King Drive is a redevelopment project that has won awards and recognition both regionally and nationwide. Its community owned shopping center alongside a light rail station has helped to raise the home values and income levels in its vicinity.

The Warehouse Historic District, nicknamed WALDO with the accompanying acronym Work And Live District Overlay, was an area of mostly empty warehouses left after three major railroads withdrew from the area. Visual artists, dancers, musicians, and writers were attracted to the neighborhood, prompting the Planning Board and City Council to pass a re-zoning ordinance which allows and encourages people to live and work in the warehouse district if they are engaged in the fine arts as a career. Sensing that too much office space would deaden the area, the new WALDO ordinance actually limits use of office space and reserves 51 percent of space for artists' live/work use.

The Saint Peter's College/McGinley Square Improvement project proposes general street repairs and improvements such as trees, better lighting, new sidewalks, upgrading McGinley Square Park, renovating the Armory Building, attractive new facades on retail structures, and a new dorm at Saint Peter's College.

Recent residential developments are many. Of note is the Gotham, a 220 unit luxury highrise with amenities such as a 24 hour concierge, two restaurants, a fitness club, and indoor and outdoor play areas for children; and Port Liberty, known as "Venice on the Hudson," which features quaint old world style townhouses and will boast a $30 million golf course overlooking the Statue of Liberty.

Commercial and industrial development centers around Greenville Yards in Port Jersey Industrial Park, which houses Summit Imports Group's food warehouse, which the company recently moved from Manhattan's TriBeCa section; a BMW vehicle preparation center; Hudson Eagle; Anheuser-Busch and Tropicana beverage distribution centers; and the 135 acre Liberty Industrial Park, home to Snow Bird bottling company, and printing facilities of the New York Daily News and Cunningham Graphics. Claremont Industrial Park and Montgomery Industrial Park also attract businesses with a skilled blue collar labor force, with access to all types of transportation, and proximity to big markets.

Economic Development Information: Jersey City Economic Development Corporation, 30 Montgomery St., Eighth Floor, Jersey City, NJ 07302; telephone (201)333-7797; fax (201)333-9323. New Jersey Economic Development Authority, CN990, Trenton, NJ 08625-0990; telephone (609)292-0369

Commercial Shipping

Jersey City, with 11 miles of waterfront on the Hudson River, is part of the bustling Port Authority of New York and New Jersey. Port Jersey's geographic location provides excellent access to the Atlantic Ocean from the Port of New York's Upper Harbor. Docks on the Hudson River and Upper New York Bay accommodate freighters, ocean liners, and coastal and river vessels. Port Jersey is divided into a 100 acre industrial park and a modern 110 acre port, with bulk capabilities, roll-on, roll-off, breakbulk facilities, and fully computerized operations. Port Jersey provides a large terminal for containerized shipping.

The Greenville Yards of Conrail are adjacent to the port, whose own railroad system services the port's seventeen

berths and its industrial complex. Truck terminals and warehousing accommodate the more than 100 motor carriers servicing the city. Jersey City is only 10 minutes away from Teterboro Airport, the nation's busiest corporate hub. Other airports certified for carrier operations nearby are the Port Authority Downtown Manhattan/Wall St. about five miles away, and Newark Liberty International, about eight miles away. Other public use airports less than 10 miles from Jersey City are the West 30th St. in New York, the Newark NR 1, and New York Skyports, Inc.

Labor Force and Employment Outlook

Jersey City has an abundance of skilled laborers of many ethnic origins. The state of New Jersey as a whole experienced record employment levels in 2004 and the state's jobless rate was well below the national average for the eighteenth straight month as of October 2004, a full one percent below the national rate at that time. Non-farm employment in an 11-county Northern New Jersey Region grew in 2004 after three years of losses, and employment in the region is expected to continue to grow moderately in 2005 and beyond. Sectors expected to enjoy the most growth in employment include government, education, health and social services, and retail trade. Construction is expected to continue steadily, while manufacturing, information, and trade, transportation and utilities are expected to continue a downward trend.

The following is a summary of data regarding the Jersey City metropolitan area (including metropolitan New York City) labor force, 2004 annual averages.

Size of nonagricultural labor force: 8,278,500

Number of workers employed in . . .
   construction and mining: 329,700
   manufacturing: 499,600
   trade, transportation, and utilities: 1,582,400
   information: 289,300
   financial activities: 769,700
   professional and business services: 1,223,500
   educational and health services: 1,358,000
   leisure and hospitality: 606,700
   other services: 346,000
   government: 1,273,000

Average hourly earnings of production workers employed in manufacturing: $13.24

Unemployment rate: 5.4% (February 2005)

Largest county employers	Number of employees
United States Post Office	4,032
The Port Authority of NY and NJ	3,900
County of Hudson	2,700

Largest county employers	Number of employees
HealthCare Staffing and Consulting	2,000
Deutsche Bank Trust Co. NJ Ltd.	1,833
Insurance Service Office Inc.	1,217
Fleet, NJ Company Development Corp.	1,000
Equiserve, Inc.	850
Provident Bank	850
Bon Secours New Jersey Health System, Inc.	818
JP Morgan Chase Bank	600
Port Authority Trans-Hudson, Inc.	600
Saint Francis Hospital, Inc.	600
National Discount Broker Group, Inc.	568
Lehman Commercial Paper, Inc.	525
US News World Report LLC	500
Top Job Personnel, Inc.	500

Cost of Living

The following is a summary of data regarding several key cost of living factors in the Jersey City area.

2004 (3rd Quarter) ACCRA Average House Price: $990,800 (Manhattan/metro NY-NJ)

2004 (3rd Quarter) ACCRA Cost of Living Index: 216.0 (Manhattan/metro NY-NJ) (U.S. average = 100.0)

State income tax rate: 1.4% to 8.97% ranging over six income brackets

State sales tax rate: 6.0%

Local income tax rate: None

Local sales tax rate: None

Property tax rate: $45.48 per each $1,000 of assessed value

Economic Information: Hudson County Chamber of Commerce & Industry, 574 Summit Ave., Suite 404, Jersey City, NJ 07306; telephone (201)653-7400; fax (201)798-3886. Jersey City Economic Development Corporation, 601 Pavonia Ave., Jersey City, NJ 07036; telephone (201)420-7755; fax (201)420-0304

Education and Research

Elementary and Secondary Schools

The Jersey City public school system, the state's second largest, was taken over by the state of New Jersey in 1989, when low test scores and high drop-out rates led officials to believe that poorer students were being disenfranchised. Now such programs as a Gifted and Talented Program in music and art, an Accelerated Enrichment Program for the academically gifted, and the Projects and Career Exploration (PACE) summer program, have turned these figures around. In just three years, the PACE program was seen to have lowered drop-out rates from 14.9 percent to 9.3 percent, and 80 percent who participated in PACE benefited from improved grades, attendance, and behavior. Dr. Ronald E. McNair Academic High School, with its all-honors curriculum, was named best high school in the state six years in a row by *New Jersey Monthly* magazine, and 15th out of 27,668 in the nation by *Newsweek* magazine in a May 2005 article.

The following is a summary of data regarding the Jersey City public schools for the 2003–2004 school year.

Total enrollment: 30,646

Number of facilities
  elementary schools: 31
  junior high/middle schools: 26
  senior high schools: 7
  other: 10

Student/teacher ratio: 17:1

Teacher salaries
  minimum: $40,000
  maximum: $47,220 base, plus $2,800 per year with more than 10 years service

Funding per pupil: $13,750

Public Schools Information: Jersey City Board of Education, 346 Claremont Avenue, Jersey City, NJ 07305-1634; telephone (201)915-6160

Colleges and Universities

New Jersey City University (NJCU) opened in 1929; after several name changes throughout the years, in 1998 the New Jersey Commission on Higher Education gave it university status and it became known by its present name. NJCU offers 32 undergraduate and 19 graduate degrees in three colleges (Arts and Sciences, Education, and Professional Studies) to about 10,000 students. In 2002, the College of Education opened University Academy Charter High School to its first ninth grade class of 125 students. In 2003 a huge new Visual Arts Building opened with a centerpiece of a sculpture by Maya Lin of Washington, D.C.'s Viet Nam Memorial fame. The Bayside Development Project features a six story Arts and Sciences building designed by renowned architect Michael Graves, which the university is building in cooperation with the city, board of education, and New Jersey Transit. It nears completion in 2005.

Saint Peter's College, a four-year Jesuit liberal arts school, offers 38 major programs leading to a bachelor's degree and numerous associate's degree programs. Saint Peter's was founded in 1872, and has a total enrollment of 3,282 and a full time enrollment of 1,926.

Hudson County Community College (HCCC) was established in 1974 and now offers a full gamut of associate degrees and certificates in business, culinary arts, education, social sciences, allied health, computer science, liberal arts, and engineering/technology. HCCC has agreements with partner colleges for students to transfer credits toward a four-year degree. It also interacts with community organizations to allow some students to begin work in their chosen fields right away, and for job placement when they complete their programs.

Jersey City Medical Center hosts the University of Medicine and Dentistry of New Jersey. Saint Francis Hospital and Christ Hospital both oversee schools of nursing in Jersey City. The Chubb Institute offers diplomas in modern technology occupations such as graphic design, computer networking and securities, and several careers in the medical field.

Libraries and Research Centers

The Jersey City Free Public Library System consists of a main library, four regional branches and seven smaller neighborhood libraries and a bookmobile. Its collection includes 400,000 print, audiovisual, and electronic materials. In 2002 the library automated its on-line catalog available from its own growing number of terminals or from the patrons's own homes. In August 2004, the library opened a new branch serving the Martin Luther King HUB area, named Glenn D. Cunningham Library after Jersey City's late Mayor and State Senator. Jersey City Free Public Library System has resources in many languages as well as music and art collections. The Jersey City Room provides information about the history, economy, and government of the area.

Other libraries in Jersey City are the Hudson County Law Library, research libraries maintained by Block Drug Company and Pershing & Company, and the libraries at New Jersey City University and other schools. In 1999 and 2000 NJCU renovated two of its libraries: the Forrest Irwin library, which was equipped with a high tech research facility, and NJCU Library, which was rededicated Congressman Frank J. Guarini Library. The Guarini Library features wide-open and well-lit study spaces, numerous PCs, including those built to accommodate physically handicapped people, laptop docking, a touch screen Library Information Kiosk, and a Bibliographic/Information literacy program centered around the Machuga Technology Center room.

The University of Medicine and Dentistry at Jersey City Medical Center specializes in eye research in its Opthalmic Facilities. It also hosts a BRANY, Biotech Research Association of New York, facility. New Jersey City University has a vast new research center in its newly renovated Forrest Irwin Library. New Jersey City University (NJCU) is also home to the Center for Public Policy and Urban Research. A 48 mile corridor in the state of New Jersey that includes

Jersey City, stretching from Newark down through Princeton, is known as the global epicenter of pharmaceutical and medical research and manufacturing. Nineteen of the 25 largest pharmaceutical companies are represented as well as over 120 biotech research companies. Just as finance companies are continuing to be attracted to the northern New Jersey region over Manhattan's high rent and utility costs, so are life science researchers from New York City's prestigious universities and research facilities.

Public Library Information: Jersey City Public Library, 472 Jersey Ave., Jersey City, NJ 07302; telephone (201)547-4500

Health Care

Health care needs are met by five hospitals in Jersey City. Liberty Health System's Jersey City Medical Center is the largest, with a 15-acre campus overlooking New York Harbor and the Statue of Liberty. It is the only designated Level II Trauma Center in the county and has the only designated Perinatal Care facility in Hudson County; there are more than 400 doctors, 100 of whom are teaching physicians. A major teaching affiliate with Mt. Sinai School of Medicine, Jersey City Medical Center includes the Fanny E. Rippel Foundation Heart Institute, the Children's Hospital of Hudson County, the Port Authority Heroes of September 11 Trauma Center, Provident Bank Ambulatory Center, (for outpatient needs such as physical therapy,) and Kazmir Family Regional Perinatal Center.

Also part of Liberty Health System, Greenville Hospital underwent recent modernization and includes a new emergency room, new patient rooms, treatment rooms, diagnostic equipment, and a renovated lobby. Liberty Health also runs two smaller Family Health Centers in Jersey City. Christ Hospital specializes in various forms of community service for seniors, women, children, and the disadvantaged. It also has a sleep disorders lab and extensive behavioral health services, Hartwood Heart Center, obstetric and oncology services, a diabetes clinic, emergency department, in- and out-patient surgery, pediatric services, and a school of nursing. Saint Francis Hospital is a 243-bed acute care hospital occupying five buildings in downtown Jersey City. The Jewish Home and Rehabilitation Center, originally the Hebrew Home for Orphans and also known as simply the Jewish Hospital, specializes in long term care and rehabilitation for senior citizens. It provides an Alzheimer's Day Care Center, Adult Medical Day Care Center, and Podiatric, Dental, and Total Eye Care clinics for the elderly.

Health Care Information: Jersey City Medical Center, 50 Baldwin Ave., Jersey City, NJ 07304; telephone (201)915-2000

Recreation

Sightseeing

Jersey City is a city of neighborhoods, many of which contain national historic landmarks. Among its most famous communities are Paulus Hook, Van Vorst Park, Hamilton Park, Harsimus Cove, Bergen Hill, and Washington Village. The Van Vorst House, the city's oldest building, is a 1740 brownstone. The Grace Van Vorst Church reflects the early English Gothic style of architecture and was built over an 11-year period in the mid-1800s. Old Bergen Reform Church is a Greek Revival structure built in 1841. Other historic buildings include the Ionic House, built between 1835 and 1840, and Old Hudson County Courthouse, opened in 1910. Apple Tree House, now a privately owned funeral home, was the site of a Revolutionary War-era supper between General George Washington and his aide, the Marquis de Lafayette.

Perhaps the most famous of Jersey City's landmarks is the Colgate Clock, located on Hudson Street facing the bay. The gigantic timepiece boasts a dial 50 feet in diameter, with a minute hand weighing 2,200 pounds and moving 23 inches every minute. The clock was erected in 1924 and is still one of the largest clocks in the world.

Jersey City's parks are known for their historical landmarks. Liberty State Park, along New York Bay and overlooking the Statue of Liberty and Ellis Island, features the restored terminal of the Central Railroad of New Jersey and the Liberty Walk along the waterfront offering panoramic views of Manhattan. Three major ferry lines run daily from Liberty State Park to both the Statue of Liberty and Ellis Island. The Liberty Science Center in Liberty State Park presents exhibits and activities exploring health, environment, and invention. Opened in 1993, the Center also houses what is billed as the world's largest OMNIMAX theater.

The Fourth Regiment Armory Arch decorates Pershing Field, while Lincoln Park boasts Earle Faser's statue of President Abraham Lincoln,, a sculpture known as ''the mystic Lincoln.'' A sunken garden, playground, and fountain also adorn Lincoln Park.

Arts and Culture

In recent years, Jersey City has experienced an arts explosion. As of 2000, there are more artists living and working in Jersey City than in New York's traditional artist haven, the SoHo district. This is most likely due to the WALDO (Work And Live District Overlay) ordinance that helped create a thriving community of various artists where there had been only empty warehouses and desolate railyards. The Friends of Music and Art of Hudson County, a nonprofit vocal and instrumental music ensemble, was formed to encourage young, gifted students to continue their work. The Friends perform at the Public Library Auditorium.

The magnificently ornate, 3,000-seat Loew's Theater in downtown Journal Square, after being closed for many years and facing demolition in the mid-1980s, recently underwent a complete renovation and is now serving as a non-profit arts and entertainment center for the city. Local volunteers, from inexperienced helpers to expert craftsmen, spent countless hours on all aspects of the renovation. New Jersey City University presents dance, musical, and dramatic productions at its Margaret Williams Theatre. Dinneen Theater at Saint Peter's College offers concerts, dance groups, repertory and traveling theater and other cultural events.

The Kennedy Dancers, a contemporary traveling company, is based in Jersey City. Other local dance troupes include the Anahi Galante Dance Company, the Carol Hayes Dance Studio, The Hudson Repertory Dance Company, and the Nai-Ni Chen Dance Company.

The Jersey City Museum is known for its exhibits of local artist's painting and sculpture, with a good representation of the more avant garde works. The museum is also known for its Otto Coctzke gem collection, and displays items of historic relevance, especially local artifacts. Once part of the Jersey City Public Library, both financially connected and physically housed on the library's fourth floor, the museum separated fiscally from the library in 1987 and began moving to its own climate-controlled building in the 1990s. In 1993 the Jersey City Redevelopment Agency donated an ideal building in the Van Vorst Historic District for the new museum, and after an $11 million overhaul, the new museum was completed in 2000 and opened its doors to the public in 2001.

The Afro-American Historical Museum concentrates on the lives of prominent African American residents of New Jersey and contains an exhibit showing a typical African American household of the 1920s. Several organizations exist to help artists in the region, including the American Artists Professional League of New Jersey, the Cultural and Historic Affairs group, Artsgenesis, and the Artist's Association, which sponsors an annual juried art show.

Twelve artists working with eight student interns produced the Columbus Drive Mural, said to be the largest mural in the eastern United States; the mural spans 10 buildings and about 15,000 square feet on the city's Columbus Drive, just

Ellis Island National Monument stands off the shores of Jersey City, New Jersey.

west of the Grove St. PATH station. The panoramic mural, whose design elements were partly decided upon by residents, is about 60 feet at its highest point and 350 feet long.

Festivals and Holidays

Jersey City is alive with festivals throughout the year, reflecting its greatly diverse population. Each April, New Jersey City University hosts a four-day Jazz Week festival with entertainment by nationally known performers. The Fourth of July is celebrated with the Jersey City Cultural Arts Festival in Liberty Park, which also offers free summer concerts. Liberty Park is again the setting for the New Jersey State Ethnic Festival in mid-September. The Annual Carribean Carnival is a new addition to the celebration scene. The July festival highlights the West Indian Community's food and lively music, arts and other entertainments. All Jersey City's ethnic neighborhoods abound with celebrations throughout the year, with Asian Indian, Filipino, Irish, Korean, and Latino parades and festivals.

Sports for the Spectator

New Jersey City University (NJCU) competes in NCAA Division III sports, with men's teams in baseball, basketball, soccer, indoor and outdoor track, cross country, and volleyball, and women's teams in bowling, softball, volleyball, basketball, cross country, and indoor and outdoor track. Saint Peter's College has NCAA Division I teams in men's and women's baseball, softball, basketball, bowling, cheerleading, football, golf, soccer, swimming and diving, tennis, track and cross country, and volleyball.

Although Jersey City does not have any professional sports team of its own, close proximity to New York City offers the full spectrum of all pro sports.

Sports for the Participant

Sports for the active participant in Jersey City center around the 70 parks and playgrounds the city maintains; its summer programs attract more than 2,000 young participants. Liberty Park is the largest recreational area, with miles of biking and running paths and its River Walk Promenade showcasing a stunning view of New York City. Lincoln Park has football fields, basketball courts, a running track, and miles of winding trails. In winter sledding and skiing can take place on the park's long hills. Pershing Field also offers tennis, track, baseball, basketball, many playground areas, and year-round indoor swimming. Two smaller parks of note are Van Vorst Park and Hamilton Park. Festivals, dance recitals, and Shakespeare in the Park programs are held in these parks, and Van Vorst hosts a Farmer's Market from June to November.

Shopping and Dining

Shoppers come to Jersey City because of the city's variety of one-of-a-kind shops and boutiques, as well as the reduced three percent sales tax available from qualified retailers in the Urban Enterprise Zones. Jersey City has 13 major shopping districts. Perhaps the most popular shopping facilities are the Hudson Mall and the Newport Mall, the latter being part of a huge waterfront development with condominiums, office buildings, and recreational facilities.

Dining in Jersey City tends to revolve around small informal eateries found in the city's many ethnic neighborhoods. Cuisines represented include those of Pakistan, India, China, Indonesia, Philippines, Germany, Italy, and Poland. One of the most popular dining spots is not in the city but on the ship *Spirit of New Jersey,* as it cruises New York Harbor, offering music and dancing on its decks. Some of the newer, more upscale additions to the restaurant scene are found in the waterfront developments, where diners can enjoy spectacular views of New York City's skyline with their food and drink.

Visitor Information: Hudson County Visitor Information, 583 Newark Avenue, Jersey City, NJ 07306; toll-free (800)542-7894

Convention Facilities

Jersey City is part of the meeting destination area known as Metro New Jersey Meadowlands, one of the state's busiest destinations; its popularity is due in part to its proximity to the attractions of Manhattan (Newark is also part of the Meadowlands destination area). Convention planners choosing Jersey City as their destination may select the Quality Inn, with 7,000 square feet of meeting space, or facilities at Jersey City State University. Of the area's many hotels, the four largest business class hotels are Doubletree Suites, which features a Business Center along with 1,830 square feet of meeting space; Candlewood Business Suites; the Hyatt Regency South Pier with a panoramic view from its Manhattan Ballroom, which is part of over 20,000 square feet of meeting space offered by the Hyatt; and the Courtyard by Marriott.

Transportation

Approaching the City

Newark International Airport, a 15 minute drive from Jersey City, offers comprehensive international and domestic travel service. Buses, trains, helicopters, and limousines all carry commuters between the airport and Jersey City. Intra- and inter- state bus lines, rapid transit, ferries, tunnels, and trains form important parts of the Jersey City transportation network. NY Waterway runs a rush hour commuter ferry route to mid-town Manhattan from Jersey City.

PATH (Port Authority Trans Hudson), the local mass transit service, connects Jersey City with Manhattan, Newark, Harrison, and Hoboken. Construction of the 20.5 mile Hudson-Bergen Light Rail Transit System, which runs from Bayonne to Ridgefield, was completed in 2000 and has won national awards and recognition for creating an excellent and innovative transit system through a public-private partnership. Its clean, electric powered 90-foot modern trolleys are intended to help air quality as well as decongest New York-New Jersey traffic.

Major east-west arteries approaching Jersey City include Interstate-280; U.S. Routes 1 and 1A, with the Pulaski Skyway alternate, and the New Jersey Turnpike, I-78, with four exits in the city. NJ Highway 440 runs north-south through the city while I-95 bypasses it to the west.

Traveling in the City

As is typical of the New York City hub, traffic is heavy throughout the day in Jersey City. Commuters to Manhattan use the Holland Tunnel, PATH rapid transit system, buses, ferries, and highway bridges. The Port Authority of New York and New Jersey operates the main passenger facility for buses and other mass transit, the downtown Journal Square Station. More than 200 buses operate on more than 35 lines within the city. Service began in 2000 on a new two mile rail spur between West Side Avenue in Jersey City and Liberty State Park.

Communications

Newspapers and Magazines

The *Jersey Journal,* Jersey City's major newspaper, is published each evening except Sundays. Other local newspapers include the *Hudson Dispatch,* the Spanish weekly *El Nueva Hudson,* and the collegiate newspaper of New Jersey City University, the *Gothic Times. This Week in Jersey City* chronicles weekly community news. New York City and New Jersey metropolitan papers also enjoy a wide readership. Older publications in the city include the *Journal of Accountancy,* a monthly publication for certified public accountants, and the weekly *Mansfield Stock Chart Service.*

Television and Radio

WFMU-FM radio station and WGKR-AM broadcast from Jersey City. While no other radio or television stations originate in Jersey City, area residents enjoy a full range of news and entertainment via New York City channels.

Media Information: *Jersey Journal,* 30 Journal Square, Jersey City, New Jersey 07306; telephone (201)653-1000

Jersey City Online

City of Jersey City. Available www.cityofjerseycity.com

Hudson County Chamber of Commerce. Available www.hudsonchamber.org

Jersey City Economic Development Corporation. Available www.jcedc.org

Jersey City Free Public Library System. Available www.jclibrary.org

New Jersey Economic Development Authority. Available www.njeda.com

Selected Bibliography

French, Kenneth. *Jersey City, New Jersey, 1940-1960* (Arcadia, 1997)

McClean, Alexander. *History of Jersey City, N.J.: A Record of Its Early Settlement and Corporate Progress* (Jersey City: Smiley, 1895)

Witcover, Jules. *Sabotage at Black Tom: Imperial Germany's Secret War in America, 1914–1917* (Chapel Hill, NC: Algonquin Books of Chapel Hill, 1989)

Newark

The City in Brief

Founded: 1666 (incorporated, 1836)

Head Official: Mayor Sharpe James (D) (since 1986; current term expires 2006)

City Population
  1980: 329,248
  1990: 275,221
  2000: 273,546
  2003 estimate: 277,911
  Percent change, 1990–2000: − .6%
  U.S. rank in 1980: 46th
  U.S. rank in 1990: 56th (State rank: 1st)
  U.S. rank in 2000: 68th (State rank: 1st)

Metropolitan Area Population

  1990: 1,915,694
  2000: 2,032,989

Percent change, 1990–2000: 6.1%
U.S. rank in 1990: 1st (NY–NJ CMSA)
U.S. rank in 2000: 1st (NY–NJ CMSA)

Area: 24.14 square miles (2000)
Elevation: 0 to 273.4 feet above sea level
Average Annual Temperature: 54° F
Average Annual Precipitation: 19.7 inches of rain; 27.6 inches of snow

Major Economic Sectors: Financial services, distribution, wholesale and retail trade, services, publishing
Unemployment Rate: 5.4% (NY–NJ MSA; February 2005)
Per Capita Income: $13,009 (1999)

2002 FBI Crime Index Total: 17,814

Major Colleges and Universities: Rutgers University-Newark Campus; New Jersey Institute of Technology; Seton Hall School of Law; University of Medicine and Dentistry of New Jersey; Essex County College

Daily Newspaper: *The Star-Ledger*

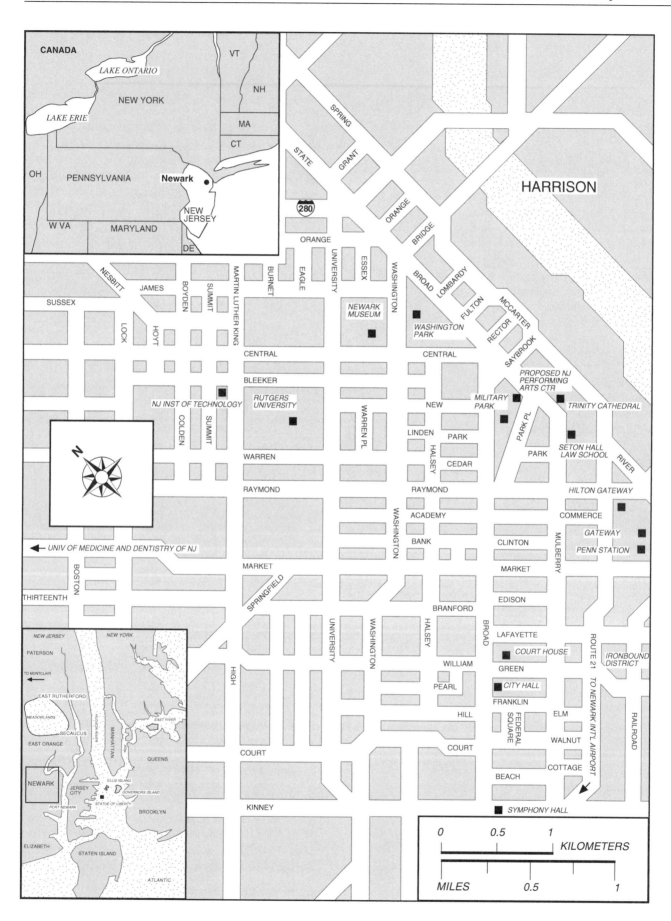

Introduction

Under the leadership of a long-serving mayor and civil rights movement veteran, Newark has recently been designated as a "Most Livable City" and an "All-America City"; Newark has also won the Environmental Protection Administrator's Award. A major east coast port of entry and the largest city in the most densely populated state in the nation, Newark is a transportation, manufacturing, and education center. Its growing service economy is dominated by medical research, insurance, and high technology research and development activities. The devastating race riots of 1967 that dominated the city's image in the twentieth century have begun to recede into history at the start of the new century. Newark has still not completely rebuilt the stores and neighborhoods destroyed in that conflagration, but efforts to do so are well underway. While the average cost of a home in Newark has remained high, the city has made notable efforts to make housing accessible to all by building handsome, affordable townhouse complexes. Success in the finance and insurance industry has spurred development of more steel towers inhabited by the headquarters of major businesses. A city once known for divisiveness and destruction is now renowned for its renaissance of construction, recycling, and civility.

Geography and Climate

Newark is located in northeastern New Jersey along the west bank of the Passaic River and Newark Bay. The city lies 8 miles west of lower Manhattan Island and is a thirty-minute drive from New York City. The Newark area, which is part of the Piedmont Region, is flat and marshy with some high points to the southwest and northeast. Newark's weather is greatly influenced by the city's proximity to the Atlantic Ocean. Winds, mostly easterly and southeasterly, can moderate temperatures, which range from very high in the summer to very low in the winter. Fall and winter storms, called "northeasters," blow off the ocean and account for much of the city's rain and snow.

Area: 24.14 square miles (2000)

Elevation: 0 to 273.4 feet above sea level

Average Temperatures: January, 30.7° F; July, 76.6° F; annual average 54° F

Average Annual Precipitation: 19.7 inches of rain; 27.6 inches of snow

History

The Real Estate Market's Early Start in Newark

During the last Ice Age about 13,000 years ago, the retreating glaciers pulled back to reveal newly fertile soil along the coast of what would become New Jersey. The nexus of rolling hills, roving rivers and endless ocean attracted the first settlers of the United States, hunter-gatherers who had followed game and fur resources to the area. At the point that the first Europeans arrived in the region surrounding present-day Newark in the 1600s, they found it occupied by Native American bands, Hackensacks and Lenni-Lenapes of the Delaware tribe, from whom the territory was purchased in 1667. Captain Robert Treat and the rest of the settlers, migrants from Connecticut's New Haven Colony in search of religious freedom and inexpensive farmland, bought the whole of Essex County from the natives. Located on the Passaic River and a sheltered Atlantic bay, the settlement was named Newark, possibly in honor of Newark-on-Trent, England; some historians, however, claim the name derives from "new ark" or "new work." While religious intolerance was the primary motivation for the move from Connecticut, Newark leaders of the Puritan Congregational Church retained a grip on community affairs for many years.

Newark's strong educational tradition dates back to 1747 when the city was home to what is now Princeton University. The city's first elementary-level school was established in 1676, followed by the laying out of a market along Washington Square and a military training ground in Military Park. The community grew slowly, hampered by its reputation for strong Puritanism. It was not until 1733 that a second church attained a foothold in Newark, when a local version of the Church of England rose up to challenge the Congregationalists' authority.

Early industry in Newark included mining, iron-making, and tanning. Newark became an important commercial site when roads and ferries connected it to New York City. During the Revolutionary War, American General George Washington used Newark as a supply base during his retreat from the British. The retreat took him across the entire state of New Jersey, across the Delaware River and into Pennsylvania. After the war, the shoe industry grew into an economic mainstay in Newark. A process for making patent leather was developed in the early 1800s by Seth Boyden. Newark was also becoming world famous by the 1830s for its jewelry, beer, and hats. The completion of the Morris Canal connected Newark to goods-producing regions to the east in New Jersey, and an expanding network of railroads brought the city into contact with the frontier.

At the outbreak of the Civil War, Newarkians were of divided loyalties. Trade with the secessionist South fueled Newark's booming economy, a circumstance that conflicted with the North's growing intolerance of slavery in the South. When the hat and shoe industries received major commissions from the Grand Army of the Potomac, the issue was settled—Newark was firmly in the Union camp, sending some 10,000 soldiers to fight for its cause.

Industry Brings Growth, New Residents

In the 1860s, Newark entered the technological age. John Wesley Hyatt invented a flexible film called celluloid in 1869, laying the basis not only for the hugely lucrative plastics industry but the motion picture industry as well. In nearby Menlo Park, Thomas Edison developed the electric light bulb; when he lived briefly in Newark, Edison also invented the stock ticker. Among the region's literary figures gaining prominence during this era were Stephen Crane, author of *The Red Badge of Courage,* and Mary Mapes Dodge, who wrote *Hans Brinker or the Silver Skates.* Several prominent newspapers were founded in the Newark area in the years following the Civil War. Also during the latter half of the nineteenth century, ships carrying European immigrants steamed into Newark Harbor. Irish, Germans, Italians, Spanish, and Portuguese came in search of plentiful jobs, many of them in Newark's newly electrified factories. The chemical industry was established in Newark during this time, as the insurance industry gained a foothold through Mutual Benefit (1845) and Prudential Companies (1873).

The Port of Newark opened around 1915, just in time for America's preparations to enter World War I. Newark led the nation's shipbuilders during the country's brief war-time period. These years were significant, too, because they brought the first large group of Southern blacks north in search of defense-related jobs; pesticides had begun to curtail agricultural employment opportunities. By the 1930s, Newark was a major East Coast transportation, retail, and manufacturing base. Newark International Airport, opened in 1930, supplemented the port, rail, and highway facilities. Huge department and specialty stores lined Broad Street. Some of the nation's first and tallest skyscrapers pierced the Newark skyline as its factories turned out machinery and thread. But while Newark enjoyed all the appearances of a boomtown, it began to suffer the first signs of increasing urban decay. A corrupt local government undermined city services, commutable highways lured city residents to homes in the suburbs, and the tax base eroded as some important industries relocated.

Newark's population peaked in 1950 at 438,000 people. Modern Newark began to take shape with the urban renewal programs of the 1950s and with the help of the city's business leaders. Newark's two major life insurance companies renewed their commitment to the city, building new headquarters downtown. Federal structures, recreational facilities, and other office buildings followed. But the burgeoning prosperity of the 1950s masked deep racial divisions and inequalities that simmered, waiting for the tipping point.

In the 1950s, the migration to the suburbs appeared mainly to involve white Newark residents leaving the bustle and increasing crime of the inner city. Middle class African Americans followed, leaving African Americans and other people of color who labored in low-paying factory jobs. By 1966, African Americans were in the majority in the general Newark population, but government offices and the police department were dominated by whites. The economic and political power imbalance was at times wielded like a club—in 1967, in a city where 70 percent of the students were African American, the Newark mayor refused to appoint an African American secretary of education. The mayor went on to raze a predominantly African American neighborhood to make room for the University of Medicine and Dentistry of New Jersey, a pricey higher education institution out of reach of most of the displaced homeowners.

Tensions reached boiling point, and the 1967 riots that commenced spanned six days and resulted in 23 deaths, 725 injured, and $10 million in property damage. However, among the riot rubble the city began to prosper again as Newark's first African American mayor entered office in 1970 as a symbol of a more unified municipality with progress in its sights.

Population Begins to Grow Once More

In 1986 Sharpe James, an ardent civic booster and veteran of the civil rights movement, was elected mayor of Newark. Downtown development in the late 1980s brought glittering office towers, though the population declined to about 275,000 by 1990. In the 1990s the city addressed the long-neglected issue of affordable housing. A number of affordably priced, suburban-style townhouses and luxury condominiums were constructed in the mid-1990s, improving the available housing stock. For example, a handsome 1,200-unit townhouse complex in the University Heights area transformed the entrance to the downtown. As of 2000, Newark's single family housing market was surging, with prices rising in all parts of the city; the population was also beginning to increase. In fact, Newark and nearby Jersey City were almost alone among the United States' historically struggling central city areas to have turned around their decline in population.

Mayor Sharpe James continues his efforts to improve the image and fiscal stability of Newark. In 2004 the city's crime rate dropped by more than 50 percent and a number of high-tech industries have been lured to the area. The insurance business has been a mainstay over the centuries, moving Newark into position as the third largest center of that industry in the U.S. The diverse population has generally shown gains since 2000 and is anticipated to surge again in coming years.

Historical Information: New Jersey Historical Society, 52 Park Place, Newark, NJ 07102; telephone (973)596-8500

Population Profile

Newark–Union PMSA Residents

1990: 1,915,694
2000: 2,032,989
Percent change, 1990–2000: 6.1%
U.S. rank in 1990: 1st (NY–NJ CMSA)
U.S. rank in 2000: 1st (NY–NJ CMSA)

City Residents

1980: 329,248
1990: 275,221
2000: 273,546
2003 estimate: 277,911
Percent change, 1990–2000: − .6%
U.S. rank in 1990: 56th (State rank: 1st)
U.S. rank in 2000: 68th (State rank: 1st)

Density: 11,495 people per square mile (2000)

Racial and ethnic characteristics (2000)
  White: 72,537
  Black or African American: 146,250
  American Indian and Alaska Native: 1,005
  Asian: 3,263
  Native Hawaiian and Pacific Islander: 135
  Hispanic or Latino (may be of any race): 80,622
  Other: 38,430

Percent of residents born in state: 50.7% (2000)

Age characteristics (2000)
  Population under 5 years old: 21,293
  Population 5 to 9 years old: 22,243
  Population 10 to 14 years old: 20,909
  Population 15 to 19 years old: 21,056
  Population 20 to 24 years old: 24,014
  Population 25 to 34 years old: 46,144
  Population 35 to 44 years old: 41,322
  Population 45 to 54 years old: 29,949
  Population 55 to 59 years old: 11,376
  Population 60 to 64 years old: 9,934
  Population 65 to 74 years old: 14,485
  Population 75 to 84 years old: 8,099

Population 85 years and over: 2,722
Median age: 30.8

Births (2002)
  Total number: 4,606

Deaths (2002)
  Total number: 2,354 (of which, 47 were infants under the age of 1 year)

Money income (1999)
  Per capita income: $13,009
  Median household income: $26,913
  Total households: 91,366

Number of households with income of . . .
  less than $10,000: 11,487
  $10,000 to $14,999: 4,852
  $15,000 to $24,999: 9,692
  $25,000 to $34,999: 8,459
  $35,000 to $49,999: 9,263
  $50,000 to $74,999: 10,167
  $75,000 to $99,999: 4,812
  $100,000 to $149,999: 2,684
  $150,000 to $199,999: 560
  $200,000 or more: 573

Percent of families below poverty level: 25.5% (27.6% of which were female householder families with related children under 5 years)

2002 FBI Crime Index Total: 17,814

Municipal Government

Newark operates with a mayor-council form of government. The mayor, who is not a voting member, serves a four-year term and executes the legislation enacted by the council. The nine council members also serve four-year terms; five council members are elected at large and four by the individual municipal wards that they represent. The council is responsible for codification and legislation for the municipality as well as budgetary compliance. Newark is the governmental seat for Essex County.

Head Official: Mayor Sharpe James (D) (since 1986; current term expires 2006)

Total Number of City Employees: 3,984 (2005)

City Information: Newark City Hall, 920 Broad Street Suite 214, Newark, NJ 07102; telephone (973)733-8004

Economy

Major Industries and Commercial Activity

Newark lies at the heart of the New York/New Jersey metropolitan area industrial economy. Newark is increasingly coming to rely on its strategic location at the center of air, sea, road, and rail transportation networks for economic growth. Manufacturing was traditionally the city's most important economic activity, but it has recently been surpassed by transportation-related industries and telecommunications firms. Seven major highways, railway routes, a world-class shipping terminal, and a busy international airport make Newark a major mid-Atlantic distribution and retail trade center. The city is one of the nation's leading centers in the wholesale trade of chemicals and machinery, and the third largest writer of life insurance policies; both Mutual Benefit and Prudential Insurance Companies are headquartered in Newark.

Items and goods produced: polymers, beer, electrical products, machinery, leather, precious metals, jewelry, electronic equipment, chemicals, textiles, paint, varnish, perfume and cosmetics, paper boxes, foodstuffs, greenhouse and nursery products

Incentive Programs—New and Existing Companies

A concerted effort between the city of Newark, state and federal governments, and business and civic groups has stimulated impressive growth and expansion within the past decade. The State of New Jersey in particular provides many incentives to entice and retain new industries and entrepreneurs to Newark and the surrounding communities.

Local programs—The Department of Economic Development, Training and Employment of Essex County provides direct financial assistance to businesses located in the county and/or guarantees of loans from banks to such businesses for building acquisition, site renovation, and equipment purchases.

In 2002 Newark was designated a Renewal Community by the U.S. Department of Housing and Urban Development. The program encourages municipal self-sufficiency through a variety of federal tax credits as opposed to grant funds. Some of the programs include a Work Opportunity Credit for businesses that hire people who've received family assistance for a long period of time, a Welfare to Work Credit, tax deductions on qualified revitalization costs, and tax credits for employing residents of the Renewal Community zone.

State programs—Newark's Urban Enterprise Zone (UEZ) program provides eligible businesses with sales tax exemption equal to 50 percent of the regular sales tax rate, employee tax credits, net worth tax exemptions, tax exemptions for most purchases of tangible personal property, sales tax exemptions for building materials, supplies, or services used in property expansions and improvements, and awards for job creation.

The New Jersey Economic Development Authority (EDA) offers a wide range of financial, real estate development, and technical services to encourage business development and growth in the state. The majority of its assistance is to small and mid-sized businesses, with a growing emphasis on high-tech enterprises. Businesses specializing in technology or biotechnology can transfer tax certificates to other New Jersey businesses, realizing up to 75 percent of their value in cash that can be spent on equipment, facilities, or for other expenses related to the business. The EDA issues bonds to provide financing at favorable interest rates for business ventures, makes low-interest loans, and guarantees loans made by private investors and lenders. It also offers a full range of real estate development services to stimulate both private and public development projects. In addition, the EDA administers a business incentive program that provides grants to expanding or relocating businesses that will create new jobs in New Jersey. Brownfields loans and grants also are available to municipalities and private property owners to encourage the clean-up and redevelopment of hazardous sites around the state.

The New Jersey Redevelopment Authority provides low-interest loans to developers and businesses seeking to construct facilities in urban areas, including small business incubators. The New Jersey Division of International Trade helps companies dependent on international commerce with advice, matchmaking, and access to trade missions and foreign trade shows. Businesses in Newark may be eligible for inclusion in Foreign Trade Zone 49, allowing for some exemptions from full U.S. Customs scrutiny for imported goods that are temporarily stored in the area.

The New Jersey Small Business Development Center (NJSBDC) network specializes in business planning, growth strategy, management strategy, and loan packaging, along with providing help in selling goods and services to government agencies, help to entrepreneurs in commercializing new technologies, linking up companies to local manufacturers who serve as mentors, and counseling for companies regarding overseas trade.

Job training programs—Workforce New Jersey is the state agency coordinating local workforce development efforts. The office assists employers in finding and training new workers, while it also helps employees with continuing education, career exploration, and job searching.

Essex County's Division of Training and Employment coordinates employment programs designed to serve families receiving social assistance. Clients receive assessment and aptitude testing, job readiness preparation, transportation assistance as needed, skill training, adult education, community work experiences, and job placement.

The New Jersey Institute of Technology offers assistance for small manufacturers, new businesses, and defense contractors through specialized programs on topics such as entrepreneurship, environmental compliance issues, and polymer processing.

Development Projects

In February of 2005 the City of Newark finalized an agreement with the New Jersey Devils hockey franchise to build an 18,000 square foot arena in Newark. The proposed facility in the downtown redevelopment district is expected to cost $355 million and should be completed by 2007. To ensure easy access to Devils games and other downtown attractions, Newark's Penn Station is undergoing a $16.1 million update of its escalators, drainage systems, and customer communication devices.

The New Jersey Schools Construction Corporation is in the process of an $8.6 billion renovation of educational buildings throughout the state, with a good portion of the resources being spent in Newark on its public school system. Aging structures are being updated to function as state-of-the-art, twenty-first century learning centers. At the same time, the City of Newark has continued to invest heavily in affordable housing that is also attractive and energy efficient, as the municipality continues to rehab its post-riot image.

Only a mile from the Newark Liberty International Airport, Catellus Development Corp. is planning an industrial warehouse project that will demolish existing structures on the acquired land and replace them with a complex that will include a 600,000 square foot distribution warehouse. Construction is expected to be complete by 2006.

Economic Development Information: City of Newark Economic Development Department, City Hall, 55 Liberty St. Room 405, Newark, NJ; telephone (201)733-6284. New Jersey Economic Development Authority, PO Box 990, Trenton, NJ 08625-0990; telephone (609)292-1800

Commercial Shipping

With 13 miles of waterfront along Newark Bay and the Passaic River, Newark is part of the nation's largest containership port—the Port of New York and New Jersey. The Port opened in 1914-15 and is now leased and operated by the Port Authority of New York and New Jersey; in 2004, more than $110 billion in goods passed through the portal. The Port Authority is equipped to deal with virtually every type of cargo, including vehicles, live animals, large containers, liquid and dry bulk loads, and more. With a main

channel 7,000 feet long, the 930-acre Port of Newark can berth 34 ships. Rail freight service is provided by Amtrak and Conrail.

Newark Liberty International Airport (NLIA) is located just south of the city center, providing passenger and cargo service to all points of the globe. Several cargo-specific businesses and structures exist at NLIA, including the FedEx Complex (a regional hub), the United Parcel Service package handling and distribution center, and the 250,000 square foot Air Cargo Center. Cargo processing is state-of-the-art, with capacity to handle sophisticated and delicate materials with a high level of efficiency. In 2003, NLIA processed 890,712 tons of cargo and served nearly 29.5 million passengers. The Port Authority maintains an administration building near the Air Cargo Center; both the Port of New York and New Jersey and the Newark Liberty International Airport reside within Foreign Trade Zone #49.

The highway system in New Jersey is the most dense in the nation, guaranteeing ample routes into, out of, and around Newark and the surrounding major metropolitan areas. Interstates 280, 80, 78, 278 and 95 link Newark to other large cities, along with a network of U.S. and state highways. Businesses have a wide choice of ground transportation vendors for cargo shipping purposes, from well-established family trucking companies to nationally-known experts such as FedEx and UPS.

Labor Force and Employment Outlook

Newark's unemployment rate remains considerably higher than the state average. Schools in Newark and the surrounding region offer an array of training in business, industrial, and vocational areas to assist workers in obtaining employment, advancing their careers, or adapting to new innovations in local industry. The region's workforce is especially well trained in communications and utilities work, finance, insurance and real estate, trade, transportation, and chemical manufacture.

It is anticipated that Newark and greater Essex County will experience continued significant growth through 2012 in the healthcare and education industries, along with management and transportation-related services. Manufacturing jobs will continue to be cut over the next decade, with anticipated losses as high as 20.8 percent of total employment in that sector. Statewide, it's expected that the pace of both commercial and residential construction will slacken, while overall employment should increase about 7.5 percent by 2012 (a slightly more gradual 10 year increase compared to the 1992-2002 statistical period).

The following is a summary of data regarding the Newark–Union, NJ–PA, metropolitan area labor force, 2004 annual averages.

Size of nonagricultural labor force: 1,028,300

Number of workers employed in . . .
   construction and mining: 41,500
   manufacturing: 93,300
   trade, transportation and utilities: 217,100
   information: 26,500
   financial activities: 81,200
   professional and business services: 162,300
   educational and health services: 137,900
   leisure and hospitality: 64,600
   other services: 44,700
   government: 159,100

Average hourly earnings of production workers employed in manufacturing: $15.67 (New Jersey; 2004 annual average)

Unemployment rate: 5.4% (NY–NJ MSA; February 2005)

Largest employers	Number of employees (2005)
Newark Liberty International Airport	24,000
Verizon Communications	17,100
Prudential Financial, Inc.	16,850
Continental Airlines	11,000
University of Medicine/Dentistry	11,000
Public Service Enterprise Group	10,800
Prudential Insurance	4,492
City of Newark	3,984
Horizon Blue Cross & Blue Shield of NJ	3,900

Cost of Living

The New Jersey area remains one of the most expensive places to live in the nation. The cost of housing is a major factor, particularly when combined with high city taxes.

The following is a summary of data regarding several key cost of living factors in the Newark area.

2004 (3rd Quarter) ACCRA Average House Price: $457,430

2004 (3rd Quarter) ACCRA Cost of Living Index: 134.6 (U.S. average = 100.0)

State income tax rate: 1.4%–8.97%

State sales tax rate: 6%

Local income tax rate: None

Local sales tax rate: None

Property tax rate: $2.26 per $100 of assessed value (2004)

Economic Information: City of Newark Economic Development Department, City Hall, 55 Liberty St. Room 405, Newark, NJ; telephone (201)733-6284

Education and Research

Elementary and Secondary Schools

The Newark Public School System, which dates back to 1676, is the largest and one of the oldest in New Jersey. In 1995, after years of deficient management and suspected corruption on the part of school administrators, the New Jersey State Department of Education assumed operating control of the district. Working with the state, a 15-member advisory board was set up to help reform the school system and reestablish sound educational policy and practices. Since 1995, the school system has purchased $3.4 million in new textbooks, begun a $4.6 million technology initiative to expand computer capabilities in the schools, and opened a new technical and vocations high school.

At present, Newark Public Schools is undergoing system-wide renovations of its aging facilities, as part of New Jersey School Construction multi-billion dollar effort. Concurrently, the school district has partnered with both Saint Barnabas Healthcare System and the Healthcare Foundation of New Jersey to establish health clinics in five more schools in Newark. The district offers other programs supportive of families as a whole, including the Citywide Parents Conference, Concerned Fathers, and the Grandparents Support Network.

Among its special programs the Newark School System offers adult education, bilingual education, special education, and an attendance/dropout prevention program. Its magnet school program includes an Arts High School, a Science High School, and a University High School. A Business Partnership program allows students to work with professionals in business, industry, medicine, and law.

The following is a summary of data regarding the Newark public schools as of the 2004–2005 school year.

Total enrollment: 42,395

Number of facilities
   elementary schools: 76
   junior high schools: 7
   high schools: 12
   other: 3

Student/teacher ratio: 12.3:1

Teacher salaries
  minimum: $40,000
  maximum: $85,000

Funding per pupil: $14,826 (2003-2004)

A number of private primary and secondary schools also operate in Newark, many of which are affiliated with a religious institution.

Public Schools Information: Newark Public Schools, 2 Cedar Street, Newark, NJ 07201; telephone (201)733-7333

Colleges and Universities

With five colleges inside the city limits and 44,000 students matriculating, Newark is one of New Jersey's premier centers of education. Perhaps the most prestigious of Newark's colleges is the city branch of Rutgers University (the state university), which offers four-year baccalaureate degrees as well as graduate degrees in law, nursing, business, and public administration to its student body of more than 30,000 men and women. The Rutgers-Newark campus is part of an urban university complex spread over 323 acres in midtown Newark, a complex that also includes a number of other schools.

As a public research institution, the New Jersey Institute of Technology (NJIT) is famous for pioneering activities in computer-integrated design and manufacturing, biotechnology, microelectronics, and computerized communications. The NJIT student body of 8,249 can pursue any of 100 undergraduate degree programs or 30 postsecondary degrees while receiving hands-on experience through the university outreach center. Seton Hall's Law School is one of the largest law schools in the country, with ethics grounded in the Catholic principles of the home university. Essex County College offers two-year degrees and certificates in vocational fields, as well as credits that are designed to transfer to four-year universities. The University of Medicine and Dentistry of New Jersey, the state's largest health education center, enrolls more than 4,500 medical, dental, and health care students and operates a 526-bed acute care teaching hospital.

Libraries and Research Centers

Newark's public library system includes a main library and 10 branch libraries. With more than 1.4 million books, periodicals, and pictures, the libraries house the most important collection in New Jersey. In addition to local and state historical collections, the library boasts excellent fine arts, business, and current affairs resources along with collections focused on the diverse cultural make-up of the city. The Peter W. Rodino, Jr., Law Library at the Seton Hall School of Law provides access to more than 45,000 law-related books and periodicals, with an emphasis on health and environmental law. Specialized libraries in Newark maintain collections relating to medicine, insurance, education, history, and utilities. The Rutgers Institute of Jazz Studies has compiled an extensive collection of recordings. All of the local universities and colleges maintain well-stocked libraries with subject matter concentrations suited to the degree programs offered.

The metropolitan Newark area is home to more research workers per capita than any other area in the country. The New Jersey Institute of Technology maintains research centers in global areas such as applied life sciences, architectural and building sciences, computer technology and telecommunications, environmental science, materials science and manufacturing, solar physics, and transportation. Specialized facilities include an Air Pollution Research Laboratory; a Building Engineering and Architectural Research Center; a Center for Biomedical Engineering, which focuses on reconstructive devices; and a Center for Information Age Technology, which assists technology transfers between academia and industry. The Institute is also home to an advanced technology center of the New Jersey Commission on Science and Technology and the computerized Manufacturing Systems Center.

The University of Medicine and Dentistry of New Jersey conducts sponsored research focusing on the health care fields, including clinical trials. Rutgers University conducts research in such varied areas as neuroscience, management, animal behavior, jazz, and finance. Also active in research are the many pharmaceutical companies in the area.

Public Library Information: Newark Public Library, 5 Washington Street, Newark, NJ 07101; telephone (973)733-7800 or (973)733-7784; fax (973)733-5648

Health Care

Newark Beth Israel Medical Center is licensed for 671 beds and functions as a teaching hospital as it provides trauma and specialized care for the northern New Jersey region. The Children's Hospital of New Jersey is an affiliate of Beth Israel, which also staffs the Heart Hospital of New Jersey. Columbus Hospital contributes another 210 beds to the community; some of its specialties include the Children's Eye Care Center of New Jersey and the Newark Eye and Ear Infirmary.

Saint James Hospital, part of the Cathedral Healthcare System, serves the Ironbound community with trilingual staff (English, Spanish, and Portuguese). A Diabetes Center, Hazardous Decontamination unit and mental health unit supplement emergency care services. Saint Michael's Medical Center is also part of Cathedral Healthcare; the 337-bed tertiary care facility is also a teaching hospital with a cardiac specialty. Hands-on experience for the doctors of tomorrow is also the aim of the hospital affiliated with the University of Medicine and Dentistry of New Jersey.

Recreation

Sightseeing

Newark, the third oldest city in the nation, exudes history, and its architecture serves as a chronological yardstick. Many buildings of interest are clustered along Broad Street, including the Blume House, which was built in 1710 and serves as a rectory for the House of Prayer Episcopal Church. Trinity Cathedral was built in 1743 and used as a hospital during the Revolutionary War. First Presbyterian Church, dedicated in 1791, remains a noted example of Georgian colonial architecture. Soaring above the buildings of the past, the New Jersey Bell Telephone Company building rises 275 feet and is adorned with colossal bas relief sculpture in Egyptian style.

The Catholic Cathedral of the Sacred Heart, begun in 1898, is as large as London's Westminster Abbey and resembles the famed basilica at Rheims. Built in the French Gothic style, the cathedral is enhanced by 200 stained-glass windows, bronze doors, and 14 church bells cast in Italy. The cathedral is near Branch Brook Park, comprising 360 acres of tranquility and cherry trees skillfully landscaped by the same firm that designed Central Park in New York. The Essex County Courthouse, a 1906 Cass Gilbert creation, is a modified Renaissance granite and marble structure. Penn Station, opened in 1935, is of neo-classical design. Newark's city hall is a good example of French Renaissance design, including a dome, balconies, and rococo decorations.

Newark's Military Park, formerly a drill field for the Colonial and Continental armies, now is famous for its monument entitled *Wars of America.* The massive sculpture is the work of Mount Rushmore artist Gutzon Borglum. The park also boasts a bust of President John F. Kennedy by Jacques Lipshitz. The history of Newark can be quietly explored at Mt. Pleasant Cemetery on Broadway; established in 1814, the burial ground is the oldest formal cemetery in Newark and has been the final resting place of many well-known residents over the centuries. Famous neighborhoods in Newark include Ironbound, a Spanish-Portuguese enclave, and historic James Street, known for its Victorian row houses.

Arts and Culture

The $150 million New Jersey Performing Arts Center, located on a 12-acre site downtown, opened its doors in 1997. It houses the 2,750-seat Great Hall and the 500-seat Victoria Theater. Symphony Hall on Broad Street has long been the performing arts heart of Newark. The fully restored 1925 Art Deco auditorium seats 2,800 patrons. Among the Hall's resident groups are the New Jersey Symphony Orchestra, the New Jersey State Opera, the Newark Boys Chorus, the Opera/Music Theatre, and an opera school.

The Cathedral Concert Series schedules classical music performances in Newark's Cathedral of the Sacred Heart. Free concerts are presented in Washington Park and in the Gateway Complex. Dance in Newark is represented by Gallman's Newark Dance Theatre, Garden State Ballet, which concentrates on classical dance, while the African Globe Theatre Works concentrates on works by African American writers. The Newark Community School of the Arts presents faculty performances, student recitals, and presentations by the Community Theatre Ensemble.

Amid a sprawling compound of galleries that include an 1885 brick-and-limestone mansion, the Newark Museum has become known for its Schaeffer Collection of antique glass, Tibetan objects, Indian relics, and African articles. On the museum property are a sculpture garden, a firehouse, and a schoolhouse. The museum adjoins historic Ballantine House, the restored mansion of a Victorian brewer. The New Jersey Historical Society, housed in a Georgian-style building maintains a collection of portraits, drawings, and prints of local personalities.

Among Newark's art galleries, the Paul Robeson Center at Rutgers' Newark campus displays changing art exhibits. Other galleries include Aljira: A Center for Contemporary Art and The Gallery, which both spotlight local artists; the Art Gallery exhibits graphics, paintings, and sculpture; City Without Walls features emerging New Jersey artists; Halsey Street Gallery focuses on African American paintings, posters and ceramics; and Richardson Gallery specializes in oil paintings, lithographs, and engravings.

Arts and Culture Information: Newark Arts Council, 17 Academy Street Suite 1104, Newark, NJ 07102; telephone (973) 643-1625

Festivals and Holidays

A city of numerous ethnic influences, Newark enjoys community parades and festivals all year long. In February, the New Year party keeps going with the Chinese Lunar New Year Celebration coordinated by the Newark Museum. The traditional Lion Dance and holiday delicacies are on hand to mark this important event. During the St. Patrick's Day

Ballentine House, built by brewer Peter Ballentine, is now part of the Newark Museum.

Parade in mid-March, everyone is Irish for a day. Each April, Branch Brook Park hosts the Newark Cherry Blossom Festival and Marathon among more than 3,000 Japanese cherry trees cultivated in the park. The Newark Museum hosts an Asian Heritage Festival in early May, with Japanese drumming, Dancing Bells, and the Indian Fold Dance taking center stage. The African American Heritage Day Parade is held in May.

The month of June is full of celebrations, starting with the Portuguese Day Parade and Festival and the Newark Festival of People. From late June until early August for the past 30-some years, the Newark Black Film Festival exposes residents and visitors to the independent film world through the eyes and talents of African American directors and actors. August stays hot with the Gospel and Africa-Newark Festivals.

Brazilian Independence Day is celebrated in September, and October is the month for the annual Columbus Day Parade and United Nations Day. The annual Sarah Vaughn Jazz Festival in November has also become a favorite event in the city.

Sports for the Spectator

The Meadowlands Sports Complex in nearby East Rutherford hosts professional sports events throughout the year. Among its home teams are the New York Giants and the New York Jets of the National Football League, and the New Jersey Nets of the National Basketball Association. The New Jersey Devils of the National Hockey League play in the Continental Airlines Arena within the grounds of the Meadowlands Sports Complex. Trotting and thoroughbred horse-racing events include the Hambletonian, the most famous event in harness racing.

In 1998, professional baseball returned to Newark when the Bears came home—the Newark Bears had originally been a farm team for the New York Yankees, warming up such hardball legends as Yogi Berra. Construction was completed in 1999 on Riverfront Stadium to welcome the Bears back in the independent Atlantic League; the roster frequently lists some former luminaries of the majors.

Rutgers-Newark University competes in nine sports at the Division III level of the National Collegiate Athletic Association, including men's and women's basketball, soccer, tennis, and volleyball.

Sports for the Participant

Famous Newark parks include Military Park and Branch Brook Park, both of which offer a full complement of recreational facilities. An ice skating rink is located at Branch Brook Park, which is also home to a roller skating center with a state-of-the-art sound system. Weequahic Park offers a golf course. Nearby facilities provide opportunities for skiing, water sports, bicycling, and horseback riding.

A number of state and national parks are within easy reach of Newark, including areas of the Atlantic seashore where visitors can swim, kayak, and play beach volleyball. The mid-Atlantic section of the Appalachian Trail system passes through the western edge of New Jersey and then traces the northern state line to the east before cutting north through New York state.

Shopping and Dining

The downtown redevelopment district encompasses a unique shopping experience, especially along discount store-lined Broad Street. Both Military Park and Market Street host open-air, seasonal farmers' markets where fresh produce, baked goods, cheeses and other items can be found. Nearby Secaucus, referred to as the outlet capital of the eastern seaboard, is home to one of the most massive concentrations of outlet stores in the world. Other communities near Newark, most notably Manhattan and other New York neighborhoods, round out the shopping experience.

A broad variety of ethnic cuisines is the hallmark of New Jersey restaurants, and in Newark the selections range from European to Asian, African, and Caribbean. The city's Ironside District is home to a smorgasbord of dining establishments featuring authentic Spanish and Portuguese cookery and some of the best sangria in the United States. A number of soul food eateries dish up traditional southern fare not often found in a northeastern city. The state of New Jersey is sometimes described as the ''diner capital of the world,'' having more diners than any other place on the planet. However, restaurant ambiance varies widely from market-side cafes on busy downtown streets to fine dining in restored historic structures. Several specialty coffee shops are sprinkled around the city.

Convention Facilities

Newark is part of the area known as Metro New Jersey Meadowlands, one of the state's busiest meeting and convention destinations; its popularity is due in part to its proximity to the attractions of Manhattan.

Downtown Newark offers the renovated 253-room Hilton Gateway Hotel, with 9,700 square feet of exhibition space, seven meeting rooms and a ballroom that can accommodate 350 people. The Gateway renewal program provided enclosed skywalks connecting Gateway projects directly to Penn Station. Other Newark convention activity focuses on Newark International Airport, where a number of nationally-known hotels offering meeting and sleeping space are located, including the 591-room Newark Airport Marriott with 20 meeting rooms and 13,200 feet of meeting space. In all, there are about 3,200 sleeping rooms at the airport hotels.

Within the Gateway Region of northern New Jersey, there are two dedicated convention centers—the New Jersey Convention and Expo Center at the Raritan Center is located in Edison and offers 150,000 square feet of exhibit space, making it New Jersey's largest venue. The facility is equipped to handle anything from banquets to trade shows and is wired for all audio-visual devices. Food service is available. At the Meadowlands Exposition Center in Secaucus, conferences and trade shows are accommodated in 61,000 square feet of exhibition space, supplemented with additional meeting rooms and a banquet facility that can seat 5,000. The MEC provides two drive-doors for offloading of equipment and is conveniently located near Newark Liberty International Airport.

Transportation

Approaching the City

Newark Liberty International Airport (NLIA), one of the world's busiest airports, annually serves more than 29 million passengers carried on more than 450,000 flights. About 60 scheduled airlines operate out of Newark. The International Arrivals Facility was completed in March 2002 and allows for efficient processing of 1,500 passengers per hour through Immigrations and Customs. Several of NLIA's terminals underwent modernization in recent times, with most of the multi-million dollar projects reaching fruition around 2002.

Approximately 450 trains arrive in and depart from Newark daily. Amtrak, Conrail, and PATH rail lines travel into Newark's recently renovated historic Penn Station. The PATH train connects downtown Newark with New York City. Interstate bus lines serving Newark include Greyhound and Trailways.

The major north-south route with access to Newark is Interstate 95, the New Jersey Turnpike. Routes from the north include Interstates 81 and 287, the Garden State Parkway, and the New York Thruway. From the west, Newark is approached by Interstates 78 and 80. Other major arteries include U.S. Highways 1, 9, and 22, and state highways 21, 24, 25, 27, 78, 82, and 280.

Traveling in the City

As is characteristic of the New York hub, traffic in Newark and on the freeways is heavy for a sizable portion of the workday. Many commuters rely on public transportation,

which consists of rapid-rail cars and buses. New Jersey Transit operates 6,000 buses on 50 lines in Newark, serving more than 40,000 commuters. Beginning in 1993 and continuing through the year 2008, New Jersey Transit is spending $67.5 million to make community rail stations accessible to disabled riders. The Newark City Subway is a tourist attraction on its own—built in a former canal bed, the subway's old-fashioned trolley cars speed past walls covered with tile murals.

Newark's business district is adjacent to the Passaic River. The downtown area is divided into four neighborhoods, each with a special identity: Market Square, Four Corners, Military Park/The Greens, and Riverfront. Broad Street and Market Street intersect in the city center and run perpendicular to each other, providing a reference point for out-of-town travelers. The city is laid out on a fairly straightforward grid pattern.

Communications

Newspapers and Magazines

Newark's major daily newspaper is the *Star-Ledger,* published each morning. Newspapers serving the city's ethnic communities include *The Brazilian Voice,* which is published in Portuguese; *The Italian Tribune;* and *Luso Americano,* a weekly. Special interest publications include the *New Jersey Law Journal* and *Healthstate,* a quarterly published for health care professionals by the University of Medicine and Dentistry of New Jersey. The New Jersey Historical Society publishes *Jersey Journeys* for children eight times a year. *The Journal of Commerce* is also published in the city.

Television and Radio

One television station originates in Newark, which also receives New York City broadcasting. Newark's Public Broadcasting System channel is the nation's largest and most productive. A cable television franchise also serves Newark. Four FM station broadcasts from Newark; many more are available to listeners from New York City.

Media Information: Newark Morning Ledger Company, Star-Ledger Plaza, Newark, NJ 07102; telephone (973)877-4141

Newark Online

City of Newark. Available www.ci.newark.nj.us

Essex County Government. Available www.co.essex.nj.us .com

Go Newark. Available www.gonewark.com

New Jersey Performing Arts Center. Available www.njpac.org

Newark Arts Council. Available www.newarkarts.org

Newark Museum. Available www.newarkmuseum.org

Newark Public Library. Available www.npl.org

Newark Public Schools. Available www.nps.k12.nj.us

The Star-Ledger. Available www.nj.com/news/ledger

Selected Bibliography

Cunningham, John T., *Newark* (Newark: New Jersey Historical Society, 1966)

Hayden, Thomas, *Rebellion in Newark, Official Violence and Ghetto Response (by) Tom Hayden* (New York: Random, 1967)

Immerso, Michael. *Newark's Little Italy: The Vanished First Ward.* *(New Brunswick, NJ: Rutgers University Press, 1999)*

Kukla, Barbara J., *Swing City: Newark Nightlife, 1925-50* (Philadelphia: Temple University Press, 1991)

Leary, Peter J., *Newark, N.J. Illustrated: A Souvenir of the City and Its Numerous Industries* (Newark: William A. Baker, 1893)

Shaw, William H., *History of Essex and Hudson Counties, New Jersey* (Philadelphia: Everts and Peck, 1884, 2 vols.)

New Brunswick

The City in Brief

Founded: 1730 (formed by royal charter) (incorporated as a town, 1736; reincorporated, 1784, 1801, 1838, 1844, 1845, 1849, 1850, 1863)

Head Official: Mayor James M. Cahill (since 1991)

City Population
1980: 41,442
1990: 41,711
2000: 48,573
Percent change, 1990–2000: 16.6%
U.S. rank in 1980: 525th (State rank: 17th)
U.S. rank in 1990: 624th (State rank: 15th)
U.S. rank in 2000: Not reported

Metropolitan Area Population (Middlesex County)
1980: 595,893
1990: 671,780
2000: 750,162

Percent change, 1990–2000: 11.7%
U.S. rank in 1980: 1st (CMSA)
U.S. rank in 1990: 1st (CMSA)
U.S. rank in 2000: 1st (CMSA)

Area: 5.2 square miles (2000)
Elevation: 86 feet above sea level
Average Annual Temperature: 52.2° F
Average Annual Precipitation: 53.3 inches of rain; 27.2 inches of snow

Major Economic Sectors: Research, business, industry
Unemployment Rate: 4.2% (April 2005; New Jersey)
Per Capita Income: $14,308 (1999)
2004 ACCRA Average Home Price: Not reported
2004 ACCRA Cost of Living Index: Not reported

2002 FBI Crime Index Total: Not reported

Major Colleges and Universities: Rutgers, The State University of New Jersey

Daily Newspaper: *Home News Tribune*

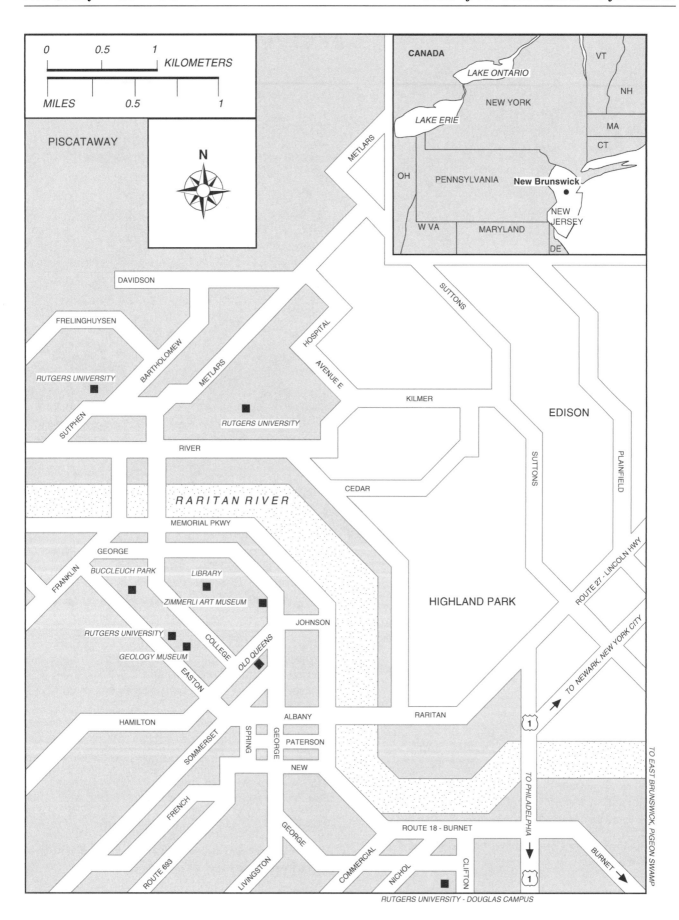

KILOMETERS

MILES

PISCATAWAY

N

CANADA

LAKE ONTARIO

NEW YORK

VT

NH

LAKE ERIE

MA

CT

OH

PENNSYLVANIA

New Brunswick

NEW JERSEY

W VA

MARYLAND

DE

METLARS

DAVIDSON

SUTTONS

FRELINGHUYSEN

HOSPITAL

BARTHOLOMEW

METLARS

AVENUE E

RUTGERS UNIVERSITY

KILMER

EDISON

SUTPHEN

RUTGERS UNIVERSITY

RIVER

PLAINFIELD

SUTTONS

RARITAN RIVER

CEDAR

MEMORIAL PKWY

ROUTE 27 - LINCOLN HWY

GEORGE

FRANKLIN

Buccleuch Park

LIBRARY

HIGHLAND PARK

ZIMMERLI ART MUSEUM

JOHNSON

RUTGERS UNIVERSITY

COLLEGE

GEOLOGY MUSEUM

OLD QUEENS

EASTON

TO NEWARK, NEW YORK CITY

HAMILTON

ALBANY

RARITAN

1

SOMMERSET

SPRING

GEORGE

PATERSON

NEW

FRENCH

TO PHILADELPHIA

GEORGE

TO EAST BRUNSWICK, PIGEON SWAMP

ROUTE 693

LIVINGSTON

COMMERCIAL

ROUTE 18 - BURNET

NICHOL

CLIFTON

1

BURNET

RUTGERS UNIVERSITY - DOUGLAS CAMPUS

Introduction

New Brunswick is a diversified commercial and retail city located on the Raritan River in the mid-eastern portion of New Jersey. Headquarters to Johnson & Johnson, New Brunswick is also notable for being the home of Rutgers University, the eighth oldest institution of higher education in the United States. The poet Alfred Joyce Kilmer, author of the widely quoted ''Trees,'' was born in New Brunswick. It is the county seat of Middlesex County, which has appeared more than once among the top 10 on *Money* magazine's list of the best places to live in America.

Geography and Climate

New Brunswick is situated in mid-New Jersey on the south bank of the Raritan River at the head of navigation, about 40 miles southwest of New York City. It lies in a line of moraines formed by glaciers in a level coastal plain. New Brunswick's is a four-season climate. The proximity of the Atlantic Ocean helps create relatively mild winters and cooling summer breezes.

Area: 5.2 square miles (2000)

Elevation: 86 feet above sea level

Average Temperatures: January, 29.7° F; July, 74.8° F; annual average, 52.2° F

Average Annual Precipitation: 53.3 inches of rain; 27.2 inches of snow

History

Raritan River a Vital Connecting Link Between Settlements

Lenni-Lenapes of the Delaware tribe crossed the Raritan River near modern New Brunswick in summertime expeditions to the Jersey Shore for fish and clamshells, long before Dutch messengers traveling between Holland's American settlements forded at the same spot, possibly as early as 1640. English settlers had been living there for about fifteen years when John Inian, an Englishman from Long Island, arrived in 1681 and established a ferry crossing linking the east and west banks of the Raritan River. At the time the place was known as Pridmore's Swamp. Known variously thereafter as Inian's Ferry, Onion's Ferry, and The River, the town was finally

named New Brunswick in 1730 to honor the House of Brunswick, then occupying the throne of England. An early visitor noted in 1730 that ''when I came to this place in 1715, there were but four or five houses in the 30 miles between Inian's Falls and the Falls of the Delaware, but now the whole way it is almost a continued lane of fences and good farmer houses'' where Dutch, English, Scottish, German, and French settlers resided. The population centered near New Brunswick, which had become a storehouse and shipping point for wheat and flour produced inland.

Revolutionary War Engages City

During the American Revolution, the third reading of the Declaration of Independence in the colonies took place in New Brunswick on July 6, 1776. The Continental army took refuge at New Brunswick after their defeat at Fort Lee. George Washington's dispirited army crossed the Raritan River on the retreat south across New Jersey that led to the Battle of Trenton, burning the bridge behind them. British and Hessian troops occupied the town from December 1776 to the following June, building hatred by robbing British and revolutionary sympathizers alike. Panic spread; as many as 300 people streamed into New Brunswick during that December to accept the British Lord Howe's offer of amnesty in return for a renunciation of revolutionary sentiments. In late spring 1777, Washington moved his troops to an area overlooking the Raritan valley; Howe was forced out, burning and pillaging on his way to add to the suffering already endured. Thereafter the town experienced little direct warfare. Washington returned in 1778 on his way to a decisive victory over Cornwallis at Yorktown.

Town Thrives as Crossroad Between New York, Pennsylvania

New Brunswick gradually became the center of Middlesex County, earning the nickname Hub City. By 1830 the population there numbered more than 5,000 people. Still a center for the transport of grain, the city was also an important stop for people traveling between New York and Philadelphia. Rough-and-tumble competition grew up among transportation companies, becoming so heated that steamships would ram into New Brunswick docks, forcing passengers to leap overboard to join the fray over competing stagecoaches. The Delaware & Raritan Canal reached New Brunswick in 1834, joining the two rivers and making way for the transport of coal from Pennsylvania and other goods being transported west. Eventually the Raritan River carried the third largest tonnage of any river in the country. The railroad era was ushered in when the Camden & Amboy Railroad linking New Brunswick to the New Jersey Railroad was completed in 1839. This development, in combination with the water power made available by the canal lock's waterfall, led to the rapid rise of industry. A wallpaper factory and a rubber plant were founded. By 1860, the population numbered 10,761 people. Elsewhere in Middlesex County, rubber also became a prime industry, supplying boots and rubbers to Union soldiers during the Civil War and afterwards. Other emerging industries were the manufacture of clay, firebrick, and terra cotta products. Industry was spurred by Thomas Edison's invention in 1879 of electric lights.

Twentieth Century Brings Modern Industry

By the early twentieth century, the rubber and wallpaper industries had begun to wane, but New Brunswick had welcomed Robert W. and James W. Johnson, who came in 1885 to establish their pioneer gauze and adhesive tape plant. Where previously Americans had reached in emergencies for old sheets or towels, soon they were reaching for Johnson & Johnson bandages. That company recruited workers from Hungary, giving the city the largest Hungarian population of any city in the country. New Brunswick also welcomed the Wright-Martin Aircraft Corporation, which supplied airplane engines during World War I. Chemical manufacturers began to produce dyes and other chemicals formerly imported from Germany. Munitions manufacturers such as E. I. du Pont moved into Middlesex County, which emerged from the war with an exhilarated feeling of expanding opportunities. County population exceeded 160,000 people by 1920, and about half the population lived in New Brunswick. Roads were built and trains raced through, making the New Brunswick to Elizabeth corridor the busiest railroad stretch in the world. Between 1950 and 1965 Middlesex County's population doubled to 560,000 people. Lately, while formerly rural areas are seeing a continuing expansion of population, New Brunswick's population remains nearly stable, in the tradition of old American cities. Industry has been drawn to the vast network of intersecting superhighways there. Efforts to reverse the decline that began after World War II resulted in the redesign of the central business district, new headquarters for Johnson & Johnson, a new hotel, and new office buildings. Rutgers University, based in New Brunswick, has become an institution vital to the entire state.

A Brief History of Rutgers

Rutgers University was first chartered in 1766 under the name Queens College. It was rechartered in 1770 when the first document had produced no results. New Brunswick was chosen as the site of the college, which, under the auspices of the Dutch Reformed Church, was set up in a former tavern with Frederick Frelinghuysen as the sole faculty member. Its first graduating class produced one graduate in 1774. British troops forced the college out of town in 1777. The college returned in 1781 and closed in 1795 due to lack of interest. Classes resumed in 1807 and closed again in 1821. Application by 30 prospective students led to the college's reopening in 1825, at which time the name Queens

was deemed unpatriotic and the college's name was changed to Rutgers, in honor of New York philanthropist Colonel Henry Rutgers. The college once again faced collapse when most of its students enlisted to serve in the Civil War. An infusion of money by the state for the establishment of an agricultural program, combined with the decision to make the school non-sectarian and to initiate an intensive scholarship and endowment campaign, revived the school yet again. It is now the State University of New Jersey and ranks among the country's major universities.

City Looks Forward

In 1999, New Brunswick and surrounding areas of New Jersey experienced damaging flooding from Tropical Storm Floyd. No lives were lost and the community pulled together to help affected residents of the city. James Cahill, New Brunswick's mayor since 1991, remains committed to focusing on New Brunswick's future growth with initiatives, programs, services, and developments.

Historical Information: Middlesex County Cultural and Heritage Commission, 703 Jersey Ave., North Brunswick, NJ 08901; telephone (732)745-4489; fax (732)745-4524; email info@cultureheritage.org

Population Profile

Metropolitan Area Residents (Middlesex County)
1980: 595,893
1990: 671,780
2000: 750,162
Percent change, 1990–2000: 11.7%
U.S. rank in 1980: 1st (CMSA)
U.S. rank in 1990: 1st (CMSA)
U.S. rank in 2000: 1st (CMSA)

City Residents
1980: 41,442
1990: 41,711
2000: 48,573
Percent change, 1990–2000: 16.6%
U.S. rank in 1980: 525th
U.S. rank in 1990: 624th
U.S. rank in 2000: Not reported

Density: 9,293.5 people per square mile (2000)

Racial and ethnic characteristics (2000)
   White: 23,701
   Black: 11,185
   American Indian or Alaska Native: 224
   Asian: 2,584

Native Hawaiian and Pacific Islander: 40
Hispanic or Latino (may be of any race): 18,947
Other: 8,780

Percent of residents born in state: 44.9% (2000)

Age characteristics (2000)
Population under 5 years old: 3,394
Population 5 to 9 years old: 2,768
Population 10 to 14 years old: 2,196
Population 15 to 19 years old: 5,623
Population 20 to 24 years old: 12,304
Population 25 to 34 years old: 8,573
Population 35 to 44 years old: 5,127
Population 45 to 54 years old: 3,455
Population 55 to 59 years old: 1,1081
Population 60 to 64 years old: 915
Population 65 to 74 years old: 1,544
Population 75 to 84 years old: 1,213
Population 85 years and over: 389
Median age: 23.6 years (2000)

Births (2004, Middlesex County)
Total number: 11,112

Deaths (2004, Middlesex County)
Total number: 5,658 (of which, 45 were infants under the age of 1 year)

Money income (1999)
Per capita income: $14,308
Median household income: $36,080
Total households: 13,053

Number of households with income of . . .
less than $10,000: 730
$10,000 to $14,999: 380
$15,000 to $24,999: 977
$25,000 to $34,999: 1,315
$35,000 to $49,999: 1,253
$50,000 to $74,999: 1,248
$75,000 to $99,999: 760
$100,000 to $149,999: 503
$150,000 to $199,999: 107
$200,000 or more: 86

Percent of families below poverty level: 16.9% (39.8% of which were female householder families with related children under 5 years)

2002 FBI Crime Index Total: Not reported

Municipal Government

New Brunswick operates under the mayor-council form of government. The mayor and five council members are elected to four-year terms. New Brunswick is the county seat of Middlesex County.

Head Official: Mayor James M. Cahill (since 1991; current term expires December 31, 2006)

Total Number of City Employees: 626 (2004)

City Information: Office of the Mayor, 78 Bayard St., New Brunswick, NJ 08901; telephone (732)745-5004

Economy

Major Industries and Commercial Activity

Research, business, and industry are the economic pillars of Middlesex County, where well over 20,000 firms are located. At the heart of research activity is Rutgers University, which maintains more than 60 research facilities. Research as well as business and industrial activities are carried out at the more than 100 *Fortune* 500 corporations that maintain plants and other facilities in Middlesex County, including Johnson & Johnson (world headquarters), Ford, General Motors, Pepsico, Cola-Cola, E. I. DuPont, General Electric, and others. Middlesex County boasts one of the largest business parks in the country, the 2,350-acre Raritan Center, which lists the presence of 20 *Fortune* 500 companies.

Rutgers University is at the northern end of the U.S. Route 1 ''high technology corridor'' that extends to Princeton University at the southern end of Middlesex County. Both universities are high technology centers in a variety of disciplines that attract research and engineering firms.

Items and goods produced: chemicals, pharmaceuticals, ceramics products, metal refining, automobiles, air conditioners, plastics, electronics

Incentive Programs—New and Existing Companies

A variety of local, state, and federal programs are available for businesses in the New Brunswick area. The Middlesex County Certified Local Development Company administers the 504 program (long-term fixed asset financing).

Local programs—The New Brunswick Department of Planning, Community and Economic Development provides programs for businesses looking to locate, expand, or upgrade their operations. The New Brunswick Small Business Loan Guarantee provides capital to small businesses located or looking to locate with the city. The New Brunswick Micro-Loan Program provides start-up businesses with modest amounts of capital. Other funds are available for facade improvement, and assistance is offered for business plan writing and site location. Certain sites within the city deemed in need of redevelopment may be eligible for favorable tax treatment and other benefits.

State programs—The New Jersey Economic Development Authority (EDA) offers a wide range of financial, real estate development, and technical services to encourage business development and growth in the state. There are 20 different programs available for businesses of all sizes, from startups to *Fortune* 500 companies. The EDA issues bonds to provide financing at favorable interest rates for business ventures, and makes low-interest loans and guarantees loans made by private investors and lenders. It also offers a full range of real estate development services to stimulate both private and public development projects. In addition, the EDA administers a business incentive program which provides grants to expanding or relocating businesses that will create new jobs in New Jersey. Loans and grants also are available to municipalities and private property owners to encourage the clean-up and redevelopment of hazardous sites around the state.

The New Jersey Urban Development Corporation provides low-interest loans to developers and businesses seeking to construct facilities in urban areas, including small business incubators. The New Jersey Small Business Development Center also provides business assistance with free consulting, affordable training, funding partners, and corporate sponsors. The Technology Help Desk & Incubator, subsidized by the state, provides inexpensive office and wet/dry lab space to small and startup technologically oriented companies.

Job training programs—Various state and federal incentive programs offer tax credit inducements based on new hires, expansion, and relocation. Employment and training programs through the federal Workforce Investment Act and the State Workforce Development Partnership reimburse employers for providing on-the-job training to certain employees.

Development Projects

As the world moves into the twenty-first century, New Brunswick is undergoing a period of tremendous redevelopment by both the public and private sectors. The Lord Sterling Elementary School, a $25-million facility completed in 2003, was built as a joint project of a private developer and the public school board, the first such venture in New Jersey history. With more than $1.5 billion in investments, the city has also seen the construction of major office and retail complexes, the development of an internationally recognized cultural center, the emergence of world-class health facilities, and the creation of affordable housing. Through 2007, more than 1.75 million square feet of new construc-

tion is expected, representing an additional investment of $325 million.

Downtown New Brunswick is a vital part of the city and one of New Jersey's most exciting urban centers. Upcoming projects in the area include the Heldrich Center, which will include a corporate conference center, hotel, apartments, and retail space in the center of downtown. Luxury apartments are to be constructed at the Highlands at Plaza Square and the Metropolitan. Expansion and renovation will be underway in late 2005 at Albany Plaza II and Civic Square IV.

Lower George Street, which connects downtown with the Douglass College area is being rejuvenated by an influx of new housing construction and rehabilitation of existing buildings. New retail areas are planned, as is an elementary school.

In the French Street neighborhood, the Robert Woods Johnson Hospital—which has been steadily expanding over the past decade—has in the planning stages a new home for its Child Health Institute, a nationally recognized research center for children's diseases. Expansion of French Street's vibrant retail area is expected to begin in 2005 with the construction of a 75,000-square-foot shopping center. Existing French Street merchants will be offered assistance as part of the city's facade improvement plan to improve their business.

Economic Development Information: New Brunswick Development Corporation, 120 Albany Street, New Brunswick, NJ 08901; telephone (732)249-2220. City of New Brunswick, 78 Bayard Street, New Brunswick, NJ 08901; telephone (732)745-5004. County of Middlesex, Office of Economic Development, 1 JFK Square, 1st Floor, New Brunswick, NJ 08901; telephone (732)745-3433; fax (732)745-5911. New Jersey Economic Development Authority, Capitol Place One, Trenton, NJ 08625; telephone (609)292-1800

Commercial Shipping

Easy access to markets has facilitated the growth of Middlesex County. Major highways directly link the county to the markets of New York, Philadelphia, and beyond. Freight is handled by more than 200 common carrier truck/van lines and a commuter rail network that includes service on the Northeast Corridor rail route. Deep water shipping is possible through facilities at the mouth of the Raritan River and the Arthur Kill, as well as the Port of New York and Port Elizabeth, a short distance away.

Labor Force and Employment Outlook

Middlesex County is home to a large, growing, and highly skilled labor pool; unskilled labor is also abundant. Businesses benefit from the presence of Rutgers University and the county-wide vocational and technical high schools there. Nearly half of the county's population has been to college. Ample space has been set aside for future industrial expansion and the outlook is considered good for continued balanced and controlled growth. Since the turn of the century, a major portion of new jobs created in Middlesex County have been in the service sector, especially accounting, personnel specialists, and engineering. The New Brunswick area benefits from its proximity to a wide array of cultural facilities.

The following is a summary of data regarding the New Brunswick labor force, 2004 annual averages (Edison, New Jersey in Middlesex County).

Size of nonagricultural labor force: 1,009,200

Number of workers employed in . . .
 construction and mining: 46,600
 manufacturing: 82,700
 trade, transportation, and utilities: 227,200
 information: 31,800
 financial activities: 63,000
 professional and business services: 163,600
 educational and health services: 129,300
 leisure and hospitality: 77,600
 other services: 40,400
 government: 147,000

Average hourly earnings of production workers employed in manufacturing: $15.30 (Statewide average)

Unemployment rate: 4.2% (April 2005; New Jersey)

Largest employers	Number of employees
Rutgers University	8,500
Robert Wood Johnson Hospital	3,500
St. Peter's University Hospital	3,500
University of Medicine & Dentistry of New Jersey	2,500
Johnson & Johnson	1,600

Cost of Living

Middlesex County boasts an expanding supply of affordable rental apartments, single-family homes, townhouses, and condominiums.

The following is a summary of data regarding several key cost of living factors for New Brunswick.

2004 ACCRA Average Home Price: Not reported

2004 ACCRA Cost of Living Index: Not reported

State income tax rate: 1.4% to 8.97%

State sales tax rate: 6%

Local income tax rate: None

Local sales tax rate: None

Property tax rate: $3.75 per $100 of assessed value (2003)

Economic Information: Middlesex County Planning Board, 40 Livingston Ave., New Brunswick, NJ 08901; telephone (732)745-3062; Middlesex County Regional Chamber of Commerce, 1 Distribution Way, Suite 101, Monmouth Junction, NJ, 08852; telephone (732)821-7700, fax (732)821-5852; email info@mcrcc.org

Education and Research

Elementary and Secondary Schools

New Brunswick Public Schools, founded in 1851, are governed by a Board of Education, whose seven members are appointed by the mayor to staggered three-year terms. Instruction in computer literacy is given to all students. There are special gifted and talented programs, and non-college-bound students may elect the Educational Investment Contracting program, which trains them on the job in local business and industry. A new high school is currently in the planning stage and is expected to be completed in time for the 2007–2008 school year.

The following is a summary of data regarding the New Brunswick public schools as of the 2004–2005 school year.

Total enrollment: 7,500

Number of facilities
 elementary schools (K-8): 11
 senior high schools: 1
 other: 1

Student/teacher ratio: 21:1

Teacher salaries
 median: $54,585

Funding per pupil: $14,533

Middlesex County Vocational and Technical High Schools were established in 1915; one of these is located in New Brunswick and four more are located throughout the county. The county also offers the New Jersey State Teen Arts program, which identifies and promotes the artistic talents of teenagers. New Brunswick is the site of three parochial schools.

Public Schools Information: New Brunswick Public Schools, 24 Bayard St., New Brunswick, NJ 08901; telephone (732)745-5414

Colleges and Universities

Although New Jersey has existed in the shadow of New York City and Philadelphia, it has made important contributions to the nation's cultural life. In colonial times, it was the only colony to have two institutions of higher learning, at Princeton and New Brunswick, where Rutgers, the State University of New Jersey, more commonly known as Rutgers University, is located. The eighth-oldest college in the United States, Rutgers is located on three regional campuses in Camden, Newark, and New Brunswick/Piscataway. Although enrollment is large (more than 50,000 students), the many colleges of small to moderate size maintain separate identities, traditions, and programs. Undergraduate programs lead to degrees in the arts, sciences, music, and fine arts. The university offers majors in more than 100 fields in its 29 degree-granting units. The Zimmerli Art Museum at Rutgers serves the creative needs of the local community, including students enrolled in the college as well as other lifelong learners. Programs focus on the interaction of the visual arts with poetry, music, dance, and science.

The Robert Wood Johnson Medical School is one of eight schools of the University of Medicine and Dentistry of New Jersey. Rated among the top 50 primary care medical schools in the country, the school's faculty numbers more than 2,500. Middlesex County College in Edison has a two-year degree program that emphasizes job skills with more than 80 degree and certificate programs.

Libraries and Research Centers

New Brunswick Free Public Library, which traces its roots back to the 1796 Union Library Company, holds about 80,000 books, more than 200 periodicals, and some 1,000 videos. One of the library's main foci is being able accommodate the multicultural nature of the community it serves. The library's children's room is said to be remembered affectionately by generations of patrons. The system maintains one bookmobile. Special collections are maintained on local history and on the Hungarian language, and the library is a U.S. government document depository.

Among the more than one dozen libraries at Rutgers University are the main university library, whose collection numbers nearly 3 million volumes, and the Center for the American Woman and Politics Library. Rutgers' library system is ranked among the top 25 in the United States. Health, pharmacology, clinical medicine, and related topics are the focus of collections at Saint Peter's Medical Center Library, E.R. Bristol-Myers Squibb Company's Pharmaceutical Institute Library, Medical Research Library, and Robert Wood

Johnson Library of Health Sciences. Gardner A. Sage Library, built in 1875, holds the archives of the Reformed Dutch Church. Middlesex County's Archives and Records Management Center in North Brunswick houses hundreds of thousands of government records and other public documents that have accumulated since 1683.

More than 60 research centers at Rutgers University study such topics as food technology, biology, economics, engineering, politics, AIDS research, computer science, shellfish, mosquitoes, and the works of Thomas Alva Edison. The William L. Hutcheson Memorial Forest, in continuous ownership by the same family from 1701 to 1955, is maintained by Rutgers as a living forest laboratory. Rutgers is one of only 11 universities in the country to be part of the establishment of a national mathematics research center, and it has been designated by the State of New Jersey as one of five academic industrial centers for high technology research. Rutgers is part of the ''super computer'' consortium that operates the ETA-10 super computer, the largest computer of its kind in the world.

Public Library Information: New Brunswick Free Public Library, 60 Livingston Avenue, New Brunswick, NJ 08901-2597; telephone (732)745-5108, fax (732)846-0226

Health Care

New Brunswick has a long tradition of attention to health care, having established the country's first medical society in 1766. Five hospitals, two of them teaching hospitals affiliated with the University of Medicine and Dentistry of New Jersey (Saint Peter's Medical Center and Robert Wood Johnson University Hospital), are located in New Brunswick. The Cancer Institute of New Jersey delivers advanced comprehensive care, conducts world class cancer research, and offers the latest clinical treatments for cancer patients. St. John's Health and Family Service Center also offers health care to New Brunswick residents.

Health Care Information: Middlesex County Health Department, telephone (732)494-6742

Recreation

Sightseeing

New Brunswick preserves many historic buildings, including nineteenth-century rubber factories, churches with pre-Revolutionary cemeteries, Buccleuch Mansion (now oper-

Historic buildings abound on the campus of Rutgers University, a popular destination for visitors.

ated as a museum), and Henry S. Guest House, a stone structure built about 1760, renovated and exhibiting shawls, old lace, and Japanese items. The birthplace of Alfred Joyce Kilmer, now used as an office, contains period furniture and photos of the Kilmer family; tours are available by appointment. The historic "Town Clock" Church, built in 1812, also offers guided tours by appointment.

The multiple campuses of Rutgers University are a popular destination for visitors. Historic buildings there include Old Queens, a brownstone designed by the man responsible for New York's City Hall; it is now the university's administrative center. On campus can also be found art, geology, and history museums. The university's 50-acre Display Gardens are notable for specimens of American holly.

New Brunswick is the eastern terminus of the Delaware & Raritan Canal, built in the 1830s. The canal is now a state park, with headquarters at Somerset, just east of New Brunswick. Along its main and feeder canals may be seen the remains of the canal and the famous Camden & Amboy railroad, as well as restored homes and stations of lock and bridge tenders.

Arts and Culture

New Brunswick Cultural Center Inc., located downtown, provides year-round programming in the visual and performing arts. Its 1,800-seat, acoustically acclaimed State Theater, home to the American Repertory Ballet, hosts symphonies performed by the New Jersey Symphony Orchestra, jazz, dance, chamber music, children's programs, and other fare. Extensive renovations began on the historic building in December 2003 and were completed in late 2004, in an attempt to restore the theater as closely as possible to its original appearance while updating sound and lighting systems to rival that of any brand new facility. For theatergoers, new plays and musicals bound for Broadway are previewed at the 367-seat George Street Playhouse; the Playhouse also features several regional theatrical productions. Crossroads Theatre, an African American professional company, offers plays, musicals, and touring programs during a September-to-May season. The Rutgers Theater Company, based at Rutgers University, offers an academic-year Subscription Series of professional theater. Rutgers is also home to the renowned children's theater group, the Shoestring Players; unfortunately the group has been on hiatus since the 2004–2005 school year because of budget cutbacks, and its future is uncertain. New Brunswick is within easy reach of the vast cultural resources of New York and Philadelphia.

Museums of note in New Brunswick include Buccleuch Mansion, built in 1739 and displaying antiques in period rooms; Hungarian Heritage Center; New Jersey Museum of Agriculture, presenting historic farming tools, household items, toys, and photographs; and Rutgers University Geology Museum. Jane Voorhees Zimmerli Art Museum, also at Rutgers, offers permanent and changing exhibits of paintings from the early sixteenth century through the present, with emphasis on the graphic arts. Considered one of the finest university museums in the country, the Zimmerli houses the university's collection of more than 35,000 art objects.

Nearby Piscataway offers East Jersey Olde Towne, a reconstructed colonial village, and the restored Cornelius Low House/Middlesex County Museum, a fine example of eighteenth-century Georgian architecture. The County Museum presents exhibits on the impact of New Jersey's people, products, and resources on American history and progress; many of these exhibits have won national awards for excellence. The Artists' League of Central New Jersey presents an annual tri-state exhibit of the works of visual artists, sculptors, and craftspeople at Cornelius Low House. At the East Brunswick Museum, fine art and historical exhibits showcase the talents of central New Jersey artists. Historic sites, museums, and theatrical performances are abundant throughout Middlesex County.

Festivals and Holidays

The annual Raritan River Festival joins New Brunswick with its cross-the-river neighbor, Highland Park, for food and fun on both sides of the Raritan. Water taxis, cabs, and buses transport participants to both cities during the festival. Boyd Park on the riverfront is the site of the annual Hispanic Riverfront Festival that celebrates the music, cuisine, and other entertainments of the city's Puerto Rican community. The annual Hungarian Festival, the first Saturday in June, features Hungarian dancing, food, crafts, and games, fencing demonstrations, a museum gift shop, and a twilight concert. The New Jersey International Film Festival, held each year in June and July, features screenings of independent, classic, international, and experimental films. October brings the Autumn in the Park Downtown Harvest Festival, with old-fashioned carriage rides, live music, and other family entertainment throughout Highland Park.

Taking place at the end of each school year, RutgersFest is an annual carnival and concert that has become a tradition for university students. A variety of musical performers, food vendors, and other amusements offer students a welcome break from exam preparation. East Brunswick presents the Middlesex County Fair during the second week in August. The holiday season is kicked off by the annual Holiday Lighting Spectacular, in which crowds fill Monument Square to see the lights come up on the city's 50-foot tree adorned with 3,200 lights. Holiday music fills the air as horse-drawn carriages take visitors for free rides on the brick-paved streets of the city.

Sports for the Spectator

Spectator sports in the region center around collegiate football and basketball competitions at Rutgers and Princeton universities. In 1869 Rutgers defeated Princeton in the world's first intercollegiate football game, held in New Brunswick. The actor Paul Robeson was a Rutgers graduate and an All-American football player there.

Middlesex County and its municipalities offer horse shows and amateur harness racing at various local parks. Year-round horse racing is also offered at nearby Meadowlands Sports Complex, home of the New Jersey Nets and Devils and host to the New York Giants and Jets.

Sports for the Participant

The New Brunswick Park System features 285 acres of parks, playgrounds, passive areas, athletic fields, facilities, lawns, and gardens. Boyd Park, located on New Brunswick's river front, was just reopened after an $11-million redevelopment. Home to numerous festivals and special events, the park now boasts views of the Raritan River and New Brunswick's skyline. The 15-acre Memorial Stadium park hosts sporting events with seating for 5,000 people. The 78-acre Buccleuch has many athletic fields, a cross country fitness trail, and sledding and skating in winter. The Colonial House, located at the park, is in the process of an historical renovation but is still open for tours on Sunday afternoons from June through October. The newly developed Alice Jennings Archibald Park includes 10.5 acres of athletic facilities for baseball, softball, soccer, football, tennis, basketball, and handball, as well as a playground and picnic area.

Also new is a 15-acre youth sports complex that hosts little league baseball and softball, as well as all youth soccer games. Still in the works at the park are a flowing brook, bridges, and picnic pavilions. Nearby is the HUB Teen Recreation Center. Scheduled for completion in 2005, the 17,000-square-foot center will offer young people the following: batting cage, golf learning center, internet cafe, computer lab, TV lounge and movie theater, dance studio, fitness gym with locker rooms, meeting rooms, game room, and a movie theater.

Recreation Information: New Brunswick Recreation Department, 65 Morris St., New Brunswick, NJ 08903; telephone (732)745-5125

Shopping and Dining

New Brunswick's major shopping areas include Albany Street Plaza, the Golden Triangle, Kilmer Square, Livingston Shopping Center, and Sears Plaza. New Jersey Designer Craftsmen, designated a resident company of the New Brunswick Cultural Center complex, displays the works of members in a gallery located there. Middlesex County is home to about 80 major shopping centers.

New Brunswick offers an array of dining establishments from the casual to the elegant. Ethnic cuisine runs the gamut from Italian to Mongolian, and includes Chinese, Japanese, Cajun, Mexican, and American fare. Several continental restaurants offer fine dining and have received both regional and national recognition in many well-known publications, such as *Gourmet* magazine and the *New York Times.*

Visitor Information: New Brunswick City Market, 120 Albany Street, 7th Floor, New Brunswick, NJ 08901; telephone (732)545-4849

Convention Facilities

New Brunswick is part of the meeting destination area known as Metro New Jersey Meadowlands (of which Newark is also a part). Its popularity is due in part to its proximity to the attractions of Manhattan. Small-meeting planners considering New Brunswick as a destination may choose from facilities at Rutgers University or at a number of hotels and motels in the city. The Rutgers Student/Conference Center provides multi-conference seminar facilities to accommodate up to 550 people, as well as an outdoor plaza for special events. The Hyatt-Regency in New Brunswick offers 288 rooms and suites, as well as 21 meeting rooms that total 28,000 square feet; there is also a 9,600-square-foot ballroom.

Convention Information: New Brunswick City Market, 120 Albany Street, 7th Floor, New Brunswick, NJ 08901; telephone (732)545-4849

Transportation

Approaching the City

Major highways crossing Middlesex County include the New Jersey Turnpike, Garden State Parkway, Interstate 287; U.S. Routes 1,9, and 130; and State Routes 18, 27, 28, 34, 35, and 440. Newark International Airport is located a short distance from Middlesex County's northern border. Amtrak and New Jersey Transit service Middlesex County.

Traveling in the City

The Cultural and Heritage Commission issues Historic Walking Tour brochures. New Jersey Transit and Suburban transit provide rail and bus service. The Hub City Local is a trolley bus that runs free throughout New Brunswick.

Communications

Newspapers and Magazines

New Brunswick's daily newspaper, the *Home News Tribune,* is published every morning. Black Voice/Carta Latina, a newspaper aimed at African American and Hispanic audiences, appears weekly. All of the major New York and Philadelphia newspapers are available locally. Rutgers University began publishing *The Targum,* the country's first college newspaper in 1869. Many scholarly journals are also published by Rutgers on a variety of topics.

Television and Radio

Two radio stations broadcast from New Brunswick. All of the major New York and Philadelphia television stations are accessible to most of the county, and cable service is available.

Media Information: *Home News Tribune,* 35 Kennedy Boulevard, New Brunswick, NJ 08816; telephone (732)246-5500

New Brunswick Online

City of New Brunswick Home Page. Available www.new brunswick.com

Home News Tribune. Available www.thnt.com

Middlesex County Office of Economic Development. Available www.co.middlesex.nj.us

Middlesex County Regional Chamber of Commerce. Available www.mcrcc.org

New Brunswick Department of Economic Development. Available www.cityofnewbrunswick.com

New Brunswick Public Schools. Available www.nbps.k12 .nj.us

Selected Bibliography

Cawley, James and Margaret, *Along the Delaware and Raritan Canal* (Rutherford, NJ: Fairleigh Dickinson University Press, 1970)

Clayton, W. Woodford, ed., *History of Union and Middlesex Counties, New Jersey, with Biographical Sketches* (Philadelphia: Everts and Peck, 1882)

McCormick, Richard P., *Rutgers: A Bicentennial History* (New Brunswick: Rutgers University Press, 1966)

McKelvey, William J. Jr., *The Delaware and Raritan Canal: A Pictorial History* (York, PA: Canal Press, 1975)

Paterson

The City in Brief

Founded: 1791 (incorporated, 1851)

Head Official: Mayor Jose Torres (since 2002)

City Population
  1980: 137,970
  1990: 140,891
  2000: 149,222
  2003 estimate: 150,782
  Percent change, 1990–2000: 5.9%
  U.S. rank in 1990: 128th (State rank: 3rd)
  U.S. rank in 2000: 147th (State rank: 3rd)

Passaic County Population

  1980: 447,585
  1990: 453,060
  2000: 489,049
  Percent change, 1990–2000: 7.9%
  U.S. rank in 1990: Not reported

U.S. rank in 2000: 115th

Area: 8.73 square miles (2000)
Elevation: 70 feet above sea level
Average Temperatures: January, 28.3° F; July, 74.6° F; annual average, 52.2° F

Average Annual Precipitation: 51.3 inches of overall precipitation; 27.6 inches of snowfall

Major Economic Sectors: Services, education and healthcare, trade, government, manufacturing
Unemployment Rate: 5.4% (NY–NJ MSA; February 2005)
Per Capita Income: $13,257 (1999)
2004 ACCRA Average House Price: Not reported
2004 ACCRA Cost of Living Index: Not reported

2002 FBI Crime Index Total: 6,842

Major Colleges and Universities: William Paterson University, Passaic County Community College, Berkeley College of Business-Garret Mountain campus

Daily Newspaper: *The Herald News, The Record*

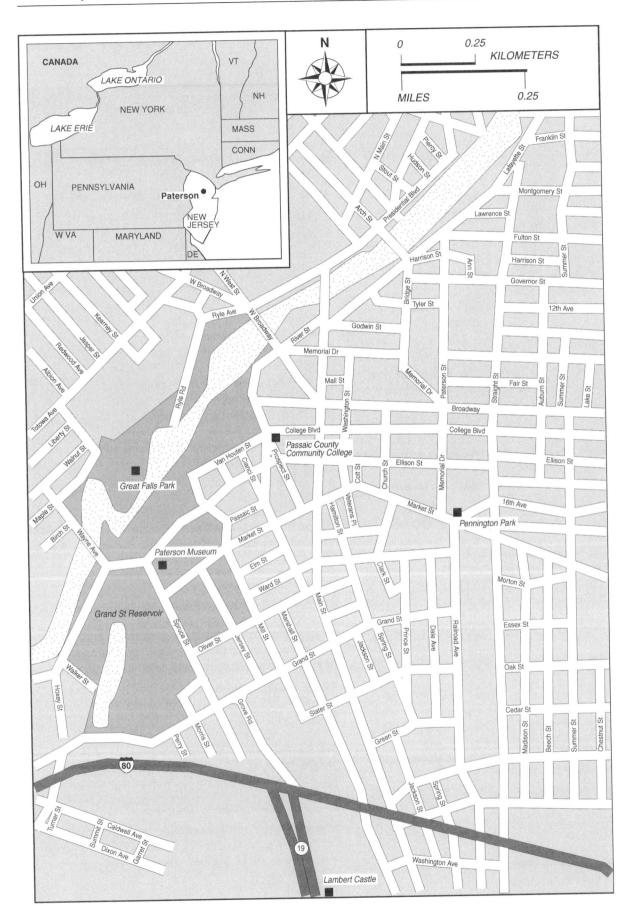

Introduction

Paterson was defined by the waterfall near which it was located, just as the river and previous glaciers had defined and refined the land of northern New Jersey. As the first planned industrial city in America, Paterson was once known as the ''Silk City'' due to the thriving textile manufacturing businesses powered by the falls. While the silk and cotton mill businesses eventually declined, Paterson has redefined itself as a regional service center and has maintained the historical thread of the industry that made Paterson part of the early fabric of the United States.

Geography and Climate

Paterson is located in what is called the Piedmont region of the United States, lying between the coastal plains and the Appalachian Mountains. The Piedmont area is characterized by rolling, low hills that are the remains of an ancient mountain range worn away by glacial action and river erosion. The city was strategically sited on the dramatic 77-foot Great Falls of the Passaic River in northern New Jersey's Passaic County, in order to capitalize on the energy of the rushing water. Several other major metropolitan areas are within easy reach of Paterson, which is 14 miles north of Newark, 11.5 miles from the George Washington Bridge, and 13 miles from the Lincoln Tunnel to Manhattan.

Paterson is in New Jersey's coastal zone, in which the continental and oceanic influences battle for dominance. In fall and early winter, Paterson's temperature is generally warmer than interior parts of the state; in spring the ocean breezes keep the temperature cooler. The effect of the ocean keeps seasonal temperature changes rather gradual, and the area is less prone to extreme temperatures than other parts of New Jersey. Humidity is high year-round, and rainstorms are most common between October and April.

Area: 8.73 square miles (2000)

Elevation: 70 feet above sea level

Average Temperatures: January, 28.3° F; July, 74.6° F; annual average, 52.2° F

Average Annual Precipitation: 51.3 inches of overall precipitation; 27.6 inches of snowfall

History

Early Industrial Development

It all started with the falls—at the end of the last Ice Age about 13,000 years ago, the retreating glaciers left a moraine in the path of the Passaic River. After initially being dammed into a glacial lake, the river managed to escape and began to carve a new route, deepening its canyon through the basalt and ultimately creating the 77-foot Great Falls. It took about 3,000 years for the area to be settled by a nomadic group of hunter-gatherers.

The Lenni-Lenape Indian people were the original inhabitants of the Paterson area. Drawn by ample opportunities for hunting, the Lenape also began to dabble in small-scale agriculture. In the 1620s, Dutch missionaries and trappers began to settle near the Great Falls on the Passaic River, intrigued by a description given by friendly Indians. Property disputes between the Dutch and the Lenape people followed, while hunting, trapping and trading of animal pelts began to deplete the formerly rich regional supplies. Exposure to previously unknown European illnesses took a toll on the Lenape, curtailing the tribe's ability to stem further encroachment by the new settlers. In 1679, the Dutch obtained the first tract of land and began farming what is now the site of the city of Paterson. The settlement stayed small for more than a century but served as a tourist attraction. During the American Revolution, visitors such as George Washington, Alexander Hamilton, and the Marquis de Lafayette stopped to have lunch at the majestic, 77-foot-high Great Falls.

In 1790, William Paterson, a signer of the Declaration of Independence, was elected governor of New Jersey. The next year, U.S. Secretary of the Treasury Alexander Hamilton, helped form the Society for Establishing Useful Manufactures (S.U.M) with the power of the Great Falls of Paterson in mind. He wanted to lessen the dependence of the United States on imported products and harness the falls in the manufacture of domestic goods. Hamilton proposed to the U.S. Congress that an industrial district be set up at the site of present-day Paterson. When Congress proved uninterested, he arranged private support for what became America's first planned industrial city, named after the state governor.

In New Jersey, the state legislature voted that the S.U.M. would ever after be exempted from county and township taxes and gave it the right to hold property, improve rivers, build canals, and raise $100,000 through the use of a lottery. The S.U.M., which continued to operate until after World War II, located its plant at the Great Falls of the Passaic River.

Early Labor Problems

Major Pierre l'Enfant, who is best known for later designing the layout of Washington, D.C., was hired to build a system of raceways in Paterson that would direct water to run and operate the mills. In 1794, the initial raceway was completed and water was brought to the first mill, which produced calico goods. This laid the foundation for a substantial textile industry that has flourished into the present.

The city grew out of the S.U.M.'s 700 acres above and below the Great Falls on the Passaic, and its first citizens were primarily workers at the local factories. In the first part of the 1800s, the town continued to grow as an industrial center. If one industry failed, it was replaced by another. By 1825 Paterson had become known as the "Cotton Town of the United States." Reportedly, oxen provided power for the first cotton spinning at a Paterson mill.

America's first factory strike took place in 1828 when Paterson cotton workers quit their looms to protest a change in the lunch hour. The mill owners had decided that it would be better for the child workers if the midday meal took place at one o'clock rather than at noon, thus making a more equal division in the workday. Employees surprised management by demanding the reduction of working hours from 13.5 to 12. Other local workers, including carpenters, masons, and mechanics working in the city, also walked out. This was the first recorded instance of a sympathy strike in the United States. The workers finally lost the strike, but it made a strong impression on the community. Afterward, the owners restored the noon lunch hour.

Paterson became more accessible in 1831 with the opening of the Morris Canal, which was dug through the coal fields of Pennsylvania. A year later the railroad steamed into Paterson, further stimulating the town's development. In 1836 gun-maker Samuel Colt opened the Patent Arms Company and began the manufacture of Colt repeating revolvers. In 1837, a machine shop owned by John Clark produced one of the earliest American locomotives, the *Sandusky,* which was modeled after an imported English model. That year, the locomotive made its first trip from Paterson to Jersey City and New Brunswick and back. Over the next 40 years, 5,871 engines were to be made in Paterson and shipped all over North and South America.

Silk Industry Blooms; Submarine Launched

Silk manufacturing first began in Paterson in 1840 when a plant was established in Paterson's Old Gun Mill. By then, cotton manufacturing had mainly been moved to New England. Within ten years, Paterson became known as the "Silk City." Except for the cultivation of silkworms, all other stages of silk production took place there. In 1841 the town of Paterson was incorporated, growing to a population of almost 20,000 twenty years later. By 1870, the city was processing two-thirds of the raw silk imported into the United States and was attracting immigrant workers from Ireland, Italy, Germany, and Russia.

Just 18 years later, Paterson's population was approaching 51,000 people. That year, a local schoolteacher and inventor named John Phillip Holland tested the first successful submarine in the Passaic River. Unlike the silk industry, the submarine model didn't immediately have a smooth ride—even when Holland surprised a U.S. Navy ship on a secret maneuver, the Navy did not take his invention seriously and many years passed before the submarine came into widespread use.

During the next decade, a three-hour strike took place in local textile factories, led by foreign workers who had been forced to flee Europe for championing liberal causes. The strike was held to protest unbearable conditions in the silk mills. However, the strike did little to change the miserable working conditions.

Citizens Face Hardships

Paterson's next major strike took place in 1902, by which time the local population had reached more than 105,000 people and the city had become the fifteenth largest in the United States. That year brought many disasters to the city. A February fire destroyed 500 buildings, including city hall and the entire business district. Local firemen, with the help of those from nearby towns, finally halted the fire a mile from its starting point.

Residents were just beginning to recover from that loss when, in March, the swollen Passaic River engulfed the lower portions of the city, sweeping away bridges, homes, and buildings. Damages reached more than one million dollars. Then a few months later a tornado struck, uprooting trees and houses and crippling vital services in the city.

Labor Difficulties Lead to Strike

Paterson's silk industry reached its peak in 1910 when the city population stood at 125,600. At that time, there were 25,000 workers in 350 large plants who wove nearly 30 percent of the silk manufactured in the United States. Three years later, all millwork came to a standstill when laborers under the leadership of the Industrial Workers of the World labor group struck in support of the continuance of the two-loom system. The owners wanted to increase the number of looms for which each worker would be responsible but the workers balked.

Workers walked out in February 1913, citing a lengthy list of longstanding abuses of labor and poor worker-management relations. The employers then declared a lockout, meaning that workers could not return without the permission of the factory owners. Supporters of the strikers began marching on picket lines in front of the mills. After the violent death of a picketer, nearly 15,000 workers joined in a funeral procession, and even children struck in support of their worker-parents. Famous American radical John Reed, who was jailed during the walk-out, staged an enormous ''Paterson pageant'' in Madison Square Garden in New York City to raise money for the striking workers. But the greatest strike in the history of Paterson ended in the defeat of the workers, who finally went back to their jobs on management's terms.

Death of the Silk Industry

By 1920, Paterson's population had reached nearly 136,000 people. After World War I, the Wright Aeronautical Corporation began manufacturing airplane motors at an old Paterson silk mill, and for a time airplane engine production became the city's primary industry. But after World War II the industry moved elsewhere.

In 1924, 20,000 silk workers began an unsuccessful battle against a proposed four-loom system. Manufacturers decided they were fed up with labor disputes and began seeking new sites in new cities with lower taxes, cheaper power, and less militant workers. By 1925, the mills began to leave Paterson. Although 700 plants still operated in the city, they were much smaller than their former size.

As the years passed, the local textile industry continued to diminish. This was primarily due to antiquated plants that were unable to compete with those in other parts of the country, the introduction of synthetic materials such as nylon and rayon, and the breakdown of large working units into smaller shops. By 1935, only 4,000 workers were weaving silk in Paterson. In time, virtually all silk production there disappeared.

By the 1930s, the fabric dyeing industry was growing and soon Paterson's plants were producing 70 percent of the nation's silk and rayon. But as the years went on, this industry shrank as most of the mills moved elsewhere. During the second half of the twentieth century, Paterson experienced a great population loss and its stature as an important industrial city was diminished, although remnants of the garment industry still remain.

Present Day Paterson: Weaving Together the Past and the Future

In 1976, Paterson's Great Falls were declared a national natural landmark, marking the swath the river and falls have cut in the actual as well as the figurative landscape of the area. The city's fascinating history is preserved in literary works by two great twentieth-century poets, William Carlos Williams and Allen Ginsberg. Williams's work entitled

Paterson was published in five books in the mid-twentieth century and is considered one the greatest philosophical poems of the century. The Passaic River serves as the thread that binds the poems together.

While labor unrest ostensibly brought down the fabric industry in Paterson, those early protests generated new legislation that addressed a multitude of workplace issues such as child labor, worker safety, a minimum wage, and limitations for the workday. The price for being a system agitator has been a 36 percent decline in manufacturing industry over the past 10 years in the greater Paterson metropolitan area, although the region maintains its role in fabric dyeing. The city also remains a cultural melting pot as a result of its industrial past.

In recent years, Paterson has managed to make use of its former industrial buildings, which are enjoying new life as historical sites. The S.U.M. historic district has become a national historic landmark, with many of the buildings converted to a variety of other uses; the Rogers Locomotive Erecting Shop has become the Paterson Museum, which highlights the city's industrial history and is known for its Native American relics and collection of New Jersey minerals. While appreciating its past, Paterson is in the process of transitioning to being a service provider to the East Coast municipalities within its reach; finance, sales, and healthcare are all areas of new economic growth for the former textile powerhouse.

Historical Information: Passaic County Historical Society, c/o Lambert Castle, Valley Rd., Paterson, NJ 07503; telephone (973)247-0085; fax (973)881-9434; email lambert castle@msn.com

Population Profile

Passaic County Residents
1980: 447,585
1990: 453,060
2000: 489,049
Percent change, 1990–2000: 7.9%
U.S. rank in 1990: Not reported
U.S. rank in 2000: 115th

City Residents
1980: 137,970
1990: 140,891
2000: 149,222
2003 estimate: 150,782
Percent change, 1990–2000: 5.9%
U.S. rank in 1990: 128th (State rank: 3rd)
U.S. rank in 2000: 147th (State rank: 3rd)

Density: 17,675.4 people per square mile (2000)

Racial and ethnic characteristics (2000)
  White: 45,913
  Black or African American: 49,095
  American Indian and Alaska Native: 901
  Asian: 2,831
  Native Hawaiian and Pacific Islander: 84
  Hispanic or Latino (may be of any race): 74,774
  Other: 41,184

Percent of residents born in state: 46.4% (2000)

Age characteristics (2000)
  Population under 5 years old: 12,578
  Population 5 to 9 years old: 12,987
  Population 10 to 14 years old: 12,173
  Population 15 to 19 years old: 11,446
  Population 20 to 24 years old: 11,937
  Population 25 to 34 years old: 24,647
  Population 35 to 44 years old: 23,082
  Population 45 to 54 years old: 16,843
  Population 55 to 59 years old: 6,222
  Population 60 to 64 years old: 4,908
  Population 65 to 74 years old: 6,937
  Population 75 to 84 years old: 4,106
  Population 85 years and over: 1,356
  Median age: 30.5 years

Births (2002)
  Total number: 2,843

Deaths (2002)
  Total number: 1,031 (of which, 18 were infants under the age of 1 year)

Money income (1999)
  Per capita income: $13,257 (1999)
  Median household income: $32,778
  Total households: 44,760

Number of households with income of . . .
  less than $10,000: 6,908
  $10,000 to $14,999: 3,379
  $15,000 to $24,999: 6,721
  $25,000 to $34,999: 6,413
  $35,000 to $49,999: 7,451
  $50,000 to $74,999: 7,536
  $75,000 to $99,999: 3,228
  $100,000 to $149,999: 2,257
  $150,000 to $199,999: 494
  $200,000 or more: 373

Percent of families below poverty level: 19.2% (25.7% of which were female householder families with related children under 5 years)

2002 FBI Crime Index Total: 6,842

Municipal Government

Paterson operates under the mayor-council form of government. The municipal council consists of nine members, six of whom are elected by and represent the six wards of the city. The remaining three at-large members of the council are elected by the general populace, as is the mayor. The mayor serves four-year terms, with primary responsibility for the day-to-day administration of the city. The council is responsible for reviewing and approving legislation that affects the municipality. Paterson serves as the seat of Passaic County, New Jersey.

Head Official: Mayor Jose Torres (since 2002; current term expires in 2006)

Total Number of City Employees: 3,000+ (2005)

City Information: City of Paterson, City Hall, 155 Market St., Paterson, NJ 07505; telephone (973)321-1500

Economy

Paterson has continued its population surge into the 21st century, adapting from its historic focus on fabric production to related industries such as dyeing and polymers. Tourism, too, has become a growth industry in the Great Falls area in specific and in New Jersey in general. The Great Falls/S.U.M. National Historic Landmark District has received $4.147 million in federal funding that will repair and stabilize bridges, preserve the upper raceway on the Falls, and create solutions for deteriorating ruins along the site.

The City of Paterson has created a Department of Community Development that has an aim of revitalizing the city and its neighborhoods through redevelopment, restoration, and attraction and retention of sustainable industries. The city is currently targeting advanced manufacturing businesses, aerospace innovators, and automotive manufacturers.

The Urban Enterprise Zone program has helped the initiation of Main Street facade treatment programs. The Paterson Small Business Development Center has provided the Department of Public Works with funds for sewer repairs, trash receptacles, street paving, and tree maintenance.

Major Industries and Commercial Activity

As the seat of Passaic County, with its Superior Court, the Roe Federal Building, and the Paterson City Hall, government is Paterson's largest single employer. It is followed in importance by health care. Textiles also remain an important industry, but hundreds of smaller industries also keep the former mills humming.

Because of the city's proximity to New York City and easy access via major highways, Paterson has been selected as the right site for many companies that conduct business in the metropolitan New York area. In addition, the city's close proximity to the Port of New York/New Jersey and Newark International Airport make it a desirable business location.

Items and goods produced: garments, textiles, electronic components, machine tools, ribbons, rubber goods, plastics, cosmetics, packaging

Incentive Programs—New and Existing Companies

Paterson is located at the crossroads of major transportation routes, close to international shipping ports, in the heart of the East Coast population center and a stone's throw from New York City. The city offers manufacturers, light industry, warehouse operations, and high-tech companies many benefits. These include tax incentives, quality real estate available at fair prices, and energy savings plans.

Local programs—Paterson's Department of Community Development functions as a one-stop resource for entrepreneurs and companies considering relocation. Services include information, assistance with permit acquisition and licensing and referrals to technical assistance and financing. The Small Business Development Center serves as a major resource for financial and planning assistance for existing small businesses and new enterprise.

Paterson has a designated Urban Enterprise Zone that covers 30 percent of the landmass of the city. Economic development within the UEZ entitles a qualified business to many tax incentives, such as a $500-$1,500 tax credit for hiring city residents or residents of other zone cities who were formerly unemployed or on public assistance.

State programs—New Jersey's Urban Enterprise Zone program allows participating businesses to receive 100 percent exemption for state sales tax for the purchase of most tangible property, including office supplies, equipment, furnishings, and services, including installation and building materials. Repairs and improvements to existing properties are also exempt, as are energy and utility services. Corporate tax credits are available to employers who hire from designated prospective employee pools.

The New Jersey Economic Development Authority (EDA) offers a wide range of financial, real estate development, and technical services to encourage business development and growth in the state. The majority of its assistance is geared toward small and mid-sized businesses and, in more recent years, the high-tech industry. Businesses specializing in technology or biotechnology can transfer tax certificates to

other New Jersey businesses, realizing up to 75 percent of their value in cash that can be spent on equipment, facilities, or for other expenses related to the business. The EDA issues bonds to provide financing at favorable interest rates for business ventures, makes low-interest loans, and guarantees loans made by private investors and lenders. It also offers a full range of real estate development services to stimulate both private and public development projects. In addition, the EDA administers a business incentive program that provides grants to expanding or relocating businesses that will create new jobs in New Jersey. A Brownfields Redevelopment Loan Program underwrites the efforts of municipalities and private property owners to remediate hazardous sites around the state.

Further tax credit programs apply to businesses that create new jobs, as well as those companies that invest in recycling equipment. The Commerce division of the State of New Jersey supports approximately 12 "incubator" businesses concentrated on science and technology activities; these businesses receive assistance in facility and equipment costs, along with essential training.

Job training programs—For more than 30 years, the Greater Paterson Opportunities Industrialization Center, Inc., has coordinated a network of employment and training programs that seek to improve the living conditions of economically challenged, unemployed, and underemployed workers through job skill training and education. Specialized programs offer assistance with childcare, transportation, driver education, and mental health services; additionally, the OIC has created a partnership with Passaic County Community College that allows the agency to offer an Opportunities Career Advancement Program with a technological spin.

The Passaic County Workforce Development Center staffs a One Stop Career Center in Paterson, where workers can improve interviewing skills, assess career aptitudes, and practice computer skills. The Workforce Investment Board of Passaic County provides easy access to a number of employment services, including labor statistics, job training, funding resources, and career counseling programs. Continuing education is also available through William Paterson University's specialized center.

All local Workforce Development offices are coordinated by the state Workforce Development Partnership program, which in turn is part of the New Jersey Department of Labor. The state agency provides training programs for new and existing businesses via its Business Resource Center.

Development Projects

In 1998, Passaic County Community College received a grant of $184,425 through the Urban Revitalization Implementation program. The college has partnered with the City of Paterson, the Hispanic Multipurpose Center, Paterson Small Development Center and others in efforts to create a Paterson Community Technology Center that will assist displaced manufacturing workers in learning new technology skills as they cross the digital divide.

In 2000, the Paterson YMCA completed a large-scale renovation of its fitness facilities, the Marcal Company moved to a local 204,000-square-foot facility, and Kirker Enterprises, Inc. purchased and renovated 165,000 square feet of office and warehouse space in the city. Also in 2000, city officials approved the construction of 34 condominiums in a former textile mill in the Great Falls Historic District, and Fairfield Textiles had plans for a 120,000-square-foot expansion of its facilities in the Bunker Hill district of the city. The Great Falls/S.U.M. National Historic Landmark District recently received $4.147 million in federal funding that will repair and stabilize bridges, preserve the upper raceway on the Falls, and create solutions for deteriorating ruins along the site. Ideally, the restoration project will stimulate increased tourism to the Great Falls area.

In late June of 2004, Barnert Hospital opened a downtown women's clinic designed to better address the health issues of a growing urban population. The new facility contributes 7,000 square feet of examination and treatment space to the community medical services available.

Economic Development Information: City of Paterson Department of Community Development, 125 Ellison St., 2nd floor, Paterson, NJ 07505; telephone (973) 321-1212

Commercial Shipping

Newark Liberty International Airport (NLIA) is located less than 15 miles southeast of Paterson, with passenger and cargo service to all points of the globe. Several cargo-specific businesses and structures exist at NLIA, including the FedEx Complex (a regional hub), the United Parcel Service package handling and distribution center, and the 250,000 square foot Air Cargo Center. Cargo processing is state-of-the-art, with capacity to handle sophisticated and delicate materials with a high level of efficiency. The Port Authority maintains an administration building near the Air Cargo Center.

The Port of New York and New Jersey provides further access, via water, to other parts of the United States and the world. The Port Authority is equipped to deal with virtually every type of cargo, including vehicles, live animals, large containers, liquid and dry bulk loads, and more. In 2004, the Port saw more than $110 billion in goods pass through its gates.

The highway system in New Jersey is the most dense in the nation, guaranteeing ample routes into, out of, and around Paterson and the surrounding major metropolitan areas of Newark and New York. Interstates 280, 80, 295 and 95 link Paterson to other large cities, along with a network of U.S. and state highways. Businesses have a wide choice of ground transportation vendors for cargo shipping purposes, from well-established family trucking companies to nationally-known experts such as FedEx and UPS.

Labor Force and Employment Outlook

Paterson has always exhibited economic strength that rests in having a diverse population of hard-working immigrant peoples. As of the 2000 census, the city's population included Latinos from more than a score of Latin American countries, people from the Middle East, Asians of Chinese and Korean descent, and African Americans, in addition to citizens of European ancestry.

It's expected that total non-farm employment in Passaic County will continue to increase through 2012 but at a more gradual rate than it has during the 10 year span from 1992 to 2002. Three particular industry sectors should account for approximately three quarters of the projected growth: education and health services, professional and business services, and retail trade. While job loss in the manufacturing sector is anticipated to decrease, about 18.4 percent of positions in that industry are expected to be sacrificed. In 2012, employment requiring a "high" level of education and experience will account for only 26.4 percent of all jobs, while positions solely requiring on-the-job training should comprise 56.4 percent of total employment.

The following is a summary of data regarding the New York–White Plains metropolitan area labor force, 2004 annual averages.

Size of nonagricultural labor force: 5,007,500

Number of workers employed in . . .
   construction and mining: 176,100
   manufacturing: 235,500
   trade, transportation and utilities: 866,200
   information: 202,100
   financial activities: 542,100
   professional and business services: 743,400
   educational and health services: 894,100
   leisure and hospitality: 368,400
   other services: 209,800
   government: 769,300

Average hourly earnings of production workers employed in manufacturing: $15.67 (New Jersey; 2004 annual average)

Unemployment rate: 5.4% (NY–NJ MSA; February 2005)

Largest employers	*Number of Employees*
St. Joseph's Reg. Medical Center	4,700
City of Paterson	3,000

Largest employers	Number of Employees
William Paterson University	1,117
Marcal Paper Products	1,000
Accurate Box	180
Frost King–Thermwell Products	No figure reported
Barnert Hospital	No figure reported

Cost of Living

The following is a summary of data regarding several key cost of living factors for the Paterson area.

2004 ACCRA Cost of Living Index: Not reported

2004 ACCRA Average House Price: Not reported

State income tax rate: 1.4%–8.97%

State sales tax rate: 6%

Local income tax rate: None

Local sales tax rate: 3%

Property tax rate: $22.97 per $1,000 assessed valuation (2005)

Economic Information: Greater Paterson Chamber of Commerce, 100 Hamilton Plaza, Suite 1201, Paterson, NJ 07505; telephone (973)881-7300

Education and Research

Elementary and Secondary Schools

In 1998, a New Jersey Supreme Court decision required that the Paterson Public School District offer students an education at the level guaranteed by the constitution, spurring whole school reform efforts throughout the district. The emphasis in all Paterson schools was on individualized learning in a civil environment; in response, a number of specialized academies and charter schools have been created. At the Martin Luther King, Jr., Educational Complex, the Coalition of Essential Schools model drives educational and student conduct services. An underpinning of democracy encourages student participation, civility, and commitment to educational resources. The Dr. Frank Napier, Jr., School of Technology is unique in its high tech offerings to elementary school-age students, preparing them both for their academic and career futures. The Roberto Clemente School, located in a predominantly African American and Latino area of Paterson, celebrates the multicultural aspects of the city and the microcosm of the classroom. The EARTH Academy (Environmental Academy for Research, House Technology and Health) is based at Eastside High School

and combines experiential learning during fieldtrips with classroom instruction. Rosa Parks High School houses the Rosa L. Parks School of Fine and Performing Arts, offering a college preparatory curriculum designed to lead students directly into degree programs in music, drama and creative writing.

Paterson Public School District is also the umbrella for several early childhood education programs, adult continuing education, and alternative schools for students whose learning styles or discipline issues make them candidates for discovery, expeditionary, and experiential education.

The following is a summary of data regarding the Paterson public school system as of the 2004–2005 school year.

Total enrollment: 27,000

Number of facilities
  elementary and middle schools: 29
  high schools: 5
  other: 3 middle school academies; 23 high school academies

Student/teacher ratio (2004): 11:1

Teacher salaries
  minimum: $40,000
  maximum: $85,000

Funding per pupil: $12,351

An assortment of religiously-based private schools also operate in the area.

Public Schools Information: Paterson Public School District, 33 Church Street., Paterson, NJ 07505; telephone (973)321-0909

Colleges and Universities

One of nine New Jersey public institutions of higher education, William Paterson University sits on 370 wooded acres in the northern part of the state. The student body of 11,409 men and women can concentrate in any of 31 undergraduate programs or 19 graduate programs within its five colleges, including Education, Business, Arts and Communication, Humanities and Social Sciences, and Science and Health. Specialized learning centers for high-tech finance and professional sales have been added to the campus, reflecting Paterson's continuing move to service industries.

Passaic County Community College (PCCC) is a two-year public college with its main campus in Paterson and branches in the New Jersey communities of Wanaque and Wayne. PCCC offers its enrollment of 6,300 the opportunity to pursue more than 40 associate degrees and certifications in such fields as allied health, business, liberal arts, criminal justice, nurse education, radiography, and technology. The school also offers extensive programs in basic skill English, reading, math, and English as a second language. Some courses are also instructed in Spanish.

The Garret Mountain campus of Berkeley College of Business confers the degree of associate in applied science in such fields as business, accounting, management, travel and tourism, paralegal studies, and various fashion fields. The school enrolls more than 700 full- and part-time students.

Libraries and Research Centers

The Paterson Free Public Library was established in 1885, making it the oldest public library in New Jersey. The system consists of a main library facility and three branches, housing more than 308,000 volumes and more than 350 periodical subscriptions. Special collections include African American history materials, collectible banknotes, genealogy materials, local history, and career resources. Local art collectors have over the years bestowed a wealth of paintings to the library, with an emphasis on late 19th and early 20th century works. In 2002 the library was the recipient of a Bill and Melinda Gates Foundation Grant, allowing for installation of 34 new computers throughout the Free Public Library system. Internet and word processing functions are available to library visitors. The library system additionally has opened a Community Learning Center that advertises GED preparation, reading and basic math tutoring, English as a Second Language instruction, and family literacy classes to the public.

The Passaic County Historical Society Library maintains special collections on Passaic County and northern New Jersey history. St. Joseph's Regional Medical Center supports its graduate medical education program with a full medical sciences library consisting of 3,000 books, 300 current periodicals and journals, and 600 audio-visual resources. Students can also tap into the National Library of Medical Databases onsite. The hospital has become more involved with clinical and basic research over the years, including clinical trials of various drug interventions. Recent research studies included exploration of a specific protein that contributes to severe bleeding disorders in patients with leukemia.

The David and Lorraine Cheng Library at William Paterson University provides access to a wealth of printed materials, including maps, atlases, newspapers, dictionaries, government publications, and almanacs. Library users can surf online databases for research and reference materials. The university also houses research facilities equipped to study biochemistry, molecular biology, neurobiology, and DNA.

Other local libraries include those of Passaic County Community College and the Passaic County Law Library.

Public Library Information: Paterson Public Library, 250 Broadway, Paterson, NJ 07501; telephone (973)321-1223

Health Care

Over the past 97 years, Barnert Hospital has grown to include 256 licensed beds serving the Bergen and Passaic county communities. Specialties run the gamut from adolescent sexual behavior issues to oncology and geriatrics. The Barnert Occupational Health Center provides diagnosis and treatment of work-related issues related to asbestos and hazardous waste, hearing loss, employment physicals, and injury prevention. Centers for pain management, sleep disorders, and breast health supplement the trauma facilities of the hospital. Outreach services include the Family and Child Education project operated in conjunction with the Paterson Public School District, with an eye toward prevention of health problems particularly among economically disadvantaged populations.

St. Joseph's Regional Medical Center, founded in 1867, is sponsored by the Sisters of Charity of St. Elizabeth in Convent Station, New Jersey, and serves the entire northern New Jersey area. The hospital is licensed for 792 beds; more than 30,000 inpatients are admitted yearly and another 350,000 outpatients are cared for. The Regional Medical Center specializes in craniofacial reconstruction and surgery, oncology, trauma care and radiology. The medical complex includes a Children's Hospital featuring a feeding and swallowing center, a child development center, and medical personnel specializing in everything from asthma to urology. A nursing home for patients requiring living assistance on a regular basis is located in Cedar Grove, New Jersey; dental and ophthalmology services are offered in addition to hospice care and physical therapy.

A number of public and private walk-in clinics operate in the northern New Jersey area as well, along with an assortment of alternative healthcare practitioners such as massage therapists, acupuncturists, aromatherapists, and hypnotherapists.

Recreation

Sightseeing

Perhaps the most spectacular sights in Paterson are Lambert Castle, perched on a mountain top, and the dramatic Great Falls. Lambert Castle, located on the Garrett Mountain Reservation, is a turn-of-the-century stone castle that once

A statue of Alexander Hamilton honors him for his pioneering vision of an industrialized America, a vision which Paterson was among the first to apply.

belonged to Catholina Lambert, a wealthy silk manufacturer. The Lambert family lived in the building from 1893 until 1923, naming it Belle Vista for its stunning vantage point. Today the castle houses a museum on park-like grounds that provide a picnic area and cross-country track. The house features hand-carved oak interior touches and a lovely terrace. In 1995 the County Freeholders began a $5 million renovation of the castle, finishing in September of 2000.

The Great Falls on the Passaic River can best be viewed from at site at McBride Avenue and Spruce Street. A brochure outlining a walking and/or driving tour and information about guided walking tours in the S.U.M. Historic District is available at the Great Falls Visitor Center, which also arranges guided walks around the Falls and the restored mill buildings that were once powered by the rushing waters.

The Paterson Museum is housed in the Thomas Rogers Locomotive Erecting shop in the Great Falls Historic District of Paterson. The museum's exhibits reflect the evolution of the city as a major U.S. industrial center. Machinery used for dyeing, winding, warping, and weaving silk are featured. The museum showcases the Paul R. Applegate, Jr., Collection of rare Colt firearms, as well as other Paterson-made firearms. Also on display are hulls of the first submersibles made by John Philip Holland, known as the "father of the submarine." The museum's simulated mine yields a fine mineral collection, including a fluorescent mineral display.

Botto House in Haledon, New Jersey, a historic landmark built in 1908, is home to the American Labor Museum. The house, which once belonged to mill worker Pietro Botto, was a meeting place for mill workers who planned the famous 1913 Paterson Silk Strike. The museum has restored period rooms, a labor library, old-fashioned gardens, and changing exhibits that highlight the lives of circa-1900 immigrant families. The museum also offers tours of sites important to the local history of the labor movement.

Ellis Island and the Statue of Liberty are only a daytrip away from Paterson, completing the history of the mills with the story of the immigrants who carried the industry on their backs while working for the labor rights enjoyed by U.S. citizens of the present day.

Arts and Culture

The Paterson Museum hosts permanent and rotating displays of the works of local artists in addition to a store of historical information about the city and region. Manuscripts, materials, looms, warping equipment, and photographic collections trace the artistry of the fabric and submarine industries in northern New Jersey. More contemporary works of art can be found year-round at the Ben Shahn Galleries located at William Paterson University.

William Paterson University (WPU) is also the scene of performances by the High Mountain Symphony, which presents three performances per season as it draws upon the combined talents of faculty and students at the university. For more than 25 years, WPU has been hosting nationally-recognized jazz performers in an ongoing musical series. Quite an ensemble of other musical offerings lie outside the bounds of the Paterson area—opera performances in Newark, off- and on-Broadway musicals in New York City, and small community theaters are plentiful.

Paterson has been portrayed by poets as diverse as Allen Ginsberg and William Carlos Williams The Paterson Poetry Center at Passaic County Community College (PCCC) is widely hailed as a leader in helping poets craft their art. The Center organizes more than 100 activities each year, including readings and presentations by internationally famous poets. The Center's Paterson Poetry Marathon each spring involves week-long workshops in the local public schools that culminate in a public program. Part of the city's historic district has become a de facto artists' colony for painters, writers, sculptors, and photographers.

PCCC's Cultural Affairs Department offers the community programs in art, music, theater, dance, and literature. The Learning Resource Gallery offers monthly art exhibits, lectures, and workshops. The Quidnunc Society also provides local residents with an opportunity to engage in cultural activities.

Arts and Culture Information: Discover Jersey Arts, PO Box 306, Trenton, NJ 08625; telephone (800)THE-ARTS

Festivals and Holidays

In September, the American Labor Museum's Annual Labor Day Celebration highlights the history and importance of the worker in northern New Jersey. Later in the month, the city's Recreation Department holds a fundraising street fair with rides, games, food, music, and arts and crafts booths. In February, Newark keeps the New Year party going with the Chinese Lunar New Year Celebration coordinated by the Newark Museum. The traditional Lion Dance and holiday delicacies are on hand to mark this important event.

In early spring Paterson sponsors a three-day Great Falls Festival that features music and entertainment from local and outside performers, skywalks over the falls and other high wire acts, crafts, rides, and games. An international food court serves dishes from the 53 ethnic groups representative of the city's various citizens. A parade from the American Labor Museum to the Great Falls is the high point of the event.

The Newark Museum hosts an Asian Heritage Festival in early May, with Japanese drumming, Dancing Bells, and the

Indian Folk Dance taking center stage. Fair weather in the month of June welcomes the Annual Sol Stein Golf Open, which is held at the High Mountain Golf Club. Throughout the summer, the Downtown Paterson Special Improvement District offers events such as music festivals, Easter promotions, and Mother's Day celebrations. In mid-July, the Passaic County Fair brings a homespun flavor back to the Silk City metropolitan area.

Sports for the Spectator

Passaic County Community College presents women's and men's basketball games, and men's soccer. William Paterson University competes in Division III of the National Collegiate Athletic Association; team sports include baseball, basketball, football, track and field, volleyball, and swimming. Nearby Newark and New York City offer major league play in all major sports. The Newark Bears professional baseball club plays in the independent Atlantic League, and the MetroStars contend in Major League Soccer play at Giants Stadium in Secaucus.

Sports for the Participant

Rifle Camp Park in Paterson contains fitness and jogging trails maintained by Passaic County government. A toboggan chute and sleigh riding hills make the park fun all year long; nature trails and a bird watching blind add education to the experience. The park offers a Nature Center and an observatory that provide special programs for local students and the general public.

The Garret Mountain Reservation abuts the Rifle Camp Park; the reservation is a 568-acre recreational area that reaches a 500 foot elevation at its topmost point. Any number of activities are available to visitors, depending on the time of year—in seasonable weather, the equestrian center can arrange for trail rides, or hikers can set off on the network of marked paths. Barbour's Pond can be fished in warmer weather or skated upon after hard freezes; in the winter, the hiking trails become cross-country ski routes.

Passaic County Recreation also oversees Tranquility Ridge Park and Friendship Park, two areas that have been left largely untouched and natural after being rescued from imminent development. Activities are more limited in these areas in order to leave little or no trace. Similarly, the 512-acre Apshawa Preserve has been carefully protected; it lies adjacent to a 68-acre parcel owned by the New Jersey Conservation Foundation.

Canoeing and rafting can be had on sections of the Passaic River, offering the opportunity to bird watch while lazily floating along.

Passaic County also operates a golf course located in Wayne, New Jersey. Two 18-hole courses are available,

along with practice greens and a shag field. The facility is open year-round, only closing on major holidays. The communities surrounding Paterson maintain additional golf courses and recreation programs that offer a selection of athletic outlets.

Shopping and Dining

Paterson's thriving downtown connects an ever-expanding array of eclectic, unique stores where shoppers can find furniture, clothing, art and collectibles, antiques, gourmet and natural foods, and linens. The city also offers two farmers' markets open all year and vending fresh produce, poultry, bakery products, grapes and wine presses, seafood, and meats. Discount stores, factory outlets, and malls are all available in or near the Paterson area.

Most any taste bud can be tantalized in Paterson and northern New Jersey, with a discernible preference for Asian cuisines such as Chinese fare and Japanese sushi. Italian and Mexican cooking are well-represented among northern New Jersey restaurants, along with basic American tastes like steaks and chops. True to its diverse immigrant history, the eatery options in the Paterson region are limitless and cover areas of the world such as India, Greece, the Middle East, Cuba, France, Ireland, New England, and Korea. An after-dinner espresso can be found at one of several locally owned coffeehouses in the city.

Convention Facilities

Within the Gateway Region of northern New Jersey there are two dedicated convention centers—the New Jersey Convention and Expo Center at the Raritan Center is located in Edison and offers 150,000 square feet of exhibit space, making it New Jersey's largest venue. The facility is equipped to handle anything from banquets to trade shows and is wired for all audio-visual devices. Food service is available. At the Meadowlands Exposition Center (the MEC) in Secaucus, conferences and trade shows are accommodated in 61,000 square feet of exhibition space, supplemented with additional meeting rooms and a banquet facility that can seat 5,000. The MEC provides two drive-doors for offloading of equipment and is conveniently located near Newark Liberty International Airport.

The theater and other meeting rooms at Passaic County Community College can also be used by the public. The theater seats 300, and a banquet facility has a 100 person capacity. Other hotels and businesses within and around Paterson can be utilized for conferences, meetings, receptions and banquets.

Transportation

Approaching the City

Paterson is located northeast of Newark on Highway 80; Newark Liberty International Airport (NLIA), located just a few more miles to the south, is one of the busiest airfields in the country. International flight service is offered by at least 20 of NLIA's resident airlines, while domestic service is handled by about 15 more providers and several air charters. Ground travelers can jump on Amtrak at Penn Station in Newark or the Greyhound/Trailways Bus Service which also serves the city.

Traveling in the City

Interstate 80 runs east and west through Paterson, which is approached from the south by State Highway 19. Market and Main Streets intersect in the city center, providing a reasonable directional reference in a municipality where the street grid bends slightly to follow the river that runs through it. Other major routes are McLean Boulevard, River Drive, and Randolph Avenue, which are laid out from north to south, and the east-west Broadway. The city is served by the Main Line of the New Jersey Transit railway and bus systems, in addition to the specialized transport programs offered through Passaic County Para Transit.

Communications

Newspapers and Magazines

The northern New Jersey area receives news from *The Herald News* or *The Record,* two daily papers that cover local, state, national, and international happenings. Both papers are part of the North Jersey Media Group, but each maintains its own personality and newsroom. An electronic newspaper, PatersonOnline.Net, focuses on local news, sports, and weather. The *Paterson Literary Review* of Passaic County Community College is published in the city, as is the *Anthonian,* a magazine of the Franciscan Order of the Roman Catholic Church.

Television and Radio

Paterson has its own Latino religious AM radio station, and Newark broadcasts National Public Radio on an FM frequency. Most radio and television programming is relayed from Newark and New York City, providing the city with full access to all national networks. Paterson has cable television service with two community access channels.

Paterson Online

City of Paterson. Available www.patcity.com

Greater Paterson Chamber of Commerce. Available www .greaterpatersoncc.org

North Jersey Regional Chamber of Commerce. Available njrcc.org

Passaic County Government. Available www.passaic countynj.org

Passaic County Historical Society. Available www .lambertcastle.org

Paterson Free Public Library. Available www.palsplus.org/ patersonpl

Paterson Public Schools. Available www.paterson.k12.nj .us/~pps

Selected Bibliography

Golin, Steve, *The Fragile Bridge: Paterson Silk Strike, 1913* (Philadelphia: Temple University Press, 1993)

Hirsch, James, *Hurricane: The Miraculous Journey of Rubin Carter* (Boston: Houghton Mifflin, 2000)

Williams, William Carlos, *Paterson* (New York: New Directions, 1963)

Trenton

The City in Brief

Founded: 1679 (incorporated, 1792)

Head Official: Mayor Douglas Palmer (NP) (since 1990)

City Population
1980: 92,124
1990: 88,675
2000: 85,403
2003 estimate: 85,314
Percent change, 1990–2000: −3.7%
U.S. rank in 1980: 158th
U.S. rank in 1990: 230th
U.S. rank in 2000: 335th (State rank: 9th)

Metropolitan Area Population (PMSA)
1980: 308,000
1990: 325,824
2000: 350,761
Percent change, 1990–2000: 7.1%

U.S. rank in 1980: 4th (CMSA)
U.S. rank in 1990: 5th (CMSA)
U.S. rank in 2000: 1st (CMSA)

Area: 7.66 square miles (2000)
Elevation: 35 to 42 feet above sea level
Average Annual Temperature: 54.7° F
Average Annual Precipitation: 42.2 inches of rain; 23 inches of snow

Major Economic Sectors: Service, government, trade, manufacturing, construction
Unemployment Rate: 3.3% (April 2005)
Per Capita Income: $14,621 (1999)
2004 ACCRA Average Home Price: Not reported
2004 ACCRA Cost of Living Index: Not reported

2002 FBI Crime Index Total: 6,199

Major Colleges and Universities: Rider University; Thomas A. Edison State College

Daily Newspapers: *The Times; The Trentonian*

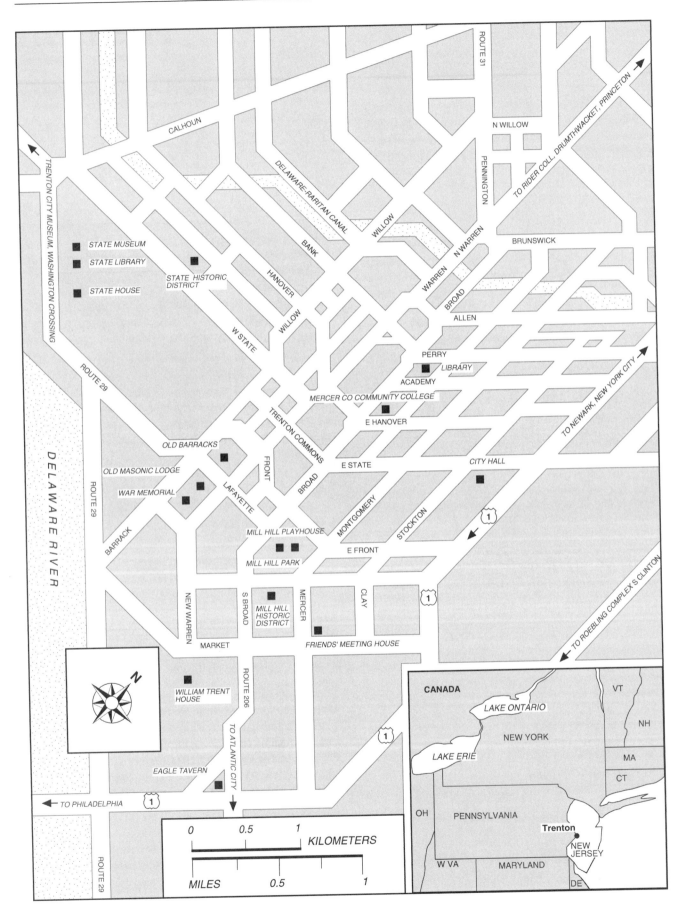

TRENTON CITY MUSEUM, WASHINGTON CROSSING

ROUTE 29

DELAWARE RIVER

CALHOUN

DELAWARE-RARITAN CANAL

BANK

HANOVER

WILLOW

W STATE

■ STATE MUSEUM

■ STATE LIBRARY

■ STATE HISTORIC
DISTRICT

■ STATE HOUSE

ROUTE 31

N WILLOW

PENNINGTON

TO RIDER COLL., DRUMTHWACKET, PRINCETON

BRUNSWICK

WILLOW

WARREN

N WARREN

BROAD

ALLEN

PERRY

ACADEMY

■ LIBRARY

MERCER CO COMMUNITY COLLEGE

■ E HANOVER

TRENTON COMMONS

OLD BARRACKS ■

OLD MASONIC LODGE

WAR MEMORIAL ■ ■

FRONT

LAFAYETTE

BARRACK

E STATE

BROAD

MONTGOMERY

STOCKTON

■ CITY HALL

TO NEWARK, NEW YORK CITY

①

MILL HILL PLAYHOUSE

■ ■

MILL HILL PARK

E FRONT

NEW WARREN

S BROAD

MILL HILL
HISTORIC
DISTRICT ■

MERCER

CLAY

FRIENDS' MEETING HOUSE ■

①

TO ROEBLING COMPLEX S. CLINTON

MARKET

N

ROUTE 206

■ WILLIAM TRENT
HOUSE

TO ATLANTIC CITY

EAGLE TAVERN

■

①

ROUTE 29

◄ TO PHILADELPHIA ①

0   0.5   1
KILOMETERS

MILES   0.5   1

CANADA

VT

LAKE ONTARIO

NH

NEW YORK

LAKE ERIE

MA

CT

OH

PENNSYLVANIA

Trenton

NEW
JERSEY

W VA   MARYLAND

DE

Introduction

Rich in colonial and industrial history, Trenton, the second oldest capital in the United States, lies on the east bank of the Delaware River north of Philadelphia. The business of Trenton is government; it is New Jersey's state capital and the Mercer County seat. The site of the first decisive American victory in the Revolutionary War, Trenton also played a supportive role in the Civil War. Trenton is famous as the home of Lenox china, vulcanized rubber, and steel made through the open-hearth process. In the 1980s, Trenton launched a vast redevelopment program that covered all sections of the city and brought about Trenton's economic rebirth. The Trenton of the twenty-first century is known for being an historic city that is proud of its past and that looks ahead to a bright future.

Geography and Climate

Trenton, located in west-central New Jersey, lies on the east bank of the Delaware River, about 30 miles northeast of Philadelphia and 60 miles southwest of New York City. Trenton is situated on a plateau at the Delaware's navigable head. The city itself is bisected by Assunpink Creek. Trenton's climate is largely continental and subject to winds from the interior of the country. To the west are the Appalachian Mountains, which temper storm activity. Annual snowfall is about 23 inches.

Area: 7.66 square miles (2000)

Elevation: 35 to 42 feet above sea level

Average Temperatures: January, 32.2° F; July, 76.2° F; annual average, 54.4° F

Average Annual Precipitation: 42.2 inches of rain; 23 inches of snow

History

Delaware River Draws Settlers

The site of modern-day Trenton was once occupied by the Sanhican, a branch of the Delaware tribe who called the area Assunpink. The name meant "stone in the water" and referred to the rocky falls in the nearby portion of the Delaware River. The first permanent European settlers arrived in 1679, when the English Quaker Mahlon Stacy arrived at what he called the "falls of the Delaware." Stacy's son sold the land in 1714 to William Trent, a Philadelphia merchant who recognized the industrial potential of the river. Trent built a stone grist mill near the falls and called the resulting community "Trent's Town," which was quickly shortened to Trenton. The town grew up at the junction of the Delaware River and Assunpink Creek.

The head of navigation on the Delaware River, Trenton became a port for shipping grain and products traveling between Philadelphia and New York City. Trenton was also a primary stopping point on the stagecoach line connecting the two larger cities. A ferry, chartered in 1727, connected Trenton with Philadelphia, completing the transportation circle. In 1750 the city's first chief burgess, Dr. Thomas Cadwalader, inoculated the population against smallpox. He later donated 50 pounds toward the founding of the state's first public library.

By the time of the Revolutionary War, Trenton was a town of about a hundred homes and mixed sentiments about the impending war. The city was captured by the British in November, 1776, and large portions of it were burned. Then, in a surprise move that was called the tactical coup of the war, American General George Washington crossed the ice-choked Delaware River on Christmas night, 1776. He marched his Continental soldiers through the night to launch a dawn attack on the Hessian troops occupying Trenton. After inflicting severe casualties on the British garrison, Washington moved his troops to a high hill near Assunpink Creek and engaged the British in the Second Battle of Trenton. Washington's successful maneuvering instilled courage in his cold and battle-weary army and resulted in the first decisive American victory in the war.

State Capital Becomes Industrial Power

Trenton was selected as New Jersey's state capital in 1790. For a time, the city had hopes of becoming the nation's capital and did in fact serve temporarily in that capacity when a yellow fever epidemic raged in swampy Washington City. Transportation continued to play an important role in Trenton's development. In 1806 a covered bridge was built across the Delaware; the structure later supported the trains of the Camden & Amboy Railroad. The Delaware Falls Company constructed the Delaware & Raritan Canal at about the same time to provide water power to Trenton's burgeoning industry. Among the entrepreneurs setting up in the city was wire manufacturer John A. Roebling, whose cables help suspend the Brooklyn Bridge. Pottery-making blossomed as an industry after 1850 and included names such as Walter Lenox and his American Belleek china. Potters were the first to unionize in Trenton, successfully striking in 1835 to win a 10-hour workday. During the Civil War, Trenton housed the U.S. Congress after the South threatened Washington, D.C. Trenton also contributed iron and rubber to the Union Army effort.

Between 1880 and 1920 Trenton's population swelled with an influx of foreign laborers seeking factory jobs. During this period the adjacent communities of Chambersburg, Wilbur, Millham Township, and parts of Ewing Township were annexed. Handcrafted Mercer motor cars were produced between 1910 and 1925, along with steel made from the open-hearth process and vulcanized rubber goods, including Goodyear tires.

In 1932 the Delaware River channel was dredged to 20 feet, making Trenton a port for sea-going vessels; the city's importance as a port has since been eclipsed by the New England and Philadelphia ports. Following World War II, Trenton's middle class population moved to suburban communities made possible through a new federal highway system and new home construction. Trenton retained its image as a smokestack town, even as some of the city's key industries moved southward. Since the 1970s Trenton has regained its reputation as an industrial leader, thanks in large part to the spate of downtown development spurred by the building of several new state structures. Trenton is also developing a reputation as a tourist attraction, a reputation built on its colonial history and its number of highly regarded restaurants. In 2005, *Forbes* magazine listed Mercer County as one of the "Best Locations for Business."

Historical Information: Trenton Historical Society, PO Box 1112, Trenton, NJ 08606; telephone (609)394-1965; New Jersey Historical Society Library, 52 Park Place, NJ 07102; telephone (973)596-8500

Population Profile

Metropolitan Area Residents (PMSA)
1980: 308,000
1990: 325,824
2000: 350,761
Percent change 1990–2000: 7.1%
U.S. rank in 1980: 4th (CMSA)
U.S. rank in 1990: 5th (CMSA)
U.S. rank in 2000: 1st (CMSA)

City Residents
1980: 92,124
1990: 88,675
2000: 85,403
2003 estimate: 85,314
Percent change, 1990–2000: −3.7%
U.S. rank in 1980: 158th

U.S. rank in 1990: 230th
U.S. rank in 2000: 335th (State rank: 9th)

Density: 11,153.6 people per square mile (2000)

Racial and ethnic characteristics (2000)
White: 27,802
Black or African American: 44,465
American Indian and Alaskan Native: 300
Asian: 716
Native Hawaiian and Pacific Islander: 199
Hispanic or Latino (may be of any race): 18,391
Other: 9,190

Percent of residents born in state: 61.1%

Age characteristics (2000)
Population under 5 years old: 6,469
Population 5 to 9 years old: 7,256
Population 10 to 14 years old: 6,521
Population 15 to 19 years old: 5,677
Population 20 to 24 years old: 6,358
Population 25 to 34 years old: 14,278
Population 35 to 44 years old: 12,978
Population 45 to 54 years old: 9,822
Population 55 to 59 years old: 3,468
Population 60 to 64 years old: 2,861
Population 65 to 74 years old: 4,939
Population 75 to 84 years old: 3,576
Population 85 years and over: 1,201
Median age: 32.2 years

Births (2002)
Total number: 1,519

Deaths (2002)
Total number: 2,819 (of which, 17 were infants under the age of 1 year; Mercer County data)

Money income (1999)
Per capita income: $14,621
Median household income: $31,074
Total households: 29,370

Number of households with income of . . .
less than $10,000: 2,266
$10,000 to $14,999: 1,078
$15,000 to $24,999: 2,745
$25,000 to $34,999: 2,992
$35,000 to $49,999: 3,065
$50,000 to $74,999: 3,700
$75,000 to $99,999: 1,639
$100,000 to $149,999: 993
$150,000 to $199,999: 269
$200,000 or more: 234

Percent of families below poverty level: 17.6% (41% of which were female householder families with children under 5 years)

2002 FBI Crime Index Total: 6,199

Municipal Government

Trenton operates under a mayor-council form of government. The seven council members serve four-year terms; three are elected at large, four elected by ward. The mayor serves a four-year term. Trenton also serves as the state capital of New Jersey and the county seat for Mercer County.

Head Official: Mayor Douglas H. Palmer (NP) (since 1990; current term expires July 1, 2006)

Total Number of City Employees: 1,750 (2005)

City Information: Mayor's Office, Trenton City Hall, 319 East State Street, Trenton, NJ 08608-1866; telephone (609)989-3030

Economy

Major Industries and Commercial Activity

Government (state, county, and municipal) forms the single largest sector in Trenton. Other significant economic areas include manufacturing, trade, and services. Trenton's set of unique circumstances contributes to its continued growth: the city benefits from the spill-over of high-technology industries and research centers locating along the Route 1 corridor; land costs, rents, and taxes in Trenton are a fraction of those in New York City, yet Trenton remains an acceptable commute for much of the Northeast Corridor; and commitment by state and local government is high.

Items and goods produced: refrigerated showcases, light bulbs, rubber goods, purses, automobile body hardware, pottery and porcelain products, chemicals, fabricated metal products, lumber and wood products, textiles, food products, electronic goods

Incentive Programs—New and Existing Companies

Local programs—The Capital City Redevelopment Corporation has all of the information a new or expanding business needs to locate or expand into the Capital District and to take advantage of all the public programs that are available. The

Mercer County Community College Small Business Development Center provides entrepreneurs and small businesses in Mercer and other counties with high quality, one-to-one management consulting, training, and the information businesses need to maximize growth in a global economy. The Mercer County One-Stop Small Business Center provides technical and finance procurement assistance and the Science & Technology Incubator helps high-tech firms get established. Trenton has a partnership with the Trenton Business Assistance Corporation, which offers merchant and micro business loan programs. In addition, Trenton is the recipient of a $2,300,000 Economic Development Administration grant made available to help in the development of the Hill Complex in the Trenton enterprise zone.

State programs—The New Jersey Economic Development Authority (EDA) offers a wide range of financial, real estate development, and technical services to encourage business development and growth in the state. The majority of its assistance is to small and mid-sized businesses. The EDA issues bonds to provide financing at favorable interest rates for business ventures, and makes low-interest loans and guarantees loans made by private investors and lenders. It also offers a full range of real estate development services to stimulate both private and public development projects. In addition, the EDA administers a business incentive program that provides grants to expanding or relocating businesses that will create new jobs in New Jersey. Loans and grants also are available to municipalities and private property owners to encourage the clean-up and redevelopment of hazardous sites around the state. The New Jersey Urban Development Corporation provides low-interest loans to developers and businesses seeking to construct facilities in urban areas, including small business incubators.

Job training programs—Mercer County Community College offers programs and services for businesses that include a business incubator, a center for training and development, international trade programs, the Network for Occupational Training & Education (NOTE), a small business development center, and New Jersey-sponsored employee training.

Development Projects

One of the primary focuses of the city's economic development strategy currently lies in the area of affordable housing, as well as plans for Trenton's first development of luxury, single-family homes in decades. The $46 million Trenton Train Station renovation is expected to attract downtown and regional development, including new office buildings and commercial projects. Plans are underway to build a new criminal courthouse and parking garage in downtown Trenton; the facility should be completed by 2008. A parking garage and office on Front Street by the Economic Development Corporation of Trenton was in the works in mid-2005.

Trenton's school district is in the midst of a several-year, $300 million project that involves construction of several new school buildings, as well as renovation of many already in existence. The recently completed Waterfront Park and the Sovereign Bank Arena have increased entertainment and trade show options in Trenton. Opened in April 2002, the $54 million Lafayette Yard Marriott Conference Hall includes a 197 room upscale hotel, a conference center with more than 16,000 square feet of meeting space, a grand ballroom, a 120-seat restaurant and lounge, and a 650-stall parking garage. The hotel is connected to the War Memorial, a historic 1,900 seat amphitheater that recently underwent a $38 million renovation, and serves as a local cultural center for the Greater Trenton Symphony, special events, and large group meetings.

Economic Development Information: New Jersey Economic Development Authority (NJEDA), PO Box 990, Trenton, NJ 08625-0990; telephone (609)292-1800; email njeda@njeda.com. Mercer County One-Stop Career Center, 650 South Broad Street, Trenton, NJ 08650; telephone (609)989-6523

Commercial Shipping

Mercer County Airport, just minutes from Trenton in Ewing Township, offers passenger, charter, cargo, and helicopter service. The Philadelphia and New York City airports, as well as Newark International Airport, are located an hour's drive away from Trenton and offer comprehensive domestic and international flight service. Rail freight service is by Conrail. Several dozen motor freight carriers service the city, taking advantage of Trenton's location along U.S. Route 1 and of the short-haul trucking to and from two of the nation's largest cities: New York and Philadelphia.

Labor Force and Employment Outlook

Mercer County's county executive, Brian M. Hughes, called 2004 "a year of extraordinary growth for our local economy," citing 7,700 new jobs added within Mercer County during that year as well as decreasing unemployment numbers. Hughes also cited partnerships with local colleges and universities as vital to the area's economic growth and future prosperity.

The following is a summary of data regarding the Trenton metropolitan area labor force, 2004 annual averages.

Size of nonagricultural labor force: 231,100

Number of workers employed in . . .
  construction and mining: 5,800
  manufacturing: 8,800
  trade, transportation, and utilities: 32,600
  information: 6,200
  financial activities: 15,900

  professional business services: 34,600
  educational and health services: 42,800
  leisure and hospitality: 14,400
  other services: 7,700
  government: 62,400

Average hourly earnings of production workers employed in manufacturing: $15.67 (New Jersey; 2004 annual average)

Unemployment rate: 3.3% (April 2005)

Largest Employers	*Number of Employees*
State of New Jersey	20,000 +

Cost of Living

The median home price in Trenton was reported as $230,080 in 2004. Several affordable housing projects are currently underway in the area, as well as the development of luxury, single-family homes, the city's first such project in decades.

The following is a summary of data regarding several key cost of living factors in the Trenton area.

2004 ACCRA Average Home Price: Not reported

2004 ACCRA Cost of Living Index: Not reported

State income tax rate: ranges from 1.4% to 8.97%

State sales tax rate: 6%

Local income tax rate: None

Local sales tax rate: None; qualified retailers in Trenton's Urban Enterprise Zone charge 3%

Property tax rate: $3.98 per $100. Equalization rate: 96.4% (2004)

Economic Information: Mercer County Chamber of Commerce, 214 West State Street, PO Box 2708, Trenton, NJ 18607-2708; telephone (609)393-4143. City of Trenton, 318 East State Street, Trenton, NJ 08608; telephone (609)989-3030

Education and Research

Elementary and Secondary Schools

Trenton's school district is the largest in Mercer County. A nine-member Board of Education is appointed for three-year terms by the mayor. The district is in the midst of a several-year project involving the construction of several new schools as well as renovation of many existing buildings.

The following is a summary of data regarding the Trenton public schools as of the 2003–2004 school year.

Total enrollment: 13,231

Number of facilities
  elementary schools: 17
  junior high/middle schools: 4
  senior high schools: 1
  other: 1

Student/teacher ratio: 19:4 (state average)

Teacher salaries
  minimum: $34,010
  maximum: $67,090

Funding per pupil: $13,803

Several parochial and private elementary and secondary schools supplement the public system in Trenton. A number of prestigious day and boarding schools are found in the nearby Princeton area.

Public Schools Information: Trenton Public Schools, 108 North Clinton Avenue, Trenton, NJ 08609; telephone (609)989-2400

Colleges and Universities

Rider University, a four-year liberal arts college founded in 1865, enrolls more than 5,000 students in four schools: business administration, continuing education, arts and sciences, and education. Thomas A. Edison State College offers adult students associate's and bachelor's degrees partially based upon life experience and equivalency examinations. Mercer County Community College, with two campuses, awards associate's degrees in 70 programs, many of them based on community needs. For instance, a portion of the college's more than 13,000 students study in training programs for business and industry.

Nearby Princeton University, one of the nation's most renowned academic institutions and a member of the Ivy League, is within commuting distance. Princeton is known for its liberal arts, medicine, education, architecture, and theology programs and is a respected research institution. The College of New Jersey, in nearby Ewing Township, serves nearly 6,000 students, offering more than 40 liberal arts and professional programs in five schools: Arts and Sciences, Business, Education, Engineering, and Nursing.

Libraries and Research Centers

Trenton's Public Library and its four branches maintain more than 600,000 volumes and special collections ranging from state and local history (the Trentonian Collection) to a large recording and print collection. The library, which houses the Arthur Holland papers on ethics in government, is also a depository for federal and state documents.

The New Jersey State Archives is the official repository for all New Jersey colonial and state government records of enduring historical value. The New Jersey State Library holds more than 750,000 volumes, maintains a Library for the Blind and Handicapped, and has special collections on law, New Jerseyana, New Jersey state government publications, U.S. government documents, and genealogy. Other special libraries in Trenton cover medical, geological, environmental, labor, legal, municipal, and technical topics.

Among Princeton University's areas of research and study are the effect of public policy on urban areas, foreign relations, population trends, and industrial relations. Princeton's Harvey S. Firestone Memorial Library is New Jersey's largest research library. Princeton also maintains the Forrestal Center, a research park employing more than 2,000 people. Drug research being conducted at Princeton Biomedical Research offers hope to sufferers of Alzheimer's disease, anxiety disorder, obsessive-compulsive behavior, and panic disorder.

Public Library Information: Trenton Public Library, 120 Academy Street, Trenton, NJ 08608; telephone (609)392-7188

Health Care

The city of Trenton benefits from health care services provided by several facilities. The St. Francis Medical Center is an acute care teaching hospital and home to Mercer County's only cardiac surgery program. The 158-bed Capital Health System Fuld Campus and the 230-bed Capital Health System Mercer Campus are part of Mercer County's largest healthcare system. Henry J. Austin Health Center offers counseling to pregnant women with substance-abuse problems. The Ann Klein Forensic Center provides both inpatient and outpatient psychiatric care.

Health Care Information: New Jersey Hospital Association, 760 Alexander Road, Princeton, NJ 08534-0001; telephone (609)275-4000

Recreation

Sightseeing

Much of Trenton's sightseeing centers around colonial and Revolutionary War sites. The State Historic District features homes built from the eighteenth to the twentieth centuries; the Mill Hill neighborhood includes the city's first grist mill.

The Old Barracks Museum commemorates its former British, Colonial, Continental, and Tory occupants.

Trenton's oldest landmark is the 1719 home of founder William Trent. During the winter of 1776 to 1777, the city played an important role in the Revolutionary War when General George Washington retook Trenton from the British. The site of Washington's crossing of the Delaware River is marked by the Washington Crossing State Park, which is also the site of the Open Air Theatre and an arboretum. The Battle of Trenton is marked with a 122-foot shaft topped by a statue of Washington. The monument, dedicated in 1893, rises from the spot where Washington's troops first fired on the British. After retaking the city, Washington held a council of war in the Douglass House, now on public view. The churchyard at the Friends' Meeting House contains the graves of many Revolutionary War heroes. The Old Masonic Lodge, built in 1793 in the Georgian colonial style, is one of the nation's oldest lodges and displays a gavel once used by George Washington. Drumthwacket, once the executive dwelling of New Jersey governors, is open to the public, as is the Soldiers and Sailors Memorial Building where the state's gubernatorial inaugurations are held. Trenton's gold-domed statehouse, erected in 1792, houses a collection of battle flags. The State House, in continuous use since 1792, is open for tours. Cadwalader Park contains a small zoo, a herd of deer, a lake and a stream, and a branch of the historic Delaware & Raritan Canal.

Arts and Culture

Trenton performance groups utilize a number of facilities. The Greater Trenton Symphonic Orchestra presents classical concerts at the War Memorial Building and at Trenton's Trinity Cathedral. Other musical groups include the Boheme Opera Company, which performs opera and musicals from September through May, and the Greater Trenton Choral Society. Dramatic productions are scheduled at Mill Hill Playhouse. Artworks Art Center of Trenton provides gallery space and art classes. Area institutions of higher education also present musical and other performances.

The New Jersey State Cultural Center in downtown Trenton consists of the State Archives, the State Museum, a planetarium, and an auditorium. The museum houses collections of New Jersey flora and fauna, fossils, and Indian relics. The Old Barracks, built in 1758, has been restored and is now a museum commemorating its various occupants: British troops fighting in the French and Indian Wars, Colonial and Continental soldiers, and Tory refugees. The Trenton City Museum at the Olmsted-designed Cadwalader Park is housed in the restored Ellarslie Mansion and exhibits the work of local artists and craftspeople. Restored Victoriana is the focus of the Contemporary Club Victorian Museum. Other collections of note include the Meredith Havens Fire Museum and the Flag Museum and Swan Collection of Revolutionary memorabilia; both of the latter are located at Washington Crossing State Park.

Among Trenton's galleries are the Library Gallery at Mercer County Community College, which yearly features shows of county artists, and the Art Porcelain Studio, which displays porcelain pieces by Boehm and Cybis.

Arts and Culture Information: New Jersey State Council on the Arts, 109 W. State St., CN 306, Trenton, NJ 08625; toll-free (800)THE ARTS

Festivals and Holidays

The festival season runs year-round in Trenton, starting in January with the Martin Luther King, Jr., Celebration, an homage to the music and oration of Dr. King. February is the month-long celebration of Black History month. The St. Patrick's Day Parade is March's highlight, with April bringing the Big Egg Hunt and an Arbor Day celebration. May Day celebrates the opening of the city's parks as well as the coming of spring with pony rides, games, and music at Cadwalader Park. The Mayor's Health Run and Walk is also held in May. Summer brings a wide variety of festivities, including the Wachovia Classic bike race and Trenton Heritage Days in June, the Independence Day Celebration in July, and the Puerto Rican Parade, Jazz Festival, and Annual Fishing Derby in August. Autumn is ushered in by the Gospel Festival and the Mayor's Cup Golf Tournament in September. The Trenton Feasts of Lights, which is a street fair held on Chambersburg, also takes place in September. October brings the Haunted Halloween Party, where children can enjoy haunted entertainment, a haunted trail, and other activities at the West Ward Recreation Center. The Thanksgiving parade launches the holiday season, which culminates in December with the Annual Tree Lighting Ceremony and the Mayor's Children Holidays Party. The Battle of Trenton Reenactment also takes place in December.

Sports for the Spectator

The AA Trenton Thunder baseball team, which is affiliated with the New York Yankees, plays its April through August home games at Trenton's Waterfront Park. The Trenton Titans of the East Coast Hockey League, a developmental league, are affiliated with the National Hockey League's Philadelphia Flyers. They play at the state-of-the-art Sovereign Bank Arena at Mercer County.

Other professional sports franchises play throughout the year in nearby Philadelphia and New York City, both of which support professional teams competing in baseball, football, hockey, and basketball. Fans of high school football look forward to the annual contest between Trenton and Notre Dame. Other high school sporting events are also enthusiastically followed by locals. Horse racing can be enjoyed at Monmouth Park Jockey Club and The Atlantic City Race Course.

Sports for the Participant

Trenton's parks offer a full complement of activities including hiking, jogging, bicycling, horseback riding, and camping. Pleasure boats can be launched from a number of public boat ramps. The city maintains a number of indoor and outdoor tennis facilities. Golf is available at Mercer County's Mountain View Golf Course, Mercer Oaks Golf Course, and other nearby clubs. Skiing, skating, tennis, swimming, and water sports can be found within a short driving distance of Trenton.

Shopping and Dining

Trenton is noted for its pottery, china, and fine porcelain from makers such as Lenox, Boehm, Cybis, and Ispanky, which may be found at outlets and showrooms throughout the area. Trenton's principal downtown shopping district encompasses four blocks on State Street and five blocks on Broad Street.

Trenton's culinary fare reflects the city's eclectic heritage; it is famous for its pizza and hoagies. Other ethnic cuisine includes the dishes of Mexico and Scandinavia. Several Italian eateries in the Chambersburg neighborhood are highly acclaimed five-star gourmet restaurants.

Visitor Information: Trenton Convention and Visitors Bureau, Lafayette and Barrack Street, Trenton NJ 08608; telephone (609)777-1770; fax (609)292-3771; email trentcvb @voicenet.com

Convention Facilities

Mercer County typically pools its resources when appealing to conference-givers. Facilities in adjacent communities include the East Windsor Hilton Inn and National Conference Center, the Hyatt Regency-Princeton, and the Henry Chauncy Conference Center in Princeton. Local corporations often rely on their own facilities for business meetings and employee training. Merrill-Lynch, for instance, maintains a 360-room resident training center outside of Trenton, and the National Training Center is located in Highstown. The $54 million Lafayette Yard Marriott Conference Hall includes a 197-room upscale hotel, a conference center with more than 16,000 square feet of meeting space, a grand ballroom, a 120-seat restaurant and lounge, and a 650-stall parking garage. The hotel, which opened in April 2002, displays a variety of fine art that reflects many of the city's historic sites.

Convention Information: Trenton Convention & Visitors Bureau, Lafayette and Barrack Street, Trenton NJ 08608; telephone (609)777-1770; fax (609)292-3771; email trentcvb@voicenet.com

Transportation

Approaching the City

Visitors traveling by air can use facilities at the Philadelphia International Airport or Newark International Airport, each about an hour's drive from Trenton. Both airports offer complete domestic and international service. Commuter plane and helicopter traffic is routed to Mercer County Airport in nearby Ewing Township, where Pan Am Airlines offers its services. New Jersey Transit, a transportation system unique in the nation, allows passengers to purchase tickets anywhere in the state, and board a train or bus to travel to any destination in the state. Amtrak schedules many daily trips to and from Boston and Washington, D.C., while Southeastern Pennsylvania Transportation Authority (SEPTA) provides daily service to Philadelphia.

Trenton lies at the heart of an extensive and heavily used network of roads. Interstate-95 passes around the city to the north while I-295 circles the eastern portion of the city and I-195 splits off toward the East Coast. Trenton is located along U.S. Route 1, which diagonally bisects the city, running northeast-southwest. Route 1 is one of the busiest in the state. U.S. Route 206 runs through the center city. U.S. Route 129 links to Route 1, I-195 and 295. The Trenton Highway complex links Route 1 and Route 29 to I-195 and I-295.

Traveling in the City

Trenton experiences moderate traffic during rush hours downtown. Major east-west thoroughfares include the John Fitch Parkway and Olden Avenue Extension while north-south arteries include Calhoun Street and Princeton Avenue. An extensive bus system services Trenton and Mercer County. Each year, the public bus system in New Jersey transports millions of passengers, many of them commuters from the Trenton area.

Communications

Newspapers and Magazines

Trenton is served by two daily morning newspapers: *The Times* and *The Trentonian*. Several local biweekly and weekly papers are issued as well. Major magazines published in Trenton include the *NJEA Review,* the state teacher's education journal, and *Area Auto Racing News.*

Television and Radio

Trenton receives the major commercial affiliates from Philadelphia and New York City television stations. Trenton itself has a local cable television franchise and receives public television and radio stations out of Philadelphia. Radio broadcasting in the area includes student-operated stations from the College of New Jersey and Mercer County Community College, as well as a variety of AM and FM stations offering music, talk shows, and religious programming.

Media Information: *The Times,* 500 Perry Street, PO Box 847, Trenton, NJ 08605; telephone (609)989-5454. *The Trentonian,* Capitol City Publishing Company, 600 Perry St., Trenton, NJ 08602; telephone (609)989-7800

Trenton Online

City of Trenton Home Page. Available www.prodworks .com/trenton or www.ci.trenton.nj.us

Greater Mercer County Chamber of Commerce. Available www.mercerchamber.org

Mercer County Home Page. Available www.mercercounty .org

New Jersey Economic Development Authority. Available www.njeda.com

New Jersey State Archives. Available www.state.nj.us/state/ darm/links/reference.html

The Times. Available www.nj.com/times

Trenton Convention and Visitors Bureau. Available www .trentonnj.com

Trenton Public Library. Available www.trenton.lib.nj.us

Trenton Public Schools. Available www.trenton.k12.nj.us

The Trentonian. Available www.the trentonian.com

Selected Bibliography

Lee, Francis Bazley, *History of Trenton, New Jersey: The Record of Its Early Settlement and Corporate Progress* (Trenton: *State Gazette,* 1895)

McMahon, William, *South Jersey Towns: History and Legend* (New Brunswick: Rutgers University Press, 1973)

Weslager, C.A., *Dutch Explorers, Traders and Settlers in the Delaware Valley, 1609–1664* (Philadelphia: University of Pennsylvania Press, 1961)

Weslager, C.A., *The English on the Delaware, 1610–1682* (New Brunswick: Rutgers University Press, 1967)

NEW YORK

The State in Brief

Nickname: Empire State
Motto: *Excelsior* (Ever upward)

Flower: Rose
Bird: Bluebird

Area: 54,556 square miles (2000; U.S. rank: 27th)
Elevation: Ranges from sea level to 5,344 feet
Climate: Cold winters, warm summers with lower temperatures in the mountains; abundant precipitation

Admitted to Union: July 26, 1788
Capital: Albany
Head Official: Governor George Pataki (R) (until 2007)

Population
    1980: 17,558,165
    1990: 17,990,455
    2000: 18,976,457
    2004 estimate: 19,227,088
    Percent change, 1990–2000: 5.5%
    U.S. rank in 2004: 3rd
    Percent of residents born in state: 65.3% (2000)
    Density: 401.9 people per square mile (2000)
    2002 FBI Crime Index Total: 537,121

Racial and Ethnic Characteristics (2000)
    White: 12,893,689
    Black or African American: 3,014,385
    American Indian and Alaska Native: 82,461
    Asian: 1,044,976
    Native Hawaiian and Pacific Islander: 8,818
    Hispanic or Latino (may be of any race): 2,867,583
    Other: 1,341,946

Age Characteristics (2000)
    Population under 5 years old: 1,239,417
    Population 5 to 19 years old: 3,971,834
    Percent of population 65 years and over: 12.9%
    Median age: 35.9 years (2000)

Vital Statistics
    Total number of births (2003): 260,844
    Total number of deaths (2003): 157,251 (infant deaths, 1,642)
    AIDS cases reported through 2003: 66,660

Economy
    Major industries: Wholesale and retail trade, transportation, finance, manufacturing, foreign trade, publishing
    Unemployment rate: 4.9% (April 2005)
    Per capita income: $36,296 (2003; U.S. rank: 6th)
    Median household income: $43,160 (3-year average, 2001-2003)
    Percentage of persons below poverty level: 14.2% (3-year average, 2001-2003)
    Income tax rate: 4.0%–7.70%
    Sales tax rate: 4.25%

Albany

The City in Brief

Founded: 1624 (chartered, 1686)

Head Official: Mayor Gerald D. Jennings (D) (since 1994)

City Population
  1980: 101,727
  1990: 101,082
  2000: 95,658
  2003 estimate: 93,919
  Percent change, 1990-2000: −5.3%
  U.S. rank in 1980: 164th
  U.S. rank in 1990: 192nd (State rank: 6th)
  U.S. rank in 2000: 277th (State rank: 21st)

Metropolitan Area Population
  1990: 861,623
  2000: 875,583
  Percent change, 1990-2000: 1.6%
  U.S. rank in 1980: 46th

U.S. rank in 1990: 49th
U.S. rank in 2000: 56th

Area: 21.84 square miles (2000)
Elevation: 29 feet above sea level
Average Annual Temperature: 47.5° F
Average Annual Precipitation: 38.6 inches of rain; 64.1 inches of snow

Major Economic Sectors: Government, services, trade, manufacturing
Unemployment Rate: 3.6% (April 2005)
Per Capita Income: $18,281 (1999)
2004 ACCRA Average Home Price: Not reported
2004 ACCRA Cost of Living Index: Not reported

2002 FBI Crime Index Total: Not reported

Major Colleges and Universities: State University of New York (SUNY) at Albany; Albany Law School; Albany Medical College; Albany College of Pharmacy

Daily Newspaper: *The Times Union*

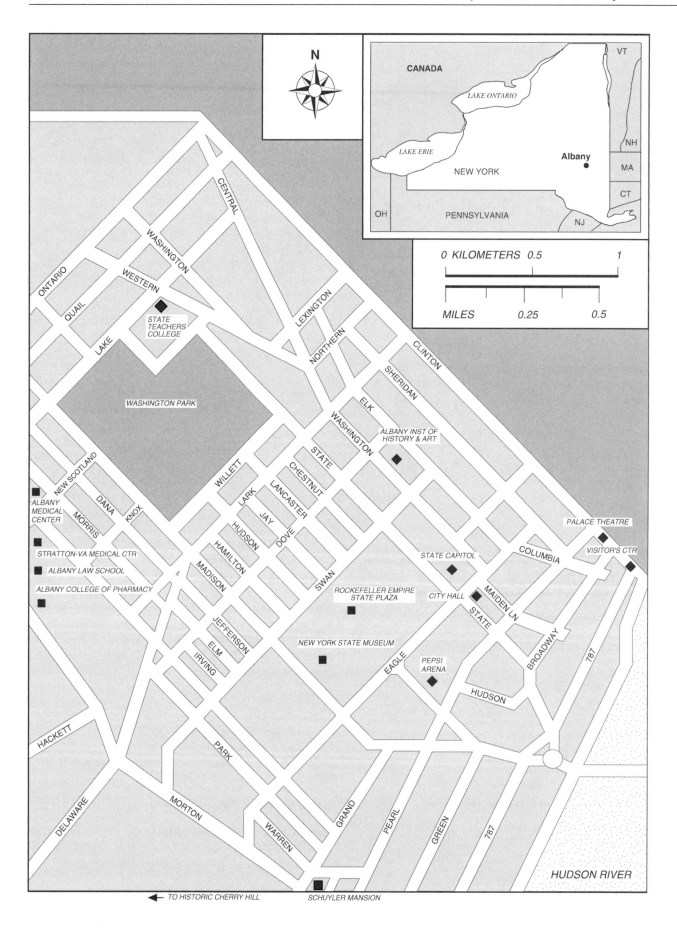

N

CANADA

LAKE ONTARIO

VT

NH

LAKE ERIE

Albany

MA

NEW YORK

CT

OH

PENNSYLVANIA

NJ

0 KILOMETERS 0.5 1

MILES 0.25 0.5

CENTRAL

WASHINGTON

WESTERN

ONTARIO

QUAIL

LAKE

STATE
TEACHERS
COLLEGE

LEXINGTON

NORTHERN

CLINTON

SHERIDAN

ELK

WASHINGTON

WASHINGTON PARK

ALBANY INST OF
HISTORY & ART

NEW SCOTLAND

WILLETT

STATE

CHESTNUT

LANCASTER

ALBANY
MEDICAL
CENTER

DANA

KNOX

MORRIS

LARK

JAY

HUDSON

DOVE

PALACE THEATRE

STRATTON-VA MEDICAL CTR

HAMILTON

COLUMBIA

VISITOR'S CTR

ALBANY LAW SCHOOL

MADISON

SWAN

STATE CAPITOL

ALBANY COLLEGE OF PHARMACY

ROCKEFELLER EMPIRE
STATE PLAZA

CITY HALL

MAIDEN LN

JEFFERSON

STATE

ELM

NEW YORK STATE MUSEUM

BROADWAY

IRVING

EAGLE

PEPSI
ARENA

787

HUDSON

HACKETT

PARK

DELAWARE

MORTON

WARREN

GRAND

PEARL

GREEN

787

HUDSON RIVER

← TO HISTORIC CHERRY HILL   SCHUYLER MANSION

Introduction

Albany is the capital and a major port and trading center for New York State. State government buildings dominate the city's skyline and governmental activities dominate the economy. One of the oldest cities in the country, Albany displays its Dutch heritage in the architecture of some of its buildings and in the narrow streets that date from colonial times. Today Albany is a thriving cultural center supporting a variety of museums, theaters, and historic buildings. In 2005 *Forbes* magazine named Albany number 34 among the nation's "Best Places for Business."

Geography and Climate

Albany is located on a steep hill at the confluence of the Mohawk and Hudson rivers in the east-central region of New York State. At the riverfront, the city is only a few feet above sea level. The terrain rises gradually, reaching a height of 1,800 feet 11 miles to the west and 2,000 feet 12 miles to the east.

Winters in Albany are usually cold and sometimes severe. In the warmer months temperatures rise rapidly during the daytime then fall rapidly after sunset, making the evenings relatively cool. The area enjoys one of the highest percentages of sunshine in the state.

Area: 21.84 square miles (2000)

Elevation: 29 feet above sea level

Average Temperatures: January, 22.2° F; July, 71.1° F; average annual temperature, 47.5° F

Average Annual Precipitation: 38.6 inches of rain; 64.1 inches of snow

History

In 1609, when explorer Henry Hudson reached the end of the river that bears his name, he found a thriving community of Mohican Indians on the site of present-day Albany. In 1624 Dutch settlers established a permanent trading community there to replace one that had burned ten years earlier, and they named it Fort Orange. The British captured the fort in 1664, renaming it Albany in honor of England's James, Duke of York and Albany. The resident Dutch were permitted to retain their own language and customs. Albany became a fur-trading center and a residence for owners of the ships that carried produce down the Hudson River to the Atlantic and on to the West Indies.

In 1754 Benjamin Franklin presented his Plan of Union, a forerunner of the U.S. Constitution, at Albany, earning the city its nickname of "Cradle of the Union." Following the American Revolution, the city served as a supply center for settlers heading west. Albany was declared the capital of New York State in 1797. Banking, iron manufacturing, and lumber trading enriched the city's economy during the nineteenth century and, with the completion of the Erie Canal in 1825 and the creation of the New York Central Railroad in 1853, Albany became an important commercial center as well.

By the early 1900s supplies of iron ore and lumber from the Adirondacks were dwindling, and Albany's industries declined. At the same time, the state of New York became increasingly important in national politics, with Albany nurturing such prominent figures as Theodore and Franklin Delano Roosevelt, Thomas E. Dewey, and Nelson A. Rockefeller. By the 1980s government had become the city's chief activity.

Albany, despite its reliance on government as its primary economic sector, was affected by the economic downturn of the late 1980s and early 1990s that resulted from a decline in the high technology sector. Gradually resurfacing through increased efforts at economic development and downtown restoration and beautification, the city recovered by the turn of the century. Republican George E. Pataki was first elected governor of New York in 1995 and was reelected to a third term in November 2002. Pataki, referred to as a catalyst for increasing New York's presence in the high technology industry, committed state funds totaling more than a billion dollars for research centers in support of this industry. Albany became the site for one of just six of these centers throughout the state, and the resulting Albany NanoTech, a university-based research facility that opened in 2003, promptly drew such high technology leaders as chip equipment manufacturer International Sematech. The first of many such partnerships, including those with Tokyo Electron Ltd. and International Business Machines Corp. (IBM), the Sematech deal was such a boon for the region that Governor Pataki stated that it " . . . could be the most important thing to happen to the upstate economy since the Erie Canal."

Historical Information: New York State Museum, Cultural Education Center, Room 3023, Albany, NY 12230; telephone (518)474-5877

Population Profile

Metropolitan Area Residents

1990: 861,623
2000: 875,583
Percent change, 1990-2000: 1.6%
U.S. rank in 1980: 46th
U.S. rank in 1990: 49th
U.S. rank in 2000: 56th

City Residents

1980: 101,727
1990: 101,082
2000: 95,658
2003 estimate: 93,919
Percent change, 1990-2000: −5.3%
U.S. rank in 1980: 164th
U.S. rank in 1990: 192nd (State rank: 6th)
U.S. rank in 2000: 277th (State rank: 21st)

Density: 4,474.6 people per square mile (2000)

Racial and ethnic characteristics (2000)
  White: 60,383
  Black or African American: 26,915
  American Indian and Alaska Native: 301
  Asian: 3,116
  Native Hawaiian and Pacific Islander: 34
  Hispanic or Latino (may be of any race): 5,349
  Other: 2,060

Percent of residents born in state: 74.8%

Age characteristics (2000)
  Population under 5 years old: 5,384
  Population 5 to 9 years old: 5,584
  Population 10 to 14 years old: 5,142
  Population 15 to 19 years old: 8,772
  Population 20 to 24 years old: 12,678
  Population 25 to 34 years old: 15,166
  Population 35 to 44 years old: 12,805
  Population 45 to 54 years old: 10,768
  Population 55 to 59 years old: 3,664
  Population 60 to 64 years old: 2,914
  Population 65 to 74 years old: 5,674
  Population 75 to 84 years old: 4,781
  Population 85 years and older: 2,326
  Median age: 31.4 years

Births (2002, Albany County)
  Total number: 3,226

Deaths (2002, Albany County)
  Total number: 2,817 (of which, 34 were infants under the age of 1 year)

Money income (1999)
  Per capita income: $18,281
  Median household income: $30,041
  Total households: 40,772

Number of households with income of . . .
  less than $10,000: 7,009
  $10,000 to $14,999: 3,712
  $15,000 to $24,999: 6,513
  $25,000 to $34,999: 5,707
  $35,000 to $49,999: 6,064
  $50,000 to $74,999: 6,005
  $75,000 to $99,999: 2,977
  $100,000 to $149,999: 1,874
  $150,000 to $199,999: 573
  $200,000 or more: 338

Percent of families below poverty level: 16.0% (54.9% of which were female householder families with related children under 5 years)

2002 FBI Crime Index Total: Not reported

Municipal Government

Albany is governed by a mayor and a sixteen-member council elected for four-year terms. The city is divided into 15 wards, with each ward represented on the council by an alderman. Albany is the focal point of Albany County, whose board of supervisors is elected by the wards and towns they represent.

Head Official: Mayor Gerald D. Jennings (D) (since 1994; current term expires 2006)

Total Number of City Employees: 1,493 (2003)

City Information: City of Albany, Office of the Mayor, City Hall, Albany, NY 12207; telephone (518)434-5100; fax (518)434-5013

Economy

Major Industries and Commercial Activity

State and local governments employ nearly a quarter of the Albany area workforce, a phenomenon that has brought long-term stability to the economy. A network of service industries, especially restaurants and food stores, law firms, and related businesses, has grown up in Albany to serve the needs of government. Area colleges and universities and an extensive healthcare network also play a dominant role in the city's economy. The presence of scientific research facilities has stimulated the growth of the high technology industries that are replacing traditional manufacturing industries.

Technology has, in fact, been targeted as a prime growth industry for Albany. The *Austin (TX) American-Statesman* declared in 2003 that the city is " . . . laying plans to storm past Austin as a high-tech hot spot.'' Albany NanoTech, a university-based research facility for nanotechnology that opened in 2003, received a large portion of the $1.4 billion that the state committed toward the establishment of research centers throughout New York. In a deal that was named one of the top economic development projects of 2002 by *Site Selection* magazine, Albany successfully attracted a new branch research center of Austin-based International Sematech. Later, Tokyo Electron Ltd., one of the world's leading makers of computer chip manufacturing equipment, decided to send researchers to Albany instead of its North American headquarters in Austin, Texas. New York City-based International Business Machines Corp. (IBM) followed suit, moving researchers to Albany.

Albany is home to a number of manufacturers, producing such items as felt products, sporting goods, and beer, but major manufacturing is represented by national companies with divisions located throughout Albany County, including General Electric Company's plastics operation in Selkirk and its silicon plant in Waterford. The sectors of finance, insurance, and real estate enjoy a strong presence in Albany, which is one of the nation's largest banking cities. As the focal point of a six-county greater metropolitan area that encompasses prime East Coast recreational areas, Albany is also affected economically by the tourists who flock to the region each year.

Items and goods produced: machine tools, paper products, felt, athletic equipment, aspirin, brake linings, cement, steel products, electrical equipment, dental products, chemicals

Incentive Programs—New and Existing Businesses

Local programs—The City of Albany's Department of Economic Development and Industrial Development Agency help coordinate incentive packages. Some of these incentives are low interest rate loans, property tax abatements, job training assistance, and tax credits. The Albany County Partnership, a venture between the Albany-Colonie Regional Chamber of Commerce and the Albany County Department of Economic Development, Conservation, and Planning, offers finance programs, loan funds, and assistance funds to qualified businesses seeking to expand, relocate, or retain operations in the region.

State programs—The Empire State Development Corporation, the state agency responsible for promoting economic development in New York State, has programs available to assist businesses that are expanding and creating jobs. Its programs range from direct financing through the Job Development Authority to low-interest subsidies and loan guarantees. Depending on the financing source, funds can be used for building construction, equipment acquisition, building purchases, and working capital. New York state's progressive tax structure combines tax credits, deductions, exemptions, and write-offs to help reduce the tax burden on businesses. State financial incentives available include those offered through the Regional Development Corporation, New York Job Development Authority, Urban Development Corporation, and locations in Economic Development Zones. As the state capital, Albany offers accessibility to information and assistance from legislators and agencies eager to assist companies locating in New York state.

Job training programs—Through the On-The-Job Training program and the Capital Region ReEmployment Center, the Albany-Colonie Regional Chamber of Commerce offers incentives to employers of qualified individuals, including reimbursement for up to 50 percent of a trainee's salary for an approved training period. In addition, prescreening of candidates can be handled by center staff so that a business is presented with only qualified applicants.

Development Projects

Between 1995 and 2005, more than $2 billion was realized in economic development projects in Albany. During 2004 alone, 30 companies committed to investing $49 million and creating 320 new jobs in the city's Empire Zone. The state government also fueled local development, particularly with Albany NanoTech, a university-based research facility for nanotechnology that opened in 2003 and has since attracted such corporate partners as International Sematech, Tokyo Electron Ltd., and International Business Machines Corp. (IBM). Other recently completed projects include the newly constructed Hudson River Way, featuring a pedestrian bridge linking downtown with the new Corning Park. The Palace Theatre received $5.5 million in renovations and improvements by 2004.

One of the largest projects underway is construction of the Albany Convention Center/Hotel complex. This $185 million project, comprised of a 300,000-square-foot convention center attached to a 400-room hotel, is scheduled for completion in the fall of 2006; it is expected to generate $3.2 billion in the local economy and create 1,740 jobs. In December 2004 an advisory committee tapped three existing library facilities, including the main library, be renovated; four new library branches be constructed in local neighborhoods; and a wireless, mobile library branch—a ''Cybermobile''—be implemented.

Economic Development Information: City of Albany Department of Economic Development, City Hall, 4th Fl., Albany, NY 12207; telephone (518)434-5192

Commercial Shipping

Albany was named one of the nation's "100 Best Metro Areas for Logistics" by *Expansion Management* magazine in September 2004. Inland 124 miles from New York City, the Port of Albany's 32-foot channel on the Hudson River admits international oceangoing vessels and serves as an important stop on the barge canal system of the state, ultimately connecting the city with the Atlantic Ocean and the Great Lakes. CIBRO Petroleum maintains a specialized installation, and the port has facilities for molasses storage and a grain elevator. The port is served by three railroads and more than 100 motor freight carriers. The cargo terminal of Albany International Airport serves FedEx, UPS, and DHL carriers. Albany is within overnight trucking distance of 35 of the country's 100 largest retail markets. The city is also the site of Foreign Trade Zone #121, an area where foreign goods bound for international destinations can be temporarily stored without incurring an import duty. The area's global presence is also facilitated by the Capital Region World Trade Center, located in nearby Schenectady, New York.

Labor Force and Employment Outlook

Albany's workforce is highly educated—the public school system is strong, the state university well-regarded. According to the 2000 U.S. Census, 17.2 percent of all residents have obtained a bachelor's degree, and 15.4 percent have achieved a graduate or professional degree. In recent years, the city has rapidly worked to redefine itself as a hub for research and high technology, further fueling the educational profile of its citizens.

The following is a summary of data regarding the Albany metropolitan area labor force, 2004 annual averages.

Size of nonagricultural labor force: 444,100

Number of workers employed in . . .
  construction and mining: 17,900
  manufacturing: 22,700
  trade, transportation and utilities: 79,200
  information: 10,900
  financial activities: 26,100
  professional and business services: 50,600
  educational and health services: 78,200
  leisure and hospitality: 31,600
  other services: 18,400
  government: 108,200

Average hourly earnings of production workers in manufacturing: $17.29 (2004; statewide figure)

Unemployment rate: 3.6% (April 2005)

Largest employers (2003, Albany County)	*Number of employees*
State of New York	30,762
General Electric Co.	9,000
United States Government	8,092
Albany Medical Center	5,269
St. Peter's Health Care Service	3,388
Northeast Health	3,059
Verizon Communications Inc.	3,000
County of Albany	2,995
Stewart's Ice Cream Co.	2,840
Knolls Atomic Power Laboratory Inc.	2,650

Cost of Living

Because a large portion of property in Albany is tax-exempt, the tax burden on individuals can be onerous. While property taxes have been lowered in recent years, school taxes tend to rise each year. The cost of housing is competitive with other metropolitan areas in the Northeast and is substantially below major areas such as Boston and New York.

The following is a summary of data regarding several key cost of living factors for the Albany area.

2004 ACCRA Average Home Price: Not reported

2004 ACCRA Cost of Living Index: Not reported

State income tax rate: 4%-7.7%

State sales tax rate: 4%

Local income tax rate: None

Local sales tax rate: 4%

Property tax rate: $22.01 per $1,000 of assessed valuation times the tax rate (2004)

Economic Information: Albany-Colonie Region Chamber of Commerce, 107 Washington Ave., Albany, NY 12210; telephone (518)431-1400; fax (518)434-1339

Education and Research

Elementary and Secondary Schools

The administration of policy for the Albany public schools is vested in an elected Board of Education, which is independent of city government and appoints officers and employees of the school district. The seven, non-paid board members each serve a four-year term.

The district's newest school, a third middle school, opened in September 2005. Earlier that year, the 99-year-old School #16 shut its operations down with plans to reopen as an elementary facility in 2007.

The following is a summary of data regarding the Albany public schools as of the 2004-2005 school year.

Total enrollment: 9,101

Number of facilities
  elementary schools: 12
  middle schools: 3
  senior high schools: 3
  other: 1 adult learning center

Student/teacher ratio: 12.5:1

Teacher salaries
  average: $55,161

Funding per pupil: $12,690

Public Schools Information: Albany City School District, Academy Park, Albany, NY 12207; telephone (518)462-7100

Colleges and Universities

Albany is home to seven colleges and universities. The State University of New York (SUNY) at Albany, one of four university centers of the SUNY system, is the largest college in the region, enrolling 11,500 undergraduate and 5,000 graduate students pursuing degrees ranging from bachelor's to doctorate. Advanced study is also available at Albany Medical College, Albany Law School, and Albany College of Pharmacy. The College of St. Rose offers bachelor's and master's degrees in liberal arts, business, education, science, and fine arts. The Junior College of Albany and Maria College both offer two-year associates degrees in a variety of disciplines.

A number of colleges and universities are located in the region outside of Albany. Schenectady is home to Union College, which offers degrees in law and pharmacy; this college houses the Dudley Observatory and is also the birthplace of the Phi Beta Kappa society. Two institutes of higher learning are located in Troy: Hudson Valley Community College and Rensselaer Polytechnic Institute, which specializes in engineering, architecture, and technology, and supports a high-technology business center. Sienna College, a Catholic and Franciscan college, is an undergraduate, liberal arts institution located in Loudonville.

Libraries and Research Centers

Founded in 1833, the Albany Public Library and its four branches hold more than 300,000 volumes, with special city and county history and oral history collections, along with a reading machine for the visually impaired. Recommendations were made in December 2004 for the construction of four new branches, renovation of three others, and the launch of cybermobile services. Thirteen New York state departments maintain libraries in Albany, as do area colleges, universities, and health centers. Of cultural and educational interest is the New York State Library, founded in 1818 and holding more than 20 million volumes; special collections focus on Dutch Colonial and Shaker history as well as the political and social history of the state. The New York State Archives contain records dating back 350 years.

Albany has dozens of research facilities. One of the newest and grandest is Albany NanoTech, a research facility for nanotechnology that has partnerships with such industry heavy-hitters as International Business Machines Corp. (IBM), International Sematech, Tokyo Electron Ltd., Advanced Micro Devices Inc., Motorola Inc., and Lockheed Martin Federal Systems. The nationally renowned Rensselaer Polytechnic Institute in Troy conducts extensive research in the fields of engineering and technology and maintains a technology park. Scientists at General Electric Research and Development in Niskayuna developed high field magnetic resonance imaging, a noninvasive diagnostic test. General Electric Company, Sterling-Winthrop Research Institute, which specializes in drug research, and other private companies in the area also conduct ongoing research. The three research universities and Albany Medical College conduct research in such areas as cancer, blood diseases, and pediatric medicine. The State University of New York (SUNY) at Albany has research institutes in law, government, management, economics, education, media, and technology.

Public Library Information: Albany Public Library, 161 Washington Ave., Albany, NY 12210; telephone (518)449-3300; fax (518)427-4321

Health Care

Albany's health care needs are served by two medical centers and 12 hospitals. The largest facility, the 651-bed Albany Medical Center, specializes in open-heart and coronary bypass surgery as well as vascular microsurgeries; it maintains trauma and burn units in addition to a children's hospital, and is affiliated with Albany Medical College. Capital District Psychiatric Center is one of the area's facilities that serve special needs. Other local hospitals include Children's Hospital, Memorial Hospital, St. Peter's Hospital, and the Veterans Affairs Medical Center. The presence of research centers in the region has made Albany a leader in the development of advanced diagnostic tools such as high field magnetic resonance imaging.

Health Care Information: Albany County Department of Health, 175 Green St., Albany, NY 12202; telephone (518)447-4580

Recreation

Sightseeing

Walking tours of renovated downtown historic sites are a popular way to see Albany. The Albany Heritage Area Visitors Center provides information about these and other programs; it also houses a hands-on exhibit detailing the city's past and present. Among the interesting sights in downtown Albany is the New York State Capitol, completed in 1898 under the supervision of five architects over a thirty-year period. Its combination of classic architectural styles contrasts with the modern complex of buildings that comprises the Nelson A. Rockefeller Empire State Plaza, encompassing cultural and recreational features as well as the state's tallest tower outside of New York City. The Empire State Plaza contains several memorials, including the Korean War Veterans Memorial, Martin Luther King Memorial, NYS Fallen Firefighters Memorial, NYS Vietnam Memorial, NYS Women Veterans Memorial, State of New York Police Officers Memorial, and World War II Memorial. Albany's other memorials located outside of the Empire State Plaza are the Henry Johnson Memorial, Moses Smiting the Rock/King Memorial Fountain, Soldiers & Sailors Monument, and Spanish-American War Monument.

Visitors can experience Albany's history by touring eighteenth-century mansions, including the Schuyler Mansion, where Betsy Schuyler married Alexander Hamilton in 1780, and Historic Cherry Hill, built in 1787 for the Van Rensselaer family and occupied until 1963 by their descendants. Several other mansions, historic churches, and government buildings are also open to the public. The Ten Broeck Mansion now contains the Albany County Historic Association. As the seat of the state's government, Albany is also home to the New York State Court of Appeals and the New York State Education Building. Another interesting sight is the *USS Slater,* a destroyer escort built in 1943; the *Slater* is one of only three remaining Destroyer Escort ships built during World War II.

Arts and Culture

As part of its effort to revitalize the downtown area, Albany has designated the area around the Palace Performing Arts Center as the "Theatre Arts District." The Palace, located in the heart of downtown, hosts a variety of events throughout the year, including Broadway shows and classical and rock concerts. It is one of two homes of the Albany Symphony Orchestra, which also performs at the Troy Savings Bank Music Hall. This music hall, located in Troy, was built in 1875 and is one of the nation's only three continuously operating nineteenth century concert halls. "The Egg" (named for its unique architectural shape) is located in the Empire State Plaza and houses two theaters: the Swyer Theatre seats 450 for chamber music concerts, cabaret, and lectures, and the Hart Theatre can accommodate up to 982 people interested in music theater and concerts. The Capital Repertory Theatre, a 250-seat facility, presents new and classic plays throughout the year. Other Albany performing groups include the Albany Ensemble and eba Dance Theater.

Albany and its environs are home to many historical, art, and specialized museums. The newly renovated and expanded Albany Institute of History and Art, founded in 1791, features an extensive permanent collection covering four centuries of regional history, art, and culture, and changing exhibits portraying life in the upper Hudson Valley through paintings, furniture, silver, and other artifacts. The New York State Museum presents multimedia exhibits dealing with everyday life through the ages in New York City, the Adirondacks, and the Upstate region, as well as the nation's first permanent exhibition of the 9-11 terrorist attacks. The Albany Heritage Area Visitors Center brings the past to the present with a museum gallery showcasing Albany's history, along with explorations of space at the Henry Hudson Planetarium.

Other notable museums in the city include the University Art Museum, which displays contemporary art dealing with diverse and challenging issues, and the Albany Center Galleries. The Plaza Art Collection, housed at the Empire State Plaza, is the world's largest collection of modern art in any single public site that is not a museum.

Festivals and Holidays

Albany's best-known celebration is the colorful Tulip Festival, held in May to commemorate the city's Dutch heritage; festivities include reenactments of the Old World tradition of scrubbing the streets, a flower show, a children's fair, and the crowning of the Tulip Queen. Also in May is the Annual Albany History Fair. June brings the Lobster Festival and the Father's Day Pops Concert. Fireworks light the sky at the Independence Day Celebration at the Empire State Plaza, which is also the setting for the Blues Fest, a weekend of blues performances held later in July. The Albany Riverfront Jazz Festival takes place in September at the Riverfront Amphitheater, while Larkfest—one of upstate New York's largest street festivals—extends along Lark Street with more than 100 vendors of arts, crafts, and cuisine. Harvest Fest is

Abstract art displays can be viewed at Empire State Plaza.

a November celebration of the state's food and wine bounty. More than 10,000 lights are set ablaze on State and Pearl streets in the Symphony of Lights, which runs from mid-November to early January. The Christmas season is further celebrated with the Capital Holiday Lights in the Park, a drive-through light display, and the Annual Holiday House Tour, featuring historic homes decorated for the holidays. The new year is ushered in by First Night Albany, a family celebration throughout downtown featuring music, art, and fireworks.

Albany hosts a number of parades throughout the year, including those that commemorate St. Patrick's Day, Memorial Day, Veterans Day, and Columbus Day. The Columbus Day Parade is followed by an Italian Festival, one of the city's many ethnic festivals. Others include May's annual Grecian Festival, July's annual Celtic Heritage Festival, and the African American Arts & Cultural Festival and LatinFest, both held in August.

Sports for the Spectator

The Albany Conquest play football at the Pepsi Arena from November through March. The Arena also hosts the Albany River Rats, a member of the American Hockey League and an affiliate of the New Jersey Devils. The Pepsi Arena is the home of the Eastern College Athletic Conference Hockey League Championship and a frequent host of the Metro Atlantic Athletic Conference tournament. The Albany Patroons play home games in the Continental Basketball Association at the Washington Avenue Armory. Fans of the New York Giants can witness practices and pre-season games at their football training camp, held during the summer at the State University of New York (SUNY) at Albany. Three area speedways present auto races from spring to fall, and the horses run at Saratoga Raceway from February through November. Saratoga Race Track is the scene of thorough-bred horseraces during August.

Sports for the Participant

Surrounded by more than 25,000 acres of state forests and many lakes, the Albany area offers recreational opportunities for all seasons. The Hudson River is now clean enough for recreational use and is connected to the city of Albany by the Hudson River Way, a pedestrian bridge that was completed in 2002. In recent years, the Erie Canal has been experiencing a renaissance of recreational use by boaters; guided tours of the canal are conducted out of Fultonville, about 35 miles west of Albany. Summer activities include golf, tennis, sailing, boating, hunting, fishing, and swimming. The area is a short distance from some of the Northeast's most popular ski centers and is within 35 minutes of Adirondack Park, at six million acres the largest wilderness area east of the Mississippi River and home of the Lake Placid Olympic facilities. State and private operators main-

tain campgrounds in the park, and other campgrounds are located at historic sites throughout the area and on islands in Lake George. One of the region's most popular recreational attractions is the Mohawk-Hudson Bikeway (35 miles), which travels along those rivers and connects the areas of Albany, Schenectady, and Troy.

Albany provides several outlets for the competitor, whether serious or recreational. Freihofer's Run for Women is a women-only 5K race held in June. The Pinebrush Triathlon invites participants age 10 and up to compete in a swimming, biking, and running event in July. FirstNight Albany, held on New Year's Eve, features both the 5K "Last Run" and the children's "Jingle Jog."

Shopping and Dining

Crossgates Mall in nearby Guilderland, is the Capital Region's premiere family shopping and entertainment complex with more than 250 shops, including Lord & Taylor, Macy's, and Filene's. There are also 30 cinemas, 22 eateries, and eight restaurants. Colonie Center Mall in downtown Albany boasts more than 120 stores, including Macy's, Sears, Boscov's and Christmas Tree Shops. It is just five minutes away from major hotels along Wolf Road. Adjacent to historic downtown, Lark Street is known as "Albany's Greenwich Village," with its unique boutiques and specialty shops.

Albany's restaurant selections span the globe. Visitors can sample the spices of Indonesia, the delicacies of France, the surprises of the Orient, the aromas of Italy, or the charm of the southwest. They can dine by candlelight, al fresco at an outdoor café, by a crackling fireplace, aboard a river cruise, or in an old-world setting.

Visitor Information: Albany County Convention & Visitors Bureau, 25 Quackenbush Square, Albany, NY 12207; telephone (518)434-1217; toll-free (800)258-3582; fax (518)434-0887

Convention Facilities

Albany is a popular site for conventions, as it combines urban attractions with proximity to recreational opportunities and scenic splendor. The 17,500-seat Pepsi Arena offers more than 55,000 square feet of exhibit space. A covered walkway connects the Pepsi Arena to the Empire State Plaza Convention Center, which houses 80,000 square feet of exhibit space, six meeting rooms, and a 982-seat theater. Construction began in the fall of 2004 on a new convention center and hotel complex. The Albany Convention Center will have 85,000 square feet of exhibition space and the attached hotel will house 400 rooms. At a cost of $185 million, the complex is scheduled for completion in late 2006.

Convention Information: Albany County Convention & Visitors Bureau, 25 Quackenbush Square, Albany, NY 12207; telephone (518)434-1217; toll-free (800)258-3582; fax (518)434-0887

Transportation

Approaching the City

Albany was one of the first cities in the nation to have its own airport. In 1928 Charles Lindbergh landed his craft at Albany International Airport in Colonie, located about seven miles west of downtown Albany. This airport accommodated more than 1.4 million enplanements in 2003.

A modern superhighway network that grew up along the shores of Albany's waterways connects the city with New York City to the south via the New York State Thruway (Interstates 90 and 87), and to the Adirondack region and Lake Champlain via the Adirondack Northway (Interstate 87). Interstate 787, the Riverfront Arterial, assists intercity travel and access to New England through connections with Interstate 90 east and U.S. Route 7. Other major highways include U.S. Routes 5, 7A, 9, 9R, and a host of county highways.

Amtrak provides intercity rail passenger service to the Northeast, Midwest, and Canadian cities. The station is located in Rensselaer, about ten minutes from downtown Albany. An increasing number of motor coaches carry tourists to the region from New England and Canada.

Traveling in the City

Two downtown bus terminals operated by Capital District Transportation Authority (CDTA) handle passenger service in the city and its environs. In addition, CDTA trolleys run a continuous loop through the downtown area, the Theatre Arts District, the waterfront, and Lark Street during the summer.

Communications

Newspapers and Magazines

Albany readers are served by *The Times Union,* which is published every morning. Albany's *Business Review* is a

weekly business publication serving the Capital Region of New York. Several special interest newspapers and magazines are also published in the city, including *The Evangelist* and *Metroland.* Locally published periodicals cover such topics as library science, law, business, employment, film literature, the food industry, organizational management, criminal justice, institutional research, dentistry, and pharmacy.

Television and Radio

Five television stations, including four network affiliates and one independent, broadcast from Albany area. The Albany area is served by more than 40 AM and FM radio stations—7 of which originate within the city—that feature a wide range of programming, including broadcasts from several area colleges.

Media Information: *Times Union,* Box 15000, News Plaza, Albany, NY 12211; telephone (518)454-5694

Albany Online

Albany City School District. Available www.albanyschools.org

Albany-Colonie Regional Chamber of Commerce. Available www.ac-chamber.org

Albany County Convention & Visitors Bureau. Available www.albany.org

Albany County Department of Economic Development. Available www.albanycounty.com

Albany County Department of Health. Available www.albanycounty.com/departments/health

Capital District Regional Planning Commission. Available www.cdrpc.org

City of Albany home page. Available www.albanyny.org

The Times Union. Available www.timesunion.com

Selected Bibliography

Kennedy, William, *O Albany! Improbable City of Political Wizards, Fearless Ethnics ...* (New York: Viking Press; Albany, N.Y.: Washington Park Press, 1983)

Killips, Tom, *New York's Capital District 1978-2003* (Mount Pleasant, SC: Arcadia, 2004)

McEneny, John J., Robert W. Arnold, and Dennis Holzman, *Albany: Capital City on the Hudson* (Sun Valley, CA: American Historical Press, 1998)

Buffalo

The City in Brief

Founded: 1803 (incorporated 1832)

Head Official: Mayor Anthony M. Masiello (D) (since 1994)

City Population
  1980: 357,870
  1990: 328,175
  2000: 292,648
  2004 estimate: 282,864
  Percent change, 1990-2000: − 10.8 %
  U.S. rank in 1980: 39th
  U.S. rank in 1990: 50th (State rank: 2nd)
  U.S. rank in 2000: 69th (State rank: 2nd)

Metropolitan Area Population

  1980: 1,243,000
  1990: 1,189,340
  2000: 1,170,111
  Percent change, 1990-2000: − 1.6 %
  U.S. rank in 1990: 33rd
  U.S. rank in 2000: 42nd

Area: 52.51 square miles total (2000)
Elevation: 599 feet above sea level
Average Annual Temperature: 47.7° F
Average Annual Precipitation: 38.5 inches of rain; 93.3 inches of snow

Major Economic Sectors: Healthcare services, transportation, manufacturing, wholesale and retail trade, tourism, research
Unemployment Rate: 5.1% (April 2005)
Per Capita Income: $14,991 (1999)

2002 FBI Crime Index Total: 19,017

Major Colleges and Universities: University of Buffalo; Buffalo State College; Erie Community College

Daily Newspaper: *The Buffalo News*

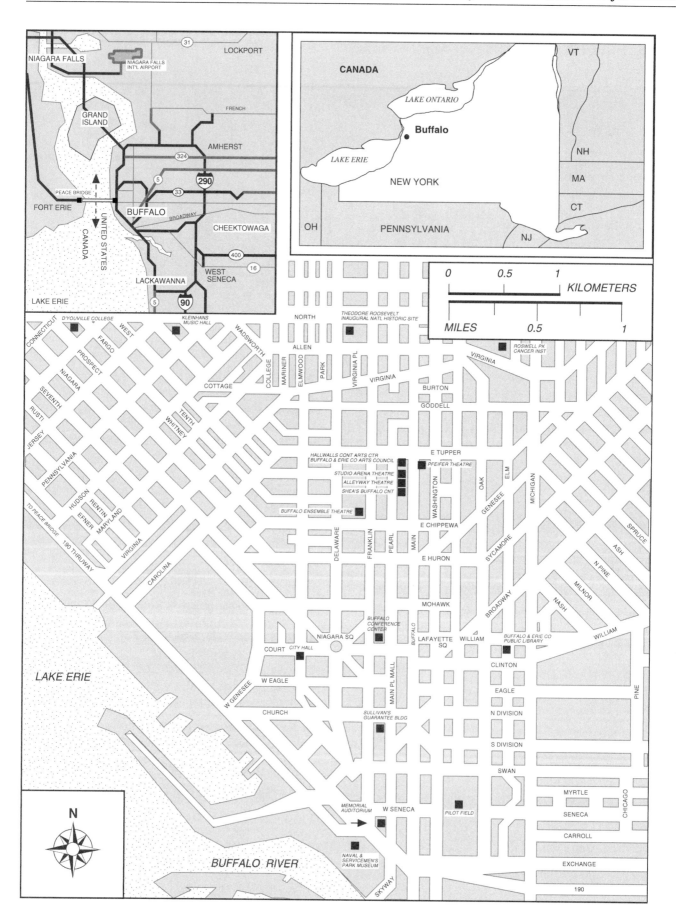

Introduction

Buffalo is the second largest city in New York State and its largest inland port. Nicknamed by Millard Fillmore as "The Queen City of the Lakes," the city derives vitality from its waterways. Buffalo is located at the eastern end of Lake Erie and at the head of the Niagara River; the lake has made the city one of the nation's leading inland ports, while the hydroelectric power supplied by Niagara Falls has attracted a diverse array of industries. Buffalo characterizes itself as the City of Good Neighbors and is a cosmopolitan municipality with strong ethnic loyalties and a record of good inter-group relationships. Its stalwart citizens, who twice rebuilt the city when it was destroyed by fire, have succeeded in creating an international lakefront city rich in culture and notable for its architecture and many beautiful parks. In 2002, the National Civic League again named Buffalo an "All-America City," designating it as one of the ten best communities in the country in which to live. In recent years, Buffalo has struggled against a declining population and a poor public perception—but the city that rebuilt after two major fires continues to look forward to its future.

Geography and Climate

Buffalo is situated on level or gently rolling terrain at the eastern end of Lake Erie at the head of the Niagara River and at the terminus of the Erie Canal.

Buffalo has a reputation for severe winters, which is slightly exaggerated. The effect of below-freezing winds gusting across the warmer lake water produces lake effect snow in amounts higher than most northern states. The lake effect also produces a somewhat longer winter season, but additionally contributes to frequent thaws. The same winds over Lake Erie create cool breezes in summer, which arrives suddenly in mid-June.

Area: 52.51 square miles (2000)

Elevation: 599 feet above sea level

Average Temperatures: January, 24.2° F; July, 70.7° F; annual average, 47.7° F

Average Annual Precipitation: 38.5 inches of rain; 93.3 inches of snow

History

Erie's Earliest Beginnings

Lake Erie was the first Great Lake to form during the retreat of the Wisconsin glacier at the close of the last ice age approximately 15,000 years ago. As the ice gradually melted, it formed lakes within its boundaries and eventually left rock moraines that acted as natural dams in the creation of the Great Lakes system. The glacier scoured and smoothed the land as it left what would become the U.S. and created channels here and there where water would flow out of the lake to carve rivers such as the Niagara. It wasn't a completely barren landscape—mammoth bones have been unearthed in western New York state, dating to the last period of glaciation. About 3,000 years after the glaciers vacated the area, early man moved in to the neighborhood. Called Folsom Man due to the arrowheads used in hunting, they were a nomadic Stone Age people and were eventually replaced by a series of primitive native peoples, the forebears of the Iroquois.

The Iroquois settled in western New York and began to develop sophisticated systems of community and architecture. These early inhabitants of Buffalo were peace-loving, matriarchal hunters and farmers who would settle in an area temporarily, farm the soil until it needed a rest, then move on to a new location. Other native tribes in the region included the Hurons, the Eries, and the Neutral-Wenro; from time to time, there were conflicts among the groups. Ultimately, though, the Iroquois were as almost as well-known for building coalitions as they were for their most famous member, Hiawatha.

The first European settler in the region of present-day Buffalo was a French trader who established a short-lived settlement in 1758 in a territory inhabited by the Iroquois tribe. At the conclusion of the French and Indian War, Great Britain took control of the entire area. In 1790 the Holland Land Company purchased four tracts of land in western New York and sent surveyor Joseph Ellicott there in 1803 to draw up a plan for a city on Lake Erie and the Niagara River, which he called New Amsterdam. Residents of the area did not approve of this choice of name, preferring the name Buffalo. One legend has it that Buffalo was a mispronunciation of the French *beau fleuve* (beautiful river), possibly referring to the nearby Niagara River.

The Price of Freedom

In the late 1700s and early 1800s, settlers in the New England area and beyond were becoming uncomfortable with British rule for a number of reasons. The U.K. wasn't allowing U.S. ships to trade with France; they were pressing

American seamen to serve in their war; the settlers in the U.S. were desirous of more territory; and, possibly of most concern to residents of early Buffalo, it was feared that the British in Canada would incite Native American violence against people living in what was then the frontier. On the east coast, there were additional concerns regarding increasingly oppressive taxation, and the United States decided it had had enough—war was declared against Britain. During the War of 1812, the British burned every building in Buffalo with the exception of a jail, a blacksmith shop, and one residence, but the town was quickly rebuilt by an undaunted citizenry. In the 1820s Buffalo was chosen as the western terminus of the Erie Canal, connecting the Great Lakes to the Hudson River and ultimately to the Atlantic Ocean, thereby opening the West to trade. By 1825 Buffalo was a major port. The city's commercial importance was increased during the Civil War of the 1860s when alternate transportation routes to the West were needed. New York State and Buffalo were part of the union, contributing materials, money, and men to the war effort. Buffalo itself became a terminus on the Underground Railroad system, hiding escaped slaves and aiding their relocation to Canada before, during, and after the war between the states.

In the mid- and late-1800s, Buffalo was becoming a heavy manufacturing center as Joseph Hibbard began building steam engines there and Joseph Dart invented the steam-powered grain elevator. The city developed into one of the largest grain storage and processing centers in the world, a distinction it still holds, attracting immigrants from throughout Europe and growing from a population of 10,000 people in 1831 to 352,000 people in 1900. The harnessing of hydroelectric power from the Niagara Falls in the early 1900s brought electricity-consuming industries to the area, including the iron and steel industries, which until the 1980s made up the city's major industrial sectors, together with the transportation-equipment manufacturers who still fill that role.

Buffalo in the Twentieth Century

The Pan-American Exposition of 1901, held in Buffalo to celebrate a century of progress in the Western Hemisphere, contributed to the city's growth as well as to its notoriety. After delivering the opening speech at the exposition on September 6, 1901, U.S. President William McKinley was shot, dying eight days later. Immediately Vice President Theodore Roosevelt took the oath of office in Buffalo, assuming the presidency.

In 1927, the Peace Bridge opened, creating an international link between Buffalo and Fort Erie, Ontario. The associated celebration hosted luminaries such as British royalty (including a couple of future kings), a prime minister or two, the U.S. Vice President, and the Governor of the State of

New York. Unfortunately, things soon took a downhill turn—after World War II, when automation began to replace heavy industrial employment and companies began to move out of the area, Buffalo suffered a severe population loss. The next big economic blow was the opening of the St. Lawrence Seaway in 1957, allowing for goods to be transported by a series of locks and canals to the St. Lawrence River and completely bypassing Buffalo. Industries began to shut down and only about 50 percent of the population at its peak was left as many fled the Rust Belt for better economic and atmospheric climes.

Buffalo Today

Efforts have been underway since the 1970s to stem the population loss and to attract new industries that will in turn attract workers who will come to Buffalo and stay. Stabilizing the tax base has been a primary mission of Buffalo city and New York state government for nearly 60 years. Progress on urban renewal began slowly, with the Buffalo Economic Renaissance Corporation leading the way. In the 1990s, Buffalo initiated a massive rebuilding of the downtown business district that enhanced historical structures, increased office space, and improved amenities. Unfortunately the terrorist attacks felt nationwide in the new century took a toll.

The repercussions of the tragedies of September 11, 2001, still are felt today in Buffalo. Aside from the city's compassion for the pain of New York City dwellers, the effects of the Patriot Act and other legislation linked to homeland security have both tightened up the U.S.-Canada border for trade purposes and have discouraged Canadian students from attending college in the nearby Buffalo region, regardless of the reputation of the local research programs.

The city is striving to level the Sun Belt and suburban flight out by creating a new niche in life science research, which utilizes much of the wisdom of the city's industrial past while keeping an eye to the future. A low cost of living, innovative employment opportunities, and the beauties of Lake Erie and Niagara Fallswill continue to keep Buffalo buoyant.

Historical Information: Buffalo and Erie County Historical Society, 25 Nottingham Court, Buffalo, NY 14216; telephone (716)873-9644

Population Profile

Metropolitan Area Residents (MSA)
1980: 1,243,000
1990: 1,189,340
2000: 1,170,111

Percent change, 1990-2000: − 1.6%
U.S. rank in 1990: 33rd
U.S. rank in 2000: 42nd

City Residents
1980: 357,870
1990: 328,175
2000: 292,648
2004 estimate: 282,864
Percent change, 1990-2000: − 10.8%
U.S. rank in 1980: 39th
U.S. rank in 1990: 50th (State rank: 2nd)
U.S. rank in 2000: 69th (State rank: 2nd)

Density: 7,205.8 people per square mile (2000)

Racial and ethnic characteristics (2000)
White: 159,300
Black or African American: 108,951
American Indian and Alaskan Native: 2,250
Asian: 4,093
Native Hawaiian and Pacific Islander: 120
Hispanic or Latino (may be of any race): 22,076
Other: 10,755

Percent of residents born in state: 77.4% (2000)

Age characteristics (2000)
Population under 5 years old: 20,768
Population 5 to 9 years old: 22,773
Population 10 to 14 years old: 21,466
Population 15 to 19 years old: 20,948
Population 20 to 24 years old: 24,031
Population 25 to 34 years old: 42,150
Population 35 to 44 years old: 43,741
Population 45 to 54 years old: 35,097
Population 55 to 59 years old: 11,976
Population 60 to 64 years old: 10,371
Population 65 to 74 years old: 19,803
Population 75 to 84 years old: 14,516
Population 85 years and over: 5,008
Median age: 33.6

Births (2002, Erie County)
Total number: 10,667

Deaths (2002, Erie County)
Total number: 10,010 (of which, 87 were infants under the age of 1 year)

Money income (1999)
Per capita income: $14,991
Median household income: $24,536
Total households: 122,720

Number of households with income of . . .
less than $10,000: 26,041
$10,000 to $14,999: 13,848
$15,000 to $24,999: 22,274
$25,000 to $34,999: 17,005
$35,000 to $49,999: 17,022
$50,000 to $74,999: 15,090
$75,000 to $99,999: 6,319
$100,000 to $149,999: 3,314
$150,000 to $199,999: 729
$200,000 or more: 1,030

Percent of families below poverty level: 23% (35% of which were female householder families with children under 5 years)

2002 FBI Crime Index Total: 19,017

Municipal Government

Buffalo, the seat of Erie County, operates under the mayor-council form of government. All nine members of the common council are elected by the individual Buffalo districts that they represent, and the mayor is elected by the general citizenry to serve a four-year term in office. The council president serves a two-year term, as do the other council members. Elections occur in odd-numbered years, with office being assumed the following January. The mayor is the head of the executive branch of the government, while the council tends to participate primarily on the legislative end of the spectrum.

The city has embarked on an aggressive campaign to cut Buffalo's deficit, including cutting the number of city employees by almost 40 percent.

Head Official: Mayor Anthony M. Masiello (D) (since 1994; current term expires 2006)

Total Number of City Employees: 2,587 (2005)

City Information: Buffalo City Hall, 201 City Hall, 65 Niagara Square, Buffalo, NY 14202; telephone (716)851-4200

Economy

Major Industries and Commercial Activity

Buffalo has suffered from a decline in population that started after the second World War, and in 2003 a state oversight authority was established to nurse Buffalo back to fiscal health. Buffalo has worked hard to capitalize on its strengths—location and natural resources—to build a diversified economy based on financial services (three major banks are headquartered there), life science research and services, and high-technology and computer equipment manufacturing. Concurrently, Buffalo has held on to some of its largest traditional employers (automotive parts manufacturers and the flour industry). The emphasis, however, has been on development of the "Byte Belt" of 700 high-tech companies in the region, with the Mayor's Information Technology Council encouraging the growth and sustenance of companies in the area. Buffalo is considered one of the most wired municipalities in the U.S., with extensive fiber optic networks that are attractive to the high-tech entrepreneur.

Situated as it is on the U.S.-Canada border, Buffalo has capitalized on the opportunity for foreign trade since 1988, when a free trade agreement was forged between the two countries. Prior to the tragedies of September 11, 2001, more than 400 foreign-owned manufacturers had established an economic presence there, with Canada a major player and increasing interest being shown by Far Eastern countries such as Japan. At present, homeland security legislation has made it more difficult for companies headquartered outside the U.S. to locate branches in this country.

Western New York is one of the state's centers of high technology and research, and retail sales is a healthy and growing segment of the region's economy. Buffalo is located about 25 miles south of Niagara Falls, one of the world's premier tourist attractions drawing more than 10 million visitors annually. Toronto, Ontario, is less than two hours away from Buffalo. Tourists, shoppers, and theatergoers visiting these popular spots add significantly to Buffalo's economy.

Of increasing importance to the area's economy are the University of Buffalo's two campuses in Buffalo and Amherst, which support more than 50 research centers, some of global importance. The university's technological resources are made available to private industry through its alliance with Insyte Consulting, Inc., part of the Western New York Technology Development Centers network. Generally speaking, Buffalo has been the source of major leaps in research and development, particularly in the life sciences; success stories include creation of the first internal cardiac pacemaker, development of the prostate cancer screening procedure, and Beta-interferon therapy for multiple sclerosis. Between Toronto in Ontario, Canada, and Syracuse, New York, there are approximately 850 companies studying life science issues, researching interventions, and developing products.

Items and goods produced: pharmaceuticals, chemicals, plastics and polymers, automotive components, fabricated metals, industrial machinery, computers, medical instruments, commercial printing, food and food products, aerospace and defense technology

Incentive Programs—New and Existing Companies

The Buffalo Economic Renaissance Corporation (BERC), a nonprofit entity, was created in 1978 by the City of Buffalo in an effort to create more jobs, recruit and retain growth-industry businesses, and provide a centralized access point for business resources. The BERC staffs three small business support centers in the city of Buffalo, with individual counseling, internet services, fax machines, and other equipment vital to a start-up operation; the BERC also provides excellent information on local incentives.

The U.S.-Canada Free Trade Agreement, which took effect on January 2, 1989, eliminated tariffs and most other trade barriers, laying the groundwork for enhanced competitiveness of both countries in the world marketplace. Buffalo has been ideally situated to benefit from the agreement.

Local programs—The Erie County Industrial Development Agency (ECIDA) offers local real property tax exemptions in certain industry sectors for new construction or purchase/renovation of an existing facility, a sales tax exemption on construction materials and non-production equipment, and a mortgage recording tax exemption. Qualified industries may be eligible for the county's Payment in Lieu of Tax (PILOT) program. ECIDA also provides assistance for businesses residing within Neighborhood Revitalization/Redevelopment boundaries. The city of Buffalo administers the Commercial Area Revitalization Effort (CARE) as a method of rehabilitating retail and commercial properties in six identified distressed communities in Buffalo. The legs of the program include Operation Facelift (providing an immediate and visible upgrade to the community), the Storefront Facade Program (offering rebates of up to 50 percent of the cost of renovations), and the Security Grant Program (up to 50 percent rebated costs for security system upgrades and installations). Finally, the University at Buffalo has established the Canada/US Trade Center, designed to facilitate the flow of trade between western New York state and southern Ontario, Canada. The center provides marketing analysis and consultation and statistical data for businesses engaging in trade with Canada.

State programs—Empire State Development (ESD), the state agency responsible for promoting economic development in New York, has programs available to assist businesses that are expanding and creating jobs. Qualified businesses that locate in an Empire enterprise zone can be exempted from sales tax, benefit from tax reductions, or receive credits on real property and business taxes. Enterprise zone businesses may additionally save money on utilities, receive technical assistance, or receive tax credits on wages for newly-created jobs. Even outside of an Empire

Zone, businesses that create new jobs can capitalize on Investment Tax Credits. Companies specializing in research and development are eligible for tax credits on 9 percent of their corporate facility tax and may receive a capital credit for their investment in emerging technologies. Machinery and equipment, facilities, property, fuels, and utilities dedicated to research and development activities may also qualify for sales tax exemptions, and the state operates more than 50 high-tech business incubators to further develop the industry. New York State has additionally partnered with electric and gas utility companies to create the "Power for Jobs" program in which companies that fulfill the requirement of retaining or generating a specified number of jobs then receive a break on their utility costs that can be as much as a 25 percent savings.

Low interest loans can be accessed through the ESD by small manufacturing enterprises, small service operations that are independently owned and operated, businesses located within an Empire zone, businesses located in "highly distressed" areas, businesses owned by women or minorities, defense industry manufacturers, and small businesses seeking to increase their export activities. Other loan programs range from direct financing through the ESD to interest subsidies and loan guarantees. Depending on the financing source, funds can be used for building construction, equipment acquisition, building purchases, and working capital. New York State's progressive tax structure combines tax credits, deductions, exemptions, and write-offs to help reduce the tax burden on businesses.

Federal funding underwrites the Renewal Communities designation of the Buffalo-Lackawanna region, providing tax incentives designed to encourage creation or relocation of businesses in eligible neighborhoods. Benefits include deductions on business expenses that contribute to commercial revitalization, increased deductions on equipment and machinery, federal tax credits for existing and new employees, and a zero percent capital gains rate for qualified businesses. The United States Small Business Association offers benefits to businesses that located within historically underutilized business zones, known as HUBZones.

Job training programs—The Buffalo and Erie County Workforce Development Consortium, Inc., is the umbrella agency for a number of local programs that train and retrain employees. The Buffalo Employment & Training Center (BETC) offers access to national job listings, computer literacy classes, tutorials, counseling, and resume assistance for job seekers. Employers can benefit from BETC's job matching and recruitment programs. The Business Services Division of the Buffalo and Erie County Workforce Development Consortium can customize training programs for businesses, coordinate on-the-job trainings, help transition displaced workers, conduct remedial workshops for ba-

sic skills, and assist in tax credit assistance for participating businesses. The Consortium also operates several youth employment centers in the Buffalo area that can offer school-to-work training, aptitude testing, GED preparatory courses, resume development, and counseling. Several area academic institutions offer programs to train and retrain prospective workers and are generally responsive to requests to develop specific programs both on and off campus. Locally, the Center for the Development of Human Services provides skill-building workshops for professionals in the state social services system, and Erie Community College's downtown campus provides retraining and workforce development programs that feature partnerships with local industries. The Buffalo Economic Renaissance Corporation offers targeted training sessions for the entrepreneur.

Development Projects

Health-related industries have become the fuel in Buffalo's economic engine. The Roswell Park Cancer Institute, which works in partnership with the University at Buffalo, is in the process of building a $60 million research facility that will add 170,000 square feet of space in which scientists will study genetics and pharmacology. In the summer of 2005, Contract Pharmaceuticals Limited decided to locate in Buffalo and will be taking over the Bristol-Myers Squibb Company facility. The packager of prescription and over-the-counter medicines will continue to contract with Bristol-Myers. As part of the Queen City Hub plan proposed by the city of Buffalo, $100 million will be poured into the new headquarters of HealthNow New York, a healthcare insurance and referral company.

The Queen City Hub strategic plan being proposed by the city of Buffalo and its economic partners has laid out development projects in five different districts of the downtown area: the Erie Canal Harbor and Waterfront, the new Downtown Education and Public Safety Campus, the Theatre District, the Financial District and Government Center, and the Buffalo Niagara Medical Campus. A primary project on the Erie Canal Harbor waterfront is renovation of the historic Memorial Auditorium, locally known as the "Aud" and reputed to be an eyesore, in an effort to create a massive mixed-use space. Tenants are expected to include specialty stores, a hotel, an Erie Canal heritage museum and interpretive center, and a theme restaurant. The city is proudest of its major committed new tenant and anchor of the space: Bass Pro Shops is a wildly popular outdoor gear retailer that attracts shoppers from miles away with its combination of vast amounts of fishing, hunting, boating, and other equipment along with outdoor education, conservation information, and entertainment.

The proposed Downtown Education and Public Safety Campus is envisioned as a consolidation of the Erie Community

College and the Buffalo and Erie County Public Library, plus a newly-constructed Public Safety Campus that will address homeland security and law enforcement in Buffalo and New York State. It is anticipated that the project will cost about $80 million and will produce hundreds of new jobs in the downtown area. On the campus of Buffalo Niagara Medical, the strategic plan calls for another $250 million in research and development facilities, matching the amount expended over the past decade in design and construction of the new Center of Excellence in Bioinformatics and the Hauptman-Woodward Research Center.

Rounding out the Queen City Hub plan will be residential construction projects creating more concentrated and affordable housing, along with supportive retail. Ultimately, the plan will play off the strengths of the radial lay-out of the city as designed by Joseph Ellicot in 1804 and the park system created by Frederick Law Olmsted, linking attractions and drawing people downtown to a safe, pedestrian-friendly zone.

In 2005 the Niagara Falls International Airport is in the process of constructing a $7.4 million Flight Research facility on the grounds of the airport. The eventual tenant will be Veridian Corporation, doing business on behalf of General Dynamics. When completed, the building will be 30,000 square feet containing office and research space in addition to an aircraft modification center and a flight operation center.

Economic Development Information: Buffalo Niagara Partnership, 665 Main Street Suite #200, Buffalo, NY 14203; telephone (716)852-7100; toll-free (800)241-0474

Commercial Shipping

In one day of travel, more than 55 percent of the U.S. population can be reached from Buffalo; approximately 65 percent of Canadians and 70 percent of Canadian manufacturing firms can be accessed within the same span of time. Buffalo is uniquely situated to transport goods by all means, including air, water, rail, and road.

Buffalo's port system maintains specialized grain storage, milling, and processing facilities and is said to rank first in the world in grain handling. The deep-water Port of Buffalo is an important shipping center for manufactured goods from the East Coast. The Welland Canal links the region to the St. Lawrence Seaway. In terms of rail service, Buffalo is one of the nation's largest railroad centers with access to major U.S. and Canadian lines such as CSX, CN, CP, and Norfolk Southern linking the area to points north, south, east, and west.

The Buffalo Niagara International Airport can handle international and domestic air cargo through any of five cargo airlines, including Airborne Express, United Parcel Service, Menlo Forwarding, FedEx, and Superior Cargo Services.

Niagara Falls International Airport, located just outside of Buffalo to the north, offers a Foreign Trade Zone next to the airport, allowing for short-term storage of imported goods without full U.S. Customs scrutiny. Within 90 miles from Buffalo is the Hamilton International Airport-Canadian, which offers customs clearance that is much faster than that available in Toronto, along with an on-site U.S. Customs service. From a sixth to a quarter of U.S.-Canadian trade clears customs at Buffalo.

Labor Force and Employment Outlook

According to the 2000 U.S. Census, approximately 74.6 percent of Buffalo citizens have achieved a high school degree or its equivalent; an additional 18.3 percent have gone on to earn a bachelor's degree or higher. For the region of western New York State, which includes Buffalo, it's anticipated that manufacturing and production jobs will continue to decline through the year 2012, with a loss of almost 5,000 jobs projected. Transportation and farming employment will remain essentially the same in number, while construction, wholesale and retail trade, food services, education, and healthcare technology, practitioner and support occupations will see growth.

The following is a summary of data regarding the Buffalo-Niagara Falls metropolitan area labor force, 2004 annual averages.

Size of nonagricultural labor force: 547,500

Number of workers employed in . . .
  construction and mining: 20,300
  manufacturing: 66,400
  trade, transportation, and utilities: 102,000
  information: 9,800
  financial activities: 34,900
  professional and business services: 64,100
  educational and health services: 84,000
  leisure and hospitality: 47,300
  other services: 22,900
  government: 95,300

Average hourly earnings of production workers employed in manufacturing: $17.78 (April 2005)

Unemployment rate: 5.1% (April 2005)

Largest employers	Number of employees (2004)
HSBC Bank USA	2,848
Roswell Park Cancer Institute	2,800
American Axle & Manufacturing Inc.	2,500
Buffalo General Hospital	2,400
M & T Bank	2,368
Ingram Micro	2,000
Verizon	2,000

Largest employers	Number of employees (2004)
Ford Motor Co.	1,840
National Fuel Gas Co.	1,425
ClientLogic	1,400
Univera Health Care	1,380
Niagara Mohawk Power Corp.	1,300

Cost of Living

Buffalo is one of the most affordable areas in the country, leading Forbes.com to rank the city #7 in the nation in regard to cost of living in 2005. Housing costs in the city remain comparatively low for the northeast region, and the real estate value per acre is high. Some experts believe that a real estate market boom will take place within the next 20 years.

The following is a summary of data regarding several key cost of living factors in the Buffalo area.

2004 (3rd Quarter) ACCRA Average Home Price: $230,914

2004 (3rd Quarter) ACCRA Cost of Living Index: 96.3 (U.S. Average = 100.0)

State income tax rate: Ranges from 4.0% to 7.70%

State sales tax rate: 4.0%

Local income tax rate: None

Local sales tax rate: 4.25% (Erie County)

Property tax rate: $37.41 per $1,000 of full valuation; county rate is $4.59 per $1,000 of assessment

Economic Information: Buffalo Niagara Partnership, 665 Main Street Suite #200, Buffalo, NY 14203; telephone (716)852-7100; toll-free (800)241-0474

Education and Research

Elementary and Secondary Schools

Buffalo operates one of the premier public school systems in New York State; it is noted for its successful model magnet school system developed in 1976 to attract students with special interests, which include science, bilingual studies, and Native American studies. Specialized facilities include the Buffalo Elementary School of Technology; the Dr. Martin Luther King, Jr., Multicultural Institute; the International School; the Dr. Charles R. Drew Science Magnet School; Build Academy; the Buffalo Academy for the Visual and Performing Arts; the City Honors School; the Riverside Institute of Technology; and the Emerson School of Hospi-

tality. Students of the public school system consistently produce high SAT scores, and the overall drop-out rate is significantly lower than that of the New York State public school average.

Buffalo Public Schools has begun to tap into its valuable university, college, and community college resources with partnership programs through which college students mentor K-12 students, provide tutoring in subjects such as math, support female K-12 students in getting and staying involved in the sciences, and much more.

In the 2002-2003 school year, five schools were closed as a cost-saving measure, addressing the declining population and enrollment in the district.

The following is a summary of data regarding the Buffalo public schools as of the 2003-2004 school year.

Total enrollment: 38,000

Number of facilities
  elementary/middle schools: 50
  senior high schools: 18

Student/teacher ratio: 13:1

Teacher salaries
  minimum: $32,000
  maximum: $60,000

Funding per pupil: $10,572 (2003)

In addition, about 70 private elementary and high schools are located in the city, including the Buffalo Seminary, a college preparatory school for girls and western New York's oldest private high school. The Nichols School is noted for its outstanding coeducational, non-denominational college preparatory program. The Academy of Theatre Arts prepares young actors between the ages of 8 through 18 for the rigors of stage, television and film performance, and production.

Public Schools Information: Buffalo Public Schools, 713 City Hall, Buffalo, NY 14202; telephone (716)851-3500.

Colleges and Universities

More than 20 public and private colleges and universities in Buffalo and its environs offer programs in technical and vocational training, graduate, and professional studies. The University at Buffalo is part of the State University of New York (SUNY) system of public institutions of higher education and is the largest public research university in the state. Millard Fillmore, who later became president of the U.S., was the first chancellor at the school, which has graduated its share of Pulitzer Prize-winning authors, journalists, and filmmakers. The university started as a medical college and it has retained its health-oriented academic focus—degrees in dental medicine, medicine and biomedical sciences, public health, nursing, and bioinformatics are available, as are concentrations in education and the arts. Buffalo State College, also in the SUNY network of schools, enrolls more than 11,000 students per year and is renowned for its programs linking the liberal arts with professional training. It also is one of only five schools in the country offering graduate programs in the preservation of neglected or aging works of art. Its "Buffalo State Works at Night" program places special emphasis on non-traditional students returning to school.

The city branch of the Erie Community College is located in downtown Buffalo and is also part of the SUNY system. The school offers associate's degrees in 58 programs and certifications in 7 areas of study; credits can also be transferred to 4-year institutions.

Other academic institutions in the Buffalo area include Canisius College (independent with a Jesuit heritage), Villa Maria College (Catholic two-year), D'Youville College (independent four-year institution), Trocaire College (two-year community college), and Medaille College (private four-year institution).

Libraries and Research Centers

Libraries have been important to Buffalonians since the city's early days, when the first library was established in 1836. In the middle of the twentieth century, the Erie County Library system merged with the City of Buffalo Public Library, becoming the Buffalo and Erie County Public Library, an impressive library network that ranks as the country's seventh largest. The library system contains 2,335,013 books, 79,316 audio items, 30,835 video materials, and about 15,970 serial subscriptions. Erie County residents are served by a central library in downtown Buffalo and another 52 facilities scattered throughout the county municipalities; a bookmobile program fills in the gaps. The Rare Book Room, established in the 1940s following a theft of valuable books, is open by appointment only; it contains more than 8,000 volumes on Americana, the manuscript of Mark Twain's *Huckleberry Finn,* and more than 2,000 volumes of American literary works, including first editions of Henry James, Ernest Hemingway, William Faulkner, and others. The library also specializes in resources for the business and academic communities, offering more than 65,000 books on business and related subjects.

The Buffalo and Erie County Historical Society maintains a 20,000-volume collection of works on Erie County and U.S. history, including the manuscript collection of Millard Fillmore. The Albright-Knox Art Gallery's Art Reference Library contains 31,000 books on modern art. Buffalo is one of seven U.S. cities to house a Karpeles Manuscript Library

Museum. The museum's comprehensive collection is the largest of its kind in the world. College, medical, law, and corporate libraries proliferate throughout the city.

A major research center in Buffalo is the University at Buffalo, which maintains more than 75 research facilities, including the Microarray and Genomics Core Facility, the Salivary Research Center, and the National Center for Geographic Information and Analysis. University of Buffalo's Center for Computational Research is considered one of the leading high-performance computing sites in the world. Perhaps the university's most ambitious research effort to date is the New York State Center of Excellence in Bioinformatics & Life Sciences. The $200 million center was completed in 2002; located on the Buffalo Niagara Medical Campus, the initiative was designed to centralize life sciences expertise in a concerted effort to study and intervene in human disease while also stimulating the economy by forging partnerships between the university and industry. Roswell Park Cancer Institute, one of the world's oldest cancer research facilities, operates in close cooperation with the University of Buffalo School of Medicine and is considered one of the top oncology research and treatment facilities in the country. The Roswell center's work focuses on the areas of immunology, cancer prevention, cancer genetics, cellular stress biology, and pharmacology and therapeutics.

Buffalo State University operates a fleet of research ships and an on-shore laboratory as part of its Great Lakes Center for Environmental Research and Education. Among the major defense- or industry-related research facilities in the area is the Cornell Aeronautical Laboratory. Major companies such as duPont and Paper Allied Industrial Chemical also conduct research in Buffalo.

Public Library Information: Buffalo and Erie County Public Library, One Lafayette Square, Buffalo, NY 14203; telephone (716)858-8900

Health Care

Nationally known as a center for medical care, research, and preventive medicine programs, metro Buffalo is home to nearly a dozen hospitals. Buffalo General Hospital, one of eight teaching hospitals affiliated with the University of Buffalo, is licensed for 511 beds and, in addition to its acute care function, has been established as a major multi-organ transplant center. Buffalo General's specialties include gastroenterology, urology, cardiac rehabilitation, and dialysis. Roswell Park Cancer Institute has been designated a comprehensive center by the National Cancer Institute; its patients may participate in clinical research on new therapies.

The institute recently completed work on its new Center for Genetics and Pharmacology, continuing Roswell Park's position on the cutting edge of cancer research, diagnosis, and treatment.

The Women & Children's Hospital of Buffalo offers services that include obstetrics and gynecology, the country's first intensive care nursery, and care of children with disabilities. The hospital is licensed for 160 juvenile patients and 60 adult maternity patients. Millard Fillmore Gates Circle Hospital's branches in Buffalo and Williamsville support a western New York State Hand Center and a Sleep Disorder Center; its Dent Neurology Center conducts ongoing research on beta interferon treatment for multiple sclerosis. The Erie County Medical Center (ECMC), which is licensed for 550 inpatient beds, has an outstanding trauma center and staffs a 156-bed skilled nursing home in the facility. ECMC is the primary teaching hospital for the University at Buffalo medical school. Mercy Hospital of Buffalo is renowned for its intensive care unit; medical services such as diagnostic imaging, cardiac rehabilitation, obstetrics, and general surgery are supported by an ethic of spiritual care along with physical care. Its sister hospital, Sisters of Charity, has a cancer care specialty and is also home to the Wildermuth Reproductive Treatment Center.

Military veterans can access the services of the VA Western New York Healthcare System at Buffalo, providing a 167-bed inpatient medical center. Surgery, cardiology, long-term care services, and comprehensive cancer care are all accessible. Inpatient substance abuse treatment is available at Brylin Hospital, and the Buffalo Psychiatric Center offers inpatient, residential, and outpatient treatment of adults diagnosed with serious mental illnesses.

A number of walk-in acute care and general medical clinics operate in Buffalo, along with a healthy supply of generalist and specialized private practitioners. Those seeking alternative health care have access to acupuncturists, massage therapists, and hypnotherapists.

Recreation

Sightseeing

Buffalo is a city noted for its architecture, and the works of such notable figures as Frank Lloyd Wright and Louis Sullivan are well represented. A great place to get the overview of Buffalo is from the Buffalo City Hall's Observation Tower, which affords an aerial view of the city and surrounding waterways. Popular sights in the downtown area include Sullivan's Guaranty Building, a 13-story skyscraper opened in 1896, and Darwin Martin House, a fine example of Wright's philosophy of "organic architecture" done in the Prairie style.

Architectural walking tours are offered by the Theodore Roosevelt Inaugural National Historical Site from April to October by reservation. The site, a Greek Revival structure that originally served as an Army officers' headquarters, contains late Victorian furniture and artifacts; in its library Roosevelt took the oath of office after the assassination of President William McKinley. The building is located on Delaware Street, Buffalo's famous promenade of mansions, most of which now house religious and charitable institutions.

The Buffalo Main Lighthouse, located on Black Rock Canal at the mouth of the Buffalo River, was built in 1818 and deactivated in 1914. The structure is open to the public and is located near Veterans Park Museum. The Peace Bridge to Fort Erie, Ontario, offers visitors a chance to celebrate this nation's unity with Canada.

The Buffalo and Erie County Botanical Gardens, open year-round, display a large collection of exotic plants in 12 greenhouses. Displays include a shrub garden, Gardens Under Glass, and the Arboretum. The Buffalo Zoo is the third oldest in the nation, and it started humbly as a deer park. The facility is committed to educational and conservation efforts; emphasis is placed on natural habitats for the animals housed at the zoo. The zoo is a participant in captive breeding programs with certain endangered species, such as clouded leopards and Puerto Rican crested toads. Special programming is coordinated throughout the year, and the zoo houses a dining experience called "The Beastro."

Visitors to Buffalo might consider the half-hour scenic car trip north to Niagara Falls, about which missionary Father Louis Hennepin wrote in 1678: "The Universe does not afford its Parallel." The falls are commonly thought to be one waterfall, but there are three distinct sections: American Falls, Bridal Veil Falls, and Canadian or Horseshoe Falls. Water plummets at the rate of 150,000 gallons per second off the 176-foot drop. Just 20 minutes east of Niagara Falls is the Lockport Cave and Underground Boat Ride, which operates a 70-minute guided tour of the hidden history of the Erie Canal. A return side trip might also include a visit to Fantasy Island, located between Buffalo and Niagara Falls and featuring rides, shows, and a water park.

Arts and Culture

Buffalo's rejuvenated Theatre District houses some of the finest facilities in the country, offering performances to suit a wide variety of tastes. The ornate Shea's Performing Arts Center, home of the Greater Buffalo Opera Company, presents Broadway shows, concerts, ballet, and opera from October to May. The renowned Buffalo Philharmonic Orchestra performs at the acoustically acclaimed Kleinhans

Several battleships, aircraft, and artifacts are on display at the Naval and Serviceman's Park Museum.

Music Hall, designed by Eliel Saarinen, and at various other sites throughout the year. Studio Arena Theatre presents seven plays during its September to May season. Pfeifer Theatre, home of the University at Buffalo theater and dance department, stages classical, modern, and experimental plays. Buffalo State College houses the Promise Theatre Company, where the cast performs in musicals that have a Christian underpinning. The nonprofit Shakespeare in Delaware Park program stages free productions of the bard's works in Delaware Park from June to mid-August. Theatre of Youth (TOY) presents a full season of child-oriented performances at the Pfeifer and other area theaters.

The Theatre District is also home to the Alleyway Theatre, an intimate facility that focuses on new and original plays and is located in the rear of a police precinct station. Other theaters in the city include Upstage New York, the Buffalo Ensemble Theatre, the Irish Classical Theatre Company, the Jewish Repertory Theatre of Western New York, the Kavinoky Theatre at D'Youville College, Pandora's Box Theatre (primarily female cast), Kaleidoscope Theatre Productions, and the Ujima Theatre Company which focuses on works by African American and Third World playwrights. The Paul Robeson Theatre company performs at the African American Cultural Center on Masten Avenue. Buffalo's only professional musical theatre troupe, the MusicalFare Theatre Company, stages its performances on the Daemon College Campus in nearby Amherst.

The Albright-Knox Art Gallery, housed in a 1905 Greek Revival building separated from a modern addition by a sculpture garden, maintains a notable collection of nineteenth and twentieth century American paintings. The works of watercolorist Charles E. Burchfield and other western New York State artists are displayed at the Burchfield-Penney Art Center at Buffalo State College; the gallery presents an annual juried display of crafts by artists from across the country. The Anderson Gallery at the University at Buffalo features a large collection of contemporary paintings, sculpture, and graphics. The Buffalo and Erie County Historical Society, located in the only building remaining from the Pan-American Exposition of 1901, contains an extensive display of western New York artifacts. The Buffalo Museum of Science features a children's discovery room and the Tifft Nature Preserve environmental education center. Other museums of note include the Buffalo and Erie County Naval and Servicemen's Park museum, the Cofeld Judaic Museum of Temple Beth Zion, the Mark Twain Musuem, and the Buffalo Fire Historical Museum. The Buffalo region is also home to unique institutions such as the Original American Kazoo Museum (in Eden, New York), the Daredevil Museum (in Niagara Falls), the Herschell Carrousel Factory Museum (in Tonawanda, New York), and Q-R-S Music Rolls, Inc., said to be the world's largest and oldest manufacturer of paper rolls for player pianos.

Festivals and Holidays

A variety of festivals and special events are celebrated throughout the year in the Buffalo area. St. Patrick's day in March is celebrated by a parade said to be the largest of its kind west of New York City. May is time for the Annual Buffalo Hellenic Festival, honoring the traditions, music, and cuisine of the Greeks. In June the Allentown Village is the scene of an outdoor art show displaying works by artists and craftspeople from across the country; and Martin Luther King, Jr., Park celebrates the freeing of the slaves in 1865 at its Juneteenth Festival, which features a basketball shootout, a parade, storytelling, and an Underground Railroad tour. Also in June, the city of Buffalo rocks with the annual Guitar Festival, with local, regional, and national musicians on display at different stages in the festival area.

In Buffalo, the July 4th holiday is observed with the Friendship Festival, planned with Fort Erie, Ontario. The date is significant for both Canada and the U.S.—Canada was formed on July 1st, and the U.S. achieved its independence on July 4th, and together the two North American countries have enjoyed 200 years of peaceful relations. The Taste of Buffalo in mid-July is a celebration of local eateries and food specialties that lasts two days and regularly sees 400,000 people savoring the eats, entertainment, and music. The Italian Heritage and Food Festival follows in mid-July; the four-day event is one of the largest Italian street fairs in the nation and spotlights the arts, crafts, music, and culinary delights of the area's Italian community. Various other ethnic festivals are scheduled throughout the year in the Buffalo area, including Dingus Day (Polish) and the Buffalo Karibana International Parade and Festival (Caribbean). August brings the Erie County Fair and Exposition, one of the oldest and largest county fairs in the country. Each August, a Teddy Bear Picnic is held at the Theodore Roosevelt Inaugural National Historic Site. Opening night for the Theatre District is marked by Curtain Up!, a black-tie event encompassing outdoor theater performances, dining, and dancing.

Fall in Buffalo signifies the National Buffalo Wing Festival in early September. The home of the buffalo wing celebrates with recipe contests, a 5K ''Running of the Chickens'' race, cooking demonstrations, and a ''Bobbing for Wings'' contest. The festival also sponsors the U.S. Chicken Wing Eating Championship semifinals. From late November to early January, Niagara Falls is the scene of the Festival of Lights, showcasing holiday decorations, animated displays, and other entertainment. First Night Buffalo, a family-friendly celebration of the arts, rings in the new year.

Sports for the Spectator

Buffalonians are sports enthusiasts, with six professional teams and one on the way. The Buffalo Bisons play in the Triple-A International League and are an affiliate of the

Major League Cleveland Indians. Minor league ball is a great place to preview the major league's future stars, as well as a chance to see some of the majors taking a break. The Bisons play baseball from April to October at Dunn Tire Park. Since 1969, the Buffalo Sabres have been scoring goals and fighting opponents in National Hockey League action. The team has employed such hockey greats as Gilbert Perreault, Dave Andreychuk, and goalie Dominik Hasek. The Sabres play their home games at the HSBC Arena during an October to April season. The 73,967-seat Ralph Wilson Stadium is home to the National Football League's Buffalo Bills, whose season extends from August to December. The Buffalo Bandits Lacrosse team plays in the National Lacrosse League from January through April, with home games at the HSBC Arena. The arena is also the home field for the Buffalo Destroyers arena football team, playing in the Arena Football League. In 2005, Buffalo started recruiting for its American Basketball Association expansion team, the Buffalo Rapids, with play expected to start in the 2005-2006 season.

Canisius College competes in Division I of the National Collegiate Athletic Association, with varsity teams in men's and women's basketball, cross-country, track, lacrosse, soccer, swimming, and diving; many other colleges and universities in the area support athletes in a variety of intercollegiate sports. The University at Buffalo boasts top-rated new athletic facilities for amateur competitions including track and field venues, and a natatorium. Buffalo State University competes in NCAA Division III play in 8 men's and 11 women's sports; Medaille College and D'Youville College also play in Division III of the NCAA.

Racing of various types is popular in the Buffalo area. Harness racing fans are entertained at Fairgrounds Gaming and Raceway in Hamburg, while auto racing is presented at Lancaster Motorsports Park (drag racing) and Holland Speedway (NASCAR).

Sports for the Participant

The New York State Canalway Trail System extends for 240 miles of multi-use recreation access, with the primary sections following the path of historic and present-day canals. The 100-mile Erie Canal Heritage Trail runs from Tonawanda to Newark in western New York, and is excellent for biking or hiking in warmer weather. All sections of the trail are open for cross-country skiing in the winter, while snowmobiling and horseback riding are allowed on some designated sections of the trail. A longer bike trip along the entire trail system is possible thanks to campsites along the route.

Held annually in late May, Buffalo Marathon participants can choose from a full marathon, half-marathon, marathon relay, or the children's mini-marathon. The course is advertised as flat, fast, and scenic. The Corporate Challenge road race draws thousands of corporate teams and individuals to run the 5K event and then party with their corporate colleagues.

Buffalo's park system, covering about 1,500 acres, affords ample space for sporting enthusiasts, offering opportunities to engage in tennis, horseback riding, camping, and sledding. Delaware Park is the largest and is home to the Buffalo Zoo; overall the city park system operates 3 ice rinks, 10 outdoor pools, 2 indoor pools, 10 recreation centers, and numerous ball fields of all varieties. Three city golf courses are available for play: Delaware Park, a par 65 course with 18 holes; Cazenovia Park, a par 35 course with 9 holes; and South Park, another par 35, 9-hole course. Other notable golf courses in the region include Glen Oak in East Amherst and the Legends of the Niagara course in Chippawa, Ontario.

A number of ski areas are located within a 90-mile radius of the city. Groomed trails are available at most resorts, and several offer cross-country and snowshoeing trails. Tubing and sledding are also great fun in the winter, and all that's needed is a simple sled and a slope. In warmer weather conditions, boaters, swimmers, and fishing fans enjoy the many lakes and rivers in the area. Lake cruises are available aboard the Miss Buffalo and Niagara Clipper Cruise ships.

Shopping and Dining

Buffalo provides a wide variety of downtown, neighborhood, and suburban factory outlet shopping experiences. In downtown Buffalo, the Main Place Mall boasts a pedestrian mall lined with department stores, specialty, and clothing shops, while Elmwood Avenue in the university district features funky small shops, bookstores, and cafes. Broadway Market is a traditional European-style market that has served the Buffalo community for more than 111 years; it offers ethnic delicacies such as kielbasa, fresh ground horseradish, bratwurst, and pierogi. The Walden Galleria in Cheektowaga contains more than 200 stores, including national chains and regional favorites, and deep discount shopping can be experienced at the 150 name-brand stores of the Prime Outlet center in Niagara Falls. East Aurora has preserved its historical flavor even when it comes to shopping on its Main Street, with art galleries, antique dealers, an ice cream shop, and an old-fashioned five-and-dime store. Buffalo's Allentown neighborhood is also good hunting ground for the antique seeker.

Buffalo boasts hundreds of restaurants with cuisines ranging from continental to ethnic, served in casual or high style according to the eater's preference. Chinese food eateries lead the way, with more than 20 restaurants listed for the area. Establishments featuring Italian, Mexican, and steaks and chops are also popular and remind the diner of the eclectic groups that together built Buffalo. Local specialties include Buffalo chicken wings served with celery sticks and blue-cheese dip, and ''beef on weck,'' a roast beef sandwich served on a Kummelweck roll with horseradish. Pizza in Buffalo is described as a cross between the thin, foldable New York-style pizza and the deep-dish variety favored in Chicago. Buffalo's proximity to lakes and rivers makes seafood a popular item on restaurant menus; Friday fish fries are enjoyed at locales ranging from restaurants to neighborhood pubs. About 14 coffeehouses are located in Buffalo, serving up sophisticated European brews and plain old java.

Visitor Information: Buffalo Niagara Convention and Visitors Bureau, 617 Main Street, Suite 200, Buffalo, NY 14203-1496; toll-free (888)228-3369

Convention Facilities

Buffalo's principal meeting facility is the Buffalo Convention Center, located downtown within easy reach of the Theatre District, shopping, restaurants, and lodging. The center features an Exhibit Hall with 64,410 square feet of space that can accommodate up to 366 booths, or which can be set up to seat 7,000 people. The Ballroom on the Marquee Level can seat 1,000 people. The center offers catering on-site and fully equipped to handle any audio-visual need. Approximately 1,250 rooms downtown and a total of more than 6,500 rooms in the greater Buffalo metropolitan area are available for conventioneers in need of rest. Just 15 minutes west of the city is the International Agri-Center in Hamburg, a 75,000 square foot facility that can accommodate conventions, exhibitions, trade shows, and other events. The exhibit space is approximately 50,000 square feet with a ceiling height of 35 feet, with space for about 250 booths. Loading docks, audio-visual capabilities, catering, and staging round out the offerings. About 20 miles east of Buffalo, in Clarence, is the Western New York Event Centre; billing itself as being closer to the western New York State population base than any other convention facility, the center provides 45,000 square feet of exhibition space that can accommodate more than 250 booths. The facility adds four smaller meeting rooms to the mix. More than a dozen major hotels in the metropolitan area maintain facilities for large and small groups.

Convention Information: Buffalo Niagara Convention and Visitors Bureau, 617 Main Street, Suite 200, Buffalo, NY 14203-1496; toll-free (888)228-3369

Transportation

Approaching the City

The Buffalo Niagara International Airport, 10 minutes northeast of the downtown area, runs more than 100 flights daily. The airport has service from major airlines such as Continental, Delta, United, Jet Blue, and Southwest. A total of 14 airlines operate out of its expanded $56 million terminal, serving more than 3 million passengers annually.

Northeast Buffalo is connected to points east by Interstate 90, which connects with Interstate 290 going south along Buffalo's eastern boundary. Northwest Buffalo is accessible via Interstate 190, which passes through the city's west side, cuts across town and connects with Interstate 90. The city can be approached from the south via a network of highways connecting with Interstate 90. The city is connected to Canada by the Peace Bridge and the Queen Elizabeth Highway (QEW).

Passenger rail service is provided by Amtrak; the city is also served by the Niagara Frontier Transit Authority bus and light rail system throughout Erie and Niagara counties. National bus service includes Greyhound, and regional bus travel can be arranged via New York Trailways.

Traveling in the City

The city's street design, based on the plan for Washington D.C., consists of broad streets branching off from the downtown area in a radial pattern. Some of the primary spokes that intersect in downtown include Cherry Street, Elmwood Avenue, the New York State Throughway, Fourth Street, and William Street. A pedestrian mall, from which many of the city's attractions are easily accessible, runs from the northern part of the city to the Naval Park in the south. A modern rail line, with 14 stations that are embellished with a million dollars' worth of art work, traverses this area and offers free rides to all attractions in the downtown area. Bus service throughout Erie County is provided by Niagara Frontier Transport Authority; buses also travel to and from Niagara Falls. Light rail service is free for passage above ground, and there is a charge for subway travel. A specialized ParaTransit program offers curb-to-curb service for riders who are unable to board the NFTA vehicles. Traffic jams are said to be rare in Buffalo, and one can reach suburban destinations from downtown in 20 minutes or less. More bike paths are being developed all the time, particularly in the vicinity of the colleges and universities in the downtown area.

Communications

Newspapers and Magazines

The Buffalo News is the city's major daily newspaper, published "all day" Monday through Friday and on weekends in the morning. The *Buffalo Criterion,* an African American community newspaper, along with several papers featuring business, lifestyle, community, religious, or ethnically-oriented topics, are published weekly. The State University of New York at Buffalo publishes a student-run paper, *The Reporter,* in print on a biweekly basis and online weekly. *The Alt Press* operates as an independent source for local, national, and international news, with a bit of a left bent; the paper is published in paper and online formats.

A number of magazines and special interest journals are published in Buffalo, including *Gun Week, The Buffalo Law Journal,* and *Free Inquiry,* a philosophical journal.

Television and Radio

Buffalo is home to television broadcasting stations affiliated with all the major networks as well as PBS, UPN, FOX, and the WB. A local independent broadcaster operates out of Buffalo, and the city has a cable company, satellite service providers, and pay-per-view companies. The city is home to a number of local radio stations, including four AM stations that focus on sports and talk radio and eight FM broadcasters with formats including jazz, urban and adult contemporary, National Public Radio, R & B, alternative, and classic rock. Radio stations reflecting a variety of cultures and religions also broadcast in or near the area. Buffalo receives radio transmissions from Canadian radio and television stations as well; the city's proximity to Toronto has encouraged greater access to international programming such as the BBC.

Media Information: The Buffalo News, One News Plaza, Box 100, Buffalo, NY 14240; telephone (716)849-3434; toll-free (800)777-8640

Buffalo Online

Buffalo and Erie County Historical Society. Available www .bechs.org

Buffalo and Erie County Public Library. Available www .buffalolib.org

The Buffalo News. Available www.buffalonews.com

Buffalo Niagara Convention and Visitors Bureau. Available www.buffalocvb.org

Buffalo Public Schools. Available www.buffaloschools.org

City of Buffalo Home Page. Available www.ci.buffalo.ny .us

Erie County Government. Available www.erie.gov

''Everything Buffalo.'' Available www.buffalo.com

Health care information. Available www.infobuffalo.com

Karpeles Manuscript Library Museum. Available www .karpeles.com

Selected Bibliography

Devoy, John, *A History of Buffalo and Niagara Falls, Including a Concise Account of the Aboriginal Inhabitants of This Region; the First White Explorers and Missionaries; the Pioneers and Their Successors* (Buffalo, N.Y., The Times, 1896)

Gerber, David A., *The Making of an American Pluralism: Buffalo, New York, 1825-60* (Urbana, IL, University of Illinois Press, 1989)

Goldman, Mark, *High Hopes: The Rise and Decline of Buffalo, New York* (Albany, N.Y., State University of New York Press, 1983)

Immigration to New York (Philadelphia, PA, Balch Institute Press; London, UK, Associated University Presses, 1991)

Siggelkow, Richard A., *Dissent and Disruption: A University Under Siege* (Buffalo, N.Y., Prometheus Books, 1991)

Snow, Dean R., *The Iroquois* (Oxford, UK; Cambridge, MA, Blackwell, 1994)

Williams, Lillian Serece, *Strangers in the Land of Paradise: The Creation of an African American Community, Buffalo, New York* (Bloomington, IL, Indiana University Press, 1999)

Ithaca

The City in Brief

Founded: 1789 (chartered 1888)

Head Official: Mayor Carolyn K. Peterson (D) (since 2003)

City Population
  1980: 28,732
  1990: 29,541
  2000: 29,287
  2003 estimate: 30,343
  Percent change, 1990–2000: −0.9%
  U.S. rank in 1990: Not reported
  U.S. rank in 2000: Not reported

Tompkins County Population
  1980: 87,085
  1990: 94,097
  2000: 96,501
  Percent change, 1990–2000: 2.6%

U.S. rank in 1990: Not reported
U.S. rank in 2000: 535th

Area: 5 square miles (2000)
Elevation: 814 feet above sea level
Average Annual Temperature: 46° F
Average Annual Precipitation: 35.3 inches of rain; 66 inches of snow

Major Economic Sectors: Shipping, manufacturing, technology
Unemployment Rate: 3.0% (May 2005)
Per Capita Income: $13,408 (1999)
2004 ACCRA Average House Price: Not reported
2004 ACCRA Cost of Living Index: Not reported

2002 FBI Crime Index Total: Not reported

Major Colleges and Universities: Cornell University, Ithaca College, Tompkins Cortland Community College

Daily Newspaper: *Ithaca Journal*

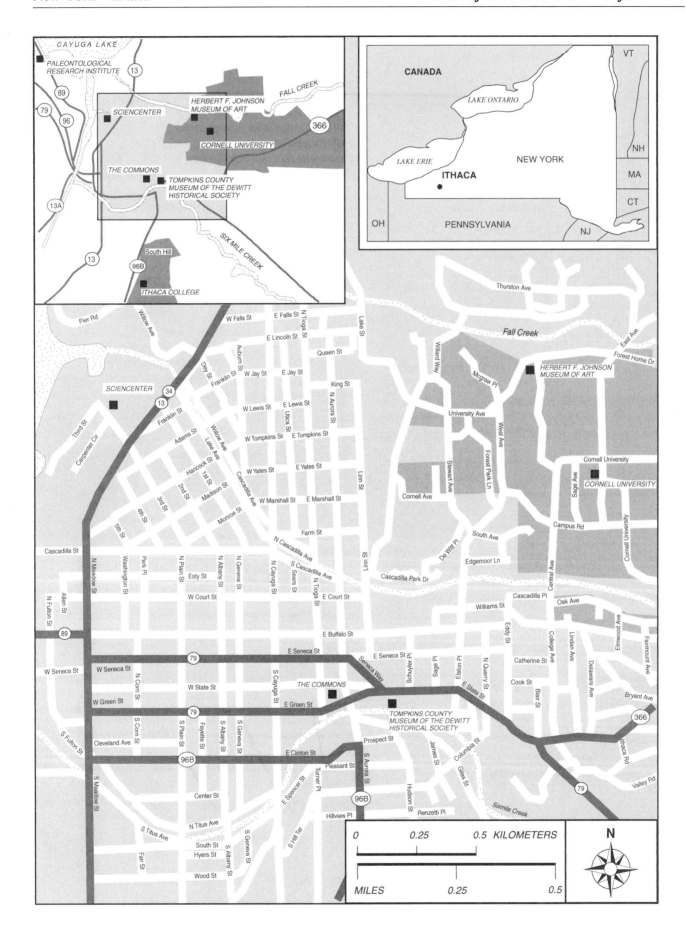

Introduction

Ithaca is a small and ethnically diverse town blessed with a beautiful glacier-carved natural setting. A progressive educational center that is home to three colleges, it enjoys a rich heritage and a thriving and sophisticated cultural life. Ithaca is a popular tourist destination in the summer and boasts New York State's premier pedestrian mall.

Geography and Climate

Ithaca is located at the southern end of Cayuga Lake, halfway between Toronto, Canada and New York City, in south-central New York's Finger Lakes region. It is 55 miles southwest of Syracuse and 28 miles northeast of Elmira. The city and surrounding area have rolling hills, forests, deep gorges, and splendid waterfalls. Reflecting these scenic treasures, a popular local bumper sticker announces, ''Ithaca is Gorges.''

Ithaca's lake location helps to temper summer's heat, but in winter, which extends from October through early May, the moisture produces an abundance of snow that totals about 66 inches annually. The month with the highest average snowfall, January, averages 16.9 inches.

Area: 5 square miles (2000)

Elevation: 814 feet above sea level

Average Temperatures: January, 21.5° F; July, 68.5° F; annual average 46° F

Average Annual Precipitation: 35.3 inches of rain; 66 inches of snow

History

Ithaca Before the Civil War

For centuries, Ithaca was a Cayuga Indian settlement. In 1779 General John Sullivan's Revolutionary War troops drove the local Indians away and burned down their orchards and cornfields. The first white settlers arrived in 1788 and set up farms in fields that had earlier been cleared by the Indians. When the title to the site was given to Revolutionary War veterans, those first pioneers were forced to move on as well. In the 1790s the first grist mill was built. Two years later, a road was cleared from Oxford in Chenango County to Ithaca.

In 1798 Simeon DeWitt, a surveyor-general of New York State, arrived in the area, and soon acquired more than 2,000 acres of land at the southern end of Caygua Lake. At that time, the land that now makes up Ithaca was part of the town of Ulysses. In 1804, DeWitt named the new town Ithaca, after the island home of Ulysses, a popular figure from Greek mythology. In 1817, Tompkins County was formed with Ithaca as its heart. In 1819, the Ithaca Paper Company Mill was built and remained in operation until 1954. In 1821 Ithaca, with a population of about 1,000 residents, was incorporated as a village.

In 1834, the Ithaca-Oswego Railroad's first horse-drawn train began service and in 1834 Ithaca's Village Hall was built. A major flood in 1857 left the city under water for several weeks. Four years later, as the Civil War began, local troops were sent off to fight for the Union cause.

Cornell University Opens, City Prospers

In 1868, Ezra Cornell founded what is now Cornell University, along with his friend Andrew D. White, who later became its first president. In 1874 Ithaca's first local public high school opened. By 1880, when the Ithaca Gun Company was founded, the city population had reached 9,105 people.

In 1888, Ithaca was incorporated and became the twenty-ninth city in the state of New York. Civic development continued with arrangements for streets, water, lighting, streetcars, traffic regulation, and social service programs.

In 1892, W. Grant Egbert founded the Ithaca Conservatory of Music, which later became Ithaca College. The year 1898 marked the incorporation of the Moore Chain Company, later to become part of the Borg-Warner Corporation, an important local employer. In 1899–1900, the first horseless carriage appeared in Ithaca and a trolley car connected downtown Ithaca to the Cornell campus. When the steamer *Frontenac* burned about that time, boat transportation came to an end in the area.

Pre-World War II Period

By 1900 Ithaca's population stood at 13,136 people. Twelve years later Ithaca's municipal airport was built at the south end of Cayuga Lake. In 1914, the Wharton brothers, who were film makers, set up a motion picture studio in the city, but the venture only lasted until the early 1920s. During that time, the films *Dear Old Girl of Mine* and *Exploits of Elaine* were filmed with Ithaca and Cornell University serving as backgrounds.

The city's population reached 20,708 people in 1930. The next year, Ithaca Conservatory of Music was reorganized and renamed Ithaca College, which in time expanded to specialize in drama and physical education as well as music. The next year, the Tompkins County Courthouse was built in Ithaca. In 1935, disaster struck the Ithaca area, which received more than eight inches of rain in less than twelve hours. As Cayuga Lake rose four and one-half feet above its normal level, a terrible flood ravaged Tompkins County, leaving eleven people dead. Ithaca's airport, golf course, and major parks and fairgrounds were submerged.

Post-War Development

In 1941, as the United States entered World War II, Ithaca's population stood at about 20,000 people. With the coming of war, Ithaca made civil defense plans. Air raid drills were held in the local schools and highway speeds were reduced to 40 miles per hour to conserve gasoline. By the time the war ended in 1945, 174 military men from Tompkins County had met their deaths.

The end of World War II ushered in a new era of development. In 1947 air passenger service started up, linking Ithaca to New York City. By 1950, the city's population stood at 29,257 people. In 1956 42 suburban school districts merged with the Ithaca City School District. In 1960, Ithaca High School opened a new nine-building campus, and from 1960 through 1965, Ithaca College constructed an entirely new campus in the city's South Hill area.

In 1961 Ithaca saw its last passenger train service as the Lehigh Valley Railroad discontinued service to the city. The next year, Mohawk Airlines, later to become part of USAir, brought jet service to the Ithaca area. In 1966, the preservationist society, Historic Ithaca, was formed and two years later a new county public library was constructed.

Ithaca began the 1970s with a population of 26,226 people. The year 1974 saw the opening of the Ithaca Commons pedestrian mall. During that decade, Pyramid Mall Ithaca was constructed and Tompkins County Hospital, later to become known as Cayuga Medical Center, opened a new building.

Events at Century's End

In 1988, Cornell opened its new Center for Theatre Arts and the Ithaca/Tompkins County Convention & Visitors Bureau became operational. By 1990 the city population stood at 29,541 people. The next decade saw the construction of the state-of-the-art Ithaca College Science Building, a new U.S. Post Office, the Sciencenter, a hands-on museum, and a new $11 million terminal at Tompkins County Airport.

USA Today ranked Ithaca number one in its list of "Emerging Cities" in March 2004. Education and tourism continue to be focal points of the Ithaca area; viniculture and technology have also emerged as local industries. It should be noted that "Ithaca" refers to two separate entities: Ithaca city is completely surrounded by, but separate from, Ithaca township. The possibility of a merger between the two entities is being discussed.

Historical Information: The DeWitt Historical Society of Tompkins County Library & Archive, 401 E. State St., Ithaca, NY 14850; telephone (607)273-8284; fax (607)273-6107

Population Profile

Tompkins County Residents
1980: 87,085
1990: 94,097
2000: 96,501
Percent change, 1990–2000: 2.6%
U.S. rank in 1990: Not reported
U.S. rank in 2000: 535th

City Residents
1980: 28,732
1990: 29,541
2000: 29,287
2003 estimate: 30,343
Percent change, 1990–2000: −0.9%
U.S. rank in 1990: Not reported
U.S. rank in 2000: Not reported

Density: 5,857.4 people per square mile (2000)

Racial and ethnic characteristics (2000)
White: 21,663
Black or African American: 1,965
American Indian and Alaska Native: 114
Asian: 3,998
Native Hawaiian and Pacific Islander: 16
Hispanic or Latino (may be of any race): 1,555
Other: 546

Percent of residents born in state: 44% (2000)

Age characteristics (2000)
Population under 5 years old: 727
Population 5 to 9 years old: 721
Population 10 to 14 years old: 729
Population 15 to 19 years old: 5,739
Population 20 to 24 years old: 10,551
Population 25 to 34 years old: 3,703
Population 35 to 44 years old: 2,179
Population 45 to 54 years old: 2,080
Population 55 to 59 years old: 593
Population 60 to 64 years old: 429
Population 65 to 74 years old: 822
Population 75 to 84 years old: 705

Population 85 years and over: 309
Median age: 22.0 years

Births (2002, Tompkins County)
Total number: 831

Deaths (2002, Tompkins County)
Total number: 565 (of which, 3 were infants under the age of 1 year)

Money income (1999)
Per capita income: $13,408
Median household income: $21,441
Total households: 10,236

Number of households with income of . . .
less than $10,000: 2,819
$10,000 to $14,999: 1,127
$15,000 to $24,999: 1,572
$25,000 to $34,999: 1,295
$35,000 to $49,999: 1,227
$50,000 to $74,999: 1,128
$75,000 to $99,999: 470
$100,000 to $149,999: 391
$150,000 or more: 207

Percent of families below poverty level: 13.5% (48.6% of which were female householders with related children under 5 years)

2002 FBI Crime Index Total: Not reported

Municipal Government

Ithaca is governed by a mayor and common council, made up of twelve members who serve two-year terms. The mayor serves a four-year term. Ithaca is the seat of south central New York State's Tompkins County.

Head Official: Carolyn K. Peterson (D) (since 2003; current term expires December 31, 2007)

Total Number of City Employees: 430 (2000)

City Information: Mayor's Office, City of Ithaca, 108 E. Green St., Ithaca, NY 14850; telephone (607)274-6501

Economy

Major Industries and Commercial Activity

Ithaca, with its ready access to the New York State Barge Canal, is an important inland shipping port. Other industries include agriculture, dairy farming, and business machine manufacturing.

High-technology firms, biotechnology, and electronics represent a rapidly growing sector of the Ithaca economic picture. The research activity at Cornell University is largely responsible for this expansion of ''clean'' industries. The University's Center for Advanced Technology-Biotechnology offers a wide range of services. In addition, Ithaca has a highly skilled work force. These factors have combined to provide many advantages on which new businesses are able to capitalize.

Traditional manufacturing remains a major industry in Ithaca. Borg Warner Automotive, Ithaca Peripherals, and Ithaca Space Systems have made major investments in technology and facilities in recent years. Local business growth is assisted by Cornell University's Center for Manufacturing Enterprise and the National Nanofabrication Facility, also at Cornell.

Agriculture represents a $90 million export industry that makes a significant contribution to the local economy. Agriculture research, plant science, and other research facilities attract start-up companies to the area. Tourism, especially prevalent in summer, adds another dimension to the local economy. The lakes, gorges, bed and breakfast inns, and wineries attract visitors from many parts of the world.

Ithaca has developed a local currency program called HOURS. Members of the local community can use HOURS bills to pay for rent, food, child care, and car and home repairs. While the currency is taxable income when it is used for trades that normally would be taxed, HOURS income does not reduce a person's eligibility for Social Security benefits. Supporters of the program say that it brings the community together and that the money supplied by the program is not tied to federal conditions. The program is so successful that as of 2004, at least 27 other communities in the United States had established currency programs modeled after that founded in Ithaca.

Items and goods produced: textiles, metal products, salt, electronic items, automobile and engine parts, scientific instruments, shotguns, chain drives, stokers, dairy, grain

Incentive Programs—New and Existing Companies

Local programs—In order to assist new and expanding businesses, the Ithaca Urban Renewal Agency offers a variety of loans, including Community Development Revolving Loans that provide below-market-rate financing to businesses throughout the city to fund activity that results in creation or retention of jobs; very low interest rate loans to encourage investment in the West State Street corridor, West End, and Downtown areas; and Community Enterprises Opportunity Micro-Enterprise Revolving Loans of up to $5,000 for persons seeking to start or expand a small business in Ithaca. Ithaca Neighborhood Housing Services (INHS) was formed in 1976 to refurbish dilapidated housing and create new rental units and homes for purchase; INHS invested $7.6 million in the community in 2003-04, refurbished 283 units, and assisted 57 families in purchasing homes.

State programs—The State of New York offers a variety of programs to provide financing for new and expanding businesses. They include assistance with site location, new facility construction, existing facility expansion, and modernizing of existing operations. The state also provides tax credits, exemptions, and abatements for business firms expanding in or relocating to New York. They include investment tax credits, research and development tax credits, sales tax exemptions, real property tax abatements, and economic development zone tax credits. The State of New York imposes property taxes on real property only, and not on personal property. Financial incentives are offered through the Regional Development Corporation, New York Job Development Authority, and Urban Development Corporation.

Job training programs—The Empire State Development Business Assistance Services section refers employers to a source of potential employees, identifies expert instructors, helps the company to develop a training program, and provides funding assistance.

Development Projects

The new $6.4 million Ithaca Public Library was completed in 2001. In 2005 Cornell University completed two new residence halls, the first in the state to earn "green" building certification under the U.S. Green Building Council's status. Under construction is the Ambulatory Care and Medical Education facility, a 330,000 square foot, multi-million dollar project of the Weill Cornell Medical College. Other projects include industrial parks at the Southwest Park and West End Development sites and the ongoing construction of the Center for Enterprise, Technology, and Commercialization. Ithaca's Ecovillage includes two neighborhoods of 30 homes each, built around a common area with emphasis on green construction and social sustainability. The third Ecovillage common house is scheduled for completion in 2005, and two other neighborhoods are planned.

Economic Development Information: City of Ithaca Planning and Development Department, 108 E. Green St., Ithaca, NY 14850; telephone (607)274-6550. Empire State Development, Southern Tier Regional Center, Room 1508, 44 Hawley St., Binghamton, NY 13901; telephone (607)721-8605

Commercial Shipping

Freight service is provided by Conrail. More than one-third of the population of the country lives within a day's drive of Ithaca.

Labor Force and Employment Outlook

Ithaca has a diverse and highly educated labor force; 26.3 percent of the members of the labor pool have bachelor's degrees, and 31.6 percent have graduate or professional degrees.

The following is a summary of data regarding the Ithaca area labor force, 2004 annual averages.

Size of nonagricultural labor force: 61,300

Number of workers employed in . . .
   construction and mining: 1,100
   manufacturing: 3,900
   trade, transportation, and utilities: 6,200
   information: 600
   financial activities: 1,600
   professional and business services: 2,700
   educational and health services: 31,200
   leisure and hospitality: 3,800
   other services: 1,300
   government: 8,600

Average hourly earnings of production workers employed in manufacturing: $17.29

Unemployment rate: 3.0% (May 2005)

Largest employers	*Number of employees*
Cornell University	8,572
Borg-Warner Automotive	1,400
Ithaca City School District	1,150
Ithaca College	985
County of Tompkins	800
Cayuga Medical Center at Ithaca	800
Wegman's Food Markets	650
Emerson Power Transmission	500

Cost of Living

The following is a summary of data regarding several key cost of living factors for the Ithaca area.

2004 ACCRA Cost of Living Index: Not reported

2004 ACCRA Average House Price: Not reported

State income tax rate: 4% to 7.7% (corporate business tax rate: 7.5%)

State sales tax rate: 4.25%

Local income tax rate: None

Local sales tax rate: 1.5%

Property tax rate: $2.026 per $100 of assessed value of real property (2005)

Economic Information: Tompkins County Chamber of Commerce, 904 East Shore Dr., Ithaca, NY 14850; telephone (607)273-7080

Education and Research

Elementary and Secondary Schools

Ithaca's public school system is large and highly diverse, with students of 80 nationalities and an enrollment that is 26 percent students of color. The system covers more than 155 square miles and serves more than 5400 students from rural, suburban, and urban communities. Approximately 88 percent of its graduates continue on to higher education. Ithaca High School students' mean combined SAT score is 200 points higher than national and statewide averages.

The following is a summary of data regarding the Ithaca public school system as of the 2003–2004 school year.

Total enrollment: 5,459

Number of facilities
  elementary schools: 8
  junior high/middle schools: 2
  senior high schools: 1
  other: 1

Student/teacher ratio: 22:1

Teacher salaries
  average: $44,037

Funding per pupil: $7,697 (2003)

Public Schools Information: Ithaca City School District, 400 Lake St., Ithaca, NY 14850; telephone (607)274-2101

Colleges and Universities

Cornell University is a world-renowned teaching and research university with a beautiful campus overlooking the city of Ithaca and Cayuga Lake. The campus includes seven undergraduate and four graduate and professional schools. Cornell has more than 13,000 undergraduates and over 5,800 graduate students on its Ithaca campus. Several national centers, including one of four supercomputing centers, make their home at Cornell. The school has developed a reputation for its strong astronomy, biotechnology, mathematics, and nuclear studies fields among others. It ranks near the top for research funding from the National Science Foundation, government, and industry.

Founded as the Ithaca Conservatory of Music in 1892, Ithaca College has five schools, including business, health sciences and human performance, humanities and sciences, music, and the Park School of Communications.

Ithaca College has over 6,000 undergraduate students and nearly 250 graduate students from 47 states and 70 different countries, who may choose from more than 100 programs. Ithaca College is ranked high among schools of its size and type.

Tompkins Cortland Community College (TC3) is part of the system of the State University of New York. Founded in 1968, it offers associate degrees and certificates in 26 program areas. The school's Business Training and Development Center offers courses in such areas as computer skills, management techniques, and licensing requirements. The school has a campus in Ithaca itself and a main campus in nearby Dryden.

Libraries and Research Centers

The Tompkins County Public Library has nearly 230,000 volumes and 265 periodical subscriptions. A new Tompkins County Public Library opened in late 2000. The 67,000-square-foot, $6.4 million structure has two main reading rooms, a large community meeting room, and a separate programming room for children. In July 2005, the Tompkins County Public Library installed a new computer catalog system which includes access in Spanish. Cornell University Library has nearly 6.5 million volumes and several departmental libraries. Other major libraries in the city include those of Ithaca College, the Finger Lakes Library System, the Cayuga Medical Center, the Paleontology Research Institution Library, and the Dewitt Historical Society of Tompkins County Library & Archive.

Cornell University is among the major research universities in the country, with approximately $300 million in annual research support. The university is home to New York State's Center for Advanced Technology in Biotechnology. The National Science Foundation has designated Cornell as the location of what may be the world's leading "Super Computer" facility, which IBM Corporation helps to co-sponsor. Cornell University also is the site of more than 75 other research centers on topics ranging from African studies, legal studies, mathematics, and social and economic research to manufacturing, agriculture, and honey bees.

Ithaca is also home to Jicamara Radio Observatory, New York Space Grant Consortium, Northeast Dairy Foods Research Center, and the USDA Agricultural Research Service Plant, Soil and Nutrition Laboratory.

Public Library Information: Tompkins County Public Library, 101 E. Green St., Ithaca, NY 14850; telephone (607)272-4557; fax (607)272-8111

Health Care

Ithaca has excellent medical facilities for a community of its size. The Cayuga Medical Center, a 204-bed acute care facility that provides inpatient and outpatient care, has the only emergency medical care facility in the area. The Medical Center serves more than 150,000 patients each year. Its 180 board certified and board eligible physicians offer specialties from neurosurgery to oncology, cardiology and rheumatology. The medical center is the only hospital in the region to have earned the Accreditation with Commendation from the Joint Commission on Accreditation of Health Care Organizations. In 2005 Cayuga Medical Center was named a Top 100 Hospital for the value it contributes to the community it serves, ranked in the top 100 of over 3,550 hospitals nationwide for the services provided compared to the cost of providing the services.

Health Care Information: Tompkins County Health Department, 401 Harris B. Dates Drive, Ithaca, NY, 14850; telephone (607)264-6674; fax (607)274-6680

Recreation

Sightseeing

Ithaca's Sciencenter offers more than 100 exhibits, including a walk-in camera, water raceway, and a moving two-story ball sculpture, as well as live demonstrations on topics such as homing pigeons and how computers work. The Sagan Planet Walk honors the late astronomer Carl Sagan with a three-quarter mile path linking downtown Ithaca and the Sciencenter. Along the walk, the sun and each planet are marked by a monument. New exhibits include Wonder Water and Crystal Creations.

The Tompkins County Museum of the DeWitt Historical Society tells the story of the City of Ithaca and Tompkins County through exhibits and the resources of a reference library. One of the nation's largest collections of fossils is showcased at the Paleontology Research Institution, which displays the diversity of life on earth. The Sapsucker Woods Sanctuary/Cornell Laboratory of Ornithology celebrates the diversity of the world of birds, with a ten-acre pond full of waterfowl, a bird-feeding garden, and a display of bird art.

A trip to Ithaca would not be complete without viewing the lovely waterfalls, cascades, and rapids that line the mile-long Fall Creek Gorge in the city center. Another must is a walking tour of Cornell University, with its wonderful ivy-covered buildings on a hill overlooking the downtown. Cornell Plantations on the university grounds includes an arboretum and botanical garden.

Arts and Culture

Ithaca prides itself on being a community of artists, writers, and performers and offers many performing and fine arts events. The Herbert F. Johnson Museum of Art at Cornell University, designed by world-renowned architect I.M. Pei, houses a large collection of art that spans 40 centuries. Its strongest areas are Asian and contemporary art. Especially notable are its funerary urns, silk paintings, and bronze Buddhas.

Ithaca has brought together some of its most fascinating features in its Discovery Trail, showcasing eight particularly noteworthy attractions for visitors. These include the Sciencenter, the Johnson Museum, and the county library, as well as Cornell's Plantations botanical gardens and arboretum and the Cornell Ornithology Center, the Museum of the Earth at the Paleontological Research Institute, the Cayuga Nature Center, and the Tompkins County History Center.

Downtown Ithaca's Firehouse Theatre presents a different play every month in its historic setting. The Kitchen Theater presents contemporary plays at its stage in the historic Clinton House. From June through August, the Hangar Theatre in Cass Park presents five Mainstage productions, eight smaller-scale productions, and a children's theater program called KIDDSTUFF.

The Cornell Center for Theatre Arts stages plays from September through May, hosts visiting performers, and presents the Cornell Dance Series. Dillingham Center on the campus of Ithaca College is the site of two college theaters that present offerings from September through May.

Music and dance are also represented by numerous groups. The Ithaca Opera Association produces two major operas annually, as well as workshops for children and adults. The Cayuga Vocal Ensemble, a professional group, performs quality music in a variety of styles. The Cayuga Chamber Orchestra ensemble of 35 musicians has a lively season with concerts, chamber concerts, and Christmas presentations for children.

Seventeenth- and eighteenth-century music is the focus of the NYS Baroque group. Outdoor concerts are held at various times throughout the year at downtown Ithaca Commons and at the art quad on the Cornell University campus. Ithaca Ballet, Upstate New York's only repertory company, presents a varied repertoire of classical and contemporary works.

Festivals and Holidays

The Apple Harvest Festival in October is a regional celebration of autumn produce, including a craft fair, music, storytelling, and dancing. Ithaca welcomes the holiday season with the coming of Santa Claus, horse-drawn wagon rides, a gingerbread house display, and performances by local groups. A wide variety of holiday craft items are on sale at the 12 Shops of Christmas, and musical and other holiday events dot the downtown area during the annual Holiday Tradition and Chili Cook Off. Holiday concerts are presented at sites throughout Ithaca, including the campuses of Cornell University and Ithaca College.

A huge book sale is the highlight of May's calendar, and the event is repeated each October at the Ithaca Public Library. The Maple Sugar Festival takes place every spring at the Cayuga Nature Center. In April, the Sciencenter challenges local residents to design packaging to protect raw eggs; the designs are then tested by being dropped 26-1/4 feet on the Commons in central Ithaca.

June's Ithaca Festival celebrates the local area through music, crafts, theater presentations, food, and fireworks. Juneteenth celebrates the freeing of the slaves at a major festival offering food, music, African drumming, and other events.

Sports for the Spectator

Ithaca is home to nationally ranked collegiate Division I-AA and Division III sports from football to softball, ice hockey to soccer, polo to lacrosse and field hockey. The Cornell Big Red hockey team is traditionally one of the country's strongest and competes regularly for the Division I national championship. Cornell teams play in the Ivy League conference. Many games take place at Cornell's Berman or Schoellkopf fields.

Sports for the Participant

The area is rich in recreational possibilities, with such activities as golf, tennis, mountain biking, hiking, hockey, skiing, rowing, canoeing, sailing, camping, and swimming, among other pursuits. The Allan H. Treman State Marine Park, the second largest inland marina in New York State, provides nearly 400 berths, and offers picnic facilities, fishing, a marina, and a pump-out station. Near downtown, Buttermilk Falls is a perfect spot for walking, with its ten waterfalls, rapids, pools, and cliffs. Robert H. Treman State Park provides an area of rustic beauty and features picnic areas, swimming, and cross-country ski trails. Taughannock Falls State park plunges 215 feet through a rock amphitheater whose walls reach nearly 400 feet. Hiking, camping, and swimming are available on the site. The city recreation department and school system provide youth in Ithaca with opportunities to ski and to play hockey, soccer, basketball, and baseball. Ithaca also features two private and one public 18 hole golf courses and one public 9 hole golf course.

Shopping and Dining

Ithaca's downtown is the site of the Commons, a pedestrian marketplace featuring specialty shops, galleries, book and music stores, and dining spots. Other downtown shopping malls are Center Ithaca and Dewitt Mall. Ithaca's largest indoor mall, with 70 stores, is Pyramid Mall Ithaca, which features three department stores and a cinema complex. Other smaller shopping areas, such as Ithaca Shopping Plaza, Triphammer Mall, Cayuga Mall, East Hill Plaza, and Collegetown dot the community landscape. Summer's Sidewalk Sale Days draws crowds on the lookout for bargains to the downtown pedestrian mall. Vendors at Ithaca's open-air Farmer's Market mall, at the foot of Cayuga Lake, sell an array of the local fruits and vegetables that grow so abundantly in the region.

A wide variety of ethnic cuisines is available in Ithaca's restaurants, ranging from Italian, Greek, Mediterranean, and Mexican to Japanese, Chinese, Thai, Vietnamese, Indian, and Middle Eastern. Popular American fare, including barbecued foods and pizza, are also available. The famous Moosewood Restaurant has gained acclaim and won many awards for its innovative vegetarian fare, and the *Moosewood Cookbook* remains popular with cooks throughout the world. The Ithaca Bakery is renowned in the area for its baked goods.

Visitor Information: Ithaca/Tompkins County Convention & Visitors Bureau, 904 East Shore Drive, Ithaca, NY 14850; telephone (607)272-1313; toll-free (800)284-8422

Convention Facilities

Meeting planners have a variety of choices for places to hold conferences in Ithaca. The Clarion University Hotel and Conference Center has 10,000 square feet of meeting space and is close to both Cornell University and Ithaca College. The Ramada Inn Executive Training & Conference Center has recently expanded to feature 13,000 square feet of dedicated meeting and training rooms. The State Theatre in the heart of downtown can seat 1,600 people.

The Statler Hotel & J. Willard Marriott Executive Education Center, located on the Cornell University campus, offers more than 20 rooms of various sizes and can handle banquets of up to 350 people and theater-style meetings for up to 889 people. The largest conference facility in Tompkins County, the Triphammer Lodge and Conference Center, can accommodate up to 400 people for banquets and 475 people for theater-style events.

Convention Information: Ithaca/Tompkins County Convention & Visitors Bureau, 904 East Shore Drive, Ithaca, NY 14850; telephone (607)272-1313; toll-free (800)284-8422

Transportation

Approaching the City

Ithaca is not located on an interstate highway, but is connected to I-90 and I-81 by a number of New York State roads. New York State (NYS) Route 79 runs east and west, and Route 96B runs from the south to the center of town. NYS Routes 13A, 34B, 38, 222, 227, 327, 366 also directly connect to I-81 and lead to the NYS Thruway.

Four miles north of Ithaca is the Tompkins County Airport, which handles nearly 40 weekday arrivals and departures. USAirways offers flights largely to many points east, connecting with its Pittsburgh hub. Northwest Airlines began service in May 2005 and offers service to its hub in Detroit. Passengers may connect to flights to many international and international destinations from either hub city. The Tompkins County Airport offers a café, conference facilities, computer jacks, and a limousine shuttle, and serviced more than 140,000 passengers in 2004. Charter flights are also available. Intercity bus transportation is provided by Greyhound, Shoreline, Trailways, Chemung County Transit, and Hampton Express. Several marinas located throughout Tompkins County provide access to Cayuga Lake and the New York State Barge Canal.

Traveling in the City

Ithaca is intersected by New York State Routes 13, 79, 89, and 96. Public transportation in Ithaca and Tompkins County is provided by Tompkins County Area Transit.

Communications

Newspapers and Magazines

Newspapers in the city include the *Ithaca Journal* (daily except Sunday), the *Cornell Daily Sun* (weekdays during the academic year), the weeklies *Ithaca Times* and *Ithaca Pennysaver,* and the weekly *Cornell Chronicle,* a university paper. Locally published magazines include *Coaching Management, New York Holstein News, Training and Condition-ing, The Cornell Hotel and Restaurant Administration Quarterly, Cornell Science & Technology Magazine, Human Ecology Forum,* and *Ithaca College Quarterly.* Journals published locally include *Administrative Science Quarterly, Agricultural Finance Review, American Journal of Botany, Cornell Focus,* a magazine on agriculture and life science, *Cornell Journal of Law and Public Policy, Cornell Law Review, Indonesia, Industrial and Labor Relations Review,* and *Philosophical Review.*

Television and Radio

Ithaca is home to a cable access provider; no television stations broadcast directly from Ithaca but many stations are available from nearby communities. Six FM and two AM stations broadcast from the city.

Media Information: *Ithaca Journal,* 123-125 W. State St., Ithaca, NY 14850; telephone (607)272- 2321; fax (607)272-4248

Ithaca Online

City of Ithaca Home Page. Available www.ci.ithaca.ny.us

Empire State Development Department. Available www.empire.state.ny.us

Ithaca City School District. Available www.icsd.k12.ny.us

Ithaca Historical Society. Available www.thehistorycenter.net

Ithaca Journal. Available www.theithacajournal.com

Ithaca/Tompkins County Convention & Visitors Bureau. Available www.visitithaca.com

Tompkins County Chamber of Commerce. Available www.tompkinschamber.org

Tompkins County Public Library. Available www.tcpl.org

Selected Bibliography

Hesch, Merrill, Richard Peiper, and Harry Letell, *Ithaca Then and Now* (Ithaca, NY: McBooks Press, 2000)

Roehl, Harvey N., *Cornell and Ithaca in Postcards* (Vestal, NY: Vestal Press Ltd., 1996)

New York

The City in Brief

Founded: 1613 (incorporated, 1898)

Head Official: Mayor Michael R. Bloomberg (R) (since 2002)

City Population
  1980: 7,071,639
  1990: 7,322,564
  2000: 8,008,278
  2004 estimate: 8,104,079
  Percent change, 1990-2000: 9.36%
  U.S. rank in 1980: 1st (State rank: 1st)
  U.S. rank in 1990: 1st (State rank: 1st)
  U.S. rank in 2000: 1st (State rank: 1st)

Metropolitan Area Population (PMSA)
  1980: 8,275,000
  1990: 8,546,846
  2000: 9,314,235
  Percent change, 1990-2000: 8.98%
  U.S. rank in 1980: 1st (CMSA)
  U.S. rank in 1990: 1st (PMSA)

U.S. rank in 2000: 1st (PMSA)

Area: 303 square miles (2000)
Elevation: 50 to 800 feet above sea level
Average Annual Temperature: 54.91° F
Average Annual Precipitation: 42.6 inches of total precipitation; 26.5 inches of snow

Major Economic Sectors: Education and health services; trade, transportation and utilities; government; professional and business services; financial services; leisure and hospitality
Unemployment Rate: 4.5% (April 2005)
Per Capita Income: $22,402 (1999)

2002 FBI Crime Index Total: 250,630

Major Colleges and Universities: City University of New York (several branches); CUNY John Jay College of Criminal Justice; Mt. Sinai School of Medicine; State University of New York's Downstate Medical Center and Maritime College; New York University; Columbia University; Juilliard School

Daily Newspapers: *The New York Times; New York Daily News; The New York Post; Newsday*

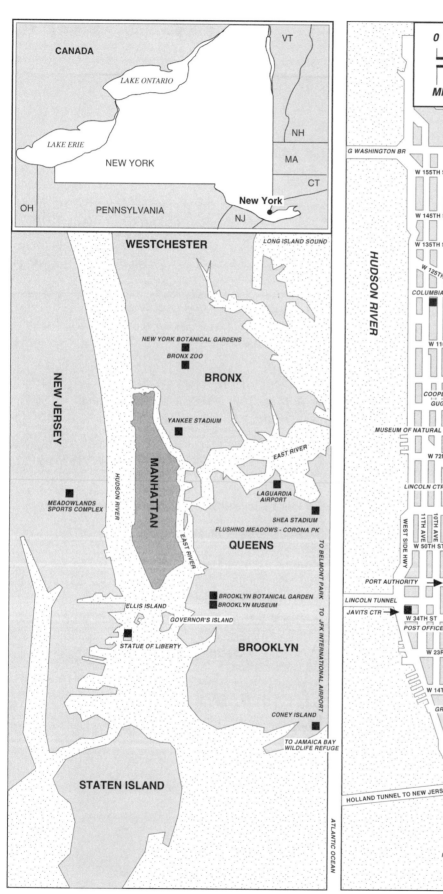

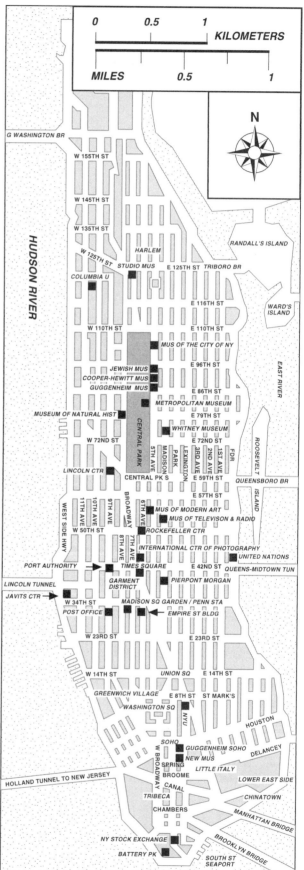

Introduction

The "Big Apple," the "City That Never Sleeps"—New York is a city of superlatives: America's biggest; its most exciting; its business and cultural capitals; the nation's trendsetter. The city seems to pull in the best and the brightest from every corner of the country. The city's ethnic flavor has been nuanced by decades of immigrants whose first glimpse of America was the Statue of Liberty guarding New York Harbor and by large expatriate communities such as the United Nations headquartered there. Just minutes from the multimillion-dollar two-bedroom co-op apartments of Park Avenue, though, lies some of the most dire urban poverty in America. But the attendant crime that affects New Yorkers and visitors alike has seen a continued dramatic reduction from 1993 to 2004—NYC has a murder rate half that of cities such as Los Angeles and Chicago, in part as the result of a concerted effort by local agencies. But for all its eight million residents, New York remains a city of neighborhoods, whether it's avant-garde Greenwich Village, bustling Harlem, the ultra-sophisticated TriBeCa, or one of the ethnic enclaves such as Little Italy or Chinatown. And a cleaner, brighter, safer New York is attracting people from around the world who are coming to enjoy the city's renaissance.

Geography and Climate

New York, located on the Atlantic Coastal Plain at the mouth of the Hudson River, is a city made up mostly of islands. Of the city's five boroughs, only the Bronx is contiguous to upstate New York. The larger metropolitan area takes in Long Island, northern New Jersey, and south-western Connecticut. Commuters now live as far away as eastern Pennsylvania. The city lies at the conjunction of the Hudson and East Rivers with New York Bay leading to the Atlantic Ocean. The weather is mostly continental with the ocean moderating summer temperatures and keeping the humidity relatively high. Due to the number of colossal buildings and the city's high level of energy use, New York City tends to have its own "micro-climate" of warmer summers and winters than surrounding areas.

Area: 303 square miles (2000)

Elevation: 50 to 800 feet above sea level

Average Temperatures: January, 32.4° F; July, 76.9° F; annual average 54.91° F

Average Annual Precipitation: 42.6 inches of total precipitation; 26.5 inches of snowfall

History

Islands Draw Native American, Dutch, and English Settlement

Imagine a New York City lacquered in ice, specifically the last ice age that covered a good part of the continent more than 15,000 years ago. As the ice began to retreat, it simultaneously scraped minerals out of the earth and deposited rocks and soil in its path. Two of the terminal moraine deposits eventually became present-day Staten Island and Long Island. Early inhabitants were drawn to the fertile ground, the abundant fauna, and the clean rivers; archeological evidence suggests that the area was first peopled around 6,000 years after the retreat of the glaciers. The abundant waterways surrounding modern-day New York eventually made the area an ideal base for Algonquian tribes, who lived on the banks of the harbor at the time of initial European discovery.

Italian explorer Giovanni da Verrazano was the first European to arrive in the region, landing at Staten Island in 1524 and mapping the region. Henry Hudson, however, became the first European to reach Manhattan in 1609 and then sailed up the river that would later bear his name. Hudson's mission had been to look for the fabled Northwest Passage to the Orient. Although English, Hudson represented a Dutch concern. The Dutch West India Company dispatched the first permanent settlers to Manhattan Island in 1624. They established Fort Amsterdam, which grew into the town of New Amsterdam as more settlers arrived. In 1626, the fledgling town's governor, Peter Minuit, bought Manhattan—meaning "Island of Hills"—from the Canarsie tribe for 24 dollars' worth of beads and trinkets; locals sometimes cite this transaction as one of the last real estate bargains in New York.

New Amsterdam's population grew to roughly 1,000 people by the 1650s, but strife between Europeans and local Native Americans—who resisted being taxed by the settlers—also escalated. The Dutch West India Company, fearing the strife could hurt its economic interests, selected the autocratic Peter Stuyvesant to end the troubles. Stuyvesant, who was fitted with a decorated wooden leg and known as "Hardheaded Pete," was able to restore peace locally, but during his seventeen-year rule the Dutch and the English fought three naval wars. The English early recognized the trading potential of the site. Finally, in 1664, English war ships arrived in New York Harbor. Stuyvesant surrendered and the town was renamed New York in honor of the Duke of York. New York prospered under English rule, as the population swelled to 7,000 people by 1700. The first newspaper, *The New York Gazette,* was published in 1725 and King's College, now called Columbia University, opened in 1754.

New York has always thrived on rough-and-tumble politics, beginning as early as the Revolutionary War era. The Stamp Act Congress, which protested unfair taxes levied by the British rulers, met there in 1765 and five years later New Yorkers first clashed with British troops. American forces took control of New York at the start of the war, but British troops recaptured the area after the Battle of Brooklyn in 1776 and held New York until the end of the war in 1783. Two years later, New York was made the temporary capital of the new nation and was the seat of Congress until 1790. New York City hosted the first presidential inauguration, as George Washington was sworn in there in 1789.

New Residents Bring Growth, Challenges

New York was once smaller than the other two colonial centers, Philadelphia and Boston. But its importance as the major East Coast port brought millions of immigrants, many of whom settled in ethnic ghettos. German, Irish, and other northern European immigrants flocked to the city throughout the 1800s, drawn by the lure of working on the city's docks and in its mills. By the last two decades of that century, Italian and many eastern Europeans also began arriving. With them came a variety of religions, including Catholicism, which heightened cultural and racial tensions between old and new residents. The immigrants, a number of whom did not speak English, came to depend on the Democratic Party-controlled Tammany Hall, a political machine that dispensed jobs and advice to immigrants in return for their votes. Led by William "Boss" Tweed, Tammany Hall eventually collapsed under the weight of its own corruption, and Tweed himself was arrested in 1871 on charges of cheating the city of as much as $200 million.

At the same time, nationwide unrest was fomenting around the issues of states' rights and slavery. New York was not a center of abolitionist sentiment during the Civil War, despite joining the Union; merchants feared trade with important Southern industries would be damaged. When army conscription was established in 1863 to fill dwindling Union ranks, riots broke out that eventually killed about 1,000 people, including many African Americans who were lynched. Order was not restored until troops arrived from Gettysburg to quell the disturbances.

Various political coalitions struggled to rule the city until Fiorello LaGuardia, nicknamed "The Little Flower," was elected mayor in 1934. LaGuardia, for whom one of the city's two major airports is now named, brought a spirit of reform to a city $30 million in debt in the middle of the Great Depression. He restored fiscal stability during his tenure, which ran until 1945, fought growing crime, and also introduced public welfare services to the city. New York's place as a world capital was bolstered in 1946 by its selection as headquarters for the United Nations. World Fairs held in

New York City, the first in 1939 featuring the introduction of television and a second in 1964, further enhanced the reputation of the metropolis.

Growth Balanced by Reform

As the science of civil engineering grew, so did the city. Brooklyn for example was fairly isolated from the rest of the area until the Brooklyn Bridge was finished in 1883. But Brooklyn and three other then-separate boroughs—the Bronx, Queens and Staten Island—did not join with Manhattan to become New York City as it is known today until 1898. Manhattan then counted the largest population, but the expanding network of bridges and tunnels leading to and from the island allowed New York City workers to spread to outlying areas.

By the 1960s, though, the city seemed nearly ungovernable. Striking transit workers shut down all subway and bus service—in a city dependent on mass transit—in 1966. A 1968 garbage workers' strike left mountains of trash to pile up on hot city streets for nine days. Police and firefighters struck in 1971 and by 1975 the city faced bankruptcy or a default on its bond payments. A bailout from the federal government helped stabilize the crisis. Into that void stepped Edward Koch. Elected mayor in 1978, Koch helped return the city to a delicate balance between competing social forces and introduced his trademark phrase: "How am I doing?" In 1989 David N. Dinkins became New York City's first African American mayor, inheriting the stewardship of a city mired in the worst recession in the post-World War era and the demise of which was predicted daily, as has been the case throughout its history. The tenure of Mayor Rudolph Giuliani in the 1990s saw a historic reduction of the city's crime rate, several years of balanced budgets, and a much-hailed improvement in the overall quality of life of city residents. Mayor Giuliani had entered office on the heels of the World Trade Center bombing on February 26, 1993, in which six people were killed, thousands more were injured, and extensive property damage was incurred. Before leaving office in January 2002, he was faced with an unimaginable tragedy—September 11, 2001.

9/11: Sadness and Solidarity

Most citizens of the United States remember exactly what they were doing on the morning of September 11, 2001, when they heard the news—a plane had struck the north tower of the World Trade Center (WTC) complex in New York City. Initial reports were that it was an accident until many of those same people watched, stunned and horrified, as live television chronicled the second plane crashing into the south tower. Thirty-five minutes later, word came that a third plane had hit the Pentagon in Washington, D.C., followed by the downing of a fourth plane in a Pennsylvania field. Compounding the tragedy was the stark realization that the weapons used against the World Trade Center buildings and the Pentagon were hijacked U.S. commercial airliners, full of travelers. The magnitude of lost lives was overwhelming, nowhere more than in the streets of New York where citizens witnessed the crashes with their own eyes. Within minutes, emergency personnel from across the massive city were mobilized to respond to the WTC crash sites.

The Twin Towers of the World Trade Center were dependent on a central structural core, and the impact and jet fuel fires from the planes had first sent shockwaves down the length of each building and then compromised the supporting structure. At 9:59 a.m., as office workers, janitors, and executives fled the World Trade Center—while rescue workers filed in to help them to safety—the south tower suddenly collapsed into a heap of rubble. The north tower followed a half-hour later. Hundreds of rescue workers and thousands of WTC workers and visitors were killed or injured. The U.S. Government ultimately determined that the four attacks on 9/11 were a symbolic strike at the financial and military emblems of the country and were coordinated through a Muslim terrorist group, al-Qaeda, under the leadership of a man named Osama bin Ladin.

In the days after 9/11, New Yorkers pulled together with a new appreciation for each other and their city. Thousands of volunteers hailing from the city and far beyond gathered to offer aid for rescue, recovery, and clean-up efforts, while donations avalanched in from across the country to support the injured and bereft. Mayor Giuliani was onsite at Ground Zero soon after the attacks, and he stayed onsite to boost the morale of workers and volunteers. The city as a whole vowed that it couldn't be brought to its knees by fear-based tactics, and plans were almost immediately put into effect to prove just that.

While the smoke was still rising, New York Governor George Pataki and Mayor Giuliani created the Lower Manhattan Development Corporation to oversee the design and construction of a lasting memorial to the victims of 9/11, while also generating a plan to rebuild and revitalize the area most profoundly affected by the horrific events. Mere months later, mayor-elect Michael Bloomberg continued the momentum and supported the previous administration's steps to remediate the damage.

Spontaneous memorials had been started soon after the collapse of the towers, and the need for a more permanent observation of the events and recognition of the victims was quickly deemed necessary. A design competition for the memorial was held in 2002, with the idea of architect David Childs being selected as the favorite. The ''Freedom Tower,'' as redesigned in 2005, will eventually surpass the height of the original Twin Towers and will feature an observation deck, office space, listings of the names of

victims of the tragedy, and a spire of light beaming endlessly into space from the top of the structure. Groundbreaking for the Freedom Tower is scheduled for 2006, with completion expected by 2010. In the meantime, Governor Pataki announced in June 2005 that construction would start on two interim memorials to the victims, survivors, and rescue workers affected by the attacks on the World Trade Center buildings. One of the memorials is an oral history project located at the Port Authority Transit Hub near the WTC site, where people can record their recollections of that day and of the loved ones they lost. The second interim memorial is the Tribute Center located across from the WTC area, housing the collected items left at the site after the tragic occurrences of 9/11.

After the smoke cleared, New York City remained the financial powerhouse of the world. The city won't forget the sacrifices made by its citizens on September 11th and on many previous occasions, and it's a city that realizes that the best memorial is to live on. The tourist trade rebounded with surprising speed, and New York City's gritty determination has pulled it through tough economic times not necessarily related to the events of 9/11. The biggest city in the country was built on the diversity of its citizenry—Irish, Jewish, Palestinian, Russian, Italian, Muslim, African, Portuguese, and so many more—and it will continue to be the cultural, financial, and educational heart of the nation.

Historical Information: New York Historical Society, 170 Central Park West, New York, NY 10024-5194; telephone (212)873-3400

Population Profile

Metropolitan Area Residents (PMSA)
1980: 8,275,000
1990: 8,546,846
2000: 9,314,235
Percent change, 1990-2000: 8.98%
U.S. rank in 1980: 1st (CMSA)
U.S. rank in 1990: 1st (PMSA)
U.S. rank in 2000: 1st (PMSA)

City Residents
1980: 7,071,639
1990: 7,322,564
2000: 8,008,278
2004 estimate: 8,104,079
Percent change, 1990-2000: 9.36%
U.S. rank in 1980: 1st (State rank: 1st)
U.S. rank in 1990: 1st (State rank: 1st)
U.S. rank in 2000: 1st (State rank: 1st)

Density: 26,402.9 people per square mile (2000)

Racial and ethnic characteristics (2000)
White: 3,576,385
Black or African American: 2,129,762
American Indian and Alaskan Native: 41,289
Asian: 787,047
Native Hawaiian and Pacific Islander: 5,430
Hispanic or Latino (may be of any race): 2,160,554
Other: 1,074,406

Percent of residents born in state: 49.5% (2000)

Age characteristics (2000)
Population under 5 years old: 540,878
Population 5 to 9 years old: 561,115
Population 10 to 14 years old: 530,816
Population 15 to 19 years old: 520,641
Population 20 to 24 years old: 589,831
Population 25 to 34 years old: 1,368,021
Population 35 to 44 years old: 1,263,280
Population 45 to 54 years old: 1,012,385
Population 55 to 59 years old: 369,105
Population 60 to 64 years old: 314,349
Population 65 to 74 years old: 494,794
Population 75 to 84 years old: 321,360
Population 85 years and over: 121,703
Median age: 34.2 years

Births (2003)
Total number: 124,345

Deaths (2003)
Total number: 59,213 (of which, 807 were infants under the age of 1 year)

Money income (1999)
Per capita income: $22,402
Median household income: $38,293
Total households: 3,021,588

Number of households with income of . . .
less than $10,000: 485,306
$10,000 to $14,999: 214,421
$15,000 to $24,999: 354,413
$25,000 to $34,999: 346,777
$35,000 to $49,999: 430,297
$50,000 to $74,999: 503,722
$75,000 to $99,999: 273,552
$100,000 to $149,999: 234,553
$150,000 to $199,999: 75,626
$200,000 or more: 103,810

Percent of families below poverty level: 18.5% (20.6% of which were female householder families with related children under 5 years)

2002 FBI Crime Index Total: 250,630

Municipal Government

New York City operates under the mayor-council form of government. The mayor is elected in a citywide election, and 51 council members are elected from as many state senate districts within the municipality; a council speaker is elected by the council membership. All officials serve four-year terms. The mayor represents the executive branch of the local government, while the council is largely responsible for legislative functions and also has sole right of approval for the city budget. The Public Advocate, who is not a member of the council, presides over meetings and may vote only in case of a tie. New York City is divided into five boroughs, each of which has its own president and district attorney.

Head Official: Mayor Michael R. Bloomberg (R) (since 2002; current term expires 2006)

Total Number of City Employees: 300,000 (approximate; 2005)

City Information: Office of the Mayor, New York City Hall, New York, NY 10007; telephone (212)788-9600

Economy

Major Industries and Commercial Activity

Despite the loss of the World Trade Center buildings, New York has remained at the core of national and international financial dealings and has continued as the global center of corporate headquarters in finance and services, media, entertainment and telecommunications, manufacturing, and trade. Profits on Wall Street, however, are not expected to equal the heights achieved in 2003, and financial services jobs are on the decline at present. Hundreds of nationwide corporations make their home in New York, from finance to insurance to advertising. New York City leads the country in the number of *Fortune* 500 and 1000 companies headquartered there, including 8 of the world's top 10 securities firms, and about two-fifths of the country's 50 leading law firms, as well as 219 banks representing every major country. The city's biggest industry is publishing, with more printing plants than anywhere else in the United States and approximately 13,000 employees. New York's clothing industry is headquartered in the Garment District near Times Square, where hundreds of factories employ more than 100,000 people.

In recent years, the high-tech and "new media" industries have taken a $9.2 billion toehold in the city, particularly in what is being termed Silicon Alley—Upper Manhattan, Brooklyn, Queens, and Staten Island. New York City has supported growth in this arena through its Digital NYC: Wired to the World program that assists with construction and remodeling efforts that result in affordable spaces with ready access to the Internet. New York City offers hundreds of thousands of miles of installed fiber-optic cable, enabling businesses to communicate with clients around the globe. Life science research and development is seeing a similar surge in activity, as the headquarters of at least three of the world's primary pharmaceutical companies have located within midtown Manhattan. Pfizer has announced ambitious expansion plans that will reportedly result in 2,000 new jobs by 2009, along with new office space and an extensive makeover for its current headquarters. Alongside cutting-edge research, professional services firms related to financial consultation or legal issues of intellectual property also flourish.

New York tourism contributes greatly to the local economy, fueled by huge advertising campaigns and interest in the site of the 9/11 tragedy. Hotel room occupancy rates are steadily increasing to more than 85 percent, and traffic through the area's airports broke the 8,000,000 mark in early 2005. Many tourists visit the city in order to experience its art and culture, resulting in a leisure and hospitality industry with more than 600,000 workers.

Television and film production in New York City constitutes another growth industry, demonstrating a significant increase in the number of overall shooting days for movies, videos, advertisements, and television programs. Almost 150 studios and stages support the industry, and film production costs in the city are now so reasonable that they rival those of Los Angeles. Three of the "Big Five" music recording businesses have headquarters in New York City.

Items and goods produced: published goods, apparel, chemicals, food products, furniture, machinery, paper products, textiles

Incentive Programs—New and Existing Companies

Mayor Bloomberg took office in January of 2002, mere months after the decimation of the World Trade Center buildings. Facing not just a public relations nightmare but also the nationwide economic downturn at that time, the mayor and his administration have expanded the city's industrial interests beyond Wall Street and into biotechnology, film production, and the recreation and tourism business. Unemployment is at its lowest point in 25 years, with 62,000 new jobs created in the city since the middle of 2003. The City of New York appears to acknowledge the value of small businesses, as reflected in its Business Improvement Districts.

Local programs—New York City has many programs available to assist eligible businesses with locating real estate, accessing capital for expansion, lowering energy costs, finding skilled employees and lowering taxes. Businesses that locate in the lower Manhattan area and who complete renovations in excess of 20 percent of the property's assessed value may qualify for the Lower Manhattan Energy Program, which can reduce energy costs up to 45 percent. Manufacturers may receive a tax credit for 3.4 percent of the money spent on utility costs, plus an additional sales tax exemption on purchases of electricity, fuel oil, steam, and natural gas.

State programs—Empire State Development (ESD), the state agency responsible for promoting economic development in New York, has programs available to assist businesses that are expanding and creating jobs. Qualified businesses that locate in an Empire enterprise zone can be exempted from sales tax, benefit from tax reductions, or receive credits on real property and business taxes. Enterprise zone businesses may additionally save money on utilities, receive technical assistance, or receive tax credits on wages for newly-created jobs. Even outside of these zones, businesses that create new jobs can capitalize on Investment Tax Credits. Companies specializing in research and development are eligible for tax credits on 9 percent of their corporate facility tax and may receive a capital credit for their investment in emerging technologies. Machinery and equipment, facilities, property, fuels, and utilities dedicated to research and development activities may also qualify for sales tax exemptions, and the state operates more than 50 high-tech business incubators to further develop the industry. New York State has additionally partnered with electric and gas utility companies to create the "Power for Jobs" program in which companies that fulfill the requirement of retaining or generating a specified number of jobs then receive a break on their utility costs that can be as much as a 25 percent savings.

Low interest loans can be accessed through Empire State Development by small manufacturing enterprises, small service operations that are independently owned and operated, businesses operating within an Empire Zone, businesses located in "highly distressed" areas, businesses owned by women or minorities, defense industry manufacturers, and small businesses seeking to increase their export activities. Other loan programs range from direct financing through the ESD to interest subsidies and loan guarantees. Depending on the financing source, funds can be used for building construction, equipment acquisition, building purchases, and working capital. New York State's progressive tax structure combines tax credits, deductions, exemptions, and write-offs to help reduce the tax burden on businesses.

Businesses that start up in or relocate to designated Commercial Expansion Areas may be eligible for a 3-5 year rent credit of up to $2.50 per square foot, dependent on lease length and company size. New York City's Commercial Expansion Areas include certain Commercial Zones and Manufacturing Zones in Bronx, Upper Manhattan, Queens, Brooklyn, and Staten Island. To qualify, businesses must occupy a building of at least 24,000 square feet and constructed prior to 1999. Businesses in these same zones may be eligible for participation in the Relocation and Employment Assistance, or REAP, program. A tax credit of $3,000 per job is allowed for up to 12 years for jobs relocated from Manhattan below 96th Street or from outside the city to Manhattan below Houston Street. Businesses that have renovated a facility at a cost of more than 50 percent of its assessed value may also be eligible, as may businesses that sign a lease of no less than three years and that spend no less than $25 per square foot improving the space.

The Printers' Relocation Fund allows for partial reimbursement of relocation expenditures to commercial printing businesses and graphic arts companies that move within New York City. Grants may be 50 percent of the qualifying moving costs or $200,000, whichever is the lesser amount.

The New York City Industrial Development Agency offers straight lease transactions and issues low-cost double and triple tax-exempt and taxable bonds on behalf of a wide range of commercial, industrial, and nonprofit companies and organizations. Many financing programs are aimed at eligible small and medium-size businesses to help them obtain financing often not available elsewhere. Various programs provide tax-exempt financing for the purchase of production equipment and machinery; tax exemptions on newly acquired property or renovations for industrial companies; venture capital funds to make capital available for companies specializing in advanced technology; funds for the expansion of nonprofit organizations; loans to small start-up city-based service, retail contracting and manufacturing businesses; and funds to assist community-based banks in making loans for which businesses may not have qualified previously.

Job training programs—In 2003, the New York City Department of Small Business Services was merged with the Department of Employment to create a single point of entry called the Division of Workforce Development. The Division staffs Workforce1 Centers throughout the boroughs of New York City, where job seekers can find extensive databases of open positions, career counseling, skills workshops, and placement programs. The centers also provide GED preparatory courses and instruction in English as a Second Language. Employers can find assistance through the Division's NYC Business Solutions Centers, where customized recruitment and training allows industries to hire workers who are already trained. The Business Solutions Centers offer advice for entrepreneurs, resources for negotiating

governmental regulations, and onsite skill development for employees.

The New York City Employment and Training Coalition has combined the resources of local community colleges, community-based organizations, and training programs associated with labor unions to create a comprehensive approach to training and retraining of the workforce. The Coalition offers employer roundtable discussions, training for management staff to facilitate recruitment and retention of quality employees, workshops and conferences, research, and technical assistance.

In 2005, the New York City Council partnered with the United Way of New York City to publicize a request for proposals for grant funding that will support programs as part of NYCWorks. The $10 million initiative will increase access to education, job readiness training, and specific job skill development for unemployed or underemployed workers in the metropolitan area.

Development Projects

New York City's Economic Development Corporation has continued its efforts to restore and reenergize the Lower Manhattan region through tax incentives that encourage retail, commercial, and residential development. Minimum amounts of investment in property improvements, minimum lease lengths, and other criteria for participation in the Lower Manhattan Revitalization Program ensure stability and commitment on the part of businesses and citizens alike.

A division of L'Oreal beauty products has decided to locate its stylist training facility in the TriBeCa neighborhood. Approximately 120 employees of the Matrix salon beauty products company will work in the 31,000 square foot space, where hairstylists will learn how to effectively use the company's products on clients.

Coney Island has meant summer fun for generations of New Yorkers; the stretch of Brooklyn beach, with its amusement park, circus sideshows, and hotdog-eating contests, has sometimes seemed to be on shaky ground, but new development in the area has bolstered the landmark yet again. In 2001, construction was completed on KeySpan Park, home of the new minor league Brooklyn Cyclones baseball team (an affiliate of the New York Mets). In 2005, the Coney Island Development Corporation chose a designer to revitalize the historic Parachute Pavilion at Coney Island, with the ultimate goal of creating a year-round attraction that will preserve the essence of the amusement park and its surroundings.

In 2004, Mayor Bloomberg announced plans for a commercial biotech research and development campus on the grounds of the city-owned Bellevue Hospital. The East River Science Park is expected to attract major players in the pharmaceutical, medical device production, and biotechnology fields. Approximately 4.5 acres have been set aside for the facility that, when completed, will encompass 870,000 square feet of research, retail, and office space. The Economic Development Corporation has committed $10 million to the project, with an expected return of 6,000 construction jobs during realization of the science park and 2,000 new permanent jobs upon completion. One of Manhattan's current pharmaceutical residents, Pfizer, also has plans in the works to renovate its existing headquarters, expand into several new buildings, and relocate thousands of employees to the downtown headquarters, at the cost of $1 billion over the next 15 years.

In the 1970s, Hunts Point (Bronx) was a crime-infested area notorious for frequent arsons in its abandoned buildings and warehouses. After being designated an In-Place Industrial Park in 1980, followed by Empire and Empowerment Zone designations in 1994, Hunts Point emerged as an industrial powerhouse, with an emphasis on food production. The City of New York and the Bronx Borough plan to capitalize on that momentum through the Hunts Point Vision Plan announced in 2005, in which the existing Produce Market on the site will be upgraded, vacant parcels in the Food Distribution Center will be developed, a buffer zone of food-related businesses will be created between the industrial park and the nearby residential neighborhood, bike paths will be constructed, rail and highway access will be enhanced, new parks will be planted, the visual appeal of the area will be heightened with new sidewalks and streetscapes, the appearance of the waterfront will be improved, and a Hunts Point Works employment and training center will be generated.

In 2005, the city of New York and the borough of Queens put a plan in motion to redevelop the former Municipal Parking Lot 1. Approximately $500 million has been set aside to turn the five-acre site into a new town square with residential spaces, a community center, retail slots, recreational facilities, and a business-class hotel. The project is called Flushing Commons and it is anticipated to generate 2,000 construction jobs during the building phase and an eventual 2,000 permanent jobs. An ancillary project in Flushing involves the construction of more than 100 affordable housing units complemented by retail spaces. The city of Flushing is also undertaking an $11 million downtown redevelopment project that will make the area more friendly for pedestrians, and a former industrial property in western Flushing will eventually be transformed into a 3.2 million square foot retail and residential area called Flushing Town Center, at a cost of about $600 million.

Economic Development Information: New York City Economic Development Corporation, 110 William Street,

New York, NY 10038; telephone (212)312-3600; toll-free (800)NYC-0100

Commercial Shipping

In 2003, the Port Authority of New York and New Jersey area handled about 4 million cargo containers and 55 million tons of bulk cargo, at a record value of $100 billion. The world's leading airport system includes LaGuardia, which transported 14,096 tons of cargo and 15,219 tons of air mail in 2004 in addition to 24,435,619 passengers. John F. Kennedy International Airport (JFK) opened two new cargo facilities in 2003, encompassing 435,000 square feet of warehouse and office space. Japan Airlines operates a sophisticated cargo structure at JFK, with 260,000 square feet of space, and the JFK Air Cargo Center is equipped to handle live animal shipments. In 2003, JFK moved 1,709,457 tons of cargo, 84,243 tons of air mail, and 31,732,446 passengers.

In 2002, New York State government and the Port Authority partnered in a rail freight service improvement project that was expected to cost about $40.195 million. Movement of goods within and outside the New York City area should be enhanced as track and yard capacity are increased in Brooklyn and Queens, vertical clearances are heightened along the Oak Point Link, cargo facilities are expanded, a new engine house is constructed for NY&A rail line, and other enhancements are instituted that will benefit rail freight service providers such as CSX and CP.

Two Foreign Trade Zones in New York City cover three major import-export sites: the Brooklyn Navy Yard, John F. Kennedy International Airport, and Howland Hook Marine Terminal (along with Port Ivory). Foreign Trade Zones are legally outside U.S. Customs territory and permit importers to store or assemble goods with minimal U.S. Customs scrutiny and no duty charges until goods enter U.S. commerce streams.

The city is bisected and surrounded by a web of interstate highways, including I-95, I-80, I-78, I-295, and I-280. More than 60 trucking companies offer local and national ground transportation of freight, and both FedEx and United Parcel Service operate air freight and package delivery services that are sited in Jamaica, NY.

Labor Force and Employment Outlook

The 2000 U.S. Census reported that 72.3 percent of New Yorkers possess a high school diploma or its equivalent; 27.4 percent of the city's population goes on to earn at least a bachelor's degree, and 11.6 percent achieve a graduate degree of some variety. Overall, this makes for a well-educated workforce. For the State of New York, labor market analysts predict that there will be marked growth in the education and training industry, with a 15.4 percent increase in available positions by the year 2012. Healthcare and healthcare support professions are expected to pick up 147,930 jobs, and community social service work is anticipated to increase by almost 20 percent. Manufacturing and administrative support positions will more than likely decrease in availability, while transportation-related and agricultural work are projected to remain essentially static. Financial services employment will continue its gradual rebound, with an 11.5 percent gain in jobs by 2012.

The following is a summary of data regarding the New York consolidated metropolitan area labor force, 2004 annual averages.

Size of nonagricultural labor force: 8,278,500

Number of workers employed in . . .
    construction and mining: 329,700
    manufacturing: 499,600
    trade, transportation and utilities: 1,582,400
    information: 289,300
    financial activities: 769,700
    professional and business services: 1,223,500
    educational and health services: 1,358,000
    leisure and hospitality: 606,700
    other services: 346,000
    government: 1,273,000

Average hourly earnings of production workers employed in manufacturing: $15.35 (April 2005)

Unemployment rate: 4.5% (April 2005)

Largest employers	*Number of employees (2004)*
City of New York	300,000
New York Public Schools	73,774
Merrill Lynch	50,600
JFK International Airport	35,000
Goldman Sachs Group, Inc.	21,928
Credit Suisse First Boston	18,341
Consolidated Edison Co. of NY	14,079
New York University	13,000
Bear Stearns Companies	10,961
HSBC Banks	10,800
Morgan Stanley Financial	9,700
Cornell University	9,200
LaGuardia Airport	8,000
Beth Israel Medical Center	7,460

Cost of Living

New York is by far the nation's most expensive city in which to live, and it ranks as the thirteenth most expensive worldwide. The city's unique rent control policies provide cheap rent to long-ensconced residents—who tend to be middle class or affluent—while leaving newcomers to fend for themselves on the open market. Areas that have been undergoing gentrification in the last decade, such as the Park Slope (Brooklyn) and Parkchester (Bronx) neighborhoods, have seen a more than 50 percent increase in rents. To deter rent inflation that may chase older residents or lower-income owners out of their properties, New York City is now offering a property tax abatement to owners of buildings comprised of less than six units and who rent to senior citizens. The city has also proposed that renters in New York City be able to benefit from the School Tax Relief program that at present only applies to property owners, and that property owners who trim the City of New York trees near their homes may qualify for a property tax credit.

The following is a summary of data regarding several key cost of living factors in the New York area.

2004 (3rd Quarter) ACCRA Average House Price: $990,800 (Manhattan only)

2004 (3rd Quarter) ACCRA Cost of Living Index: 216 (Manhattan only, U.S. average = 100.0)

State income tax rate: Ranges from 4% to 7.7%

State sales tax rate: 4%

Local income tax rate: Graduated, from 1.5% to approximately 4.45%

Local sales tax rate: 4.375%

Property tax rate: Class 1 (single-family dwelling) in Manhattan, 15.094% of assessed value; Class 4 in Manhattan, 11.558% of assessed value (2004-2005)

Economic Information: Manhattan Chamber of Commerce, 1375 Broadway, Third Floor, New York, New York, 10018; telephone (212)479-7772; fax (212)831-4244

Education and Research

Elementary and Secondary Schools

New York City's public school system is the largest in the nation, serving more than one million children. Until recently, school district activities were dictated by the New York City Board of Education, which gained a reputation for poorly serving its student population. Soon after taking office, Mayor Bloomberg abolished the Board of Education and assumed mayoral control of New York Public Schools under a school governance agreement. One of Bloomberg's campaign promises was to create special classrooms that would keep students with multiple disciplinary infractions involved in education but in a controlled setting. As a result, the district opened 20 New Beginnings Centers by 2004 along with five off-site Suspension Centers that operate in partnership with community-based organizations to provide a complete range of student support services.

The school system leans toward the magnet model, with a variety of specialized learning institutions within the elementary, middle, and high school strata. Concentrations include leadership studies, writing and communication, culinary arts, technology, computer science, international relations, performing arts, law, social justice, aerospace, and sports professions to name just a few. In the fall of 2005, the Department of Education plans to open more than 50 new small secondary schools across the city, in an effort to broaden the academic choices available to students and their parents or guardians. The new schools will concentrate on an academically rigorous curriculum, personalized to each student and enhanced with community partnerships. In addition, there are 48 charter schools in operation within the district, which is divided into 10 regions that are loosely based on sections of the five New York City boroughs.

New York City public schools tend to have fewer teachers, administrators, and librarians than the state average; spending per pupil also lags behind the state average. Approximately 54.3 percent of the city's public school students graduate from high school, while the district sends about 71.5 percent of that diminished group on to an institution of higher education.

Many private K-12 schools operate in the New York City area, some of which are secular and some of which are religiously based. Since the city is a major television and film production center, a number of acting and technical schools related to the industry have been created.

The following is a summary of data regarding the New York City public schools as of the 2004–2005 school year.

Total enrollment: 1,047,156

Number of facilities
  elementary schools: 616
  junior high schools: 221
  senior high schools: 295
  special education schools: 57

Student/teacher ratio: 12.5:1

Teacher salaries (2004)
  minimum: $39,900
  maximum: $81,232

Funding per pupil: $11,627

Public Schools Information: Chancellor's Office, New York City Department of Education, New York, NY 10007; telephone (212)374-5115

Colleges and Universities

New York is the only U.S. city with a large public-university system. The City University of New York (CUNY) offers open admission at its 20 sites to all New York City residents with a high school degree. With branches in all five boroughs, CUNY embraces eight liberal arts colleges, the John Jay College of Criminal Justice, the Mount Sinai School of Medicine, the New York City College of Technology, the City University School of Law, business programs, and graduate degree programs. The extensive State University of New York (SUNY) system operates several specialized branches in the city, such as the Fashion Institute of Technology, the Downstate Medical Center, the State College of Optometry, and the Maritime College.

More than two dozen private colleges in New York City provide access to associate, baccalaureate, masters, and doctoral degrees. New York University is one of the largest private institutions of higher education in the country, enrolling almost 40,000 students in undergraduate and graduate programs with a focus on the arts. Columbia University belongs to the Ivy League and is the city's oldest college. Columbia is renowned for its journalism program and has gained a reputation for its medical research work. Yeshiva University, a private Jewish academic research institution, enrolls almost 7,000 students in graduate and undergraduate programs in its Albert Einstein School of Medicine and the Benjamin N. Cardozo School of Law. The Julliard School is considered one of the best music, dance, and theater schools in the country. In recent years, Juilliard has begun to focus on community outreach, the interface of technology and art, and interdisciplinary programming. Fordham University is a Jesuit institution with a specialty in medieval studies, while Rockefeller University is famous for its biomedical sciences. The Bard Graduate Center for Studies in the Decorative Arts, which opened in 1993, offers a master of arts degree. The New School in New York was formerly the New School for Social Research, and it has retained that academic bent.

Libraries and Research Centers

The New York Public Library system, like the city itself, is immense. Five central libraries, four specialized research libraries, and 80 branch facilities hold collections of more than 19 million books system-wide, in addition to 1.6 million audio resources, 205,074 video materials, and more than 85,000 periodicals. The Science, Industry and Business Library (SIB), which opened in 1996, is the nation's largest public information center dedicated to science and business. The SIB houses more than 2 million volumes and 60,000 periodicals and provides users with broad access to electronic science and business content via 150 networked computer work stations. Among the research centers' special collections are the Henry W. and Albert A. Berg Collection of English and American Literature, which includes the Vladimir Nabakov Archive; manuscripts and archives of the Schomburg Center for Research in Black Culture; and the Theater on Film Archive, which preserves videotapes of live theater performances accumulated for more than 25 years.

In addition to the city library system, more than a thousand other libraries are operated in the city by schools, private groups, and most museums. The Pierpont Morgan Library is known for its collection of rare books and manuscripts. The Morgan Library is on the grounds of a 45-room Victorian brownstone, connected to the library by a glass-enclosed conservatory. In 2005, the library temporarily closed for a major expansion effort that will improve the entrance, internal circulation, the galleries, and auditorium space. Masonic literature, history, and relics are collected in the Chancellor Robert R. Livingston Masonic Library of Grand Lodge, while the New Historical Society houses a fine collection of materials relevant to New York's role in early United States history. At the United Nations, the Dag Hammarskjold Library specializes in international affairs and world peace with an aim of getting U.N. members the best information possible as quickly as possible. The U.S. National Archives for the Northeastern United States houses such items as court records from the Rosenberg and Hiss cases, limitation of liability suits involving the *Titanic,* and census records since 1790 on microfilm.

With its universities and industry research campuses, New York City has become a global contributor in practically all areas of research and development. On average, the city receives $1.2 billion in funding from the National Institute of Health, underwriting the efforts of its 128 resident Nobel Laureates and other members of the scientific community. The New York State Energy Research and Development Authority assesses public utilities, conducts research on energy efficiency and alternative power, and supports projects in schools, municipalities, and local industries. New York University is a leading research center with programs in medicine and health fields, international studies, urban affairs, and Latin America. The State University of New York maintains a research foundation that supports efforts across the SUNY system of universities. Recent projects include a study of brain cell behavior and methods of preventing blindness. Columbia University's Center for Environmental Research and Conservation studies nature and wildlife issues nationally and globally. Among the independent organizations researching health areas are those focusing on drug addiction, blood disorders, hearing problems, genetic disorders, and psychiatric issues. The New York Botanical Garden studies the flora of the New World, catalogs five million

samples in its herbarium, and publishes the *Botanical Review.* Offering research and consultation on government public policy is the Institute of Public Administration. The New York Public Interest Research group conducts consumer-interest, environmental, energy, governmental system, social justice, and health research. The United Nations Institute for Training and Research studies all aspects of United Nations policy, operation, and organization.

Public Library Information: The New York Public Library, 188 Madison Ave #1, New York, NY 10016; telephone (212)930-0800; fax (212)921-2546

Health Care

New York City offers the opportunity for world-class medical care and has one of the highest concentrations of hospitals on the planet, with 111 facilities that span the spectrum from smaller neighborhood hospitals to major medical centers. The city is served by more than 30 teaching hospitals, a number of medical schools, more than 10 cardiac rehabilitation centers, and 6 cancer treatment centers. The New York City Health and Hospitals Corporation—by far the largest public hospital system in the country—employs thousands of workers at 11 acute care hospitals, 6 diagnostic and treatment centers, 4 long-term care facilities, 1 home health agency, and 100 community health clinics.

According to *U.S. News & World Report,* a number of the top hospitals in the country in 2005 are located in New York City, including: New York-Presbyterian University Hospital of Columbia and Cornell (third in neurology, second in psychiatry, and fourth in kidney disease); Hospital for Special Surgery (second in orthopedics and third in rheumatology); Memorial Sloan-Kettering Cancer Center (first in cancer care); Mount Sinai Medical Center (third in geriatrics and seventh in digestive disorders); and Rusk Institute for Rehabilitation Medicine at New York University Medical Center (eighth in rehabilitation). Other specialized services can be obtained at the New York State Psychiatric Institute, Kirby Forensic Psychiatric Center, the Orthopaedic Institute, and the New York Ear and Eye Infirmary. Residents of New York City can also access a wide variety of holistic healthcare, including homeopathy, hypnotherapy, massage therapy, and acupuncture. Diagnosis and treatment for pets and exotic animals is available from the nearly 400 veterinarians and animal hospitals operating in the five boroughs.

Health Care Information: The New York Health and Hospitals Corporation, 125 Worth Street, New York, NY 10013; telephone (212)788-3339

Times Square, called The Great White Way, is known for its neon, movie houses, theaters, stores, and crowds.

Recreation

Sightseeing

An energetic visitor could keep busy for weeks in Manhattan alone. A good place to start is where the Dutch explorers first settled—in Battery Park on the southernmost tip of Manhattan, which offers spectacular views of the harbor and the Statue of Liberty, itself accessible by boats leaving from the park. The American Museum of Immigration at the base of the statue—the largest of modern times—traces the history of the men and women who sailed into the harbor for a new future. Ellis Island processed more than 12 million European immigrants before it was shuttered in 1954; it is once again open to the public and drawing visitors from around the country and the globe.

A natural sightseeing transition might be a trip to the New York City Hall, the oldest in the nation still housing the city's governmental functions. Back in 1802, a design team consisting of a Frenchman and a native New Yorker won a competition to create the then-new City Hall; the resulting building reflects the Federal style of architecture, with noticeable French influences. Ten Corinthian columns, a soaring rotunda, arched windows, and a cupola crowned by a copper statue of Justice make the building a dramatic sight. The Governor's Room in the City Hall contains a museum with relics from the civic development of the U.S. and New York; its visitors have included Albert Einstein and President Abraham Lincoln, who later lay in state in the room following his assassination.

The New York Stock Exchange offers free tours and a visitor's gallery to observe the hectic activity; for a more peaceful perspective, the sightseer can look down on the city from the observation platform of the fabled Empire State Building, once the world's tallest building. Grand Central Station is a destination in itself; since it opened in 1913, the station whose name has become synonymous with bustle has added shops, restaurants, and entertainment. Group and individual tours can be arranged. Rockefeller Center is not just a place to see but to be seen—the NBC network produces "The Today Show" in the historic complex of buildings that includes the Rainbow Room and the Radio City Music Hall.

Ground Zero, the former site of the World Trade Center complex, is a powerful experience. Interim memorials are located near the site to keep alive the memory of the tragedy of September 11, 2001. The absence of the towering buildings themselves, in a city that uses every available space, is haunting.

The United Nations meets for about three months beginning on the third Tuesday of September, and free tickets to the General Assembly are distributed about an hour before each conclave. Guided tours of the building are also available in at least 16 languages. Visitors should also take time to stroll through New York's many neighborhoods. Chinatown abounds with restaurants and stores. Greenwich Village retains much of its Bohemian charm with bookstores, nightlife, and specialty boutiques. The Garment District, still a headquarters for the clothing trade, teems with workers pushing racks of clothing down the street.

In the Bronx, the 250-acre New York Botanical Garden owns one of the world's biggest plant collections in an herbarium with four million specimens. The Bronx Zoo is home to more than 4,000 animals in natural environments. The zoo is active in preservation activities, having been the home of the Wildlife Conservation Society since 1895. Some of the realistic habitats include the Himalayan Highlands Habitat, the Congo Gorilla Forest, and an Asian rainforest. The zoo also contains a butterfly garden, a tiger exhibit that puts visitors within a whisker of the cats, and a bug carousel for the kids.

The Brooklyn Botanical Garden cultivates 900 varieties of roses and is undergoing a series of improvements and restorations in 2005. Astroland, near the Coney Island Boardwalk, is a family fun center with rides, games, and other amusements. Also nearby, the New York Aquarium highlights a shark tank, dolphin and sea lion shows, Beluga whales, and thousands of other fish and varieties of marine life. The Brooklyn Bridge, one of the world's most beautiful suspension bridges, is open to pedestrians for a memorable view of lower Manhattan.

The Jamaica Bay Wildlife Refuge in Queens is nearly as large as Manhattan and is a beautiful site for nature walks. On Staten Island, the William T. Davis Wildlife Refuge offers similar opportunities. The Staten Island Zoo is small, but maintains an excellent reptile collection.

New York is famous around the world for its glittering nightlife, from jazz clubs in Harlem to discos and nightclubs in Manhattan. Comedy clubs, improvisational theater, and singles lounges are key New York attractions.

Arts and Culture

New York City is the ultimate destination for performers in and consumers of all aspects of the arts. The city's rich culture attracts fans to the fabled lights of Broadway (and off-Broadway) theaters and the all-night clubs of Greenwich Village. The Theater District in Manhattan offers 36 theaters and a ton of talent in a small strip of land. Performance venues named for luminaries such as Ethel Barrymore, the Gershwins, and Helen Hayes line the streets and entertain millions every year. The artistic heart of the city literally beats at the Lincoln Center for the Performing Arts, home of cultural icons such as the New York Philharmonic Orchestra, the School of American Ballet, the New York City Opera, The Chamber Music Society, the New York City Ballet, and the Metropolitan Opera. The 268-seat Walter Reade Theater located within the Lincoln Center is the first permanent home of the Film Society. The Dance Theatre of Harlem started as an initiative to give underserved children the opportunity to study a wide variety of dance forms and has now become one of the best-known multicultural professional companies in the world.

Cultural and historical museums in New York City are as diverse as the populace. El Museo del Barrio has evolved into a primary ethnic institution for New York's Latino residents and is a must-see within Manhattan's Museum Mile on Fifth Avenue. Both the Museum of the City of New York and the collections of the New York Historical Society illustrate how the ''Big Apple'' developed into the metropolis it is today. The Museum of Television and Radio keeps a vault of 16,000 radio and television tapes that visitors can select by computer and then watch in private booths. The museum also holds special screenings and is a center for radio, television and film research efforts. The Jewish Museum is devoted to Jewish culture both ancient and modern, as is the Yeshiva University Museum. The South Street Seaport Museum is actually a historical district that is several blocks long and features exhibits relating to New York's marine past. A fleet of ships from the late 1800s and early 1900s is docked at the museum pier and can be boarded by the public. The American Museum of Natural History in Central Park features permanent exhibits on peoples from around the globe, meteorites, gems, primates, birds and reptiles, and is probably best known for its dramatic dinosaur reconstructions. The 563-carat sapphire called Star of India is on display at the museum, and the museum's Hayden Planetarium presents frequent lecture series, weekly galaxy explorations, and daily astronomy demonstrations. The New York City Fire Museum resides in a circa-1903 firehouse built in the Beaux Art fashion and contains historical articles, equipment, and memorabilia related to firefighting. The New York City Police Museum contains one of the world's biggest collections of police and emergency services memorabilia.

The Museum of Modern Art, or MoMA as it's popularly known, is the largest art museum in the country with 135,000 specimens of painting, sculpture, photography, films, and drawings. The building itself recently underwent an expansion and remodeling that increased both the total square footage and the exhibit space by approximately a third. The collections within MoMA include some of mankind's greatest art treasures ranging from classical Greek sculpture to avant-garde photography. The permanent collection features artists such as Raphael, El Greco, Vermeer, Van Gogh, Hopper, Dali, and Pollock. The Whitney Museum of American Art holds the largest collection of twentieth-century American work and is now amassing pieces from the twenty-first century. The museum has collected the works of Hopper, O'Keefe, and Calder extensively and has dedicated rooms to each of these artists. The Solomon R. Guggenheim Museum, housed in a Frank Lloyd Wright building, is a masterpiece itself and specializes in modern painting, sculpture, and graphic arts. The now-public collections started as the private holdings of the Guggenheim family; Peggy Guggenheim was known for her appreciation for and support of contemporary art and was instrumental in the careers of several modern artists, including Jackson Pollock. The New Museum of Contemporary Art (NMCA) exhibits some of the most current trends in the art world. In 2005, the NMCA will begin construction of a 60,000 square foot facility on Prince Street to allow for expanded collections and programming. A temporary location for viewing will be established on the ground floor of the Chelsea Art Museum on West 22nd Street. The American Folk Art Museum (AFAM) opened exactly two months after the terror attacks on the World Trade Center in 2001, and the building itself has won several awards for its architecture. The AFAM collection includes 4,000 paintings, quilts, sculptures, and weathervanes. The Studio Museum in Harlem collects culturally relevant works in a variety of media and offers educational workshops. The Dahesh Museum has concentrated its collection efforts on the works of nineteenth and early-twentieth century European artists such as Bonheur, Vernet, and Picou. The younger set will appreciate the Children's Museum of the Arts, where a hands-on experience in visual and performing arts awaits. The Museum of African Art, located on SoHo Museum Row, seeks to increase public awareness and appreciation of the works of African artisans. The Cooper-Hewitt Museum, part of the Smithsonian Institution, is the nation's only museum devoted to contemporary and historical design.

Festivals and Holidays

Practically every day is a party somewhere in New York City. The St. Patrick's Day Parade (Irish) and the Columbus Day Parade (Italian) remain the city's two biggest ethnic celebrations. Others include the German Steuben Day Parade, the Muslim Day Parade, the Brooklyn Latinos Unidos Parade, the Mexican Day Parade, and the Polish Pulaski Day Parade. The Great 4th of July Festival explodes with fireworks by Macy's Department Store and a street fair. Toward the end of July, the River to River Festival at the waterfront in Manhattan honors the arts in all forms. In August, the New York Fringe Festival is an alternative celebration of visual and performing arts. The Festival of the Americas in mid-August expresses the diversity of the continent from north to south. The Macy's Thanksgiving Day Parade, broadcast nationwide, features huge cartoon-character balloons that drift over city streets and has figured largely in movies such as "Miracle on 34th Street." Since 1933, the lighting of the communal tree in Rockefeller Center has drawn New Yorkers and visitors in a kick-off for various cultural observations occurring in December. New Year's Eve is celebrated in a raucous party that centers on Times Square where the "Big Apple" and the ageless Dick Clark have for many years marked the start of a new year.

Sports for the Spectator

A Big League city demands Big League sports heroes and New York's professional teams have provided those for generations. The New York Yankees of professional baseball's American League East play in the "House That (Babe) Ruth Built," Yankee Stadium in the Bronx. The National League New York Mets play their baseball games at Shea Stadium in Queens. The New York Rangers of the National Hockey League, the New York Liberty of the Women's National Basketball Association, and the New York Knicks of the National Basketball Association all play home games at Madison Square Garden in Manhattan. The National Hockey League's New York Islanders host their hockey matches at Nassau Coliseum on Long Island, which is also the scene for arena football action with the New York Dragons. From the National Football League, the New York Giants and the New York Jets both play their home games across the river in New Jersey at Giants Stadium within the Meadowlands complex.

While New York City was unsuccessful in its bid for the 2012 Olympic Games, there are still plenty of amateur sporting events to enjoy in the metropolis. Minor league baseball is represented by the Brooklyn Cyclones, an affiliate of the Mets, and the Yankees' farm team in Staten Island. Columbia University competes in Division I of the National Collegiate Athletic Association in a number of sports such as basketball, cross-country, and soccer.

Aqueduct Race Track in Queens attracts horseracing fans as do nearby Belmont Park Race Track in Elmont and the Meadowlands in New Jersey. For almost 140 years, the Belmont Stakes have been one leg of the Triple Crown thoroughbred horserace series. The U.S. Open Tennis Championships are played annually in August and early September at the Arthur Ashe Stadium in the Flushing Meadows-Corona Park area of Queens.

Sports for the Participant

Recreational sports for hundreds of thousands of Manhattan residents center on gigantic Central Park, an 840-acre green oasis of rolling hills, ponds, and biking and running paths. Many roads through the park are closed on weekends and certain hours during the week to allow cyclists to pedal in peace. Rowboats can be rented from Loeb Boathouse for a small fee. Runners, walkers, and rollerbladers have unlim-

ited access to miles of footpaths in Central Park, but should exercise caution at night and in isolated areas of the park.

New York City's Parks and Recreation Division administers more than 1,700 parks and facilities scattered throughout the five boroughs that constitute the city. With 614 ball fields, 991 playgounds, 53 outdoor swimming pools, 14 miles of beaches, and 550 tennis courts, the city offers something for everyone. A plethora of city-sponsored sporting opportunities are available for individuals and groups, and the Police Athletic League operated by the police department coordinates sporting events for more than 70,000 children every year.

The Jamaica Bay Wildlife Refuge in Queens is nearly as large as Manhattan, with 9,155 acres of natural habitats and hiking trails that aren't overly demanding. On Staten Island, the William T. Davis Wildlife Refuge covers 2,500 acres where hikers can hit either the Blue or White trails as they pass through diverse ecosystems. Outside of New York City, the Adirondack Forest Preserve contains more than 2,000 miles of established trails that can challenge hikers of all ages and abilities. The Adirondacks offer opportunities for backpacking and camping, rock climbing and bouldering, or canoeing in the lake country. In the winter, there's skiing at Whiteface Mountain and hiking trails convert to cross-country skiing use. A number of resorts with downhill and cross-country trails are within easy driving distance of the city.

The New York City Marathon, held annually, is one of the biggest races in the country, attracting thousands of professional and amateur participants from around the globe. In the winter, ice skaters can glide on rinks at Rockefeller Center and at the Wollman Memorial Skating Rink in Central Park. Open all year is the New York City Building rink at Flushing Meadows-Corona Park where rentals are available. There are eight golf courses within the vicinity, including Rock Hill, Montauk Downs, Spook Rock, and Swan Lake.

Shopping and Dining

The iconic Macy's in Herald Square, the world's largest store, covers 2.1 million feet of space and offers 500,000 different items for the shopper's consideration. Macy's has a visitors center that conducts tours in several languages and the department store houses a gourmet food shop in The Cellar. Flagship stores for Calvin Klein, Chanel, Versace, Prada, Dolce and Gabbana, Tommy Hilfiger, and others have led to a designer boom on Fifth and Madison avenues and 57th Street. SoHo (short for the area south of Houston Street) remains a favorite destination for its unique boutiques and stylish art galleries.

Fifth Avenue, New York's avenue of fashion, includes Bergdorf Men, located across from Bergdorf Goodman and featuring clothing for men only. The venerable Henri Bendel resides in a beautifully restored Beaux Arts building; nearby, Saks Fifth Avenue still caters to upscale shoppers. Also nearby is FAO Schwarz toy emporium, where kids of all ages come to be amazed and entertained. Rare toys, collectibles, faux vehicles, and stuffed animals run rampant in a store that invites visitors to play with the merchandise.

Designer clothing at bargain prices can be found at Woodbury Common Premium Outlets, located about an hour outside of Manhattan in upstate New York. Vendors include Dolce and Gabbana, Gucci, Neiman Marcus, Barney's, Banana Republic, The Gap, and Chanel. A shuttle bus service is available to and from the city.

The Crystal District is a five-block expanse of Madison Avenue that houses the world's greatest collection of luxury crystal. Baccarat, a French crystal company, maintains a flagship store in that area, along with Steuben, Swarovski, and Lalique. More sparkly things can be found at the perennial source for engagement and wedding rings, Tiffany and Co. The most extensive offering of Lladro ceramics in the United States is available at Lladro U.S.A. Inc. on 57th Street. New York is also home to world-famous auction houses Christie's and Sotheby's.

Books are a popular and readily available item, sold in general bookstores, specialty shops for specific subject matter, and at sidewalk stands. International goods are the bailiwick of the United Nations Gift Center, and Greenwich Village has continued to be a source for hip and happening music or golden oldies found in its plentiful record and CD shops. All five boroughs also host greenmarkets, some of which are seasonal and some year-round.

Dining options in New York are limited only to one's pocketbook. The more than 18,000 possibilities include everything from posh four-star restaurants to sidewalk cafés and Kosher delicatessens. Continental cuisine coexists with soul food in Harlem, pasta in Little Italy, and Asian specialties in Chinatown. Several restaurants atop New York's skyscrapers offer meals with a breathtaking view. There are a number of time-honored eateries that deserve individual mention: The Four Seasons combines luxurious surroundings with sumptuous food that continually pushes the envelope of American cuisine; the Russian Tea Room is a New York institution which recently reopened and is enjoying a renaissance; Tavern on the Green has been feeding its flocks since 1934—before that, it was a sheepfold; Tom's Restaurant was featured on the comedy series "Seinfeld" and serves up cheap eats.

Visitor Information: NYC & Company, Convention and Visitors Bureau, 810 Seventh Avenue, New York, NY 10019; telephone (212)484-1200; fax (212)245-5943

Convention Facilities

New York has been named one of the world's "Best Cities" by *Travel + Leisure* magazine, and in 2002 *Conde Nast Traveler* designated it a "Hot City." The combination of 71,000 hotel rooms, cultural attractions, world-class professional sports teams, and proximity to the world's financial powers makes New York City an extremely attractive choice for conventions and tradeshows. Venues range from traditional convention halls to unique accommodations in museums, ships, racetracks, and universities.

The Jacob Javits Convention Center is named for the former United States senator from New York and was designed by renowned architect I. M. Pei. The stunning glass facade of the building mirrors the city's skyline by day and glows from within at night. It offers 814,000 square feet of exhibition space including the largest single hall in the Western Hemisphere at 410,000 square feet, supplemented by more than 100 other rooms.

Pier 94 New York styles itself as "The Unconvention Center" as it offers a 175,000 square foot space that can be flexed to meet the needs of any event. The Show Piers on the Hudson offers 225,000 square feet of space on the waterfront for tradeshows, exhibits, and conferences. Other major convention destinations are Madison Square Garden, the Hilton New York, Lincoln Center, the Waldorf Astoria, and the American Museum of Natural History.

Convention Information: NYC & Company, Convention & Visitors Bureau, 810 Seventh Avenue, New York, NY 10019; telephone (212)484-1200; fax (212)245-5943

Transportation

Approaching the City

The two major New York City airports saw a combined total of 54,215,216 passengers pass through their gates in 2003. Thousands of flights depart each day from New York to more than 500 destination cities around the world. John F. Kennedy International Airport (JFK) handles the most international flights—more than 200 a day—of any other airport, in addition to domestic traffic. LaGuardia Airport, somewhat closer to Manhattan, offers mostly domestic connections. Newark Liberty International Airport in New Jersey also serves the metropolitan area. A rapid rail link to Newark Liberty was completed in 2001 and construction on the JFK and LaGuardia branches of the AirTrain system are expected to be complete within the next few years, creating easier access to the airfields while reducing traffic.

Interstate, U.S., and state highways form a virtual web around and through the New York City area, with I-495, I-95, and U.S. 1 being primary routes. The New Jersey Turnpike (Interstate 95) is the major artery leading into the city from the south. From the north, the New York Thruway (Interstate 87) connects with the Major Deegan Expressway, which follows the east side of the Harlem River through the Bronx. The New England Thruway (another part of I-95) also leads into the city from the north. Interstate 80 from western New Jersey parallels I-95 as it approaches New York City.

The two main train stations, Pennsylvania and Grand Central, serve as both commuter and long-distance terminals for more than 600,000 people every day, as well as providing Amtrak connections. In the past decade, Grand Central Station underwent a renovation that restored it to its previous magnificence, with a gourmet food market, five restaurants and lounges, entertainment, and updated information kiosks. The Port Authority Bus Terminal—the largest in the world—is the main station for bus transportation locally and nationally.

Traveling in the City

New York City consists of a collection of islands, making bridges and tunnels an important aspect of navigation. The Lincoln Tunnel connects Interstate 495 to Manhattan, and Queens links up via the Long Island Expressway. The Brooklyn Bridge in the southern part of Manhattan crosses the water to the eponymous borough, and the Holland Tunnel gets commuters to New Jersey. In all, there are 12 major bridges or tunnels connecting the boroughs.

Traffic in New York is probably the heaviest in the nation. The term "gridlock," a traffic jam out of which no one can move, was invented there and many intersections are clogged during any given day. Many residents do not own cars, relying instead on plentiful taxis or public transportation. A $100 million system of sensors has been installed under the city's roadways to enable the New York City Transportation Department to monitor congestion, identify trouble spots, and control the flow of traffic by changing the duration of traffic lights. Much of Manhattan is laid out in a grid pattern, but other boroughs require a good street map for visitors. Broadway Avenue runs from north to south through the city, intersecting the numbered east-west streets. Parking in a garage in Manhattan ranges from $6.00 to $15.00 per hour.

Subways are one of the best bargains in the city. A $1.50 token or Metrocard fare payment permits travel on more than 704 miles of subway track, including local and express trains. The subway system is well-maintained and policed so

that it is much safer and cleaner than its somewhat unshakeable 1970s-era reputation would indicate. Subways and buses are the only sure way to beat Manhattan's numbing gridlock on surface streets. Many New Yorkers walk or ride bikes to their destinations.

Communications

Newspapers and Magazines

More than 200 newspapers have offices in New York, including the city's major daily newspapers: *The New York Times,* one of the world's most influential newspapers, *Newsday,* and the *The New York Daily News.* Many other English- and foreign-language dailies and weeklies and more than 100 scholarly journals serve specialized readerships, including the *Wall Street Journal* and the *Amsterdam News,* which focuses on African American issues.

Hundreds of local and national magazines are published in New York. *Newsweek* and *Time* are both based in the city. Other magazines include *Flying, Psychology Today, Sports Illustrated, Parade, Cosmopolitan, People Weekly, Ladies Home Journal, Better Homes and Gardens, Bon Appetit, Cycle World, Forbes, GQ,* and *Glamour.*

Television and Radio

Eight television stations broadcast from New York City, including the three major networks of CBS, ABC, and NBC. Appearing in the background of the morning news programs has become a competitive sport for residents and visitors alike. Throughout the history of television, many programs have been created, produced, and set in New York City, including "The Ed Sullivan Show," "Late Night With David Letterman," "I Love Lucy," "That Girl," "Kojak," "All in the Family," "Mad About You," "Sex and the City," "Seinfeld," and "Law & Order: SVU." Hundreds of radio stations broadcast from the city, covering all major radio formats from all-talk to urban contemporary music to classical music on both AM and FM bands. Other radio stations cater to those with a taste for Spanish music and news, Caribbean music, Christian music, and soul.

Media Information: The New York Times Company, 1 New York Times Plaza, Flushing, NY 11354-1200; telephone (718)281-7000

New York Online

City of New York. Available www.nyc.gov

Manhattan Chamber of Commerce. Available www.manhattancc.org

New York City Department of Education. Available www
.nycenet.edu

New York City Economic Development Corporation. Available www.newyorkbiz.com

New York City Health and Hospitals Corporation. Available
www.nyc.gov/html/hhc/home/home.shtml

The New York Historical Society. Available www.nyhistory
.org

New York Public Library. Available www.nypl.org

NYC & Company, Convention & Visitors Bureau. Available www.nycvisit.com

Port Authority of New York and New Jersey. Available
www.panynj.gov

Selected Bibliography

Bull, Chris and Sam Erman (eds.). *At Ground Zero: Young Reporters Who Were There Tell Their Stories.* (New York, NY: Thunder's Mouth Press, 2002)

Burrows, Edwin G. and Mike Wallace. *A History of New York City to 1898.* (Oxford University Press, 1998)

Ellis, Edward Robb and Jeanyee Wong. *The Epic of New York City: A Narrative History.* (Kodansha America, 1997)

Goodwin, Doris Kearns. *Wait Till Next Year: A Memoir.* (Touchstone Books, 1998)

Homberger, Eric, and Alice Hudson (Illustrator). *The Historical Atlas of New York City: A Visual Celebration of Nearly 400 Years of New York City's History.* (Henry Holt & Co., 1998)

Murphy, Dean E. (compiled by). *September 11: An Oral History.* (New York, NY: Doubleday, 2002)

Osofsky, Gilbert. *Harlem: The Making of a Ghetto. Negro New York, 1890-1930.* (Elephant/Ivan R. Dee, 1995 reprint)

Remnick, David and Susan Choi, eds. *Wonderful Town: New York City Stories from the New Yorker.* (Random House, 2000)

Rosenzweig, Roy, and Elizabeth Blackmar. *The Park and the People: A History of Central Park.* (Ithaca, NY: Cornell University Press, 1992)

Rochester

The City in Brief

Founded: 1803 (incorporated, 1834)

Head Official: Mayor William A. Johnson, Jr. (since 1994)

City Population
  1980: 241,741
  1990: 230,356
  2000: 219,773
  2003 estimate: 215,093
  Percent change, 1990–2000: −4.8%
  U.S. rank in 1990: 66th
  U.S. rank in 2000: 91st

Metropolitan Area Population
  1980: 971,230
  1990: 1,062,470
  2000: 1,098,201
  Percent change, 1990–2000: 3.4%

U.S. rank in 1990: 38th
U.S. rank in 2000: 47th

Area: 36 square miles (2000)
Elevation: ranges from 246 feet to 748 feet above sea level
Average Annual Temperature: 56.8° F
Average Annual Precipitation: 33.98 inches total; 92.3 inches of snow

Major Economic Sectors: Services, trade, manufacturing, government
Unemployment Rate: 4.5% (April 2005)
Per Capita Income: $15,588 (2000)
2004 ACCRA Average House Price: Not reported
2004 ACCRA Cost of Living Index: Not reported

2002 FBI Crime Index Total: 16,911

Major Colleges and Universities: University of Rochester; Rochester Institute of Technology

Daily Newspaper: *Democrat and Chronicle*

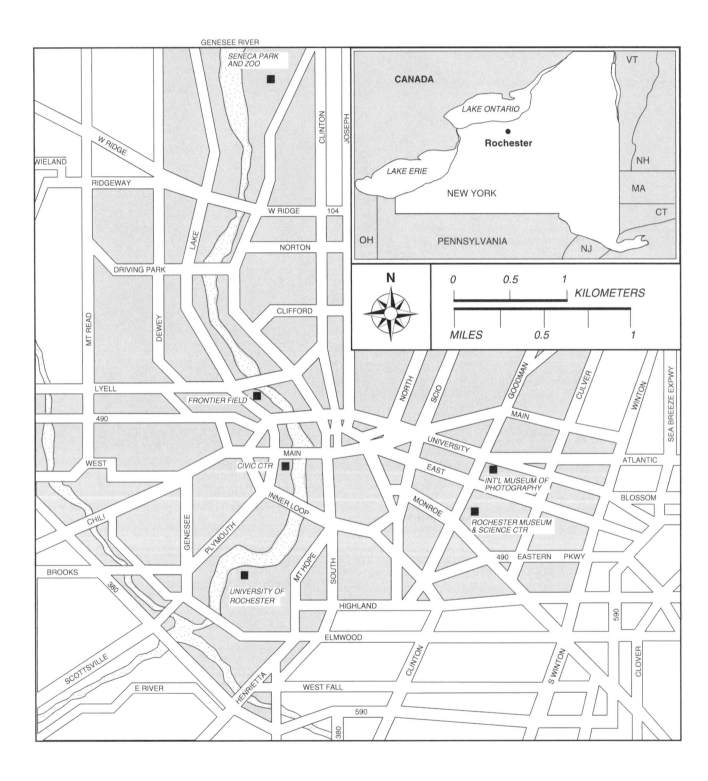

Introduction

Rochester, the third largest city in New York State, is the economic and cultural center of the Genesee River-Finger Lakes region and gateway to the fertile Lake Ontario Fruit Belt. Known as the Flower City because of its nurseries, parks, and gardens, Rochester is also renowned for its museums, schools, and many cultural amenities. The city is probably best known for George Eastman's Kodak camera; it is also a world leader in the high technology and telecommunication sectors.

Geography and Climate

Rochester is located at the mouth of the Genesee River, which bisects the city, at the approximate mid-point of the south shore of Lake Ontario. Lake Ontario, which remains unfrozen in winter, plays a major role in the city's weather. Its cooling effect in summer prevents the temperature from rising much above the mid-90s, and in winter it usually prevents temperatures from falling below − 15.0° F. Precipitation is fairly evenly distributed throughout the year.

Area: 36 square miles (2000)

Elevation: Slopes from a lakeshore elevation of 246 feet to 748 feet above sea level

Average Temperatures: January, 31.2° F; August, 79.1° F; annual average, 56.8° F

Average Annual Precipitation: 33.98 inches total; 92.3 inches of snow

History

Location Favorable for Flour Milling

The Five Nations of the Iroquois hunted, fished, and foraged for minerals in the Genesee River region until 1779, when, weakened by the destruction of their villages by Revolutionary War General John Sullivan, they were induced to sell to speculators a large tract of land known as the Phelps and Gorham Purchase. Part of this tract was the site of a flour mill acquired by Nathaniel Rochester of Maryland in 1803. More flour mills were built, powered by the Genesee River and its falls; by the time the Erie Canal reached the area in 1825, Rochester's concentration of flour mills caused the settlement to be dubbed Flour City. The pioneering horticul-

tural efforts of George Ellwanger and Patrick Barry, begun in the 1840s, brought the city international recognition; many beautiful parks and gardens were developed, and Rochester's nickname became Flower City.

Rochester has been home to a remarkable collection of Americans. In 1853 John Jacob Bausch and Henry Lomb opened a small optical shop there; today the company they started, Bausch & Lomb, is a world leader in optics and health care. In 1888 George Eastman introduced the camera he had developed in his mother's Rochester kitchen. Susan B. Anthony, a prominent suffragist, made Rochester her home for the last 40 years of her life. Frederick Douglass, escaped slave, abolitionist orator, and newspaper publisher (*The North Star*), lived in Rochester for 25 years until his home burned down in 1872.

Throughout the nineteenth century Rochester was a thriving commercial center. The men's clothing industry there was given a boost by the Civil War of 1861 to 1865 and by the subsequent demand for ready-made suits in the West; eventually this industry ranked second only to flour milling in importance. In 1866 the Vacuum Oil Company, which later became Mobil Oil, was founded in Rochester, and in 1906, the Haloid Company, now known as Xerox Corporation, began in a loft above a shoe factory.

City Responds to Twentieth-Century Challenges

While these new industries were developing, music and art were flourishing in Rochester, assisted greatly by the philanthropy of George Eastman, whose Eastman Kodak Company was expanding rapidly. But industrial growth was taking its toll on the Genesee River; by the early twentieth century this once beautiful resource had become little more than an open sewer lined with decaying industrial buildings.

The increasing attainability of the automobile in Rochester prompted a middle-class exodus to the suburbs. By the 1950s the city's population consisted largely of the poor and jobless. Rochester's reputation was tarnished by violent race riots in 1964. In response to those riots and the forces behind them, city leaders began major renovations of the downtown area. The long-neglected Genesee River was cleaned up. The expansion of Eastman Kodak, Bausch & Lomb, and Xerox Corporation protected upstate New York from the economic problems that beset many other industrial cities in the 1970s. In recent years many middle- and upper-income residents of the suburbs have been lured back to the city, which today thrives as a high-technology center and a cosmopolitan oasis surrounded by outstanding natural beauty.

Rochester is currently implementing a comprehensive renewal strategy called Rochester 2010: The Renaissance Plan. Affordable health care, attractive neighborhoods, progressive public schools, and an appealing downtown are just a few target of this ambitious campaign; the goal is to transform Rochester into a world-class cultural, social and economic center by the end of the decade.

Historical Information: Rochester Historical Society, 485 East Avenue, Rochester, NY 14607; telephone (585)271-2705. City historian Ruth Rosenberg Naparsteck, Office of the City Historian, 115 South Ave., Rochester, NY 14604-1896; telephone (585)428-8095; fax (585)428-8098

Population Profile

Metropolitan Area Residents
1980: 971,230
1990: 1,062,470
2000: 1,098,201
Percent change, 1990–2000: 3.4%
U.S. rank in 1990: 38th
U.S. rank in 2000: 47th

City Residents
1980: 241,741
1990: 230,356
2000: 219,773
2003 estimate: 215,093
Percent change, 1990–2000: −4.8%
U.S. rank in 1980: 57th
U.S. rank in 1990: 66th
U.S. rank in 2000: 91st

Density: 6,104.8 people per square mile (2000)

Racial and ethnic characteristics (2000)
White: 106,161
Black or African American: 84,717
American Indian and Alaska Native: 1,033
Asian: 4,943
Native Hawaiian and Pacific Islander: 104
Hispanic or Latino (may be of any race): 28,032
Other: 14,452

Percent of residents born in state: 68.8% (2000)

Age characteristics (2000)
Population under 5 years old: 17,227
Population 5 to 9 years old: 18,733
Population 10 to 14 years old: 17,233
Population 15 to 19 years old: 15,699
Population 20 to 24 years old: 18,432
Population 25 to 34 years old: 37,652
Population 35 to 44 years old: 33,057
Population 45 to 54 years old: 25,014

Population 55 to 59 years old: 8,395
Population 60 to 64 years old: 6,354
Population 65 to 74 years old: 9,992
Population 75 to 84 years old: 8,179
Population 85 years and older: 3,806
Median age: 30.8 years

Births (2002, Monroe County)
Total number: 8,883

Deaths (2002, Monroe County)
Total number: 6,273 (of which, 61 were infants under the age of 1 year)

Money income (1999)
Per capita income: $15,588
Median household income: $27,123
Total households: 89,093

Number of households with income of . . .
less than $10,000: 17,228
$10,000 to $14,999: 8,611
$15,000 to $24,999: 15,717
$25,000 to $34,999: 12,650
$35,000 to $49,999: 13,372
$50,000 to $74,999: 12,170
$75,000 to $99,999: 5,202
$100,000 to $149,999: 2,839
$150,000 to $199,999: 607
$200,000 or more: 697

Percent of families below poverty level: 23.4% (56.6% of which were female householder families with related children under 5 years)

2002 FBI Crime Index Total: 16,911

Municipal Government

Rochester, the seat of Monroe County, operates under a mayor-council form of government. The mayor and five council members are elected by the citizens at large, and four council members are elected by district.

Head Official: Mayor William A. Johnson, Jr. (since 1994; current term expires 2005)

Total Number of City Employees: 3,003 (full time, 2004-2005)

City Information: City of Rochester, City Hall, 30 Church Street, Rochester, NY 14614; telephone (585)428-5990

Economy

Major Industries and Commercial Activity

Rochester is one of the leading manufacturing centers in the United States, dominated by Eastman Kodak, Bausch & Lomb, Inc., Delphi Automotive Systems and Xerox Corporation. The area is home to more than 1,500 small and medium-sized manufacturing companies, most of which are involved in high technology sectors such as computer and electronic products, machinery and chemicals. In 2004, companies in Greater Rochester exported more than $14 billion worth of products and services, exceeding 40 states. Rochester also benefits from the Monroe County Foreign Trade Zone, which offers tax advantages for international trade.

Items and goods produced: photographic and optical products, telecommunication system software, pharmaceuticals, automotive equipment, fibres and plastics

Incentive Programs—New and Existing Companies

A variety of incentives is available from city and county government organizations. The County of Monroe Industrial Development Agency (COMIDA) offers funding for industrial and non-industrial projects through tax-exempt bonds and sale/leaseback transactions; it also administers the JobsPlus tax abatement program for employers who increase full-time employee base by 10 percent or more. Over the last two decades COMIDA has financed more than 500 projects totaling $2 billion in investment and thousands of new jobs. The Monroe County Industrial Development Corporation (MCIDC) provides long-term financing for the purchase of land or equipment through the SBA 504 Program, interest rate subsidies on loans or capital leases, equipment purchase rebates, and gap financing. The Monroe Fund is a private venture capital fund investing in startup and turnaround businesses. Monroe County Economic Development provides customized advice, connecting businesses with the most advantageous programs or incentives.

Local programs—The City of Rochester offers a range of incentives for new and growing businesses. Loans from $25,000 to $500,000 are available to manufacturing or industrial businesses seeking to expand; approved projects must create or retain jobs and promote investment in the city. Similar loans are available to companies in the service, wholesale or retail sectors. The city offers 90/10 matching grants for exterior improvements in distressed commercial districts and will match up to $5,000 in advertising funds for businesses in low- or moderate-income areas. The City of Rochester administers the U.S. Department of Housing and Urban Development Section 108 Loan Program, which provides fixed asset and working capital financing to eligible businesses. The city also offers job growth credits which can be used to reduce payments on city loans.

State programs—The New York State Empire Zone Program offers incentives for developing new businesses, expanding existing operations or increasing human resources; incentives include wage tax credits, sales tax refunds, utility discounts, investment tax credits, and property tax abatements. New York also offers tax credits to businesses that create jobs and invest in production property or equipment. A nine percent corporate tax credit is available to businesses investing in research and development, and such companies may also be eligible for three-year job creation credits. Sales tax exemptions may be granted on equipment purchases, research and development property, and fuels or utilities. Empire State Development administers the Export Marketing Assistance Service, which helps businesses find distributors overseas, and the Global Export Market Service, which provides up to $25,000 of export marketing consultant services for small and medium sized businesses. New York State's Division of Minority- and Women-owned Business Development provides access to capital, procurement assistance, and loans from $20,000 to $500,000.

Job training programs—New York State offers funding for up to 50 percent of any employee training project and its Workforce Development Liaison helps coordinate employers and job seekers. RochesterWorks! provides on-the-job training incentives for companies who hire or retrain employees lacking in experience or credentials. The Rochester Corporate Training Initiative provides access to internal training programs of successful local companies as well as funding opportunities. Specialized job training programs are also available through Monroe Community College and various other agencies throughout the area.

Development Projects

The $230 million Renaissance Square project is underway on East Main Street; plans call for a performing arts center, underground bus terminal, and Monroe Community College satellite to revitalize the downtown area. The Strong Museum has begun a $33 million expansion that will double its current size, making it the second-largest children's museum in the nation. The museum's new "whimsical" design is a nod to its mission of learning through play. Eastman Theatre has completed a $5 million renovation to improve acoustics, lighting and rigging and enlarge the orchestra pit. A $52 million renovation of Xerox Tower is scheduled for completion in 2005. The Hyatt Regency Rochester Hotel will complete a $4 million renovation in 2006. Bausch & Lomb has announced a $35 million expansion of its research and development center, creating 200 new jobs.

Economic Development Information: Monroe County Department of Planning and Development, Economic Development Division, 50 West Main Street, Suite 8100, Rochester NY 14614; telephone (585)428-2970. County of Monroe Industrial Development Agency, 50 West Main Street, Suite 8100, Rochester NY 14614; telephone (585)428-5260

Commercial Shipping

Greater Rochester International Airport is served by a number of air cargo companies. Rail freight service is available from CSX, Norfolk Southern and Canadian Pacific railways. Rochester boasts an extensive network of highways. Shipping of oversize and bulk commodities can be arranged through the Lake Ontario New York State Barge Canal system.

Labor Force and Employment Outlook

According to the *Manpower Employment Outlook,* Greater Rochester has the third-highest job growth rate in the nation. More than half of the region's employers expect to increase staffing in the immediate future. Telecommunications is one of the fastest growing sectors, with over 85 companies in Rochester's "Telecom Valley." Manufacturing continues to play a major role in the local economy, while Rochester's high-tech output ranks 20th out of 319 metropolitan areas in the United States.

The following is a summary of data regarding the Rochester metropolitan area labor force, 2004 annual averages.

Size of nonagricultural labor force: 508,300

Number of workers employed in . . .
   construction and mining: 17,900
   manufacturing: 78,600
   trade, transportation and utilities: 84,500
   information: 12,300
   financial activities: 21,800
   professional and business services: 56,700
   educational and health services: 98,600
   leisure and hospitality: 38,700
   other services: 18,800
   government: 79,800

Average hourly earnings of production workers employed in manufacturing: $17.29 (statewide, 2004)

Unemployment rate: 4.5% (April 2005)

Largest employers	Number of employees
Eastman Kodak Company	23,900
University of Rochester	12,690
Xerox Corporation	12,150
ViaHealth	7,052
Wegmans Food Markets	5,469
Excellus Inc.	3,100
Unity Health System	3,073
Delphi Automotive Systems Corp.	3,000
Valeo S.A.	2,601
Rochester Institute of Technology	2,555

Cost of Living

Rochester prides itself on offering a high quality of life, from affordability of homes to recreational opportunities. In 2003, Rochester was one of three cities in the nation to receive top honors in the City Livability Awards Program, which recognizes mayors for their efforts to improve quality of life.

The following is a summary of data regarding several key cost of living factors in the Rochester area.

2004 ACCRA Average House Price: Not reported

2004 ACCRA Cost of Living Index: Not reported

State income tax rate: 4–6.85%

State sales tax rate: 4%

Local income tax rate: None

Local sales tax rate: 4%

Property tax rate: $37.11 per $1,000 of assessed value

Education and Research

Elementary and Secondary Schools

Rochester City School District has begun reorganizing its elementary, middle and high schools into a two-tiered system comprised of elementary (grades pre-K to 6) and secondary (grades 7-12) facilities. The redesign is expected to provide a more stable learning environment for students, alleviate overcrowding, and help develop a strong base for increased academic achievement.

Despite challenges such as high poverty rates and student mobility, Rochester's public school system was ranked among the ten best in the U.S. by *Places Rated Almanac.* Fourteen Rochester elementary schools were named among the state's most improved in language arts or math in 2005; and *Newsweek* listed Wilson Magnet High School 49th among the nation's top 100 high schools based on advanced curriculum.

The following is a summary of data regarding the Rochester public schools as of the 2003–2004 school year.

Total enrollment: 35,659

Number of facilities
  elementary schools: 39
  secondary schools: 16

Student/teacher ratio: 11:1

Teacher salaries
  average: $41,825

Funding per pupil: $12,552

The Rochester City School District also supports approximately 200 private, parochial and charter schools, urban-suburban sites, and home-based schools.

Public Schools Information: Rochester City School District, 131 West Broad Street, Rochester, NY 14614; telephone (585)262-8100

Colleges and Universities

Rochester's best-known institution of higher education is the University of Rochester, which includes the renowned Eastman School of Music, the School of Medicine and Dentistry, the School of Nursing, and the William E. Simon Graduate School of Business Administration, considered one of the best in the country.

Rochester Institute of Technology offers graduate and undergraduate degrees, certificates and diplomas through its eight colleges. The school is internationally known for its College of Imaging Arts and Sciences, School for American Crafts, and National Technical Institute for the Deaf.

Monroe Community College offers 83 professional degree and certificate programs; students may also transfer to a four-year institution. Other post-secondary facilities in the city include Rochester Business Institute, St. John Fisher College, Nazareth College of Rochester, and Roberts Wesleyan College.

Libraries and Research Centers

The Rochester Public Library System is made up of the Central Library and ten branch libraries, with a yearly circulation of nearly 1.7 million titles. The Central Library, housed in the Bausch and Lomb Public Library Building and the Rundel Memorial Library Building, includes a reading garden, children's center, and meeting space; special collections are maintained on such topics as art, business, education, history, local history, science and technology. The Toy Resource Center at the Lincoln Branch offers educational toys for infants, young children, and children with special needs. Rochester Public Library is part of the Monroe County Library System.

Among the dozens of special libraries in Rochester are the collections of the Rochester Institute of Technology on the

topics of chemistry, graphic arts, deafness, and printing technology, and Eastman Kodak's collection on various topics, including business, photography, chemistry, engineering, health and environment, and computer science. More than a dozen libraries are operated by the University of Rochester, focusing on such topics as Asian history and literature, chemistry, art history, music, engineering, geology, laser energetics, management, microcomputers, astronomy, and medicine. The University maintains an extensive rare book collection dating from the seventh century. The Sibley Musical Library at the University of Rochester is one of very few libraries in the country devoted exclusively to music.

The International Museum of Photography at George Eastman House contains a large research library of more than 43,000 volumes on photography and cinematography and special collection of rare books and images. Visual Studies Workshop maintains a research library on the topic of contemporary imaging. The Rochester Civic Garden Center has a 4,000-volume library dedicated to horticulture.

The concentration of scientists and technicians engaged in research in Rochester is said to place the region on a par with California's Silicon Valley. A major center for this activity is the University of Rochester, which has committed funding for the construction of new biotechnology research facilities. Among the more than two dozen other research facilities at the University are the Laboratory for Laser Energetics, the Rochester Theory Center for Optical Science and Engineering, and the Wireless Communication and Networking Group.

More than a dozen research centers at the Rochester Institute of Technology conduct studies in such areas as user-controlled video applications, imaging sciences, microelectronic and computer engineering applications, printing, and photographic preservation.

Public Library Information: Rochester Public Library, 115 South Avenue, Rochester, NY 14604; telephone (585)428-7300

Health Care

Rochester's health system remains a model for success, with an uninsured population well below state and national rates and better-than-average access to medical and dental care. Cooperation between large employers and health care providers kept costs low through the 1990s; although this structure is less evident today, statistics indicate Rochester citizens have a higher satisfaction level with their health system than most of the nation.

Strong Health is the largest health care provider in Rochester, with a network of hospitals, outpatient services and community clinics across upstate New York. The 750-bed Strong Memorial Hospital is its flagship facility, consistently ranking among the nation's top hospitals in an annual survey by *U.S. News and World Report.* Strong Memorial offers highly specialized services, such as a heart transplant unit, and a 24-hour emergency department. Other facilities include Highland Hospital, known for its women's services, joint center, and gastric bypass program; and Golisano Children's Hospital, one of the nation's leading pediatric hospitals. Strong Health is affiliated with the University of Rochester School of Medicine and Dentistry and the School of Nursing.

Other health care providers in the area include Rochester General Hospital, a 526-bed acute care teaching hospital; Park Ridge Hospital, a 521-bed non-profit hospital recognized for its quality Intensive Care Unit; and Monroe Community Hospital, a 566-bed long-term care facility.

Health Care Information: Monroe County Medical Society, 1441 East Avenue, Rochester, NY 14610; telephone (585)473-7573

Recreation

Sightseeing

The city of Rochester is especially noteworthy for its architecture—both new and historic—and for its scenic parks. Rochester's City Hall, a national landmark, is a Romanesque structure featuring an elaborate three-story atrium where concerts and other entertainments are often staged. The East Avenue Preservation District, where the city's manufacturers and businessmen built their homes after the Civil War, offers a mix of architectural styles popular in the period, the most common being American Tudor. It was in this district that George Eastman built his 49-room Georgian mansion in 1905, designed from photographs he had taken of other homes; it is now part of the International Museum of Photography & Film. The Woodside Mansion, built in the Greek Revival style in 1839, is now the headquarters of the Rochester Historical Society. The society's collection includes nineteenth-century paintings, costumes, furnishings, and toys.

On the west side of the city, the Corn Hill district is a neighborhood of restored nineteenth-century homes, including Campbell-Whittlesey House, a fine example of the Greek Revival style. Nearby is Susan B. Anthony House, the site of her arrest in 1872 for attempting to cast her vote. Now a National Historic Landmark, it contains original furnishings, photos, and documents relating to her work. Anthony and Frederick Douglass are buried in Mount Hope Cemetery, one of the oldest Victorian cemeteries in the country. Mount Hope is noted for its funereal art, pastoral landscaping, and cobblestone pathways; guided tours are offered on Sunday afternoons during the summer.

Many visitors to Rochester make it a point to visit the area's parks, some of which were designed by noted landscape architect Frederick Law Olmsted. Highland Park and Maplewood Park are famous for their stunning floral displays. Ellwanger Garden, the former private garden of famed horticulturalist George Ellwanger, is known as a ''living museum.'' Cobbs Hill Park offers a view of Lake Ontario and the Finger Lakes region. The 96-foot waterfall of the Genesee River is known as High Falls and is in an urban cultural park area and part of the High Falls Entertainment District. The River of Light laser, light, and sound show at High Falls runs Thursday, Friday and Saturday nights, mid-May through September. Boat tours and bike trails along the Erie Canal allow quiet thoughts in a peaceful setting.

Sightseeing Information: Greater Rochester Visitors Association, 45 East Avenue, Suite 400, Rochester, NY 14604-2294; toll-free (800)677-7282

Arts and Culture

Rochester is a music-oriented city. The Eastman School of Music, one of the country's most prestigious, presents symphonic, wind, chorale, jazz, chamber, and opera concerts year-round at the Eastman Theatre. Eastman Theatre is also home to the acclaimed Rochester Philharmonic Orchestra, founded by George Eastman in 1922. The orchestra is heavily involved in community outreach and education programs; it also offers a wide variety of performances ranging from children's concerts to Broadway shows during its extensive season. The Rochester Opera Factory is a volunteer, not-for-profit opera chorus featuring local, professional-quality musicians. Hochstein School of Music and Dance offers regular recitals and performances. Area parks offer free concerts during the summer.

Theater offerings range from small groups to Rochester's major professional theater, Geva, which presents eight productions annually, including *A Christmas Carol,* in a renovated historic building. Shipping Dock Theatre presents award-winning plays at a new location in the Visual Arts Workshop. Downstairs Cabaret Theatre is a not-for-profit troupe with a focus on non-traditional material.

The star of the Rochester dance scene is the Tony Award-winning Garth Fagan Dance Troupe, one of the most famous modern dance companies in the world. Rochester City Ballet performs classic favorites with the Rochester Philharmonic Orchestra.

The George Eastman House, built in 1905, is home to the International Museum of Photography.

Rochester offers a variety of museums and historical sites. The International Museum of Photography & Film at George Eastman House contains a massive collection of prints, negatives, films, movie stills, and cameras. The Strong Museum, gift of Margaret Woodbury Strong, an avid collector who sometimes acquired items by the freight-car load, features more than 500,000 items documenting late nineteenth- and early twentieth-century middle-class lifestyles. The collection also includes the National Toy Hall of Fame. The natural and cultural history of Upstate New York is depicted through exhibits at the Rochester Museum & Science Center; the center's Strasenburgh Planetarium offers daily and nightly shows combining theater and astronomy. Many smaller museums are located near the city, including the Stone-Tolan House in Brighton, a 1792 pioneer homestead, the Genesee Country Village and Museum in Mumford, an authentic nineteenth-century village, and the Victorian Doll Museum, located in North Chili.

Rochester's major art museum, the Memorial Art Gallery of the University of Rochester, explores art through the ages in a collection ranging from ancient relics to Rembrandts and Monets. Recent traveling exhibitions included works by Maxfield Parrish and Edgar Degas.

Festivals and Holidays

Rochester's famous Lilac Festival takes place each May in Highland Park. In June, the nine-day Rochester International Jazz Festival draws thousands of fans. Maplewood Rose Festival is also held each June in historic Maplewood Rose Garden. The Corn Hill Arts Festival brings more than a quarter million people to the city in July; this two-day event features the country's finest artists and craftspeople, outdoor music and acrobatics, and food from around the world. Rochester MusicFest takes place in July at Genesee Valley Park. August brings the Park Avenue Summer Art Fest, one of the city's most popular summer events; and the Fiddler's Fair, featuring continuous fiddling and dancing on four stages. Rochester's longest-running event, the Memorial Art Gallery Clothesline Festival, has taken place each September since 1957.

Sports for the Spectator

Rochester loves baseball—it is said that the first curve ball in history was launched there by Red Wings' pitcher Richard Willis. Today this team, an International League affiliate of the Minnesota Twins and the first municipally-owned baseball team in the country, entertains fans at Frontier Field from April to September. Frontier Field is also home to the Raging Rhinos minor league soccer team from May through August. From January to March the Blue Cross Arena is home to the Knighthawks, Rochester's indoor lacrosse team. The Rochester Rattlers play major league outdoor lacrosse at Bishop Kearney Field. The Rochester Americans, an Ameri-

can Hockey League affiliate of the Buffalo Sabres, call the Blue Cross Arena home. Bowling fans are treated to an annual Lilac City Bowling Tournament, and the men's Professional Bowlers Tournament and women's pro circuit make annual stops in the city. Nearby racetracks offer horse and auto racing as well as off-track betting.

Sports for the Participant

Recreational opportunities abound for water sports enthusiasts in the Rochester-Finger Lakes region. The Genesee River is a popular canoeing site; canoeing and rowing are also possible at several other locations, including the Erie Canal. For sailors, Lake Ontario is favored for large craft; many yacht clubs, launches, and lakeside parks are available for smaller craft. Anglers may take advantage of Lake Ontario and local bays, ponds, and lakes, as well as the Genesee River, which is stocked with salmon. Rochester is the scene of the Empire State-Lake Ontario Trout and Salmon Derbies, held in fall and spring; this competition awards more than $80,000 in cash and prizes annually.

Golf enthusiasts will find over 50 golf courses in the area; Rochester also maintains 66 baseball fields, 47 tennis courts, 7 soccer pitches and an extensive network of walking, jogging and bicycling paths. Cold weather brings opportunities for ice skating, cross-country and downhill skiing, and snowboarding.

Shopping and Dining

Shoppers may choose from a wide variety of experiences in the Rochester area. Several major malls, factory outlets, and discount designer stores are located throughout the region. Off East Main and North Union streets is Rochester's open-air Public Market. The parallel ''Avenues''—Park and Monroe—offer an eclectic mix of fashionable boutiques, specialty shops, and restaurants. Of unique interest is Village Gate Square, a collection of antique, leather, and jewelry shops and art galleries housed in a historic printing factory. Northfield Common and Schoen Place offer boutiques, boating, and dining along the Erie Canal in the village of Pittsford.

Rochester diners may choose from an assortment of cuisines ranging from American to Cajun, Thai, Italian, Greek, Chinese, French, and Indian. Settings vary from modern to historic; an 1848 gristmill, an 1842 railroad station, an 1818 Erie Canal tavern, and a gas station are among the structures that Rochester restaurateurs have converted to dining establishments.

Visitor Information: Greater Rochester Visitors Association, 45 East Avenue, Suite 400, Rochester, NY 14604-2294; toll-free (800)677-7282. Arts & Cultural Council for Greater Rochester, 277 North Goodman St., Rochester, NY 14607; telephone (585)473-4000

Convention Facilities

Riverside Convention Center is an award-winning facility featuring 100,000 square feet of flexible meeting and exhibit space for up to 5,000 people. Located downtown, it is connected by an enclosed skywalk to the Four Points by Sheraton Hotel (466 rooms and 20,000 square feet of meeting space), the Hyatt Regency Rochester (336 rooms and 13,500 square feet of meeting space), enclosed parking and a local retail area. The Clarion Riverside Hotel offers 30,000 square feet of meeting space and 465 rooms. The Dome Center is minutes from Rochester and offers nearly 60,000 square feet of meeting space in three buildings; a grandstand is available for outdoor events. The Blue Cross Arena can seat 13,500 people and accommodate groups of various sizes. More than a dozen major hotels in the area provide more than 6,000 rooms.

Convention Information: Greater Rochester Visitors Association, 45 East Avenue, Suite 400, Rochester, NY 14604; telephone (585)546-3070

Transportation

Approaching the City

The Greater Rochester International Airport, located ten minutes from downtown, is served by several major carriers and feeder lines. High-speed ferry travel to Toronto is available daily for passengers and cars. Rail service is provided by Amtrak and Conrail. NY State Trailways and Greyhound bus terminals are located downtown. A convenient network of highways, inner- and outer-loop arterial expressways, and the New York State Thruway facilitate auto travel. From Interstate 490 at the Clinton Avenue and Plymouth Avenue exits, a color-coded sign system directs visitors to five major downtown areas of interest.

Traveling in the City

Walking tours of Rochester are a popular way to explore the city. ARTWalk is a "permanent urban art trail" connecting arts centers and public spaces downtown; the outdoor space itself features benches, sidewalk imprints and light pole art by local artists. The Landmark Society offers six self-guided walking tours in downtown Rochester and three neighborhood walking tours. The Rochester-Genesee Regional Transportation Authority operates a bus service. Rochester's free blue and yellow EZ Rider shuttle buses circle the downtown area every evening except Sunday. Taxi and limousine service is also available.

Communications

Newspapers and Magazines

Gannett Rochester Newspapers publishes the city's daily newspaper, the morning *Democrat and Chronicle. City Newspaper* is a weekly alternative journal. Other locally published newspapers include *Golden Times*, a publication aimed at mature citizens, *The Daily Record*, for business and legal professionals, as well as *Greater Rochester Advertiser, The Greece Post,* and several religious newspapers. About a dozen magazines are published in Rochester on topics ranging from antiques to business.

Television and Radio

Five television stations—four network affiliates, and one public—serve Rochester. Time Warner Communications provides cable service. The city is served by five AM and eight FM radio stations. Two college stations broadcast alternative music. Rochester Radio Reading Service on WXXI sponsors a program of readings for the sight-impaired from local and national newspapers and magazines.

Media Information: Democrat and Chronicle, 55 Exchange Blvd., Rochester, NY 14614; telephone (585)232-7100. *City Newspaper*, 250 North Goodman St., Rochester, NY 14607; telephone (585)244-3329

Rochester Online

Arts & Cultural Council for Greater Rochester. Available www.artsrochester.org

City of Rochester. Available www.ci.rochester.ny.us

Greater Rochester Visitors Association. Available www.visitrochester.com

Monroe County Industrial Development Agency. Available www.growmonroe.org

Monroe County Planning & Economic Development. Available www.monroecounty.gov

Rochester Business Alliance. Available www.rochesterbusinessalliance.com

Rochester City School District. Available www.rcsdk12.org

Rochester *Democrat and Chronicle*. Available www.democrat andchronicle.com

Rochester Public Library. Available www.rochester.lib.ny.us

Selected Bibliography

DuBois, Eugene E. *The City of Frederick Douglass: Rochester's African-American People and Places* (Landmark Society of Western New York, 1994)

Johnson, Paul E. *A Shopkeeper's Millennium: Society and Revivals in Rochester, New York, 1815-1837* (New York: Hill & Wang, 1990)

Lanni, Clement Garibaldi, *George W. Aldridge, Big Boss, Small City* (Rochester, N.Y., Rochester Alliance Press, 1939)

Syracuse

The City in Brief

Founded: 1805 (chartered, 1848)

Head Official: Mayor Matthew J. Driscoll (D) (since 2001)

City Population
1980: 170,105
1990: 163,860
2000: 147,306
2003 estimate: 144,001
Percent change, 1990–2000: −10.1%
U.S. rank in 1980: 86th
U.S. rank in 1990: 106th
U.S. rank in 2000: 160th

Metropolitan Area Population
1980: 722,865
1990: 742,237
2000: 732,117

Percent change, 1990–2000: −1.4%
U.S. rank in 1980: 53rd
U.S. rank in 1990: 57th
U.S. rank in 2000: 60th

Area: 25 square miles (2000)
Elevation: 414 feet above sea level
Average Annual Temperature: 47.4° F
Average Annual Precipitation: 36 inches total; 114 inches snowfall

Major Economic Sectors: Services, trade, government, manufacturing
Unemployment Rate: 4.6% (April 2005)
Per Capita Income: $15,168 (1999)

2002 FBI Crime Index Total: 9,791

Major Colleges and Universities: Syracuse University; LeMoyne College

Daily Newspaper: *The Post Standard*

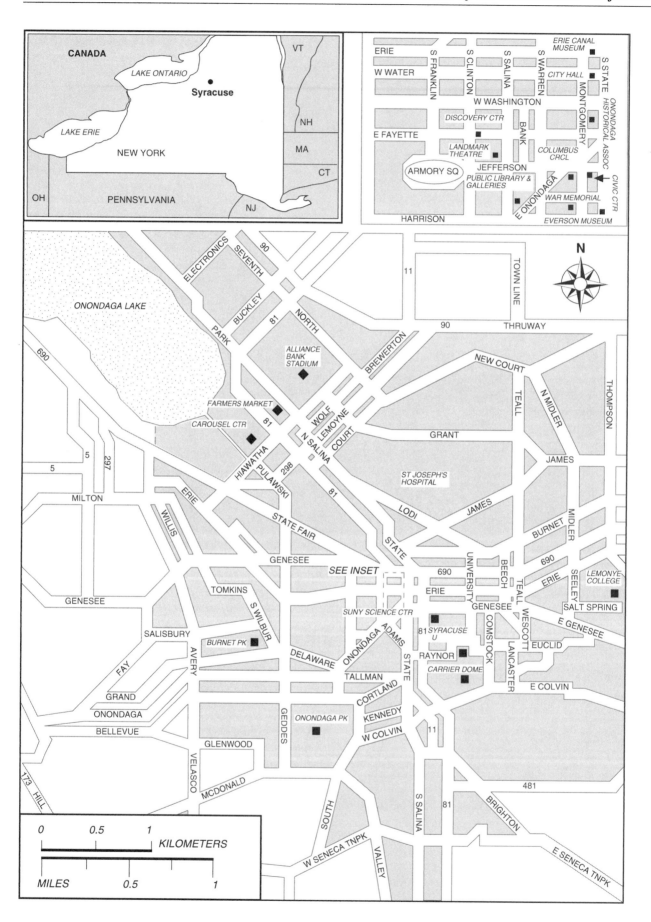

CANADA

LAKE ONTARIO

Syracuse

VT

NH

MA

CT

LAKE ERIE

NEW YORK

OH

PENNSYLVANIA

NJ

ERIE
W WATER
S FRANKLIN
S CLINTON
S SALINA
S WARREN
ERIE CANAL MUSEUM
CITY HALL
S STATE
ONONDAGA HISTORICAL ASSOC
W WASHINGTON
MONTGOMERY
DISCOVERY CTR
E FAYETTE
BANK
COLUMBUS CRCL
LANDMARK THEATRE
CIVIC CTR
ARMORY SQ
JEFFERSON
PUBLIC LIBRARY & GALLERIES
E ONONDAGA
WAR MEMORIAL
HARRISON
EVERSON MUSEUM

ELECTRONICS
SEVENTH
90
11
TOWN LINE
N
PARK
BUCKLEY
81
NORTH
90
THRUWAY
ONONDAGA LAKE
ALLIANCE BANK STADIUM
BREWERTON
NEW COURT
TEALL
N MIDLER
THOMPSON
690
FARMERS MARKET
81
WOLF
LEMOYNE
COURT
GRANT
JAMES
CAROUSEL CTR
HIAWATHA
N SALINA
5
PULAWSKI
298
81
ST JOSEPH'S HOSPITAL
JAMES
297
5
MILTON
ERIE
STATE FAIR
LODI
STATE
JAMES
BURNET
MIDLER
WILLIS
GENESEE
UNIVERSITY
BEECH
TEALL
690
ERIE
SEELEY
LEMONYE COLLEGE
GENESEE
SEE INSET
690
ERIE
GENESEE
SALT SPRING
TOMKINS
SUNY SCIENCE CTR
ONONDAGA
ADAMS
81
SYRACUSE U
COMSTOCK
WESCOTT
E GENESEE
GENESEE
S WILBUR
SALISBURY
DELAWARE
STATE
RAYNOR
LANCASTER
EUCLID
BURNET PK
FAY
TALLMAN
CARRIER DOME
E COLVIN
GRAND
CORTLAND
GEDDES
ONONDAGA PK
KENNEDY
ONONDAGA
AVERY
W COLVIN
11
BELLEVUE
GLENWOOD
VELASCO
MCDONALD
481
173
HILL
SOUTH
S SALINA
81
BRIGHTON
0   0.5   1
KILOMETERS
W SENECA TNPK
VALLEY
E SENECA TNPK
MILES   0.5   1

Introduction

Syracuse, once the capital of the powerful Iroquois Confederacy under Chief Hiawatha, is located in the heart of New York State. The city's strategic central location and well developed transportation network have earned it the nickname "Crossroads of New York State." An important industrial and commercial hub, Syracuse also boasts an excellent education network and cultural and recreational opportunities to rival any major city. Massive urban renewal programs begun in the 1960s have transformed the downtown area into a bustling commercial and residential center. Syracuse lies near Onondaga Lake in the famed Finger Lakes region; the Iroquois believed that the lakes were formed when the Great Spirit placed his hand on some of the most beautiful land ever created.

Geography and Climate

Syracuse is located in the center of New York State on the south shore of Lake Ontario in a region of rolling hills, flat plains, lakes, and streams. The salt springs discovered there when Native Americans first settled the area have since disappeared. The city itself lies on a rise at the south end of Onondaga Lake. During the nineteenth century, Syracuse was important for its location as a port at the junction of the Oswego and Erie canals. Syracuse enjoys a four-season climate with marked seasonal changes. Cold air masses from the Great Lakes make for cold, snowy winters. During the summer and parts of spring and autumn, temperatures rise rapidly in the daytime and fall rapidly after sunset, so the nights are relatively cool. Excessively warm spells are rare and precipitation is well distributed throughout the year.

Area: 25 square miles (2000)

Elevation: 414 feet above sea level

Average Temperatures: January, 24° F; July, 71° F; annual average, 47.4° F

Average Annual Precipitation: 36 inches total; 114 inches snowfall

History

Location Favorable for Saltworks, Transportation

In 1570, attracted in part by the naturally occurring brine springs on Lake Onondaga, Chief Hiawatha chose the village of the Onondaga Nation as the capital of the Iroquois Confederacy. In 1658 the French built Fort Sainte Marie de Gannentaha on the lake shore but abandoned it two years later because of Native American hostility. Pioneers who arrived in the late 1700s established saltworks, starting an industry that thrived for nearly 100 years; for many years most of the salt used in the country came from this area. At the same time, Thomas Wiard began making wooden plows, and the region began to prosper. The opening of the Erie Canal in 1819 and the arrival of the railroad in the late 1830s brought new industries, further spurring economic growth. Over the years the community went by a succession of names; when it was incorporated as a village in 1825, the name Syracuse was chosen after an ancient Sicilian town that also lay near salt springs.

In 1851 Syracuse was the scene of what came to be known as the Jerry Rescue when Jerry, a slave who had escaped 30 years earlier, was reclaimed by his former master. He was freed from jail by a band of abolitionists, who smuggled him into Canada. When Charles Dickens visited Syracuse in 1869 he described it as "a most wonderful out-of-the-world place, which looks as if it had begun to be built yesterday, and were going to be imperfectly knocked together with a nail or two the day after tomorrow."

City Responds to Twentieth-Century Challenges

By the early 1900s the salt brine springs of Onondaga Lake were depleted and salt production in the city once known as "Salt City" declined. Talented inventors emerged, helping build Syracuse's manufacturing legacy; their creations included the first air-cooled engine in the world, the first synthetic penicillin, the first loafer, and the Brannock Device for measuring feet. Post World War II, an influx of GIs to Syracuse University created a need for affordable housing and prompted a trend towards moving to the suburbs. The creation of the Interstate Highway System replaced the railroad as a primary means of transportation and accelerated suburban growth. Renewal programs begun in the 1960s have since revitalized the downtown area, which has become Central New York State's primary commercial center as well as the area's center for entertainment and cultural activities. Syracuse is well poised to meet the challenges of the twenty-first century; a diversified market structure protects the city as it moves from manufacturing towards a knowledge- and service-based economy.

Historical Information: Onondaga Historical Association, 321 Montgomery Street, Syracuse, NY 13202; telephone (315)428-1862

Population Profile

Metropolitan Area Residents

1980: 722,865

1990: 742,237
2000: 732,117
Percent change, 1990–2000: − 1.4%
U.S. rank in 1980: 53rd
U.S. rank in 1990: 57th
U.S. rank in 2000: 60th

City Residents
1980: 170,105
1990: 163,860
2000: 147,306
2003 estimate: 144,001
Percent change, 1990–2000: − 10.1%
U.S. rank in 1980: 86th
U.S. rank in 1990: 106th
U.S. rank in 2000: 160th

Density: 5,892.2 people per square mile (2000)

Racial and ethnic characteristics (2000)
  White: 94,663
  Black or African American: 37,336
  American Indian and Alaska Native: 1,670
  Asian: 4,961
  Native Hawaiian and Pacific Islander: 72
  Hispanic or Latino (may be of any race): 7,768
  Other: 3,284

Percent of residents born in state: 71.6% (2000)

Age characteristics (2000)
  Population under 5 years old: 10,209
  Population 5 to 9 years old: 10,929
  Population 10 to 14 years old: 10,129
  Population 15 to 19 years old: 13,356
  Population 20 to 24 years old: 16,874
  Population 25 to 34 years old: 21,349
  Population 35 to 44 years old: 19,795
  Population 45 to 54 years old: 16,134
  Population 55 to 59 years old: 5,358
  Population 60 to 64 years old: 4,225
  Population 65 to 74 years old: 8,507
  Population 75 to 84 years old: 7,527
  Population 85 years and older: 2,914
  Median age: 30.5 years

Births (2002, Onondaga County)
  Total number: 5,627

Deaths (2002, Onondaga County)
  Total number: 4,125 (of which, 51 were infants under the age of 1 year)

Money income (1999)
  Per capita income: $15,168
  Median household income: $25,000
  Total households: 59,568

Number of households with income of . . .
  less than $10,000: 12,718
  $10,000 to $14,999: 6,288
  $15,000 to $24,999: 10,778
  $25,000 to $34,999: 7,957
  $35,000 to $49,999: 8,351
  $50,000 to $74,999: 7,195
  $75,000 to $99,999: 3,315
  $100,000 to $149,999: 2,027
  $150,000 to $199,999: 400
  $200,000 or more: 539

Percent of families below poverty level: 21.7% (64.1% of which were female householder families with related children under 5 years)

2002 FBI Crime Index Total: 9,791

Municipal Government

Syracuse, the county seat of Onondaga County, is governed by a mayor elected for a four-year term, and an independent policy-making nine-member council, headed by a president. District councilors and councilors-at-large are elected for two-year and four-year terms respectively. The mayor has broad administrative powers, including the appointment of all city department heads.

Head Official: Mayor Matthew J. Driscoll (D) (since 2001; current term expires 2008)

Total Number of City Employees: 1,800 (2005)

City Information: Office of the Mayor, 203 City Hall, Syracuse, NY 13202-1473; telephone (315)448-8005; fax (315)448-8067

Economy

Major Industries and Commercial Activity

Syracuse is a major commercial, industrial, and transportation center for the Northeast. The economy is highly diversified; this enabled the city to weather a recession in 2001. While manufacturing remains significant to the local market, the service industry is experiencing record growth. Subsectors leading the trend include call centers, finance, education services and retail trade.

Syracuse has been recognized as an excellent place to work and live; its Cost of Doing Business Index is sixth-lowest in the nation at 87.7 (a score of 100 is average), and *Expansion Management* magazine listed Syracuse among the country's top 50 cities for business relocation and expansion. Recent studies indicate Syracuse is leading the state in job growth.

Items and goods produced: automotive components, air conditioning and heating equipment, medical instruments, pharmaceuticals, military electronics, specialty metals, telecommunication devices

Incentive Programs—New and Existing Companies

A range of state, county and municipal programs are available to new and expanding businesses in the Syracuse area.

Local programs—The City of Syracuse offers tax exemptions and permanent low-cost financing, loans up to $10,000 for high-risk startups and $50,000 for specific projects, and regulatory or technical assistance. The Greater Syracuse Chamber of Commerce provides a variety of services from business startup advice to government lobbying. The Chamber also manages the Greater Syracuse Business Development Corporation, a private, not-for-profit organization that provides financial assistance to new and expanding businesses. The Onondaga County Industrial Development Agency has invested more than $1 billion on 190 projects since 1970, creating or retaining nearly 30,000 jobs in the region. Its municipal counterpart, the Syracuse Industrial Development Agency, finances manufacturing, research, commercial, industrial or pollution control projects within city limits. The Urban Business Opportunity Center provides entrepreneurial training and loans up to $10,000 for women- and minority-owned small businesses in financial need. Syracuse Technology Garden is a newcomer to the field of economic development and acts as an incubator for high-tech startups. Successful applicants receive mentorship and networking, access to venture capital, and state-of-the-art office space. The Samuel W. Williams, Jr. Business Center has provided similar incubator services to small business since 1986; more than two dozen local companies call it home.

State programs—The State of New York offers financing for new or expanding businesses to acquire land or capital, improve infrastructure, increase exports, or enhance productivity. Various incentives include loans and grants, interest rate subsidies, and low cost utilities. New York State's Empire Zone program provides special assistance to companies relocating or expanding in specific areas; two of the state's Empire Zones are found in the Syracuse region. Successful applicants in an Empire Zone may pay no state sales taxes for 10 years and can also receive wage tax or investment tax credits. The Central New York Enterprise Development Fund supports small manufacturing and service companies by providing working capital and fixed asset loans up to $100,000; commercial loan guarantees for up to $160,000 are also available. The New York Job Develop-

ment Authority provides funding to local economic development agencies for re-lending.

Job training programs—New York's Empire State Development Corporation provides up to half the cost of a workforce training project, reimbursement for training programs that create or retain at least 300 jobs, and opportunities for on-the-job training in new skills and technologies. The Onondaga County Industrial Development Agency provides matching grants up to $12,500 to train production or first-line supervisory staff. CNY Works is a federally-funded organization that arranges educational programs for incumbent, underemployed and unemployed workers. Onondaga Community College works with local employers to develop specialized training programs to meet specific needs. Dozens of local universities, colleges, vocational and technical schools offer training in a variety of professional disciplines.

Development Projects

A groundbreaking ceremony was held in June 2005 for the Syracuse Center of Excellence in Environmental and Energy Systems headquarters, a $25.5 million project designed to create jobs and promote investment in the Central New York region. The 60,000-square-foot facility is expected to open in spring 2007. Syracuse University (SU) will renovate the former Dunk & Bright warehouse at Armory Square into a multi-use space; plans call for community art gallery, auditorium and classroom space. SU has also announced plans to build a three mile "Connective Corridor" linking the campus with downtown's entertainment, arts and cultural venues; $4.5 million in public and private funding has been committed. University Hospital is expected to complete a $35 million children's hospital in 2006. Crouse Hospital is in the planning stages for a new $30 million operating room suite. The $3.25 million Syracuse Technology Garden, a business incubator for high-tech startups, was completed in 2004. Syracuse Research Corp. is undergoing a $1.3 million, 16,000-square-foot expansion of headquarters in order to employ 65 new engineers. The Inner Harbor project, adapting the old barge canal terminal for recreational use, remains in the planning stages.

Economic Development Information: Greater Syracuse Chamber of Commerce, 572 Salina St., Syracuse, NY 13202-3320; telephone (315)470-1800; fax (315)471-8545

Commercial Shipping

Syracuse's strategic central location and well developed transportation network, including road, water, rail, and air services, make it a distribution hub for the Northeast. More than 50 percent of U.S. and Canadian manufacturing establishments are located within a 750-mile radius. Syracuse is located at the junction of two major interstate highways, east/west I-90 and north/south I-81. More than 150 trucking companies service the area, including the top 12 general freight carriers in the nation. CSX provides direct rail service to a number of Northeastern markets with more than 70 trains per week. Six major air freight companies operate out of Syracuse Hancock International Airport, as well as a variety of regional carriers. The Port of Oswego and the New York Barge Canal system provide water access to the Great Lakes, the St. Lawrence Seaway and the Hudson River. The Syracuse area is a foreign trade zone.

Labor Force and Employment Outlook

Greater Syracuse offers a pool of educated, productive and affordable employees. Although Syracuse's employment rate is growing faster than any other city in upstate New York, approximately 75,000 qualified workers have been identified as underemployed, representing a large selection of potential hires. Over the next few years Syracuse is expected to transition from a manufacturing center to a services and knowledge-based economy.

The following is a summary of data regarding the Syracuse metropolitan area labor force, 2004 annual averages.

Size of nonagricultural labor force: 317,900

Number of workers employed in . . .
   construction and mining: 12,300
   manufacturing: 33,100
   trade, transportation and utilities: 64,800
   information: 7,000
   financial activities: 17,300
   professional and business services: 33,800
   educational and health services: 53,400
   leisure and hospitality: 26,400
   other services: 12,600
   government: 56,800

Average hourly earnings of production workers employed in manufacturing: $17.29 (statewide, 2004)

Unemployment rate: 4.6% (April 2005)

Largest employers	Number of employees
SUNY Upstate Medical University	6,305
Syracuse University	4,640
Wegmans	3,775
New Process Gear Inc.	3,400
St. Joseph's Hospital Health Center	3,365
P & C Food Markets	2,500
Lockheed Martin	2,300
Crouse Hospital	2,200
Loretto	2,115
Niagara Mohawk A National Grid Co.	2,010

Cost of Living

Parenting Magazine lists Syracuse among the nation's top 10 small cities in which to raise a child, based on affordable housing, a strong economy, good schools, low crime, and a clean environment. The following is a summary of data regarding several key cost of living factors in the Syracuse area.

2004 (3rd Quarter) ACCRA Average House Price: $230,914

2004 (3rd Quarter) ACCRA Cost of Living Index: 96.3 (U.S. average = 100.0)

State income tax rate: 4%–6.85%

State sales tax rate: 4%

Local income tax rate: None

Local sales tax rate: 4%

Property tax rate: $34.836 per $1,000 of assessment

Economic Information: New York State Department of Labor, 677 S. Salina Street, Syracuse, NY 13202; telephone (315)479-3390

Education and Research

Elementary and Secondary Schools

The City of Syracuse School District is administered by a superintendent appointed by a seven-member policy-making Board of Education. In 2004, the school board and the municipal government announced a $665 million district-wide renovation project, which will modernize all Syracuse schools within the next 10 years. The district was also awarded $14 million in federal funding to bring Internet access to each of its facilities.

The following is a summary of data regarding the Syracuse public schools as of the 2003–2004 school year.

Total enrollment: 22,455

Number of facilities
   elementary schools: 21
   middle schools: 9
   senior high schools: 4
   other: 5

Student/teacher ratio: 13.5:1

Teacher salaries
   average: $44,176

Funding per pupil: $11,074

Public Schools Information: Syracuse City School District, 725 Harrison Street, Syracuse, NY 13210; telephone (315)435-4499

Colleges and Universities

The Greater Syracuse Region boasts 44 private and state colleges with a combined enrollment of 215,000. Syracuse University attracts students from all 50 states and a number of other countries; its 13 schools and colleges offer a range of undergraduate and graduate degrees. LeMoyne College offers 24 different undergraduate majors in a Catholic and Jesuit tradition, and has been recognized as the fourth-best liberal arts college in the Northeast. SUNY Upstate Medical University offers degrees in medicine, nursing and other health professions; together with Syracuse University and SUNY College of Environmental Science and Forestry, it forms a student hub known as University Hill. Nearby two-year colleges include Bryant & Stratton Business Institute, Onondaga Community College and Cayuga Community College.

Libraries and Research Centers

The Onondaga County Public Library system consists of a central location, eight city branches and two community satellites with an annual circulation of 1.5 million titles. Central Library moved to its present location in the downtown Galleries of Syracuse in 1988; its main entrance features the ''Browse-About,'' a 12,000-square-foot bookstore-like layout. The library offers branch-to-branch deliveries, family literacy programming, and a 24-hour reference service.

The Erie Canal Museum maintains a collection of artifacts, books and photographs about canal life. The Onondaga Historical Association maintains one of the largest regional history collections in the nation. Onondaga County's Supreme Court Law Library is located in Syracuse. Area colleges, universities, and corporations also maintain libraries.

Research in a variety of areas is carried out by universities and private companies in Syracuse. Syracuse University research units focus on digital commerce, computer and software engineering, cancer, gerontology, public policy and psychology. State University of New York sponsors research through the College of Environmental Science and Forestry and the Health Science Center. Bristol-Myers Squibb Company's Industrial Division maintains a pharmaceutical research facility. Other research sites in the city conduct research on cancer treatment and on industrial issues.

Public Library Information: Onondaga County Public Library, The Galleries of Syracuse, 447 South Salina Street, Syracuse, NY 13202-2494; telephone (315)435-1800

Health Care

Syracuse has one of the lowest hospitalization rates in the nation, thanks to an efficient local health care system. Almost 1,500 physicians and 6,000 registered nurses serve the population of Syracuse and Onondaga County. More than 2,000 inpatient beds are available in five hospitals.

Crouse Hospital is a not-for-profit facility with 576 beds, including a 51-bed neonatal intensive care unit. It also offers high-risk maternity care, pediatric services, cardiac care and the region's only substance abuse program. It is currently undergoing a renovation of its Intensive Care and Dialysis Units with completion expected in 2006. Community General Hospital operates 306 acute-care beds and 50 nursing care beds; in addition to medical, surgical and emergency care it also runs three specialty centers dedicated to wound care, breast health and sleep. St. Joseph's Hospital Health Center is Syracuse's busiest hospital based on patient volume; it offers emergency and intensive care, ambulatory surgery, dialysis, mental health programs, maternity care and rehabilitation. University Hospital operates four Centers of Excellence in Oncology, Pediatrics, Neuroscience and Cardiovascular Health; it is the region's only teaching hospital. Syracuse VA Medical Center offers acute medical and surgical services, a variety of specialty services and short-term nursing care. Psychiatric care is offered at Hutchings Psychiatric Center and Benjamin Rush Center.

Recreation

Sightseeing

Those interested in architecture are advised to take a stroll through downtown Syracuse for an opportunity to see the imposing Hotel Syracuse as well as fine old churches and other structures. Columbus Circle contains a statue of the explorer. Syracuse Urban Cultural Park downtown highlights the city's past as a transportation center through interpretive signs. The Parke Avery House, a mid-nineteenth century residence built by the salt baron whose name it bears, hosts various events and exhibits throughout the year. The old Syracuse Savings Bank building was designed by prominent architect Joseph L. Silsbee in Gothic Revival style; other structures of note express Art Deco, Queen Anne and Neoclassical motifs. Hanover Square was the site of the original village well and the city's first commercial district; today it is a National Historic District featuring a variety of nineteenth century buildings.

Hiawatha Lake and gazebo in Upper Onondaga Park.

The Rosamond Gifford Zoo is open year-round and very popular with visitors to Syracuse. The zoo displays about one thousand domestic and exotic animals in simulations of their natural settings, including the $3.7 million "Penguin Coast" exhibit which opened in June 2005 and features a breeding group of endangered Humboldt penguins. Special exhibits trace animal history through the ages.

Onondaga Park, an historic landscape designed by Frederick Law Olmsted to incorporate landscape and architecture, features a gazebo and a Fire House. Boat tours down the Erie Canal and tram trips along the shore of Onondaga Lake are also available.

The Bristol Omnitheater at the Milton J. Rubenstein Museum of Science and Technology (MOST) is the only IMAX Domed Theater in New York State; MOST is central New York's largest hands-on science center. Museum-goers can navigate through a human cell, discover the underlying faults of earthquakes, learn about the rhythms of the human body, and visit the Space Gallery.

Arts and Culture

The performing arts are very much alive in Syracuse, which boasts Broadway-quality entertainment at a fraction of the price. The focal point of this activity is the John H. Mulroy Civic Center, said to be the first building complex in the western hemisphere to combine a performing arts center with a government complex. The center houses three theaters and is home to the Syracuse Opera Company, which stages three productions a year as well as community outreach and education programs, and to the Syracuse Symphony Orchestra, whose ambitious 39-week season encompasses classics and pops, dance performances, a family series, and a concert series featuring works by minority composers and artists. The Syracuse Area Landmark Theatre, opened in 1928 and described as an "Indo-Persian fantasy palace," was saved from demolition and refurbished in 1975; it hosts performances by popular entertainers and Broadway touring companies. The Regent Theatre Complex, which contains an infrared lighting system for the hearing impaired, is home to Syracuse Stage, Central New York's only professional theatre group. Syracuse Stage shows seven plays and one children's touring production each year; actors, designers, directors, and technicians from Broadway and other professional theaters across the country are recruited to work on the performances. The Regent Theatre Complex is also home to the Syracuse University Drama Department. The forty thousand-seat Carrier Dome at Syracuse University showcases internationally known musical performers, as does the smaller War Memorial. Salt City Center for the Performing Arts presents a year-round season of musicals, drama, and comedies, as well as adult and children's classes.

Syracuse is home to a number of distinctive art and historical museums. The Everson Museum of Art, designed by I. M. Pei, houses American nineteenth and twentieth century paintings, sculptures and prints, and one of the nation's finest collections of ceramic art. Syracuse University's Lowe Art Gallery features a large permanent collection of modern art. LeMoyne College's Wilson Art Gallery, located at the college library, offers various exhibits throughout the year. The Erie Canal Museum, located in the country's only remaining weighlock building, features interactive exhibits as well as a 65-foot canal boat. Open Hand Theater's International Mask and Puppet Museum is housed in an 1890 castle. Onondaga Lake Parkway contains the Salt Museum, including a reconstructed 1856 boiling block, and Sainte Marie among the Iroquois, a recreation of the original French Jesuit settlement, now a living-history museum. The Onondaga Historical Association provides local and regional history through a series of changing exhibits. In all there are more than forty museums and galleries in the Syracuse area.

Festivals and Holidays

Syracuse is home to the New York State Fair, the oldest state fair in the country. Featuring agriculture and livestock competitions, an International Horse Show, business and industrial exhibits, and tractor pulls, this 10-day event attracts more than a million people from across the Northeast each year. It takes place at the end of August.

The Syracuse Polish Festival takes place in June, as well as the Taste of Syracuse Festival, a two-day event featuring dollar samples from Syracuse's finest restaurants and continuous entertainment on three stages. Juneteenth honors the end of slavery in the United States. Other cultural festivals in Syracuse include the Jewish Music and Cultural Festival, the Bavarian Festival, the Irish Festival, La Festa Italiana and Oktoberfest.

Musical events in Syracuse include the M & T Jazz Fest in June, the NYS Rhythm and Blues Festival in July, and the CNYBA Apple Valley Bluegrass Festival in July.

Sports for the Spectator

Spectator sports in Syracuse center around the Carrier Dome, a $27 million domed complex completed in 1980 where the Syracuse University Orangemen play lacrosse, football and basketball. The dome is also the scene of the Empire State Games and other amateur sports competitions. LeMoyne College supports 16 NCAA varsity sports teams, while Onondaga Community College hosts NJCAA athletic events.

The Syracuse Sky Chiefs, a minor league affiliate of the Toronto Blue Jays baseball team, compete at the 12,000-seat

P & C Stadium from April to mid-September. The Syracuse Crunch Hockey Team, an American Hockey League affiliate of the Columbus Blue Jackets, plays in the War Memorial arena. Baseball fans in Syracuse may enjoy side trips to Cooperstown, home of the Baseball Hall of Fame.

South of Syracuse, auto racing fans are entertained at the Watkins Glen International. Onondaga Lake is the scene of various rowing competitions.

Sports for the Participant

Lakes, rivers, and sporting clubs in the Syracuse area offer abundant opportunities for fishing, boating, rafting, camping, swimming, and hunting. More than 50 parks and nature areas are located in Syracuse, providing facilities for baseball, tennis, swimming, skating, and golf. Several ski facilities and at least 40 golf courses are located in the region.

Shopping and Dining

Syracuse's newest mall is the Carousel Center overlooking Onandaga Lake. It features 170 shops, 13 eateries, five sit-down restaurants and a 12-screen cinema. It also has a fully restored 1909 antique carousel that gives the mall its name and invokes the days when the area was famed for the fine quality and craftsmanship of its carousels. The centerpiece project of downtown Syracuse's revitalization, the Galleries of Syracuse, houses approximately 80 high quality stores. The Armory Square Historic District, a few blocks away, is also a popular place to browse with a variety of shops, galleries and pubs. The Shoppingtown Mall, with 140 stores, and the Great Northern Mall, with 125 stores, are also major shopping destinations. The Downtown Farmers' Market, open Tuesdays from June to mid-October, features fresh produce from growers and dealers. There are more than 400 restaurants in the Syracuse area, including 20 fine dining establishments.

Visitor Information: Syracuse Convention and Visitors Bureau, 572 South Salina Street, Syracuse, NY 13202-3320; telephone (315)470-1910; toll-free (800)234-4797

Convention Facilities

Syracuse boasts a range of convention and meeting facilities. Over the last five years the city has hosted an annual average of 125,000 delegates from a variety of groups, from the American Baptist Churches to the National Roller Skating Association. Downtown's Oncenter Complex includes a 208,000-square-foot convention hall, a 6,200-seat arena, several performing arts theatres and a parking complex; in 2003 it hosted 32 trade shows and 26 conventions. Meeting

rooms are available at Syracuse University's Carrier Dome while the arena itself is suited for large rallies and concerts. The Marx-Radisson offers 9,000 square feet of meeting space including presentation technology and catering. Most other meeting facilities can be found in three areas of the city: the Carrier Circle area (Thruway Exit 35), the 7th North Street/Buckley Road Area (Thruway Exits 36 and 37), and the Downtown/University Area. More than 6,200 hotel rooms are located in Greater Syracuse.

Convention Information: Syracuse Convention and Visitors Bureau, 572 South Salina Street, Syracuse, NY 13202-3320; telephone (315)470-1910; toll-free (800)234-4797

Transportation

Approaching the City

Syracuse Hancock International Airport, located minutes from the downtown area, serves more than 200 passenger flights daily on 8 major airlines and 4 commuter lines.

Two major four-lane highways intersect Syracuse. Interstate 81, a north-south route, passes through the center of the city. Interstate 90 (the New York State Thruway), an east-west route, crosses Interstate 81 a mile north of the city.

Amtrak provides passenger rail service. Greyhound, Onondaga Coach, Syracuse & Oswego and Trailways provide intercity and interstate bus travel.

Traveling in the City

The downtown business district is bounded by Interstate 81 and Interstate 690 and is easily accessible by car. CENTRO, described as one of the nation's best mid-sized transit systems, provides bus service throughout the city on 24 routes. It also operates Call-a-Bus services for the elderly and disabled.

Communications

Newspapers and Magazines

The major daily newspaper in Syracuse is the morning *The Post-Standard,* with a circulation of 400,000. The area is also served by more than a dozen weekly newspapers, including *News for You,* a literary newspaper, *Nor'easter Leadership News,* published by the Presbyterian Church, and the *Syracuse New Times,* a tabloid highlighting area arts and entertainment. Magazines published in Syracuse include *Agway Cooperator* (for farm cooperatives), *The Business*

Record, Central New York Business Journal, the ecology journal *Clearwaters, Dairynews,* and the quarterly *American Journal of Mathematical & Management Sciences.*

Television and Radio

Syracuse television viewers are served by four national networks and one public station. Cable service is available through Time Warner. Nineteen AM and FM radio stations cover the broadcast spectrum.

Media Information: The Post-Standard, PO Box 4915, Syracuse, NY 13221; telephone (315)470-0011

Syracuse Online

City of Syracuse home page. Available www.syracuse.ny.us

Greater Syracuse Chamber of Commerce. Available www.syracusechamber.com

New York State Education Department. Available www.emsc.nysed.gov

Onondaga County Public Library. Available www.onlib.org

Syracuse Convention and Visitors Bureau. Available www.visitsyracuse.org

Syracuse Online. Available www.syracuse.com

Selected Bibliography

Beauchamp, William Martin, *Past and Present of Syracuse and Onondaga County, New York, From Prehistoric Times to the Beginning of 1908* (New York, Chicago: S. J. Clarke Publishing, 1908)

Bernardi, Roy A., Fred Wilson, Kevin Wilson, and Charles F. Wainwright. *Greater Syracuse: Center of an Empire* (Towery Publishing, 1998)

Bruce, Dwight H. (Dwight Hall), *Memorial History of Syracuse, N.Y., From Its Settlement to the Present Time* (Syracuse, N.Y.: H.P. Smith & Co., 1891)

Chase, Franklin Henry, *Syracuse and Its Environs: A History* (New York and Chicago: Lewis Historical Publishing, 1924)

Hand, Marcus Christian, *From a Forest to a City. Personal Reminiscences of Syracuse, N.Y.* (Syracuse: Masters & Stone, 1889)

PENNSYLVANIA

The State in Brief

Nickname: Keystone State
Motto: Virtue, liberty, and independence

Flower: Mountain laurel
Bird: Ruffled grouse

Area: 46,055 (2000; U.S. rank: 33rd)
Elevation: Ranges from sea level to 3,213 feet
Climate: Cold winters, warm summers, abundant precipitation

Admitted to Union: December 12, 1787
Capital: Harrisburg
Head Official: Governor Ed Rendell (D) (until 2007)

Population
   1980: 11,863,895
   1990: 11,881,643
   2000: 12,281,054
   2004 estimate: 12,406,292
   Percent change, 1990–2000: 3.4%
   U.S. rank in 2004: 6th
   Percent of residents born in state: 77.7% (2000)
   Density: 274 people per square mile (2000)
   2002 FBI Crime Index Total: 350,466

Racial and Ethnic Characteristics (2000)
   White: 10,484,203
   Black or African American: 1,224,612
   American Indian and Alaska Native: 18,348
   Asian: 219,813
   Native Hawaiian and Pacific Islander: 3,417
   Hispanic or Latino (may be of any race): 394,088
   Other: 188,437

Age Characteristics (2000)
   Population under 5 years old: 727,804
   Population 5 to 19 years old: 2,542,780
   Percent of population 65 years and over: 15.6%
   Median age: 38 years (2000)

Vital Statistics
   Total number of births (2003): 142,287
   Total number of deaths (2003): 126,404 (infant deaths, 981)
   AIDS cases reported through 2003: 15,178

Economy
   Major industries: Manufacturing, services, tourism, transportation, mining, high technology, agriculture
   Unemployment rate: 4.9% (April 2005)
   Per capita income: $31,706 (2003; U.S. rank: 18th)
   Median household income: $43,869 (3-year average, 2001-2003)
   Percentage of persons below poverty level: 9.9% (3-year average, 2001-2003)
   Income tax rate: 3.07%
   Sales tax rate: 6%

Allentown

The City in Brief

Founded: 1762 (incorporated, 1867)

Head Official: Mayor Roy Afflerbach (D) (since 2002)

City Population
 1980: 103,758
 1990: 105,301
 2000: 106,632
 Percent change, 1990–2000: 1%
 U.S. rank in 1980: 155th
 U.S. rank in 1990: 184th
 U.S. rank in 2000: 240th (State rank: 3rd)

Metropolitan Area Population
 1980: 635,481
 1990: 595,081
 2000: 637,958
 Percent change, 1990–2000: 7.5%

 U.S. rank in 1980: 54th
 U.S. rank in 1990: 64th
 U.S. rank in 2000: 65th

Area: 17.4 square miles (2000)
Elevation: 387 feet above sea level
Average Annual Temperature: 49° F
Average Annual Precipitation: 45.6 inches of rain; 32.4 inches of snow

Major Economic Sectors: Manufacturing, services, retail trade
Unemployment Rate: 4.4% (April 2005)
Per Capita Income: $16,282 (1999)
2004 ACCRA Average Home Price: Not reported
2004 ACCRA Cost of Living Index: Not reported

2002 FBI Crime Index Total: 5,944

Major Colleges and Universities: Cedar Crest College, Muhlenberg College

Daily Newspaper: *The Morning Call*

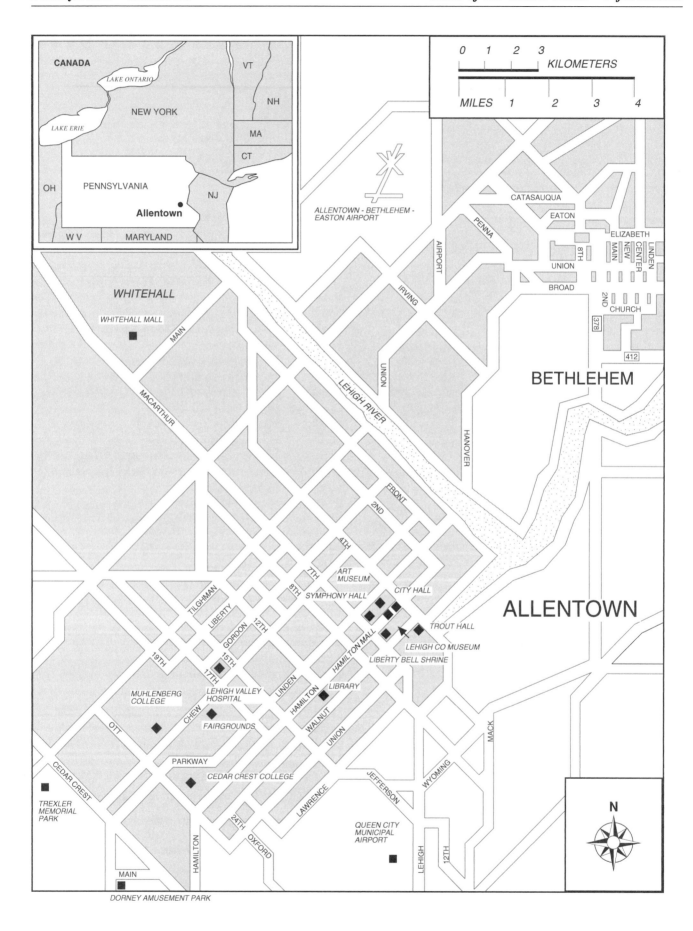

Introduction

Allentown, Bethlehem, and Easton comprise Pennsylvania's Lehigh Valley, the state's third largest metropolitan area. The Lehigh Valley is a thriving community characterized by bustling metropolitan areas surrounded by scenic countryside. In recent years, the city has gone from a primarily manufacturing-based financial system to a community with a diverse economy and a wealth of service industries.

Geography and Climate

Allentown is located in the east central section of Pennsylvania in the Lehigh River Valley between Blue Mountain to the north and South Mountain. The terrain is rolling with many small streams. Temperatures are usually moderate, although because of the mountain ranges winter temperatures are sometimes 10 to 15 degrees lower than in Philadelphia, just 50 miles to the south. Freezing rain is a common problem in winter. Precipitation is ample, especially during the summer, when high humidity can cause periods of discomfort.

Area: 17.4 square miles (2000)

Elevation: 387 feet above sea level

Average Temperatures: January, 26.9° F; August, 71° F; annual average, 49° F

Average Annual Precipitation: 45.6 inches of rain; 32.4 inches of snow

History

Eight thousand years before European settlers crossed the Atlantic, ancestors of the Delaware tribe were thriving in the Lehigh Valley. The city now known as Allentown stands on a tract of land purchased in 1735 by William Allen from a friend of the family of William Penn, founder of Pennsylvania. William Allen, who served for several years as chief justice of Pennsylvania, built a hunting and fishing lodge on the geographically isolated site, which was first known as ''Allen's little town.'' Allen and his son had hoped to turn the lodge into a trading center but the river was too shallow for boat traffic and the American Revolution of 1776 intervened. When the British captured Philadelphia in 1777, the Liberty Bell was carried to Allentown where it was concealed in a local church and later returned to Philadelphia upon British evacuation of that city.

By the early 1800s Allentown was little more than a sleepy marketing town for local farmers. However, when the Lehigh Canal was opened in 1829 to carry coal from the area north to the Delaware Canal and east to New York, and south to Philadelphia, Allentown for the first time had access to outside markets. Even more important was the availability of water power, and a growing number of businesses began to settle in the Lehigh Valley, including the country's first commercially successful iron furnace powered by anthracite coal. The resulting boom in the production of pig iron began to fade by the turn of the century when English advances in steel technology lessened the demand for iron. Nearby Bethlehem Iron was the only Lehigh Valley metals industry to successfully make the transition from iron to steel. Allentown, earlier than other northeastern industrial areas, was forced to diversify its economic base. With the arrival of the silk industry in the 1880s Allentown came to be known as ''silk city.'' Other light industries followed and Allentown leaders determined to never again depend on one business for the city's survival. In the early 1900s Mack Trucks, Inc., moved to the city and remained one of the city's largest employers for most of the century.

World War II gave a boost to the Lehigh Valley's economy, but thereafter synthetics began to replace silk in the manufacture of clothing, the cement works phased out many operations, and the steel companies began to lay off workers. As has been the case with many industrial cities, improved highways, large tracts of available, affordable land, and the demand for larger homes encouraged development outside the city. The 1980s saw expansion in suburban shopping centers, industrial parks, and office buildings. Allentown and the surrounding region have benefitted from the completion of an interstate highway in 1989, which has promoted economic development, and from an influx of persons fleeing high prices and overcrowding in New York City, Philadelphia, and elsewhere.

Today the Lehigh Valley supports a diversity of businesses and industries, having moved from what was once a primarily manufacturing base. The city has also begun an intensive revitalization of its downtown area, which includes plans for a multi-purpose complex on what was once industrial property along the Lehigh River. Numerous industrial facilities will be renovated at the same time, providing the area with a much-needed facelift and tying into Mayor Afflerbach's plan to create a ''safer, cleaner, more prosperous city in which to live, work, play, and invest.''

Historical Information: Lehigh County Historical Society and Museum, Old Courthouse, PO Box 1548, Allentown, PA 18105; telephone (610)435-1074

Population Profile

Metropolitan Area Residents
1980: 635,481
1990: 595,081
2000: 637,958
Percent change, 1990–2000: 7.5%
U.S. rank in 1990: 64th
U.S. rank in 2000: 65th

City Residents
1980: 103,758
1990: 105,301
2000: 106,632
Percent change, 1990–2000: 1%
U.S. rank in 1980: 155th
U.S. rank in 1990: 184th (State rank: 4th)
U.S. rank in 2000: 240th

Density: 6,011.5 people per square mile (2000)

Racial and ethnic characteristics (2000)
White: 77,361
Black: 8,370
American Indian and Alaska Native: 356
Asian: 2,421
Native Hawaiian and Other Pacific Islander: 78
Hispanic (may be of any race): 26,058
Other: 14,260

Percent of residents born in state: 64% (2000)

Age characteristics (2000)
Population under 5 years old: 7,586
Population 5 to 9 years old: 7,723
Population 10 to 14 years old: 7,288
Population 15 to 19 years old: 7,301
Population 20 to 34 years old: 15,777
Population 35 to 44 years old: 15,988
Population 45 to 54 years old: 12,415
Population 55 to 59 years old: 4,282
Population 60 to 64 years old: 3,722
Population 65 to 74 years old: 7,587
Population 75 to 84 years old: 6,326
Population 85 years and over: 2,228
Median age: 34.5 years (2000)

Births (2002, Lehigh County)
Total number: 13,956

Deaths (2003, Lehigh County)
Total number: 3,186 (of which, 29 were infants under the age of 1 year)

Money income (1999)
Per capita income: $16,282 (1999)
Median household income: $32,016
Total households: 42,051

Number of households with income of . . .
less than $10,000: 2,305
$10,000 to $14,999: 1,572
$15,000 to $24,999: 3,885
$25,000 to $34,999: 3,969
$35,000 to $49,999: 4,688
$50,000 to $74,999: 5,328
$75,000 to $99,999: 1,989
$100,000 to $149,999: 1,234
$150,000 to $199,999: 157
$200,000 or more: 229

Percent of families below poverty level: 14.6% (55.7% of which were female householder families with children under the age of 5 years)

2002 FBI Crime Index Total: 5,944

Municipal Government

The city of Allentown operates under the strong-mayor form of government. Voters at large elect the mayor and a seven-member council to four-year terms.

Head Official: Mayor Roy Afflerbach (D) (since 2002; current term expires December 2005)

Total Number of City Employees: 964 (2004)

City Information: Allentown City Hall, 435 Hamilton St., Allentown, PA 18101, telephone (610)437-7546

Economy

Major Industries and Commercial Activity

Manufacturing, at one time the dominant activity in the Allentown metropolitan area, continues to decline to just 15 percent of total employment in the area. The service sector now dominates employment in the area, concentrated in the area of health services. Jobs in this sector continue to grow at a rapid pace; many businesses report having trouble finding qualified workers available positions. According to the Lehigh Valley Economic Development Corporation, 33,000 new jobs were created between 1996 and 2004. The metropolitan area has been selected as the headquarters or principal plant locations for major corporations such as Mack Trucks and Bethlehem Steel, as well as *Fortune* 500 companies Air Products and Chemicals, and PPL Corporation.

Items and goods produced: steel products, industrial equipment, food products, electrical and mechanical equipment, clothing and textiles, trucks, chemical and mineral processing equipment, fabricated metals, furniture

Incentive Programs—New and Existing Companies

Local programs—The Allentown Economic Development Corporation (AEDC), a nonprofit corporation managed by a board of directors representing the leaders of business, industry, civic groups, and city government, has as its mission the long-range economic growth and diversity of the city of Allentown. AEDC operates the Bridgeworks Enterprise Center, a facility that offers tenants shared centralized services such as educational business counseling and management and financial assistance. Relocation assistance is available for those companies that outgrow the incubator space. The Lehigh Valley Economic Development Corporation (LVEDC) offers a variety of financing options, education and training venues, and technology support services. Three enterprise zone programs are available in the region to help stimulate growth. These programs emphasize assisting industrial, manufacturing, and export service firms. Tax credits of up to $250,000 are also available for eligible projects. The Small Business Development Center at Lehigh University and the Team Pennsylvania Lehigh Export Network also help companies with expansion and growth.

State programs—Funding programs offered by the state include bond financing, grants, loans and loan guarantees, tax credits and abatements, and technical assistance. The Lehigh Valley Keystone Opportunity zone consists of 642 acres of land within Lehigh and Northampton counties, including a technology-ready corridor in downtown Allentown. These areas will remain virtually tax-exempt until 2013. Four state Enterprise Zones in Philadelphia are eligible for numerous incentives, including state tax credits, security rebates, low-interest loans, and technical assistance. The state's Job Creation Tax Credits program provides $1,000-per-job tax credit to approved businesses that agree to create jobs within three years.

Job training programs—The region has available a network of specialized training programs, numerous recruitment assistance packages, connections to a variety of workforce training providers and innovative partnerships between education and industry, including Eastern Pennsylvania Training WORKS Partnership, Lehigh Valley Team Pennsylvania CareerLink, and WEDNet Pennsylvania's Guaranteed Free Training Program. The most widely used state and federal programs to help employers reduce the costs of hiring and training workers include the federal Workforce Investment Act (WIA),

customized job training funded by the Commonwealth of Pennsylvania, Targeted Jobs Tax Credit Program, and a state tax credit Employment Incentive Payment Program.

Development Projects

Plans are underway in Allentown for an ambitious downtown revitalization project that includes a new attraction, Lehigh Landing. One of the projects planned is a multipurpose complex on a former industrial property along the Lehigh River. Several turn-of-the-century industrial facilities will be renovated for the complex, using a combination of public and private funds. The anchor for this project will be the America On Wheels Transportation Museum, to be located in a former Lehigh Valley Transit Company building. A ground-breaking ceremony was held for the museum in April 2005. Over-the-road transportation exhibits have already been promised by the Smithsonian Institution, as well as from Mack Trucks, whose headquarters is located in Allentown. The Lehigh Landing project includes a river walk and a tie-in to the Delaware and Lehigh Canal, as well as boating activities along the river.

The Pennsylvania Expo Center at Lehigh Valley is the region's newest and largest exhibition facility. This state-of-the-art facility offers more than 95,000 square feet of contiguous ground-level exhibition space.

In March 2005, Lehigh Valley Economic Development Corporation (LVEDC) announced the approval of funding for the development of the Allentown Brew Works. The building's first three floors will house the restaurant, microbrewery, and a banquet facility for up to 200 people, along with a lounge in the basement. The fourth and fifth floors will be converted into commercial office space.

In August 2006, Olympus, a technology leader in healthcare and consumer electronics, will relocate its North American headquarters facility and distribution centers to the Lehigh Valley. The high-tech firm CryOptics, which designs, develops, and manufactures optical engines, has also announced plans to relocate its headquarters to the area.

Economic Development Information: Allentown Economic Development Corporation, 718 Hamilton Street, Allentown, PA 18101; telephone (610)435-8890

Commercial Shipping

Twenty-five percent of the nation's population lives within a 250-mile radius of the Allentown-Bethlehem-Easton metropolitan area, linked to it by major highways, Lehigh Valley International Airport, and Queen City Municipal Airport. More than 50 motor freight carriers provide daily service in the area, and Norfolk Southern operates a major rail classification yard in Allentown.

Labor Force and Employment Outlook

The labor pool in the Lehigh Valley is described as highly skilled and possessing a strong work ethic. Jobs in the business services sector have accounted for a large increase in the area's employment. Severe workforce shortages of qualified candidates in the healthcare occupations continue in the region. Employment projections for the area show a continuing decline in the number of jobs in manufacturing, agriculture, and mining, though a recent burst of new construction projects has meant a slight increase in some manufacturing jobs. Jobs in the retail and service sectors are projected to increase, particularly high-tech jobs.

The following is a summary of data regarding the Allentown metropolitan area labor force, 2004 annual averages.

Size of nonagricultural labor force: 329,100

Number of workers employed in . . .
construction and mining: 15,800
manufacturing: 45,300
trade, transportation, and utilities: 66,700
information: 7,700
financial activities: 16,200
professional and business services: 35,300
educational and health services: 57,500
leisure and hospitality: 29,000
other services: 15,200
government: 40,300

Average hourly wage of production workers employed in manufacturing: $14.54

Unemployment rate: 4.4% (April 2005)

Largest employers	Number of employees
Lehigh Valley Hospital and Health Network	7,364
St. Luke's Hospital	4,963
Air Products & Chemicals	4,246
U.S. Government	2,740
PPL Corporation	2,351
Giant Food Stores, Inc.	2,217

Cost of Living

The following is a summary of data regarding key cost of living factors in the Allentown area.

2004 ACCRA Average Home Price: Not reported

2004 ACCRA Cost of Living Index: Not reported

State income tax rate: 3.07%

State sales tax rate: 6%

Local income tax rate: 1%

Local sales tax rate: None

Property tax rate: $7.31 per $1,000 of market value

Economic Information: Allentown Economic Development Corp., 718 Hamilton St., 7th Floor, PO Box 1400, Allentown, PA 18105-1400; telephone (610)435-8890. Allentown City Planning Commission, 435 Hamilton St., Allentown, PA 18101; telephone (610)437-7611

Education and Research

Elementary and Secondary Schools

The Allentown School District (A.S.D.) is the fourth largest in the state. The district is said to have pioneered the neighborhood school concept and has offered a program for gifted students since 1924. A.S.D. is in the high range of national norms in the percentage of students testing at high IQ levels.

The following is a summary of data regarding the Allentown public schools as of the 2002–2003 school year.

Total enrollment: 15,966

Number of facilities
elementary schools: 17
secondary schools: 4
high schools: 2

Student/teacher ratio: 18.8:1

Teacher salaries
average: $50,831

Funding per pupil: $7,207

Public Schools Information: Allentown School District, 31 South Penn Street, PO Box 328, Allentown, PA 18105; telephone (610)821-2641

Colleges and Universities

The Lehigh Valley is home to 11 colleges and universities, 3 of them located within Allentown city limits. Lehigh University, located in Bethlehem, is nationally recognized for its science, engineering, business, and economic programs. Muhlenberg College in Allentown offers numerous undergraduate majors, including a premedical program. Cedar Crest College and Lehigh College Workforce Training Center are also located in the city. A campus of Pennsylvania State University is located near Allentown.

Libraries and Research Centers

The Allentown Public Library's two branches house nearly a half-million volumes, and offers free public access to the

Internet. The Lehigh County Historical Society Library maintains a collection of the publications of local history scholars, and a Frank Lloyd Wright Library is part of the Allentown Art Museum.

The Lehigh Valley's colleges and universities maintain extensive holdings, including the Lehigh University collection of more than 870,000 volumes featuring a special collection of engineering laboratory research project reports. Muhlenberg College's library houses 330,000 volumes, including a special collection of "best" works of fiction and nonfiction.

At the heart of the Lehigh Valley's research activities is Lehigh University, one of the country's leading technological universities. The university is home to the North East Tier Ben Franklin Advanced Technology and the Advanced Technology for Large Structural Systems program, the first large-scale structure testing facility in the country. A number of private companies maintain research and development programs, including Rodale, of organic gardening fame, whose center is located in Kutztown.

Public Library Information: Main Library, 1210 Hamilton St., Allentown, PA 18102; telephone (610)820-2400

Health Care

Allentown's health care needs are served by four acute-care hospitals offering a full range of services and one psychiatric hospital. Lehigh Valley Hospital is a regional trauma center with a MedEvac helicopter. Lehigh Valley Hospital's Allentown site is ranked among the nation's best hospitals for heart surgery, cardiac care, urology, and geriatric care, hospice, pediatric, emergency, outpatient, dental, diabetes, and radiology care and rehabilitation services. St. Luke's Hospital and Health Network has been named as one of the nation's top hospitals. Its Regional Heart Center is the area's most nationally honored heart-care center. Home health care is available, as is treatment for substance abuse. The region as a whole supports eight hospitals.

Recreation

Sightseeing

One of the most popular sights in Allentown is the Liberty Bell Shrine Museum in the Zion Reformed Church, which contains a replica of the bell. Trout Hall, built in 1770 by the son of the founder of Allentown, is the city's oldest building; Lehigh County Historical Society sponsors tours of it. Tours

are available at the Frank Buchman House, founder of the Moral Rearmament movement, and the Haines Mill Museum, an operating grist mill, adjacent to a county park. Two railroads offer nostalgic rides through the area's scenic wonders, and the Covered Bridge (driving) Tour culminates at the Trexler-Lehigh County Game Preserve, where native and exotic fauna roam 1,500 acres of rolling countryside. Several historic structures in nearby Bethlehem, which was a center for the religious group known as Moravians, are open to tourists. Easton also preserves historic buildings and homes.

Arts and Culture

Allentown has long been supportive of artistic and cultural activities. Symphony Hall is home to the Allentown Band, which has been providing musical entertainment since 1829. Concerts are presented by the Allentown Symphony Orchestra at Symphony Hall; the Pennsylvania Sinfonia Orchestra is the only year-round orchestra in the Valley. The Lehigh Valley Chamber Orchestra performs great music from the traditional to the contemporary. A Community Concert series brings nationally-known artists to the city, and musical and theatrical performances are sponsored by area colleges. The Theatre Outlet is the Lehigh Valley's award winning "Off Broadway" company, performing at its own arts center. Rounding out the musical, theatrical, and dance offerings are the Civic Theatre of Allentown, and the Cedar Crest College Stage Company, the State Theatre, and Muhlenberg College's Center for the Arts.

The Allentown Art Museum houses the Samuel H. Kress collection of Renaissance paintings. Lehigh County Historical Museum displays artifacts pertaining to local history and traditions and maintains a Geology Garden. The Open Space Gallery offers juried exhibitions of contemporary regional arts and crafts. The Lenni Lenape Historical Society of Pennsylvania has restored an eighteenth-century stone farmhouse to display Indian artifacts. It is called the Museum of Indian Culture and features a traditional village and garden.

Festivals and Holidays

The Lehigh Valley offers an array of annual festivals, primarily during the summer months, that appeal to a broad range of interests. Allentown's Mayfair, a three-day celebration of the arts, is held over the Memorial Day weekend at various city parks. All activities, which range from dancing to crafts to musical performances and fiddling competitions, are free. July brings the traditional Independence Day fireworks celebration, as well as SportsFest. This action-packed sporting event featuring more than 25 competitive events attracts athletes from all over the world. Lehigh County Council on the Arts sponsors an Arts Festival each summer. August is an event-filled month as Allentown presents the Great Allentown Fair, and Das Awkscht Fescht (The August Festival), featuring an antique car show, and Bethlehem celebrates its nine-day Musikfest. From the Wednesday before Thanksgiving until January 1, more than a half-million visitors enjoy holiday displays at Lights In the Parkway. Bethlehem is a popular destination during the Christmas season, which is celebrated there in the serene, noncommercial style traditional to the Moravians, a group of religious, middle-European missionaries.

Sports for the Spectator

At the Lehigh Valley Velodrome, national and international bicycle racing meets are held annually on its Olympic standard cycling track. Adjacent to the Velodrome is the Bob Rodale Cycling & Fitness Park. Live horse racing via satellite is offered year round at the Downs at Lehigh Valley. The Allentown Ambassadors minor league baseball team is also located in Allentown.

Sports for the Participant

Allentown's park system, which at 13 percent of the city's acreage is said to consist of more acres per capita than any other city its size, and a network of area tennis courts, swimming pools, golf courses, ski slopes, and campgrounds offer year-round recreational opportunities for the sports enthusiast. Cedar Creek Parkway's 127 acres include Lake Muhlenberg, where pedal boating, fishing, and picnicking go on; also located there is the Rose Garden, with its old-fashioned gardens and lagoons. The proximity of the Poconos and other ski resorts make the Lehigh Valley a popular winter destination. Among the more than 100 rides at Dorney Park and Wildwater Kingdom is one of the world's tallest wooden roller coasters; at Wildwater, families enjoy giant slides, river rides, and an enormous wave pool. Gymnastic and exercise programs are offered at Parkettes National Training Center. The Lehigh Valley's streams, forests, and winding roads offer sites for fishing, swimming, hunting, hiking, ice skating, water skiing, and cycling. Allentown is home to SportsFest, an annual event featuring local, national, and international competitors who participate in team and individual sporting events.

Shopping and Dining

Essential and luxury items are available in the Lehigh Valley's many malls and shopping centers. Dozens of national brand factory outlets operate within a short drive of the area, as do several farmers' markets, featuring a wide variety of local produce. Bethlehem and its environs offer many unusual shops specializing in Christmas items, candles, and silk flowers; one is housed in an 1803 mansion.

Restaurants in Allentown offer varied cuisines and entertainment.

Visitor Information: Lehigh Valley Convention and Visitors Bureau, PO Box 20785, Lehigh Valley, PA 18002-0785; telephone (610)882-9200; toll-free (800)633-8437

Convention Facilities

The Pennsylvania Expo Center at Lehigh Valley is the region's newest and largest exhibition facility. This state-of-the-art facility, which offers more than 95,000 square feet of contiguous ground-level exhibition space, is quickly becoming home to many of the region's largest trade and consumer shows. The Agri-Plex at the Allentown Fairgrounds offers 58,000 square feet, and the Stabler Arena at Lehigh University in nearby Bethlehem can seat up to 6,000. There are more than 40 hotels and motels in the area, most of which provide courtesy shuttle service to and from the airport.

Convention Information: Lehigh Valley Convention and Visitors Bureau, PO Box 20785, Lehigh Valley, PA 18002-0785; telephone (610)882-9200; toll-free (800)633-8437; fax (610)882-9200

Transportation

Approaching the City

Air travelers to the Lehigh Valley are served by the Lehigh Valley International Airport, a modern, full-service facility located minutes from downtown Allentown and providing coast-to-coast service by major airlines.

The Pennsylvania Turnpike's Northeast Extension, Interstate 78, Interstate 476, and U.S. Routes 22, 222, 309, and 33 provide easy access by car to Allentown from the East Coast. The city can be approached from the South by Interstate-95 and from the West by interstates 76 and 80. The region is served by four interstate bus lines. Freight rail service in the Lehigh Valley is provided by several operators.

Traveling in the City

Allentown is laid out in a basic grid pattern. The downtown area is the center of the city's retail, banking, lodging, entertainment, and cultural activities. The Lehigh and Northampton Transit Authority (LANTA) operates a fleet of buses serving the city and its environs.

Communications

Newspapers and Magazines

Two daily newspapers are published in the Lehigh Valley: Allentown's *The Morning Call* is published Monday–Sunday,

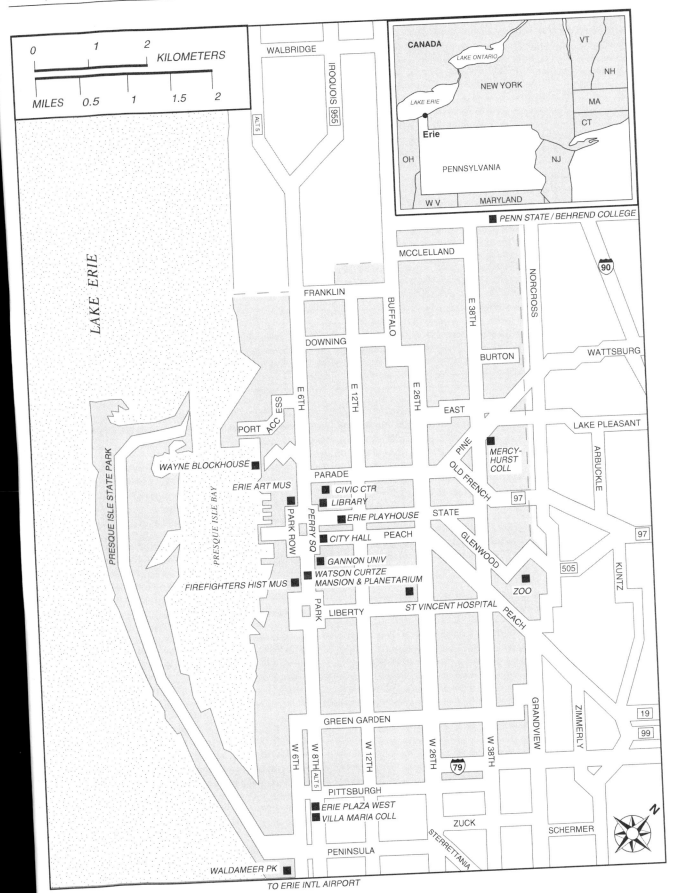

and Easton's *The Times-Express,* published Monday–Sunday. Also published in Allentown are the *Eastern Pennsylvania Business Journal,* a weekly publication, *East Penn Press,* a weekly local newspaper, and *Allentown Times,* which is also a weekly publication.

Television and Radio

Network broadcasts from Philadelphia supplement television coverage by an independent television station in the Lehigh Valley. Public television service features local and Public Broadcasting Service programs. Several cable companies also serve the area. More than 30 AM and FM radio stations, including a public radio station, offer a variety of programming; 11 of them broadcast from Allentown.

Media Information: The Morning Call, 101 N. 6th Street, Allentown, PA 18105; telephone (610)820-6500

Allentown Online

Allentown Public Library. Available www.allentownpl.org

Allentown School District. Available www.allentownsd.org

City of Allentown home page. Available www.allentownpa .org

Lehigh Valley Convention and Visitors Bureau. Available www.lehighvalleypa.org

Selected Bibliography

Hoffman, Richard, *Half the House: A Memoir* (New York: Harcourt- Brace, 1995)

The City in Brief

Founded: 1795 (incorporated, 1851)

Head Official: Mayor Richard E. Filippi (since 2002)

City Population
 1980: 119,123
 1990: 108,718
 2000: 103,717
 Percent change, 1990–2000: −4.2%
 U.S. rank in 1980: 130th
 U.S. rank in 1990: 175th
 U.S. rank in 2000: 247th (State rank: 3rd)

Metropolitan Area Population
 1980: 280,000
 1990: 275,572
 2000: 280,843
 Percent change, 1990–2000: 2%

 U.S. rank in 1980: 111th
 U.S. rank in 1990: 124th
 U.S. rank in 2000: 135th

Area: 22 square miles (2000)
Elevation: 710 feet above sea level
Average Annual Temperature: 51.9° F
Average Annual Precipitation: 38.1 inches of rain; inches of snow

Major Economic Sectors: Manufacturing, services, r trade
Unemployment Rate: 4.9% (April 2005)
Per Capita Income: $14,972 (1999)
2004 ACCRA Average House Price: Not reported
2004 ACCRA Cost of Living Index: Not reported

2002 FBI Crime Index Total: 3,560

Major Colleges and Universities: Penn State Erie Camp Gannon University

Daily Newspapers: *Erie Daily Times; Erie Morning N*

Introduction

Erie, the third largest city in Pennsylvania, is a major manufacturing and shipping center. Located on the southeast shore of Lake Erie, the city is the only lake port in the state. Its shoreline and protected harbor, and the availability of fresh water, offer the city unique advantages as a center of shipping and manufacturing in Pennsylvania. With numerous building projects and renovations taking place over the past decade, Erie continues to emerge as a top contender for job growth and livability.

Geography and Climate

Erie, the northernmost city in Pennsylvania, is located on the southeast shore of Lake Erie. Presque Isle, a 7-mile-long peninsula, curves around the city's harbor. The terrain rises gradually in a series of ridges.

Cold air masses moving south from Canada in the winter are modified by the relatively warm waters of Lake Erie, but the temperature difference between air and water produces cloudiness and frequent snow from November through March. Spring weather is usually cloudy and cool. Summer heat waves are tempered by cool lake breezes, and autumn, with its long dry periods and an abundance of sunshine, is usually the most pleasant season. Precipitation is well distributed throughout the year.

Area: 22 square miles (2000)

Elevation: 710 feet above sea level

Average Temperatures: January, 28.2° F; July, 70.9° F; average annual temperature, 51.9° F

Average Annual Precipitation: 38.1 inches of rain; 77.9 inches of snow

History

Erie was named after the Eriez tribe, which was destroyed by a combination of pestilence and the Seneca nation under Chief Cornplanter in the mid-seventeenth century. The first European settlers in the area were the French, who built Fort Presque Isle on the city's site in 1753. The French abandoned the fort to the English, who lost it in 1763 at the start of Pontiac's Rebellion. When General "Mad" Anthony Wayne induced the native tribes to make peace in 1794, the area was opened to settlement. The city was laid out in 1795 and became a port, engaged principally in the salt trade, in 1801.

The city's history throughout the nineteenth century was dominated by harbor activity. In 1813, in what is often referred to as Erie's proudest historical moment, Commodore Oliver Perry defeated the British in the Battle of Lake Erie. Most of Commodore Perry's ships were built in Erie.

The importance of the city and its port gradually diminished throughout the nineteenth and twentieth centuries as the development of automobiles, the railroad, and airplanes eroded the lake trade. The 1980s saw Erie's residents engaged in heated debates over the question of how they saw their city's future: Should Erie remain a "provincial" town devoted to waterfront activity, or should it reform its image into that of a "progressive" town? The debate continues today. Whatever the answer, Erie is respectful of its reputation as a rising entrepreneurial hotspot determined to maintain quality of life while making room for mindful progress. As the twenty-first century is well underway, Erie continues to improve economically; the city has seen new jobs and new business startups, as well as a reversal of urban sprawl and a reinvestment in city living.

Historical Information: Erie County Historical Society, 419 State Street, Erie, PA 16501; telephone (814)454-1813

Population Profile

Metropolitan Area Residents
1980: 280,000
1990: 275,572
2000: 280,843
Percent change, 1990–2000: 2%
U.S. rank in 1980: 111th
U.S. rank in 1990: 124th
U.S. rank in 2000: 135th

City Residents
1980: 119,123
1990: 108,718
2000: 103,717
Percent change, 1990–2000: −4.2%
U.S. rank in 1980: 130th
U.S. rank in 1990: 175th
U.S. rank in 2000: 247th (State rank: 3rd)

Density: 4,722.9 people per square mile (2000)

Racial and ethnic characteristics (2000)
White: 83,550

Black: 14,724
American Indian and Alaska Native: 232
Asian: 776
Native Hawaiian and Pacific Islander: 42
Hispanic (may be of any race): 4,572
Other: 1,991

Percent of residents born in state: 79.7% (2000)

Age characteristics (2000)
Population under 5 years old: 7,849
Population 5 to 9 years old: 7,844
Population 10 to 14 years old: 6,978
Population 15 to 19 years old: 7,615
Population 20 to 24 years old: 8,418
Population 25 to 34 years old: 14,854
Population 35 to 44 years old: 14,722
Population 45 to 54 years old: 12,109
Population 55 to 59 years old: 4,283
Population 60 to 64 years old: 3,474
Population 65 to 74 years old: 7,395
Population 75 to 84 years old: 6,409
Population 85 years and over: 2,127
Median age: 34.1 years (2000)

Births (2002, Erie County)
Total number: 3,372

Deaths (2003, Erie County)
Total number: 2,695 (of which, 23 were infants under
the age of 1 year)

Money income (1999)
Per capita income: $14,972
Median household income: $28,387
Total households: 40,908

Number of households with income of . . .
less than $10,000: 2,166
$10,000 to $14,999: 1,638
$15,000 to $24,999: 4,091
$25,000 to $34,999: 3,896
$35,000 to $49,999: 5,136
$50,000 to $74,999: 5,115
$75,000 to $99,999: 1,763
$100,000 to $149,999: 626
$150,000 to $199,999: 153
$200,000 or more: 162

Percent of families below poverty level: 13.8% (54.4% of
which were female householder families with children
under the age of 5 years)

2002 FBI Crime Index Total: 3,560

Municipal Government

Erie operates under a mayor-council form of government,
with the mayor and seven council members elected for four-
year terms.

Head Official: Mayor Richard E. Filippi (D) (since 2002;
current term expires December 31, 2005)

Total Number of City Employees: 800 (2005)

City Information: City of Erie, Municipal Building, 626
State St., Erie, PA 16501; telephone (814)870-1234

Economy

Major Industries and Commercial Activity

Erie has a diverse economy, which helps buffet it against
national downturns. Manufacturing jobs make up more than
one-quarter of the Erie area workforce. Erie has the highest
concentration of toolmakers of any place in the nation. More
than 10 percent of the nation's plastics injection molding is
done in Erie, and four of the nation's top 50 plastics companies are located there. Products in well over 135 different
classifications are made in Erie. Erie is also a major retail
center, drawing shoppers from the tri-state area and Canada.
Major service providers include the headquarters of Erie
Insurance Group, large regional hospitals, several telemar-
keting companies, and the Gertrude Barber Center. Erie has
a large tourism industry with visitors drawn by the beaches
and unique nature of Presque Isle State Park, the U.S. Brig
Niagara, a maritime museum, and other historical and recreational attractions. Agriculture is still a viable industry; Erie
County produces cherries and grapes.

Items and goods produced: plastics products, locomotives,
boilers, engines, meters, turbines, castings, forgings, pipe
equipment, motors, diesel engines, paper, grapes, cherries

Incentive Programs—New and Existing Companies

Local programs—The Erie Area Chamber of Commerce is
the first stop for companies considering relocating or expanding to the Erie area. The Chamber sends information
and sits down with company representatives to determine
their needs; it serves as a clearinghouse and referral agent to
other businesses and agencies that can help with commercial
real estate, financing, business planning, and regulations.
The Local Economic Revitalization Tax Assistance
(LERTA) program was designed in 2002. The city, school
district, and county adopted ordinances to provide for a

beneficial investment incentive for commercial and residential properties throughout the city of Erie. The ordinances provide for a 10-year period of 100 percent eligible tax exemption.

State programs—Funding programs offered by the state include bond financing, grants, loans and loan guarantees, tax credits and abatements, and technical assistance. The Keystone Opportunity Zone has designated some areas as exempt from state and local business taxes; these areas will remain virtually tax-exempt until 2013. The state's Job Creation Tax Credits program provides $1,000-per-job tax credit to approved businesses that agree to create jobs within three years.

Job training programs—State funding provides for programs such as Customized Job Training, School-to-Work initiatives, and the Dislocated Workers Unit. In Erie, the Regional Occupational Skill Center offers training in such areas as basic machining, tool-and-die pre-apprenticeships, and industrial maintenance. Northwest Pennsylvania Technical Institute offers technical training ''without walls'' in partnership with local colleges and other educational institutions. Training is based on worker needs and industry specifications.

Development Projects

Warner Theatre, showcase for the performing arts in Erie, recently completed renovations designed to upgrade the facility, as well as preserve its historical character. In addition to the restoration of the opulent furnishings that make the theater a community landmark, the loading dock was expanded and the stage area was improved. Erie's landmark downtown Boston Store (with its famous clock) was renovated to include affordable apartments and numerous offices. It is also home of the Erie Chamber of Commerce and several locally owned radio stations where disc jockeys can be observed through the windows.

More than $25 million in federal and state funding has been obtained by the city, including $12 million for Erie's new Bayfront Convention Center as well as $5 million from the governor's economic surplus package for the next phase of improvements of the Koehler Brewery Square. The convention center is expected to be completed by 2007 and will provide an additional 120,000 square feet of exhibit and convention space to the already existing three-building Civic Center Complex. A hotel will also be added.

New home construction increased by 538 percent in 2003 with the residential Local Economic Revitalization Tax Assistance program. The development of a new Wal-Mart was negotiated in a vacant plaza on the east side of town, which created more than 300 jobs and additional reinvestment in what had been a blighted neighborhood.

Splash Lagoon Indoor Water Park Resort, Pennsylvania's only indoor water park, opened in February 2003. This resort complex comprises the water park and a Lazer Tag arena, as well as numerous hotels from which guests can access the park without having to go outside. Ground was broken in 2002 for the 58,000-square-foot Tom Ridge Center at Presque Isle State Park. The recently completed facility serves as a new regional learning, research, and visitor-information facility directly outside the park entrance.

Erie's Intermodal Transportation Center was officially opened in November 2002. The $8.9-million project serves as a hub for many modes of transportation, including buses, taxi cabs, limousines, and bicycle. The 33,500-square-foot heated space also provides parking for 151 vehicles. Plans are underway for a $53-million runway expansion at the Erie International Airport, Tom Ridge Field.

Economic Development Information: Erie Area Chamber of Commerce, 208 E. Bayfront Parkway, Suite 100, Erie, PA, 16507; telephone (814)454-7191; fax (814)459-0241

Commercial Shipping

The Port of Erie, Pennsylvania's only lake port, handles imports and exports through the St. Lawrence Seaway to the Atlantic Coast and is a major distribution center for shipping and receiving goods to and from foreign countries.

Erie is served by Conrail, some 60 truck and motor freight companies, and several air cargo companies, providing convenient access to large metropolitan centers throughout the United States and Ontario, Canada. Interstates 79 and 90, intersecting just south of the city, provide easy access to all points in the country.

Labor Force and Employment Outlook

Erie ranks high in the United States in the diversity of its industry and has a history of good labor-management relations. According to Mayor Richard Filippi, more than 1,000 new jobs were created in 2003, as well as more than 30 business startups.

The following is a summary of data regarding the Erie metropolitan labor force, 2004 annual averages.

Size of nonagricultural labor force: 131,100

Number of workers employed in . . .
   construction and mining: 4,800
   manufacturing: 24,400
   trade, transportation, and utilities: 22,700
   information: 2,700
   financial activities: 6,800
   professional and business services: 11,200
   educational and health services: 23,600

leisure and hospitality: 12,600
other services: 6,200
government: 16,200

Average hourly wage of production workers employed in manufacturing: $14.72

Unemployment rate: 4.9% (April 2005)

Largest employers
(in Erie County)   *Number of employees*

Largest employers (in Erie County)	Number of employees
General Electric Company (locomotives, D.C. Motors)	5,500
St. Vincent Medical Center	2,700
Hamot Medical Center	2,500
Plastek Industries	2,000
Erie Insurance Group	1,750
Erie School District	1,425
Giant Eagle (supermarkets)	1,350

Cost of Living

The following is a summary of data regarding several key cost of living factors for the Erie area.

2004 ACCRA Average House Price: Not reported

2004 ACCRA Cost of Living Index: Not reported

State income tax rate: 3.07%

State sales tax rate: 6.0%

Local income tax rate: 1.0%

Local sales tax rate: None

Property tax rate: 49.45 mills per 100% of assessed value, which is typically 25 to 30% of market price (2004)

Economic Information: Erie Area Chamber of Commerce, 208 E. Bayfront Parkway, Suite 100, Erie, PA, 16501; telephone (814)454-7191; fax (814)459-0241

Education and Research

Elementary and Secondary Schools

Community support for quality education is strong in Erie County, where several new schools have recently been built or renovated. Erie's East High and Millcreek's Belle Valley Elementary and Walnut Creek Middle School have won various awards.

The following is a summary of data regarding Erie public schools as of the 2001–2002 school year.

Total enrollment: 12,886

Number of facilities
  elementary schools: 14
  junior high/middle schools: 3
  senior high schools: 3
  other: 1

Student/teacher ratio: 15.5:1

Teacher salaries
  minimum: $28,500
  maximum: $66,000

Funding per pupil: $7,042 (2001–2002)

The Catholic diocese of Erie oversees 22 elementary and secondary schools in the area.

Public Schools Information: The School District of the City of Erie, PA, 148 W. 21st Street, Erie, PA 16501; telephone (814)874-6000

Colleges and Universities

Erie has four colleges and a medical school: Edinboro University of Pennsylvania (approximately 7,500 students), Gannon University (more than 3,300 students), Mercyhurst College (about 3,000 students), Lake Erie College of Osteopathic Medicine (more than 600 students), and Penn State Erie (The Behrend College, with nearly 4,000 students). Career and technical training are offered at the Northwestern Pennsylvania Technical Institute and the Erie Business Center.

Libraries and Research Centers

The Erie County Library is headquartered in Erie; the main facility is the Raymond M. Blasco, M.D., Memorial Library. The library's four branches house well over a half-million volumes, and bookmobile service is available to rural areas. General Electric Company, Hammermill Paper Company, and Lord Corporation maintain technical libraries in the city. Erie's two largest health care organizations maintain medical libraries, and Mercyhurst College's collection includes the records of Erie County industries.

Erie is also home to the Erie County Historical Society Library/Archives, with its extensive holdings; the Erie County Law Library; and the Northwest Institute of Research Library. Research centers in the area include Mercyhurst College Cancer Research Unit, Gannon University's Center for Economic Education and Engineering Research Institute; Hamot Medical Center's research unit; and the Mercyhurst Archaeological Institute.

Public Library Information: Erie County Public Library System, 160 E. Front Street, Erie, PA 16507; telephone

(814)451-6900; fax (814) 451-6907; email reference @erielibrary.org

Health Care

Saint Vincent Health Center is the Erie area's largest health care provider. More than 400 staff physicians offer a full range of health care services. In addition, the staff specializes in peripheral vascular and intra-abdominal laser surgery. Its maternity center delivers more than 2,000 babies each year.

Hamot Medical Center, with a staff of more than 200 physicians, is Erie's second largest hospital. It offers total patient care and specializes in trauma, cancer, and high-risk infant care. Hamot offers specialty services through the Cardiopulmonary Center, Sports Medicine Center, the Institute for Behavioral Health, the Endoscopy Center and others. It is ranked among the nations top cardiovascular hospitals.

Erie's Millcreek Community Hospital is 135-bed acute-care teaching facility; it also provides 24-hour emergency care, physical therapy, laboratory, pharmacy, respiratory therapy, and other services. The Shriners Hospital for Children is one of 22 in the United States that accepts and treats children with orthopedic problems, utilizing the latest treatments and technology.

Erie's nationally known Dr. Gertrude A. Barber Center has four facilities in Pennsylvania that provide education, research, and state-of-the-art services for individuals with disabilities and their families.

Recreation

Sightseeing

Erie's most popular historical site is Commodore Perry's ship, the USS *Niagara,* a brig reconstructed for the centennial of the battle that took place in 1813 which was restored in 1990. In 1998, the *Niagara*'s berth moved a few hundred yards to the new Erie Maritime Museum, where it is on display when in port. The Shipwright Gift Shop is located there as well. The Bicentennial Tower offers an aerial view of Erie's Harbor, and a tour is available from 16 stations at the observation level of the tower.

The city's most notable buildings—the Old Custom House, now the Erie Art Museum; and Cashiers House, home to the collection of the Erie County Historical Society—stand side-by-side on State Street. Several other historical sites and turn-of-the-century mansions are located throughout the area. The Erie History Center presents changing exhibits on industry, architecture, and local history. The Battles Museums of Rural Life allows visitors to explore 130 acres of farmlands and woodlands, two houses, and a bank. Walking tours are sponsored by The Erie County Historical Society.

The 3,200-acre Presque Isle State Park attracts more than four million visitors annually. The park offers spectacular views of the sun setting over Lake Erie in addition to the usual park amenities. Near the entrance to the park is Waldameer Park and Water World, open mid-May until Labor Day.

The 15-acre Erie Zoological Park and Botanical Garden of Northwest Pennsylvania welcomes some 400,000 visitors each year. The main building transports visitors to Africa, as all the animals are from Africa or Madagascar. Visits to wineries in the outlying areas are also popular with visitors to Erie. The Experience Children's Museum provides hands-on fun for children and adults at its Gallery of Science and Gallery of the Human Experience. Visitors might also consider a trip to historic Chautauqua, located just east of Erie, which offers a summer program of concerts and educational and spiritual pursuits in a 750-acre park-like setting. The new Splash Lagoon is a $21-million indoor water park that is open year-round.

Arts and Culture

Several cultural organizations make up the Erie Arts Council. Among these are the Erie Philharmonic, which conducts symphonic and pops programs, and the Erie Civic Music Association, which presents concerts at the elegant Warner Theatre in the Civic Center complex. The Warner Theatre is a major cultural arts center in the region. The 2,500-seat facility is undergoing renovation in 2005 to upgrade and preserve the historic building. The Roadhouse Theatre presents ''dark, intense drama and outrageous comedy.'' The Erie Playhouse presents local talent in a variety of theatrical works at its renovated downtown theater; it has been cited as one of the top ten community theaters in the country. The Erie Chamber Orchestra provides free Friday concerts at bayfront churches and cathedrals. The Lake Erie Ballet Company's annual presentation of ''The Nutcracker'' is considered a community classic.

The 800-seat Mary D'Angelo Performing Arts Center at Mercyhurst College offers outstanding acoustics and a schedule of world-class entertainers using state-of-the-art computerized sound and lighting systems and a performance stage of 3,400 square feet.

The Erie Art Museum, which offers exhibits, classes, concerts, children's activities and tours, is located in the historic

Old Customs House. The Anthony Wayne Memorial Blockhouse Museum is a replica of the blockhouse where the general died in 1796. The museum is located on the grounds of the Pennsylvania Soldiers' and Sailors' Home. Other popular sights in Erie include the Erie Historical Museum and Planetarium, housed in a restored Victorian residence; Lake Shore Railway Museum; and the Firefighters Historical Museum.

Festivals and Holidays

Among Erie's major annual celebrations is the Erie Summer Festival of the Arts, which offers free performances and art exhibits at the Liberty Park and Pepsi Amphitheater. July brings Harborfest at Harborcreek Community Park. The Wattsburg (Erie County) Fair takes place in August and the Wine Country Harvest Festival is held in September. Erie's winter festival features holiday events including a Festival of Trees, ZooLumination at the Erie Zoo, and "The Nutcracker" ballet performance. First Night is an alcohol-free New Year's Eve celebration for children and adults.

Sports for the Spectator

The Erie Otters, a professional team in the Ontario Hockey League, entertain fans at the Erie Civic Center. At the 6,000-seat Jerry Uht Ball Field, the Erie SeaWolves, AA affiliates of the Detroit Tigers, play professional baseball from June until September.

Sports for the Participant

Erie's Presque Isle State Park, one of the most popular tourist attractions in Pennsylvania and the state's only beach park, draws more than 5 million visitors annually. The park offers a full array of year-round recreational opportunities, including swimming, boating, and skiing. The now-clean waters of Lake Erie contain more than 20 species of freshwater fish, and fishing can be enjoyed throughout the year. The Erie area supports a thriving boat rental industry. The City Parks Department operates a variety of indoor and outdoor facilities offering 107 tennis courts, 27 golf courses, and 128 swimming pools, among other amenities. U.S. Route 6, an official bicycle route, passes through the Erie area. Just outside the city is a ski resort, and the Allegheny National Forest is nearby.

Shopping and Dining

Erie has become a regional shopping center attracting shoppers from the tri-state area and Canada. Shopping venues have expanded considerably in recent years. The city has two huge plazas off upper Peach Street near I-90, and a third one, Erie Marketplace Plaza, anchored by a Target store, opened in 2001. The Millcreek Mall underwent a 1.5-million-square-foot expansion and is now home to more than 150 stores. More than 2,000 retail establishments are located in Erie, in

12 large shopping centers and 54 smaller centers. On the west side of town, Village West offers specialty stores in a New England style atmosphere. Various outlet and discount stores and antique shops are located throughout the Erie County area.

American and Italian cuisines are well represented on Erie area bills of fare, as are several other ethnicities. Pubs, grills, and café's are among the most popular eateries in the area; fast food and fine dining establishments round out the offerings.

Visitor Information: Erie Area Tourist and Convention Bureau, Inc., 208 E. Bayfront Parkway, Suite 103, Erie, PA 16507; telephone (814)454-7191

Convention Facilities

Erie's Civic Center Complex is a three-building, $20-million complex. The complex includes the Louis J. Tullio Convention Center, which seats more than 7,000 people for concerts, conventions, and sporting events; an adjacent Exhibit Hall, which features 36,000 square feet of exhibit/convention space and state-of-the-art audiovisual equipment; and the Warner Theatre. By 2007 a fourth addition is expected to open—the new $45-million Bayfront Convention Center. This 120,000-square-foot facility will overlook Presque Isle Bay. A new hotel will be added that connects it to the convention center. Some 3,200 area hotel and motel rooms support these facilities.

Convention Information: Erie Area Chamber of Commerce, 208 E. Bayfront Parkway, Suite 100, Erie, PA, 16507; telephone (814)454-7191; fax (814)459-0241

Transportation

Approaching the City

Erie International Airport, Tom Ridge Field, is located 6 miles from downtown and serves 170,000 passengers annually. For those approaching the city by car, access is made easy by a network of superhighways and access roads. Amtrak carries train passengers to the city.

Traveling in the City

Erie was laid out in a grid pattern based on a modified plan of Washington, D.C., by two surveyors who were associated with the designer of the nation's capital. Bus service is provided by the Erie Metropolitan Transit Authority. Over the past five years, $270 million has been spent on improvements to Interstates 79, 86, and 90.

Communications

Newspapers and Magazines

The Times Publishing Company provides newspaper readers with the dailies the *Erie Morning News* and the *Erie Daily Times,* and the weeklies the *Erie Sunday Times, Weekender* on Saturday morning, and *Your Money* on Thursday. Magazines published in Erie include *Erie & Chautauqua Magazine, Pax Christi USA,* the *Fraternal Leader,* a Christian family magazine, and two business trade publications, *Builder/Dealer* and *Business Systems Dealer.*

Television and Radio

Television viewers in Erie are entertained by four television networks. Cable service is also available. Four AM and 10 FM radio stations broadcast from Erie.

Media Information: Times Publishing Company, 205 West 12th Street, Erie, PA 15634; telephone (814)870-1600

Erie Online

City of Erie Home Page. Available www.cityoferiepa.com

Erie Chamber of Commerce. Available www.eriechamber.com

Erie County Public Library. Available www.erielibrary.org

Erie School District. Available esd.iu5.org

Erie Tourist Information. Available www.visiteriepa.com

School District Profile. Available www.paprofiles.org

Selected Bibliography

Daughters of the American Revolution, *Soldiers of the American Revolution Who at Some Time Were Residents of, or Whose Graves . . .* (Erie, PA: 1929)

Erie Yesterday, *Erie County, Pennsylvania* (Arcadia Tempus Publishing Group, 1997)

Harrisburg

The City in Brief

Founded: 1791 (incorporated as city, 1860)

Head Official: Mayor Stephen R. Reed (D) (since 1982)

City Population
1980: 53,264
1990: 52,376
2000: 48,950
2003 estimate: 48,322
Percent change, 1990–2000: −6.5%
U.S. rank in 1980: 447th
U.S. rank in 1990: 473rd
U.S. rank in 2000: Not reported (State rank: 17th)

Metropolitan Area Population
1980: 556,000
1990: 587,986
2000: 629,401
Percent change, 1990–2000: 7%

U.S. rank in 1980: 62nd
U.S. rank in 1990: 67th
U.S. rank in 2000: 66th

Area: 11.44 square miles (2000)
Elevation: Ranges from 100 to 358 feet above sea level
Average Annual Temperature: 52.9° F
Average Annual Precipitation: 40.5 inches of rain; 34.3 inches of snow

Major Economic Sectors: Manufacturing, services, retail trade, state government
Unemployment Rate: 3.6% (April 2005)
Per Capita Income: $15,787 (1999)

2002 FBI Crime Index Total: 2,928

Major Colleges and Universities: Harrisburg Area Community College, Penn State Downtown Center, Penn State Eastgate Center, Temple University at Harrisburg, Dixon University Center at Harrisburg

Daily Newspaper: *The Patriot-News*

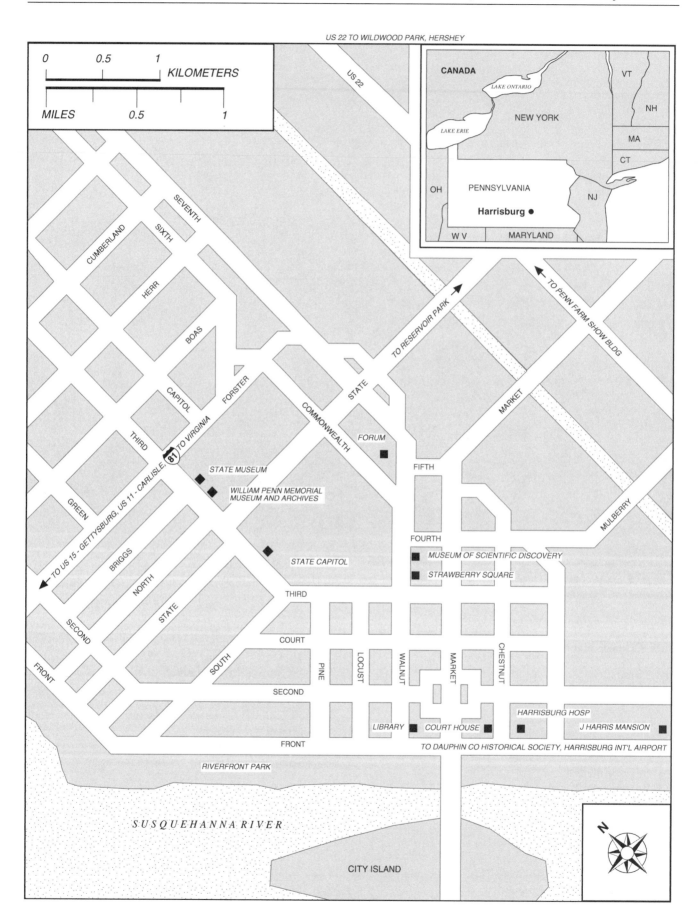

US 22 TO WILDWOOD PARK, HERSHEY

US 22

0   0.5   1
KILOMETERS

MILES   0.5   1

CANADA

LAKE ONTARIO

NEW YORK

VT

NH

LAKE ERIE

MA

CT

OH

PENNSYLVANIA

NJ

Harrisburg ●

W V   MARYLAND

SEVENTH

SIXTH

CUMBERLAND

HERR

BOAS

TO RESERVOIR PARK →

← TO PENN FARM SHOW BLDG

CAPITOL

FORSTER

STATE

MARKET

THIRD

COMMONWEALTH

FORUM

TO VIRGINIA

81

STATE MUSEUM

FIFTH

MULBERRY

WILLIAM PENN MEMORIAL MUSEUM AND ARCHIVES

GREEN

FOURTH

MUSEUM OF SCIENTIFIC DISCOVERY

STATE CAPITOL

STRAWBERRY SQUARE

← TO US 15 - GETTYSBURG, US 11 - CARLISLE, US 11

BRIGGS

THIRD

NORTH

COURT

CHESTNUT

SECOND

STATE

PINE

LOCUST

WALNUT

MARKET

SOUTH

SECOND

FRONT

HARRISBURG HOSP

LIBRARY   COURT HOUSE

J HARRIS MANSION

FRONT

TO DAUPHIN CO HISTORICAL SOCIETY, HARRISBURG INT'L AIRPORT

RIVERFRONT PARK

SUSQUEHANNA RIVER

N

CITY ISLAND

Introduction

Harrisburg is the capital of the Commonwealth of Pennsylvania and a major distribution center for the northeastern United States. Located on the Susquehanna River near the beautiful Blue Mountains, it offers the amenities of a big city with the ambiance of a small town. Harrisburg has received top national awards for budgeting, water pollution control, law enforcement, and conservation for several years running. The prosperity of the business climate can be seen in the area's selection in June 2004 as one of the ''country's hottest up & coming cities'' for populations between 500,000 to one million by *Money* magazine.

Geography and Climate

Harrisburg is located on the eastern bank of the Susquehanna River, 100 miles west of Philadelphia, at a gap in the Blue Mountains between the Cumberland and Lebanon valleys created by the river. The terrain is rolling, with a band of flat land in the southern part of Dauphin County ranging up to a mile wide along the Susquehanna River. The region is underlain by limestone which, combined with the gently rolling terrain, creates an ideal farming environment.

Harrisburg's climate is humid continental; there are four distinct but mild seasons. Summers are warm to occasionally hot with relatively high humidity; winters are comparatively mild for the region's latitude.

Area: 11.44 square miles (2000)

Elevation: Ranges from 100 to 358 feet above sea level

Average Temperatures: January, 28.6° F; July, 73.5° F; average annual temperature, 52.9° F

Average Annual Precipitation: 40.5 inches of rain; 34.3 inches of snow

History

Susquehanna River a Crossing for Indians, Europeans

Native Americans occupied what is now Harrisburg as early as 5,000 years ago. The first European contact with Native Americans in Pennsylvania was made by the Englishman, Captain John Smith, who journeyed from Virginia up the Susquehanna River in 1608 and visited with the Susquehanna tribe. The Shawnees, a nomadic tribe, and members of the Algonquin nation came to the Susquehanna Valley from the southwest in the 1690s. The Swedes and the French used the Susquehanna River as a route during their explorations of the Middle Atlantic Region but did not settle there. The Englishman, John Harris, was the first white man to appreciate the region's strategic location. He established a trading post at the site in about 1710 and began ferry service in 1733. After Harris' death in 1748, his son, John, continued his father's liberal policies with the natives so there was considerable settlement of the region by the time of the French and Indian Wars of 1753–58.

Thousands of German settlers were attracted by the rich farmlands, and their industriousness contributed to the region's prosperity. The iron industry became so important that workers were forbidden to leave work to join the militia during the American Revolution unless they had special permission. Following the Revolution, the Pennsylvania state assembly created Dauphin County out of a portion of Lancaster County and directed the establishment of a county seat near Harris's Ferry. They temporarily named the county seat Louisburg in honor of the French king who had been so helpful during the Revolution. But John Harris refused to sell the land for the county seat under these terms, and it was agreed that the new name would be Harrisburg, in honor of his father.

City Becomes State Capital, Transportation Hub

Harrisburg's location on major east-west routes and the importance of the Susquehanna River as a gateway north and south quickly established the city as a business center. At the same time, there was growing sentiment in the Commonwealth of Pennsylvania against what were seen as the aristocratic goals of the Federalists in Philadelphia, capital of the United States from 1790 to 1800. When it came time to select a state capital, the choice of Harrisburg became official in 1812.

Stagecoach lines from Philadelphia had reached Harrisburg by 1776. By the 1830s Harrisburg was part of the Pennsylvania canal system and an important railroad center as well. Steel and iron became dominant industries. To the original German settlers were added people from the rest of the nation and immigrants from throughout the Old World, especially Scots-Irish, Welsh, French, and Huguenots. Because farming was still the predominant industry, Harrisburg did not develop in the arts, music, and science as did Philadelphia—the lack of leisure time and concentration of population hindered that development. Settlers in Harrisburg and environs did bring with them aspects of European culture that flourished, including the fashioning of pottery, furniture, glass works, and pewterware, and the use of brass instruments.

Harrisburg's population had grown to more than 13,000 people by 1860, when it was incorporated as a city. Its industrial power played a decisive role in the Civil War, and it also served as a Union Army training center. Harrisburg was the target of a Confederate Army invasion in 1863, but General Robert E. Lee stopped his troops a few miles from the city and ordered them to proceed to nearby Gettysburg, where the battle ensued that was to be the turning point of the Civil War.

Prosperity, Building, Culture Distinguish City

Steel and other industries continued to play a major role in the local economy throughout the latter part of the nineteenth century. The city was the center of enormous railroad traffic and supported large furnaces, rolling mills, and machine shops. The Pennsylvania Steel Company plant, which opened in nearby Steelton in 1866, was the first in the country; it is now operated by Bethlehem Steel. Harrisburg Car Manufacturing Company began as a railroad car manufacturer in 1853; in 1935 the firm changed its name to Harrisburg Steel Company then in 1956 to Harsco, a diversified *Fortune* 500 company. Many fine schools and churches were built; banks and other institutions were founded. Stately residences were erected overlooking the Susquehanna River. The first three decades of the twentieth century saw the building of high-rise department stores and opulent hotels. A $12.5-million expansion of the state capitol complex was completed in 1906, and many cultural institutions were founded.

Decline Followed by Rebirth

As was the case throughout the industrialized Northeast, Harrisburg began to decline after World War II as residents moved to the suburbs. The decline continued into the early 1980s, when Harrisburg was regarded as one of the most distressed cities in the country. The area's economic troubles were heavily influenced by the nuclear accident at the nearby Three Mile Island power plant in 1979 that resulted in mass evacuations and a loss of billions of dollars. Small amounts of radiation entered the atmosphere, though no deaths were ever attributed to the partial meltdown.

A revitalization spurred by business and industrial development led to residential restoration and new building. During the period 1982–2003, over $3.4 billion in new investment was undertaken in Harrisburg, one of the highest investment rates in the country for a city its size. After 30 years of suburban flight, the city realized its first net population gain in 1995 as thousands of new residents joined a burgeoning "back-to-the-city" movement. Although the population declined by the 2000 Census, Harrisburg, which remains an important transportation hub for every mode of travel, is enthusiastic about its prospects as a rejuvenated city in a stunning natural setting on the Susquehanna River with its abundance of beautiful isles.

Harrisburg boasts a pro-business, reform mayor in Stephen R. Reed, whose initiatives since he took office in 1982 related to economic development, creation of non-tax revenue sources, and the improvement of the operations of local government that have helped to turn around a city that at the start of the 1980s was considered the second most distressed in the nation under the Federal distress criteria. In the period from 1981 to 2003, the city experienced a crime rate reduction of 56.5 percent while the fire rate fell by 76.3 percent. This change put the city in the eleventh spot for "Best Crime Rate in the Nation" on *Forbes* 2004 Rankings for Performance list. Central business district revitalization has resulted in nearly 9.2 million gross square feet of developed business land in the downtown, or Center City area, figures that led to *Inc.* magazine's ranking Harrisburg eighteenth on its March 2004 "Top 25 for Doing Business in America" for medium-sized cities.

This growth contributed to a record number of 6,951 businesses in 2005 for the city. According to Mayor Reed, "The City of Harrisburg has become an example of urban resurgence at a time when many of America's cities continue to undergo further decline and serious economic stress. Harrisburg's renewal has been multi-faceted, touching virtually every area of city governmental and community endeavor."

Historical Information: Dauphin County Historical Society, 219 S. Front St., Harrisburg, PA 17104; telephone (717)233-3462; fax (717)233-6059; email hsdc@paonline .com. Pennsylvania Historical and Museum Commission, State Museum Bldg., 300 North St., Harrisburg, PA 17120; telephone (717)787-3362

Population Profile

Metropolitan Area Population
1980: 556,000
1990: 587,986
2000: 629,401
Percent change 1990–2000: 7%
U.S. rank in 1980: 62nd
U.S. rank in 1990: 67th
U.S. rank in 2000: 66th

City Residents
1980: 53,264
1990: 52,376
2000: 48,950
2003 estimate: 48,322
Percent change, 1990–2000: −6.5%
U.S. rank in 1980: 447th
U.S. rank in 1990: 473rd
U.S. rank in 2000: Not reported (State rank: 17th)

Density: 6,035.6 people per square mile (2000)

Racial and ethnic characteristics (2000)
    White: 15,527
    Black or African American: 26,841
    American Indian and Alaska Native: 183
    Asian: 1,384
    Native Hawaiian and Pacific Islander: 35
    Hispanic or Latino (may be of any race): 5,724
    Other: 3,199

Percent of residents born in state: 68.3% (2000)

Age characteristics (2000)
    Population under 5 years old: 3,968
    Population 5 to 9 years old: 4,158
    Population 10 to 14 years old: 3,794
    Population 15 to 19 years old: 3,139
    Population 20 to 24 years old: 3,228
    Population 25 to 34 years old: 7,593
    Population 35 to 44 years old: 7,561
    Population 45 to 54 years old: 6,459
    Population 55 to 59 years old: 2,140
    Population 60 to 64 years old: 1,590
    Population 65 to 74 years old: 2,807
    Population 75 to 84 years old: 1,808
    Population 85 years and over: 705
    Median age: 33.0 years (2000)

Births (2002)
    Total number: 849

Deaths (2003)
    Total number: 565 (of which, 11 were infants under
    the age of 1 year)

Money income (1999)
    Per capita income: $15,787
    Median household income: $26,920
    Total households: 20,613

Number of households with income of . . .
    less than $10,000: 3,786
    $10,000 to $14,999: 2,054
    $15,000 to $24,999: 3,790
    $25,000 to $34,999: 3,215
    $35,000 to $49,999: 3,151
    $50,000 to $74,999: 2,691
    $75,000 to $99,999: 1,045
    $100,000 to $149,999: 581
    $150,000 to $199,999: 145
    $200,000 or more: 155

Percent of families below poverty level: 23.4% (53.4% of
    which were female householder families with related
    children under 5 years)

2002 FBI Crime Index Total: 2,928

Municipal Government

Harrisburg's is a strong mayor form of government, with separate executive and legislative branches. The mayor and seven council members are elected to four-year terms.

Head Official: Mayor Stephen R. Reed (D) (since 1982; current term expires January 2006)

Total Number of City Employees: 721 (2003)

City Information: Office of the Mayor, City of Harrisburg, City Government Center, 10 N Second St., Ste. 202, Harrisburg, PA 17101; telephone (717)255-3040; fax (717)255-3036; email mayor@cityofhbg.com

Economy

Major Industries and Commercial Activity

Harrisburg is the metropolitan center for some 400 communities. Its economy and more than 6,900 businesses are diversified with a large representation of service-related industries (especially health) and growing technological industry to accompany the dominant government field inherent to being the state's capital. National firms either headquartered in the region or with major operations there include Tyco Electronics Corp. (components), IBM, Hershey Foods, Harsco Corp., and Rite Aid Corp. (retailers). The largest employer, state government, provides stability to the economy and attracts attendant services. Excellent roads and rail transportation contribute to the city's prominence as a center for trade, warehousing, and distribution.

Items and goods produced: shoes, books, computer products, food products, textiles, apparel, leather goods, machinery, railway equipment

Incentive Programs—New and Existing Companies

Local programs—The Mayor's Office of Economic Development (MOED), created in 1983, supports new and expanding businesses in site selection and securing financing. The city also offers tax abatement on new investment, lower property tax millage on improvements, below-market-rate financial assistance, investment tax credits, and more. The MOED directs business and industrial development programs, including the Division of Contract Compliance and Minority and Female Business Enterprises which offers certification programs, financial counseling, and bid assistance. City incentives designed to increase residential sales in Harrisburg include the Mortgage Tax Credit Certification Program, real estate tax abatements, special financing, and investment tax credits, among others.

The Harrisburg Regional Chamber, through the Capital Region Economic Development Corporation (CREDC), is an active association offering a variety of services to enhance business growth, including lobbying at all levels of government, sponsoring an annual business fair, offering financing programs including small business loans, and providing training programs.

State programs—The state of Pennsylvania provides about 100 programs for new and existing businesses that are searchable at the Pennsylvania Department of Community & Economic Development's (dubbed NewPA) website, which works with new and existing companies and community leaders to foster development and growth for businesses and neighborhoods. Ben Franklin Technology Partners operates four centers throughout the state with Harrisburg and Dauphin County under the central and northern district that provides assistance to entrepreneurs via investments, information, and solutions. The Team Pennsylvania Foundation (more commonly referred to as Team PA) was founded in 1997 to bolster the state's business environment by collaborating the efforts of business and government leaders to feed into the creation of initiatives and programs.

Job training programs—The most widely used state and federal programs to help employers reduce the costs of hiring and training workers include the federal 1998 Workforce Investment Act (WIA), Customized Job Training (CJT) funded by the Commonwealth of Pennsylvania and maintained by the Pennsylvania Workforce Development department, Work Opportunity Tax Credit (WOTC) Program, and a state-tax-credit Employment Incentive Payment (EIP) Program. Harrisburg Area Community College (HACC) offers customized training programs for business and industry and in 2001 opened a new Technology Training Center. Shippensburg University, accredited by the American Assembly of Collegiate Schools of Business, offers custom-tailored programs through its Frehn Center for Management. The Mayor's Office of Economic Development (MOED) also helps in identifying training programs for local businesses.

Development Projects

Harrisburg claims national recognition for its strong economy and high quality of life. City planners continue to follow a comprehensive land use plan titled "Forum 2000" that covers a wide array of different elements of the community including downtown, commercial, and neighborhood development along with recreational opportunities, transportation resources, and parking availability.

In its recent history, Harrisburg has witnessed the opening of the $52.7 million Whitaker Center for Science and the Arts in

1999 and the $10 million conversion of a Ramada Inn in 2000 to the Crowne Plaza Harrisburg hotel and conference center. In the planning stages is the "Entertainment Crossroads" that will encompass several streets and blend existing and new entertainment and nightlife amenities into various corridors and bolster the availability of hospitality and commercial services. The future creation of "Neighborhood Service Centers" will allow residents nearby availability of convenience shopping, personal and business services, professional services, and recreational centers which will recreate an old-time, small-town feel.

Economic Development Information: City of Harrisburg, Mayor's Office of Economic Development, City Government Center, 10 N. 2nd St., Ste. 405, Harrisburg, PA 17101; telephone (717)255-3027; fax (717)255-6432; email moed @cityofhbg.com. Harrisburg Regional Chamber, 3211 N. Front St., Ste. 201, Harrisburg, PA 17110-1342; telephone (717)232-4099; fax (717)232-5184

Commercial Shipping

Located midway between Philadelphia and Pittsburgh, Harrisburg grew up from its earliest days as a transportation center and has long been an important freight center. All major air, rail, and highway arteries linking the markets of the East, Midwest, and South pass through the region. There are eight public airports in the region, the largest being Harrisburg International Airport (HIA), a modern facility where twice the national average of freight and mail (in excess of 61,000 tons annually) are handled by five air freight forwarders. The Susquehanna Area Regional Airport Authority (SARAA) and the city are in the process of establishing HIA as a Foreign Trade Zone (FTZ), which would facilitate in the delivery of local goods to the international market. Several major interstate and U.S. highways connect the region to major metropolitan areas, and local roads are well maintained. Norfolk Southern operates two intermodal freight facilities within the city, which also opened up the rail for freight service between Canada and the Gulf of Mexico.

Labor Force and Employment Outlook

The Capital Region boasts a growing pool of talented, productive, and educated workers. While the city's population decreased by more than six percent, the metropolitan area's population increased seven percent between 1990–2000. Wages paid in the region are reported to be competitive. The state provides resources to area residents through its Pennsylvania Workforce Development department as does the Capital Region Economic Development Corporation (CREDC).

The following is a summary of data regarding the Harrisburg-Carlisle metropolitan area labor force, 2004 annual averages.

Size of nonagricultural labor force: 323,000

Number of workers employed in . . .
  construction and mining: 12,100
  manufacturing: 25,500
  trade, transportation, and utilities: 69,100
  information: 6,400
  financial activities: 24,800
  professional and business services: 35,200
  educational and health services: 42,900
  leisure and hospitality: 26,900
  other services: 17,200
  government: 63,000

*Average hourly earnings of workers employed in manu-
  facturing:* $15.15

Unemployment rate: 3.6% (April 2005)

Largest employers
(Harrisburg metropolitan
statistical area)	*Number of employees*
Commonwealth of Pennsylvania	31,200
U.S. Government	11,600
Hershey Food Corp.	5,600
Highmark Blue Shield	5,600
Tyco Electronics Corp.	5,332
Hershey Medical Center	4,251
PinnacleHealth	3,587
EDS Corp.	2,708
Rite Aid Corp.	2,375
County of Dauphin	2,175

Cost of Living

The following is a summary of data regarding several key cost of living factors for the Harrisburg area.

2004 (3rd Quarter) ACCRA Average Home Price: $240,280

2004 (3rd Quarter) ACCRA Cost of Living Index: 98 (U.S. average = 100.0)

State income tax rate: 3.07%

State sales tax rate: 6%

Local income tax rate: none

Local sales tax rate: none

Property tax rate: in the two-rate system, 24.414 mills on land; 4.069 mills on building and improvements

Economic Information: Capital Region Economic Development Corporation, 3211 N. Front St., Ste. 201, Harrisburg, PA 17110-1342; telephone (717)232-4099; fax (717)232-5184

Education and Research

Elementary and Secondary Schools

The Harrisburg Public Schools offer special programs in remedial and special education and for the gifted and handicapped along with courses toward English as a second language. A collaborative high school with the Harrisburg University of Science and Technology focuses on math and science studies; there is one vocational-technical school. The district is operated by an unpaid five-member board that is appointed by the mayor.

The following is a summary of data regarding the Harrisburg public schools as of the 2003–2004 school year.

Total enrollment: 7,663

Number of facilities
  elementary/middle schools: 12
  high schools: 1
  other: 1 alternative school

Student/teacher ratio: 13:1

Teacher salaries
  average: $49,123

Funding per pupil: $10,754

Private school education is offered at seven parochial institutions and at Harrisburg Academy, as well as a number of other secular institutions.

Public Schools Information: Harrisburg School District, 2101 N Front St., Bldg. 2, Harrisburg, PA 17110-1081; telephone (717)703-4000. Pennsylvania Department of Education, Division of Data Services, 333 Market St., Harrisburg, PA 17126-0333; telephone (717)787-2644; fax (717)787-3148; email ra-ddsadmin@state.pa.us

Colleges and Universities

Ten colleges, five community/junior colleges, and three graduate schools are located in the Harrisburg area. Among these are branches of three major universities—Penn State, Temple University, and Widener University. Institutions located in the city limits are Harrisburg Area Community College (HACC), founded in 1964 and the state's first community college, offering more than 100 associate degrees, certificates, and diploma programs; Penn State's Downtown and Eastgate Centers; Temple University at Harrisburg; Dixon University Center at Harrisburg, part of the State System of Higher Education and offering graduate degrees in Business Administration, Library Studies, Public Administration, and Safety Science; and the Pittsburgh-based Computer Tech.

Penn State's College of Medicine at Hershey offers graduate programs for doctors, nurses, and medical researchers. Carlisle is home to the Army War College and Penn State's Dickinson School of Law. Shippensburg University specializes in business; its campus looks out on the Blue Mountains.

Libraries and Research Centers

The Dauphin County Library System, founded in 1889, is headquartered in downtown Harrisburg on Walnut Street and also maintains a facility in Colonial Park (East Shore Area Library) along with six additional branches located throughout the region. The system holds more than 321,000 items including periodical subscriptions, tapes, videos, and maps. Special collections focus on local history and grantsmanship. Internet access is available at all locations.

The State Library of Pennsylvania serves the reference needs of state government and acts as the regional library resource center for public, college, and special libraries. It holds about one million general interest volumes along with 6,500 serials and maintains special genealogy, periodical, and law libraries. At the State Archives, created in 1903, are government and private papers relating to Pennsylvania history that includes 195 million pages of documents and manuscripts, 20,000 reels of microfilm, and one million special collection items. Also located in Harrisburg are the collections of many libraries of state agencies, available for use by researchers and others through special arrangement. Rare medical books are housed at George T. Harrell Library at Pennsylvania State University College of Medicine at nearby Hershey. The Alexander Family Library, part of the Dauphin County Historical Society, features genealogy and local history resources.

Government-related research centers in Harrisburg include the Legislative Office for Research Liaison (LORL), which coordinates the research needs of legislators using the capabilities of academic researchers. Pennsylvania Family Institute studies family issues as they relate to government policy.

Milton S. Hershey Medical Center conducts AIDS and cancer research, as well as an artificial heart research project, biostatistics, and epidemiology. Hershey Foods Corp. maintains an Information Analysis Center.

Public Library Information: Dauphin County Library System, 101 Walnut St., Harrisburg, PA 17101; telephone (717)234-4961; fax (717)234-7479; email HDBweb@dcls.org

Health Care

PinnacleHealth is a community-based system offering comprehensive services and programs for people of all ages and backgrounds in Central Pennsylvania, from prenatal and maternity services to gerontology. Care is provided through four hospitals in Harrisburg: Community General Osteopathic, Harrisburg, Polyclinic, and Seidle, as well as the Fredricksen Outpatient Center, a network of family practice and urgent care centers, managed care entities, home healthcare, hospice, and an array of other healthcare services. PinnacleHealth's medical staff is comprised of more than 800 primary care physicians supported by more than 4,000 skilled nurses and technicians.

Since 1845 Harrisburg has been the home of the Harrisburg State Hospital, a psychiatric facility, which is located on 200 acres and comprised of 50 buildings. With most mental health patients being cared for at community-based centers, it was announced in January 2005 that the hospital would close. The decision will impact approximately 250 patients and 540 staff members, although patient numbers have steadily declined since the early 1990s.

Health Care Information: PinnacleHealth System, PO Box 8700, Harrisburg, PA 17101-8700; telephone (717)782-5678

Recreation

Sightseeing

Harrisburg can be conveniently divided into five districts for sightseeing purposes: Center City, the Shipoke Historic District, the Capitol district and complex, Old Uptown Historic District, and Allison Hill.

Highlights of Center City, where most historic buildings were spared in rebuilding, include Riverfront Park, a scenic five-mile stretch that features a sunken flower garden, and City Hall, where sightseeing brochures can be obtained and perused at an outdoor plaza bedecked with sculptural works.

In the Front Street area of Center City, Governor's Row preserves several townhouses that housed early state chief executives. Also of interest are the art-deco Dauphin County Courthouse and a number of nineteenth-century churches.

The Shipoke Historic District, a late nineteenth-century residential area overlooking the Susquehanna River, contains the John Harris/Simon Cameron Mansion as well as restored townhouses interspersed with modern dwellings.

The Capitol district and complex contains the Capitol Building, an Italian Renaissance structure covering two acres and surrounded by a 13-acre park. Considered by many to be the finest such structure in the country, the Capitol Building features a dome modeled after St. Peter's basilica in Rome and stairs patterned after those at the Grand Opera in Paris.

Hershey Park is a popular attraction for children.

Also located in the district are the State Museum of Pennsylvania, with exhibits relating to the state's history from earth's beginning to the present time, and the beautiful churches and mansions preserved on State and Front streets.

The Old Uptown Historic District encompasses the Historic Midtown District. Highlights there include late nineteenth- and early twentieth-century residences of various architectural styles and, a short distance away, Italian Lake, created from a swamp in the 1930s and spanned by a picturesque Italian Bridge. Contained in the baroque park setting is the Obelisk, a memorial to Dauphin County's Civil War soldiers.

Allison Hill is the name used for the portion of the city that rises above the Susquehanna Valley. In the area are found the Mount Pleasant Historic District (Allison Hill's oldest section); Bellevue Park, an early planned residential community laid out in 1910; and McFarland House, an Italianate residence built in 1876 and later home to J. Horace McFarland, horticulturist, environmentalist, and publisher. State Street East is a grand boulevard that descends from Allison Hill to the Soldiers and Sailors Memorial Bridge and State Capitol Complex.

Of special interest to children are the Museum of Scientific Discovery (on the third level of the Strawberry Square Mall) with a variety of exhibits on subjects such as aviation, Earth and space, and biology along with the Fire Museum of Greater Harrisburg, Indian Echo Caverns in Hummelstown, and Hersheypark in Hershey. Known as the most beautiful "company town" in the country, Hershey is the headquarters of Hershey Foods Corporation and was conceived as a story-book-like town for company employees. Sights there include Chocolate World, Hersheypark, Zooamerica, Hershey Gardens, and the Hershey Museum. The Hessian Powder Magazine Museum of Carlisle describes the contributions of Hessian soldiers to the American Revolution.

Arts and Culture

A major venue for the performing arts in Harrisburg is the 1,763-seat State Forum, an art-deco edifice located in the state government built in 1931. There the Harrisburg Symphony Orchestra, founded in 1930, presents seven classical and three pops series, three outdoor summer concerts, and special concerts and guest artists. Market Square Concerts brings national and international performing artists to Harrisburg between September and May with most concerts held in the Market Square Presbyterian Church. Central Pennsylvania Friends of Jazz sponsors several performances at varied locations. Rounding out the musical offerings are performances by the Harrisburg Opera Association, the Harrisburg Singers, Chamber Singers of Harrisburg, Harrisburg Choral Society, and the Susquehanna Folk Music Society.

Theatre Harrisburg, formerly known as Harrisburg Community Theatre and founded in 1926, has its own playhouse

and stages full-scale productions. Rose Lehrman Arts Center at Harrisburg Area Community College holds concerts and theatrical events and is home to Open Stage of Harrisburg, which presents works reflecting the area's multicultural population. One of the Central Pennsylvania Youth Ballet studios resides in Harrisburg while a lively network of local theater groups, historical societies, literary and music clubs, and art associations complete the city's rich cultural landscape.

The Art Association of Harrisburg (AAH) offers 10 annual exhibitions of works in all styles and mediums by artists from around the world. In Reservoir Park is a restored 1898 mansion that contains an art gallery as well as the National Civil War Museum at Harrisburg, the nation's largest Civil War museum, with artifacts and collections from both the Union and the Confederacy. One of the world's largest paintings, "The Battle of Gettysburg: Pickett's Charge," is displayed at the State Museum of Pennsylvania, home to an extensive collection of state historical documents and artifacts. Other museums in Harrisburg are John Harris/Simon Cameron Mansion, home of the Dauphin County Historical Society and its collections and library; and Fort Hunter Mansion and Park.

Festivals and Holidays

Harrisburg proper is the site of the well-attended Greater Harrisburg ArtsFest at Riverfront Park in May; the Central Pennsylvania Commerce Bank Jazz Festival and Harrisburg Shakespeare Festival in June; American MusicFest at Riverfront Park for the Fourth of July and Pennsylvania Pump Primers Muster in mid-July; and the Dauphin County 4-H Fair in August and the official Labor Day celebration, known as Kipona Festival, at Riverfront Park. The Harrisburg Holiday Parade opens the holiday season, and a New Year's Eve Celebration is held on Market Square. In addition, many arts and crafts fairs with juried exhibitions and ethnic festivals are held throughout the region.

The Pennsylvania State Farm Show Complex, a 25-acre exposition hall that is one of the largest of its kind in the country, hosts the Pennsylvania Farm Show and Pennsylvania Auto & Boat Show in January, the Eastern Sports & Outdoor Show in February, Annual Spring Craft Show in March, the Pennsylvania Relief Sale of Mennonite crafts in early April, the Eastern National Antique Show in late April, the RV and Camping Show in mid-September, the All-American Dairy Show in late September, the Pennsylvania State 4-H Horse Show in October, and the Pennsylvania and Gift Show in early December.

Sports for the Spectator

City Island, in the Susquehanna River, contains Commerce Bank Park, home of Harrisburg's Eastern League Class

Double-A minor league baseball team the Senators (affiliated in 2005 with Major League Baseball's Washington Nationals), whose season extends from April to Labor Day. Spectators gather downtown each June for the Faulkner Honda Harrisburg Criterium international cycling event.

Hersheypark Arena is home to the Hershey Bears, an American Hockey (AHL) team that entertains fans from October through April. The arena also hosts the Ice Capades and the Harlem Globetrotters. Hershey Country Club is home to the Reese's Cup Classic in May, although this was cancelled in 2005 due to ongoing renovations at the club. Sprint-car racing goes on at area tracks, and Penn National Race Course in Grantville offers the opportunity for betting on thoroughbred horses.

Sports for the Participant

Harrisburg's Department of Parks and Recreation maintains a network of 17 recreational sites, 27 parks and playgrounds, two pools, and tennis courts. The city's recreational showpiece is City Island, located in the Susquehanna River only 400 yards from downtown. In addition to the usual park facilities, the Island offers riding stables, miniature golf, swimming, jogging and nature trails, volleyball courts, multipurpose playing fields, and much more. Recreational facilities are also available at Italian Lake Park, Reservoir Park, and Riverfront Park. Wildwood Park, a wildlife haven, has bike and hiking trails and picnic areas. Harrisburg sponsors the Harrisburg Marathon & Relay and other running events throughout the year. Fifteen public and private golf courses are located in the region. Fishing on the Susquehanna River is a popular pastime, and islands in the river may be explored by boat or canoe. Nearby Carlisle boasts the best fly-fishing streams in the East while Ski Roundtop has facilities for the winter (skiing and snowboarding) and summer (rock climbing and paintball) sports enthusiast.

Recreation Information: Department of Parks and Recreation, City of Harrisburg, 10 N 2nd St., Ste. 401, Harrisburg, PA 17101; telephone (717)255-3020; fax (717)255-6554

Shopping and Dining

Downtown shopping in Harrisburg centers around the Shops at Strawberry Square, two floors of enclosed shopping located in a huge office complex. More than 40 shops and galleries along with 10 food emporiums are contained in about 170,000 square feet of retail space. Harrisburg East Mall is the city's other main shopping area, a 90-store complex anchored by Hecht's, Bass Pro Shops, and Boscov's. Specialty stores can also be found at adjacent Walnut Place and along a number of streets in Center City. Broad Street Farmers Market, dating back to 1860, offers fresh produce Thursday through Saturday. It is located in the Historic Midtown Market District, a neighborhood shopping area that also features antique and art shops. Harrisburg is a major East Coast outlet shopping center—bus charters bring in thousands of shoppers annually.

Downtown dining opportunities have expanded to accommodate increased tourism and convention business. Cuisine ranges from Philadelphia steaks to seafood. One local establishment, The Fire House at Hope Station, is located on the first floor of an 1871 firehouse.

Visitor Information: Harrisburg-Hershey-Carlisle Tourism and Convention Bureau, 415 Market St., Rm. 208, Harrisburg, PA 17101; telephone (717)231-7788; toll-free (800)955-0969

Convention Facilities

Harrisburg's largest convention facility is the 341-room Hilton Hotel & Towers. Located at Market Square and linked by an overhead walkway to Strawberry Square, the Hilton offers the 9,472-square-foot Harrisburg Ballroom with a reception capacity of about 1,200 guests; overall, the facility provides 17,000 square feet of meeting space. The Harrisburg Holiday Inn Hotel and Conference Center, with 299 rooms, has 21,000 square feet of meeting space. The State Farm Show Complex, one of the largest exhibition halls in the country, offers space for large shows and hosts more than 200 events annually. The 43,000-square-foot Wildwood Conference Center at the Harrisburg Area Community College (HACC) can facilitate more than 300 events annually for a variety of group sizes. With its mountain views, the Ski Roundtop is a picturesque setting for meetings, company outings, and conferences.

Convention Information: Harrisburg-Hershey-Carlisle Tourism and Convention Bureau, 415 Market St., Rm. 208, Harrisburg, PA 17101; telephone (717)231-7788; toll-free (800)955-0969

Transportation

Approaching the City

Harrisburg International Airport (HIA), eight miles south of Center City, offers 7 major airlines to 13 domestic stops along with one international destination as well as short-hop commuter service. Services at HIA, operating under the Susquehanna Area Regional Airport Authority (SARAA), continue to expand to accommodate increasing traffic (about 750,000 enplanements per year). Also under SARAA's ownership is the Capital City Airport, which is available for charters and business and pleasure craft. Philadelphia International Airport, 100 miles from Harrisburg, may be the most convenient destination for visitors flying in from distant locations.

Harrisburg is easily accessible by car. Interstate highways 76 (Pennsylvania Turnpike), 78, 81, and 83 cross in the region and connect it to major metropolitan areas. Other major highways are U.S. 11, 15, 22, 322, and 422.

Amtrak's main east-west line carries passengers into the restored Harrisburg Transportation Center (formerly the 1884 Pennsylvania Railroad Station) on 16 daily departures. The center is a hub for a planned light-rail, commuter transit system and a cross-state high-speed rail line. The Southeastern Pennsylvania Transportation Authority (SEPTA) provides commuter and high-speed rail service out of Philadelphia. Bus lines carrying passengers into the region from other locales include Greyhound, Fullington Trailways, and Capitol Trailways. Capital Area Transit provides local bus service.

Traveling in the City

Harrisburg's downtown Center City comprises the original 80-acre borough laid out in a grid pattern by John Harris in 1785. East-west streets are named and north-south streets are numbered. Market Street, running east-west, is the dividing point between north and south street designations. Sightseeing is probably best done on foot downtown and by car or bicycle elsewhere. The Capitol Area Transit (CAT) maintains 67 buses for 26 regular routes along with four express routes for 2.1 million annual riders.

Communications

Newspapers and Magazines

Harrisburg's daily newspaper, *The Patriot-News,* has a daily morning edition; Patriot-News Company also publishes the *Sunday Patriot-News* and a weekly tabloid examining area business, arts, and entertainment. Another daily, the *Press and Journal,* is published in Middletown. Other newspapers published in Harrisburg are *The Catholic Witness* and *Community Affairs.* Journals published there include *The New Social Worker* (by White Hat Communications), *The PBA Quarterly,* and *Pennsylvania Heritage* (by the Pennsylvania

Heritage Society). Many other magazines are published in Harrisburg, including *Country Journal* and several magazines focusing on sports and hobbies, law and medicine.

Television and Radio

Harrisburg receives two major network affiliates and public television; cable service is available. A Harrisburg educational television station presents Public Broadcasting Service (PBS) series as well as programs of local interest, especially those relating to issues arising at the state capital. Four AM and six FM radio stations broadcast from Harrisburg, which also receives stations from Philadelphia, Lancaster, and York.

Media Information: Patriot-News Company, 812 Market St., Harrisburg, PA 17101; telephone (717)255-8100; toll-free (800)692-7207

Harrisburg Online

Capital Region Economic Development Corporation. Available www.harrisburgregionalchamber.org

City of Harrisburg. Available www.harrisburgpa.gov.

Dauphin County Historical Society. Available www.dauphincountyhistoricalsociety.org

Dauphin County Public Library. Available www.dcls.org

Harrisburg-Hershey-Carlisle Tourism & Convention Bureau. Available www.visithhc.com/capcity.shtml

Harrisburg Regional Chamber. Available www.harrisburgregionalchamber.org

Harrisburg School District. Available www.hbgsd.k12.pa.us

Pennsylvania Historical and Museum Commission. Available www.phmc.state.pa.us

PinnacleHealth System. Available www.pinnaclehealth.org

Selected Bibliography

Del Tredici, Robert, *The People of Three Mile Island: Interviews and Photos* (San Francisco: Sierra Club Books, 1980)

Eggert, Gerald E. *Harrisburg Industrializes: The Coming of Factories to an American Community* (Pennsylvania State University Press, 1993)

Seitz, Blair (photographer) and John Hope, ed.. *Harrisburg: Renaissance of a Capital City* (Rb Books, 2000)

Lancaster

The City in Brief

Founded: 1718 (incorporated 1818)

Head Official: Mayor Charlie Smithgall (R) (since 1998)

City Population
  1980: 54,725
  1990: 55,551
  2000: 56,348
  2003 estimate: 55,351
  Percent change, 1990–2000: 1.1%
  U.S. rank in 1980: 384th
  U.S. rank in 1990: 429th (State rank: 8th)
  U.S. rank in 2000: 597th (State rank: 11th)

Metropolitan Area Population
  1980: 362,000
  1990: 422,822
  2000: 470,658
  Percent change, 1990–2000: 11.3%

U.S. rank in 1980: 91st
U.S. rank in 1990: 85th
U.S. rank in 2000: 88th

Area: 7 square miles (2000)
Elevation: 368 feet above sea level
Average Annual Temperature: 52.2° F
Average Annual Precipitation: 43 inches of rain; 31 inches of snow

Major Economic Sectors: Manufacturing, services, retail trade
Unemployment Rate: 3.5% (May 2005)
Per Capita Income: $13,955 (1999)
2004 ACCRA Average House Price: Not reported
2004 ACCRA Cost of Living Index: Not reported

2002 FBI Crime Index Total: 2,785

Major Colleges and Universities: Franklin and Marshall College; Pennsylvania School of Art and Design; Harrisburg Area Community College-Lancaster

Daily Newspaper: *Intelligencer Journal; Lancaster New Era*

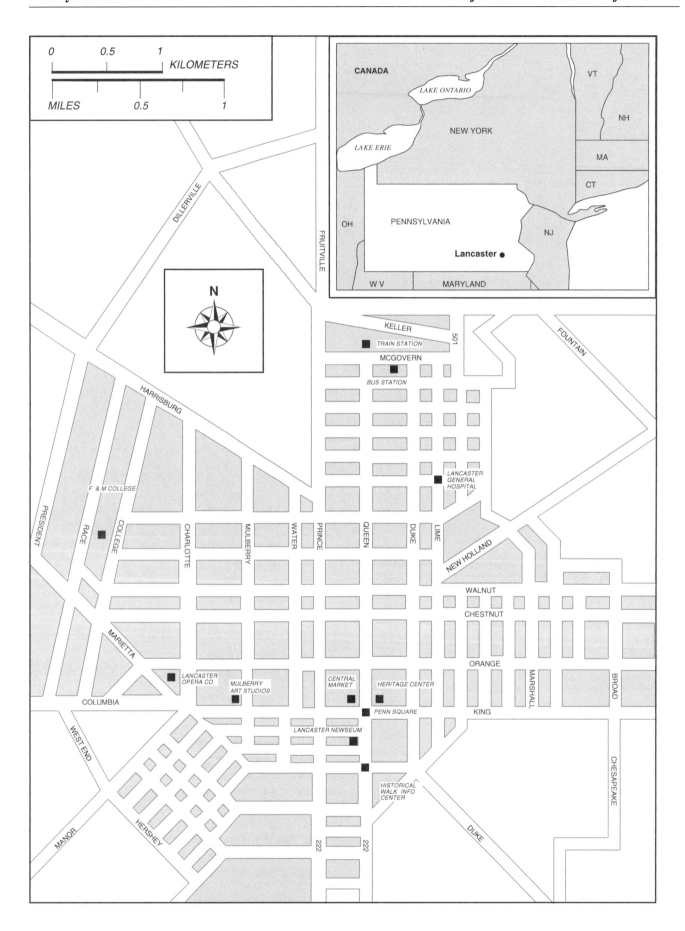

Introduction

Lancaster, an important industrial and business center in southeastern Pennsylvania, is located in the heart of Pennsylvania Dutch country. It is the county seat of Lancaster County, where the "Plain" people—Amish, Mennonite, and Brethren—living without benefit of automobiles, electricity, or television, practice a lifestyle that vanished from most areas of this country generations ago. The historic city of Lancaster, known for its strong work ethic and community spirit, won the All-America City Award in 2000 for its outstanding community-building programs.

Geography and Climate

Lancaster is part of the middle Susquehanna River Basin in the southeastern section of Pennsylvania. It is located near the center of Lancaster County in one of the most fertile agricultural lowland areas in the United States. The surrounding terrain is generally rolling, with some low ranges of hills. To the west lie the Susquehanna River and the South Mountains. The climate is classified "humid continental." The southeast corner of Pennsylvania lies in the path of Caribbean hurricanes that occasionally bring high winds and heavy rains to the area.

Area: 7 square miles (2000)

Elevation: 368 feet above sea level

Average Temperatures: January, 29.1° F; July, 74.4° F; annual average, 52.2° F

Average Annual Precipitation: 43 inches of rain; 31 inches of snow

History

Rich Farm Land Attracts Religious Refugees

The Susquehanna, Shawnee, and Iroquois tribes inhabited the area around Lancaster when William Penn and his Quaker followers took up residence in nearby Philadelphia in 1682. The second influx of immigrants to Philadelphia was comprised of Germans, some of them Mennonites (German-speaking religious refugees). Around 1710, a number of these Germans moved beyond Philadelphia to take advantage of the rich farm land stretching along the Susquehanna River to the foothills of the Appalachian Mountains. The Germans were

followed by a group of Amish (orthodox Anabaptists) from Switzerland and Bohemian Moravians (Protestants) from Czechoslovakia. The descendants of the Germans, known as the Pennsylvania Dutch (a corruption of *Deutsch,* meaning German) and the Amish are still there, many living on the farms which have made the area one of the top five agricultural counties in the country in terms of value per acre.

The first European settler of record in Lancaster was George Gibson, who in 1721 opened a tavern in the area of town now known as Penn Square. In his honor the town was called Gibson's Pasture until 1741, when it was renamed Lancaster after a town in England. Frontiersmen bought farm tools and the famous Kentucky rifle, actually a Lancaster product, as they passed through the city on their way west. The city became known as "the arsenal of the colonies" during the American Revolution of the 1770s for the guns it produced. Lancaster was the capital of the American colonies for one day in 1777, when the Continental Congress interrupted its flight from the British out of Philadelphia on its way to (New) York. From 1799 to 1812, Lancaster was the capital of Pennsylvania.

Economy Thrives, Diversifies

In addition to farming, other ventures carried out in Lancaster city and county were iron mining and furnace operations as well as quarrying. By 1789 Lancaster supported saddlers, shoemakers, furriers, forges, rolling mills, slitting mills, sawmills, brass foundries, rope makers, brush makers, silversmiths, steelwrights, printers, and other artisans and manufacturers, laying the foundation for the diverse economy for which the city is still known. By 1840, the population was 8,417; by 1860, that figure had more than doubled.

Traffic between Lancaster and Philadelphia became so heavy that a road was built between the two cities, using a technique of crushed stone paving developed by James McAdam (hence the word macadam). The turnpike, the first major paved road in the country, opened in 1794, having taken four years and $450,000 to complete.

Today, Lancaster County is famous for the high quality of the agricultural products supplied by the many family farms located throughout the county and for the diversity and quality of its manufactured goods. As the hub of the county the city is a center of government, arts and culture, education, professional and financial services, business, manufacturing, and health services. Combining sophistication with a reverence for its historic past, Lancaster is considered one of the Northeast's best cities for growing a business. In addition, Lancaster continues to be one of the most popular tourist destinations in the country, bringing in thousands of visitors each year to experience the county's cultural uniqueness; as a result, tourism continues to be a major economic factor to the financial success of Lancaster.

Famous Lancastrians include F. W. Woolworth, who opened his first store in Lancaster around 1879, pricing every item at five cents; Robert Fulton, co-inventor of the steamboat; Pennsylvania's only president of the United States, James Buchanan; and Susanna Wright, raiser of silkworms and maker of the first pair of silk stockings in Pennsylvania.

Historical Information: Lancaster County Historical Society, 230 N. President Ave., Lancaster, PA 17603; telephone (717)392-4633. Lancaster Mennonite Historical Society, 2215 Millstream Rd., Lancaster, PA 17602; telephone (717)393-9745. Historic Preservation Trust of Lancaster County, 123 N. Prince St., Lancaster, PA 17603; (717)291-5861

Population Profile

Metropolitan Area Residents
1980: 362,000
1990: 422,822
2000: 470,658
Percent change, 1990–2000: 11.3%
U.S. rank in 1980: 91st
U.S. rank in 1990: 85th
U.S. rank in 2000: 88th

City Residents
1980: 54,725
1990: 55,551
2000: 56,348
2003 estimate: 55,351
Percent change, 1990–2000: 1.1%
U.S. rank in 1980: 384th
U.S. rank in 1990: 429th (State rank: 8th)
U.S. rank in 2000: 597th (State rank: 11th)

Density: 7,614.6 people per square mile (2000)

Racial and ethnic characteristics (2000)
  White: 36,347
  Black or African American: 9,195
  American Indian and Alaska Native: 549
  Asian: 1,602
  Native Hawaiian and Pacific Islander: 114
  Hispanic or Latino (may be of any race): 17,331
  Other: 10,908

Percent of residents born in state: 63.8% (2000)

Age characteristics (2000)
  Population under 5 years old: 4,445
  Population 5 to 9 years old: 4,488
  Population 10 to 14 years old: 4,258

Population 15 to 19 years old: 4,602
Population 20 to 24 years old: 5,502
Population 25 to 34 years old: 8,795
Population 35 to 44 years old: 8,366
Population 45 to 54 years old: 6,193
Population 55 to 59 years old: 2,115
Population 60 to 64 years old: 1,651
Population 65 to 74 years old: 2,994
Population 75 to 84 years old: 2,216
Population 85 years and over: 723
Median age: 30.4 years

Births (2002, Lancaster County)
  Total number: 6,749

Deaths (2003, Lancaster County)
  Total number: 4,337 (of which, 61 were children under the age of 4 years)

Money income (1999)
  Per capita income: $13,955
  Median household income: $29,770
  Total households: 20,928

Number of households with income of . . .
  less than $10,000: 2,926
  $10,000 to $14,999: 1,948
  $15,000 to $24,999: 3,842
  $25,000 to $34,999: 3,364
  $35,000 to $49,999: 4,090
  $50,000 to $74,999: 3,069
  $75,000 to $99,999: 1,026
  $100,000 to $149,999: 447
  $150,000 to $199,999: 91
  $200,000 or more: 125

Percent of families below poverty level: 17.9% (54.9% of which were female householder families with related children under 5 years)

2002 FBI Crime Index Total: 2,785

Municipal Government

Lancaster, the county seat of Lancaster County, operates under the mayor-council form of government.

Head Official: Mayor Charlie Smithgall (since 1998; current term expires January 1, 2006)

Total Number of City Employees: 610 (2005)

City Information: City of Lancaster, 120 N. Duke St., PO Box 1599, Lancaster, PA 17608; telephone (717)291-4711

Economy

Major Industries and Commercial Activity

Lancaster County has a widely diversified economy; industries range from manufacturing to agriculture, tourism to health care, and retail trade to wholesale distribution. Many firms in the county have existed there for at least 50 and some for more than 100 years, including the oldest tobacco store in the country.

Lancaster County is known for the incredible diversity of its agriculture. The county's 4,500 farms make it one of the top farming counties in the United States. Together, these farms raise 45 million broiler chickens, 10 million laying hens, 95,000 dairy cows, 250,000 beef cattle, and 335,000 hogs annually. The county also leads all Pennsylvania counties in the value of its livestock, dairy products, wheat, corn, hay, tobacco, eggs, and milk, earning $725 million a year in agricultural revenue. Farmland preservation is a top priority for Lancaster County planners, who are struggling to preserve farmland even as the population grows and development continues. In 1999, Lancaster County had more than 30,000 acres of preserved farmland and 375 preserved farms, more preserved farms than any other county in the nation. The state of Pennsylvania has allocated millions of dollars to the farm preservation effort, which offers farmers economic incentives when they sign over development rights to the state so that the farmland can never be sold for development.

Lancaster County's industrial base is supported by hundreds of manufacturers and distributors. Service industries account for millions of dollars in revenue. More than 11,000 businesses employ more than 250,000 local residents.

Millions of tourists visit Lancaster County every year to tour its historical communities, view its rich architectural heritage, and witness life in its picturesque and culturally distinct farming communities. This influx of visitors provides jobs and income for thousands of local workers and businesses.

Items and goods produced: television tubes and electronic equipment, textiles, watches, farm machinery, building materials, linoleum, steel containers, ball bearings, locks, aluminum products, pharmaceuticals, toys, furniture, candy and food products

Incentive Programs—New and Existing Companies

Through economic development organizations like the Economic Development Company of Lancaster County and other community organizations, a wide array of public financing programs are available to local businesses. Resources include funding for start-up and business development projects, technical assistance, business counseling and training, and access to local, state, and federal funding programs.

Local programs—Lancaster's Economic Company Finance Corporations administers a number of funding programs for area businesses. The Pennsylvania Small Business First Fund provides low-interest financing to manufacturing and industrial businesses with less than 100 employees; companies can borrow up to $200,000 for land acquisition, construction, machinery, and working capital. The Community First Fund offers fixed-rate loans up to $50,000 and business counseling to small businesses, nonprofit organizations, and housing development agencies for use in real estate, machinery and equipment, and leasehold improvements. The Penn Southeast Mezzanine Fund is for firms with high growth and earnings potential; it extends loans of up to $750,000 for acquisitions, equipment purchase, working capital, and real estate.

State programs—Pennsylvania's Department of Community and Economic Development is the main source of funding and other economic growth programs for state businesses. Funding programs offered by the state include bond financing, grants, loans and loan guarantees, tax credits and abatements, and technical assistance. The state's tools include the Job Creation Tax Credit Program, which provides a $1,000-per-job tax credit for businesses that create new jobs; 25 percent of the tax credits allocated each year must go to businesses with less than 100 employees. The Opportunity Grant Program provides funds needed to create or preserve Pennsylvania jobs to businesses involved in manufacturing, exporting, agriculture, and research and development. The First Industries Fund is a grant and loan program aimed at strengthening Pennsylvania's agriculture and tourism industries. Loans up to $200,000 can be used for land acquisition and construction, machinery purchase, and working capital. The state also runs a number of technology investment programs, which are designed to help create and bolster new and existing technology companies within the state. Program areas include funding, assistance programs, industry initiatives, and research and development.

Job training programs—The Lancaster County Career and Technology Center offers a wide range of trade and skill-development opportunities to students in Lancaster County. The center has been renovated and its facilities offer modern, state-of-the-art laboratories and training programs geared to today's labor market needs. The Career and Technology Center's Work Keys program helps employers with job applicant selection and provides businesses with assessment services to determine where additional training would help increase employee performance.

Development Projects

The city of Lancaster has been involved in numerous development projects. Many of them include renovations and additions to Lancaster's cultural and recreational venues, including the city's multi-purpose baseball stadium, the Academy of Music, the Quilt Museum, and the Franklin and Marshall Life Sciences Building. Transportation improvements include work on the Red Rose Transit Center, the Amtrak Station, and the Fruitville Pike Bridge. Recent expansion and renovation also took place at the Lancaster General Hospital and the premises of the Susquehanna Association for the Blind.

Economic Development Information: Economic Development Company of Lancaster County, Southern Market Center, 100 S. Queen St., PO Box 1558, Lancaster, PA 17608; telephone (717)397-4046. City of Lancaster Economic Development Department; telephone (717)291-4760

Commercial Shipping

Air transportation facilities are provided by Lancaster Airport; air cargo lines include American, Continental, Delta, Northwest, United, Airborne Express, FedEx, and UPS. Norfolk Southern Rail serves as the area's primary freight railroad; daily service is available. Small freight and air cargo service is also available. The Philadelphia Regional Port Authority, 68 miles east of Lancaster County, handles more than 5 million tons of cargo each year.

Labor Force and Employment Outlook

Lancaster's widely diversified economy is expected to continue to stand the city in good stead. The city lays claim to a skilled labor force with a Pennsylvania Dutch work ethic. More than 11,000 companies employ a workforce of more than 250,000 people, in sectors including manufacturing, services, retail, tourism, and agriculture. Lancaster's nonagricultural labor force has diminished over the last decade, while jobs in the construction and tourism industries have increased significantly.

The following is a summary of data regarding the Lancaster metropolitan area labor force, 2004 annual averages.

Size of nonagricultural labor force: 232,100

Number of workers employed in . . .
  construction and mining: 16,400
  manufacturing: 45,700
  trade, transportation and utilities: 50,800
  information: 4,000
  financial activities: 10,100
  professional and business services: 21,400
  educational and health services: 32,400
  leisure and hospitality: 20,200
  other services: 10,400
  government: 20,800

Average hourly earnings of production workers employed in manufacturing: $15.35

Unemployment rate: 3.5% (May 2005)

Largest employers (2003)	*Number of employees*
Lancaster General Hospital	(no employee
R. R. Donnelley & Sons Co.	figures available)
Mutual Assistance Group	
Armstrong World Industries, Inc.	
Lancaster County	
Manheims PA Auction Services Inc.	
Ephrata Community Hospital	
Federal Government	
School District of Lancaster	
Weis Markets, Inc.	
QVC, Inc.	
Masonic Homes	
Dart Container Corporation	
Tyson Poultry, Inc.	
Lancaster Lebanon Intermediate Unit	

Cost of Living

According to the Economic Development Company of Lancaster County, the median rent within the county was $572 in 2000. The 2000 median housing value for the county was $119,300. Pennsylvania also has the lowest maximum income tax rate, 3.07%, of any state that imposes a personal income tax.

The following is a summary of data regarding several key cost of living factors for the Lancaster area.

2004 ACCRA Average House Price: Not reported

2004 ACCRA Cost of Living Index: Not reported

State income tax rate: 3.07% includes earned income plus interest

State sales tax rate: 6.0%

Local income tax rate: Lancaster County assesses an earned income and an occupational assessment tax that vary from municipality to municipality. It is based on one's occupation (therefore, an accountant would pay a different tax from a farmer, for example)

Local sales tax rate: None

Property tax rate: 2.96 mills based on 100% of fair market value (2005)

Economic Information: Lancaster Chamber of Commerce and Industry, Southern Market Center, 100 S. Queen St., PO Box 1558, Lancaster, PA 17608; telephone (717)397-3531; fax (717)293-3159

Education and Research

Elementary and Secondary Schools

The School District of Lancaster, established in 1836, is the second oldest school district in the state, and enrolls approximately 1,400 staff members. The district services a diverse student population which is approximately 50 percent Hispanic, 23 percent African American, and 22 percent Caucasian. Thirteen percent of the district's students are enrolled in its English as a second language program. The average school district attendance rate in 2003 was 92 percent, and high school students had a graduation rate of 71.1 percent in 2003. Over 67 percent of high school graduates intended to go on for post-secondary education.

The following is a summary of data regarding the Lancaster public schools as of the 2004–2005 school year.

Total enrollment: 11,300

Number of facilities
   elementary schools: 13
   junior high/middle schools: 4
   high schools: 1
   other: 1 alternative school

Student/teacher ratio: 14.4:1 (2002)

Teacher salaries
   average: $50,599 (2001-02 statewide average)

Funding per pupil: $9,653 (2002-2003)

Lancaster offers a diverse selection of private, parochial, and specialized schools, including Dayspring Christian Academy, Lancaster Catholic High School, Lancaster Christian School, Lancaster Country Day School, Linden Hall School for Girls, Lancaster Mennonite School, Montessori Academy of Lancaster, New School of Lancaster, and Pennsylvania Academy of Music, which offers instruction in orchestral instruments, voice, and piano.

Public Schools Information: School District of Lancaster, 251 S. Prince St., 3rd Fl., Lancaster, PA 17603; telephone (717)291-6148; email communications@lancaster.k12.pa.us

Colleges and Universities

Franklin and Marshall College, founded in 1787, is a selective liberal arts institution that grants degrees in more than 30 disciplines. The school has a student/teacher ratio of 11 to 1, and was cited as offering one of the 100 best values in private college education in the U.S. by *Kiplinger's* magazine in 2004. The Pennsylvania College of Art and Design offers bachelor of fine art programs in graphic design, fine art, illustration, and photography; they also offer professional programs in digital design, mural painting, and folk art studies. Institutions with a religious focus are the Lancaster Theological Seminary and the Lancaster Bible College and Graduate School.

The Penn State Lancaster Campus, with more than 2,000 students, offers continuing education programs for adults, business, and industry. Graduate courses in education and business management are also available. Spread out amongst four campuses, Lancaster's Harrisburg Area Community College offers a number degree, certificate, and diploma programs in liberal arts and business concentrations. Among the three vocational-technical schools in the region is Thaddeus Stevens College of Technology, which offers two-year associates degrees in 17 programs. Enrollment averages 500 students per year.

Libraries and Research Centers

The Lancaster County Library, headquarters for the Library System of Lancaster County, opened in 1759. The County Library maintains 17 public libraries in the area, including the Duke Street main facility and the libraries in Leola, Mountville, and Manheim Township. Its collection numbers about 300,000 fiction and nonfiction books, more than 300 periodicals and newspapers, and hundreds of videocassettes, films, and records. Special facilities and programs at the main library include a summer reading program, a Spanish language section, the Cooperating Collections program, family activities, literacy programs, and a Library Center for Youth. Special collections include books on the preservation of historic architecture, local and regional history resources in the Gerald S. Lestz Reading Room, and a Business Information Center.

The Lancaster County Historical Society is an internationally recognized historical and genealogical research facility; its library contains more than 15,000 volumes, including maps, family files, microfilm, and CDs. The Lancaster Mennonite Historical Society also maintains a genealogical research library. Among the several libraries at Franklin and Marshall College is the Shadek-Fackenthal Library, containing 450,000 volumes and 400,000 government documents, with special emphasis on topics such as the theater, Lincoln, and Napoleon.

Public Library Information: Lancaster County Library, 125 N. Duke St., Lancaster, PA 17602; telephone (717)394-2651

Health Care

Three main hospitals cater to the health care needs of Lancastrians. City health care facilities include Lancaster General Hospital, with more than 550 beds and 470 physicians; the hospital's emergency room treats more than 68,000 patients each year, and the hospital's Lancaster General Heart Center performs more than 600 open heart surgeries annually. For more than 60 years, Ephrata Community Hospital has been providing preventative services, primary care, diagnostic services, and rehabilitation services to area residents. Other available services include an active wellness program, a pain management center, and a women's health services center. Lancaster Regional Medical Center, a 268-bed acute-care community hospital, offers care in 32 specialties, including dermatology, orthopedics, gynecology, psychiatry, and urology. Lancaster Cleft Palate Clinic, affiliated with Lancaster General Hospital, conducts research on children with cranio-facial anomalies, and provides medical, dental, speech, and hearing services.

Lancaster's health care facilities are booming with new projects. In 2005, Lancaster General Hospital opened its Lancaster General-Norlanco facility in order to service residents of northwestern Lancaster County. The facility offers radiology, laboratory, and rehabilitation services. Ephrata Community Hospital recently renovated its CardioVascular Laboratory, including the purchase of the Siemens Axion Artis, a piece of diagnostic equipment that produces high-quality images through very low radiation doses.

Health Care Information: Lancaster General Hospital, 555 N. Duke St., Lancaster PA; telephone (717)544-5511. Ephrata Community Hospital, 169 Martin Ave., PO Box 1002, Ephrata, PA 17522; telephone (717)733-0311

Recreation

Sightseeing

Lancaster and its environs maintain many buildings of historic interest. Among them are the 1852 Fulton Opera House, which has been restored and houses a wooden statue of Robert Fulton; the 1889 Central Market, which is the oldest publicly-owned continually operating farmers market in the country; Rock Ford Plantation, a Georgian mansion built in 1792 for General Edward Hand; Wheatland, the 1828 country estate of President James Buchanan; and 1719 Hans Herr House, the oldest house built by European settlers in the county and the Western Hemisphere's oldest Mennonite meeting house.

The Heritage Center Museums of Lancaster County, including the Lancaster Cultural History Museum and the Lancaster Quilt and Textile Museum, provide information about the cultural history of Lancaster County and have attractive displays of decorative and fine arts produced by generations of local artists and craftspeople. Lancaster Newspapers' Newseum explores the history of newspapers. At the Charles Demuth House and Garden, visitors can tour the eighteenth century home, studio, and gardens of world-famous artist Charles Demuth; the Demuth Tobacco Shop, located next door, was founded in 1770 and is the oldest tobacco shop in the U.S. The city also offers the Historic Lancaster Walking Tour, which concentrates on Revolutionary War era sites; the Pennsylvania Railroad Museum, which displays more than 100 locomotives and cars; the Ephrata Cloisters, one of the country's earliest and most influential religious communities; and the Robert Fulton Birthplace.

The countryside surrounding Lancaster is a favorite destination of visitors, who have made Lancaster County one of the top ten tourist attractions in the country. By car, bicycle, bus, buggy, or steam train, passing through covered bridges, one can tour re-created Amish farms and visit farmers' markets and Pennsylvania Dutch restaurants. Visitors interested in learning more about Pennsylvania Dutch Country can do so through a multimedia attraction at the Amish Experience Theater, located at Plain & Fancy Farm on Route 340. The production combines special effects with the traditional story of the Amish people and their centuries-old culture. The theater presents an original and critically acclaimed screenplay called ''Jacob's Choice,'' which chronicles the saga of an Amish family from its flight from religious persecution in sixteenth century Europe to modern-day Lancaster County.

For those looking to explore nearby communities, a number of attractions in and near Hershey are worth a visit. Hersheypark offers amusement rides, shopping, food, and other forms of family fun. Hershey's Chocolate World serves as Hershey Food Corporation's official visitors center, and offers chocolate-making tours. For nature enthusiasts, Indian Echo Caverns gives guided tours of underground caves. And in nearby Kennett Square, Longwood Gardens allows visitors to tour one of America's most famous horticultural showplaces.

Arts and Culture

Lancaster Symphony Orchestra makes its home at the beautifully restored 1852 Fulton Opera House, a national historic landmark. There the orchestra performs 20 yearly subscription concerts in addition to a special New Year's Eve celebration and an outdoor patriotic concert at Long's Park. Also performing at the Fulton is Opera Lancaster, one of just a few non-profit, all-volunteer opera companies in the U.S. They boast an active performing membership of more than 100. The Fulton is a focal point for theatrical productions of all kinds, presented by groups sponsored by high schools and colleges as well as by touring professionals and community-based enterprises. These groups include the Actors Company at the Fulton, Youtheatre, and the Theatre for Young Audiences.

Recreated Amish farms can be toured in the countryside surrounding Lancaster.

Outdoor concerts at Long's Park Amphitheater and other locales are presented during the summer months by Lancaster Symphony Orchestra and other groups under the auspices of the Long's Park Free Summer Entertainment Series. Both women and men participate in local barbershop choruses that perform from time to time throughout the area, as does Wheatland Chorale, a group of 36 singers specializing in close ensemble a capella singing.

Co-Motion, Hole-In-The-Wall Puppet Theatre, and First Stage Theatre provide family entertainment. Lancaster's Theater of the Seventh Sister has been in operation for more than 15 years, and offers a range of performances from new dramatic works, to plays of the old masters, to live musical performances. Dutch Apple Dinner Theater presents professional musicals and comedies accompanied by a large buffet dinner; Broadway comedies and hearty dinners are the bill of fare at Rainbow Dinner Theatre. Sight & Sound Theatres, one of the largest theatres in the U.S., has been offering musicals with a religious theme for more than 25 years. Philadelphia, with its rich array of cultural offerings, is 65 miles from Lancaster.

Landis Valley Museum is considered one of the most important living history museum complexes in the country. The complex's numerous exhibit areas, interpreting Pennsylvania rural life, include original structures such as the 1800s Landis Farmstead and the 1856 Landis Valley House Hotel, and other historically significant structures that were either moved to the site or are period reconstructions. The North Museum of Natural History and Science, on the campus of Franklin and Marshall College, is filled with hands-on displays and one of the largest planetariums in the state.

The Heritage Center Museums of Lancaster County are located in two historic buildings on Penn Square: the Lancaster Quilt and Textile Museum exhibits folk and decorative arts and crafts; the Lancaster Cultural History Museum collects items important to the area's history. Folk art and crafts are also on display at the Kauffman Museum of Pennsylvania Folk Arts and Crafts, located on the grounds of Rock Ford Plantation. Sheldon's Gallery in nearby Ephrata features original paintings, prints, photographs, and sculptures, while Garthoeffner Gallery specializes in painted furniture, folk art, and vintage toys. A number of art galleries in downtown Lancaster present permanent and changing exhibits; offered are works of local craftspeople, including Amish quilts, as well as national and international art.

Festivals and Holidays

Throughout the year, the Downtown Investment District coordinates many downtown Lancaster events, including Art in the Park, a Puerto Rican Festival, LancasterFest, a Classic Car and Auto Show, a Jazz and Blues Festival, and New Year's Eve's Count Down Lancaster. Winter visitors to the Lancaster area enjoy maple sugaring beginning in February. The Quilters' Heritage Celebration, held in early spring, is one of the largest quilting conventions in the world; the event showcases hundreds of quilts entered in a juried and judged contest. A Rhubarb Festival is held in Intercourse in mid-May, paying homage to a crop that grows abundantly in Pennsylvania Dutch country. Early June brings the Lancaster Spring Show of Arts and Crafts, displaying the works of artisans from around the country in a juried exhibition. The Kutztown Pennsylvania German Festival, held in Kutztown in late June and early July, celebrates the Pennsylvania Dutch way of life; arts, crafts, and quilts are displayed and sold, and regional and ethnic food is available in abundance.

The Pennsylvania Renaissance Faire, held at Mount Hope Estate and Winery 15 miles north of Lancaster, is a re-creation of a sixteenth-century English country fair. Costumed entertainers, jousting, Shakespearean presentations, crafts, and more appear each weekend from early July through mid-October. In late July and early August, Franklin and Marshall College hosts the Pennsylvania State Craft Show and Sale. Arts and crafts are also the focus of Long's Park Art & Craft Festival held in Lancaster on Labor Day Weekend. The Christmas season is celebrated in downtown Lancaster during Downtown Holiday Weekends, featuring food, tree lightings, music, gingerbread displays, and carriage rides. The season is celebrated throughout the region with special holiday tours at Rock Ford Plantation, Hans Herr House, and the Ephrata Cloister in Ephrata; Victorian Christmas Week at Wheatland; and Christmas at Landis Valley.

Sports for the Spectator

One of two spring highlights in downtown Lancaster is the Wachovia Cycling Series, which brings more than 200 of the world's top professional cyclists through the town's downtown on their way to Philadelphia. It is billed as the longest running and richest single-day cycling race in the U.S. The springtime five-mile Red Rose Run also draws hundreds of spectators, and has been an area event for more than 25 years. Lancastrians are also avid supporters of Philadelphia and Baltimore professional teams.

Sports for the Participant

Lancaster maintains nearly 300 acres of land in the form of community parks. The Lancaster Recreation Commission operates an active year-round schedule of adult and child-oriented sports and recreation programs. Park and recreation facilities include athletic fields, a street hockey rink, tennis courts, basketball courts, children's play equipment, and picnic areas. Dozens of state ski areas are accessible from Lancaster.

Shopping and Dining

Downtown Lancaster is a thriving and architecturally interesting district supporting hundreds of businesses that offer distinctive jewelry, home decorations, apparel, books, antiques, music, crafts, and gifts. A favorite among tourists and locals is Central Market, where baked goods, crafts, flowers, fresh produce, and Pennsylvania Dutch food and other ethnic delicacies are abundant. Park City Center, located in the city, is one of the largest malls in the state with 1.4 million square feet of space and about 170 stores. The northern end of the county is known for its weekend flea markets and antiques mall. With almost 1,000 Amish "micro enterprises" in existence, it's possible to locate everything from traditional handcrafted quilts to rolltop desks and Adirondack chairs—all within a few miles of each other in the surrounding countryside. Some shops are in family homes; other businesses have showrooms filled with beautiful handcrafts.

With the dozens of restaurants located in Lancaster's downtown area, diners can choose from a casual pub experience to elegant dining, as well as enjoy Thai, Chinese, Jamaican, Italian, and other ethnic cuisines. Pennsylvania Dutch specialties such as chicken pot pie, schnitz and knepp (dried apples with ham and dumplings), apple butter, and shoofly pie (actually a molasses sponge cake baked in a crust) are served in restaurants located throughout the nearby countryside; some of these restaurants are housed in eighteenth- and nineteenth-century inns that lined the country's first paved road.

Visitor Information: Pennsylvania Dutch Convention and Visitors Bureau, 501 Greenfield Rd., Lancaster, PA 17601; telephone (800)PADUTCH; email info@padutchcountry .com.

Convention Facilities

Meetings are a tradition among the Amish, and convention personnel in Lancaster County/City promise a traditional commitment to hospitality for the millions of visitors the area receives annually. Within the city of Lancaster, the Hotel Brunswick, located downtown, offers excellent facilities within close proximity to historic sites, specialty shops, and the oldest continuously operating farmer's market in the United States; its facilities cover 28,000 square feet of meeting space and 20 different meeting rooms. The county's largest meeting facility, the Lancaster Host Resort and Conference Center, occupies 225 acres and offers an 18-hole golf course, tennis, basketball, volleyball, swimming pools, and a fitness trail. Meeting and exhibit space of more than 80,000 square feet includes 25 flexible function rooms, a grand ballroom for 1,000 guests, and a 23,000 square foot expo center. Sleeping rooms total 330 with many overflow properties within close proximity.

The Best Western Eden Resort Inn & Conference Center offers 25,000 square feet of first-class flexible meeting space and thirteen distinctive banquet rooms. Residential suites for important clients, two pools, wireless internet access, and a total of 276 deluxe guest rooms are available. The Netherlands Inn and Spa, a 102-room retreat location nestled amidst farmland, offers more than 7,000 square feet of meeting space for a unique and peaceful experience. The Willow Valley Resort & Conference Center can accommodate groups of 15 to 1,000 people in a 342-room resort with 16 meeting rooms totaling more than 20,000 square feet. This resort also has amenities such as golf, indoor and outdoor swimming pools, a fitness facility, tennis, family activities, and outstanding cuisine.

Convention Information: Pennsylvania Dutch Convention and Visitors Bureau, 501 Greenfield Rd., Lancaster, PA 17601; toll-free (800)PADUTCH; email info@padutch country.com

Transportation

Approaching the City

Airline service into Lancaster Airport is provided by USAir Express, from Pittsburgh and Philadelphia, and from surrounding airports in Harrisburg, Baltimore, Washington, D.C., and Philadelphia. Limousine and taxi service, as well as free long and short term parking are available. Baltimore/Washington International Airport and Philadelphia International Airport are both less than two hours away. Three Amtrak stations are located in Lancaster county—in the city of Lancaster, and in the boroughs of Mount Joy and Elizabethtown; Amtrak's Chicago to New York City service passes through Lancaster. Greyhound and Capitol Trailways offer service to points across the country. All of the state's major highways converge in the city with the exception of the Pennsylvania Turnpike, which encompasses interchanges at U.S. 222, PA 72, and PA 23, 15 miles north of the city. The convenience of these highways make Lancaster a three-hour drive from New York City, a 90-minute drive from Philadelphia, and a two and a half hour drive from Washington, D.C.

Traveling in the City

Walking is a popular pastime in Lancaster, and Historic Lancaster Walking Tours, led by guides in colonial costumes, are offered daily from April through October. Red Rose Transit Authority services 2.5 million passengers with city and county buses on 16 routes.

Communications

Newspapers and Magazines

Lancaster Newspapers, Inc., provides citizens with the *Intelligencer Journal* in the mornings Sunday through Friday, the *Lancaster New Era* in the afternoons Monday through Saturday, and the *Sunday News.* Although all three newspapers are owned by the same corporation, they have completely separate staffs and the publications actively compete with each other. *La Voz Hispana,* a bimonthly, tabloid-sized newspaper, caters to Lancaster's Hispanic and Latino communities with local, national, and international news and events written in both Spanish and English.

Television and Radio

Two AM and seven FM radio stations are based in Lancaster, with reception from Philadelphia and other cities in the state. One radio station is college-owned, and one presents Hispanic programs. Two television stations, Channel 15 and Channel 8, broadcast from Lancaster as well.

Media Information: Lancaster Newspapers, Inc., P.O. Box 1328, Lancaster, PA 17608; telephone (717)291-8622

Lancaster Online

City of Lancaster. Available www.cityoflancasterpa.com

Economic Development Company of Lancaster County. Available www.edclancaster.com

Lancaster Chamber of Commerce and Industry. Available www.lcci.com

Lancaster County Library. Available www.lancaster.lib.pa .us

Lancaster Newspapers, Inc. Available www.lancasteronline .com

Lancaster Pennsylvania Dutch Convention and Visitors Bureau. Available www.padutchcountry.com

The Pennsylvania Manual online. Available www.dgs.state .pa.us/PAManual

School District of Lancaster. Available www.lancaster.k12 .pa.us

Selected Bibliography

Hostetler, John Andrew, *Amish Children: Education in the Family, School, and Community* (Fort Worth: Harcourt Brace Jovanovich, 1991, 2nd ed.)

Kaiser, Grace H., *Dr. Frau: A Woman Doctor Among the Amish* (Intercourse, Pa: Good Books, 1986)

Kraybill, Donald B., and Steven M. Nolt, *Amish Enterprise: From Plows to Profits* (Johns Hopkins University Press, 2004, 2nd ed.)

Lestz, Gerald S., *To Lancaster With Love* (Lancaster: Stemgas Publishing, 1992)

Reninger, Marion Wallace, *Orange Street* (Lancaster: Stemgas Publishing, 1954)

Rupp, I. Daniel, *History of Lancaster County, Pennsylvania: To Which Is Prefixed a Brief Sketch of the Early History of Pennsylvania* (Spartanburg, S.C.: Heritage Books, 1990)

Philadelphia

The City in Brief

Founded: 1682 (incorporated, 1701)

Head Official: Mayor John F. Street (D) (since 2000)

City Population
   1980: 1,688,210
   1990: 1,585,577
   2000: 1,517,550
   2003 estimate: 1,423,538
   Percent change, 1990–2000: −4.5%
   U.S. rank in 1980: 4th
   U.S. rank in 1990: 5th
   U.S. rank in 2000: 6th (State rank: 1st)

Metropolitan Area Population (CMSA)
   1980: 4,717,000 (PMSA)
   1990: 5,892,937
   2000: 6,188,463
   Percent change, 1990–2000: 5%
   U.S. rank in 1980: 4th (CMSA)
   U.S. rank in 1990: 5th (CMSA)
   U.S. rank in 2000: 6th (CMSA)

Area: 135.09 square miles (2000)
Elevation: Ranges from 5 feet to 431 feet above sea level
Average Annual Temperature: 53.6° F
Average Annual Precipitation: 45.7 inches of rain; 20.5 inches of snow

Major Economic Sectors: Pharmaceuticals; biotechnology; healthcare; communications; manufacturing; retail trade; finance, insurance, and real estate; services; government
Unemployment Rate: 4.5% (April 2005)
Per Capita Income: $16,509 (1999)
2004 ACCRA Average House Price: Not reported
2004 ACCRA Cost of Living Index: Not reported

2002 FBI Crime Index Total: 83,392

Major Colleges and Universities: University of Pennsylvania; Drexel University; Thomas Jefferson University; Temple University; Philadelphia University; Philadelphia College of the Arts; University of the Sciences in Philadelphia; La Salle University; Haverford College; Swarthmore College

Daily Newspaper: *Philadelphia Inquirer; Philadelphia Daily News*

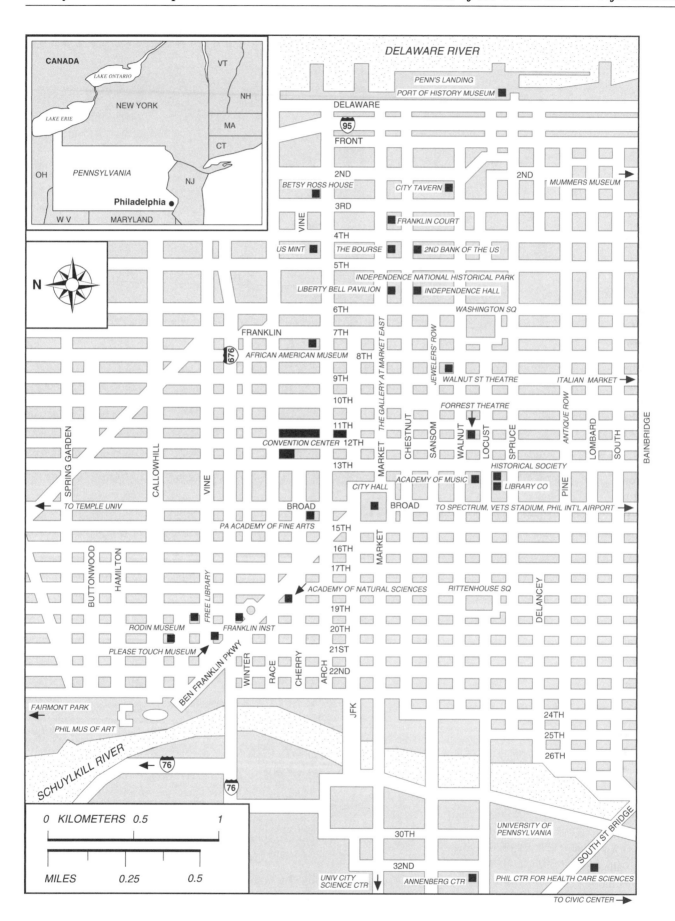

CANADA

LAKE ONTARIO

NEW YORK

LAKE ERIE

VT

NH

MA

CT

OH

PENNSYLVANIA

NJ

W V

MARYLAND

Philadelphia

N

DELAWARE RIVER

PENN'S LANDING

PORT OF HISTORY MUSEUM

DELAWARE

95

FRONT

2ND

2ND

MUMMERS MUSEUM

BETSY ROSS HOUSE

CITY TAVERN

3RD

VINE

FRANKLIN COURT

4TH

US MINT

THE BOURSE

2ND BANK OF THE US

5TH

INDEPENDENCE NATIONAL HISTORICAL PARK

LIBERTY BELL PAVILION

INDEPENDENCE HALL

6TH

WASHINGTON SQ

FRANKLIN

7TH

676

AFRICAN AMERICAN MUSEUM

8TH

9TH

WALNUT ST THEATRE

ITALIAN MARKET

10TH

FORREST THEATRE

11TH

CONVENTION CENTER

12TH

13TH

HISTORICAL SOCIETY

CITY HALL

ACADEMY OF MUSIC

LIBRARY CO

BROAD

BROAD

TO SPECTRUM, VETS STADIUM, PHIL INT'L AIRPORT

TO TEMPLE UNIV

PA ACADEMY OF FINE ARTS

15TH

SPRING GARDEN

CALLOWHILL

VINE

MARKET

CHESTNUT

SANSOM

WALNUT

LOCUST

SPRUCE

ANTIQUE ROW

PINE

LOMBARD

SOUTH

BAINBRIDGE

THE GALLERY AT MARKET EAST

JEWELERS' ROW

16TH

17TH

ACADEMY OF NATURAL SCIENCES

RITTENHOUSE SQ

DELANCEY

19TH

RODIN MUSEUM

FREE LIBRARY

FRANKLIN INST

20TH

PLEASE TOUCH MUSEUM

21ST

BUTTONWOOD

HAMILTON

WINTER

RACE

CHERRY

ARCH

22ND

BEN FRANKLIN PKWY

FAIRMONT PARK

PHIL MUS OF ART

JFK

24TH

25TH

26TH

SCHUYLKILL RIVER

76

76

0   KILOMETERS   0.5   1

MILES   0.25   0.5

UNIVERSITY OF
PENNSYLVANIA

SOUTH ST BRIDGE

30TH

32ND

UNIV CITY
SCIENCE CTR

ANNENBERG CTR

PHIL CTR FOR HEALTH CARE SCIENCES

TO CIVIC CENTER

Introduction

Rich in history and culture, Philadelphia has been in the forefront of the nation's intellectual, economic, and humanitarian development for more than three hundred years. Today its efforts are being directed to restoration with an emphasis on preserving the best of the past while allowing for the development of a vigorous new city. A city of neighborhoods, trees, parks, and open spaces, Philadelphia offers the advantages of living in a big city while maintaining a small-town atmosphere and preserving reminders of its dignified past. The Greater Philadelphia area has been on numerous best city lists as a good place to balance work and family life.

Geography and Climate

Philadelphia is located at the confluence of the Delaware and Schuylkill rivers on the eastern border of Pennsylvania. The Appalachian Mountains to the west and the Atlantic Ocean to the east moderate the climate, eliminating extremes of hot and cold weather. Occasionally during the summer months the city becomes engulfed in ocean air that brings high humidity. Precipitation is fairly evenly distributed throughout the year, with maximum amounts during the summer months occasionally flooding the Schuylkill River. Snowfall is usually higher in the northern suburbs than in the city, where snow often turns to rain. High winds sometimes prevail during the winter months.

Area: 135.09 square miles (2000)

Elevation: Ranges from 5 feet to 431 feet above sea level

Average Temperatures: January, 32.0° F; August, 75.3° F; annual average, 53.6° F

Average Annual Precipitation: 45.7 inches of rain; 20.5 inches of snow

History

Quakers Receive Pennsylvania Grant

At the time the first settlers of European descent arrived in the area now known as Philadelphia, it was inhabited chiefly by Native Americans who called themselves Lenni-Lenape; settlers called them Delawares. Intertribal warfare had weakened the native tribes, and the advance of colonial settlement pushed them farther west, causing great hostility.

The Netherlands laid claim to the area in 1609 when Henry Hudson, an Englishman in the Dutch service, sailed into Delaware Bay, and around 1647 the Dutch began to build trading posts. The Dutch were ousted by the English in 1664.

In 1681 England's King Charles granted William Penn the territory now known as Pennsylvania in exchange for a debt owed Penn's father. Penn, wealthy and well educated, had committed himself to the Society of Friends, also called Quakers, who practiced a form of religion generally regarded by society with suspicion because of its tenets and its insistence upon simplicity in speech and dress. Penn himself had been imprisoned four times for voicing his beliefs, and King Charles was only too happy to be rid of him and his followers.

Although he had been granted all the land in Pennsylvania, Penn chose to buy the claims of any native people still living there, which set a new standard in colonial settlers' relations with Native Americans. Penn dispatched his cousin to lay out a city, which he called Philadelphia, from the Greek for ''brotherly love,'' and which Penn envisioned as a haven for his fellow Quakers to enjoy freedom of worship and the chance to govern themselves. He charged his cousin with laying out a ''greene Country Towne, which will never be burnt, and always be wholesome.'' The city was laid out in a grid, with large lots, wide streets, and a provision for five city parks, four of which still survive. Historians note that Philadelphia was one of the first cities in the New World built according to a plan.

The Quakers were not only humanitarians but shrewd businesspeople as well. They offered large tracts of land at reasonable prices and advertised throughout Europe for settlers. Attracted by the liberality and tolerance of the Quaker government, and looking for better economic opportunities, thousands of immigrant families soon began arriving, including a group of German Quakers who established the first German settlement in America.

Prosperity and Culture Distinguish City

From the beginning Philadelphia was a leading agricultural area, and because of its location at the confluence of the Delaware and Schuylkill rivers, shipyards flourished. Farm products were exchanged for sugar and rum in the West Indies, and these in turn were exchanged for English manufactured goods. Abundant natural resources, including coal and iron, helped Philadelphia become an early industrial leader. Other significant early industries included home manufacture of textiles, printing, publishing, and papermaking. By the 1770s Philadelphia was one of the most important business centers in the British Empire.

This prosperity and William Penn's principles attracted the best minds of the day to Philadelphia. Among the city's illustrious early residents was the young Benjamin Franklin, scientist and intellectual. His many accomplishments include the publication of the *Pennsylvania Gazette,* one of the best of the colonial newspapers; he also established the colonies' first hospital, first free library, and first learned society, the American Philosophical Society. Perceiving the need for higher education, Franklin was instrumental in the founding of the institution that later became the University of Pennsylvania.

During the late 1700s many fine private and public buildings were constructed in Philadelphia, such as Andrew Hamilton's Independence Hall. Oil painting flourished, and Philadelphia came to be known as an "Athens of America." By 1774 a sophisticated populace was chafing at the restrictions placed on them by the British king. Because of Philadelphia's strategic location near the middle of colonial settlement, and the importance of winning Quaker support, the delegates who formed the First Continental Congress in 1774 chose Philadelphia as the site for their discussions. The Second Continental Congress proclaimed the colonists' Declaration of Independence in Philadelphia, and when the Revolutionary War broke out in full force, Philadelphia became the capital of the revolutionary movement. Following the American patriots' victory at Yorktown, the Constitutional Convention delegates met in Philadelphia, and in 1787 they framed the document that was to become the basis of America's governmental structure. Philadelphia then served as the capital of the United States from 1790 to 1800.

In the early 1800s Philadelphia began an ambitious program of building canals and railroads and developing coal fields, thus laying the foundation of its industrial power. Philadelphia's railroad lines, which by 1834 comprised a quarter of the nation's total, expedited the development of industry.

New Residents Meet Modern Challenges

When the issue of slavery became acute, many African American leaders centered their activities in Philadelphia, and the city became the focal point of one of the most important African American communities in the nation. Philadelphia's industrial strength contributed to the Union's military and economic advantage over the South during the Civil War of 1861 to 1865.

Pennsylvania had been one of the first colonies to admit Catholics and Jews. The increasing demand for factory workers in the late 1800s and early 1900s attracted hundreds of thousands of immigrants of Irish, German, Italian, and Polish descent, who created many distinctive ethnic neighborhoods throughout the city. At the same time, the development of the railroad made commuting easier, and the city's elite began moving to the suburbs that—as they grew up along the main line of the Pennsylvania Railroad—became known as the "Main Line." By the 1930s the modern city

had emerged, with outlying residential districts segregated by income, race, and ethnic origin.

Philadelphia's industrial progress brought with it the exacerbation of differences in wealth. After the Great Depression of the 1930s Philadelphia became a union town, and labor strikes were common. Political machines that had emerged after the Civil War became sophisticated in the ways of manipulating the political processes, particularly through the new immigrant groups. Discrimination in housing resulted in overcrowded African American districts. During the 1960s Philadelphia was shaken by race riots born of decades of inadequate housing and discriminatory practices.

A reform movement, begun in 1939, prompted Philadelphia in 1951 to adopt a new city charter and elect Mayor Joseph Clark, who began a vast urban renewal program. Slated for completion in the early 21st century, this program called for the improvement of highways and the transportation system, housing projects, and the building of more libraries, parks, and shopping and recreation centers. However, a recession and mounting social problems saw Philadelphia teetering on the edge of bankruptcy by the early 1990s.

Economic Woes Reversed

A former prosecutor, Edward G. Rendell, was sworn in as the mayor in 1992, promising "dramatic change from top to bottom." On his watch Rendell was credited with bringing labor costs into line, rallying Philadelphia's business community, bringing back strong bond ratings, and securing the 2000 Republican National Convention, as well as spurring a resurgence in development in the city, from a new $500 million convention center, to the $330 million Avenue of the Arts.

In 2000, John Street became mayor of Philadelphia. The former Philadelphia city council president had worked with Rendell and helped save the city of Philadelphia from bankruptcy, turning a $250 million deficit into the largest surplus in Philadelphia history in 1998. A lawyer and one-time activist, Street is the city's second African American mayor. Now entering his second term, Street continues to serve as a role model for his teenage son and all the city's young people of color.

Historical Information: Historical Society of Pennsylvania, 1300 Locust Street, Philadelphia, PA 19107; telephone (215)732-6200; fax (215)732-2680; email library@hsp.org

Population Profile

Metropolitan Area Residents (PMSA)
1980: 4,717,000 (PMSA)

1990: 5,892,937

2000: 6,188,463

Percent change, 1990–2000: 24.5%

U.S. rank in 1980: 4th (CMSA)

U.S. rank in 1990: 5th (CMSA)

U.S. rank in 2000: 6th (CMSA)

City Residents

1980: 1,688,210

1990: 1,585,577

2000: 1,517,550

2003 estimate: 1,423,538

Percent change, 1990–2000: −4.5%

U.S. rank in 1980: 4th

U.S. rank in 1990: 5th

U.S. rank in 2000: 6th (State rank: 1st)

Density: 11,233.6 people per square mile (2000)

Racial and ethnic characteristics (2000)
   White: 683,267
   Black or African American: 655,824
   American Indian or Alaska Native: 4,073
   Asian: 67,654
   Native Hawaiian and Pacific Islander: 729
   Hispanic (may be of any race): 128,928
   Other: 72,429

Percent of residents born in state: 71.7% (2000)

Age characteristics (2000)
   Population under 5 years old: 98,161
   Population 5 to 9 years old: 112,111
   Population 10 to 14 years old: 112,726
   Population 15 to 19 years old: 110,701
   Population 20 to 24 years old: 117,609
   Population 25 to 34 years old: 224,864
   Population 35 to 44 years old: 219,910
   Population 45 to 54 years old: 182,530
   Population 55 to 59 years old: 67,280
   Population 60 to 64 years old: 57,936
   Population 65 to 74 years old: 107,048
   Population 75 to 84 years old: 79,335
   Population 85 years and over: 27,339
   Median age: 34.2 years

Births (2002)
   Total number: 21,380

Deaths (2003)
   Total number: 16,506 (of which, 231 were infants under the age of 1 year)

Money income (1999)
   Per capita income: $16,509 (1999)
   Median household income: $30,746
   Total households: 600,740

Number of households with income of . . .
   less than $10,000: 109,237
   $10,000 to $14,999: 49,035
   $15,000 to $24,999: 89,059
   $25,000 to $34,999: 79,532
   $35,000 to $49,999: 91,683
   $50,000 to $74,999: 92,326
   $75,000 to $99,999: 42,495
   $100,000 to $149,999: 25,092
   $150,000 to $199,999: 5,639
   $200,000 or more: 6,185

Percent of families below poverty level: 18.4% (47.4% of which were female householder families with children under 5 years)

2002 FBI Crime Index Total: 83,392

Municipal Government

Philadelphia city and county are the same entity. The city passed what is widely considered to be the nation's first modern big-city charter in 1951; under this charter the city council was removed from its administrative role and the staff and powers of the mayor were increased. Elections are held every four years, at which time the mayor and seven council members are elected by all the voters and 10 council members are elected by districts. The mayor may serve an unlimited number of terms but not more than two consecutively.

Head Official: Mayor John F. Street (D) (since 2000; current term expires January 2008)

Total Number of City Employees: 30,000 (2005)

City Information: City Hall, Room 215, Philadelphia, PA 19107; telephone (215)686-2250

Economy

Major Industries and Commercial Activity

Manufacturing and the related distribution sector were traditionally the backbone of the Philadelphia economy. Since the end of World War II this industrial base has declined, as it has in many of the established industrial cities of the Northeast and upper Midwest, as many firms moved to new locations in the suburbs or migrated to other regions of the country. Today, the region has evolved into a more diverse economy geared toward information and service-based businesses.

Computer-based businesses, finance, telecommunications, insurance companies, and the printing and publishing industries are doing well. The biomedical field, encompassing hospitals, medical schools, pharmaceutical firms, research institutions, manufacturers of medical instruments and supplies, and medical publishing, is flourishing in Philadelphia. As manufacturing continues to recede, the city's educational and health institutions have come forward as important drivers of the regional economy. Education currently represents about 12 percent of city and 7 percent of suburban employment. Health services constitute about 18 percent of city jobs and 12 percent of those in the suburbs.

Few cities in the country can match Philadelphia's historic attractions, and the city plays host to millions of tourists each year. Thus, tourism remains an important segment of the local economy.

The Greater Philadelphia region has become one of the major corporate centers in the United States. Many companies are locating or expanding facilities in the area. They are attracted by the area's location at the center of the country's largest market, the access to transportation, the availability of medical, engineering, and business schools to supply technical talent, and the open land for industrial park development. Center City is still the financial, governmental, and cultural hub of the region. Concerted efforts over the last several years by government, business leaders, and concerned citizens to improve Philadelphia's reputation as a corporate host have borne fruit, and the city is continuing to be discovered as an attractive place to live and work.

Items and goods produced: chemicals, pharmaceuticals, office and computing equipment, telecomunications from fiber optics to celluar technology, instruments, biomedical products, fabricated metal products, paper products, processed foods, clothing, petrochemicals, machinery

Incentive Programs—New and Existing Businesses

Both Philadelphia and Pennsylvania sponsor programs to encourage business retention and growth.

Local programs—The city's three empowerment zones provide additional tax incentives and financing to transform these areas into thriving neighborhoods for businesses and workers. Philadelphia Industrial Development Corporation enables the city to provide low-cost financing for acquisition, construction, and equipment. The city is eligible to receive state grants for site preparation and infrastructure for industrial development. Other programs provide individual businesses with low interest loans.

State programs—Funding programs offered by the state include bond financing, grants, loans and loan guarantees, tax credits and abatements, and technical assistance. The Key-

stone Opportunity Zone has designated some 500 acres in a dozen zones throughout the Philadelphia area as exempt from state and local business taxes; these areas will remain virtually tax-exempt until 2013. Four state Enterprise Zones in Philadelphia are eligible for numerous incentives, including state tax credits, security rebates, low-interest loans, and technical assistance. The state's Job Creation Tax Credits program provides $1,000-per-job tax credit to approved businesses that agree to create jobs within three years.

Job training programs—The Philadelphia Industrial Development Corporation (PIDC) assists in the development of the workforce by partnering with the Philadelphia Workforce Development Corporation (PWDC), the Delaware Valley Industrial Resource Center, and the Collegiate Consortium to provide job training, program funding, and technical assistance. The PIDC offers a broad spectrum of qualified workers, and can customize programs such as on-the-job training, for which the employer receives some reimbursement; targeted programming for specific populations; customized training for specific job skills; recruitment, and referral and assessment aid. The PWDC Transitional Workforce Division provides training, support, education, employment, and other services to some of the region's most needy job seekers.

Development Projects

Since the completion of new international and commuter terminals, along with enhanced airport roadways at Philadelphia International Airport, other improvements included the consolidation of Terminals B and C, which resulted in a new food, beverage, and retail gallery.

The University of the Arts, on the heels of a new academic building with a recital hall, classrooms, a studio theater, dance studios, and lecture halls, has $379 million worth of new and planned investments proposed for the Avenue of the Arts District. A nearly $200 million family-oriented entertainment complex at Penn's Landing, to serve as the locus of a revitalized waterfront, opened in mid-2001. The $255 million Regional Performing Arts Center, a 5,000-seat venue on the Avenue of the Arts, opened in 2002. A $65 million master site plan for Independence National Historic Park was completed in late 2002.

In 2004 the School District of Philadelphia, in cooperation with the Microsoft Corporation, broke ground on the School of the Future, ushering in a new era of technology and education. The school, which is the first of its kind designed to be a model for improved instructional development through the use of technology, is expected to open in 2006 and cost an estimated $50 million. After receiving a $30 million commitment from the City of Philadelphia, the Free Library is preparing to renovate its Beaux Arts building and add 160,000 square feet of additional space. Final plans for the project were expected to be in place by December 2005.

The city's Neighborhood Transformation Initiate has gained national attention as one of the most comprehensive neighborhood revitalization strategies ever attempted. The plan has created a framework for making neighborhoods cleaner and safer. A $100 million neighborhood revitalization project in the Cecil B. Moore Avenue area of North Philadelphia resulted in the completion of nearly 300 new homes. Plans are currently underway for a new mixed-use community along the Delaware River. The mayor's new Livable Neighborhoods Program focuses on improving Philadelphia's older neighborhoods.

The New River City initiative involves stimulating private investment along the city's waterfront. During 2004, the mayor and the Philadelphia Industrial Development Corporation announced a master plan that includes the potential for $2 billion of private investment and the creation of 25,000 new jobs. The lower Schuylkill River will be home to a newly constructed River Park and Trail as well as a host of new residential projects and a 700,000-square-foot office tower. Also underway are redevelopment plans for the Civic Center and main Post Office. Improvements are also planned for the North and Central Delaware riverfront zones.

The Pennsylvania Convention Center will soon undergo major new construction that will double the existing facility. When the project is completed, the Center will have 541,000 square feet available, two ballrooms totaling 93,000 square feet, 87 meeting rooms, and a fully equipped main kitchen.

Economic Development Information: Philadelphia City Planning Commission, One Parkway Bldg., 1515 Arch Street, 13th Floor, Philadelphia, PA 19102; telephone (215)683-4615; fax (215)683-4630; email info@philaplanning.org. Philadelphia Industrial Development Corporation, 2600 Centre Square West, 1500 Market Street, Philadelphia, PA 19101; telephone (215)496-8020

Commercial Shipping

Philadelphia's port, together with the ports in southern New Jersey and Delaware, form the Ports of Philadelphia. The Ports of Philadelphia, the largest freshwater shipping complex in the world, handle the largest volume of international tonnage on the East Coast. Major imports include crude oil, fruits, iron, steel, and paper. Exports include scrap metal and petroleum products. Most of the terminals in the city are owned by the Philadelphia Regional Port Authority. With an infusion of state funds for capital improvements and the development of a new intermodal yard to serve three railroads—the Chessie, CSX, and the Canadian Pacific—the Philadelphia terminals are poised for growth. Philadelphia's Port, Penn's landing, is the largest freshwater port in the United States.

Labor Force and Employment Outlook

In the past, Philadelphia's economy was dominated by manufacturing, providing half of the city's jobs. But as manufactur-

ing decreases, now accounting for just 5 percent of the city's employment, education and health have emerged as principal drivers of the local economy, accounting for 12 percent and 18 percent of the city's jobs, respectively. In addition, Philadelphia promotes itself as a center for biomedical and pharmaceutical companies. Few cities have the historical past of Philadelphia, and it remains a mecca for tourists.

The following is a summary of data regarding the Philadelphia city/county area labor force, 2004 annual averages.

Size of nonagricultural labor force: 655,800

Number of workers employed in . . .
construction and mining: 11,200
manufacturing: 32,100
trade, transportation, and utilities: 90,400
information: 13,500
financial activities: 48,300
professional and business services: 84,100
educational and health services: 182,700
leisure and hospitality: 53,400
other services: 28,000
government: 112,200

Average hourly earnings of production workers employed in manufacturing: $15.73

Unemployment rate: 4.5% (April 2005)

Largest employers	Number of employees
Federal Government	52,000
City of Philadelphia	30,000
Philadelphia School District	26,000
University of Philadelphia (incl. hospital)	22,605
Jefferson Health System	14,317
Temple University	12,000
MBNA	11,000
Merck and Company	10,000
DuPont	10,000

Cost of Living

Housing prices in Philadelphia tend to be lower than those in comparably sized cities, and are among the lowest in the Northeast, with a median home price of just $59,700 in 2002. The housing stock dates from the 18th and 19th centuries and the city encourages preservation of the existing stock with federal, state, and private aid. The tax burden overall is high relative to other large cities nationwide.

The following is a summary of data regarding several key cost of living factors for the Philadelphia area.

2004 ACCRA Average House Price: Not reported

2004 ACCRA Cost of Living Index: Not reported

State income tax rate: 3.07%

State sales tax rate: 6.0%

Local income tax rate: 2.8%

Local sales tax rate: 1.0%

Property tax rate: 8.26% on every $100 assessed

Economic Information: Greater Philadelphia Chamber of Commerce, Business 200 S. Broad St., Suite 700, Philadelphia, PA 19107; telephone (215)545-1234

Education and Research

Elementary and Secondary Schools

Authority for Philadelphia's school system, the seventh largest in the nation by enrollment, is vested in a nine-member board of education appointed by the mayor. The city was one of the first in the nation to recognize the needs of gifted children, and it supports a range of special admission schools providing programs for students ranging from academically gifted to talented in the creative and performing arts.

In 2004, the District in cooperation with the Microsoft Corporation broke ground on the School of the Future, ushering in a new era of technology and education. The school, which is the first of its kind designed to be a model for improved instructional development through the use of technology, is expected to open in 2006.

The following is a summary of data regarding the Philadelphia public schools as of the 2003–2004 school year.

Total enrollment: 196,309

Number of facilities
  elementary schools: 175
  junior high/middle schools: 43
  other: 55, including 43 neighborhood and magnet high schools, vocational-technical and special schools

Student/teacher ratio: 19:1

Teacher salaries
  average: $53,390

Funding per pupil: $7,669 (elementary)

The Roman Catholic Archdiocese of Philadelphia oversees one of the largest parochial school systems in the country, with more than 250 elementary and secondary schools in the city. About a third of elementary and secondary school students attend these and other private schools run by a variety of secular and religious groups such as the Society of

Friends. Philadelphia is also home to the High School for the Creative and Performing Arts.

Public Schools Information: The School District of Philadelphia, 21st and Parkway, Philadelphia, PA 19103-1099; telephone (215)299-7000

Colleges and Universities

More than 80 degree-granting institutions operate in the Philadelphia region, offering the highest concentration of colleges and universities in America. Nearly 30 of them are located in the city. Suburban to Philadelphia are prestigious Swarthmore, Haverford, and Bryn Mawr colleges. The Philadelphia region's six medical schools graduate nearly 20 percent of the nation's physicians. Degrees are offered in many disciplines, including nursing, dentistry, biological sciences, business, law, and design.

The University of Pennsylvania, which provides more than 100 academic departments, is rated among the top three schools in the United States.

Libraries and Research Centers

Philadelphia's public library, the Free Library of Philadelphia, consists of the Central Library, 54 branch libraries throughout the city, Homebound Services, and a Library for the Blind and Physically Handicapped. Collections number more than 8 million bound volumes (more than a million of which are in the Central Library), and more than 6 million non-book items, including photographs, maps, microfilms, manuscripts, government documents, and other materials. The staff supports service to nearly a half-million registered borrowers; circulation totals almost 6,500,000 items annually. A $30 million expansion of the Central Library underway in 2005 will offer an additional 160,000 square feet of space, including a 600-seat auditorium. Notable special collections in the Central Library include the Automotive Reference Collection; the Theatre Collection of more than a million items; the Edwin A. Fleisher Music Collection, reportedly the world's largest library of orchestral scores with complete parts; the Rare Book Collection, which includes several original manuscripts of Edgar Allan Poe; and the Children's Literature collections, including the Beatrix Potter Collection. The Free Library of Philadelphia serves the area business community with comprehensive collections of resource materials. In particular, the Central Library and Northeast Regional Library provide specialized information services relating to business, industry, and finance.

The Philadelphia area is rich in special library collections on the topic of American history. Examples of these are the Library Company of Philadelphia, founded in 1731 and holding more than 450,000 volumes on pre-1860 Americana and Philadelphia subjects; and the library of the American Philosophical Society, holding 230,000 volumes and 5 million manuscripts on Americana and the history of American science. Philadelphia is also home to many institutional collections on the subjects of medicine, pharmacy, and science and technology, as well as corporate special libraries dealing with such topics as insurance, law, finance, computers, chemicals, and transportation.

From Ben Franklin's studies on electricity in the 1740s to the development 200 years later of ENIAC (Electronic Numerical Integrator and Computer), the world's first electronic digital computer, Philadelphia has enjoyed a long tradition as a leader in research and technology. Temple University, the University of Pennsylvania, and other area educational institutions support a total of more than 100 formal research centers. Several dozen of these specialize in the medical sciences, although a variety of other studies is also pursued, ranging from insect biocontrol to federalism. Philadelphia is also known for its corporate research activities, such as those of the Philadelphia Electric Company.

Public Library Information: Free Library of Philadelphia, 1901 Vine Street, Philadelphia, PA 19103; telephone (215)686-5322

Health Care

There are 373 physicians per 100,000 residents in the Greater Philadelphia reagion. Within a 100-mile radius of Philadelphia is the nation's largest concentration of health care resources. The area is home to several medical schools, dental schools, nursing schools, pharmacy colleges, and schools offering advanced degrees in biological sciences. World-class health care facilities, such as Children's Hospital of Philadelphia (ranked number one in U.S. children's hospitals), Alfred I. Du Pont Hospital for Children, Wills Eye Hospital (the first and largest hospital devoted to eye care), the Deborah Heart and Lung Center (site of the first open-heart surgery), and Fox Chase Cancer Center. The University of Pennsylvania houses a Comprehensive Cancer Center, and the city is served by more than a dozen regional trauma centers. The growth of the biotechnology companies in the last two decades has gained the area the reputation as the nation's foremost pharmaceutical and technology center.

Recreation

Sightseeing

Philadelphia ranks third in the nation among cities with the greatest number of historic sites. Notable among them are Independence National Historical Park, dubbed ''the most historic square mile in America,'' where the many landmarks either remain intact as they existed 200 years ago or have been restored. Independence Hall—where the Declaration of Independence and the Constitution were written—is among the park's 26 interesting sites, which also include the Liberty Bell Pavilion, the Second Bank of the United States, and City Tavern, a reconstruction of the Revolutionary-era inn that operates today, serving visitors fare commonly prepared 200 years ago.

Historic homes throughout the city are open to the public—including Franklin Court and the Betsy Ross House—and many architectural styles are represented. Several historic churches also remain in Philadelphia. Other points of interest are the United States Mint and Penn's Landing, where harbor tours are available. The city is known, too, for its fine parks, including Fairmount Park, reportedly the largest landscaped urban park in the world and site of the nation's first zoo. The Park contains more than 200 pieces of sculpture. Philadelphia and its environs can be toured by bus or trolley.

Arts and Culture

Philadelphia's efforts to strengthen its downtown artistic attractions are centered on a 3.5-mile-long stretch along Broad Street dubbed the Avenue of the Arts. The Academy of Music, opened in 1857, is located there in the Kimmel Center for the Performing Arts, which includes Verizon Hall, Perelman Theater, Innovation Studio, and the Merck Arts Education Center. The Kimmel Center is also home to the world-class Philadelphia Orchestra, Philly Pops, Opera Company of Philadelphia, Pennsylvania Ballet, Chamber Orchestra of Philadelphia, American Theater Arts for Youth, and several others.

The Arden Theater is a professional regional theater, offering theatrical and educational programs and productions. Other leading Philadelphia theater groups include the Philadelphia Theatre Company, the Venture Theatre, Freedom Theatre, Hedgerow Theatre, Society Hill Playhouse, and the Media Theater for Performing Arts. Broadway and off-Broadway productions are presented at Forrest Theater and at the Merriam Theater at the University of the Arts. The Annenberg Center at the University of Pennsylvania presents the annual Dance Celebration, children's shows, and other performances in its three theaters. Several other university-affiliated theaters stage productions as well.

The Pennsylvania's Ballet's annual performance of *The Nutcracker* has become a holiday tradition. Dance performances are also presented at the Annenberg Center and by other leading troupes such as Philadanco and the Leon Evans Dance Theatre.

The Declaration of Independence and the Constitution were signed at Independence Hall.

Considered one of the world's great art museums, the Philadelphia Museum of Art houses more than 500,000 works dating from the Western Middle Ages onward; Asian art is also represented. The Museum also runs the Rodin Museum, said to possess the largest collection of that artist's sculptures outside of Paris, and historic houses in Fairmount Park (seven of these are open to the public at Christmas, decorated as they might have been when built). The Pennsylvania Academy of the Fine Arts, one of the oldest art museums and schools in the country and deemed an architectural masterpiece, displays more than seven thousand works of American art dating from 1750. The Barnes Foundation Gallery features more than 1,000 rarely seen works by the Impressionists and other nineteenth-century painters. The Academy of Natural Sciences Museum, the nation's oldest institution of its kind, features such exhibits as "Butterflies" and "Raptors: Hunter of the Sky". A national memorial to Benjamin Franklin, the Franklin Institute Science Museum and Planetarium features fascinating exhibits that move and can be moved, and it houses many of Franklin's personal effects. Philadelphia's newer museums include the Afro-American Historical and Cultural Museum, the Mummers Museum, and the Port of History Museum at Penn's Landing; the latter features changing local and international exhibits of arts and crafts and photography. The Perelman Antique Toy Museum and the Please Touch Museum specialize in childrens' interests. In addition, many small museums are housed in restored buildings throughout the city.

Arts and Culture Information: Greater Philadelphia Cultural Alliance, 1616 Walnut, Suite 600, Philadelphia, PA 19103-5306, telephone (215)557-7811

Festivals and Holidays

Philadelphia welcomes the new year with its famous New Year's Day parade, featuring 30,000 Mummers (costumed and/or masked musicians and actors). February features the Philadelphia's Pepsi String Band Show of Shows, an indoor musical extravaganza, which leads to March's Philadelphia Flower Show (considered the top such event in the country), the St. Patrick's Day Parade, and the Book and Cook Festival, which teams famous cookbook authors with local chefs to create culinary wonders. The arrival of spring is heralded in Philadelphia by Valborgsmassoafton (Spring Festival), a Swedish tradition. During its annual Sunoco Welcome America! Philadelphia celebrates the Fourth of July—Independence Day—with gusto: four nights of music, fireworks, a food festival, and a parade culminate in the Mummers' performance of a special summer "strut" at Independence Hall. The Philadelphia Festival in August, one of the country's oldest outdoor musical events, has become an end-of-summer ritual for "folkies" from around the country. The Craft Show at the Pennsylvania Convention Center in November, sponsored by the Philadelphia Museum of Art, has had a great influence on the current American crafts revival. Philadelphia's Thanksgiving Day Parade in November is the oldest of its kind in the country.

The city in addition hosts the PECO Energy Jazz Festival, Jam on the River, Army-Navy Football Game, and many other ethnically-related festivals, music festivals, and art fairs.

Sports for the Spectator

With more than 200 years of athletic competition history, Philadelphia is considered a premier sports city. Along with a busy annual sports calendar, first-class facilities, 10 professional teams, and more than 60 intercollegiate athletic programs, the city has also hosted many premiere sporting events such as the 2002 NBA All-Star Game. The nation's fourth largest media market, Philadelphia boasts extensive athletic facilities, including the Liacouras Center at Temple University and Wachovia Complex, where the National Hockey League Flyers host games during the season. Two new state-of-the-art facilities contribute to Philadelphia's reputation as a top sports location: the National Football League Eagles' new home, Lincoln Financial Field, opened in August 2003, while the Major League Baseball Phillies' new ballpark, Citizens Bank Park, opened in April 2004.

Suburban to Philadelphia are a number of racetracks offering thoroughbred racing from summer through winter and trotter racing in the summer only. The Wings indoor lacrosse team add variety to the city's sports offerings.

Collegiate athletic events of all kinds are regularly scheduled at the many colleges and universities in the area.

Sports for the Participant

While Philadelphia's park system includes hundreds of parks and playgrounds, Fairmount Park is the center of the city's recreational activities. Located throughout its 9,204 landscaped acres are 215 miles of trails; baseball diamonds and tennis courts; football, soccer, cricket, field hockey, and rugby fields; golf courses; a rowing course and a stocked trout stream; and a variety of other recreational opportunities. The RiverRink at Penn's Landing offers public skating days and evenings from November through February.

The city maintains six municipal golf courses. Indoor tennis is available at the University of Pennsylvania's Robert P. Levy Tennis Pavilion.

Shopping and Dining

Philadelphia is a city of shops rather than huge merchandising outlets. From major department stores, such as Strawbridge's, to complexes such as The Shops at Liberty Place, to the boutiques and specialty shops of Rittenhouse

Row, the city is brimming with fine shopping. A downtown area renaissance has attracted many new stores and shopping areas. Casual South Street offers a colorful variety of galleries, avant garde fashions, antique shops, and bookstores. Society Hill, a restored colonial neighborhood, is home to a waterfront shopping complex. The Bourse, across from Independence Hall, houses a collection of specialty shops and restaurants in a restored Victorian stock exchange. A few blocks away is Pine Street's Antique Row. The Gallery at Market East contains more than 230 shops and restaurants. Jewelers' Row is one of the world's largest and oldest diamond centers. The stretches north, south, and west of downtown contain several shopping centers, including the Shops of Chestnut Hill in the historic Germantown neighborhood, and the lively Italian Market.

Philadelphia has been called one of the best restaurant cities in the country, and its Le Bec Fen is a local favorite. New restaurants are proliferating in Philadelphia, and national and international cuisines are well represented in the city's restaurants, where dining styles range from casual to elegant. Seafood is a local favorite, as are Philadelphia cheesesteaks and soft pretzels with mustard. Early in colonial history, Pennsylvania Dutch scrapple—an aromatic mixture of cornmeal and pork scraps formed into a loaf—became essential to the proper Philadelphian's breakfast menu, and this specialty can still be found on regional bills of fare, as can Philadelphia Pepper Pot, a peppery tripe soup. At the Reading Terminal Market, formerly a hub for trains and food distributors, 80 merchants cater to the lunchtime crowd, offering unusual multiethnic fare ranging from Mexican mole to Mennonite-made shoo-fly pies.

Visitor Information: Philadelphia Convention and Visitors Bureau, 1700 Market Street, Suite 3000, Philadelphia, PA 19103; telephone (215)636-3300

Convention Facilities

The Pennsylvania Convention Center covers six city blocks in the heart of the city and offers 440,120 square feet of exhibit space, including a 32,000-square-foot ballroom and more than 50 meeting rooms. It encompasses historic Reading Terminal Market. The facility will soon undergo major new construction that will provide the Northeast with the largest continuous space in the region. When the project is completed, the Center will have 541,000 square feet available, two ballrooms totaling 93,000 square feet, 87 meeting rooms, and a fully equipped main kitchen. Another major convention facility is the Civic Center, with 382,000 square feet of exhibit space, auditorium seating for 12,500 people,

and 30 meeting rooms. Ample hotel space is available to accommodate guests and meetings.

Convention Information: Philadelphia Convention & Visitors Bureau, 1700 Market Street, Suite 3000, Philadelphia, PA 19103 (215)636-3330

Transportation

Approaching the City

Northeast Philadelphia Airport and Philadelphia International Airport operate within Philadelphia's city limits; the latter, located about seven miles from Philadelphia, offers service to more than 100 foreign and domestic cities and is connected with the city by the high-speed SEPTA Airport Rail Line. Fourteen other airports are located within commuting distance of Philadelphia.

The city is served by the Pennsylvania and New Jersey turnpikes and by Interstate-95 and I-76. These highways and their connections allow easy access to the city from many parts of the country.

Amtrak provides rail service to and from Philadelphia on a variety of daily routes. An ambitious rail network links 13 area rail lines into a 272-mile system by which passengers can reach any commuter station from any other within a 50-mile radius. Luxury overnight trains operate between Philadelphia and a number of major cities in the Northeast, South, and Midwest.

Traveling in the City

Philadelphia is laid out in a basic grid pattern. The commercial, historic, and cultural center is 24 blocks long—stretching from the Delaware River on the east to the Schuylkill on the west and 12 blocks wide from Vine Street on the north to South Street.

The Southeastern Philadelphia Transportation Authority (SEPTA) operates a large fleet of buses throughout the city and suburbs. The Authority's DayPass allows travelers unlimited rides on the public transportation system for $5.50. The city is served by two subway lines: The Market Frankford (east-west) and Broad Street (north-south). Because the streets are narrow in the Center City, traffic is often congested, and travel on foot or by taxi is recommended. The PHLASH-Downtown Loop purple buses provide a safe and convenient way for visitors to travel day and night to the city's most popular tourist destinations.

Communications

Newspapers and Magazines

Philadelphia's major daily newspaper, the *Philadelphia Inquirer,* circulates as a morning edition. The *Philadelphia Daily News* is distributed every evening except Sunday. *The Philadelphia Spotlite,* published weekly, focuses on visitor information and entertainment. Well over a hundred scholarly journals are published in Philadelphia, including publications of the Philadelphia Historical Society; several law journals are published in the city as well.

Television and Radio

Philadelphia is served by seven television stations and at least three cable operations. Stations originating in New York and New Jersey, and in nearby communities, are also accessible to Philadelphia viewers, as is cable service. Thirteen AM and FM radio stations broadcast a wide variety of radio programming ranging from classical to hard rock, gospel, Caribbean, big band, and jazz.

Media Information: Philadelphia Inquirer and *Philadelphia Daily News,* 400 North Broad St., Philadelphia, PA 19101; telephone (215)548-2000

Philadelphia Online

City of Philadelphia. Available www.phila.gov

Free Library of Philadelphia. Available www.library.phila.gov

Greater Philadelphia Chamber of Commerce. Available www.gpcc.com

Historical Society of Pennsylvania. Available www.hsp.org

Philadelphia City Planning Commission. Available www.philaplanning.org

Philadelphia Convention and Visitor's Center. Available www.pcvb.org

Philadelphia Industrial Development Corporation. Available www.pidc-pa.org

Philadelphia Visitors Center. Available www.phillyvisitor.com

School District of Philadelphia. Available www.philsch.k12.pa.us

Selected Bibliography

Anderson, Elijah, *Code of the Street: Decency, Violence, and the Moral Life of the Inner City* (Norton, 1998)

Bissinger, Buzz G. and Robert Clark, *A Prayer for the City* (New York: Random House, 1998)

Johnson, Gerald W., *Pattern for Liberty: The Story of Old Philadelphia* (New York: McGraw-Hill, 1952)

Pennypacker, Samuel W., *Pennsylvania Dutchman in Philadelphia* (Philadelphia, no.pub., 1897)

Weigley, Russell F., Edwin Wolf, and Nicholas B. Wainwright, eds., Joseph E. Illick and Thomas Wendel, *Philadelphia: A 300-Year History* (Norton, 1982)

Pittsburgh

The City in Brief

Founded: 1758 (incorporated, 1816)

Head Official: Mayor Tom Murphy (D) (since 1994)

City Population
    1980: 423,959
    1990: 369,879
    2000: 334,563
    2003 estimate: 325,337
    Percent change, 1990–2000: −9.5%
    U.S. rank in 1980: 30th
    U.S. rank in 1990: 40th (State rank: 2nd)
    U.S. rank in 2000: 54th (State rank: 2nd)

Metropolitan Area Population
    1980: 2,219,000
    1990: 2,394,811
    2000: 2,358,695
    Percent change, 1990–2000: −1.5%

U.S. rank in 1980: 13th
U.S. rank in 1990: 19th
U.S. rank in 2000: 20th

Area: 58.35 square miles (2000)
Elevation: Ranges from 696 feet to 1,223 feet above sea level
Average Annual Temperature: 50.3° F
Average Annual Precipitation: 36.85 inches of rain; 43 inches of snow

Major Economic Sectors: medical services, research and technology, government, wholesale and retail trade, manufacturing
Unemployment Rate: 4.8% (April 2005)
Per Capita Income: $18,816 (1999)

2002 FBI Crime Index Total: 19,737

Major Colleges and Universities: University of Pittsburgh; Carnegie Mellon University; Duquesne University

Daily Newspaper: *Pittsburgh Post-Gazette*

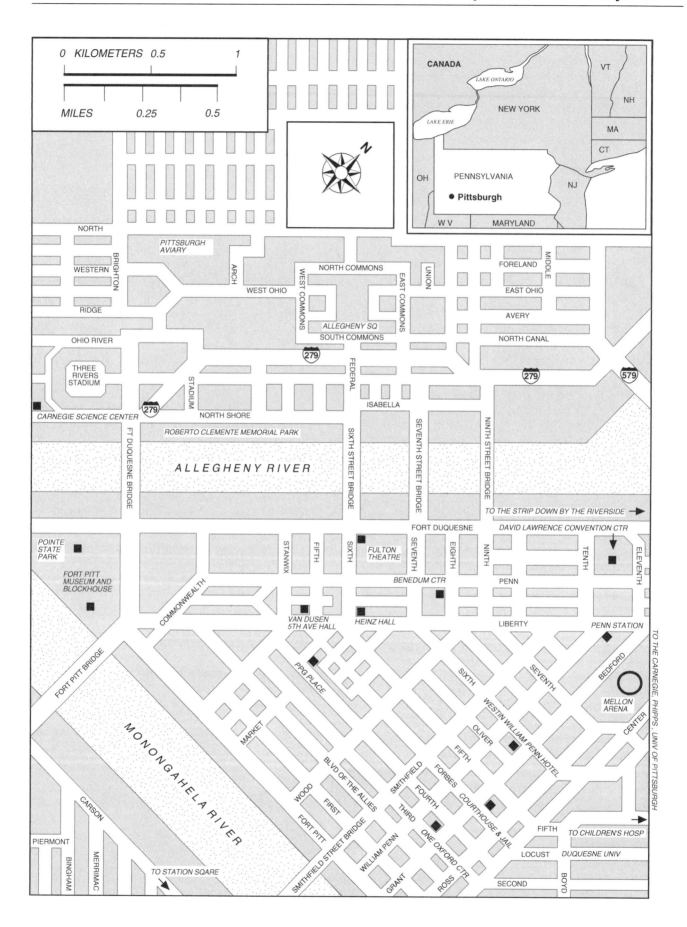

Introduction

Pittsburgh, once referred to as "the smoky city" and "hell with the lid off" because of its sooty factories, is a modern success story. Air quality controls, stream purification laws, and the razing and redesign of congested areas since World War II have resulted in a city that surprises first-time visitors. Nestled among the forested hills of southwestern Pennsylvania at the point where the Allegheny and Monongahela Rivers form the Ohio River, the new Pittsburgh is a city of skyscrapers, parks, fountains, more than 700 bridges, and close-knit neighborhoods with a vibrant cultural life. The city has over 70 miles of urban riverfront—more than any other inland port city in America. The transformation of Pittsburgh from an industrial center to a leader in science and technology and the success of its rehabilitation efforts have moved President George W. Bush to call it "Knowledge Town," and the *Wall Street Journal* to rank it as one of the top technology markets (going so far as to nickname it "Roboburgh").

Geography and Climate

Pittsburgh is located in the southwestern corner of Pennsylvania, at the foothills of the Allegheny Mountains, where the Allegheny and Monongahela Rivers join to form the Ohio. The city's humid climate is modified slightly by its relative proximity to the Atlantic Seaboard and the Great Lakes. The Pittsburgh area experiences extremes of all four seasons, with temperatures ranging from zero to 90° F or so. Precipitation is distributed well throughout the year, with a good bit of the precipitation occurring as snow during the winter months. From April through October, the sun shines more than 50 percent of the time.

Area: 58.35 square miles

Elevation: 696 feet above sea level at river base; 1,223 feet above sea level at highest point

Average Annual Temperatures: January, 28.4° F; July, 73.1° F; annual average, 50.3° F

Average Annual Precipitation: 36.85 inches of rain, 43 inches of snow

History

Early History

The first humans to live in what is now southwestern Pennsylvania were descendants of Asians who had crossed the Bering Straight and spread down through North America, hunting, gathering, and migrating, around 12 to 18 thousand years ago. About six thousand years ago, these Native Americans developed canoes and better tools for hunting and fishing; three thousand years ago, they learned to cultivate maize (corn), an agricultural revolution which led from a nomadic life to permanent villages. In another thousand years, agriculture was thriving and so was trade between villages and even tribes. Trade was carried out via either individuals carrying goods over a complex system of footpaths throughout densely forested Pennsylvania, or by canoes up and down rivers.

The coming of Europeans is what is likely to have wiped out the original native tribe of the Pittsburgh region, the Monongahela. Spread of European diseases to which the natives had no resistance, plus the fur trade resulting in depleted game supply, are theorized to have contributed to the disappearance of all humans from vast sections of western Pennsylvania in the 1600s. Soon, however, other displaced tribes from the south and east of Iroquois and Algonquian origins, especially the Shawnee, Seneca, Susquehannock, and the Lenni Lenape (Delaware), moved in to take their place.

French And British Vie For Strategic Location

Even in these early days, both British and French realized the strategic value of the wilderness location at the forks of the Ohio, a meeting place to trade for furs with the Indians. The French saw the Ohio River Valley as the only way to connect New France (Canada) with their Louisiana Territory. They claimed the Great Lakes, the Mississippi, and any river that flowed into it. The British had colonized the East Coast and were now hungry to push westward. A young Colonel George Washington, sent on a surveying mission to the area in 1755, observed that it was "extremely well situated for a fort, having command of both rivers." Washington's party left a tiny group of men to build Fort Prince George for the British, which the French easily outnumbered and captured without bloodshed later that same year. The French troops built a stronger Fort Duquesne there at "the Point," and held it for three years. Again without bloodshed, the English took back control in 1758 as the treaty ending the French and Indian War was signed in Europe. The French simply burnt down the fort and vacated the region. The English then built Fort Pitt, in honor of William Pitt, their Prime Minister; Fort Pitt was the largest and most elaborate fort in the colonies at that time. A small village that was first known as ''Pittsborough'' sprouted up around the fort. A 1763 addition, the Fort Pitt Blockhouse, still stands as the oldest building in Pittsburgh today.

The Whiskey Rebellion

The Pittsburgh region's economy was largely agricultural through most of the 1700s, growing from mere subsistence to having a surplus, especially in grains. Farmers found they could make better profits, especially in shipping, by turning their surplus grain into alcohol and bartering it. President George Washington, who had at age 23 noted the importance of Pittsburgh, had to face his first real challenge as President and the first challenge to the new country's Constitution, in a conflict over that alcohol that became known as the Whiskey Rebellion. The fledgling Federal government had decided to levy its first tax against whiskey, but the farmers argued they didn't have cash to pay taxes on bartered goods, and marched in protest. Washington had to send troops to squelch the protest and enforce the tax laws.

Gateway to the West

Because travel was quite difficult over the Allegheny Mountains, Pittsburghers learned it was better to produce goods themselves rather than pay and wait for items to be shipped from the east. The city's population was only about 300 by the 1790s, but many were skilled craftsmen such as blacksmiths, weavers, shoemakers, saddlers, tanners, brewers, cabinet makers, tinsmiths, and other artisans who could transform the region's agricultural products into goods that could be used or easily shipped and sold downriver. The first and largest industry emerging in the 1800s was boat building—both flatboats to transport waves of pioneers and goods downriver, and keelboats, which a strong crew could propel upstream as well.

In 1795 James O'Hara and Isaac Craig started a glass factory, an important development since glass was the hardest material to transport. Its success prompted other glass factories to crop up around the area, becoming its second biggest industry.

Pittsburgh increasingly became known as the ''Gateway to the West,'' a jumping-off point for people to more easily continue down the river after the arduous crossing of the mountains. Travel both ways on the rivers became easier in 1811 when Robert Fulton, with Nicholas Roosevelt, launched his first steamboat on western waters, the Pittsburgh-built *New Orleans*. The 116-foot vessel reached its self-named destination safely, then continued to run regularly between New Orleans and Natchez. The amazing Pennsylvania Mainline Canal reached its terminus in Pittsburgh in 1830, further facilitating migration from Philadelphia westward by offering an easier alternative to crossing

the daunting Allegheny Ridge. Plentiful natural resources of the region were constantly shipped in to the city, including enormous lumber rafts from northern forests, and barge after barge of coal pushed by steamboats up and down the Monongahela. In addition to being situated on one of the world's biggest coal deposits, Pittsburgh was also surrounded with oil, clay, limestone, natural gas, and sand suitable for glass. To supply iron needs for the War of 1812, foundries, rolling mills, machine shops, and forges sprang up on flat land along the rivers. With the growth of these factories and improved transportation, the population grew to allow Pittsburgh to incorporate as a city in 1816. Although Brownsville, Pennsylvania and Wheeling, West Virginia were early rivals to Pittsburgh's ''Gateway to the West'' title, Pittsburgh clinched it with the arrival of the Pennsylvania Railroad in 1852.

''Hell With The Lid Off''

As the 1800s wore on, Pittsburgh became known as the ''Smoky City'' due to manufacturing, steamboats, and household heating, all fueled with coal. The continued growth of the railroads plus demands of the Civil War increased the need for manufacturing. Earlier, iron furnaces had been run by charcoal, and thus were mostly located in rural places where wood was plentiful. However, when the coke-fueled blast furnace was invented, factory owners could consolidate and move their operations right to the riversides where coal, of which coke is a purified byproduct, could be conveniently delivered. This consolidation allowed them to keep prices down and remain competetive, even though iron making was still a small business of master craftsmen and not yet the huge operations of later years. Near the end of the 1800s, Birmingham, now Pittsburgh's South Side, had about 70 glass factories and was the world's largest supplier of glass. With railroad and river transportation boosting industry, other types of factories flourished as well, including five large and several small textile mills which employed about 3,000 workers in the late 1850s. In the 1860's, Pittsburgh was the world's largest refiner of petroleum products. The oil lamp, which in pre-electricity days was standard wherever gas lighting was unavailable, had been powered by increasingly rare and expensive whale oil, until it was found that the petroleum in the ground in western Pennsylvania could be put to similar uses. The refinery boom was brief, ending when John D. Rockefeller's Standard Oil attracted the business to Cleveland.

Steel City

With the invention of the Bessemer Converter, the making of steel changed from an expensive, high quality metal worked by a skilled artisan to being mass produced by relatively unskilled labor. Andrew Carnegie opened the Edgar Thomson Works in Braddock in 1875 and brought inexpensive, mass-produced steel to the Pittsburgh area. Carnegie had been an executive with the Pennsylvania Railroad, but quit to take the opportunity to manufacture the stronger Bessemer steel rails he knew the railroad intended to use. He hired engineers to further streamline and mechanize the steel making process so as to maximize the profits of mass production.

Carnegie's meeting and dealing with another major entrepreneur of the day, Henry Clay Frick, etched an important page in history. Frick was a self-made millionaire before he turned 30; he had formed a company to buy land rich in coal, which he processed into industrial coke, an essential steel making ingredient. Frick managed to buy out many of his competitors and became a major supplier to the burgeoning steel industry. The two formed a union that soured, ending in what is called the Homestead Strike, a lockout that ended in 10 deaths and many injuries, even necessitating intervention by the Pennsylvania National Guard. Carnegie and Frick became bitter enemies over the episode, a feud they took to their graves. Still, the Carnegie and Frick names are nearly synonymous with philanthropic causes in Pittsburgh today; their legacies bestowed priceless gifts to the city in the form of libraries, schools, parks, and museums, in addition to bridges, railroads, and factories. Somewhat less prominent but equally important, other local employers such as Westinghouse, Alcoa, and Heinz were also on the forefront of improving working conditions and of supporting cultural life in the community.

A Modern Pittsburgh Emerges

From the late 1800s, Pittsburgh's population more than doubled to more than a million people in the metropolitan area by 1910, and the character of its downtown began to change from factories and residences to more office buildings. Banking activity increased so much to keep up with the booming economy that a section along Fourth Avenue became known as Pittsburgh's Wall Street. This period also saw great progress in public works, as water filtration and sewer systems were completed and electric lines and pipes for natural gas installed. Because commuting was still a luxury most mill workers could not afford, people continued to live, shop, and worship in the same self-sufficient communities where they worked. Pittsburgh today remains a city of neighborhoods, many of which still strongly reflect varied ethnic roots.

The coming of the trolleys in the late 1890s and of the automobile soon after helped to connect neighborhoods a bit more, and allowed some of the white collar manager's families to begin to populate the city's first middle class suburbs such as Shadyside, Dormont, and West View. Some were concerned about this city that held such great wealth for some, yet squalid conditions for many others. A boom in

social programs, instituting hospitals and other services and general cleaning up of the city began, but was hindered by local events such as a devastating flood in 1936, and national events including the Great Depression and World Wars I and II.

After World War II, Pittsburgh began to concentrate on giving itself a make-over, including river clean-up and air pollution controls, and new building projects under the umbrella heading Renaissance I. Democrats and Republicans, led by Mayor David Lawrence and banker Richard King Mellon, actually worked together on the face-lift. Some of the Renaissance projects were successful, such as Gateway Center, an office tower complex completed in the 1950s; and Point State Park at the end of Downtown's "Golden Triangle," officially opened in 1974, with a fountain foaming high into the air at the very point where the rivers join. Others were considered less successful, such as the razing of the Lower Hill District in order to build the Civic Arena, which was highly criticized for breaking up a tightly knit and artistically thriving African American community and leaving the neighborhood far worse off than it had been. Throughout the 1960s many major construction projects continued to revamp the city in East Liberty and Allegheny Center neighborhoods as well as downtown. In 1970, the last game was played at the Pittsburgh Pirate's Forbes Field, and Three Rivers Stadium, along with the U.S. Steel Building, (later changed to USX Tower) were the last buildings to be completed under Renaissance I.

By the late 1970s to the early 1980s, Pittsburgh's reign as one of the titans in the world of Big Steel had neared its end. The number of steel workers in the Pittsburgh area dropped from 90,000 in 1980 to 44,000 in just four years. U.S. Steel, formed when Elbert Gary and J.P. Morgan bought Carnegie Steel, lost $561 million in only one quarter in 1980. The city's population, which had peaked in 1950 at over 676,000, dropped to about 423,000 by 1980. Unemployment rates soared as the city's leaders scrambled to reinvent the local economy on a new base of service, health, and education fields; high tech industries; riverfront development; and regional tourism. Despite fluctuations in the economy, Renaissance II forged ahead through the 1980s, giving the city many of its signature skyline buildings such as Mellon Bank Center, One Oxford Center, PPG Plaza, Fifth Avenue Place, and the USX (U.S. Steel) Building. Through the 1990s, the transition from heavy manufacturing to new, mostly high tech industries took place, as Pittsburgh today stands at the forefront of medical research and computer and robotics technologies, as well as a center for arts and culture.

Historical Information: Historical Society of Western Pennsylvania, 1212 Smallman St., Pittsburgh, PA 15222; telephone (412)454-6000

Population Profile

Metropolitan Area Residents
1980: 2,219,000
1990: 2,394,811
2000: 2,358,695
Percent change, 1990–2000: −1.5%
U.S. rank in 1980: 13th
U.S. rank in 1990: 19th
U.S. rank in 2000: 20th

City Residents
1980: 423,959
1990: 369,879
2000: 334,563
2003 estimate: 325,337
Percent change, 1990–2000: −9.5%
U.S. rank in 1980: 30th
U.S. rank in 1990: 40th (State rank: 2nd)
U.S. rank in 2000: 54th (State rank: 2nd)

Density: 6,019 people per square mile (2000)

Racial and ethnic characteristics: (2000)
White: 226,258
Black or African American: 90,750
American Indian and Alaska Native: 628
Asian: 9,195
Native Hawaiian and Pacific Islander: 111
Hispanic or Latino (may be of any race): 4,425
Other: 2,218

Percent of residents born in state: 78.1% (2000)

Age characteristics (2000)
Population under 5 years old: 17,607
Population 5 to 9 years old: 19,004
Population 10 to 14 years old: 18,907
Population 15 to 19 years old: 25,881
Population 20 to 24 years old: 34,570
Population 25 to 34 years old: 48,860
Population 35 to 44 years old: 46,870
Population 45 to 54 years old: 41,082
Population 55 to 59 years old: 14,142
Population 60 to 64 years old: 12,606
Population 65 to 74 years old: 26,483
Population 75 to 84 years old: 21,362
Population 85 years and older: 7,189
Median age: 35.5 years old

Births (2002, Allegheny County)
Total number: 13,469

Deaths (2002, Allegheny County)
Total number: 15,100 (of which 106 were infants under the age of 1 year)

Money income (1999)
Per capita income: $18,816
Median household income: $28,588
Total households: 143,752

Number of households with income of . . .
Less than $10,000: 25,927
$10,000 to $14,999: 13,668
$15,000 to $24,999: 24,606
$25,000 to $34,999: 19,228
$35,000 to $49,999: 21,441
$50,000 to $74,999: 20,482
$75,000 to $99,999: 8,366
$100,000 to $149,999: 5,843
$150,000 to $199,999: 1,797
$200,000 or more: 2,394

Percent of families below poverty level: 15% (57.9% of which were female householder families with children under 5 years)

2002 FBI Crime Index Total: 19,737

Municipal Government

The City of Pittsburgh operates under a mayor-council form of government, with the mayor elected by popular vote every four years and nine council members elected by district, also for four year terms. Because the city has recently been in financial trouble while Allegheny County has remained solvent, there has been a movement to consolidate the 130 municipalities and 43 school districts under one central county government, or at least to increase cooperation among them. The issue is being studied and debated, but most studies agree that some form of consolidation would benefit all the municipalities. Allegheny County is run by a County Chief Executive and 15 county council members, 13 of whom are elected by district, and two elected at large, all for staggered four-year terms. This is a fairly recent change in the county government, from the Home Rule Charter of 1998, when voters approved shifting from having three county commissioners to the present executive/council form of government.

Head Official: Mayor Tom Murphy (D) (since 1994; current term expires 2005)

Total Number of City Employees: 3,412 (2005)

City Information: Mayor's Office, 414 Grant St., Room 512, City County Building, Pittsburgh, PA 15219; telephone, (412)255-2626; fax (412)255-2687

Economy

Major Industries and Commercial Activity

The southwestern Pennsylvania region, especially the city of Pittsburgh, showed great resiliency and resourcefulness in shifting from an industrial economy to one based on health care, research, hospitality and tourism through the 1990s. Nevertheless, the local economy mirrored the national recession for various reasons following the events of September 11, 2001. U.S. Airways, a major employer, suffered serious losses from decreased travel due to fear or terrorism and the SARS (Severe Acute Respiratory Syndrome) epidemic. Although U.S. Airways came out of bankruptcy in 2003, it cut more than 300 jobs and reduced service by about a third in 2004; Pittsburgh, which had once been the airline's largest hub, was reduced in status and Pittsburgh International Airport lost jobs to U.S. Airway's other hub cities such as Philadelphia and Charlotte. In January 2005, Southwest Airlines, the nation's largest discount carrier and sixth largest airline, announced it would start service at Pittsburgh International Airport in May, helping to fill the gap left by the loss of leases by U.S. Airways. Local officials are also trying to lure JetBlue, Frontier, and Spirit.

Losses in manufacturing jobs were not completely replaced by high tech jobs, as the latter account for only about six percent of jobs in the Pittsburgh MSA. Another reason for loss of jobs and the region's general downward economic trend is that Pittsburgh has one of the highest corporate tax rates in the nation. Not only do high taxes increase the cost of production for companies, they also discourage new businesses from locating in the area and may force established businesses to relocate to places with more favorable tax structures. The City of Pittsburgh was forced to file for financially distressed status under Pennsylvania's Act 47 in December of 2004. In the wake of this alternative to bankruptcy, the state Department of Community and Economic Development appointed a recovery team to compile a five year plan for economic recovery for the city. Financial analysts are cautiously optimistic as the unemployment rate seems to have peaked at 6.8 percent in January of 2003 and has come back down to 4.8 percent in April of 2005.

By far, the largest employment sector for the Pittsburgh area is in health, educational, and social services. Though heavy manufacturing continues to play a part, it employs only 12.3 percent of the work force as of May 2005. Health care, construction, and education all added jobs in 2004. Financial analysts predict continued modest growth in 2005, with finance, business services, and health care again providing key support. Research is now the third largest industry; the Pittsburgh area is home to 150 laboratories and over 7,500 scientists and engineers. Service, hospitality, and tourism jobs are growing fast as well, adding more than 10,000 jobs in these sectors since 1994, and 5,400 jobs in May 2005 alone. Education and state government employment declined slightly during that same month.

Film making is another emerging industry. Major motion pictures made in Pittsburgh include the original *Angels in the Outfield, Night of the Living Dead, The Deer Hunter, Flashdance, Gung Ho, The Silence of the Lambs, Lorenzo's Oil, Hoffa, Groundhog Day, The Wonder Boys,* and *The Mothman Prophecies.* Overall, the size of the labor force and the number of jobs, as defined by the Commonwealth of Pennsylvania, have both increased during the first half of 2005 resulting in a slightly lowered unemployment rate.

Items and goods produced: fabricated metal products, primary metals, glass products, machinery, food and related products, medical equipment, chemicals, plastics, electronics, software, robotics

Incentive Programs—New and Existing Companies

In keeping with the style of having many small municipal governments and school districts, Pittsburgh metro area's economic development groups number at least 27 different agencies. Typically, local incentives are used to augment traditional funding sources, federal and state assistance for which companies may be eligible. For example, the Pittsburgh Urban Redevelopment Authority administers the Pittsburgh Business Growth Fund, which is designed to provide "gap financing" for small businesses that create and keep jobs in the City of Pittsburgh, providing loans at competitive rates for leasehold renovations, equipment, and working capital.

Local programs—Among the many programs offering business incentives in the Pittsburgh area are the Community Loan Fund of Southwestern Pennsylvania, Inc., a $16 million fund that offers capital to manufacturing firms and businesses, job training, and early funding to chosen entrepreneurs; Pittsburgh Partnership for Neighborhood Development, which attempts to unite a network of community development corporations with public and private investors; the Port of Pittsburgh Commission, which is concerned with a 10 county, 200 mile network of waterways and the promotion of travel and industrial development along them; the Regional Development Funding Corporation, which acts on behalf of the U.S. Small Business Administration, Pittsburgh District Office in various economic development activities; and the Regional Industrial Development Corporation (RIDC) of Southwestern Pennsylvania, a private, not-for-profit corporation that coordinates local, state and federal funding programs for environmental assessment and renovations, working capital, infrastructure and new building construction and equipment, and administrates the Pennsylvania Industrial Development Authority's funding for land and building acquisition and improvements.

The Allegheny County Department of Economic Development's Redevelopment Authority of Allegheny County runs four programs: the $50 million Economic Development Fund, which assists local companies; redevelopment assistance; the Tax Increment Financing program; and the Housing Division, which administers the Home Improvement Program of Allegheny County and the Vacant Property Recovery Program.

State programs—The Commonwealth of Pennsylvania has the Department of Community and Economic Development to implement its Economic Stimulus Package, with 18 components or programs that assist in everything from site selection to loans for equipment, Enterprise Zone grants, tax credits, brownfield development financing, and more.

Job training programs—Carnegie Library's Job Training and Workforce Development catalogue lists 22 job training and related services in Pittsburgh, six given by Pennsylvania, and the U.S. Department of Labor's Employment and Training Administration. Several of the regional services are associated with Pittsburgh's colleges and universities. The Greater Pittsburgh Supported Employment Association helps those with severe disabilities get vocational rehabilitation and supported jobs. The Allegheny County Department of Human Services helps determine if individuals are qualified for federal funding. Some programs focus on minority youth, some on military veterans, some on displaced factory workers. Many help dropouts get a GED (high school equivalency diploma). Some agencies of note are Pittsburgh Job Corps, YouthWorks, the Urban League of Pittsburgh, Three Rivers Workforce Investment Board, and Carnegie Mellon University's Infolink.

Development Projects

Of the many development projects of recent years, the largest and those with the biggest economical impact have been the completion of the David L. Lawrence Convention Center downtown; and the two new stadiums on the North Side, the stunningly beautiful PNC Park for MLB's Pittsburgh Pirates, and Heinz Field for NFL legends Pittsburgh Steelers. Then-governor Tom Ridge broke ground for the Convention Center in April 2000, and its 1.5 million square feet was opened in three stages even as construction continued. Phase I was completed in February 2002; May 2002 saw Phase II completed with four exhibition halls and 18 meeting rooms; and in March 2003 the grand opening cere-

mony was held with all 5 exhibition halls, 51 meeting rooms, and the huge Grand Ballroom. PNC Park opened March 31, 2001 with an exhibition game with the New York Mets. Although it is the next to smallest ballpark in Major League Baseball with 38,127 seats, it is considered to be one of the most beautiful, designed to offer amazing views of the city skyline and intimate views on the field. Heinz Field opened August 25, 2001; it is a 65,000 seat, horseshoe shaped stadium with the open end at the south end zone facing the fountain at Point State Park. New hotels, restaurants and retail outlets have sprung up near the new stadiums and convention center.

Pittsburgh Urban Redevelopment Authority handles many projects but there are six showcase projects of note. South Side Works involved riverside development and brownfield renewal around Carson Street and the Hot Metal Bridge, resulting in a mixed use development with offices, a hotel, retail, and restaurants, a sports medicine complex and practice fields, and housing. Summerset at Frick Park, also known as Nine Mile Run, revived an environmentally ravaged slag heap into a 238 acre, 713 home community. Bedford Hill area housing developments were made possible when the Pittsburgh Housing authority received a $26.6 million HOPE VII grant. The Pittsburgh Technology Center is the result of Carnegie Mellon University and the University of Pittsburgh joining forces with the business community to create an interdisciplinary research center to advance studies in biotechnology, robotics, artificial intelligence, bioengineering, and computer applications. Washington's Landing is a development on a small island in the Allegheny River about two miles upstream from the downtown Golden Triangle. Herr's Island was transformed from garbage heap into an exclusive community with townhouses on the west end, businesses, a rowing center, and tennis courts in the middle, with a portion of the 17 mile Heritage Trail skirting the trees and fields along the perimeter. Crawford Square is an 18 acre residential development on the eastern edge of downtown Pittsburgh, bordering the mostly African American Hill District neighborhood.

In the southern end of Oakland and extending eastward to the Hazelwood neighborhood, an abandoned factory and brownfield area is being recovered as the Pittsburgh Technology Center Office and Research Park takes over the old LTV Coke plant. When complete, the LTV Coke Works Redevelopment Project will result in 700,000 square feet of office and research and development space, accompanied by around 1,000 residential units of various types. The city hopes the project will encourage businesses to locate near the universities in Oakland. Another research center is under construction in south Oakland on the edge of Carnegie Mellon's campus, the Junction Hollow Research and Development Technology Center, which will create 300,000 square feet for high technology companies that spin off from interaction with CMU. Both the Junction Hollow and the LTV Coke Works projects hope to qualify for funding from the Keystone Innovation Zone Program, which funds joint ventures of universities and corporations.

In the heart of Pittsburgh's downtown, the "Golden Triangle," the African-American Cultural Center Project is scheduled to be completed in 2007. A performing arts and exhibition center, the project will include a hotel and parking, and will add a sixth theater to the downtown "Cultural District." The Pittsburgh Riverfront Trail Connections Projects is an ongoing effort to improve, maintain, lengthen, and add connections to the 17-mile Three Rivers Heritage Trail System, which is used both recreationally and for commuting on foot, by bike, or by rollerblade. Pittsburgh's Three Rivers Heritage Trail System is acknowledged to be a national model for urban trail design and economic benefits thereof. North Shore Transportation Improvements Project has evolved with the new stadiums to include a new riverfront park, a 900 space parking garage, and a revamp of the pre-colonial street grid to improve traffic flow. Future developments on the North Shore will be new office buildings for Del Monte Foods and Equitable Gas, an expansion of Carnegie Science Center, a 6,000 seat public amphitheater, more retail and residential developments, another parking garage of 1,000 spaces, and an extension of the light transit rail. In Lawrenceville, another East End neighborhood, St. Francis Hospital has been bought out by University of Pittsburgh Medical Center, which has a new pediatric research center under construction and plans to move its Children's Hospital facility there. It is expected to be completed in 2007, with the current Children's hospital in Oakland remaining open until that time.

Other ongoing projects include Magee-Women's Hospital Research Center, a seven story addition to the hospital of the same name. A much needed upgrade of Schenley Plaza at the juncture of the Oakland neighborhood's University of Pittsburgh and Carnegie Mellon campuses, as well as upgrades to Schenley Park, is underway.

One of the major projects outside Pittsburgh city limits but within the greater metropolitan area is The Waterfront, another renewed brownfield area where the infamous Homestead Steel Works once flourished. It is a $300 million mix of commercial, retail, and residential use that the Allegheny County Department of Economic Development convinced three municipalities to share the financing and tax revenues. The Airside Business Park and Airport Cargo Center are two very important economic developments, the business park being a 273,000 square foot multi-use office space/warehouse facility in Moon Township near Pittsburgh International Airport. The newest completed development in the area is the Pittsburgh Mills mall in east suburb Frazer Township, which held a grand opening in July 2005. The

Galleria section of the mall features more than a million square feet of space including a 165,000 square foot Kaufmann's, a 98,000 square foot JCPenney, an entertainment and sports wing with bowling lanes, and a state of the art 16 screen theater.

Finally, a more controversial means of developing revenue in Pittsburgh is coming: gambling. In 2004, Governor Ed Rendell persuaded the state to pass the slots law, which approves 14 casinos to be built around Pennsylvania, 7 at horse racing tracks (one of which is The Meadows in nearby Washington County), 5 "stand-alone" locations, and 2 in resort areas. Pittsburgh is allotted one of the stand-alone casinos, and in mid-2005 several groups were vying for the Pennsylvania Gaming Control Board to grant them the license for their proposed sites. The 23-member Pittsburgh Gaming Task Force was appointed by Mayor Tom Murphy to study the social and economic impact of a casino, provide input on the aesthetic look it should have, and determine how it should interact with its neighbors. The licenses are expected to be given out some time in 2006, with casinos opening in 2007.

Economic Development Information: Allegheny County Department of Economic Development, 425 Sixth Avenue, Eighth Floor, Pittsburgh, PA 15219; telephone (412)350-1010; toll-free (800)766-6888; fax (412)612-2217. Urban Redevelopment Authority of Pittsburgh, 200 Ross Street, Pittsburgh, PA 15219; telephone (412)255-6600; fax (412)255-6617; email info@ura.org. Pennsylvania Department of Community and Economic Development, 400 North Street, Fourth Floor, Commonwealth Keystone Building, Harrisburg, PA 17120-0225; toll-fee (866)466-3972

Commercial Shipping

The Port of Pittsburgh is the country's largest inland port in terms of tonnage originating and passing through it. More than 50 million tons of cargo, primarily coal, are shipped annually on its three-river system. The port offers convenient access to the nation's inland waterway system on 8,000 miles of navigable rivers flowing through 24 states. The port system affects almost a half million water-dependent jobs. There are two Class I railroads and five Class II, with several connecting rails near industrial sites. Pittsburgh is served by more than 100 trucking firms with access to four major interstate highways. Air freight services are available at Pittsburgh International Airport and Allegheny County Airport.

Labor Force and Employment Outlook

Factors such as a low crime rate, high quality public education, and a skilled labor force with a strong work ethic continue to attract new employers to Pittsburgh. However some workers are struggling with the economic shift from heavy industry to more high tech occupations, as many lower-paying service jobs have replaced the higher-paying factory jobs of yesterday. Even in the fall of 2002, a time of recession for the nation and the region, Pittsburgh area employers had a hard time filling positions for more skilled workers, managerial and professional posts. However, overall, the unemployment rate has come down steadily in the past couple years so economic prognosticators are somewhat optimistic.

The following is a summary of data regarding the Pittsburgh metropolitan area labor force, 2004 annual averages.

Size of nonagricultural labor force: 1,134,700

Number of workers employed in . . .
  construction and mining: 58,900
  manufacturing: 103,300
  trade, transportation and utilities: 233,700
  information: 24,100
  financial activities: 69,600
  professional and business services: 138,900
  educational and health services: 213,500
  leisure and hospitality: 105,100
  other services: 59,500
  government: 128,100

Average hourly earnings of production workers employed in manufacturing: $16.37

Unemployment rate: 4.8% (April 2005)

Largest county employers	Number of employees
UPMC Health Systems	26,700
U.S. Government	20,400
Commonwealth of Pennsylvania	15,900
West Penn Allegheny Health Systems	10,200
University of Pittsburgh	10,100
Mellon Financial Corp.	8,404
PNC Financial Services Group, Inc.	6,959
Allegheny County	6,695
USX Corp.	6,300
Giant Eagle, Inc.	5,700
Highmark Blue Cross Blue Shield	5,600
Eat'n' Park Hospitality Group	4,600
Verizon Communications	4,400
USAirways Group, Inc.	4,000

Cost of Living

Pittsburgh's cost of living is slightly lower than the national average as is the price of housing. The following is a summary of data regarding several key cost of living factors for the Pittsburgh area.

2004 (3rd Quarter) ACCRA Average House Price: $226,663

2004 (3rd Quarter) ACCRA Cost of Living Index: 94.9 (U.S. average = 100.0)

State income tax rate: 2.8%

State sales tax rate: 6%

Local income tax rate: 3%

Local sales tax rate: 1%

Property tax rate: $24.72 per $1,000 assessed value (2005)

Economic Information: Allegheny County Department of Economic Development, 425 Sixth Avenue, Eighth Floor, Pittsburgh, PA 15219; telephone (412)350-1010; toll-free (800)766-6888; fax (412)612-2217. Pittsburgh Regional Alliance, Regional Enterprise Tower, 425 Sixth Avenue, Suite 1100, Pittsburgh PA 15219

Education and Research

Elementary and Secondary Schools

Pittsburgh Public School System's nine-member Board of Public Education underwent recent upheaval, seeking a new superintendent in 2005. Despite the temporary disruption of the change in leadership, Pittsburgh Public Schools remains dedicated to enabling its veteran, well-trained staff to give each individual child whatever is needed to help him or her grow into not only a successful student, but a socially adjusted adult who will contribute to society. In addition to the excellent mainstream education, the district offers a variety of support programs for special education needs, including speech/language support, visually impaired support, deaf or hard-of-hearing support, autistic support, multiple disabilities support, emotional and life skills support, learning support, physical support, and programs for the gifted and for early intervention. Creatively and scholastically gifted students have the Pittsburgh Gifted Center for kindergarten through eighth grade levels, then in high school the Center for Advanced Studies program is available. All gifted students get a custom-made Gifted Individualized Education Program (GEIP) designed for them in coordination with the school and the student's family. Magnet school options include the structured atmosphere of traditional academies, international studies, Montessori method schools, a baccalaureate program, vocational-technical training in computer sciences and such fields, and the CAPA program for Creative and Performing Arts. About 78 percent of teachers hold advanced degrees.

The following is a summary of data regarding the Pittsburgh Public School District as of the 2003–2004 school year.

Total enrollment: 34,167

Number of facilities
  elementary schools: 53
  junior high/middle schools: 17
  senior high schools: 10
  other: 4

Student/teacher ratio: 11.4:1

Teacher salaries
  minimum: $35,500
  maximum: $104,020

Funding per pupil: $15,514

The Diocese of Pittsburgh administers a large network of grade schools and high schools; there are more than 250 private schools and more than 85 vocational and trade schools in the region.

Public Schools Information: Pittsburgh Public Schools, 341 South Bellefield Avenue, Pittsburgh, PA 15213; telephone (412)622-3870

Colleges and Universities

The University of Pittsburgh, or "Pitt," was founded in 1787 near Fort Pitt. Originally known as Pittsburgh Academy, it is one of the nation's oldest universities. It is the area's largest four year school with a total enrollment of 26,795 in 2004. Pitt offers 118 programs including liberal arts, law, business, engineering, information science, and international studies. The University of Pittsburgh School of Medicine and Medical Complex, located in Oakland in the northwest of Pitt's campus, is foremost in the world in health administration, sports medicine, and bioresearch, and pioneered in organ transplants with the first combination heart, liver, and kidney transplant in 1989. The University of Pittsburgh spans a 132-acre urban campus with the majestic Cathedral of Learning as its centerpiece.

Carnegie Mellon University (CMU) began as Carnegie Technical Schools in 1900 by local steel magnate and philanthropist Andrew Carnegie and became known as Carnegie Mellon University after a merger with Mellon Institute in 1967. CMU offers nearly 200 bachelor's, master's, and doctoral degree programs, specializing in robotics, computer sciences, a strong fine arts department with a famous drama school, and the Tepper School of Business, rated by the *Wall Street Journal* as the number two business school in the world. Carnegie Mellon University has a campus in Silicon Valley, California, and one in the nation of Qatar. CMU seeks to expand its global connections with educational partnerships around the world. Its roughly 2,000 international students make up almost a quarter of the student body.

Other institutions of higher learning in Pittsburgh are Duquesne University, a Catholic University founded in 1878; Carlow College, another Catholic school, primarily for women; Robert Morris University, which emphasizes business studies and whose interns work and study at prestigious firms; Chatham College, one of the country's oldest women-only colleges having been founded in 1869; and Point Park University, a small, private, liberal arts school recently raised from college to university status. Community College of Allegheny County has four campuses and seven community centers, offers flexible scheduling and affordability, and allows thousands of students each year to transfer credits to a four-year college.

Libraries and Research Centers

The heart of Pittsburgh's library systems is the Carnegie Libraries of Pittsburgh, another gift of Andrew Carnegie. It consists of the main branch in Oakland, 18 other neighborhood branches, a Library for the Blind and Physically Handicapped, and three bookmobiles. The library has an extensive children's department and is believed to have had the first children's "storytime" in a library in 1899. On October 3, 2004, the Main Branch of the Carnegie Library held a ribbon cutting celebration for its newly renovated first floor; the Bookmobile Center was also recently remodeled. The library holds more than two million books and a plethora of computer terminals, all "Free to the Public," as Carnegie had enscribed above the doors to the Main Branch. Other features of Carnegie Libraries are a special Teens section in the new Main Branch first floor, which features a multimedia information desk, an indoor/outdoor reading deck, and a library shop and café. The library offers a Music Collection with more 12,000 books, scores, and periodicals and 30,000 recordings, featuring nineteenth and twentieth century Pittsburgh musicians prominently in the collection; an Art Collection, with more than 72,000 books, 200 periodicals, over 100,000 slides and pictures, and a growing video and DVD collection; and a Dance Collection of about 2,000 books and videos.

Carnegie Libraries of Pittsburgh also maintain a Job and Career Education Center and a Business Foundation Center. Because Pennsylvania's 2003-2004 budget reduced the library's funding by 50 percent, a nominal fee is charged for some computer classes.

The Pittsburgh area is one of the most active research and development sites in the United States, in part due to its two biggest universities, the University of Pittsburgh and Carnegie Mellon University. A joint venture of the two plus Westinghouse Electric Corp. is the Pittsburgh Supercomputing Center, established in 1986 and still continuing to develop and provide innovative software for scientific researchers nationwide.

University of Pittsburgh Medical Center (UPMC) operates most of the medical research centers in the region, including the Children's Hospital General Clinical Research Center, the Cooperative Research Center for Muscular Dystrophy, the Center for Injury Research and Control, Magee-Women's Research Center (for gynecology, obstetrics, and reproductive health studies), the Center for Neuroscience, a new Center For BioSecurity, and many others. Non-medical research involving the University of Pittsburgh includes a variety of centers, such as the Learning Research and Development Center, the Center for Urban and Social Research, the Chevron Science Center (for chemistry), the Small Business Development Center, and the Joseph M. Katz School of Business Institute for Entrepreneurial Excellence.

Carnegie Mellon University has no less than 77 research centers of all disciplines under its umbrella, some of which are jointly operated with the University of Pittsburgh and/or local businesses. Some of note are its Robotics Engineering Consortium, Art Conservation Research Center, Bosch Institute for Applied Studies in International Management, the Steinbrenner Institute for Environmental Education and Research, and the Institute for Complex Engineered Systems. A few of the most recent and most important research centers are CyLab, which has launched a security initiative to protect PC users from cyber terrorists and hackers; four separate Robotics research facilities, and the Software Engineering Institute (SEI), which was founded by a grant from the U.S. Department of Defense. Among other research institutes are Seagate, a computer and electronics company; the federal government's Pittsburgh Rehabilitation Research and Development Center; the Pittsburgh Research Laboratory; the National Energy Technology Laboratory; and the Pennsylvania Cooperative Fish and Wildlife Research Unit. Pittsburgh today is home to more than 200 institutional and commercial research centers and laboratories.

Public Library Information: Carnegie Library of Pittsburgh, 4400 Forbes Avenue, Pittsburgh, PA 15213-4080, telephone (412)622-3114

Health Care

More than 50 hospitals in the Pittsburgh region, including 20 in the city, offer a full range of traditional health services. The University of Pittsburgh Medical Center (UPMC) is the premier health care system in the region and its largest employer. UPMC consists of 19 hospitals including Western Psychiatric Institute; two surgery centers, a diagnostic center, and 17 assisted living facilities; the system has been ranked as a top hospital system for six years by *U.S. News and World Report.* The medical school and its research affiliates attract more than $375 million a year in National Institute of Health grants. UPMC is committed to biotech-

nology and is concentrating on research fields such as minimally invasive robotic surgery, genetic therapy, cancer, muscular dystrophy, chronic pain, arthritis, heart disease, regenerative medicine, and pharmaceutical discovery. In a 29-county western Pennsylvania region, UPMC employs more than 40,000 workers, has an annual budget of over $5 billion, and contributes over $200 million each year in community and charitable services.

The West Penn Allegheny Health System consists of six hospitals, two of which are in Pittsburgh—the Western Pennsylvania Hospital in the Bloomfield neighborhood and Allegheny General Hospital on the North Side. Western Pennsylvania provides 524 beds and handled more than 30,000 emergency visits in 2004. Allegheny General has 625 beds and 3,876 employees, 817 of whom are medical staff. The system's medical specialties include geriatric care, emergency trauma, children's health, surgery and transplants, sports medicine, and heart, cancer, and diabetes care.

Pittsburgh Mercy Health System has two hospitals, a mental health personal care home named Outlook Manor, and an outpatient clinic run by Catholic Health East. Mercy was the first hospital in Pittsburgh, established in 1847 by seven Sisters of Mercy nuns. Mercy is dedicated to bringing health care to even the poorest patients, and provides a number of community minded charitable services, such as domestic violence and child abuse programs, a state of the art trauma and burn emergency center, programs that fight drug and alcohol addictions, the Carol Sue Rocker Health Education Center, and Operation Safety Net, an outreach program for the city's homeless.

Recreation

Sightseeing

A logical starting place for a tour of Pittsburgh is downtown at Point State Park, where a 150-foot fountain symbolizes the confluence of the Allegheny, Monongahela, and Ohio Rivers. Located within the park is the Fort Pitt Blockhouse, the only remaining structure of Fort Pitt. Throughout the Golden Triangle, Pittsburgh's downtown area, sightseers can observe turn-of-the-century skyscrapers and other architecturally interesting modern and historic buildings, such as Pennsylvania Station, the Frick Building, the Union Trust Building, and the Omni William Penn Hotel. Among the city's most famous structures are the Allegheny County Courthouse and Jail, completed in 1888 and connected by the "Bridge of Sighs." In Oakland, the architectural jewel of Pitt's campus is the Cathedral of Learning, which looks like a cross between a French Gothic church and a sky-

The Cathedral of Learning at the University of Pittsburgh is the centerpiece of Pittsburgh's Civic Center.

scraper. This 42-story building houses 24 Nationality Class-rooms designed by artists and architects from the nations represented. The cathedral was designed by Charles Zeller Klauder, as was adjacent Heinz Chapel. A more recent attraction is the Senator John Heinz Pittsburgh Regional History Center, which houses a comprehensive archive of America's early 20th century push to progress.

South of downtown Pittsburgh, across the Monongahela, is Mount Washington, formerly called Coal Hill, from which a spectacular view of the city is provided by means of cable car rides on the Duquesne and Monongahela Inclines. The Carnegie Science Center on the North Shore offers many scientific curiosities including a planetarium, an OmniMax theater, and a claustrophobia-inducing tour of a World War II submarine. In Oakland at the entrance to Schenley Park, Phipps Conservatory and Botanical Gardens encloses more than two acres of floral exhibits, including a Butterfly Forest with 300 living chrysalises and butterflies at any given time. The conservatory opened a Welcome Center on March 31, 2005, a 10,885 square foot entrance with a shop and a café. Completion of the Welcome Center marked the completion of a $36.6 million expansion plan for Phipps.

The Pittsburgh Zoo and PPG Aquarium display more than 4,000 animals representing 475 species in naturalistic habitats over its 77 acres in hilly Highland Park. Part of the facility, Kids Kingdom is considered to be among the nation's top three children's zoos. The crown jewel is the $17.4 million PPG Aquarium that opened in June 2000. The 45,000 square foot aquarium houses a two-story Amazon Rainforest Exhibit around a 100,000 gallon tank with sharks, other fish, and simulated coral, recreating a diverse ecosystem.

The National Aviary on the North Side has about 600 birds in various simulated habitats. It offers close encounters with large birds of prey, and walk-through Wetlands of the Americas and Tropical Rain Forest exhibits, among many other activities. Kennywood Park, touted as "America's Favorite Traditional Amusement Park" and "the Roller Coaster Capital of the World," is in West Mifflin, 10 miles southeast of downtown Pittsburgh. Kennywood was established in 1898 and offers a range of rides from vintage wooden roller coasters to the new Phantom's Revenge, with a 230 foot drop and reaching speeds of about 85 miles per hour, one of the fastest coasters in the world. Sandcastle Waterpark is Kennywood's sister park across the Monongahela in Homestead; same-day passes to use both parks are available.

The famous Frank Lloyd Wright house built over a waterfall, Fallingwater, is only about an hour's drive from Pittsburgh in Ohiopyle, Pennsylvania. An offbeat way to see Pittsburgh sights is to embark upon a World War II amphibious vehicle and take in a Just Ducky tour. For those who prefer a larger vessel, the Gateway Clipper Fleet is a collec-

tion of riverboats offering tourists a view of the city from the water while they enjoy fine dining, dancing, and entertainment. Once docked back in Station Square, visitors can enjoy more dining and shopping there in the old railroad station turned office building, mall, and nightlife center. Behind the new Hard Rock Café in Station Square's latest extension, Bessemer Court, is the "Dancing Waters" 130-foot high water jet display synchronized with lighting and music.

Arts and Culture

The Pittsburgh community is strongly supportive of the visual and performing arts. Heinz Hall, internationally acclaimed for its outstanding acoustics, is home to the renowned Pittsburgh Symphony Orchestra and it also presents Broadway shows and other performances. One street over from Heinz Hall in the Golden Triangle's Cultural District is the Benedum Center, a $42 million dollar renovation of the old Stanley Theater in response to demand on Heinz Hall for performing space and time. Benedum Center is now home for Pittsburgh Ballet, Opera, Dance Council, and Civic Light Opera. Also located in the Cultural District are the Byham, O'Reilly, and Harris theaters, the former two being rebuilt vaudeville venues and the latter being leased by Pittsburgh Filmmakers Institute. Near the theaters in the Cultural District is Wood Street Galleries, which promotes multidisciplinary artists and provides space and equipment to smaller arts organizations; the galleries also share office space with the Pittsburgh Cultural Trust, which oversees arts matters in the city.

The Post-Gazette Pavillion at Star Lake, about 40 miles southwest of the city; Hartwood Acres in the north suburbs; and the Chevrolet (formerly I.C. Light) outdoor amphitheater in Station Square are the main venues for rock concerts or other large outdoor events. Pittsburgh's River City Brass Band performs at various locations from September through May. Pittsburgh Theater groups and acting companies include the Pittsburgh Playhouse, City Theatre, the Gemini Theater, Pittsburgh International Children's Theater, Civic Light Opera, PNC Broadway in Pittsburgh, Pittsburgh Public Theater, South Park Theatre, and Kuntu Repertory Theater. The universities have their own acting venues; Carnegie Mellon's drama department produces musicals and dramas at its Purnell Center for the Arts while Pitt's troupers perform at the Stephen Foster Memorial Theater. The Mattress Factory on the North Side is a unique combination of working and living space for artists, museum, gallery, and performance space.

To fulfill his dream of bringing together the disciplines of art, music, literature, and science, Andrew Carnegie gave the city The Carnegie, a building constructed in two styles—Italian Renaissance and Beaux Arts—with an elaborate foyer that Carnegie is said to have insisted cost more than a throne room. Another Oakland landmark, The Carnegie houses the Museum of Natural History on one side and the Museum of Art on the other, as well as the main branch of the Carnegie Library with a separate side street entrance around the corner at the other end of this vast edifice. The Carnegie Museum of Natural History boasts one of the best dinosaur collections of any museum in the world, with the first T. rex ever discovered and the third largest fossil collection. Its 10,000 or so items and specimens on display are not even one percent of its entire collections. The Carnegie Museum of Art's permanent collections includes outstanding pieces of impressionist art such as Monet's Water Lilies, as well as American paintings and artifacts and changing exhibitions of exciting new art from around the world. Also housed within The Carnegie is the Hall of Music, which regularly presents entertainment by locally and internationally known performers. On the North Side is the Andy Warhol Museum, the Children's Museum, and Carnegie Science Center. In the east end is the Frick Art and Historical Center with a museum, shop, and café, and the Henry Clay Frick mansion, Clayton.

In the Strip District bordering downtown is the Heinz Regional History Center, devoted to the heritage of western Pennsylvania. Other attractions of note in the area are the Pennsylvania Trolley Museum in Washington; the Western Pennsylvania Model railroad Museum in Gibsonia; and Old Economy Village, created in 1824 by the Harmony Society, a group similar to the Amish who settled here to escape religious persecution in Germany. Also of interest are the Allegheny Cemetery Historical Society, the Alle-Kiski Historical Society, the Center for American Music at the Stephen C. Foster Memorial at the University of Pittsburgh, Braddock's Field Historical Society, the Depreciation Lands Museum, the George Westinghouse Museum, the Kerr Museum, the Rachel Carson Homestead, the Rivers of Steel National Heritage Area, Soldiers and Sailors Memorial Hall, the University Art Gallery at Pitt, and the circa 1785 Neville House.

Festivals and Holidays

Locals start the New Year off with a family-oriented First Night celebration. An eight dollar charge admits one to various buildings and theaters all over downtown to enjoy live drama, music, dance, comedy, puppets, and more, while outside there is a parade followed by fireworks at midnight. Come spring, even the non-Irish enjoy the St. Patrick's day parade and subsequent Bourbon Street-like party in downtown Pittsburgh in March. In April is the Pittsburgh International Science and Technology festival. May brings the Pittsburgh Folk Festival and the International Children's Festival.

The rivers, parks, entertainment centers, and neighborhoods of Pittsburgh are host to a wide variety of fairs and festivals

throughout the year. The most ambitious of all of them is the 17-day extravaganza known as the Three Rivers Arts Festival. Held in June, it offers arts and crafts, free concerts, food, and children's activities. Also in June is the Mellon Jazz Festival, the Pennsylvania Microbrewers Fest, and in the neighboring county to the north one can visit the Butler County Rodeo and Big Butler Fair. From late May to mid-August the Stephen Foster Memorial Theater presents the Three Rivers Shakespeare Festival. The Three Rivers Regatta, held in July in the waters around Point State Park, celebrates the industrial and recreational importance of the city's rivers. The Pittsburgh Blues Festival is held every July to benefit the Greater Pittsburgh Community Food Bank. July also sees the Wings over Pittsburgh air show, which features the USAF Thunderbirds and showcases a Stealth bomber. Beginning in 2005, the Bassmaster Classic fishing tournament in late June will highlight how the area's rivers have been cleaned up enough, allowing previously endangered species return. The Greater Pittsburgh Renaissance Festival is held in the Laurel Highlands resort area in August, as are two Shadyside Arts Festivals and the Three Rivers Storytelling Festival. Labor Day weekend is time for another breath-taking fireworks display. The holiday season starts in late November with Light Up Night and free parking, carolers, horse-drawn carriage rides, ice skating at PPG Plaza, hot apple cider and other old fashioned holiday experiences for the season.

Sports for the Spectator

Pittsburghers have long been ardent sports fans. The city is home to three major sports teams; black and gold is worn by its baseball, football, and ice hockey teams, making Pittsburgh the only city in the United States to have all their major sports teams in the same colors. The National League's Pittsburgh Pirates play in the new PNC Park from April to October. The National Football League's Pittsburgh Steelers, four-time Super Bowl champions, use Heinz Field as their battle ground. The National Hockey League's Pittsburgh Penguins, owned by legendary center Mario Lemieux who led them to back-to-back Stanley Cups in the early 1990s, play from September to April at the Mellon Arena. Pro soccer offers the Pittsburgh Riverhounds, whose Falconi Field is actually in nearby Washington, Pennsylvania.

College sports are very much alive at the University of Pittsburgh and Duquesne University. The Pitt Panthers have men's teams in football, basketball, wrestling, cross country, swimming and diving, soccer, baseball, and track and field, and women's teams in basketball, cross country and track, gymnastics, volleyball, softball, swimming and diving, and tennis. The Panthers are a Big East team that has been a national contender in football and basketball of late. Panthers Football is played at Heinz Field, while other sports are played on the university campus at Petersen Events Center or the Fitzgerald Field House. The Duquesne Dukes teams compete at their uptown A.J. Palumbo facility. Harness track racing is offered at the Meadows in Washington County.

Sports for the Participant

Every season offers a variety of choices for the sports-minded in the Pittsburgh area. The rivers and many parks provide cycling and running paths, and water sports such as swimming, rowing, whitewater rafting, skiing, and fishing. The surrounding hilly country offers recreational opportunities to campers, hikers, and spelunkers, and within a two-hour drive of the city are 10 ski resorts and numerous cross country ski and snowmobile trails, as well as 800,000 acres of game land to entice hunters. Much work was done through the Rails to Trails program in the 1990s and today Pittsburgh enjoys a 17-mile Three Rivers Heritage Trail system and other trails in the area such as the Montour Trail in Robinson Township. The Montour Trail is currently about 40 miles long and will eventually connect Pittsburgh to Washington, D.C. Although running is a popular activity in the area, the city has had trouble financing its Pittsburgh Marathon, a 26.2-mile race that attracted the top distance runners in the world, finally shutting down the race for good in 2003. Another popular event (also cancelled due to financial woes, but reinstated in 2003) is the Great Race, a ten kilometer foot race in late September that attracts world-class competition—Mayor Tom Murphy has run every Great Race since the first one in 1976.

Pittsburgh Parks and Recreation Department (CitiParks) operates many other educational and sports and fitness activities year-round, including aquatics, bicycling, tennis, senior games, lawn bowling, ice skating, and BIG League sports, a collection of baseball and softball leagues and tournaments. Another popular sport is golf; the *Pittsburgh Post-Gazette* lists over 150 golf courses in the greater Pittsburgh area, and the PGA Senior Championships are held every June in nearby Verona. *Golf Digest* magazine ranked Pittsburgh the fourth best urban area for golfers.

Shopping and Dining

The Golden Triangle's eleven square blocks house major department stores and a myriad of specialty stores and boutiques. PPG Place, a stunning multi-block structure rendered entirely in glass, contains 20 specialty stores and restaurants. One Oxford Center features five levels of restaurants and upscale shops. Fifth Avenue Place has a mix of specialty shops on its first floor and a fast food court with one fine dining restaurant, Caffe Amante, adjacent to it. A popular destination is across the Smithfield Street Bridge from downtown in Station Square, original site of the Pittsburgh and Lake Erie Railroad headquarters, which has been restored and now has more than 50 shops; more than 25 restaurants, bars, comedy clubs, and nightclubs; a Sheraton hotel; Hard Rock

Café; the dock for the Gateway Clipper Fleet; and access to the Monongahela Incline cable car up to Mt. Washington, where several fine dining establishments take advantage of the spectacular view to accompany the cuisine.

Pittsburgh's many neighborhoods each have their own shopping district with its own unique character. The Strip District has grown from being the city's warehouse center for fresh meat, fish, produce, and ethnic delicacies to include restaurants and entertainment complexes, of which a newer development is the Boardwalk, an enormous nightclub that floats on the Allegheny River. Squirrel Hill and Shadyside neighborhoods are both reminiscent of Greenwich Village with its unique boutiques and art shops. The Bloomfield neighborhood is known as Pittsburgh's Little Italy. For micro-brew aficionados, visits to the Church Brew Works in Lawrenceville and the Penn Brewery in Troy Hill are a must. At the Pittsburgh International Airport, travelers can find good food and duty free shopping in over 100 outlets at the Airside Mall. The largest shopping malls in the suburban areas are Century III and the Galleria in the south, Ross Park Mall in North Hills, Monroeville Mall and the huge new Waterfront development in Homestead to the east; farther east is the brand new Pittsburgh Mills Mall in Frazer Township.

Visitor Information: Greater Pittsburgh Convention and Visitor's Bureau, 4 Gateway Center, Pittsburgh PA 15222; telephone (412)281-7711; toll-free (800)359-0758. Pittsburgh History and Landmarks Foundation, One Station Square, Suite 450, Pittsburgh PA 15219; telephone (412)471-5808

Convention Facilities

Conventioneers are allured by the Pittsburgh's accessability, its relatively low costs, low crime rate, and variety of attractions. The new David L. Lawrence Convention Center is the cornerstone of convention and tourism business in the region. It spans three city blocks in one corner of the Golden Triangle between the Cultural District and the Strip District, offering 313,400 square feet of exhibit space, 236,900 square feet of which are column-free; a Grand Ballroom that can hold up to 4,000 attendees; 51 meeting rooms, two 175-seat lecture halls, and a secondary exhibit hall; a 12,000 square foot main kitchen; 37 convenient loading docks; and pedestrian walkways to nearby hotels with 3,000 rooms available and to a riverside park and trail. Heinz Field, PNC Park, and Mellon Arena are also available for conventions and meetings. The Pittsburgh ExpoMart in Monroeville, about 9 miles from downtown, has 106,000 square feet for groups up to 2,000, and is connected to the Radisson Monroeville hotel, which offers additional flexible meeting space for groups of 10 to 600.

Clusters of hotels—old and new, and economy and luxury—are located around the airport, the Oakland university and hospital complex, Monroeville and other suburban locations, near the stadiums on the North Side, and downtown. Major downtown hotels include the Omni William Penn, Pittsburgh's oldest hotel with original 1916 grandeur and 596 guest rooms; the 616-room Westin Convention Center and the 182-room Courtyard Pittsburgh, which both connect to the David L. Lawrence Convention Center; and the Hilton, downtown's largest hotel with 713 rooms and more than 40,000 square feet of meeting space. Others include the Ramada Plaza Suites, Marriott City Center, and the Renaissance in the newly renovated 1906 Fulton Building. Also within walking distance to downtown are the Sheraton Station Square on the South Side, and the Priory and SpringHill Suites on the North Side.

Convention Information: Greater Pittsburgh Convention and Visitor's Bureau; 4 Gateway Center, Pittsburgh, PA 15222; telephone (412)281-7711; toll-free (800)359-0758

Transportation

Approaching the City

The 3-million-square-foot Pittsburgh International Airport opened in 1992. This state-of-the-art facility moves more than 14 million travelers in nearly 400,000 aircraft each year; it has 100 gates served by 20 passenger and 9 freight airlines. Taxis and buses provide transportation to the Golden Triangle, about 15 miles away.

The Pittsburgh area is at the center of an extensive highway system focused around Interstates 70, 80 and 76/376 (the Pennsylvania Turnpike) which run east and west, and Interstate 79/279 that runs north and south. Improvements to the Southern Beltway, the Findlay Connector, and the Mon-Fayette Expressway south of the city were recently completed and improvements to I-279 from the city to the airport area are ongoing. A recent renovation of the Fort Pitt Tunnels, which go through the base of the cliff of Mt. Washington connecting I-279 north of the city to south, was completed in early 2005 and greatly helped traffic congestion. Amtrak provides train service and Greyhound provides bus service into Pittsburgh.

Traveling in the City

The city center is confined in size by the three rivers and may be traversed on foot. The Port Authority Transit of Allegheny county (PAT) serves the city of Pittsburgh, all of Allegheny County and portions of five neighboring counties with 1,066 buses, 83 light rail vehicles, 4 incline cars, 75 other vehicles, and 457 ACCESS vehicles for elderly and handicapped riders. PAT services 228,454 passengers on an average weekday and had an approximate ridership of 68 million in 2004. There are 15,879 stops of which 256 are shelters or stations, and 64 Park and Ride lots with 14,850 parking spaces. Bus fare for adults is $1.75 for a one-way trip, and just 50 cents more buys one a transfer to a connecting line or a ride back home.

Communications

Newspapers and Magazines

The Pittsburgh Post-Gazette, the city's daily paper, appears Monday through Sunday mornings. *Pittsburgh Magazine* is published monthly. *Carnegie Magazine* focuses on culture, emphasizing the collections at the Carnegie Museums and Library. In addition, several publications of interest to the African American community and various religious groups, as well as a variety of foreign language periodicals are published in Pittsburgh. The *Pittsburgh Business-Times* provides weekly coverage of the region's business community. More than two dozen other magazines and newspapers of local interest are published in and around Pittsburgh.

Television and Radio

Pittsburgh is served by four major networks and a public television station, and 13 smaller independent stations. Two of these are historic firsts in television history: WQED is home of Mr. Rogers Neighborhood and the first publicly funded television station in the U.S., and KDKA, which had the honor of broadcasting the first electronic image through the air in 1929. DIRECTV sells satellite dish service in the area and Comcast is the cable TV company for Pittsburgh.

Thirteen AM and at least 20 FM radio stations broadcast programs whose content ranges from news and talk to R&B, rock, and country music. Westinghouse-owned station KDKA was granted the world's first commercial radio license in Pittsburgh in 1920.

Media Information: Pittsburgh Post-Gazette, 34 Boulevard of the Allies, Pittsburgh, PA 15222; telephone (412)263-1743; toll-free (800)228-NEWS (6397). *Pittsburgh Magazine,* QED Communications, 4802 Fifth Avenue, Pittsburgh PA 15213; telephone (412)622-1360

Pittsburgh Online

Allegheny County home page. Available www.county.pa .us/index.asp

The Carnegie Museums and Library. Available www.clpgh .org

City of Pittsburgh home page. Available www.city.pgh.pa .us

Pittsburgh Chamber of Commerce. Available www.pittsburgh chamber.com/public/cfm/homepage_chamber/index.cfm

Pittsburgh Greater Convention and Visitors Bureau. Available www.visitpittsburgh.com

Pittsburgh Post-Gazette. Available www.post-gazette.com

Pittsburgh Public Schools. Available www.pghboe.net

Pittsburgh Radio and TV Online. Available www.pbrtv.com

Pittsburgh Regional Alliance. Available www.pittsburgh region.org

Urban Redevelopment Authority. Available www.ura.org

Western Pennsylvania History. Available www.qed.org/erc/ pghist/units/WPAhist/wpa1.shtml

Selected Bibliography

Baldwin, Leland Dewitt, *The Delectable Country* (New York, L. Furman, 1939

Demarest, David P., Jr. And Fannia Weingartner, eds., *The River Ran Red* (Pittsburgh, University of Pittsburgh Press, 1992)

Innes, Lowell, *Pittsburgh Glass, 1797-1891: A History and Guide for Collectors* (Boston: Houghton-Mifflin, 1976)

Krause, Paul, *The Battle for Homestead 1880-1892* (Pittsburgh, University of Pittsburgh Press, 1992)

O'Meara, Walter, *Guns at the Forks* (Englewood Cliffs, New Jersey, Prentice-Hall, 1965)

Serrin, William, *Homestead: The Glory and Tragedy of an American Steel Town* (New York: Times Books/Random House, 1992)

Stanford, Les, *Meet You in Hell: Andrew Carnegie, Henry Clay Frick, and the Partnership that Transformed America* (New York, Crown Publishing, 2005)

Scranton

The City in Brief

Founded: 1786 (incorporated, 1866)

Head Official: Mayor Christopher A. Doherty (D) (since 2002)

City Population
1980: 88,117
1990: 81,805
2000: 76,415
2003 estimate: 74,320
Percent change, 1990–2000: −6.7%
U.S. rank in 1980: 199th
U.S. rank in 1990: 261st (State rank: 5th)
U.S. rank in 2000: 394th (State rank: 7th)

Metropolitan Area Population
1980: 728,796
1990: 638,524
2000: 624,776
Percent change, 1990–2000: −2.2%

U.S. rank in 1980: 49th
U.S. rank in 1990: 61st
U.S. rank in 2000: 67th

Area: 25.2 square miles (2000)
Elevation: 754 feet above sea level
Average Annual Temperature: 49° F
Average Annual Precipitation: 38.8 inches of rain; 48.7 inches of snow

Major Economic Sectors: Services, manufacturing, retail trade
Unemployment Rate: 5.3% (Metropolitan area; April 2005)
Per Capita Income: $16,174 (1999)
2004 ACCRA Average House Price: Not reported
2004 ACCRA Cost of Living Index: Not reported

2002 FBI Crime Index Total: 2,549

Major Colleges and Universities: University of Scranton, Marywood University

Daily Newspapers: *The Scranton Times-Tribune*

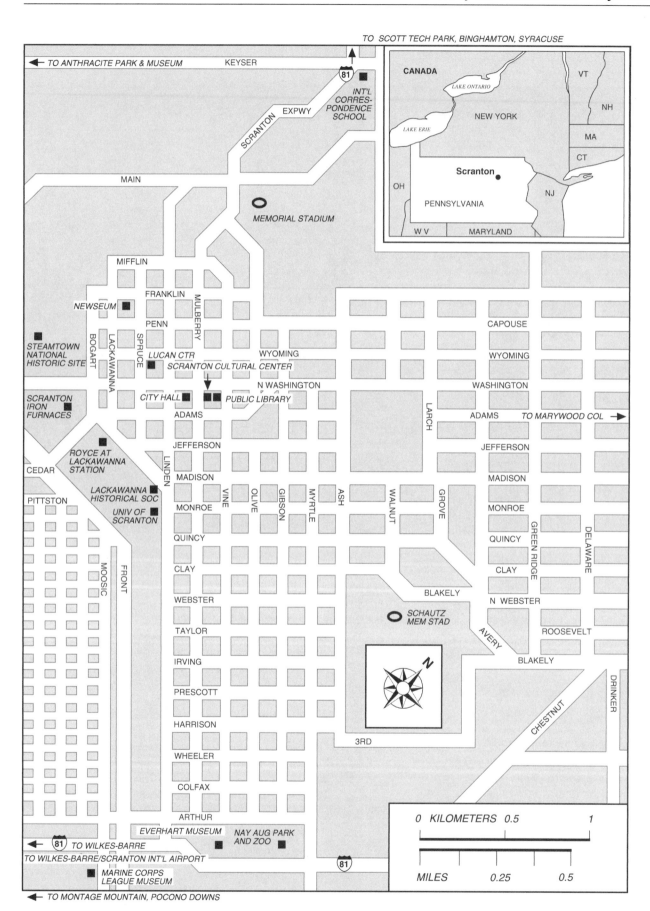

TO SCOTT TECH PARK, BINGHAMTON, SYRACUSE

← TO ANTHRACITE PARK & MUSEUM   KEYSER

81

INT'L
CORRES-
PONDENCE
SCHOOL

SCRANTON   EXPWY

MAIN

MEMORIAL STADIUM

CANADA

LAKE ONTARIO

LAKE ERIE

NEW YORK

VT

NH

MA

CT

Scranton

OH

NJ

PENNSYLVANIA

W V   MARYLAND

MIFFLIN

FRANKLIN

NEWSEUM

PENN

MULBERRY

CAPOUSE

STEAMTOWN
NATIONAL
HISTORIC SITE

BOGART

LACKAWANNA

SPRUCE

LUCAN CTR

SCRANTON CULTURAL CENTER

WYOMING

WYOMING

SCRANTON
IRON
FURNACES

CITY HALL

N WASHINGTON

PUBLIC LIBRARY

WASHINGTON

ADAMS

LARCH

ADAMS   TO MARYWOOD COL →

ROYCE AT
LACKAWANNA
STATION

JEFFERSON

JEFFERSON

CEDAR

LINDEN

MADISON

VINE

OLIVE

GIBSON

MYRTLE

ASH

WALNUT

GROVE

MADISON

PITTSTON

LACKAWANNA
HISTORICAL SOC

UNIV OF
SCRANTON

MONROE

MONROE

GREEN RIDGE

DELAWARE

QUINCY

QUINCY

MOOSIC

FRONT

CLAY

CLAY

WEBSTER

SCHAUTZ
MEM STAD

BLAKELY

N WEBSTER

TAYLOR

ROOSEVELT

IRVING

N

AVERY

BLAKELY

PRESCOTT

DRINKER

HARRISON

3RD

CHESTNUT

WHEELER

COLFAX

ARTHUR

EVERHART MUSEUM

NAY AUG PARK
AND ZOO

← 81   TO WILKES-BARRE

TO WILKES-BARRE/SCRANTON INT'L AIRPORT

81

MARINE CORPS
LEAGUE MUSEUM

← TO MONTAGE MOUNTAIN, POCONO DOWNS

0   KILOMETERS   0.5   1

MILES   0.25   0.5

Introduction

Scranton, formerly known as the Anthracite Capital of the World, is one of the largest cities in Pennsylvania and site of the Steamtown National Historic Site. In the early 1990s the city found itself in the peculiar position of simultaneously emerging from a 40-year decline while having to file what amounted to a bankruptcy petition with the state. The loss of its manufacturing base and nearly half its population without an accompanying reduction in city services forced The Pennsylvania Economy League in 1992 to develop a three-year plan to rescue Scranton from insolvency.

By the late 1990s, hundreds of millions of dollars were being spent on development projects and surveys rank the city highly as a desirable place to live and locate a business. Today, the professional services, health, education, retail, and tourism industries are the basis of the economy. Scranton is traditionally linked with Wilkes-Barre, the seat of neighboring Luzerne County, and is conveniently located near some of the Northeast's finest ski slopes and the beautiful Poconos Mountains.

Geography and Climate

Scranton stands in a valley bordered by the ridges of the Allegheny Mountains; the Pocono Mountains are to the southeast. The mountains protect the city from high winds; they also influence the temperature and precipitation throughout the year. The climate is relatively cool in the summer with frequent showers; winter temperatures are not severe, but when snowstorms do occur they approach blizzard conditions.

Area: 25.2 square miles (2000)

Elevation: 754 feet above sea level

Average Temperatures: January, 25.5° F; August, 69.5° F; annual average, 49° F

Average Annual Precipitation: 38.8 inches of rain; 48.7 inches of snow

History

The first European settlers in Scranton were the Abbott brothers, who founded a gristmill there in 1786. In 1800 the Slocum brothers took the mill over, named the area

Slocumville, and began a charcoal furnace for iron manufacturing. When the Scranton brothers arrived in 1840, they built the iron furnace that would later grow into the Lackawanna Iron and Steel Company. The community was named Harrison in honor of President William Henry Harrison in 1845; later the name was changed to Scrantonia then shortened to Scranton. The abundance of coal in the region attracted many other industries. In the 1880s the Scranton Steel Company was founded; it later merged with the Lackawanna Iron and Coal Company to become Lackawanna Iron and Steel Company. This company's move to Buffalo in 1902 dealt a heavy blow to Scranton's economy, but the growing importance of anthracite (hard) coal eventually earned the city the nickname "Anthracite Capital of the World." In the early 1900s, most of the hard coal mined in the country came from the Scranton area. The declining demand for coal after World War II forced Scranton, earlier than other industrial centers, to endeavor to find ways to diversify its economy. Its Scranton Plan, a revitalization plan devised in 1945, has been used as a model for other cities in decline. However, the plan had limitations.

By the end of 1991, after running a deficit for more than three years and projecting a 1992 deficit exceeding 23 percent of its $33 million budget, Scranton was designated a distressed municipality by the Commonwealth of Pennsylvania. A financial plan drawn up by the state and intended to prevent Scranton's imminent insolvency called for state technical assistance and aid in return for Scranton allowing the state to reorganize municipal government, raise temporary taxes, and dictate terms of labor contracts while the plan was in effect. After implementing these measures, the situation brightened in the mid-1990s. Scranton had more projects, more revitalization, and more economic development than almost any other city its size in the country, and tourism was on the increase. Today, Scranton has recovered from its past troubles and is a thriving town with a diverse economy, involved community, and rich cultural attractions. Each year, more and more visitors discover this hidden gem at the foothills of the Poconos Mountains.

Historical Information: Lackawanna Historical Society, The Catlin House Library and Archives, 232 Monroe Ave., Scranton, PA 18510; telephone (570)344-3841

Population Profile

Metropolitan Area Residents
1980: 728,796
1990: 638,524
2000: 624,776
Percent change, 1990–2000: −2.2%

U.S. rank in 1980: 49th
U.S. rank in 1990: 61st
U.S. rank in 2000: 67th

City Residents
1980: 88,117
1990: 81,805
2000: 76,415
2003 estimate: 74,320
Percent change, 1990–2000: −6.7%
U.S. rank in 1980: 199th
U.S. rank in 1990: 261st (State rank: 5th)
U.S. rank in 2000: 394th (State rank: 7th)

Density: 3,032.3 people per square mile (2000)

Racial and ethnic characteristics (2000)
  White: 72,200
  Black or African American: 2,744
  American Indian and Alaska Native: 236
  Asian: 961
  Native Hawaiian and Pacific Islander: 34
  Hispanic or Latino (may be of any race): 1,999
  Other: 1,125

Percent of residents born in state: 82.9% (2000)

Age characteristics (2000)
  Population under 5 years old: 4,035
  Population 5 to 9 years old: 4,422
  Population 10 to 14 years old: 4,631
  Population 15 to 19 years old: 6,007
  Population 20 to 24 years old: 6,217
  Population 25 to 34 years old: 9,011
  Population 35 to 44 years old: 10,509
  Population 45 to 54 years old: 9,574
  Population 55 to 59 years old: 3,442
  Population 60 to 64 years old: 3,204
  Population 65 to 74 years old: 6,876
  Population 75 to 84 years old: 6,231
  Population 85 years and over: 2,256
  Median age: 38.8 years

Births (2002, Lackawanna County)
  Total number: 2,043

Deaths (2002, Lackawanna County)
  Total number: 2,820 (of which, 13 were infants under the age of 1 year)

Money income (1999)
  Per capita income: $16,174
  Median household income: $28,805
  Total households: 31,307

Number of households with income of . . .
  less than $10,000: 4,592

$10,000 to $14,999: 3,514
$15,000 to $24,999: 5,610
$25,000 to $34,999: 4,571
$35,000 to $49,999: 5,004
$50,000 to $74,999: 4,749
$75,000 to $99,999: 1,971
$100,000 to $149,999: 895
$150,000 to $199,999: 194
$200,000 or more: 207

Percent of families below poverty level: 10.7% (56.4% of which were female householder families with related children under 5 years)

2002 FBI Crime Index Total: 2,549

Municipal Government

Scranton is the county seat of Lackawanna County. The mayor and five council members are elected to four-year terms.

Head Official: Mayor Christopher A. Doherty (since 2002; current term expires January 2006)

Total Number of City Employees: 550 (2005)

City Information: City of Scranton, Municipal Building, 340 N. Washington Ave., Scranton, PA 18503; telephone (570)348-4100

Economy

Major Industries and Commercial Activity

Once a one-industry town, Scranton is still dominated by manufacturing enterprises, primarily in the nondurable goods sector for companies such as Proctor & Gamble and Techneglas. However, between 1995 and 2000, major financial and professional services corporations such as AT&T, Fleet Financial Group, Cigna Health Care, and Alliance Fund Services opened large offices locally. Since that time, there has also been a marked increase in the number of people employed in the health, education, and social services industry—close to 25 percent of Scranton's employed population. Defense contractors also play an important role in the region's diversified economy, and construction, utilities, retail trade, and government make up a large part of the economic base. Tourism is also a growing industry.

Items and goods produced: apparel and related products, plastics, compressors, automotive components, heating and air conditioning equipment, candy, fabricated metal products, records and compact discs, caskets, books, furniture, chemicals, electrical equipment, glass products, tank parts, ordnance supplies, and other products for the Armed Forces

Incentive Programs—New and Existing Companies

Many programs available in Lackawanna County can be combined to form a comprehensive funding package for an eligible project. The primary programs are administered through SLIBCO (Scranton Lackawanna Industrial Building Company), PEDFA (the Pennsylvania Economic Development Financing Authority), PIDA (the Pennsylvania Industrial Development Authority), and SIDCo (the Scranton Industrial Development Company). Working together under the auspices of the Greater Scranton Chamber of Commerce, these organizations coordinate public and private sector resources to purchase industrial sites, construct shell buildings for lease to outside industry, develop raw land into industrial parks, and generally promote the region to corporate officials worldwide and assist expanding local businesses and industries.

Local programs—The University of Scranton McDade Technology Center serves as a resource for high technology businesses seeking to locate or expand in the Scranton area. Skills in Scranton, a business/education partnership run by the Greater Scranton Chamber of Commerce since 1989, has created a forum of communication between business and education to address the employment needs of Northeastern Pennsylvania's employers. The organization helps businesses with job training and re-training, and helps new graduates with making the school-to-work transition.

State programs—Pennsylvania's Department of Community and Economic Development is the main source of funding and other economic growth programs for state businesses. Funding programs offered by the state include bond financing, grants, loans and loan guarantees, tax credits and abatements, and technical assistance. The state's tools include the Job Creation Tax Credit Program, which provides a $1,000-per-job tax credit for businesses that create new jobs; 25 percent of the tax credits allocated each year must go to businesses with less than 100 employees. The Opportunity Grant Program provides funds needed to create or preserve Pennsylvania jobs to businesses involved in manufacturing, exporting, agriculture, and research and development. The First Industries Fund is a grant and loan program aimed at strengthening Pennsylvania's agriculture and tourism industries. Loans up to $200,000 can be used for land acquisition and construction, machinery purchase, and working capital. The state also runs a number of technology investment programs, which are designed to help create and bolster new and existing technology companies within the state. Program areas include funding, assistance programs, industry initiatives, and research and development.

Job training programs—There are a number of widely used state and federal programs to help employers reduce the costs of hiring and training workers. The Customized Job Training Program reimburses local employers for up to 75 percent of certain job training expenses, including instructional costs, supplies, contracted services, and travel costs. In return, companies must demonstrate an increase in employment opportunities, improved wages, and job retention. The Workforce Investment Act brings together area employers and unemployed or dislocated workers and trains those workers for employment with those companies at no expense to either party. Funds from this program can be used for job placement, skills assessment, labor market information, and training services.

Development Projects

A variety of projects are underway or have been completed in the Scranton area since the early 2000s. Almost $300 million has been invested in a variety of city improvement projects; recent construction projects include the $16 million Southern Union Headquarters, the $2.3 million Marquee Theaters, the $11.5 million Hilton Parking Garage, the $3.5 million police headquarters, and the $4 million Riverfront Sports complex. Infrastructure improvements include a number of road paving and improvement projects, the Meadow Avenue Flood Protection Project, the renovation of a number of area bridges, and the rehabilitation of the Merrifield Pumping Station.

Scranton's Nay Aug Park recently underwent a major renovation, including work to the Harlon's Grove Amphitheater, John Cleland Greenhouse, Rose Garden Fence, and Wildlife Center. The park's electric service and heating were also upgraded, the Davis Trail was restored, and workers installed safety rails along various pathways and constructed observation decks. Other neighborhood parks that have undergone rehabilitation include Weston Park, Weston Field, Crowley Park, Robinson Park, Jackson Street Playground, and Dorothy Street Playground. Scranton's downtown revitalization projects alone have totaled more than $26 million in improvements.

Economic Development Information: Greater Scranton Chamber of Commerce, 222 Mulberry St., PO Box 431, Scranton, PA 18501; telephone (570)342-7711. Pennsylvania Department of Labor and Industry, Room 1700, 7th and Forster Sts., Harrisburg, PA 17120; telephone (717)787-5279

Commercial Shipping

Scranton's proximity to Northeast Corridor markets is enhanced by an excellent transportation network. Five major interstate highways are accessible within 30 miles of the city's center, and both Manhattan and Philadelphia are two hours's drive from Scranton. Rail customers have access to Norfolk Southern, the Canadian Pacific Railway, and several other short lines, including the Lackawanna County Railroad Authority. Dozens of major trucking terminals and package delivery companies also service the area. Wilkes-Barre/ Scranton International Airport, a full-service facility located nine miles south of Scranton in Avoca, maintains inland port-of-entry facilities and an adjacent foreign trade zone, enabling Scranton to accommodate a growing international market. The northeast Pennsylvania area has a number of general service airports, heliports, and private service airports.

Labor Force and Employment Outlook

In recent years the city has experienced an influx of financial and service companies lured there by low costs and easy access to New York and Philadelphia. Scranton has also seen a large increase in jobs available in the fields of education, health, and social services; a number of hospitals that serve the area are located in Scranton. The city also draws an increasing amount of tourism traffic from visitors of the nearby Pocono Mountains resort area and visitors to the Steamtown National Historic Site.

The following is a summary of data regarding the Scranton metropolitan area labor force, 2004 annual averages.

Size of nonagricultural labor force: 255,700

Number of workers employed in ...
    construction and mining: 10,300
    manufacturing: 35,200
    trade, transportation, and utilities: 57,500
    information: 6,400
    financial activities: 14,100
    professional and business services: 20,800
    educational and health services: 47,600
    leisure and hospitality: 21,900
    other services: 10,200
    government: 31,700

Average hourly earnings of production workers employed in manufacturing: $13.87 (metropolitan area average)

Unemployment rate: 5.3% (metropolitan area; April 2005)

Largest employers (2003)	Number of employees
Tobyhanna Army Depot (electronics)	2,712
Proctor & Gamble (paper products)	2,500
Diocese of Scranton	2,377
Allied Services (health care)	2,196
WEA Manufacturing (CDs and DVDs)	1,800
Community Medical Center	1,800

Largest employers (2003)	Number of employees
Lackawanna County	1,438
Techneglas (glass TV screens)	1,300
Mercy Hospital	1,300
Moses Taylor Hospital	1,200

Cost of Living

Lackawanna County is a family-oriented, non-transient community. Housing costs are relatively low, with one-bedroom, one-bath apartments typically renting for less than $800 a month, and houses for purchase range from $100,000 to $300,000.

The following is a summary of data regarding several key cost of living factors in the Scranton area.

2004 ACCRA Average House Price: Not reported

2004 ACCRA Cost of Living Index: Not reported

State income tax rate: 3.07%

State sales tax rate: 6%

State property tax rate: none

Local income tax rate: 3.4% (city of Scranton)

Local sales tax rate: none

Local property tax rate: 82.122 mills on land, 17.86 mills on improvements (city of Scranton), 29.7293 mills on real estate (Lackawanna County)

Economic Information: Greater Scranton Chamber of Commerce, 222 Mulberry St., PO Box 431, Scranton, PA 18501; telephone (570)342-7711

Education and Research

Elementary and Secondary Schools

Elementary and secondary public education in Scranton is monitored by the Northeast Educational Intermediate Unit, one of many such agencies in Pennsylvania. The Scranton metropolitan educational system is considered to be among the best in the country. More than 60 percent of public high school graduates go on to higher education; the rate is even higher for private school graduates in the area. Average class sizes are small, with an average graduating class size of 187. More than 85 percent of high school seniors graduated in 2003, and that same year the attendance rate was over 93 percent.

The following is a summary of data regarding the Scranton public schools as of the 2004–2005 school year.

Total enrollment: 8,560

Number of facilities
  elementary schools: 13
  secondary schools: 3
  high schools: 2

Student/teacher ratio: 15:1

Teacher salaries
  average: $54,315

Funding per pupil: $9,100 (2002-2003)

The Diocese of Scranton operates a parochial school system that spreads across multiple counties. Private schools include Yeshiva High School, Hebrew Day School, Baptist High School, and Scranton Preparatory School (Jesuit).

Public Schools Information: Scranton School District, 425 N. Washington Ave., Scranton, PA 18503; telephone (570)348-3402. Pennsylvania Department of Education, 333 Market St., Harrisburg, PA 17126; telephone (717)783-6788

Colleges and Universities

Scranton, known as the world's center of education by mail, is home to Education Direct, one of the oldest and largest distance learning institutions in the world. Founded in 1890, the school has provided credit courses and personal enrichment studies to more than 13 million students in nearly every country in the world. The University of Scranton, a Jesuit institution, is noted for its outstanding academics and progressive campus and technology. The school was founded in 1888 and serves approximately 4,800 students. For eight years in a row, *U.S. News & World Report* has ranked the University of Scranton among the 10 finest master's universities in the North. Marywood University, a Catholic co-ed institution established in 1915, offers 60 academic programs including the arts, sciences, fine arts, social work, nursing, and music. Its 115-acre campus in suburban Scranton is said to be one of the prettiest in the state.

Scranton is also home to a technical school and a junior college. Lackawanna College, in operation for more than 100 years, offers associate's degrees in science, applied science, and arts, and also offers a variety of certificate programs for its 1,000 students. Johnson College offers twelve associate's degree programs and specializes in technical skills and general education. It boasts small class sizes and an attractive 65-acre campus. A number of other higher education institutions are located near Scranton, including Baptist Bible College, King's College, East Stroudsburg University, and Bloomsburg University.

Libraries and Research Centers

The Scranton Public Library is housed in the Albright Memorial Building, an early-Renaissance-design structure noted for its stained glass windows depicting the art of bookbinding and its marble floors and fireplaces. The library's holdings include thousands of volumes as well as U.S. government documents, compact and laser discs, and videotapes. The library maintains a special collection on local history; special services include free computer classes, teen and children's programs, and Books by Mail. The Lackawanna County Children's Library is housed in the renovated Marion M. Isaacs Building next to the main library; there are six other branches county-wide and a bookmobile servicing outlying areas.

The Lackawanna Historical Society Library also offers a wide range of research materials, much of it related to genealogy and local history. The library holds more than 6,000 books, more than 5,000 photographs, more than 1,200 maps, an extensive manuscript and scrapbook collection, and local newspapers.

The Harry and Jeanette Weinberg Memorial Library at the University of Scranton offers a collection of more than 450,000 books in a technology-rich environment. Its special collections include rare books and historical documents, and the library's electronic resources include an online catalog, 110 internet databases, and access to more than 13,000 full-text journals. Marywood College's library holds more than 200,000 volumes plus thousands of items on microform and various other media. It also offers a wide variety of computer training workshops.

Public Library Information: Albright Memorial Library, 500 Vine St., Scranton, PA, 18509; telephone (570)348-3000; fax (570)348-3020

Health Care

Five hospitals in Greater Scranton offer advanced treatment in rehabilitation therapy, oncology, and heart, kidney, and neonatal care. Moses Taylor Hospital founded in 1892, has 176 beds in addition to a fourteen-bed inpatient rehabilitation unit. It has a full-service emergency department as well as medical/surgical and other acute care specialty services. Mercy Hospital, specializing in cardiovascular treatment, is part of Catholic Healthcare Partners, the seventh largest nonprofit healthcare system in the country. Community Medical Center, with 310 beds, is a full-service hospital with an accredited regional trauma center and family and specialty practices. These three hospitals, the largest in the area, are all located within minutes of each other in Scranton's Hill Section. Other area hospitals include Marian Community Hospital in Carbondale and Mid Valley Hospital in Peckville.

Scranton's Allied Services, one of the largest rehabilitation facilities in the country, treats people who have suffered strokes, head trauma, and spinal cord injuries, as well as those with communications disorders and Alzheimer's disease. Affiliated with the University of Scranton, the Northeast Regional Cancer Institute is a network of six hospitals that run programs to benefit people living with and affected by cancer. Lourdesmont/Good Shepherd Youth and Family Services treats adolescents with mental health and substance abuse problems.

Recreation

Sightseeing

The historic Scranton Iron Furnaces, located in the heart of the city, are a potent reminder of the city's industrial past. The four interconnected stone blast furnaces, once operated by the Lackawanna Iron & Steel Company, closed in 1902; they were rededicated in the 1980s and have been completely rehabilitated. The National Park Service runs the Steamtown National Historic Site, located on 40 acres of the Scranton yard of the Delaware, Lackawanna & Western Railroad. This facility houses one of the nation's largest collections of standard-gauge steam locomotives. The collection includes the 1.2 million-pound 1941 Union Pacific Big Boy, one of the largest steam locomotives ever built, and a tiny 1937 H.K. Porter industrial switcher. Steamtown's Technology Museum and History Museum are housed in existing portions of the Roundhouse, dating from as early as 1902. The History Museum displays a timeline of railroading as well as exhibits that detail life on early railroads. The Technology Museum features a sectioned steam locomotive, caboose, and boxcar for visitors to explore.

The Houdini Museum is the only museum in the world devoted entirely to the escape artist Harry Houdini, and features antiques, memorabilia, magic, and artifacts. Three miles outside the center city, McDade Park is the site of the Lackawanna County Coal Mine Tour, considered one of the area's premier tourist attractions. The tour features an underground rail car trip 300 feet below the earth to the floor of the mine and exploration of three coal veins. The area also offers tours of interesting architectural sites and of the area's first commercial winery.

Arts and Culture

The Greater Scranton area hosts a variety of artistic and cultural events throughout the year. The striking Masonic

Temple and Scottish Rite Cathedral, located downtown, was designed by architect Raymond M. Hood following a Neo-Gothic and Romanesque design. The cathedral is home to the Community Concerts Association, the Broadway Theater League, and the Northeastern Pennsylvania Philharmonic. The Philharmonic, dance troupes, and other professional entertainers also appear at the F. M. Kirby Center for the Performing Arts in Wilkes-Barre. The Scranton Public Theatre performs comedies, drama, and original plays at the intimate Lucan Center for the Arts downtown from fall through spring. In summer, this professional repertory company sponsors the Pennsylvania Summer Theatre Festival at McDade Park, five minutes from the center city.

The history of the Scranton region is interpreted through exhibits at the Pennsylvania Anthracite Heritage Museum. Its collections highlight the lives and living conditions of the people who worked in the area's anthracite mines and textile factories, including replications of a family kitchen, a local pub, and a church. Another destination of historical significance is the Catlin House, headquarters of the Lackawanna Historical Society. Inside this 1912 English Tudor-style manor, visitors can view an extensive collection of books, photographs, clothing, and furnishings. A pictorial history U.S. Marine Corps from the American Revolution to the present can be traced at the U.S. Marine Corps League Museum. Founded in 1908, the Everhart Museum at Nay Aug Park features fine arts and natural history exhibits. The history of a local newspaper is presented in an outdoor display of artifacts and pictures known as the Scranton Times Newseum.

Festivals and Holidays

Scranton is a city that loves festivals and special events. The city starts out the year with First Night Scranton, a visual and performing festival that is punctuated by a fireworks display at midnight. In March, the town celebrates holds the nation's fourth largest St. Patrick's Day parade. Spring brings cherry blossom and wine tasting festivals, outdoor concerts, and music festivals. The Lackawanna Arts Council arranges festivals, exhibits, and special attractions, including the annual fall Arts Festival. Various ethnic and church festivals are scheduled during spring and summer, culminating in La Festa Italiana on Labor Day Weekend, which draws thousands of revelers to downtown's Courthouse Square. And in June, the U.S. Navy performs at the Wilkes-Barre/Scranton International Airport's Airshow.

Sports for the Spectator

Summer nights are perfect for taking in a game of professional baseball, so area residents head to Lackawanna County Stadium to watch the Scranton/Wilkes-Barre Red Barons, an affiliate of the Philadelphia Phillies. The team

The Lackawanna Coal Mine Tour is one of Scranton's premier tourist attractions.

plays 72 home games each season. Auto racing fans are drawn to Pocono International Raceway, considered one of NASCAR's most competitive speedways; it is located just 30 minutes from downtown Scranton and features a 2.5-mile tri-oval track. Horse racing fans are entertained at Pocono Downs in nearby Luzerne County, where harness racers compete on what is said to be the fastest five-eighths-mile track in the world. The Wilkes-Barr/Scranton Penguins, the American Hockey League affiliate of the Pittsburgh Penguins, delight hockey fans during their 40 home games at the First Union Arena at Casey Plaza. The Scranton Eagles play fifteen semi-pro football games each year in the Empire Football League, and the University of Scranton's sports teams compete in the NCAA Division III.

Sports for the Participant

Scranton is at the center of one of the Northeast's most popular skiing areas. Facilities for the expert and novice alike are available at Montage Mountain Ski Resort, just five miles from downtown Scranton; skiers can also choose from more than thirteen other ski areas within driving distance. Montage Mountain features a number of challenging ''black diamond slopes,'' snowboarding facilities, scenic chairlift rides, an ice skating rink, tubing, and hiking and picnic areas for summer entertainment. Cross-country skiing and snowmobiling are a few of the other popular wintertime activities; in the summer, residents and visitors enjoy water sports in the many area lakes and streams. Golfing, biking, fishing, hunting, and hiking are also popular pastimes. In October, the Steamtown Marathon attracts 1,500 entrants to a race given 14 of a possible 15 stars on marathonguide.com, with particular praise for the race's organization and volunteers. The city maintains dozens of indoor/outdoor sports and leisure areas.

Shopping and Dining

Downtown Scranton recently underwent a burst of commercial growth, bringing a number of new national chains to the area. A variety of specialty stores, antiques shops, and independent boutiques are also located in downtown Scranton. The area has also developed a reputation as an outlet center. The Mall at Steamtown offers two levels of specialty shops and a food court, and Viewmont Mall, anchored by major department stores, features dozens of specialty stores. From mid-July to Thanksgiving, local produce and baked goods are sold at Scranton Co-op Farmers Night Market, minutes from downtown Scranton.

Scranton's population is ethnically diverse and the city supports a number of ethnic restaurants, including Asian, French, German, Greek, Italian, Middle Eastern, and Mexican fare. Local ethnic favorites include pierogies, halluski, and halupkies. Diners can also enjoy a range of other restaurants, from fine dining establishments to classic dinners, steakhouses, cafes, and pubs.

Visitor Information: Greater Scranton Chamber of Commerce, 222 Mulberry St., PO Box 431, Scranton, PA 18501; telephone (570)342-7711. Lackawanna County Convention & Visitors Bureau, 99 Glenmaura National Blvd., Scranton, PA 18507; telephone (570)963-6363; email info@visitnepa .org

Convention Facilities

The new Hilton Scranton & Conference Center, located in downtown Scranton, features 19 meeting rooms—the largest of which is more than 7,000 square feet. Facilities also include a 75-seat amphitheater and a grand ballroom that accommodates up to 500 guests. The hotel portion contains 175 guest rooms with complimentary high speed internet access and free local calls. A business center is also available.

The Radisson Lackawanna Station, the result of a multi-million dollar renovation of the 1908 Erie-Lackawanna Terminus building, is Scranton's other main downtown meeting facility. A stately structure built in the Neo-Classical style, the Radisson provides 146 guest rooms, two ballrooms, four executive boardrooms, three meeting rooms, and hospitality suites. Guests can also take advantage of the hotel's complimentary high speed internet access, fitness center, and airport shuttle. Dozens of hotels and motels in the metropolitan area provide additional accommodations to the thousands of visitors Scranton attracts each year.

Convention Information: Lackawanna County Convention & Visitors Bureau, 99 Glennamura National Blvd., Scranton, PA 18507; telephone (570)963-6363; email info @visitnepa.org

Transportation

Approaching the City

The Wilkes-Barre/Scranton International Airport, located nine miles south of Scranton, is served by United, Delta, Northwest, Continental, and U.S. Airways, and offers nonstop service to selected cities with connections nationally.

Scranton is connected to the Canadian border and Maryland by Interstate 81; Interstate 84 extends to the Massachusetts Turnpike; the northeast extension of the Pennsylvania Turnpike leads to Philadelphia. Interstate 380 provides a link to the Poconos and connects the area with Interstate 80, a principal east-west route from New York City to California.

Scranton is just over a two-hour drive from both Manhattan and Philadelphia.

Passenger rail service between Scranton and the metropolitan New York/New Jersey area is scheduled to return in 2006. A multi-million dollar intermodal transportation center is being built downtown to service rail passengers.

Traveling in the City

Scranton is laid out in a grid pattern. Bus transportation is provided by the County of Lackawanna Transit System. Taxi service is available. Martz Trailways has a bus depot in downtown Scranton.

Communications

Newspapers and Magazines

The Scranton Times-Tribune is the city's daily newspaper. The *Sunday Times* appears weekly. A number of religious and ethnically-oriented newspapers and magazines are also published in Scranton.

Television and Radio

Six television stations broadcast from Scranton; four AM and seven FM radio stations also service the area, playing a variety of formats. Cable service is available.

Media Information: The Scranton Times-Tribune, 149 Penn Ave., Scranton, PA 18503; telephone (570)348-9100

Scranton Online

City of Scranton. Available www.scrantonpa.gov

Greater Scranton Chamber of Commerce. Available www .scrantonchamber.com

Lackawanna County Convention & Visitor's Bureau. Available www.visitnepa.org

Lackawanna County Government. Available www .lackawannacounty.org

Pennsylvania Department of Education. Available www.pde .psu.edu

Scranton Public Library at Albright Memorial Building. Available www.albright.org

Scranton *Times-Tribune.* Available www.thetimes-tribune .com

Selected Bibliography

Craft, David, J. Woolridge, William A. Wilcox, and Alfred Hand, *History of Scranton, Pennsylvania* (Heritage Books, 1996)

Hitchcock, Frederick L., *History of Scranton and Its People* (New York: Lewis Historical Publishing, 1914)

Throop, Benjamin H., *A Half Century in Scranton* (Scranton, PA: Press of the Scranton Republican, 1895)

RHODE ISLAND

The State in Brief

Nickname: The Ocean State
Motto: Hope

Flower: Violet
Bird: Rhode Island red hen

Area: 1,545 square miles (2000; U.S. rank 50th)
Elevation: Ranges from sea level to 812 feet
Climate: Warm summers, abundant rainfall; long winters with occasional heavy snowfall; moderated by ocean

Admitted to Union: May 29, 1790
Capital: Providence
Head Official: Governor Don Carcieri (R) (until 2007)

Population
1980: 947,154
1990: 1,003,464
2000: 1,048,319
2004 estimate: 1,080,632
Percent change, 1990–2000: 4.5%
U.S. rank in 2004: 43rd
Percent of residents born in state: 61.4% (2000)
Density: 1003.2 people per square mile (2000)
2002 FBI Crime Index Total: 38,393

Racial and Ethnic Characteristics (2000)
White: 891,191
Black or African American: 46,908
American Indian and Alaska Native: 5,121
Asian: 23,665
Native Hawaiian and Pacific Islander: 567
Hispanic or Latino (may be of any race): 90,820
Other: 52,616

Age Characteristics (2000)
Population under 5 years old: 63,896
Population 5 to 19 years old: 218,720
Percent of population 65 years and over: 14.5%
Median age: 36.7 years (2000)

Vital Statistics
Total number of births (2003): 13,081
Total number of deaths (2003): 10,064 (infant deaths, 76)
AIDS cases reported through 2003: 1,103

Economy
Major industries: Trade, services, manufacturing, research, agriculture
Unemployment rate: 4.7% (April 2005)
Per capita income: $31,937 (2003; U.S. rank: 17th)
Median household income: $45,205 (3-year average, 2001-2003)
Percentage of persons below poverty level: 10.7% (3-year average, 2001-2003)
Income tax rate: 25% of federal income tax liability
Sales tax rate: 7%

Newport

The City in Brief

Founded: 1639 (incorporated 1784)

Head Official: Mayor John J. Trifero (since 2005)

City Population
  1980: 29,259
  1990: 28,227
  2000: 26,475
  2004 estimate: 25,879
  Percent change, 1990-2000: −6.2%
  U.S. rank in 1990: 958th (State rank: 7th)
  U.S. rank in 2000: 1,223rd (State rank: 7th)

Metropolitan Area Population (Newport County)
  1980: 81,383
  1990: 87,194
  2000: 85,433
  Percent change, 1990-2000: −2.0%
  U.S. rank in 1990: Not reported

U.S. rank in 2000: 611th

Area: 11.47 square miles (2000)
Elevation: From 6 to 96 feet above sea level
Average Annual Temperature: January, 30.4° F; July, 71.0° F; annual average, 50.78° F
Average Annual Precipitation: 44.7 inches rainfall; 35.7 inches snowfall

Major Economic Sectors: U.S. Navy-related activities, tourism and related activities, education and healthcare
Unemployment Rate: 4.8% (April 2005)
Per Capita Income: $25,441 (1999)
2004 ACCRA Average House Price: Not reported
2004 ACCRA Cost of Living Index: Not reported

2002 FBI Crime Index Total: Not reported

Major Colleges and Universities: Salve Regina University, U.S. Naval War College, Community College of Rhode Island-Newport

Daily Newspaper: *Newport Daily News*

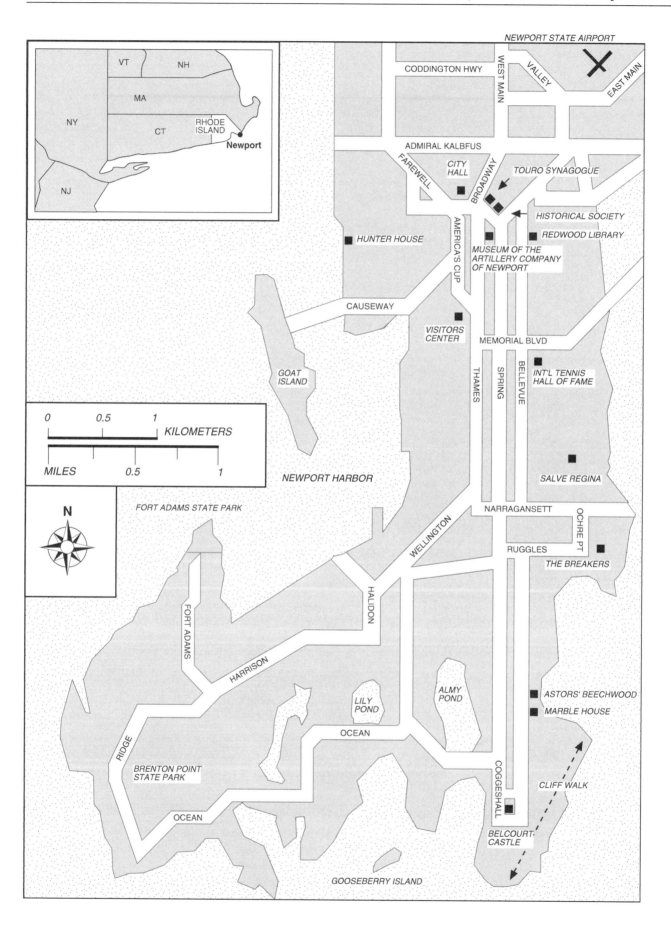

NEWPORT STATE AIRPORT

CODDINGTON HWY

WEST MAIN

VALLEY

EAST MAIN

ADMIRAL KALBFUS

FAREWELL

CITY HALL

BROADWAY

TOURO SYNAGOGUE

HISTORICAL SOCIETY

HUNTER HOUSE

AMERICA'S CUP

REDWOOD LIBRARY

MUSEUM OF THE ARTILLERY COMPANY OF NEWPORT

CAUSEWAY

VISITORS CENTER

MEMORIAL BLVD

GOAT ISLAND

THAMES

SPRING

BELLEVUE

INT'L TENNIS HALL OF FAME

NEWPORT HARBOR

SALVE REGINA

FORT ADAMS STATE PARK

WELLINGTON

NARRAGANSETT

OCHRE PT

RUGGLES

THE BREAKERS

HALIDON

FORT ADAMS

HARRISON

ALMY POND

ASTORS' BEECHWOOD

LILY POND

MARBLE HOUSE

RIDGE

OCEAN

BRENTON POINT STATE PARK

COGGESHALL

CLIFF WALK

OCEAN

BELCOURT CASTLE

GOOSEBERRY ISLAND

VT
NH
MA
NY
RHODE ISLAND
CT
Newport
NJ

0   0.5   1   KILOMETERS

MILES   0.5   1

N

Introduction

Historic Newport is best known as a summer resort colony. Three distinct communities comprise its population: the settled, predominantly Catholic community, the summer colony, and the United States Navy. The city has been called "The Birthplace of the Navy;" the presence of navy personnel builds on the distinctly nautical flavor of the seaside town. Newport is located on Aquidneck Island, which has expanded its role in naval activities in recent years, resulting in the growth of high technology industries and support services in the development of sophisticated communications and defense weaponry systems. Newport's beautifully preserved architectural heritage, including the summer "cottages"—actually late nineteenth-century mansions built by wealthy New York families—have made the city a warm-weather capital of American "high society" and a mecca for tourists interested in the colonial history of the United States. Newport's past is a fascinating mix of religious tolerance, slave trade, the military, and the very wealthiest of U.S. capitalists.

Geography and Climate

Newport is located at the southern end of Aquidneck Island in Narragansett Bay and is bounded on the east by the Atlantic Ocean, on the north by Massachusetts, on the south by the Rhode Island Sound, and on the west by mainland Rhode Island. The bay moderates the climate, making this area of the state somewhat warmer in the winter and cooler in the summer. The weather is of the kind described by meteorologists as humid continental.

Area: 11.47 square miles (2000)

Elevation: From 6 to 96 feet above sea level

Average Temperatures: January, 30.4° F; July, 71.0° F; annual average, 50.78° F

Average Annual Precipitation: 44.7 inches rainfall; 35.7 inches snowfall

History

Earliest Newport

Ironically, Newport and the rest of Rhode Island started out as part of the western coast of Africa—more than 500 million years ago. Tectonic forces gradually moved what is now Rhode Island toward the North American continent, where it collided and stuck, creating the Appalachian Mountains in the process. A series of ice ages changed the landscape over time through the approach and retreat of glaciers, which scraped a channel into the earth that separated Aquidneck Island from the mainland. About 3,000 years after the glaciers cleared out, humans moved in; evidence indicates that people have been living in the greater Newport area for somewhere between 10,000 and 12,000 years. These hunter-gatherers transitioned into the native tribes more familiar today, with the Narragansett (members of the Algonquian tribe) and Wampanoag Indians being the primary occupants of the Rhode Island area before the new neighbors moved in.

The first European known to have visited the Narragansett Bay area was Giovani Verrazzano, who briefly touched down in the region during an expedition in 1524. Fur traders came next, peacefully doing business with the native people for many years. A defining moment for Newport was the advent of religious dissidents who had been expelled from Massachusetts and many of whom were following Anne Hutchinson, who in 1638 founded Pocasset (later Portsmouth) on the northern end of Aquidneck Island with a small group led by William Coddington and John Clarke. In 1639 Coddington and Clarke moved south and established Newport.

As more settlers moved south to Newport, they adopted the predominant beliefs that church and state should be separated and that all people should be free to practice the religion of their choice. This atmosphere of tolerance attracted an eclectic mix of religious refugees, including members of the Society of Friends (also known as Quakers), Irish Catholics, and the Jewish community. In 1663 Newport and three other towns were chartered by England's King Charles II as the Colony of Rhode Island and Providence Plantation, which free-thinking Newporters didn't much care for.

Pirates, Slaves, and Civil Unrest

By the 1690s, Newport was one of the principal ports in North America. Most of the trade was legitimate, but pirates were a common sight in Newport. The state's reputation as a haven for individualists and pirates earned it the nickname "Rogues Island." By the 1760s Newport was also notorious for being the major slave-trading port in the British Empire—the "Triangular Trade" was an endless cycle of Caribbean molasses being imported to Newport, where it was made into rum that was shipped to Africa to trade for slaves, who were transported to the Caribbean to be sold for molasses that would make its way back to Newport. "Surplus" slaves who weren't traded for molasses were brought back to North America and sold in the south to work on plantations. Freedom appeared to be a limited commodity in colonial times.

During the 1700s Newport rivaled Boston, New York, and Philadelphia as a major trade and cultural center. It also developed as a resort colony, attracting vacationers from the Carolinas and Caribbean seeking to escape the heat and humidity of summers there. At the same time Rhode Island merchants chafed at the restrictions placed upon them by the British government. This tension came to a head in 1763 when the British sent vessels to police Narragansett Bay against smuggling activities. Several skirmishes broke out between the colonists and the British Navy; the British exacted their revenge in 1765 during the American Revolution by seizing the town of Newport and occupying it for nearly three years. As a result of this occupation, Newport's maritime trade collapsed. Although the city ranked as a leading whaling center from 1775 to 1850, its economy did not fully recover for nearly a century.

With the aid of the French, Newport was regained by the United States; French troops remained in the area until 1783 to ensure that it stayed in U.S. control. This time of instability left the city out of the industrial leaps that had occurred in other parts of the country, and Newport began to rely increasingly on its image as a summer resort. Writers, architects, scientists, and artists converged on the scenic area.

An End to the Triangle Trade

In 1774, Newport outlawed slavery, shattering the Triangular Trade. As part of the Union during the Civil War, Newport was designated the site of the U.S. Navy; the Naval Training Station, the Torpedo Station (now the Naval Underwater Systems Center) and Naval War College were established there during the 1880s, creating an important naval presence that continues to this day. Following the Civil War, in a time Mark Twain called the Gilded Age (1890 to 1914), income tax was an unknown concept. Wealthy families such as the Astors, Vanderbilts, and Morgans began to build opulent mansions they referred to as cottages in Newport to entertain each other during the brief summer season. At the cottage of Mrs. William Astor, where the ballroom held exactly 400 people, the legend of the Four Hundred was born, becoming America's first social register.

Newport's economy was given another boost by World War I as its shipyards built combat and cargo ships, but the city suffered heavily when the stock market crashed in 1929. The decline continued through the 1970s as the Newport Naval base was closed and the city lost 15 percent of its population. However, modern Newport is still a center of naval activities, housing the Naval War College and other training schools.

The New Newport

Newport today retains the cachet of a seaside resort, but the city today has more affordable housing than any other community in Rhode Island, and the military presence remains influential in the culture and the economy. The city has reinvented itself as a destination for all tourists, not just the wealthy, offering family-oriented activities and sightseeing excursions. Restoration of historic buildings has been a priority in recent years, from the Cliff Walk past staggeringly massive mansions to the downtown Brick Market. Newport hosts yachting events, tennis tournaments, golf championships, and a broad variety of festivals that honor the city's ethnic heritage.

In the summer of 2007, tall ships will again dock at Newport; the accompanying festival will include concerts, art exhibits, block parties, and fireworks as well as the breathtaking spectacle of dozens of towering ships parading on Narragansett Bay, in celebration of Newport's seafaring history and future.

Historical Information: Newport Historical Society, 82 Touro St., Newport, RI 02840; telephone (401)846-0813

Population Profile

Metropolitan Area Residents
1980: 81,383
1990: 87,194
2000: 85,433
Percent change, 1990-2000: −2.0%
U.S. rank in 1990: Not reported
U.S. rank in 2000: 611th

City Residents
1980: 29,259
1990: 28,227
2000: 26,475
2004 estimate: 25,879
Percent change, 1990-2000: −6.2%
U.S. rank in 1990: 958th (State rank: 7th)
U.S. rank in 2000: 1,223rd (State rank: 7th)

Density: 3,336.3 people per square mile (2000)

Racial and ethnic characteristics (2000)
    White: 22,272
    Black or African American: 2,053
    American Indian and Alaska Native: 225
    Asian: 353
    Native Hawaiian and Pacific Islander: 23
    Hispanic or Latino (may be of any race): 1,467
    Other: 638

Percent of residents born in state: 45.6% (2000)

Age characteristics (2000)
Population under 5 years old: 1,526
Population 5 to 9 years old: 1,465
Population 10 to 14 years old: 1,412
Population 15 to 19 years old: 1,986
Population 20 to 24 years old: 2,671
Population 25 to 34 years old: 4,229
Population 35 to 44 years old: 4,117
Population 45 to 54 years old: 3,481
Population 55 to 59 years old: 1,276
Population 60 to 64 years old: 904
Population 65 to 74 years old: 1,646
Population 75 to 84 years old: 1,261
Population 85 years and over: 501
Median age: 34.9

Births (2000)
Total number: 318

Deaths (2000)
Total number: 222 (of which none were infants under
the age of 1 year)

Money income (1999)
Per capita income: $25,441
Median household income: $40,669
Total households: 11,562

Number of households with income of . . .
less than $10,000: 1,343
$10,000 to $14,999: 941
$15,000 to $24,999: 1,400
$25,000 to $34,999: 1,440
$35,000 to $49,999: 1,632
$50,000 to $74,999: 2,271
$75,000 to $99,999: 1,090
$100,000 to $149,999: 923
$150,000 to $199,999: 233
$200,000 or more: 289

Percent of families below poverty level: 12.9% (55% of
which were female householder families with children
under 5 years)

2002 FBI Crime Index Total: Not reported

Municipal Government

Newport is governed by a council and a city manager under
a home rule charter. The council consists of seven members,
one elected from and representing each of three city wards

and four that are elected at-large. A mayor is chosen by the
four at-large councilors. The council is seated for two-year
terms. The City Manager directs all administrative departments for the municipality.

Head Official: Mayor John J. Trifero (since 2005; current
term expires 2007); City Manager James C. Smith (since
2002)

Total Number of City Employees: 346 (2005)

City Information: Office of the Mayor, City Hall, 43 Broadway, Newport, RI 02840; telephone (401)846-9600

Economy

Major Industries and Commercial Activity

Since the days of the Civil War, Newport has been an
important naval base, and the United States Navy is still a
major employer in spite of the closing of several installations in the 1970s. Today, the Naval War College, the Naval
Education and Training Center, and the Naval Underwater
Systems research center continue to stimulate the economy
in Newport, particularly in the area of technological research
and application related to national defense. The adjacent
communities of Middletown and Portsmouth experienced a
high-tech boom in the 1980s spurred in part by the location
of the Naval Underwater Systems Center in Newport, and
Aquidneck Island as a whole is becoming a high-technology
hub with more than 80 software and engineering firms
employing a large portion of the labor force.

Internationally known as a summer resort and yachting center, Newport depends heavily on wholesale and retail trade
and services catering to summer residents and tourists. Some
light industry plus fishing and lobstering also contribute to
Newport's economy.

Items and goods produced: electronic equipment, health and
beauty aids, fabrics

Incentive Programs—New and Existing Companies

Most incentive programs for development in Newport are
offered at the state level. The Rhode Island Economic Development Corporation provides direct access to state economic and business resources including finance, export
trade, federal procurement, and marketing. The Rhode
Island Small Business Development Center provides services to businesses with fewer than 500 employees, including the presentation of training seminars and workshops in
business planning, marketing, financing, and other business
subjects, as well as free consultations by experts in all
aspects of business.

Local programs—The City of Newport offers private businesses access to low cost capital through the Economic Development Revolving Loan Fund, with the intent of creating and retaining jobs. Businesses that are just starting up or expanding can utilize the funds to come up to compliance with the State Fire Code. Recipients can take up to 5 years to pay back the loan at 3.5 percent interest. Newport City also provides tax relief to encourage the reuse of historic properties, including expansion, renovation and development that fit within the Historic District Commission standards. To be eligible for the tax exemption, the property must increase in value no less than $100,000. Newport has consistently been a recipient of a pool of Community Development Block Grant (CDBG) monies that it has parceled out to support development projects that benefit low and moderate income residents.

State programs—Rhode Island provides a corporate income tax rate reduction for those firms increasing employment. Manufacturers and traded service firms paying above average wages or investing significantly in work training are able to take a 10 percent credit on purchased or leased equipment. Businesses may also take a significant credit for expenses for approved job training programs. Creativity is rewarded by income tax exemption for writers and artists who sell their works. Research and development activities may also be eligible for tax credits under a variety of programs administered by the Rhode Island Economic Development Corporation. Restoration of historic buildings as businesses or residences may qualify for tax breaks, as may businesses residing in certified mill buildings. Other state programs offer benefits to businesses that provide adult education, that create apprenticeship opportunities, or that are engaged in manufacturing, particularly within the areas of defense, medical instruments, or pharmaceuticals.

Job training programs—The Rhode Island Department of Labor & Training provides employers and small businesses with counseling and direct access to federal and state training, labor market information, recruitment and skills enhancement programs, and grants. The state additionally coordinates services to dislocated workers, foreign workers, youth who wish to be employed, and military veterans. The state maintains a large database of available jobs that can be accessed by those seeking employment. The Workforce Partnership of Greater Rhode Island supports the Department of Labor & Training by assisting businesses and industries in grant writing, goal-setting, job fair coordination, creation of school-to-work linkages, and employee training to address critical skill shortages.

Development Projects

In the early part of the twenty-first century, Newport and other Aquidneck Island communities received a $50,000 grant as part of the Aquidneck Island Planning Commission

(AIPC), allowing for a thoroughly researched and thoughtfully implemented plan for the former Navy lands on the west side of the island. Stated goals include preservation of open space and ocean views, economic development that is controlled and compatible with Naval Station Newport, increased passive and active recreation opportunities, and affordable housing. The planning process, which began in 2000, was ongoing as of 2005.

An associated project involves analysis of the island's primary water source, Bailey Brook; funding from the Natural Resources Conservation Services has allowed the AIPC to develop an environmental management plan that will ultimately lead to cleaner drinking water. The AIPC has a Transportation Improvement Plan prepared for implementation in 2006-2007, involving a study of current traffic patterns and usages of existing roads and paths, analysis of the data, rerouting of vehicular traffic to maximize efficiency, and creation of bike paths to encourage use of alternate modes of transportation.

The Washington Square Historic Restoration Project seeks to revitalize the historic downtown area with improved parking and traffic flow, restored historic buildings, enhanced signage that will better connect destinations and facilitate traffic movement, and to overall beautify area amenities. Construction started in 2004 and, accounting for cessations in work due to winter weather, the project is expected to be complete by fall of 2005.

The City of Newport has continued its ambitious North End Redevelopment Plan, which will promote jobs, education, and housing opportunities. By 2005 the city created space for a Newport branch of the Community College of Rhode Island, completed work on the Maple Avenue Ball Fields, and realigned the Pell Bridge. Ongoing projects include redevelopment of the old Navy Hospital facility, market analysis for the entire area, an enterprise zone, Pell Bridge land redevelopment, and affordable housing replacement unit construction. Altogether, millions of dollars have been allocated to restoration and renewal projects such as reinforcement of the Cliff Walk, updating of Goldberg Field, paving of historic Southern Thames Street, construction of quality affordable housing within Newport Heights, redevelopment of former military housing, and creation of a new harbor shuttle system to alleviate vehicle congestion.

Economic Development Information: Newport County Chamber of Commerce, 45 Valley Rd., Middleton, RI 02842; telephone (401)847-1600. City of Newport Planning, Zoning, Development and Inspection, City Hall, 43 Broadway, 3rd Floor, Newport, RI 02840; telephone (401)846-9600

Commercial Shipping

Logan International Airport is approximately two hours from Newport and provides access to a number of national and international cargo carriers. On an annual basis, Logan moves more than 364,000 metric tons of cargo and mail. The airport is part of Foreign Trade Zone #27, allowing for temporary storage of imported goods that are exempt from full U.S. Customs scrutiny. The Port of Providence, easily accessible from Newport, has been increased to a 40-foot depth in order to accommodate medium and deep-draft vessels. The Port can handle any type of cargo, has approximately 300,000 square feet of warehouse capacity, and offers twenty-five wharves and docks. In addition, Newport offers docking facilities suitable for barge transportation or smaller ships. Excess Navy bases operated by the Rhode Island Economic Development Corporation in Portsmouth, Middletown, and North Kingston can handle bulk and general cargo. Two trucking firms serve the area.

Labor Force and Employment Outlook

Approximately 87 percent of Newport's residents possess a high school diploma or its equivalent; about 41 percent hold a bachelor's degree or higher, making for a well-educated workforce. Statewide, it's anticipated that overall employment will increase by 11.5 percent by the year 2012, with significant gains in construction, professional and technical services, healthcare and social assistance, leisure and recreation businesses, and accommodation and food service industries. It is anticipated that manufacturing jobs will fall by approximately 13.5 percent by 2012, the only employment sector in which there are projected losses.

The following is a summary of data regarding the Providence-Fall River-Warwick, RI-MA metropolitan statistical area labor force, 2004 annual averages.

Size of nonagricultural labor force: 581,300

Number of workers employed in . . .
   natural resources and mining: 300
   construction: 25,600
   manufacturing: 75,700
   trade, transportation, and utilities: 102,700
   information: 11,700
   financial activities: 37,200
   professional and business services: 60,900
   educational and health services: 106,900
   leisure and hospitality: 58,900
   other services: 26,500
   government: 74,900

Average hourly earnings of production workers employed in manufacturing: $13.45 (April 2005)

Unemployment Rate: 4.8% (April 2005)

Largest employers (2004)	*Number of employees*
Naval Underwater Services Center	2,824
Naval Station Newport	950
Newport Hospital	804
James L. Maher Center	700
Salve Regina University	460
Newport Public Schools	380
City of Newport	346
Naval War College	250
WalMart	225

Cost of Living

The following is a summary of data regarding several key cost of living factors in the Newport area.

2004 ACCRA Average House Price: Not reported

2004 ACCRA Cost of Living Index: Not reported

State income tax rate: 3.75 to 9.9%

State sales tax rate: 7%

Local income tax rate: None

Local sales tax rate: None

Property tax rate: $13.72 per $1,000 of assessed value (2004)

Economic Information: Newport County Chamber of Commerce, 45 Valley Rd., Middletown, RI 02842; telephone (401)847-1600

Education and Research

Elementary and Secondary Schools

Newport Public School District bills itself as a "student-centered learning community" that provides an academically rigorous experience for students from kindergarten through grade 12. The district has one of the highest amounts of total spending per pupil in the nation, with a well-developed visual and performing arts program, advanced technology in preparation for careers or college, and a community literacy program utilizing volunteer tutors. Up until 2002, Thompson Middle School was located in a circa-1897 building; a new facility was built from the ground up on the original site, opening in 2002.

Newport Public Schools also operates the Aquidneck Island Adult Learning Center, designed to serve youth and adults with GED and alternative diploma programs. The agency provides job skill development and work transition activities, arranges job shadowing opportunities, and cultivates adult literacy. Assessment for learning disabilities is available as well. The Newport Area Career and Technical Center is another program under the Newport Public Schools umbrella.

The following is a summary of data regarding the Newport Public School District as of the 2004-2005 school year.

Total enrollment: 2,826

Number of facilities
 elementary schools: 6
 junior high/middle schools: 1
 senior high schools: 1
 other: 2

Student/teacher ratio: 13:1 (statewide)

Teacher salaries:
 minimum: $32,769
 maximum: $58,443

Funding per pupil: $12,500 (2004)

Several charter and private schools are open for enrollment in the Newport County area, including the Meadowbrook Waldorf School in West Kingston, Rhode Island, and St. George's School, a college preparatory institution in Newport. The List Academy of Music and Arts is a nonprofit visual and performing arts institution offering enrichment classes to students of all ages and abilities.

Public Schools Information: Newport Public Schools, 437 Broadway, Newport, RI 02840; telephone (401)847-2100

Colleges and Universities

Newport is home to one private Catholic coeducational four-year university of arts and sciences, Salve Regina University, which offers baccalaureate degrees in 44 areas of concentration. Thirteen masters programs are available, and a PhD can be earned in Humanities. Enrollment in the 2004-2005 academic year stood at 2,479 students representing 34 states and 14 countries. Salve Regina has well-respected nursing and elementary, secondary, and special education programs.

The Naval War College (NWC) operates a military leadership institution in Newport, with a core curriculum that addresses national security decision making, strategy and policy, and joint military operations. NWC works on a trimester system; its student body of mid- and upper-level officers can earn baccalaureate degrees in any of five colleges, while a masters of arts degree is available in National Security and Strategic Studies. The NWC is part of the Naval Education and Training Center, as is the Naval Justice School that trains judge advocate generals and other military legal experts.

Civilians can also gain hands-on experience with boats at the International Yacht Restoration School in Newport, where students learn the history of yachts while honing their skills

in restoration and boat-building. The school coordinates an annual Summer Gala in celebration of the yacht. Newport is also home to a branch of the Community College of Rhode Island, the main campus of which is located in Warwick. Students of CCRI-Newport can pursue a variety of associate degrees, certifications, or transfer credits for four-year institutions of higher education.

Libraries and Research Centers

The Newport Public Library has served the community for more than 130 years; the library operates a bookmobile service, offers a number of programs tailored to youth and teen readers, and maintains a collection of more than 124,000 volumes supplemented by upwards of 4,000 audiovisual materials. In 2005 the library received a grant of $27,500 to strengthen technological resources available to patrons. Through a reciprocal borrowing agreement, patrons have access to library materials in communities throughout the state.

Special libraries in Newport include those coordinated by various departments of the U.S. Navy on such topics as military science and antisubmarine warfare. Libraries are maintained by Salve Regina University, Newport Hospital, Newport Historical Society, the U.S. Naval War College, and the International Tennis Hall of Fame. Of unique interest is the Redwood Library and Athenuaeum, founded in 1747 and said to be the oldest continuously circulating library in the United States. The library contains a valuable collection of rare books, paintings, furnishings, and historical items. The building itself is reminiscent of a Grecian temple; services have been relocated in 2005 while the structure undergoes restoration.

The library and museum materials housed within the Newport Historical Society can jumpstart genealogical and local history research with access to more than 200,000 photographs, 12,000 volumes and 10,000 collectible objects. The U.S. Naval War College conducts war games research, hosts strategic think tank sessions and houses a Naval Underwater Systems research center, all of which contribute to the future direction of the Navy.

Public Library Information: Newport Public Library, 300 Spring St., Newport, RI 02840; telephone (401)847-8720

Health Care

Most health care needs in Newport are attended to at Newport Hospital, a general hospital containing 217 beds. The facility features the Drexel Birthing Center, a renovated surgical floor (Turner 2), emergency services, cardiac rehabilitation, and cancer care. The hospital conducts outreach to the community via the Newport Alliance, a workplace-based substance abuse and immunization program. The Naval Ambulatory Care Center (NACC) offers a range of service to Navy personnel, including emergency and acute care, dental health, immunizations, occupational therapy and an aviation medicine clinic. NACC provides inpatient services through an External Resources Sharing Agreement with Newport Hospital.

A number of walk-in and acute care clinics also operate in Newport, along with a plethora of private practitioners of medical specialties. Alternative healthcare seekers can find massage therapists, acupuncturists, and other holistic service providers in and around the city.

Health Care Information: Newport Hospital, 11 Friendship St., Newport, RI, 02840; telephone (401)846-6400

Recreation

Sightseeing

Newport is best known for its splendid mansions, located mainly along Bellevue Avenue, Ocean Drive, and Harrison Avenue; the area is known as Historic Hill, a living museum of history and architecture. Kingscote, one of the more modest structures, was built in 1839 in the Gothic Revival style. It features a mahogany and cherry dining room illuminated by natural light shining through a wall of Tiffany glass. The most opulent structure is Breakers, built in 1895 for Cornelius Vanderbilt in the style of a sixteenth-century Italian palace. The firm of Frederick Law Olmsted designed the landscape. Perhaps the most extravagant of the mansions is Marble House, commissioned by William Vanderbilt for his wife. The house cost $2 million to build and $9 million to furnish; it was awarded to Mrs. Vanderbilt in a divorce settlement. Other mansions include the Astors' Beechwood, where the Gilded Age is recreated through live theatrical performances, and Belcourt Castle, a French castle built in 1894 for Oliver Hazard Perry Belmont and his wife, the former Mrs. William Vanderbilt.

Cliff Walk, a three-mile path winding along the coast, offers views of the mansions and of Rhode Island Sound. In 2000, Rough Point on Bellevue Avenue, the summer home of the late heiress Doris Duke, was opened to the public and allows viewers to see one of the finest private art collections in the area. Newport boasts more pre-1830 buildings still standing than any city in the country. Many are open to the public, such as Colony House—built of English bricks, the structure was a rarity in 1739 and was the scene of a reading of the Declaration of Independence and a Newport visit by

George Washington. Touro Synagogue, the oldest Jewish house of worship in the country, was built in 1763. Hunter House, considered one of the most beautiful eighteenth-century mansions in the country, displays porcelain, silver, paintings, and furniture.

A quiet history of Newport can be traced at the Common Burying Ground and Island Cemetery, affectionately known as "God's Little Acre." Headstones dating back to the 1600s reveal the ebb and flow of life in the colonies, with some particularly poignant remembrances for African American slaves. Some of the gravestones were hand-carved with great artistry by slave Zingo Stevens, and there are Europeans laid to rest among the African Americans who contributed to the creation of Newport.

In cooler weather, Newport and its fauna can be experienced from the sea, on the weekly Seal Safaris and Newport Harbor Seal Watches. However, anytime of year is a good time to view Newport from the ocean; motorized and sailboat charter tours are offered throughout the year or can be arranged.

Both President Eisenhower and President Kennedy maintained a Summer White House in Newport; the Eisenhower House, used by the president from 1958 to 1960, is located within the bounds of Fort Adams State Park. Fort Adams itself deserves a visit; the fortification was created between the Revolutionary War and the War of 1812, undergoing frequent revisions as theories of coastal defense revised over time. The Museum of Yachting features a small crafts collection, the America's Cup Gallery, and a Single-Handed Hall of Fame. Science and technology are the focus of the Thames Science Center, while the art and science of tennis are celebrated at the International Tennis Hall of Fame and Museum at the Newport Casino. For a real taste of the local flavor, a visit to the Newport Vineyard provides samples of homegrown wines aged in French oak barrels. The vineyard is about 10 minutes outside of Newport along Route 138.

Sightseeing Information: The Newport Convention and Visitors Bureau, 23 America's Cup Avenue, Newport, RI 02840-3050; telephone (401)849-8048; toll-free (800)976-5122. Newport Historical Society, 82 Touro St., Newport, RI 02840; telephone (401)846-0813; fax (401)846-1853

Arts and Culture

The Fireside Theatre in Newport stages a minimum of five plays during its year-round performance season, mounting productions that range from comedies to drama. The Beechwood Theatre Company puts on historical vignettes that transport visitors to the Astors' Beechwood Mansion back to its heyday. Dinner and a theatrical production can be experienced year-round at the Newport Playhouse and Cabaret, a family-owned dinner theater that has been entertain-

Newport's Trinity Church, built from 1724 to 1726, houses an organ that was tested by G.F. Handel before it left England in 1733.

ing the city for more than 20 years. Musical entertainment ranging from rock and roll to disco, jazz, and Broadway tunes is offered at local bars, nightclubs, and restaurants. For aspiring young actors, the Newport Children's Theatre coordinates activities, games and performances to build confidence and skills.

The Swanhurst Chorus has been entertaining Newport since 1928; the ensemble performs several major pieces each season, including a sing-along to Handel's *Messiah.* The Newport Baroque Orchestra specializes in seventeenth and eighteenth century music using period instruments; the orchestra also sponsors the Newport Children's Choir and the Newport Youth Symphony Orchestra. The Island Moving Company puts on contemporary ballet performances in Newport while also providing outreach to local schools and corporations.

The works of famous Newport cabinetmakers are displayed at Samuel Whitehorne House and at the headquarters of the Newport Historical Society, which also features permanent and changing exhibits on various aspects of Newport's past. The society's marine museum, also at this location, depicts the history of the Merchant Marine. The history of American and foreign militia and of naval warfare can be studied at the Military Museum and at the Naval War College Museum. The Museum of Newport History, in the renovated Brick Market, highlights the city's past in interactive displays and local artifacts. Newport is also the home of the International Tennis Hall of Fame Museum, housed in the Newport Casino, once a fashionable resort. The Rhode Island Fishermen and Whale Museum allows firsthand experiences with whale bones and with skippering a ship.

The Newport Art Museum is located in the former Griswold Mansion, itself a major example of late Victorian domestic architecture; the museum displays permanent and changing exhibits of nineteenth and twentieth century American art. Sculptural works are displayed on the museum grounds, and the Museum additionally hosts an art school within the Coleman Center for Creative Studies. A powerful piece of sculpture depicting the ''triangular'' slave trade in Newport is housed in the lobby of the Newport Public Library. Island Arts coordinates a large exhibition space for local artists and also offers a Creative Arts Camp for children between 6 and 12 years of age. After-school arts programs are available for teens. Project One is a public arts initiative, and the Four Corners Arts Center oversees a variety of arts programs for the Aquidneck Island region. Artists also run the Deblois Gallery space for professionals as well as beginning exhibitors.

Just north of Newport, in Middletown, are the Norman Bird Sanctuary and Museum and Whitehall Museum. The Norman Bird Sanctuary consists of 300 acres of preserved open space

with 7 miles of trails that take hikers through a variety of habitats. Hooded warblers, black-crowned night herons, Caspian terns, and salt marsh sharp-tailed sparrows can all be viewed within the grounds of the sanctuary. The Whitehall museum, used at various times as a farm house, a tavern, and as a residence for British officers during the American Revolution, is of architectural and historic interest.

Festivals and Holidays

The Newport year kicks off with Opening Night, the city's New Years Eve Arts Celebration, which can be followed up with the New Year's Day Polar Bear Plunge. February brings 10 days of food and festivity with the Newport Winter Festival. March celebrations include Newport Irish Heritage Month. The St. Patrick's Day Parade is bolstered by a Kinsale Ireland Festival of Fine Food, quite fitting as Newport is a sister city of Kinsale.

April's festivities include the Newport Metaphysical Faire, while the month of May offers the Newport Fun Cup Windsurfing Regatta and the Newport Spring Boat Show, featuring hundreds of used and new boats. Food and film festivals abound in June, which first dishes up the Great Chowder Cook-Off and the Newport Film Festival.

Summer offers the Newport Fourth of July Celebration and Public Clambake. Later in the month, the Black Ships Festival commemorates the signing of a treaty between Japan and the U.S. that ended 200 years of isolationism. Asian cuisine, arts, dance, and music are coordinated by the Japan-America Society and Newport's Japanese sister city, Shimoda. Fine summer weather greets the Newport Kite Festival, with the sky full of demos and instruction; then the air is filled with music as the city hosts the Newport Music Festival in mid-July. The Dunkin' Donuts Folk Festival-Newport happens in late July or early August, and the JVC Newport Jazz Festival takes off in mid-August.

In September, the Taste of Rhode Island allows attendees to sample the best flavors of the Ocean State on the waterfront, accompanied by music and children's programs. October is a time of ethnic celebrations such as Festa Italiana, with food and music reflecting Newport County's Italian heritage, and Oktoberfest's Bavarian music, German food, and biergarten. October's Haunted Newport presents 10 days of Halloween activities like ghost tours, pirate tales, a horror film festival, and the Sea Witch Ball. In November, local restaurants show off their chops at Taste of Newport. Later in the month, Christmas in Newport features concerts and candlelight tours in local mansions, a Festival of Trees, a Holly Ball, and visits by St. Nicholas. The festival extends from late November through December. The Newport year winds up with FirstNight Newport, a family-friendly celebration of the new year.

Sports for the Spectator

Special sporting events take place throughout the summer in the Newport area. Professional tennis at the Newport Casino includes the Campbell's Hall of Fame Tennis Championship tournament in July, where 32 of the top male players in the game will compete for the Van Alen Cup. From June through August every year, the Newport International Polo Series takes place, with competition between teams from France, Scotland, India, Egypt, Jamaica, Barbados, and many more. Games are held at Glen Farm in nearby Portsmouth.

From 1851 to 1983 the America's Cup yacht races were held in the waters around Newport; today the city is the scene of many boating competitions, including a Mini America's Cup Race, scheduled throughout the summer. In mid-June, the New York Yacht Club's Annual Regatta is held, as it has been for the past 150 years. More than 100 yachts compete in a variety of races testing skill and speed. The Rolex Swan America Regatta is held toward the end of July and features more than 50 Swan yachts.

In 2001, the Newport Gulls brought New England Collegiate League baseball to the city. The nonprofit team competes in Cardines Field, a historic stadium that has been home to amateur baseball since the early 1900s. Satchell Paige at one point sat in a rocking chair near one of the dugouts while he waited to pitch. From February through December, the Spanish Basque sport of jai alai, a competition similar to handball, and parimutuel betting are offered at Newport Jai Alai.

Sports for the Participant

Newport's most popular outdoor sport is sailing, and boat rentals can be arranged locally. Excellent sea kayaking opportunities abound in Newport Harbor, and other water-related activities can be had at Easton Beach, which is maintained by the city of Newport. A boardwalk lines the beach, where boogie boards, surfboards, beach chairs, umbrellas, and bathhouses are all available for rent. From April to November, anglers may take advantage of some of the best saltwater fishing in the Northeast in Narragansett Bay, the Sakonnet River, and along the Atlantic coastline; many local ponds offer freshwater fishing; spear fishing and scuba diving are also available. When the water freezes, the Born Family Outdoor Skating Center at the Newport Yachting Center offers up family fun.

The International Tennis Hall of Fame offers grass and court tennis open to the public, along with professional instruction. There are several golf courses in the area and, in 2006, the United States Women's Open Golf Championship will be held at the Newport Country Club. Newport National Golf Club has been named the top course in Rhode Island in 2004 according to *Golf Digest,* offering 18 holes and greens that were designed to play fast. The Recreation Department oversees nine soccer, baseball and softball fields, two outdoor basketball courts, and five tennis courts.

Several state parks are within an easy drive from or just outside of Newport, including Fort Adams State Park and Brenton Point State Park. Hiking trails, fishing holes, and overlooks where visitors can view the Atlantic are highly recommended.

Shopping and Dining

Downtown Newport offers the Brick Market, originally a market and granary and now a center for specialty, gift, and antique shops. Thames, Spring, and Franklin streets also offer antiques; there are more than three dozen antique shops in Newport County. Cadeaux du Monde specializes in handmade folk art from the Caribbean, Latin America, Asia, and Africa. The Long Wharf Mall features jewelry, gift items, men's apparel, and leather goods. Galleries and shopkeepers at Bannister's Wharf offer a variety of upscale gift items, along with a real Newport dining experience in the Clarke Cooke House Restaurant's eighteenth century dining rooms. Another historic waterfront shopping site is located at Bowen's Wharf, with top-shelf clothing, jewelry and art shops. In reflection of its immigrant history, Newport hosts several Irish import stores. Aquidneck Island's only enclosed mall houses 25 stores, and there are two large malls in nearby Warwick.

From June to October, Newport puts on two farmers' markets with fresh produce, breads, cheeses and other goods sold in an open-air setting. The Aquidneck Growers Market II is held Wednesdays on Memorial Boulevard, while the Newport Farmers Market takes place on Thursdays and Saturdays on Marcus Wheatland Blvd.

As might be expected, seafood figures largely on restaurant plates in Newport. Lobster and quahog (hardshell clams) are local favorites; the quahog is the state symbol. A traditional Rhode Island clambake, featuring layers of clams, mussels, potatoes, onions, corn, sausage, fish, and lobster cooked over hot stones and seaweed, can be arranged. Catering to the tastes of the many immigrants who created the town, Newport serves up an array of restaurants offering Irish, French, Japanese, Italian, Lebanese, and Chinese cuisines. Ambience ranges from chain fast-food spots to delis to bistros; some restaurants are located in historic buildings and many are located harborside. The Newport Dinner Train offers a three-hour dinner excursion as the luxury train meanders along the Narragansett Bay coast. Specialty coffees can be found at a variety of locales throughout Newport, and dessert really ought to be had at the Newport Creamery, which has been scooping up ice cream in Rhode Island since 1928.

Visitor Information: Newport County Convention & Visitors Bureau, 23 America's Cup Avenue, Newport, RI 02840; telephone (401)849-8048; toll-free (800) 976-5122. Rhode Island Tourism Division, 1 West Exchange St., Providence, RI 02903; telephone (401)222-2601; toll-free (800)556-2484

Convention Facilities

Conference facilities in Newport offer a combined total of 80,000 square feet of exhibition space. A principal meeting facility in Newport is the Newport Marriott, overlooking the harbor. It features 11 function rooms, a 7,800-square foot ballroom, and can accommodate more than 1,100 people in its 12,000 square feet of space. The Hotel Viking, located downtown, recently underwent an extensive renovation that updated facilities while retaining the historic character of the building. The Viking contains more than 13,400 square feet of flexible meeting space that includes the 5,880-square foot Viking Ballroom and the 4,032-square foot Bellevue Ballroom. Five elegant, permanent executive boardrooms are fitted with wireless internet access. The Hyatt Regency Newport on Goat Island in Newport Harbor offers 27,000 square feet of meeting space and 3,000 square feet of exhibit space within its 16 meeting rooms, an amphitheater, boardrooms, and a grand ballroom that can accommodate up to 1,000 attendees. Newport's many hotels, motels, and guest houses contain more than 1,500 rooms; in addition, there are many small guest houses.

The Newport Regatta Club is a dramatic setting for banquets and corporate retreats, with a Grand Ballroom that can accommodate 250 people, with room for an additional 150 guests on the waterfront patio area off the ballroom. Located about 10 minutes outside of the city, the Newport Vineyard has tent and outdoor spaces available for special events, with convenient access to the 1,000 square foot tasting room located in the winery.

Convention Information: Newport County Convention and Visitors Bureau, 23 America's Cup Avenue, Newport, RI 02480; telephone (401)849-8048; toll-free (800)-976-5122

Transportation

Approaching the City

Theodore Francis Green Airport in Warwick is located approximately 40 minutes from Newport and is served by a number of major airlines such as American and Continental,

in addition to several charters. Newport State Airport in Middletown provides private and charter service with feeder flights to Warwick, Boston, and New York. Boston's Logan International Airport is approximately two hours from Newport and provides access to all points across the country and the globe. In 2003, the airport saw 22,778,495 passengers move through its portals.

Highway access from the west is via Interstate 195 to state highways 138 and 114. Access from Boston in the north is via Route 128 to Route 24 South to the Sakonnet River Bridge via routes 138 or 114 into the city. Bonanza Bus Lines was started in Newport 50 years ago and connects the Aquidneck Island area to a number of major New England cities. Rhode Island Public Transit Authority links Newport back to the continental U.S., and Amtrak provides passenger service.

Traveling in the City

The streets in Newport have conformed to the shape of the island on which it's located, giving the grid a slightly northeast orientation. Farewell Street and Bellevue Avenue intersect in the city center, providing a reference point for further navigation; Memorial Boulevard West provides another major artery as it crosses the Easton Bay. Traffic congestion is an ongoing problem in Newport, and a number of studies and rerouting projects are underway to address that issue.

Walking and bicycling tours of Newport are a popular way to see the city. The Chamber of Commerce offers taped walking and auto tours and maps outlining self-guided tours. Bicycles can be rented locally. Narrated harbor tours are also available. The Block Island ferry departs from Newport to Block Island daily in the summer. The City of Newport has received grants totaling 1.58 million dollars for implementation of a harbor shuttle system that will decrease street congestion. Landing areas are anticipated to include Perotti Park, Goat Island, Fort Adams, and the International Yacht Restoration School; the project is hoped to be complete by summer of 2006.

Communications

Newspapers and Magazines

The Newport Daily News is published Monday through Friday evenings and Saturday morning. *The Newport Mercury,* a community newspaper, is published weekly and provides subscribers with a summary of local events, news and sports, as does *Newport This Week.* The monthly *Newport Traveler* serves residents and tourists in southern

New England. Magazines published in Newport include *Cruising World, Sailing World Magazine,* and *The Yacht,* all marketed to the resident and visiting watercraft afficianados. *The Newport Navalog* is a weekly newspaper serving the local Navy community.

Television and Radio

Radio and television programming on Aquidneck Island is largely provided by way of Providence, Rhode Island and larger municipalities in Massachusetts. Television viewers in Newport are served by three major networks, a public television station, and a cable franchise. The Newport Musical Arts Association operates a low-power FM radio station that broadcasts a diverse mix of music and programming, including jazz, blues, ska and funk. Another local FM station focuses on swing music, while its AM affiliate provides news and talk radio to Newport residents.

Media Information: The Newport Daily News, 101 Malbone Rd., PO Box 420, Newport, RI 02840; telephone (401)849-3300

Newport Online

City of Newport. Available www.cityofnewport.com

Newport County Chamber of Commerce. Available www .newportchamber.com

Newport County Convention &Visitors Bureau. Available www.gonewport.com

Newport Public Library. Available www.newportlibraryri .org

Newport Public Schools. Available http://newportrischools .org

Rhode Island Convention Center. Available www .riconvention.com

Rhode Island Economic Development. Available www .riedc.com

Rhode Island Tourism Division. Available www.visit rhodeisland.com

Selected Bibliography

Amory, Thomas C., *Siege of Newport* (Cambridge, Mass: J. Wilson and Son, 1888)

Cahoone, Sara S., *Sketches of Newport and its Vicinity: With Notices Respecting the History, Settlement and Geography of Rhode Island* (New York: J. S. Taylor, 1842)

Dow, Charles H., *Newport: The City by the Sea. Four Epochs in Her History. An Age of Shadowy Tradition* (Newport: J. P. Sanborn, 1880)

O'Connor, Richard, *The Golden Summers: An Antic History of Newport* (New York: Putnam, 1974)

Sirkis, Nancy, *Newport Pleasures and Palaces* (New York: Viking, 1963)

Providence

The City in Brief

Founded: 1636 (incorporated, 1832)

Head Official: Mayor David N. Cicilline (D) (since 2003)

City Population
    1980: 156,804
    1990: 160,281
    2000: 173,618
    2003 estimate: 176,365
    Percent change, 1990–2000: 8.3%
    U.S. rank in 1980: 99th
    U.S. rank in 1990: 110th (State rank: 1st)
    U.S. rank in 2000: 119th (State rank: 1st)

Metropolitan Area Population (PMSA)
    1980: 919,000
    1990: 1,134,350
    2000: 1,188,613

Percent change, 1990–2000: 4.8%
U.S. rank in 1980: 41st (CMSA)
U.S. rank in 1990: 35th (CMSA)
U.S. rank in 2000: 40th (CMSA)

Area: 18.5 square miles (2000)
Elevation: 80 feet above sea level
Average Annual Temperature: 51.1° F
Average Annual Precipitation: 46.45 inches total; 36.0 inches snowfall

Major Economic Sectors: Health care, information, manufacturing, tourism, wholesale and retail trade, services
Unemployment Rate: 4.3% (May 2005)
Per Capita Income: $15,525 (1999)

2002 FBI Crime Index Total: 12,478

Major Colleges and Universities: Brown University; Rhode Island School of Design; Providence College; Johnson and Wales University; Rhode Island College

Daily Newspaper: *The Providence Journal*

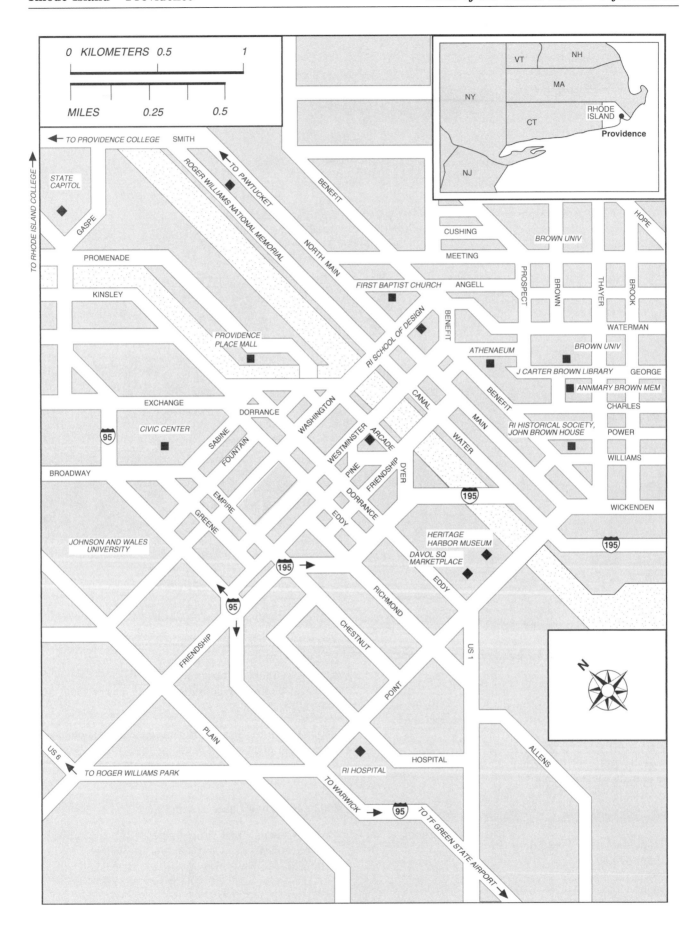

Introduction

Providence is the state capital, the largest city in Rhode Island, and one of the first cities established in America. Once a seafaring and trading town, the city has survived the economic decline that began after World War II to become one of New England's major commercial, financial, and industrial centers as well as one of the largest jewelry manufacturers in the country. A relaxed and cosmopolitan city, Providence in recent years turned two rivers back to their natural courses and created a riverwalk and a downtown park called Waterplace.

Geography and Climate

Providence is located at the head of Narragansett Bay on the Providence River near the Atlantic coast. The city is intersected by two rivers and is built on three hills. Summer weather is seasonably warm and tempered by ocean breezes. Spring and autumn are mild and sunny, and winters are moderately cold.

Area: 18.5 square miles (2000)

Elevation: 80 feet above sea level

Average Temperatures: January, 28.7° F; August 71.9° F; annual average, 51.1° F

Average Annual Precipitation: 46.45 inches total; 36.0 inches snowfall

History

Religious Freedom Establishes Providence

Providence was founded in 1636 by Roger Williams, who had been exiled from Massachusetts for his radical espousal of the doctrine of separation of church and state powers. He called his new settlement Providence Plantations, believing that God had guided him there. At the time Providence was the only settlement in America assuring religious freedom and it became a haven for dissenters. The title to the area was secured from the Narragansett tribe, who knew Williams as a friend fluent in their language.

At first Providence developed as an agricultural community, but when the first wharf was built in 1680, the stage was set for its becoming a major commercial center. By 1700 Providence had begun to take part in the lucrative trade in West Indies and African rum, molasses, and slaves, rivaling Newport in this activity. Many taverns were constructed, and townspeople gathered there to voice their increasingly bitter complaints about restrictive British laws. In 1772 a British ship sent to prevent evasion of navigation acts was destroyed at Providence, and on May 4, 1776, two months before the American colonies proclaimed the Declaration of Independence, the Rhode Island Independence Act was signed there. The city was saved from British attack during the American Revolution of the 1770s by a series of forts built along the Providence River.

Following the Revolutionary War, trade with China, led by John Brown and his brothers, contributed greatly to Providence's prosperity. Huge fortunes were amassed, great mansions were built, and the city flourished socially, culturally, and economically. In 1790 the country's first water-powered cotton-spinning device was built in nearby Pawtucket and, financed by the Brown brothers, Providence became the center of the nation's textile industry. The jewelry industry, for which it is known to this day, began in 1794 when a method was discovered of covering cheap metals with precious metals.

State Capital Welcomes Renewal

By the time of the Civil War in 1861, during which Providence enthusiastically favored the Union, industry had replaced commerce as the city's economic foundation with Providence leading the country in textile and jewelry manufacture. Large numbers of Italian, Swedish, Portuguese, and French-Canadian immigrants arrived to supply labor for shops and mills. Banks, insurance companies, and the coming of the railroad in the latter part of the century supported industrial development. From being one of several Rhode Island capitals since 1663, Providence became the sole capital of the state in 1900.

When World War I broke out in 1914, Providence factories produced war materials, its shipyards built combat and cargo vessels, and the city prospered. These capabilities were again mobilized for World War II in the 1940s. In the 1950s, Hurricanes Carol (1954) and Diane (1955) brought tremendous flooding to the city and state, causing more than $260 million in damage statewide. As many industries moved to the South to defray expenses, the city's population began to decline from its 1950 high of 248,674 people, and the 1960s saw the economy stagnating. An urban renewal project initiated at that time resulted in the restoration of historic areas and the construction of many new buildings. The blizzard of 1978 brought the city to a standstill, and it took over a week for traffic to be allowed back in downtown Providence. By 1980 the population had dipped to 156,804 people.

In the 1990s, the two rivers that run through downtown Providence were uncovered and moved. In place of the pavement that once buried them, now graceful bridges span streams which are flanked by cobblestone sidewalks. In concert with the construction of the Rhode Island Convention Center, the river relocation project has transformed the city's downtown.

In recent years, Providence, during its history a leader in agriculture, shipping, and industry, has benefitted greatly from the high-technology boom that originated in Boston. The city is proud that the beginning of the new century sees it securely ensconced as a national leader in its fourth stage of economic development. Recent national surveys have named Providence the second safest city in America, and among the most livable cities. In 2002, David N. Cicilline was elected mayor, and he has the distinction of being the first openly gay mayor of a state capitol.

In his 2005 State of the City Address, Mayor Cicilline said "... the City of Providence can become the jewel of the Northeast. It can become America's first metropolis on a human scale—a cultural and economic force with a personal face. It can be an incubator for the kinds of ideas and innovations that boost economies into the next dimension, yet still be a city of neighborhoods and of families that go back generations. It can be both a hub of opportunity and haven of livability."

Historical Information: Rhode Island Historical Society, 110 Benevolent St., Providence, RI 02906; telephone (401)331-8575, fax (401)351-0127

Population Profile

Metropolitan Area Residents
1980: 919,000
1990: 1,134,350
2000: 1,188,613
Percent change, 1990–2000: 4.8%
U.S. rank in 1980: 41st
U.S. rank in 1990: 36th (CMSA)
U.S. rank in 2000: 40th

City Residents
1980: 156,804
1990: 160,281
2000: 173,168
2003 estimate: 176,365
Percent change, 1990–2000: 8.3%
U.S. rank in 1980: 99th
U.S. rank in 1990: 110th (State rank: 1st)
U.S. rank in 2000: 119th

Density: 9,401.7 people per square mile (2000)

Racial and ethnic characteristics (2000)
White: 94,666
Black or African American: 25,243
American Indian and Alaska Native: 1,975
Asian: 10,432
Native Hawaiian and Pacific Islander: 270
Hispanic or Latino (may be of any race): 52,146
Other: 30,477

Percent of residents born in state: 42.8% (2000)

Age characteristics (2000)
Population under 5 years old: 12,607
Population 5 to 9 years old: 13,463
Population 10 to 14 years old: 12,290
Population 15 to 19 years old: 17,957
Population 20 to 24 years old: 21,766
Population 25 to 34 years old: 27,165
Population 35 to 44 years old: 22,570
Population 45 to 54 years old: 17,281
Population 55 to 59 years old: 5,741
Population 60 to 64 years old: 4,623
Population 65 to 74 years old: 8,476
Population 75 to 84 years old: 6,856
Population 85 years and older: 2,823
Median age: 28.1 years

Births (2000)
Total number: 8,934

Deaths (2000)
Total number: 3,457 (of which, 28 were infants under the age of 1 year)

Money income (1999)
Per capita income: $15,525
Median household income: $26,867
Total number of households: 62,327

Number of households with income of . . .
less than $10,000: 13,430
$10,000 to $14,999: 6,173
$15,000 to $24,999: 9,749
$25,000 to $34,999: 7,842
$35,000 to $49,999: 8,704
$50,000 to $74,999: 8,143
$75,000 to $99,999: 3,917
$100,000 to $149,999: 2,312
$150,000 to $199,999: 861
$200,000 or more: 1,196

Percent of families below poverty level: 23.9% (52.1% of which were female householder families with related children under 5 years

2002 FBI Crime Index Total: 12,478

Municipal Government

Providence is the county seat of Providence County, the largest in the state. The mayor and fifteen council members are elected to four-year terms.

Head Official: Mayor David N. Cicilline (D) (since 2003; current term expires January 2007)

Total Number of City Employees: 6,500 (2004)

City Information: Providence City Hall, 25 Dorrance Street, Providence, RI 02903-3215; telephone (401)421-7740

Economy

Major Industries and Commercial Activity

Providence is a major industrial, commercial, medical, and financial center for New England with an economy based on manufacturing and service enterprises. The city is a major supplier of jewelry and silverware to the United States and Europe. Providence is home to four multibillion-dollar financial concerns and many smaller ones. Tourism and conventions are emerging industries. As the capital of Rhode Island, Providence supports a number of government-related jobs.

Items and goods produced: jewelry, silverware, and related products; electrical equipment, textiles, transportation equipment, fabricated metals, rubber and plastic goods, supplies for the Department of Defense and federal government, machinery, instruments, primary metals

Incentive Programs—New and Existing Companies

The Rhode Island Economic Development Corporation (RIEDC) serves as a one-stop clearing house for a variety of financing plans and financing agencies to assist enterprises in all phases of economic development. RIEDC is making it easier, faster and more efficient for businesses to access such tools as: financing, permitting and job training assistance; real estate and site location analysis; export and government contract assistance; enterprise zone counseling; information on economic issues and tax incentives; and creative problem-solving.

Local programs—The support services of the Providence Department of Planning and Development include research and feasibility studies; site planning and design review; help in obtaining low-cost financing and other incentives, through federal, state, city and private programs. The Providence Economic Development Corporation administers the Providence Economic Development corporation Revolving Loan Program, with a choice of rates pegged below the prime rate of interest for a period of 10 years. The Providence Neighborhood Business District Program oversees infrastructure improvements; it also offers market research and planning services for new and existing businesses, and grants for related improvements.

State programs—Rhode Island provides a corporate income tax rate reduction for those firms increasing employment. Manufacturers and traded service firms paying above average wages or investing significantly in work training are able to take a ten percent credit on purchased or leased equipment. Businesses may also take a significant credit for expenses for approved job training programs. The Jobs Development Act permanently reduced companies' corporate income tax rate. Companies with 100 employees or more receive a quarter-point reduction for every 50 full-time jobs created. Companies with fewer than 100 employees will receive a quarter-point reduction for every 10 jobs created during a three-year period

Rhode Island offers tax credits for investment, new employment, interest, and donations made in areas designated as Enterprise Zones. Two of those zones are situated in the city of Providence. Many enterprise zone benefits extend to those who develop any of the state's designated historic industrial mill structures or historic preservation areas. Other sectors which have special tax incentives are the financial services, telecommunications, and insurance industries.

Job training programs—Rhode Island has job training tax credits equal to half of a company's training expenditure, and job training grants that can be customized to the company's needs. There are also tax credits for apprenticeship programs and adult education classes. Providence/Cranston Job Training, through netWORKri centers helps disadvantaged workers find jobs, provides job search skills and job training, and has a summer youth employment program.

Development Projects

Capital Center, the downtown area of Providence, is experiencing a residential building boom, with $1.8 billion in projects either under construction or in the planning stages as of 2005. A new $80 million addition to the Westin hotel broke ground in 2005, consisting of a 31-story tower with 200 hotel rooms and 100 luxury condominiums. The Hotel Dolce Villa boutique hotel—formerly a jewelry manufacturing company—opened in 2005 after a $2 million makeover. Currently under construction is GTECH Holding Corporation's new 12-story headquarters in Capital Center, downtown Providence, the first new corporate office building to be constructed there since 1988. Waterplace, also begun in 2005, is a $100 million, two-tower condominium project, and will be one of the tallest buildings in Waterplace

Park. Capitol Cove, a project also in Capital Center, will consist of 255 high-end apartments in two towers. In 2005, Roger Williams University put its Providence branch up for sale for the booming redevelopment market.

Economic Development Information: Rhode Island Economic Development Corporation, One West Exchange Street, Providence, RI 02903; telephone (401)222-2601; fax (401)222-2102. Greater Providence Chamber of Commerce, 30 Exchange Terrace, Providence, RI 02903, telephone: (401)521-5000; fax (401)751-2434, email chamber @provchamber.com. City of Providence Department of Planning and Development, 400 Westminster St., Providence, RI 02903; telephone (401)351-4300; email planning@ids.net

Commercial Shipping

Excellent transportation facilities, including the Port of Providence, New England's second largest deepwater port and a Foreign Trade Zone, make Providence a major industrial center. The principal waterborne commodities handled at the port are petroleum products, cement, scrap metal, lumber, automobiles, and conventional and containerized general cargo. Theodore Francis Green State Airport, with a new 323,000-square-foot, multilevel terminal, has 15 gates and has incorporated a cargo development facility. Direct trucking service is available to every state, Mexico and most of Canada on a multimillion-dollar highway system. Daily rail service to Rhode Island industrial sites is provided by the Providence & Worcester Railroad, which allows access to the entire United States and Canadian rail systems.

Labor Force and Employment Outlook

Rhode Island boasts the highest number of trained workers per square mile in the country. The labor force is described as mature, skilled in diverse areas, educated, efficient, and offering high productivity at reasonable wage levels. The fastest-growing occupational groups are professional and technical workers in new and varied industries; opportunities are expanding in the service and financial sectors, as well as in hospitality. Providence looks forward to continued expansion of technological fields.

The following is a summary of data regarding the Providence metropolitan area labor force, 2004 annual averages.

Size of nonagricultural labor force: 581,300

Number of workers employed in . . .
   natural resources and mining: 300
   construction: 25,600
   manufacturing: 75,700
   trade, transportation and utilities: 102,700
   information: 11,700
   financial activities: 37,200
   professional and business services: 60,900

   educational and health services: 106,900
   leisure and hospitality: 58,900
   other services: 26,500
   government: 74,900

Average hourly earnings of production workers employed in manufacturing: $13.37 (2004)

Unemployment rate: 4.3% (May 2005)

Largest employers (2004)	Number of employees
Rhode Island Hospital	5,853
Brown University	4,450
U.S. Postal Service	4,000
Women & Infants Hospital of Rhode Island	2,640
Miriam Hospital	1,993
Bank of America/Fleet Bank (Providence only)	1,725
Verizon	1,400
Roger Williams Medical Center	1,340
Johnson & Wales Uninversity	1,200
Blue Cross and Blue Shield of Rhode Island	1,198
Providence Journal Co.	1,100

Cost of Living

The following is a summary of data regarding several key cost of living factors in the Providence area.

2004 (3rd Quarter) ACCRA Average House Price: $472,818

2004 (3rd Quarter) ACCRA Cost of Living Index: 127.7 (U.S. average = 100.0)

State income tax rate: 3.75% to 9.9%, applied only to the Federal Adjusted Gross Income, minus deductions

State sales tax rate: 7%

Local income tax rate: None

Local sales tax rate: None

Property tax rate: $29.65 per $1,000 of assessed valuation for residential properties, $37.00 for commercial properties.

Economic Information: Rhode Island Economic Development Corporation, One West Exchange St., Providence, RI 02903; telephone (401)222-2601; fax (401)222-2102

Education and Research

Elementary and Secondary Schools

The overall responsibility for public education in Rhode Island is delegated to the Board of Regents for Elementary and Secondary Education, consisting of nine members appointed by the mayor. School committees govern local schools, meeting uniform standards set by the board. Providence secondary schools are part of the College Board's "Pacesetter" pilot program, which uses the latest consensus by educators on what students should know in mathematics, English, science, Spanish, and world history to develop a curriculum and test for high school students.

The following is a summary of data regarding the Providence public schools as of the 2004–2005 school year.

Total enrollment: 25,742

Number of facilities
   elementary schools: 22
   junior high/middle schools: 6
   senior high schools: 7
   charter: 2

Student/teacher ratio: 26:1

Teacher salaries
   minimum: $33,521
   maximum: $63,185

Funding per pupil: $11,592

Public Schools Information: Providence School Department, 797 Westminster St., Providence, RI 02903; telephone (401)456-9100

Colleges and Universities

Providence is home to seven institutions of higher education and is within 50 miles of dozens more. Brown University, the nation's seventh oldest college and a member of the Ivy League, is noted for its medical school and its engineering, liberal arts, and science programs; it contains more than 40 academic departments. The Rhode Island School of Design, founded in 1877, offers programs in art, architecture, and design, and it shares a cooperative arrangement with Brown University. Providence College offers liberal arts and science programs under the auspices of the religious order of Dominicans. Johnson and Wales University is noted for its culinary arts program. Technical and career education is provided by New England Institute of Technology and Rhode Island College. Roger Williams University's continuing education department provides part-time classes for adult learners. The University of Rhode Island's College of Continuing Education is in Providence, while its main campus is in Kingston.

Libraries and Research Centers

The Providence Public Library, second largest public library in New England, maintains collections on whaling, printing, architecture, Civil War and slavery, ship models, early chil-

dren's books, and Irish and Italian culture. It consists of a main library and 10 branches, with holdings of more than 800,000 items. It is a Patent Depository Library with computer access to the U.S. Patent and Trademark Office, and is also a U.S. and State Documents Depository.

Among the 15 private and public libraries in Providence are those maintained by Brown University, such as the John Carter Brown Library, a center for advanced research in the humanities, and the Annmary Brown Memorial, which exhibits early printed matter. The renovated John Hay Library is the location of most of Brown's rare books, manuscripts, special collections, and archives. The Providence Athenaeum, where Edgar Allan Poe courted the woman who later did not become his wife, is a private library built in 1838 to resemble a Greek temple. The Rhode Island Historical Society maintains a library containing printed and graphic materials relating to state history and genealogy. The Rhode Island School of Design Library is an important resource for art, architecture, and design information in the state.

A major center for research activity is Brown University, where research is being carried out in areas such as medicine, sociology, astronomy, political science, and psychology. Rhode Island College studies evaluation and research, and nature conservancy. Medical research is performed by the Veterans Administration Medical Center Research Service and Roger Williams Cancer Center.

Public Library Information: Providence Public Library, 225 Washington St., Providence, RI 02903; telephone (401)455-8000, Fax (401)455-8080

Health Care

Rhode Island's largest health care system is Lifespan, which serves as an umbrella for several hospitals and related services. Providence hospitals within Lifespan are Rhode Island Hospital, the Miriam Hospital, Hasbro Children's Hospital, and Bradley Hospital. Care New England, the other major network of local hospitals, recently announced its intention to be part of the Lifespan system, pending regulatory approval. Care New England's Providence partners include Women and Infants' Hospital and Butler Hospital.

Rhode Island Hospital is the state's oldest (built in 1863) and largest health care facility. It is the region's trauma center and referral hospital for complex specialty surgical procedures, including open heart surgery, kidney transplants, and non-invasive procedures performed with the gamma knife—one of only 20 in the world. Hasbro Children's Hospital, named in recognition of a major financial gift by the Rhode Island-based toy manufacturer, is an 87-bed child- and family-centered pediatric medical facility. HCH is the region's referral hospital for complex pediatric cases. The Miriam Hospital was founded by the Jewish community in 1926 and is the major teaching affiliate of Brown University. Its research programs include studies in cardiovascular disease, shock and trauma, and behavioral disorders. St. Joseph Health Service, the state's only Roman Catholic hospital, offers a complete range of acute inpatient and outpatient care, specializing in ambusurgery, orthopedic neurosurgery, and maternity services.

Women and Infants' Hospital is the eleventh largest hospital in the country for obstetrics, with over 9,700 births in 2003. It is home to several centers for clinical care and research including the Breast Health Center, the Program in Women's Oncology, and the Division of Reproductive Endocrinology. Butler Hospital is the only psychiatric and substance abuse hospital in the state offering short-term specialty programs for children, adolescents, and adults. In 2004 it was named by *US News & World Report* as one of the top 30 psychiatric hospitals in the country.

Roger Williams Medical Center is noted for its oncology, bone marrow transplant, and clinical pharmacology research programs. The 220-bed acute-care hospital also operates the Roger Williams-Edgehill Substance Abuse Treatment Center, and has taken its services to the community with affiliations into extended care and assisted living facilities. The U.S. Veterans Medical Center is also located in Providence.

Brown University currently has affiliations with six Providence Hospitals: Rhode Island, Miriam, Bradley, New England Medical Center, Womens and Infants', and Butler. There is no Brown University-owned hospital.

Recreation

Sightseeing

The Providence River partially separates the commercial district on the west side from the historic district on the eastern bank. A good place to begin a tour of the historic district is at the State Capitol, which stands on Smith Hill overlooking the downtown area. An impressive structure built of Georgian marble, the capitol is surmounted by what is believed to be the second largest self-supported dome in the world. A statue of the Independent Man atop the dome represents Rhode Islanders' independent spirit. The building contains historic relics, flags, cannons, and a Gilbert Stuart portrait of George Washington. Nearby, the Roger Williams National Memorial contains a Visitor Center featuring exhibits and slides about Williams's life and the history of Providence. Historic buildings in the area include the Old

State House, the First Baptist Church, where Brown University commencement ceremonies are held, and the Joseph Brown House. Benefit Street, laid out in the 1750s, preserves a mile-long stretch of historic houses in a variety of styles, including John Brown House, considered one of the finest eighteenth-century houses in the country and now the headquarters of the Rhode Island Historical Society. The College Green at Brown University is lined with Colonial and Greek Revival buildings. Market House in Market Square was the focal point of colonial Providence where townspeople gathered to buy produce and exchange news and gossip. The Governor Henry Lippitt House Museum, an impeccably preserved Renaissance Revival mansion, is available for tours on Fridays or by appointment.

West of the downtown area, the 430-acre Victorian-style Roger Williams Park contains a chain of 10 lakes; flower gardens; 9 miles of drives; and a zoo with an aviary, tropical greenhouses, and an African Savannah exhibit. The zoo is the third oldest zoo in the country, and works with the American Zoo and Aquarium Association to protect and breed endangered species, including red wolves and Madagascar lemurs. *Juliett 484,* a former Soviet cruise missile submarine, is open for tours at Collier Point Park.

Arts and Culture

Providence has been hosting concerts and dramatic performances since 1761. Continuing this tradition, the Providence Performing Arts Center and the Providence Civic Center offer Broadway shows, classical, rock, and pop music concerts, and dance performances throughout the year. The Rhode Island Philharmonic presents concerts throughout the year at Veteran Memorial Auditorium. The nationally acclaimed Trinity Repertory Company, the largest and oldest permanent ensemble in the country and recipient of a Tony award, presents classic and contemporary works at the restored Lederer Theater during a 12-production season. The Providence Performing Arts Center, a former Loews theater built in 1928, hosts touring Broadway productions, music, dance and film programs. Other performing groups include the Festival Ballet, Newgate Theater, the Sandra Gamm-Feinstein Theatre, and the Perishable Theatre, at the AS220 Arts Complex.

The history, architecture, and decorative arts of Rhode Island are interpreted through changing exhibits at the Museum of Rhode Island History, housed in an 1822 Federal mansion. The Museum of Art of the Rhode Island School of Design features a wide-ranging collection of works from ancient to modern times from cultures around the world. The Providence Children's Museum features hands-on exploration exhibits in a former textile factory in the Jewelry District. The Museum of Natural History and Planetarium Rhode Island Black Heritage Society holds periodic displays on local history and sponsors discovery tours of African American roots in the state. A small collection of American furniture, silverware, and paintings is on display at Pendleton House adjacent to the museum. The school also maintains Woods-Gerry Mansion as an example of nineteenth-century residential architecture; exhibit galleries are located on the ground floor. At Brown University, the David Winton Bell Gallery presents permanent and loan exhibits of historical and contemporary art.

Many of the local galleries and museums have banded together to create a monthly event called Gallery Night. A free art trolley loops throughout the city and stops at participating galleries, art shops, and museums for visitors to come and go as they please.

Festivals and Holidays

Gardeners eager for the planting season await the the Rhode Island Spring Flower and Garden Show at the Convention Center in February. Providence begins its festival season with Columbus Day on Federal Hill, celebrating the city's Italian community. June brings the Festival of Historic Houses, including candlelight house and garden tours, and Convergence X, a week-long celebration of the arts. Also in June is Festival del Sancocho, celebrating Latino culture, music and food. On select evenings throughout the spring and summer, the city's Waterfire exhibit features about 100 ''singing bonfires'' mounted along the newly revitalized riverfront in downtown Providence. Burning torches are accompanied by music designed specifically for the display. Volunteers move up and down the river on a small barge rekindling the torches as they burn during the course of an evening's performance. In August the juried Rhode Island International Film Festival is held in various venues in the area.

In late October or early November is the Great International Beer Competition, held at the Rhode Island Convention Center. Special holiday festivities are held throughout the month of December, culminating in First Night Providence on December 31, a city-wide, family-oriented welcome to the New Year featuring music, art, dance, parades, and fireworks.

Sports for the Spectator

The Providence Civic Center is home to the American Hockey League's Providence Bruins, playing in the Atlantic Division. It is also home to the Providence College Friars basketball team. Rhode Islanders enthusiastically follow the University of Rhode Island, Brown University, and Providence College intercollegiate football and basketball teams. Nearby Pawtucket is the home of the Pawtucket Red Sox Triple-A farm team of baseball's American League Boston Red Sox. The dogs run year-round at Lincoln Greyhound Park in nearby Lincoln. The Montfgolfier Day Balloon Regatta is held in November.

Sports for the Participant

An abundance of fresh and salt water make Rhode Island and the Providence area a boating, swimming, fishing, and skin diving paradise. More than 60 percent of the state is woodlands and meadows, and Providence itself maintains 104 parks, offering opportunities for camping, picnicking, horseback riding, hiking, bicycling, tennis, and golf. Facilities for winter sports of all kinds are easily accessible from Providence. The Harvard Health Downtown 5-K run is held in October. The Fleet Skating Center, a rink twice the size of the one in New York's Rockefeller Center in the heart of downtown at Kennedy Plaza, is a 14,000-square-foot year-round outdoor facility which offers both ice-skating and roller-skating, as well as skating lessons.

Shopping and Dining

America's first enclosed shopping mall, the Arcade, built in 1820, is located in downtown Providence. Cited by the Metropolitan Museum of Art as one of the finest commercial buildings in historic American architecture, the three-story Grecian structure offers 40 shops and restaurants. The Providence Place Mall features anchor stores Nordstrom's, Filene's, and Lord & Taylor, and houses a food court, a restaurant complex, a 16-screen movie complex, and a 400-seat IMAX theater.

Providence's Little Italy section is a friendly neighborhood of Italian shops and restaurants. The Davol Square Marketplace, formerly a rubber factory, has been restored and now houses upscale shops and restaurants. The area around the Rhode Island School of Design has grown into a thriving art community. Nearby towns Lincoln, Cranston, and Warwick contain large malls.

Providence's ethnic tradition is reflected in the wide variety of ethnic restaurants in the city, featuring Italian, Greek, Portuguese, and Chinese cuisines, among others. Because of the city's proximity to the Atlantic coast, seafood is a local specialty.

Visitor Information: Providence/Warwick Convention and Visitors Bureau, 1 Exchange Street, Providence, RI 02903; telephone (401)274-1636. Rhode Island Tourism Division, One West Exchange, Providence, RI 02903; telephone (401)222-2601; toll-free (800)556-2484

Convention Facilities

The Rhode Island Convention Center offers a total of 365,000 square feet, with 100,000 square feet of exhibit space, a 20,000-square-foot ballroom, and an additional

17,000 square feet of meeting space. The Center is within walking distance of 1,500 hotel rooms. Five major hotels in the city offer meeting space; a 345-room Westin Hotel offers 17,000 square feet of meeting space, including two ball-rooms, and can accommodate groups up to 800 people. Another interesting facility is the Roger Williams Park Casino, a historic preserved social hall, with the park's bandstand available and a seating capacity of 300.There are dozens of lodging establishments within a short distance of the downtown area. Campus meeting facilities at area colleges are also available.

Convention Information: Providence/Warwick Convention and Visitors Bureau, 1 West Exchange Street, Providence, RI 02903; telephone (401)274-1636; toll-free (800)233-1636. Rhode Island Convention Center Authority, telephone (401)458-6000; fax (800)458-6500

Transportation

Approaching the City

Theodore Francis Green State Airport, 10 miles south of Providence, handles all of Rhode Island's commercial air traffic. The airport, rebuilt in 1996, is serviced by 12 carriers with more than 200 incoming and outgoing flights daily. Boston's Logan Airport is also fairly accessible from Providence for international travel. Providence is served by Amtrak on the Regional line, and the Acela high-speed train service connects Providence to Boston, New York, Philadelphia, and Washington D.C., stopping in cities along the way. The city is also served by the Massachusetts Bay Commuter Rail, which travels to Boston's South Station. Several bus lines provide interstate service. Interstate routes 95, 195, and 295 provide easy access by car.

Traveling in the City

The east side of Providence, although hilly, is compact, and walking tours of historic sites are possible. A series of public improvements, completed in 1994 as part of the Capital Center Project, has facilitated the movement of buses, pedestrians, and automobiles in downtown Providence. The Rhode Island Public Transit Authority provides bus service in the city and across the state. The Providence LINK is comprised of two trackless trolley lines, the Green Line and the Gold Line, and connects major attraction and shopping areas. A special way to see the city is by Venetian gondola trip along the Woonasquatucket and Providence rivers, through La Gondola.

Communications

Newspapers and Magazines

The city's principal daily newspaper is *The Providence Journal,* which is published mornings. *Providence Business News,* a weekly tabloid, covers business, politics, and the arts in southeastern New England. Other publications include *Rhode Island Monthly,* the *Providence Phoenix,* and *College Broadcaster.* The American Mathematical Society publishes several journals in Providence.

Television and Radio

Television viewers in Providence may choose from five network affiliates, one public broadcasting station, and two independent stations. Cable service is also available. Twelve AM and FM radio stations, including a college station, provide formats ranging from big band music to progressive rock, talk, ethnically-oriented, and public radio programming.

Media Information: The Providence Journal, 75 Fountain Street, Providence, RI 02902; telephone (401)277-7000

Providence Online

City of Providence home page. Available www.providenceri.com

Greater Providence Chamber of Commerce. Available www.provchamber.com

Providence *Journal.* Available www.projo.com

Providence Public Library. Available www.provlib.org

Providence Schools. Available www.providenceschools.org

Providence/Warwick Convention and Visitors Bureau. Available www.providencecvb.com

Waterfire. Available www.waterfire.org

Selected Bibliography

Arnold, James N., ed. *Narragansett Historical Register: A Magazine Devoted to the Antiquities, Genealogy and Historical Matter Illustrating the History of the State of RI and Providence Plantations* (Heritage Books, 1994)

Avi, *The Man Who Was Poe: A Novel* (New York: Orchard Books, 1989)

Warwick

The City in Brief

Founded: 1642 (incorporated 1931)

Head Official: Mayor Scott Avedisian (R) (since 2000)

City Population
1980: 87,123
1990: 85,427
2000: 85,808
2004 estimate: 87,683
Percent change, 1990-2000: 0.4%
U.S. rank in 1990: 255th (2nd in state)
U.S. rank in 2000: 328th (2nd in state)

Metropolitan Area Population (Providence-Fall River-Warwick, RI-MA)
1980: 1,072,725
1990: 1,134,352

2000: 1,188,613
Percent change, 1990-2000: 4.8%
U.S. rank in 2000: 39th

Area: 20.53 square miles (2000)
Elevation: 64 feet above sea level
Average Annual Temperature: 48.7° F
Average Annual Precipitation: 19 inches rain; 35.5 inches snowfall

Major Economic Sectors: Education and health services, financial services, wholesale and retail trade, manufacturing
Unemployment Rate: 4.8% (April 2005)
Per Capita Income: $23,410 (1999)

2002 FBI Crime Index Total: 2,931

Major Colleges and Universities: Community College of Rhode Island, New England Institute of Technology

Daily Newspapers: *The Kent County Daily Times*

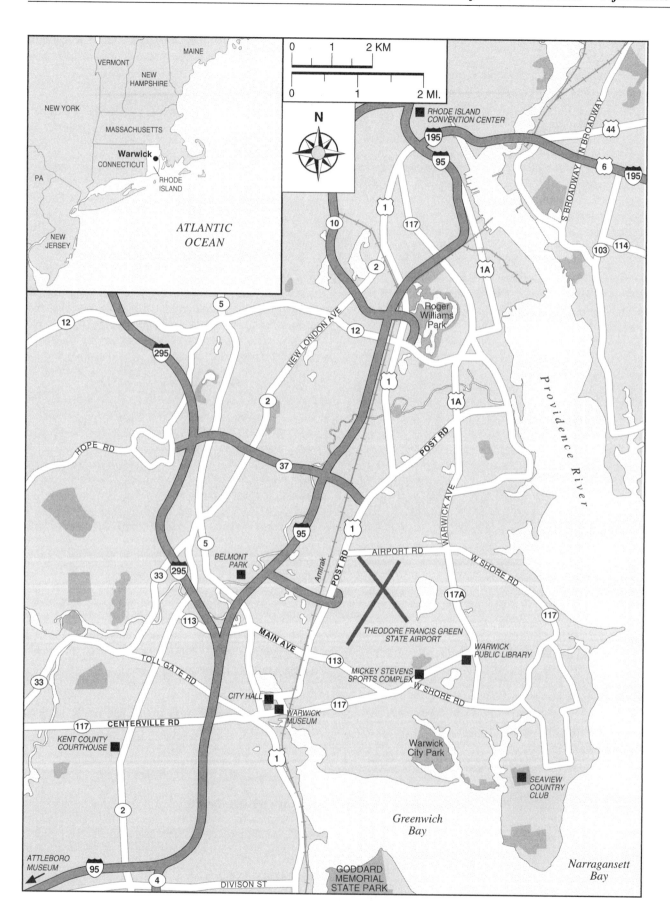

Introduction

Warwick may at first glance seem ''connected at the hip'' to nearby Providence, but the small city has a long, proud history as a colonial outpost, a roost for revolutionary rabble-rousers, and a mecca for manufacturing. Like the rest of Rhode Island, Warwick was founded by independent and free-thinking people seeking a refuge from religious intolerance. What they found in Warwick was a site of transcendental beauty and power, situated on a saltwater bay and fast-flowing rivers. The pioneer qualities that created Warwick have served it well in its evolutionary journey over the decades, as it has transformed from a rough manufacturing town to a sophisticated city attracting financiers and tourists while still appreciating a home-town atmosphere.

Geography and Climate

Warwick is located in central Rhode Island on the northwest end of the Narragansett Bay, a natural harbor to the north of the Rhode Island Sound. Thirty-nine miles of coastline distinguish the city, including the shore along the Providence River that borders the northern and eastern edges of Warwick. Thirty separate villages make up the municipality of Warwick.

The entire state experiences four distinct seasons; the bay moderates the climate, making this area of the state somewhat warmer in the winter and cooler in the summer. The weather is of the kind described by meteorologists as humid continental. Hurricanes occur every 15 years or so, and hail is infrequent.

Area: 20.53 square miles (2000)

Elevation: 64 feet above sea level

Average Temperatures: January, 28.7° F; July, 73.3° F; annual average, 48.7° F

Average Annual Precipitation: 19 inches rain; 35.5 inches snowfall

History

Going Its Own Way

Warwick and the rest of Rhode Island started out as part of the western coast of Africa more than 500 million years ago.

Tectonic forces gradually moved what is now Rhode Island toward the North American continent where it collided and stuck, creating the Appalachian Mountains in the process. A series of ice ages changed the landscape over time through the approach and retreat of glaciers, which scraped a channel into the land that separated an archipelago from the mainland and filled what is now Narragansett Bay. About 3,000 years after the glaciers cleared out, humans moved in; evidence indicates that people have been living in the greater Warwick area for somewhere between 10,000 and 12,000 years. These hunter-gatherers transitioned into the native tribes more familiar today, with the Narragansett (members of the Algonquian tribe) Indians being the primary occupants of the Rhode Island area before Europeans settled the area.

The first European known to have visited the Narragansett Bay area was Giovani Verrazzano, who briefly touched down in the region during an expedition in 1524. Dutch explorer Adriaen Block navigated and mapped the Narragansett Bay about 80 years later, and Dutch fur traders followed to capitalize on the abundant resources in the region. Exposure to European-borne diseases began to take a toll on the resident native tribes, and the debilitated Indians started to let go of territories to willing buyers. In 1642, the Narragansett tribe sold the site where Warwick now stands to a group led by Samuel Gorton. Gorton was a man of extreme religious views, and he not only quarreled with authorities in Massachusetts but also with his fellow religious refugees in the newly-formed Rhode Island colony. So, Gorton and his followers found their own corner of Rhode Island, soon to be joined by other independent-minded or persecuted groups.

The state's reputation as a haven for individualists earned it the nickname ''Rogues Island,'' particularly when coupled with Rhode Island's encouragement of privateering during wartime. Warwick also contributed to the notorious ''Triangular Trade'' perpetrated in Newport in which Caribbean molasses was imported to Newport, where it was made into rum that was shipped to Africa to trade for slaves, who were then transported to the Caribbean to be sold for molasses that would make its way back to Newport. Rhode Island remained the leading slave trader of the colonies until a partial ban was placed on importation of slaves in 1774; in 1784, Rhode Island enacted legislation that declared free all children born to slaves in the state, thus gradually emancipating the enforced workers about 55 years before the Civil War.

In the 1760s the Triangular Trade and maritime industries were flourishing along coastal Rhode Island, interesting the British government. A series of laws were enacted to limit the molasses, sugar, and rum trades; Rhode Island entrepreneurs responded by taking to smuggling. British customs officials stepped up enforcement activities, until one particularly aggressive British ship, *The Gaspee,* ran aground in the

Narragansett Bay while chasing smugglers. Warwick locals set fire to the ship as a protest against British interference with the trade of the colonies—this was a seminal event leading up to the American Revolution.

Warwick gave the American War of Independence one of its most noted patriots in Nathanael Greene, who was second in command to General George Washington. With a victory in the War of Independence, the colonies had to figure out how to organize themselves; Rhode Island was the last of the original 13 colonies to ratify the proposed constitution, out of concern for loss of state's rights and because the dominant Quaker culture was opposed to the compromise it required on the issue of slavery. But sign Rhode Island did, independently deciding to ban slavery over the ensuing five years. Ironically, the cotton mill spurred the area's industrial revolution in the late 1700s, using materials gained by the back-breaking forced labor of imported Africans.

In spite of the contradiction, Warwick and other towns on water (which functioned then as the primary source of power) built textile and metalworking mills. The War of 1812 and other conflicts made goods from abroad difficult to obtain, making Rhode Island cloth, lace, jewelry and other items the only available in town. Warwick and similar communities benefited from their position near ports that could move their wares up and down the coast. The expansion of railroad systems later in the 1800s facilitated movement of Rhode Island-produced goods to points west. Jobs in the mills pulled in former agricultural workers seeking a better pay-off for their labor and recent immigrants, particularly the Irish, who were looking for work. The incoming homogenous groups created the villages that comprise modern-day Warwick, as they settled in separate communities that retained the flavor of homes far away.

The mid-1800s were a time of prosperity and industrial progress for Warwick and Rhode Island. The Triangular Trade had been replaced by the China Trade, with locally-produced goods such as textiles and crops being traded in Asia for exotic items. Here at home, the country had begun to fracture, however, and Rhode Island was somewhat torn when it came to picking a side. Warwick and a number of other Rhode Island towns had woven themselves wealth and reputation in textile mills supplied by southern, slave-owning plantations. Concurrently, Rhode Island had preemptively abolished slavery and had a large contingent of Quakers pushing for the state to join the Union. When the war commenced in 1861, Rhode Island sided with the blue and again contributed mightily to the war effort, while also seeing a marked increase in need for cloth and worked metal produced in its factories.

A Modern Warwick Emerges

Warwick industry continued to boom after the Civil War; at the same time, the region became more accessible to more

people with the development of the automobile and continued expansion of passenger train service. Warwick's lovely beaches started to generate a buzz as a tourist destination, no doubt assisted by the proximity of Newport and its yachting set. World War I took a toll on the population of Warwick, but local industry received another boost that lasted until the Great Depression hit in the late 1920s. Mills closed abruptly, and displaced workers found themselves building local schools and roads as part of government aid programs.

World War II stimulated the economy again to some extent, and Warwick was back to moderate levels of industrial production and residential construction. T.F. Green Airport was commandeered by the U.S. Army in a move that, along with Newport's Naval installation, generated a major military presence in the small state that is still felt today. Control of the airfield was returned to the State of Rhode Island in 1946.

The end of the war heralded a significant shift in Warwick—families from the Providence area, attempting to escape the travails of big city life, started to migrate into Warwick, creating a need for expanded infrastructure, housing, and schools. Retail trade gradually began to develop into the fastest growing economic sector; the Midland Mall (now called the Rhode Island Mall) and the Warwick Mall put Warwick on the map and attracted shoppers from across the New England region.

After enduring a series of natural disasters—hurricanes in 1954 and 1955, and a record snowfall in 1978 that shut down the city for several days—Warwick continues to hum along, not to the sound of factories and mills but to the whir of cash registers at the largest malls in the state. Even more than the siren call of good shopping deals, visitors and new residents are drawn to Warwick by the water, the ebb and flow of which reflect the history of this tough, adaptable town.

Historical Information: Warwick Historical Society, 25 Roger Williams Circle, Warwick, RI 02888; telephone (401)467-7447. Rhode Island Historical Society, 121 Hope Street, Providence, RI 02906; telephone (401)273-8107

Population Profile

Metropolitan Area Residents (MSA)
1980: 1,072,725
1990: 1,134,352
2000: 1,188,613
Percent change, 1990-2000: 4.8%
U.S. rank in 2000: 39th

City Residents

1980: 87,123
1990: 85,427
2000: 85,808
2004 estimate: 87,683
Percent change, 1990-2000: 0.4%
U.S. rank in 1990: 255th (2nd in state)
U.S. rank in 2000: 328th (2nd in state)

Density: 2,417.2 people per square mile (2000)

Racial and ethnic characteristics (2000)
 White: 81,695
 Black or African American: 996
 American Indian and Alaskan Native: 213
 Asian: 1,281
 Native Hawaiian and Pacific Islander: 15
 Hispanic or Latino (may be of any race): 1,372
 Other: 506

Percent of residents born in state: 75.8% (2000)

Age characteristics: (2000)
 Population under 5 years old: 4,640
 Population 5 to 9 years old: 5,222
 Population 10 to 14 years old: 5,670
 Population 15 to 19 years old: 4,958
 Population 20 to 24 years old: 4,074
 Population 25 to 34 years old: 10,994
 Population 35 to 44 years old: 14,804
 Population 45 to 54 years old: 12,738
 Population 55 to 59 years old: 4,583
 Population 60 to 64 years old: 3,567
 Population 65 to 74 years old: 7,101
 Population 75 to 84 years old: 5,629
 Population 85 years and over: 1,828
 Median age: 40 years

Births (2000)
 Total number: 917

Deaths (2000)
 Total number: 961 (of which, 6 were infants under the age of 1 year)

Money income (1999)
 Per capita income: $23,410
 Median household income: $46,483
 Total households: 35,517

Number of households with income of . . .
 less than $10,000: 2,441
 $10,000 to $14,999: 2,197
 $15,000 to $24,999: 3,997
 $25,000 to $34,999: 4,332
 $35,000 to $49,999: 6,234
 $50,000 to $74,999: 8,349
 $75,000 to $99,999: 4,326
 $100,000 to $149,999: 2,651
 $150,000 to $199,999: 528
 $200,000 or more: 488

Percent of families below poverty level: 13.7% (15% of which were female householder families with children under 5 years)

2002 FBI Crime Index Total: 2,931

Municipal Government

The city of Warwick functions under the mayor-council form of government, with nine council members elected by and representing the nine city wards. Elections for both the mayor and council members are held every November in even-numbered years, making terms in office two years in duration. The mayor is elected by the general populace of Warwick.

Head Official: Mayor Scott Avedisian (R) (since 2000; current term expires 2006)

Total Number of City Employees: 900 (2005)

City Information: City of Warwick, Warwick City Hall, 3275 Post Road, Warwick, RI 02886; telephone (401)738-2000

Economy

Major Industries and Commercial Activity

Warwick is one of Rhode Island's major manufacturing zones, home to textile factories, metal fabrication centers, and electronic plants. However, Rhode Island's retail trade industry has increasingly centered in Warwick and the city has become more of a bedroom community for Providence workers. As the city moves into the twenty-first century, finance and high-tech industries are gaining a foothold and appear, along with tourism, to be the wave of the future in Warwick.

In 1996, the nonprofit Central Rhode Island Development Corporation (CRIDCO) was formed to counter downsizing in the local defense industry. The Corporation is dedicated not just to the support of existing manufacturers and industries, but also to the identification and attraction of growth-oriented industries. To this end, CRIDCO offers a Manufacturers Roundtable, during which business owners can discuss strategies, brainstorm problems, and develop joint projects. The Food Manufacturers Network brings together local food producers to cut costs by sharing resources and consult with experts in the field. CRIDCO is in the process of creating a Hi-Tec/Bio-Tec Network that will provide support for entrepreneurs and small business owners.

Items and goods produced: Diecast machinery and tools; human resource, finance, and inventory control software technology; jewelry; seafood

Incentive Programs—New and Existing Companies

Both the city of Warwick and the state of Rhode Island are invested in attracting and keeping viable businesses, with a particular emphasis on companies that are doing international business or who are in the high-tech industry.

Local programs—The municipal government offers the Warwick Export Development Program as a support for businesses that are engaging or would like to engage in international trade. Services included are an international trade data network, seminars, consulting reports, and a global link program. The U.S. Small Business Administration has housed local Small Business Development Centers within chambers of commerce across Rhode Island. The Central Rhode Island Chamber of Commerce in Warwick assists businesses in accessing capital, provides professional development workshops, helps with marketing strategies, and coordinates trade shows.

State programs—Rhode Island provides a corporate income tax rate reduction for those firms increasing employment. Manufacturers and trade service firms paying above average wages or investing significantly in work training are able to take a 10 percent credit on purchased or leased equipment. Businesses may also take a significant credit for expenses for approved job training programs. Creativity is rewarded by income tax exemption for writers and artists who sell their works. Research and development activities may also be eligible for tax credits under a variety of programs administered by the Rhode Island Economic Development Corporation. Restoration of historic buildings as businesses or residences may qualify for tax breaks, as may businesses located in certified mill buildings. Other state programs offer benefits to businesses that provide adult education, that create apprenticeship opportunities, or that are engaged in manufacturing, particularly within the areas of defense, medical instruments, or pharmaceuticals.

Job training programs—The Rhode Island Department of Labor & Training provides employers and small businesses with counseling and direct access to federal and state training, labor market information, recruitment and skills enhancement programs, and grants. The state additionally coordinates services to dislocated workers, foreign workers, youth who wish to be employed, and military veterans. The state maintains a

large database of available jobs for those seeking employment. The Workforce Partnership of Greater Rhode Island supports the Department of Labor & Training by assisting businesses and industries in grant writing, goal-setting, job fair coordination, creation of school-to-work linkages, and employee training to address critical skill shortages.

The Tech Collective marshals the resources of high-tech companies and educational institutions across the state of Rhode Island, in an effort to provide workforce development in support of technology businesses. In the Warwick area, the nonprofit agency has partnered with the Central Rhode Island Chamber of Commerce and the Warwick Career and Technical Center to coordinate programs such as the Groundhog Job Shadow Day, technology partnerships that train workers in innovative industries such as biomanufacturing, a Grrl Tech program that encourages young women to enter and remain in the field, and Principal for a Day, in which a business or civic leader has the opportunity to get to know a local school.

Among other services, the Central Rhode Island Development Corporation also offers training assistance for the local workforce.

Development Projects

In 2004 the state of Rhode Island received $856,000 in federal money to create a wireless communication system to increase security of ports in the Narragansett Bay area. The U.S. Department of Homeland Defense supplied the funds, and Lockheed-Martin acted as consultant in the design of the project, which ultimately will employ video cameras, text messaging, and voice communication capabilities linked with motion, biochemical, and underwater sensors. Once complete, the system could serve as a model for other ports across the nation.

T.F. Green State Airport handles the bulk of passenger air travel in Rhode Island and the number of people passing through its gates is expected to double within the next 20 years. As a result, airport authorities have formulated a 20-year master plan that identifies facilities necessary for the airfield to remain in compliance with the Federal Aviation Administration. The master plan lists an expanded terminal with twice the current capacity, a new 500-foot main runway, a new parallel runway, additional terminal road access, and enhanced parking structures. The plan is not without its detractors—a Concerned Airport Neighbors group has been involved in public meetings regarding noise issues, and an environmental impact study is being conducted to determine how the proposed expansions will affect wetlands and traditional tribal grounds in the path of construction.

The Rocky Point Amusement Park gave Warwick thrills since original developer Captain William Winslow began to add attractions in 1847. Over time, the park saw a virtual parade of carnival acts and rides, including rollercoasters, houses of horror, flumes, and a saltwater pool. The park was decimated by a hurricane in 1938 and was rebuilt, only to face closure in the 1990s. Now, the site is being reborn via an ambitious redevelopment project to build a resort that will incorporate some of the amusement park's entertainment aspects. The project will cost an estimated $175 million and will include a holistic healing center, a tribute to Rocky Point Amusement Park, a retail mall, an artist village, "A Taste of Rhode Island" cuisine center, an amphitheater, a hiking trail system, and other features. Planning and discussion have been ongoing since 2003, and construction was expected to be complete in summer of 2007.

Commercial Shipping

T.F. Green Airport in the Warwick/Providence area offers some shipping resources, with airlines such as Continental, American and United onsite. Boston's Logan International Airport is approximately 70 minutes from Warwick and provides access to a number of national and international cargo carriers. On an annual basis, Logan moves more than 364,000 metric tons of cargo and mail. The airport is part of Foreign Trade Zone #27, allowing for temporary storage of imported goods that are exempt from full U.S. Customs scrutiny. For water transport, Warwick is only minutes away from the Port of Providence, which has been increased to a 40-foot depth in order to accommodate medium and deep-draft vessels. The Port can handle any type of cargo, has approximately 300,000 square feet of warehouse capacity, and offers 25 wharves and docks.

Located at the center of the state's superhighway system, Warwick is a hub for ground transportation of goods. Interstates 95 and 295 serve as the primary access to and from the Warwick area. A number of over-the-road freight transporters operate in the Warwick-Providence area. The United Parcel Service maintains a huge presence in Warwick and is one of the area's largest employers. The Providence & Worcester Railroad hauls cargo regionally, with a focus on waste and scrap and the capacity to carry stone, chemicals, and fabricated materials.

Labor Force and Employment Outlook

Warwick's population tends to be educated, a little older on average, and more experienced vocationally as a result. The 2000 U.S. census reported that 85 percent of Warwick residents had earned a high school diploma or its equivalent, while more than a quarter of the citizens went on to earn a bachelor's degree or higher. Statewide, it is anticipated that overall employment will increase by 11.5 percent by the year 2012, with significant gains in construction, professional and technical services, healthcare and social assistance, leisure and recreation businesses, and accommodation

and food service industries. It is anticipated that manufacturing jobs will fall by approximately 13.5 percent by 2012, the only employment sector in which there are projected losses.

The following is a summary of data regarding the Providence-Fall River-Warwick, RI-MA metropolitan statistical area labor force, 2004 annual averages.

Size of nonagricultural labor force: 581,300

Number of workers employed in ...
  natural resources and mining: 300
  construction: 25,600
  manufacturing: 75,700
  trade, transportation and utilities: 102,700
  information: 11,700
  financial activities: 37,200
  professional and business services: 60,900
  educational and health services: 106,900
  leisure and hospitality: 58,900
  other services: 26,500
  government: 74,900

Average hourly earnings of production workers employed in manufacturing: $13.45 (April 2005)

Unemployment rate: 4.8% (April 2005)

Largest employers	*Number of employees (2004)*
Kent Memorial Hospital	2,300
Citizens Bank Warwick Call Center	1,000
United Parcel Service	1,000
Metropolitan Life Insurance	950
City of Warwick	900
Leviton Manufacturing Co., Inc.	840
WalMart	800
Community College of Rhode Island	687
J.C. Penney Co., Inc.	550
Kenney Manufacturing Company	550
Metlife Auto and Home Insurance	500
Autocenter Imports (Inskip)	350

Cost of Living

In a small state like Rhode Island, housing is at a premium and housing costs reflect that scarcity. The local legislature is continually under pressure to reduce the amount of property taxes that are paid in Rhode Island. When combined with salaries that aren't significantly higher than other states across the nation, it would appear that Warwick has a relatively high cost of living.

2004 (3rd Quarter) ACCRA Average House Price: $472,818 (Providence, RI)

2004 (3rd Quarter) ACCRA Cost of Living Index: 127.7 (U.S. average = 100.0) (Providence metro)

State income tax rate: 3.75% to 9.9%

State sales tax rate: 7%

Local income tax rate: None

Local sales tax rate: None

Property tax rate: $14.81 per $1,000 assessed market value

Economic Information: Central Rhode Island Chamber of Commerce, 3288 Post Road, Warwick, RI 02886; telephone (401)732-1100. Rhode Island Economic Development Corporation, One West Exchange Street, Providence, RI; telephone (401)222-2601

Education and Research

Elementary and Secondary Schools

Warwick Public Schools (WPS) expresses in its mission statement its desire to create individualized learning experiences for its diverse students while preparing them for the higher-tech workplace of today. The school district has cultivated relationships with institutions of higher learning in an effort to facilitate the transition from high school to college, and the district has additionally created the Warwick Area Career and Technical Center as a resource for both preparing students in grades 10 through 12 for college coursework as well as providing students with skills that will serve them well immediately in employment. In total, WPS graduated 93 percent of its students in 2003.

Warwick Public Schools also administers an Adult Learning Center that is housed at the Warwick Area Career and Technical Center facility. The center offers GED preparation, English as a Second Language instruction, and vocational training for adult learners.

The following is a summary of data regarding the Warwick public schools as of the 2004–2005 school year.

Total enrollment: 11,993

Number of facilities
  elementary schools: 20
  junior high schools: 3
  high schools: 3
  other: 2

Student teacher ratio: 13:1

Teacher salaries
  minimum: $31,025
  maximum: $55,973

Funding per pupil: $11,132

Five private Catholic schools and three independent private schools operate in the Warwick area, along with one school

for students of all ages with special needs. The J. Arthur Trudeau Center provides respite care, case management, an applied behavior analysis program for children with autism, vocational skills training, community support service, and home-based therapy for clients.

Public Schools Information: Warwick Public Schools, 34 Warwick Lake Avenue, Warwick, RI 02889; telephone (401)734-3000

Colleges and Universities

The main campus of the Community College of Rhode Island (CCRI) is located in Warwick, operating as a public two-year institution of higher education that offers associate's degrees and certifications in nursing, legal studies, computer science, chemistry, dental health, foreign languages and cultures, mathematics, and more. Most credits can be transferred to a four-year university if desired. CCRI enrolls approximately 16,000 students per year and has a faculty of 300. The New England Institute of Technology (NEIT) in Warwick was founded in 1940; during the past 60-some years, technology has progressed at astonishing speed, and NEIT is designed to assist students in keeping up the pace. The private, nonprofit institution offers bachelor's of science and associate's degrees in 29 programs including mechanical engineering, architectural building engineering, programming technology, interior design, digital recording arts, software engineering, video and radio production, and business management technology. NEIT strongly emphasizes practical application of theoretical concepts as its primary teaching strategy.

Nearby Providence, Rhode Island, is home to a number of vocational schools, community colleges, and universities, including Johnson & Wales, a private nonprofit institution with a student body of 16,084 and 58 undergraduate degree programs. Associate's and bachelor's degrees can be obtained in business, technology, education, and hospitality. The culinary arts program at J & W is renowned for turning out chefs such as Emeril Lagasse of Food Network fame. The university also offers graduate programs such as a Masters in the Art of Teaching, a Doctorate in Education, and a Masters in Business Administration. Brown University in Providence enrolls 7,595 students in undergraduate and graduate degree programs as well as its medical school. The Rhode Island School of Design, a private art and design institution, offers undergraduate and graduate degrees in 18 disciplines such as apparel design, ceramics, photography, sculpture, and furniture design. Providence is also home to several schools focusing on the medical professions of radiology, sonography, nuclear medicine, and nursing.

Libraries and Research Centers

The Warwick Public Library contains approximately 200,000 texts, more than 8,000 audio-visual materials, and more than

500 periodic subscriptions. The central library branch is located on Sandy Lane, and three branch libraries are situated in Warwick villages such as Apponaug. The library coordinates story hours and children's activities throughout the year. Located in another of Warwick's many villages, the Pontiac Free Library offers 20,000 books, 500 audio-visual materials and 50 subscriptions to its public. The Free Library has been serving Pontiac and surrounding villages since 1884; programming now includes storytelling for children, summer reading challenges, and a book discussion group. The modern library offers patrons internet access.

The Warwick campus of the Community College of Rhode Island has access to more than 100,000 volumes and 600 periodicals through the interlibrary loan system, which allows students at one campus to borrow materials from other campuses. Specialized collections include Academy Award-winning movies from 1990 to the present.

Brown University in Providence coordinates a library system containing more than six million items. Humanities and social sciences resources are located in the university's John D. Rockefeller Jr. Library, while medical students conduct their literature reviews in the Sciences Library. Special collections, such as rare books and Americana, are housed in the John Hay and John Carter Brown Libraries. The university received $110 million in research dollars during fiscal year 2003, funding projects through NASA, the National Science Foundation and the Departments of Defense and Energy, to name a few. Increased lab space, completed in 2004, has enhanced the university's ability to participate in research in the areas of marine biology, life science, and computational molecular biology. Other specialized libraries are within easy reach of Warwick, with the Health Library at Kent County Hospital, the U.S. Naval War College Library in Newport, and the Rhode Island State Law Library in Providence.

Public Library Information: Warwick Public Library, 600 Sandy Lane, Warwick, RI 02889; telephone (401)739-5440

Health Care

Kent Hospital in Warwick has been serving the Kent County area since 1951 as an acute care nonprofit medical facility. Expansions over the years have brought the number of licensed beds at the hospital to 359 at present, and a major renovation of the emergency department in 2004 has increased the patient care bays to 46. The hospital's Women's Care Center is in the process of remodeling in 2005, with the postpartum rooms being updated with a more homey, welcoming feel. Kent Hospital's hyperbaric medicine chamber is a resource for all of southeastern New England for the treatment of carbon monoxide poisoning. The hospital additionally provides extended coronary care, wound recovery treatment, oncology and chemotherapy services, and diagnostic imaging.

The Visiting Nurse Association of Care New England provides home healthcare options such as preventive, short-term, chronic, and terminal care. Nutritional consultation, occupational and physical therapy, spiritual counseling, and respite services are available along with general nursing attention to patients' medical issues. Warwick is also served by two walk-in medical clinics, a variety of specialists, several veterinary practices, and a range of alternative healthcare providers including acupuncturists, massage therapists, reflexologists, and naturopaths.

The Kent Center in Warwick coordinates outpatient, day treatment and partial hospitalization for the treatment of alcoholism and substance abuse. The program accepts adolescent and adult clients from a variety of referral sources and specializes in treatment of dually diagnosed clients.

Recreation

Sightseeing

Each of Warwick's 30 distinctive villages has something to offer the sightseer—historic Pawtuxet Village is the oldest in New England and was home to the rabble-rousers who burned the British customs ship, *The Gaspee,* at the start of the American Revolutionary War. Pawtuxet also served as a stop on the Underground Railroad for escaped slaves prior to and during the Civil War. Warwick City Park is located in the Buttonwoods district, with more than 120 acres of nature trails, beaches, and bike routes. Buttonwoods beaches hosted parties in the 1800s that made New England clambakes popular. The Oakland Beach neighborhood provides access to more beaches and seashore activities, while the Conimicut Village features Conimicut Point Park and Lighthouse. The lighthouse is still operational and in use, thus not open to the public; however, it remains a picturesque and historical structure in a wild and beautiful setting. Apponaug Village once abutted the western wilderness beyond the original Warwick settlement but now is considered the downtown and houses the Victorian-era Warwick City Hall with its six-story clock tower. The Warwick Museum is located in Apponaug as well, with historical exhibitions and displays arranged in the circa-1912 Kentish Artillery Armory building which was built with two wall openings for its Revolutionary War-era cannons.

The Warwick Neck Lighthouse is the last traditional lighthouse built in Rhode Island. Located at the bottom of Warwick Neck, the 1827 lighthouse is still in use today, and also not open to the public. Regardless, its history, dramatic location, and charming exterior continue to attract visitors. The John Waterman Arnold House is a fine example of architecture in the late 1700s; the clapboard house has two stories containing a beehive oven, wall niches in the winding stairwell, a fireplace, and paneled walls. This structure is now home to the Warwick Historical Society.

The Industrial Revolution started spinning at Slater Mill in nearby Pawtucket. A living history museum acknowledges the contribution Samuel Slater made to the manufacturing industry locally when he constructed the first cotton mill in the state. Demonstrations of nineteenth-century waterpower, arts, crafts, and gardening take place during daily tours from March through October.

The Roger Williams Park Zoo in Providence is the third oldest zoo in the country and now contains a polar bear habitat, a collection of bison, and the Marco Polo Trail. The Trail recreates Marco Polo's three-year exploration through Asia and combines the zoological experience with history and culture.

The State of Rhode Island has developed a Heritage Trail system that provides sightseers with efficient, educational, and fun routes to follow throughout the state. The Warwick Heritage Trail runs from the upper Narragansett Bay into the western hills of Rhode Island, encompassing a number of the historical sites mentioned above. Trail maps can be obtained from Warwick City Hall. Tours by water can be an excellent way to get the big picture of Warwick and can be arranged for small or large groups.

Arts and Culture

The Warwick Museum of Art in the downtown Apponaug Village coordinates showings by Rhode Island painters, sculptors, photographers, and ceramicists in addition to exhibitions by artists from across the nation and the globe. Performance art shows also are held in the museum, including poetry and prose readings and comedy troupe acts. The Museum School provides art workshops and classes for students of all ages throughout the year. Complements Art Gallery in Warwick offers art consultation services, exhibitions, and art sales to private individuals and corporations.

In nearby Providence, the Waterfire exhibit must be seen to be believed. The award-winning "fire sculpture" consists of 100 bonfires suspended just above the surface of the three rivers that run through downtown, illuminating an expanse of urban public spaces and parks. Fire tenders silently maintain the blazes, dressed all in black for increased drama, and the entire experience is a feast for the senses. The Rhode Island School of Design in Providence is home to an eclectic collection of art ranging from antiquarian times to the contemporary. The nearly 80,000 works are international and are in every variety of media, including sculpture, textiles, painting, and photography.

Also in Providence and recently restored to its original 1928 opulence, the Providence Performing Arts Center (PPAC) was originally a Loew's Movie Palace and now is home to touring Broadway shows, theatrical offerings of all sorts, current and classical movies, and concerts. The PPAC contains a rare Mighty Wurlitzer organ to accompany screenings of silent films. The Providence Black Repertory Company stages performances year-round at its theatre center, with professional productions that celebrate the creativity and unique view of black theatre in the U.S. The Trinity Repertory Company in Providence produces annual performances of *A Christmas Carol* and a summer Shakespeare Project, along with seven other shows throughout its season. The Trinity stages its productions in the restored 1917 Majestic Theatre and provides educational outreach programs to local schools.

The Narragansett Bay Chorus makes its home in Providence at the Providence Performing Arts Center, but the group sings throughout Rhode Island and neighboring states. Performances are *a capella* in the barbershop quartet style. Opera Providence is in its sixth season as a professional-level opera company, staging comic and tragic operas such as *Carmen, La Boheme,* and *Porgy and Bess.* Festival Ballet of Providence puts on four performances per season in addition to its annual production of *The Nutcracker.*

Arts and Culture Information: Providence/Warwick Convention and Visitors Bureau, One West Exchange Street, Providence, RI 02903; telephone (401)274-1636; toll free (800)233-1636

Festivals and Holidays

BrightNight Providence is the biggest New Years party in Rhode Island, with more than 160 performers such as jugglers, acrobats, musicians, and magicians. At the end of March or in early April, Shawomet Baptist Church's Easter sunrise services are held at the Warwick Neck Lighthouse. The Warwick area then kicks off summer with frequent clambakes, seafood festivals, and the Gaspee Days Festival, held over the Memorial Day weekend. The colonial history of Pawtuxet and Warwick's other villages is celebrated with costume contests, fireworks, an arts and crafts fair, reenactment of the burning of *The Gaspee,* and a golf scramble. The same weekend, Oakland Beach puts on a festival as well. Pawtuxet hosts a Kayak Regatta in mid-June, with prizes awarded in several categories. The June Festival Del Sanchoco in Providence showcases the Latino community in a party centered around a flavorful stew. Recipe competitions, music, booths, crafts, and entertainment make this a family-friendly event. Warwick's Summer Concert Series is held on Wednesday nights from mid-June through mid-August. Also in mid-August, cinema buffs can cool off in an air-conditioned theater while enjoying the Rhode Island International Film Festival, a six-day juried art show with entries from across the planet in categories such as animated short, documentary, and feature presentations. The festival is accompanied by the Providence Film Festival, which acknowledges local film producers.

Downtown Warwick welcomes fall with the Apponaug Festival, held in the historic village at the center of the city in September, followed by the three-day St. Gregory the Great Parish Festival. Providence welcomes the Halloween season with the Rhode Island International Horror Festival in late October. Short films, documentaries, and scary cinema of all varieties are screened at the Columbus Theatre, with a juried competition among entrants. The Great International Beer Competition and Festival takes place in November; Providence is home to this celebration of the grain, in which more than 50 local, regional, national and international breweries compete for top honors in 10 categories. November is also the month for the Warwick Annual Indoor Powwow, featuring dances, costumes, and foods of the native people who first populated the region. The weekend of Veterans Day features the historical remembrances of the Warwick Heritage Festival.

Sports for the Spectator

Baseball fans may need to commute a short distance to get their fix, but just north of Providence is the home of the Pawtucket Red Sox, a AAA affiliate of the Boston Red Sox baseball franchise. The stars of tomorrow (and sometimes yesterday) play home games at McCoy Stadium. For fans who want to see the baseball stars of today, the 2004 champion Boston Red Sox and storied Fenway Park are a mere 50 miles to the north.

The Providence Bruins compete in minor league hockey in the American Hockey League. An affiliate of the Boston Bruins, the Providence team plays its home games in the Dunkin' Donuts Center. The Boston Bruins play in the National Hockey League and over the years have featured standout players such as Bobby Orr and Ray Borque, who went on to win the Stanley Cup as part of the Colorado Avalanche. Other professional teams in Boston are the Celtics (NBA basketball), the New England Patriots (NFL football and winners of three recent Superbowls), and the New England Revolution (Major League Soccer).

Brown University in Providence competes in the Ivy League of Division I of the National Collegiate Athletic Association, with men's and women's programs in basketball, crew, ice hockey, lacrosse, soccer, fencing, track, and swimming. Boston's universities and colleges also sponsor varsity sports.

Sports for the Participant

Warwick boasts 39 miles of coastline and dozens of marinas, making boating one of the major recreational activities. Anchorage is good in Greenwich Cove and Warwick Cove, where sailors can pilot their own vessels, rent a boat, or take instruction. Rental canoes and kayaks can also be obtained for exciting or leisurely outings on the bay or rivers, depending on the section attempted. Many of the city and state parks are excellent spots for fishing, and anglers can either go after marine varieties like swordfish, bluefin tuna, and striped bass or freshwater fish such as black bass, rainbow trout, and yellow perch. Saltwater swimming, surfing and boogie boarding can be enjoyed at Goddard Memorial State Park, Oakland Beach Park, and City Park Beach. For a more leisurely water experience, take a lazy float down the Providence River on a gondola, leaving from Citizens Plaza in Providence.

The City of Warwick coordinates more than 850 acres of recreational facilities, including bike paths, 56 ball fields, 39 tennis courts, 32 basketball courts, 2 ice rinks, 8 parks, 53 playgrounds, and an Olympic-sized swimming pool. The Mickey Stevens Sports Complex alone houses two bocce courts, two basketball courts, a baseball field, two indoor ice rinks, an indoor pool, six tennis courts, and a jogging track. Local golf courses are located at Goddard State Park (a nine-hole public course), Potowomut Golf Club (an 18-hole private course), the Seaview Country Club (nine holes that are semi-private), and the Warwick Country Club (private course with 18 holes).

Hiking and bird-watching can be had both at Goddard State Park near Warwick and across the Narragansett Bay at the Prudence and Patience Islands Wildlife Management Area in Bristol, Rhode Island.

Shopping and Dining

Warwick has become a retail trade monster, home to two of Rhode Island's largest malls. The Warwick Mall on Bald Hill Road is anchored by four department stores—Macy's, JCPenney, Filene's and Old Navy. An expansive food court and hundreds of national chain shops draw shoppers from throughout the New England region. The somewhat smaller and more discount-oriented Rhode Island Mall next door on Bald Hill Road contains a WalMart and a Kohl's department store. Pontiac Mills adds a historical touch to the shopping experience—an eclectic mix of shops, boutiques, galleries, antique stores, art dealers, and custom furniture purveyors are now resident in the renovated former textile mill that once housed the Fruit of the Loom company. Pawtuxet Village has also cultivated a quaint feel in its shops, coupled with an unbeatable harbor view. Ann & Hope Outlet Plaza is a Warwick original; opened as the first discount self-service store, Ann & Hope has evolved into a collection of deep-discount retail outlets. Other shopping meccas include Bald Hill Commons, Bald Hill Plaza, CompUSA Plaza, Greenwich Village, Marketplace Center, Summit Square, and Warwick Commons.

Seafood is big in Warwick, both literally and figuratively—chowder houses, fish 'n' chips stands, clam shacks, and lobster eateries abound. A local delicacy, the quahog is a large and tasty hard-shell clam that is often featured in Warwick clambakes. As a reflection of Warwick's immigrant past, a wide menu of ethnic cuisines are served, with an emphasis on Chinese fare and Italian dishes. Restaurant ambience ranges from fast-food sites to fine bistros in upscale settings. Several locally-owned coffeehouses round out the offerings, and a visit to Johnson & Wales' fine culinary institute in Providence might yield the opportunity to get a foretaste of great chefs to come.

Convention Facilities

The place for exhibitions and tradeshows is the Rhode Island Convention Center in Providence; four halls offer a combined 100,000 square feet of space in which up to 500 booths can be erected. The space can be modified to accommodate small meetings or massive tradeshows as required, and the facility is equipped to handle all related audio-visual needs. In-house catering is available, and a loading dock and parking garage complete the arrangements for large-scale events.

The historic Aldrich Mansion overlooking Narragansett Bay in Warwick offers an elegant alternative meeting site, with a 230-seat capacity and a European cuisine dining. In nearby Cranston, groups from 50 to 2,500 people can participate in meetings, tradeshows, seminars, or social functions at Rhodes-on-the-Pawtuxtet, a ballroom and gazebo that were once part of a resort-class complex of facilities. The ballroom offers 22,000 square feet of flexible space and fine in-house cuisine is available for events.

Transportation

Approaching the City

T.F. Green State Airport handles more than a million passengers yearly, making it the busiest airfield in Rhode Island. The airport is served by major airlines such as American, Continental, Delta, and United in addition to regional charters. The city of Warwick is in the process of

developing plans to build an Amtrak station near the airport. Amtrak currently passes through Warwick and provides passenger rail service. Boston's Logan International Airport is approximately two hours from Newport and provides access to all points across the country and the globe. In 2003, the airport saw 22,778,495 passengers move through its portals. Travelers coming to Warwick by car primarily access the city via Interstates 95 and 295. Regional bus service is coordinated through the Rhode Island Public Transit Authority, and Greyhound Bus Company caters to the national traveler.

Traveling in the City

Warwick was built on a section of land that projects out into Narragansett Bay, and its street grid reflects this with a slight bent to the northeast. Warwick Neck Avenue and Tidewater Drive are two primary north-south arterials within the city center, and state highway 117, Sandy Lane, and Rocky Point Avenue run east-west. Bus service within Warwick is coordinated by the Rhode Island Public Transit Authority, while the City of Warwick operates the Transwick program, providing rides to residents 55 years of age or older who have a disability or who lack access to other means of transportation. Taxi service is readily available through a menu of providers, and efforts are being made to improve existing bike paths that run along the Washington Secondary rail line from West Warwick, through Warwick, to Cranston. The vision of bike path advocates is to join the Washington Secondary trail with the Blackstone River Bikeway that runs through Providence. The Warwick-East Greenwich Bicycle Network links the north end of Warwick with the southeast village via a system of bike paths.

Communications

Newspapers and Magazines

The daily paper serving Warwick and the greater Kent County area is *The Kent County Daily Times,* which is published Monday through Saturday in West Warwick and provides local, state, national, and international news coverage. Folks in Warwick get their community news from *The Warwick Beacon,* which is published two times every week and concentrates on local news, sports, entertainment, and events. *The Narragansett Times* also reports on local news and is published twice a week.

Television and Radio

Television programming is primarily relayed from the Providence area, which is home to a Fox affiliate (WPRI) and an ABC affiliate (WLNE). An NBC affiliate, WJAR, broadcasts out of Cranston. Other networks and cable channels are available through the cable company that serves the Warwick region.

Warwick is served by one Christian AM radio station, WARV; other AM and FM stations in a broad range of formats are accessible via Providence and Boston.

Media Information: *The Kent County Times,* 1353 Main Street, West Warwick, RI 02893; telephone (401)821-7400

Warwick Online

Central Rhode Island Chamber of Commerce. Available www.centralrichamber.com

City of Warwick. Available www.warwickri.gov

Providence/Warwick Convention & Visitors Bureau. Available www.pwcvb.com

Rhode Island Convention Center. Available www.riconvention.com

Rhode Island Economic Development. Available www.riedc.com

Rhode Island Public Transit Authority. Available www.ripta.com

Rhode Island Tourism Division. Available www.visitrhode island.com

Warwick Public School District. Available www.warwick schools.org

Selected Bibliography

Bamberg, Cherry Fletcher and Jane Fletcher Fiske, eds.; transcribed by Marshall Morgan, *More Early Records of the Town of Warwick, Rhode Island* Boston, MA: New England Historic Genealogical Society (2001)

Fuller, Oliver Payson, *The History Of Warwick, Rhode Island* Providence, RI: Angell, Burlingame and Co. (1875)

Gorton, Samuel, *Simplicity's Defence Against Seven-Headed Policy* Providence, RI: Marshall, Brown and Co. (1835)

Vaughan, Alden T, ed., *New England Encounters: Indians and Euroamericans ca. 1600-1850*, Boston, MA: Northeastern University Press (1999)

VERMONT

The State in Brief

Nickname: Green Mountain State
Motto: Vermont, freedom, and unity

Flower: Red clover
Bird: Hermit thrush

Area: 9,614 square miles (2000; U.S. rank: 45th)
Elevation: Ranges from 95 feet to 4,393 feet
Climate: Long, cold winters; warm summers

Admitted to Union: March 4, 1791
Capital: Montpelier
Head Official: Governor James H. Douglas (R) (until 2007)

Population
    1980: 511,456
    1990: 562,758
    2000: 608,827
    2004 estimate: 621,394
    Percent change, 1990–2000: 8.2%
    U.S. rank in 2004: 49th
    Percent of residents born in state: 54.3% (2000)
    Density: 65.8 people per square mile (2000)
    2002 FBI Crime Index Total: 15,600

Racial and Ethnic Characteristics (2000)
    White: 589,208

Black or African American: 3,063
American Indian and Alaska Native: 2,420
Asian: 5,217
Native Hawaiian and Pacific Islander: 141
Hispanic or Latino (may be of any race): 5,504
Other: 1,443

Age Characteristics (2000)
    Population under 5 years old: 33,989
    Population 5 to 19 years old: 132,268
    Percent of population 65 years and over: 12.4%
    Median age: 37.7 years (2000)

Vital Statistics
    Total number of births (2003): 6,546
    Total number of deaths (2003): 5,068 (infant deaths, 32)
    AIDS cases reported through 2003: 250

Economy
    Major industries: Services, manufacturing, tourism
    Unemployment rate: 3.3% (April 2005)
    Per capita income: $30,534 (2003; U.S. rank: 23rd)
    Median household income: $43,212 (3-year average, 2001-2003)
    Percentage of persons below poverty level: 9.4% (3-year average, 2001-2003)
    Income tax rate: 3.6–9.5%
    Sales tax rate: 6.0%

Burlington

The City in Brief

Chartered: 1763 (incorporated, 1865)

Head Official: Mayor Peter A. Clavelle (NP) (since 1989)

City Population
  1980: 37,712
  1990: 39,127
  2000: 38,889
  2003 estimate: 39,148
  Percent change, 1990–2000: −0.6%
  U.S. rank in 1980: 590th
  U.S. rank in 1990: 675th
  U.S. rank in 2000: Not reported (State rank: 1st)

Metropolitan Area Population
  1980: 115,308
  1990: 151,506

  2000: 169,391
  Percent change, 1990–2000: 11.8%
  U.S. rank in 1980: 224th
  U.S. rank in 1990: 218th
  U.S. rank in 2000: 183rd

Area: 15.48 square miles (2000)
Elevation: 112 feet above sea level
Average Annual Temperature: 44.6° F
Average Annual Precipitation: 34.5 inches of rain; 78.3 inches of snow

Major Economic Sectors: Services, manufacturing
Unemployment Rate: 3.1% (April 2005)
Per Capita Income: $19,011 (1999)

2002 FBI Crime Index Total: 1,871

Major Colleges and Universities: University of Vermont; Champlain College

Daily Newspaper: *The Burlington Free Press*

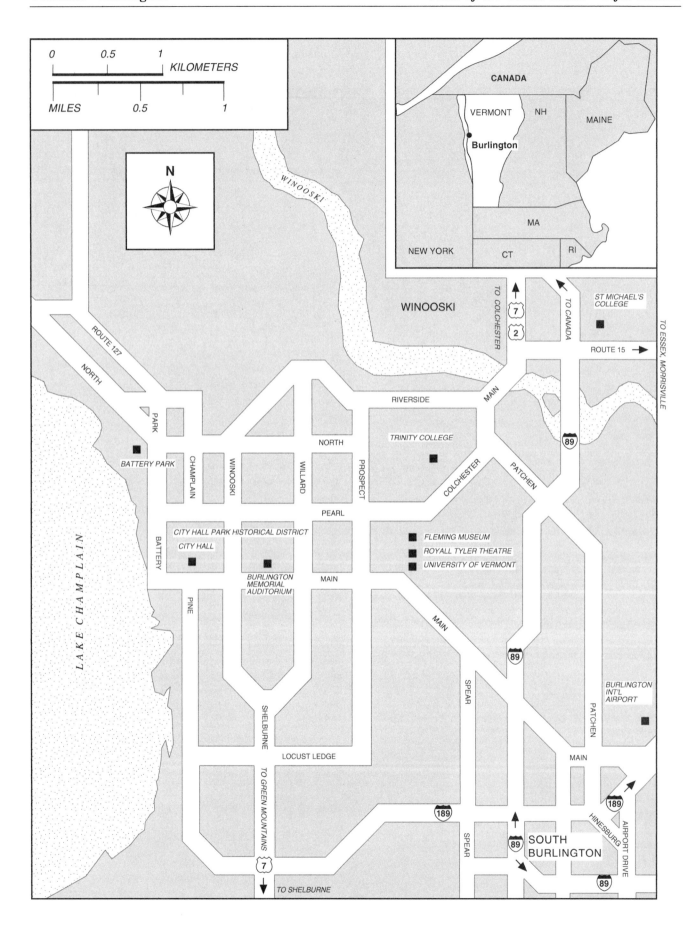

Introduction

Burlington is the largest city in Vermont and is the state's business, industrial, educational, financial, and cultural center. Situated on the eastern shore of beautiful Lake Champlain near the Green Mountains, Burlington is a port city offering spectacular scenery and year-round recreational opportunities. In the Greater Burlington area, the old lives in harmony with the new as farms that have been in the same family for centuries coexist with industries engaged in space-age technology. The region's population is thriving while the high-level labor force leads to the prosperity of the overall business climate. Burlington's successes have frequently been cited: in 1999, by the Arts & Entertainment Network (A&E) that proclaimed it as "No. 1 of Top 10 Cities to Have it All," along with the 2004 presentation of "Outstanding Achievement Award" by the U.S. Conference of Mayors as part of its annual "City Livability Awards."

Geography and Climate

Burlington is built on three terraced slopes on the shores of Lake Champlain in northern Vermont. The lake moderates temperatures, relative to the rest of the state, by creating little variance during the four seasons; summers are cool while winter temperatures remain fixed below the freezing mark.

Area: 15.48 square miles (2000)

Elevation: 112 feet above sea level

Average Temperatures: January, 16.3° F; July, 70.5° F; annual average, 44.6° F

Average Annual Precipitation: 34.5 inches of rain; 78.3 inches of snow

History

Lumber Industry Supports Early Economy

Samuel de Champlain, adventurer and captain in the French Navy, was one of the first Europeans to explore the Burlington area. In the spring of 1609 Champlain was led on an expedition by a young Algonquian chief to the great lake of the Iroquois that now bears the name Lake Champlain. When the Iroquois caught sight of the party, a battle ensued into which the French were reluctantly drawn, inspiring the Iroquois animosity that caused them to align with the British against the French during the hostilities that occupied the territory for nearly 150 years over control of the area. In 1764 England's King George III ruled that the disputed land in Vermont, at various times claimed by kings, governors, and land speculators, belonged to New York. Burlington had been chartered a year earlier but few people lived there. Among them was Ethan Allen who, to prevent Vermont from being annexed by any other state, formed the Green Mountain Boys. This group began to drive New Yorkers off the disputed lands, but their efforts were interrupted by the outbreak of the American Revolution in 1775. The Green Mountain Boys were called upon to assist Connecticut Captain Benedict Arnold in seizing the cannon at nearby Fort Ticonderoga for transport to Boston, where the rebels required artillery for their battle against the British. Despite this assistance, Vermont as a whole remained a fiercely independent territory, and following the signing of the Declaration of Independence in 1776 by the original 13 colonies, Vermont declared itself an independent republic. In 1791, however, Vermont agreed to join the Union, becoming the first new state after the original colonies.

By the early 1800s Burlington, which had been laid out by Ethan Allen's brother Ira, was capitalizing on the abundant lumber in the region, carrying on a lively export business with Canada. The War of 1812 disrupted the city's economic life when President Thomas Jefferson ordered an extension on the trade embargo with the British to include trade with Canada, thus foreclosing the major economic outlet of the Burlington region. Citizens ignored the embargo, smuggling goods across the border. This situation, which might have resulted in Vermonters aligning themselves with Canada against the United States government, was resolved when the British were defeated on Lake Champlain in 1814.

By 1830 lumber supplies in the Burlington area were nearly depleted; the city shifted to importing timber for finishing into boards and wood products for shipment elsewhere. By the mid-nineteenth century, Burlington was the third largest lumber mart in the country, attracting many settlers of French-Canadian descent. In 1850 St. Joseph's in Burlington became the first French-Catholic parish in the United States. At the same time, the arrival of the railroad in Burlington portended the decline of water-borne commerce. The railroads brought products that could be sold for less than the small manufacturers in Burlington needed to stay solvent, and the trains made it easier for citizens to leave the city for the West, thus beginning Burlington's population decline.

Progressive History Greets High-Technology Industry and Future Economic Stability

Vermont's constitution, based on the liberal views of William Penn, founder of Pennsylvania, included a then-unique provision prohibiting slavery. During the Civil War of 1861 to 1865 Vermonters proved their dedication to the anti-slavery cause when the state suffered more casualties per capita than any other northern state. Vermont appropriated the then-enormous sum of $8 million to the war effort. The economic effect of that decision was felt for many long, hard years; many more young people moved West.

Burlington's fortunes took a dramatic turn for the better in 1957 when IBM Corporation chose the city as the site of its new plant for the design and production of computer memory chips. Immediately 4,000 jobs were created, and by 1980 the plant provided over 7,000 jobs. The economic wave continued as new recreational facilities and dozens of light industrial firms were built. The state launched a newspaper campaign urging former Vermonters to return home; many of them did.

As Burlington grew, so did concern over the impact of this growth on the environment. In 1969 Vermont voters passed Act 250, a stringent land-use law to restrict the expansion; billboard and bottle bans followed. Act 250 was invoked by Burlington to block a proposed shopping mall backed by New York State developers.

Burlington entered the 2000s a comparatively small and appealing city with an interest in attracting high-technology, manufacturing, and service industries while preserving control of its future. The city continues to be consistently rated highly for its quality of life: a diverse cultural scene, annual festivals, scenic views, historic neighborhoods, and recreational opportunities. These factors have helped to maintain the city's population between 1980 and 2000 as well as fuel the dramatic growth of the region during that same time (47 percent). In turn, residents and business leaders enjoy the positive effects that economic growth and a positive business climate bring.

Historical Information: Vermont Historical Society, 60 Washington St., Barre, VT 05641-4209; telephone (802)479-8500; fax (802)479-8510; email vhs@vhs.state.vt.us

Population Profile

Metropolitan Area Residents
1980: 115,308
1990: 151,506
2000: 169,391
Percent change, 1990–2000 11.8%
U.S. rank in 1980: 224th
U.S. rank in 1990: 218th
U.S. rank in 2000: 183rd

City Residents
1980: 37,712
1990: 39,217
2000: 38,889
2003 estimate: 39,148
Percent change, 1990–2000: −0.6%
U.S. rank in 1980: 590th
U.S. rank in 1990: 675th
U.S. rank in 2000: Not reported (State rank: 1st)

Density: 3,682 people per square mile (2000)

Racial and ethnic characteristics (2000)
   White: 35,883
   Black or African American: 693
   American Indian and Alaska Native: 182
   Asian: 1,031
   Native Hawaiian and Pacific Islander: 8
   Hispanic or Latino (may be of any race): 546
   Other: 211

Percent of residents born in state: 45.1% (2000)

Age characteristics (2000)
   Population under 5 years old: 1,788
   Population 5 to 9 years old: 1,826
   Population 10 to 14 years old: 1,690
   Population 15 to 19 years old: 3,566
   Population 20 to 24 years old: 7,343
   Population 25 to 34 years old: 6,822
   Population 35 to 44 years old: 5,244
   Population 45 to 54 years old: 4,073
   Population 55 to 59 years old: 1,387
   Population 60 to 64 years old: 1,058
   Population 65 to 74 years old: 1,936
   Population 75 to 84 years old: 1,451
   Population 85 years and older: 705
   Median age: 29.2 years

Births (2002, Chittenden County)
   Total number: 1,600

Deaths (2002, Chittenden County)
   Total number: 984 (of which, 2 were infants under the age of 1 year)

Money income (1999)
   Per capita income: $19,011
   Median household income: $33,070
   Total households: 15,869

Number of households with income of . . .
   less than $10,000: 2,016
   $10,000 to $14,999: 1,225
   $15,000 to $24,999: 2,665
   $25,000 to $34,999: 2,389
   $35,000 to $49,999: 2,706

$50,000 to $74,999: 2,469
$75,000 to $99,999: 1,316
$100,000 to $149,999: 693
$150,000 to $199,999: 170
$200,000 or more: 220

Percent of families below poverty level: 10.4% (45.4% of which were female householder families with related children under 5 years)

2002 FBI Crime Index Total: 1,871

Municipal Government

Burlington operates under a weak-mayoral form of government. The mayor is elected to a 3-year term while the 14 members of the city council receive 2-year terms. Burlington is the seat of Chittenden County.

Head Official: Mayor Peter A. Clavelle (NP) (since 1989; current term expires April 2006)

Total Number of City Employees: 654 (2005)

City Information: City of Burlington, City Hall, 149 Church St., Burlington, VT 05401; telephone (802)865-7000

Economy

Major Industries and Commercial Activity

Greater Burlington is the industrial, tourist, and financial center of the state. Manufacturing is the largest industry in Burlington, led by the electronics industries that had fueled an industrial boom during the 1990s. This region of Vermont supports nearly one-third of the state's manufacturing employment. The 20-block downtown shopping and residential district alone accounts for 9,000 workers in positions such as service, government, and retail, making it the second largest employment area in the state. The Greater Burlington region contains hundreds of small manufacturers producing a wide variety of products; many national and international manufacturing businesses have plants there that also support attendant service businesses. Tourism is the area's second largest industry; several banks are also headquartered there.

Items and goods produced: electronics and computer parts; food products; textiles; apparel; lumber; paper and wood products; furniture and fixtures; chemicals and allied products; petroleum, coal, rubber, plastic, leather, stone, clay, and glass products; toys; jewelry; primary and fabricated metals; machinery and electrical equipment; instruments.

Incentive Programs—New and Existing Companies

Local programs—Vermont, under the Regional Economic Development Program, has been organized into development districts to provide in-depth assistance to existing businesses and industries interested in locating in the area. Each of these nonprofit development corporations coordinates economic development efforts in the region. The agency responsible for Burlington is the Greater Burlington Industrial Corporation (GBIC). Also assisting local businesses is the Community and Economic Development Office, a department of the city of Burlington, that maintains business guides, offers tax incentives and loans, and advises on general business planning matters.

State programs—The Vermont Economic Development Authority (VEDA) consists of nine members appointed by the governor who facilitate several funding programs, while the State of Vermont's Department of Economic Development fosters business development and overseas trading. In 1998, Vermont passed Act 71, an Act Relating to Education, Taxation and Education Financing that contains a package of financial incentives, the most comprehensive in Vermont's history, designed to stimulate quality growth throughout the State of Vermont. Unlike incentive programs adopted by many states, Vermont's program incorporates a strategic framework that emphasizes quality jobs and symbolizes the state's core values with regard to meaningful employment opportunity. Facilitated by the Vermont Economic Progress Council (VEPC), the statute creates an innovative approval process for awarding tax incentives to both businesses and municipalities for economic development activity. Applications will be approved if they compare favorably to a set of guidelines and show that they will have a net positive fiscal effect. The incentives program is designed to benefit companies that already call Vermont home, with a special focus on small businesses.

Job training programs—The State of Vermont Department of Labor (VDOL) operates Career Resource Centers throughout the state for job-seekers, a free jobs database at Vermont JobLink, and the Workforce Education and Training Fund for both new and active workers while giving employers tax incentives for hiring displaced workers. The Lake Champlain Regional Chamber of Commerce's Learn to Earn program, as part of the Vermont School-to-Work collaborative, strives to enhance economic development and quality of life by focusing on improving the quality of education in the Lake Champlain region through business-education partnerships, School-to-Work transition initiatives, and workforce preparation strategies. It provides Learn to Earn opportunities in a variety of industry-certified programs including building trades, culinary studies, aviation technology, printing trades, dental assisting, childcare, and others. Students entering these programs receive advanced credits and placements when they enroll in college. Graduates of these partnership programs receive education and training that enables smooth transition into high paying jobs in the community.

The Vermont Small Business Development Center (VtSBDC), partially funded by the federal Small Business Administration (SBA), is available to assist new and existing small businesses with basic training courses and individual counseling; the Chittenden County branch worked with 170 clients in 2003. A field office of the Vermont Manufacturing Extension Center (VMEC) is in Burlington, and offers workshops and counseling to small- and medium-sized manufacturers. The VMEC collaborates with the National Institute of Standards & Technology (NIST), state colleges, and other state agencies.

Development Projects

The city's Community and Economic Development Office (CEDO) creates detailed annual action plans that focus on particular projects and programs throughout the area. Recent developments reported by the CEDO in their 2003–2004 plan include the Innovation Center of Vermont, the Burlington Town Center, and waterfront growth (including a $14 million project involving an inn, theaters, and retail and office space). The vitality of the downtown area can be seen in the planning of 300 new housing units by 2008, and a condominium project. And, according to the proposed 2005 city budget, nearly $1 million in developmental monies have been set aside for improving the ascetics of the downtown area. In transportation, the Burlington International Airport began a $24.8 million expansion in 2003 that included a new parking garage, expansion of a terminal, and the addition of gates; the third phase is still in progress in 2005.

Economic Development Information: Greater Burlington Industrial Corporation, 60 Main St., PO Box 786, Burlington, VT 05402; telephone (802)862-5726; toll-free (800)942-4288; fax (802)860-4288; email gbic@vermont.org. Lake Champlain Regional Chamber of Commerce, 60 Main St., Ste. 100, Burlington, VT 05401; telephone (802)863-3489; toll-free (877)686-5253; fax (802)863-1538; email vermont@vermont.org

Commercial Shipping

Once perceived as a rural area far removed from transportation networks and cut off from important markets, supplies and services, the Greater Burlington area has solidified its position in telecommunications, road, rail, air, and waterborne transport of goods to all areas of the United States, Canada, and worldwide.

An excellent—and scenic—highway system is used by a number of local and long-distance trucking companies offering overnight service to cities as distant as Washington, D.C., Pittsburgh, and Toronto, Canada—roughly 80 million consumers are located within a 500-mile radius of the city. Rail freight service is provided by Vermont Railway, which connects Burlington with three interline carriers including the Canadian Pacific Railway System, and Central Vermont Railway. Modern Burlington International Airport (BTV) offers air freight and expedited air service. Tugboats, barges, and tankers on Lake Champlain and its canals carry cargo to the Port of Montreal, the St. Lawrence Seaway, and south to the Port of New York.

Labor Force and Employment Outlook

Workers in the Greater Burlington area have been described as industrious, dependable, ingenious, and self-motivated. Its labor force has witnessed consistent growth in recent years with the total amount in 2002 of 106,500, representing nearly a third of Vermont's workers. Meanwhile, the city of Burlington's employment level of over 31,000 in 2002 also accounted for a third of Chittenden County's workforce. The greatest gains have been in the service industry which have helped to offset some losses in the manufacturing sector.

One of Vermont's biggest growth industries in the 1990s and 2000s was the "captive insurance" business, wholly-owned subsidiaries of large corporations that enable them to control insurance costs. Vermont passed its captive insurance law in 1981 and one captive was formed that year; by 1986 there were 69, and in 1990 there were 215; the number ballooned to more than 700 by the end of 2004.

The following is a summary of data regarding the Burlington and South Burlington, Vermont metropolitan area labor force, 2004 annual averages.

Size of nonagricultural labor force: 113,300

Number of workers employed in . . .
construction and mining: 6,100
manufacturing: 15,300
trade, transportation and utilities: 22,000
information: 3,200
financial activities: 5,400
professional and business services: 10,000
educational and health services: 18,100
leisure and hospitality: 10,700
other services: 3,700
government: 19,100

Average hourly earnings of production workers employed in manufacturing: $15.15

Unemployment rate: 3.1% (April 2005)

Largest employers
(Burlington metropolitan area)   *Number of employees*

IBM Corporation	6,000
Fletcher Allen Health Care	4,086
University of Vermont	3,137
Chittenden Corp.	1,208
IDX Systems Corporation	750
Ben & Jerry's Homemade, Inc.	735
Napoli Group	680
City of Burlington	654
Verizon	650
Goodrich Corp.	645

Cost of Living

The following is a summary of data regarding several key cost of living factors in the Burlington area.

2004 (3rd Quarter) ACCRA Average House Price: $339,117

2004 (3rd Quarter) ACCRA Cost of Living Index: 117.6 (U.S. average = 100.0)

State income tax rate: 3.6–9.5%

State sales tax rate: 6%

Local income tax rate: None

Local sales tax rate: None

Property tax rate: $2.7162 per $100 of value (2005)

Economic Information: Lake Champlain Valley RMO, The Lake Champlain Regional Marketing Organization, 60 Main St., Ste. 100, Burlington, VT 05401; telephone (802)863-3489; toll-free (877)686-5253; fax (802)863-1538; email vermont @vermont.org. Greater Burlington Industrial Corporation, 60 Main St., PO Box 786, Burlington, VT 05402; telephone (802)862-5726; toll-free (800)942-4288; fax (802)860-4288; email gbic@vermont.org. Vermont Department of Labor, PO Box 488, 5 Green Mountain Dr., Montpelier, VT 05601; telephone (802)828-4000; fax (802)828-4022. Community & Economic Development Office, City Hall, 149 Church St., Rm. 32, Burlington, VT 05401; telephone (802)865-7144; fax (802)865-7024; fd@ci.burlington.vt.us

Education and Research

Elementary and Secondary Schools

Burlington's is the largest and most diverse school district in Vermont. The system is overseen by the Board of School Commissioners whose 14 members are elected to two-year terms. Connections with five institutions of higher educa-

tion, including the University of Vermont and partnerships with a variety of businesses, including IBM, support the high standards for learning in the Burlington schools. On average, teachers in the district hold master's degrees coupled with 15 years of experience.

The following is a summary of information regarding the Burlington public schools as of the 2004–2005 school year.

Total enrollment: 3,532

Number of facilities
  elementary schools: 6
  junior high/middle schools: 2
  senior high schools: 1
  other: 4

Student/teacher ratio: 11.8:1

Teacher salaries
  average: $50,754

Funding per pupil: $7,264

Chittenden County is also home to a number of parochial elementary and secondary schools along with several dozen private institutions.

Public Schools Information: Superintendent of Schools, Burlington School District, 150 Colchester Ave., Burlington, VT 05401; telephone (802)865-5332; fax (802)864-8501

Colleges and Universities

Burlington is home to the University of Vermont, founded in 1791, which offers more than 90 fields of study in 8 undergraduate divisions and graduate programs, including medicine. The campus resides on 450 acres and educates 8,000 undergraduates, nearly 1,300 graduate students, and about 400 medical students. The College of Medicine received a ninth-place ranking (of 125 medical schools nationwide) in a 2006 survey by *U.S. News and World Report* for its primary care training. Established in 1878, the private Champlain College provides its 1,700 fulltime students 29 undergraduate-degree programs and two master's degree programs. Also located in the city is Burlington College, an alternative liberal arts private college; St. Michael's College, renowned for its theater program; and the Community College of Vermont.

Libraries and Research Centers

Burlington's Fletcher Free Library contains more than 100,000 books along with CDs, audio books, videos, and children's materials. The Romanesque-style Billings Library, built in 1885 and rededicated in 1962 as the Billings Student Center, houses the 12,000-book collection assembled by George Perkins Marsh, author of *Man and Nature,* still regarded as the ecologist's bible. Four libraries at the

University of Vermont boast 1.4 million volumes and 20,000 periodicals along with a variety of other resources, while Champlain College features 60,000 volumes and 6,000 electronic books. Libraries are also maintained by Trinity College, Planned Parenthood of Northern New England, and the National Gardening Association.

Research on heart disease, cancer, and other illnesses is conducted by Fletcher Allen Health Care in conjunction with the University of Vermont College of Medicine. The university also conducts research in such areas as international studies, rural studies, art objects, maple trees and other flora, water needs of cold areas, engineering, business, chemistry, and product development.

Public Library Information: Fletcher Free Public Library, 235 College St., Burlington, VT 05401; telephone (802)863-3403; fax (802)865-7227

Health Care

SELF magazine selected Burlington as the healthiest city in the country in November 2003. In 1995 Fletcher Allen Health Care formed via the integration of former entities Fanny Allen Hospital, Medical Center Hospital of Vermont, and University Health Center. A teaching facility, it includes more than 700 physicians and 1,200 registered nurses and provides a full range of tertiary level inpatient and outpatient services at the Colchester and Burlington campuses. Services offered include cardiology, radiology, kidney dialysis and transplant, rehabilitation, occupational and physical therapy, and a regional laboratory. The Howard Center for Human Services is based in Burlington and offers regional families mental health and crisis support services.

Health Care Information: Fletcher Allen Health Care, Medical Center Campus, 111 Colchester Ave., Burlington, VT; telephone (802)847-0000

Recreation

Sightseeing

The Greater Burlington area offers many architectural landmarks. Examples of distinctive nineteenth-century styles can be seen in the Pearl Street Historic District and the Head of Church Street Historic District. City Hall Park Historic District in downtown Burlington preserves significant buildings from the city's early history, such as Ethan Allen Fire Station and City Hall. The University Green Historic District at the University of Vermont is surrounded by 29 historic buildings; the land was donated by Ira Allen, brother of Ethan, with the stipulation that it be preserved.

Battery Park, the scene of a battle between British and American troops during the War of 1812, offers scenic vistas and sunsets. Ferry cruises of Lake Champlain depart from Burlington Harbor in the Battery Street-King Street Historic District, the city's earliest settled area.

At Shelburne Farms, a 1,000-acre landscape designed by Olmsted offers breathtaking lake and mountain vistas. Vermont products are sold at its visitor's center.

Arts and Culture

A major showcase for the performing arts in Burlington is the 2,600-seat Memorial Auditorium, which holds about 12 major concerts a year, augmented by about 6 to 8 local concerts. Burlington City Arts operates the Firehouse Center for the Visual Arts, displaying a variety of exhibits at the renovated Ethan Allen Firehouse. The Vermont Symphony Orchestra is based in Burlington and performs 50 concerts annually at different venues across the state.

Burlington offers a rich schedule of artistic events throughout the year. The summer music season includes the Vermont Mozart Festival, offering a series of chamber music concerts at varying locales in the region. Banjo and fiddle contests as well as bandshell concerts are also popular. The University of Vermont's 295-seat Royall Tyler Theatre provides a variety of offerings. Summer professional theatrical performances are presented at St. Michael's Playhouse, while the Art-Deco style, 1,453-seat Flynn Theatre is the scene of performing arts events of all kinds all year long. The Lyric Theatre of Burlington and the Lane Performing Artist Series at the University of Vermont are also popular.

The university is home to Robert Hull Fleming Museum, a $15-million collection of more than 20,000 paintings, sculptures, and decorative arts. The Shelburne Museum in nearby Shelburne, a 100-acre complex housing one of the largest collections of Americana in the country, features 39 early American buildings and an extensive display of 150,000 eighteenth- and nineteenth-century artifacts. The Discovery Museum of Essex specializes in hands-on exhibits oriented toward children, and includes a planetarium. For all ages the ECHO at the Leahy Center provides an educational and enjoyable day at the lake aquarium and science center, highlighted by 100 interactive exhibits and 60 species of animals.

Artisans of all kinds have long been attracted to the natural beauty of Vermont, and their works are on display at several arts and crafts galleries in and around Burlington.

Arts and Culture Information: Burlington City Arts, 149 Church St., Burlington, VT 05401; telephone (802)865-7166

The University of Vermont, considered one of the best undergraduate institutions in the country, was founded in 1791.

Festivals and Holidays

Festivals abound in greater Burlington as the area hosts the Lake Champlain Balloon Festival, the Vermont Mozart Festival, and Ben & Jerry's One World One Heart Festival. St. Patrick's Day is marked by the week-long Burlington Irish Heritage Festival. Vermont is the country's leading producer of maple syrup, and the sugaring season is celebrated in nearby St. Albans at the annual Vermont Maple Festival in early April. A parade, art, and activities make for a fun-filled Kids' Day festival in early May for some 15,000 attendees.

At the Green Mountain Chew-Chew, held in June, local eateries prepare ethnic specialties in what is billed as northern New England's largest smorgasbord, attracting about 60,000 people. Also in June is the Discover Jazz Festival with music at various locations throughout the city, and the Art's Alive Annual Juried Festival of Fine Art which presents workshops and demonstrations. July begins with a Fourth of July celebration; the middle of the month features samplings from 25 breweries at the Vermont Brewers Festival. The summer wraps up with the state's largest county fair, the 10-day Champlain Valley Fair for 300,000 people.

Autumn in Vermont is an unofficial festival, when spectacular fall foliage draws visitors from all over the world. Winter brings the Vermont Handcrafters Fair in November in South Burlington at the Sheraton Conference Center, and a Christmas celebration at the Shelburne Museum in early December with music, an old-fashioned magic show, and craftmaking. The holiday season is also celebrated by a lighting ceremony of 100,000 lights at the Church Street Marketplace, followed by First Night on New Year's Eve, when downtown Burlington is the scene of a gala featuring parades, fireworks, music, and other family-friendly performances at 32 venues. In February, the Winter Festival offers indoor and outdoor fun highlighted by ice sculpting, sledding, and other events.

Sports for the Spectator

Affiliated with Major League Baseball's (MLB) Washington Nationals, the Class A Vermont Expos, founded in 1994, play from June through September at Centennial Field, located on the campus of the University of Vermont in the New York-Penn League. The Catamounts of the University of Vermont are part of the National Collegiate Athletic Association's (NCAA) Division I with men's and women's programs in hockey, soccer, basketball, baseball, and track events.

Sports for the Participant

Burlington's location on the shore of Lake Champlain, the nation's sixth largest freshwater lake, near the Green Mountains provides a wide spectrum of year-round recreational opportunities. Summer offers boating, golfing, hiking, horse-back riding, swimming, and tennis. An eight-mile bike path curves along the lake, traversing parks and three public beaches. Within the city, 30 parks and natural areas occupy 531 acres and offer residents a variety of options. Fishing is popular winter and summer. Burlington is the hub of downhill skiing in the East; cross-country skiing night and day on miles of scenic trails is also possible, as are sleigh rides and snow boarding. Ice skaters can choose among six different outdoor venues as well as indoors at the Gordon H. Paquette Arena in Leddy Park, which also hosts local hockey leagues.

Shopping and Dining

Constructed in 1981, the centerpiece of downtown Burlington is the Church Street Marketplace, a bustling four-block outdoor pedestrian mall lined with more than 100 shops along with restaurants and cafés; among the wares offered are original works by local artists along with retailers such as Banana Republic, Eddie Bauer, and Old Navy. Adjoining the marketplace is Burlington Square Mall, offering 60 specialty stores on 150,000 square feet of space including Filene's Department Store, Gap, and Victoria's Secret. University Mall in South Burlington is the state's largest indoor mall with more than 70 stores and restaurants and featuring major retailers such as JCPenney, Sears, and the Children's Place. Several indoor and outdoor malls and factory outlet stores are located within a seven-mile radius, as are the types of stores for which Vermont is most famous—crafts, antiques, and Vermont-made products.

Burlington's growing sophistication has resulted in a restaurant renaissance, and many establishments, from small chef-owned to classic country inns, offer Vermont-made dairy and other products; fresh lake trout is a local specialty. After dinner visitors may enjoy a stroll to Ben and Jerry's Ice Cream Parlor for a sampling of what a national magazine described as ''the best ice cream in the world.'' On Saturdays between May and October, the Burlington Farmers' Market in City Hall Park brings out an abundance of food from local farmers and bakers along with the wares of craftsmakers.

Visitor Information: Lake Champlain Regional Chamber of Commerce, 60 Main St., Ste. 100, Burlington, VT 05401; telephone (802)863-3489; toll-free (877)686-5253; fax (802)863-1538; email vermont@vermont.org

Convention Facilities

Meeting and convention business is one of the largest segments of Vermont's economy. The Burlington area offers more than 3,000 guest rooms in 34 hotels and motels along with a variety of meeting facilities encompassing about 385,000 square feet to accommodate large and small groups.

A principal meeting place is Memorial Auditorium in downtown Burlington, offering two levels of exhibit space totaling nearly 17,000 square feet. The 1,453-seat Flynn Theatre, also located downtown, is available for lectures, award ceremonies, and live performances. Conferences can be held on the 500-passenger Spirit of Ethan Allen III cruise ship and dining yacht from May through October. Other unique function space is provided at Fleming and Shelburne museums and Shelburne Farms.

Convention Information: Vermont Convention Bureau, 60 Main St., Ste. 100, Burlington, VA 05401; telephone (802)863-3489; toll-free (877)686-5253; fax (802)863-1538; email meetings@vermont.org

Transportation

Approaching the City

Burlington is the air hub of Vermont. Burlington International Airport (BTV), three miles east of the city, is served by seven major airlines traveling to major destinations in New England and the Midwest; about one-half million passengers are served yearly. Amtrak and Green Mountain Railroad provide rail service throughout New England and the New York area. Major highway routes are interstates 89 and 91, and U.S. 7 and U.S. 2. Greyhound/Vermont Transit offers bus service; passenger and auto ferries travel across Lake Champlain between Vermont and upstate New York at three locations, provided by the Lake Champlain Transportation Company.

Traveling in the City

Driving tours of Burlington and its environs are a popular way to see the area, but rush-hour bottlenecks and traffic jams do occur and the prudent visitor may wish to carry a map. The downtown area has ample parking for those who do wish to venture about with 4,000 spaces in lots and garages. A fleet of 47 buses carry about 1.6 million passengers annually and connects Burlington to the surrounding areas, courtesy of Chittenden County Transportation Authority (CCTA); all buses are equipped with bike racks and paratransit services are available.

Communications

Newspapers and Magazines

Burlington's daily newspaper, *The Burlington Free Press,* is published every morning, and the *Vermont Times, VOX*

(an arts newspaper), and *Seven Days* (politics and culture) appear weekly while *The Vermont Catholic Tribune* is produced biweekly. Magazines published monthly in Burlington include *National Gardening, Vermont Business Magazine, Vermont Outdoors Magazine,* and *Kids VT,* published 10 times per year.

Television

Television viewers in Burlington may choose from two network affiliates, one public station, and cable service. Four FM radio stations, including one owned by the University of Vermont and another featuring National Public Radio (NPR) programming, and three AM stations broadcast from Burlington.

Media Information: *The Burlington Free Press,* PO Box 10, Burlington, VT 05402; telephone (802)863-3441

Burlington Online

Burlington City Arts (events). Available www.burlington cityarts.com

The Burlington Free Press. Available www.burlington freepress.com

Burlington School District. Available www.bsdvt.org

City of Burlington Home Page. Available at www.ci .burlington.vt.us

Community & Economic Development Office, City of Burlington. Available www.cedoburlington.org

Greater Burlington Industrial Corporation. Available www .vermont.org/gbic

Lake Champlain Regional Chamber of Commerce. Available www.vermont.org

State of Vermont, Department of Labor. Available www.det .state.vt.us

Vermont Convention Bureau. Available www.vermont.org/ groups

Vermont Department of Economic Development. Available www.thinkvermont.com

Vermont Department of Education School Report (Burlington). Available crs.uvm.edu/schlrpt

Vermont Department of Tourism. Available www.1-800-vermont.com

Vermont Historical Society. Available www.vermonthistory .org

Vermont Life Magazine. Available www.vtlife.com

Vermont Living. Available www.vtliving.com

Selected Bibliography

Baruth, Philip E., *The Dream of the White Village: A Novel in Stories* (Winooski, Vt.: R.N.M. Inc., 1998)

Montpelier

The City in Brief

Founded: 1791 (incorporated, 1895)

Head Official: City Manager William J. Fraser (since 1995)

City Population
   1980: 8,240
   1990: 8,247
   2000: 8,035
   2003 estimate: 7,945
   Percent change, 1990–2000: −2.5%
   U.S. rank in 1990: Not reported
   U.S. rank in 2000: Not reported

Metropolitan Area Population (Washington County)
   1980: 52,393
   1990: 54,928
   2000: 58,039
   Percent change, 1990–2000: 5.7%
   U.S. rank in 1980: 758th

U.S. rank in 1990: 796th
U.S. rank in 2000: 824th

Area: 10.3 square miles (2000)
Elevation: 484 feet above sea level
Average Annual Temperature: 42.8° F (statewide Vermont)
Average Annual Precipitation: Approximately 30 inches of rain; 100 inches of snow

Major Economic Sectors: Government, services, finance, insurance and real estate, manufacturing, tourism
Unemployment Rate: 3.1% (Statewide average, 2005)
Per Capita Income: $22,599 (1999)
2004 ACCRA Average House Price: Not reported
2004 ACCRA Cost of Living Index: Not reported

2002 FBI Crime Index Total: Not reported

Major Colleges and Universities: Vermont College of Norwich University; Woodbury College; New England Culinary Institute; Community College of Vermont

Daily Newspaper: *Barre-Montpelier Times-Argus*

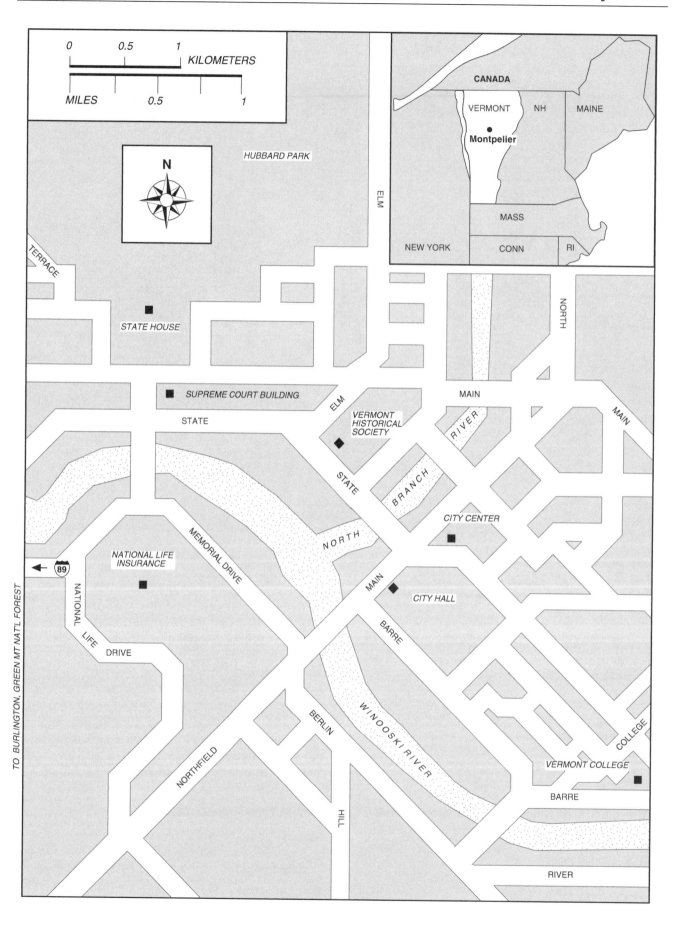

Introduction

Montpelier is the capital of Vermont and the center of the state's insurance industry. The smallest and possibly most livable of United States capital cities, Montpelier is a cosmopolitan and dignified oasis in a rural and scenic setting. The city's downtown is on the National and State Registers of Historic Places, and *Inc.* magazine recently named it the Top Small City for Doing Business in the United States. The city is traditionally linked to the larger town of Barre, home of the world's largest granite quarry. Montpelier has been recognized as one of the top 100 art towns in the United States.

Geography and Climate

Montpelier is located in a valley on the Winooski and North Branch rivers, which trisect the city, in central Vermont. The city enjoys a four-seasons climate. More than 40 inches of precipitation fall each year, with 30 inches coming as rain and the other 10 in the form of snow, which translates to an annual snowfall of more than 100 inches and a great benefit to the region's long-established ski industry.

Area: 10.3 square miles (2000)

Elevation: 484 feet above sea level

Average Temperatures: January, 19.0° F; August, 69.0° F; annual (statewide) average, 42.8° F

Average Annual Precipitation: Approximately 30 inches of rain; 100 inches of snow

History

Montpelier was settled relatively late in comparison to other Vermont towns. The first permanent settler was Colonel Jacob Davis in 1789. In 1791, the year Vermont entered the union, Montpelier organized itself as a town. It is not known why a town notable for an unusually large number of whiskey distilleries chose the name of a French town notable for wine and brandy, and there are various theories about why Montpelier was chosen by the state legislature in 1805 as the permanent state capital. The theories range from Montpelier's central location to promises of land and money. Some local historians hold that topography explains the development of Montpelier, as four branches of the Winooski River come together there to form what is gener-

ally regarded as Vermont's most important river. Since in Vermont roads follow rivers, they explain, the coming together of many roads caused it to become a meeting place for both government and commerce.

The town carried on a thriving trade during the early nineteenth century, attracting craftsmen, factories, sawmills, and ironworks. Nearby Barre's quarries attracted granite workers and sculptors from Italy and Sweden; stonecutters from Spain settled in Montpelier. The coming of the railroad in the mid-1800s stimulated business and brought in the first tourists. At the same time, Dr. Julius Dewey, father of Spanish-American War hero Admiral George Dewey, decided that selling life insurance would be more lucrative than practicing medicine and founded the National Life Insurance Company, now one of the oldest life insurance companies in the world. Following the Civil War of 1861–1865, resort hotels such as the Pavilion in Montpelier attracted visitors from throughout the country, further stimulating Montpelier's economy. The first state publicity service in the country was established in Montpelier in 1891, hurrying the flow of tourism. When the first rope tow in the country powered by a Model T engine was rigged up in Vermont in 1935, the ski industry was born. Montpelier is located near three of Vermont's largest ski areas.

In March 1991, ice floes acting like a dam altered the course of the Winooski River, sending much of it rushing through downtown Montpelier and leaving some areas under six feet of water. Damage was estimated at tens of millions of dollars. Montpelier, in many ways a classic small town, saw its ambitious plans for a riverfront and office park development take shape when construction began in 1997 on the Winooski Riverfront Redevelopment Project. Besides adding acres of parkland, including several hiking and cross-country ski trails, the city has developed some pocket parks. At the dawn of the new millennium Montpelier quietly enjoys its reputation as one of America's most livable cities, with a strong local economy, easy access to beautiful natural surroundings, and minimal growth.

Historical Information: Vermont Historical Society, Pavilion Building, Montpelier, VT 05602; telephone (802)828-2291

Population Profile

Metropolitan Area Residents
1980: 52,393
1990: 54,928
2000: 58,039
Percent change, 1990–2000: 5.7%

U.S. rank in 1980: 758th
U.S. rank in 1990: 796th
U.S. rank in 2000: 824th

City Residents
1980: 8,240
1990: 8,247
2000: 8,035
2003 estimate: 7,945
Percent change, 1990–2000: −2.5%
U.S. rank in 1990: Not reported
U.S. rank in 2000: Not reported

Density: 780.1 people per square mile (2000)

Racial and ethnic characteristics (2000)
White: 7,758
Black or African American: 52
American Indian and Alaska Native: 19
Asian: 66
Native Hawaiian and Pacific Islander: 1
Hispanic or Latino (may be of any race): 113
Other: 31

Percent of residents born in state: 48.1% (2000)

Age Characteristics (2000)
Population under 5 years old: 364
Population 5 to 9 years old: 432
Population 10 to 14 years old: 549
Population 15 to 19 years old: 548
Population 20 to 24 years old: 505
Population 25 to 34 years old: 970
Population 35 to 44 years old: 1,292
Population 45 to 54 years old: 1,448
Population 55 to 59 years old: 411
Population 60 to 64 years old: 316
Population 65 to 74 years old: 557
Population 75 to 84 years old: 447
Population 85 years and older: 196
Median age: 40.5 years

Births (2002, Washington County)
Total number: 636

Deaths (2002, Washington County)
Total number: 500

Money income (1999)
Per capita income: $22,599
Median household income: $37,513
Total households: 3,735

Number of households with income of . . .
less than $10,000: 390
$10,000 to $14,999: 282
$15,000 to $24,999: 509

$25,000 to $34,999: 569
$35,000 to $49,999: 688
$50,000 to $74,999: 624
$75,000 to $99,999: 339
$100,000 to $149,999: 235
$150,000 to $199,999: 63
$200,000 or more: 36

Percent of families below poverty level: 7.2% (70% of which were female householder families with related children under 5 years)

2002 FBI Crime Index Total: Not reported

Municipal Government

Montpelier operates under a city-manager form of government. The mayor and six aldermen are elected to two-year terms and appoint the city manager for an unspecified term.

Head Official: City Manager William J. Fraser (since 1995)

Total Number of City Employees: 100 (2005)

City Information: Montpelier City Hall, 39 Main Street, Montpelier, VT 05602; telephone (802)223-9502

Economy

Major Industries and Commercial Activity

Montpelier's economy is dominated by state governmental activities. Approximately 2,300 state employees work in Montpelier—truly remarkable in a city of its size. The presence of state government has led to a large service and retail industry. Higher education and insurance, including the headquarters of National Life Insurance Company, which is among the nation's largest insurance providers, also are significant economic presences. Due to its position at the center of a popular East Coast resort area, as well as being the state capital, Montpelier supports a thriving tourism industry; the Sugarbush and Mad River Glen ski areas are known throughout the northeast. In the Central Vermont region, which includes Montpelier, are manufacturers known worldwide for the production of granite memorials, manufacturers of machinery and instruments for the semiconductor industry, an expanding food-processing industry including the headquarters of Ben & Jerry's Ice Cream, and many other small manufacturers.

Incentive Programs—New and Existing Companies

Local programs—The Central Vermont Economic Development Corporation (CVEDC), one of 12 regional development agencies in Vermont, assists new and existing businesses through programs such as mortgage loans, industrial revenue bonds, and low-interest loan guarantees. The CVEDC is one of just three U.S. Small Business Administration certified development companies in Vermont, and has helped bring more than $46 million in capital investment and 1,200 permanent jobs to the region since its inception in 1976. The City of Montpelier Planning and Development office guides entrepreneurs through the approval process. Through its Community Development Agency, the city administers a business development revolving loan fund, a handicap accessibility loan fund, and other economic development programs, including support of the Montpelier Downtown Community Association. The city also administers several successful housing renovation and home ownership programs to benefit persons of low and moderate income.

State programs—Vermont's tax incentive program offers incentives based on quality jobs. These tax incentives are available based on whether or not the proposed economic development meets certain guidelines, and whether a cost/benefit model analysis points to a positive net fiscal effect on Vermont's tax revenue. The cost benefit model and other functions of the program are mainly coordinated by the Vermont Economic Progress Council. Vermont's Downtown Development Act is an incentive to help benefit Vermont's downtowns with programs for rehabilitation of certified historic or older buildings, sprinkler system rebates, reallocation of sales tax on construction materials, downtown transportation, related capitol improvement fund, planning grant for qualifying for designation, and other state and federal incentives.

Vermont's Act Relating to Education, Taxation and Education Financing provides financial incentives to grow businesses that are the most comprehensive in the state's history. The statute awards tax incentives to both businesses and municipalities for economic development activity, with a special focus on small businesses. The state also offers sales tax exemptions on certain resources vital to industry, including electricity, building materials in excess of $1 million, industrial fuels, and heavy machinery and equipment.

Development Projects

The City of Monptelier and the State of Vermont, working jointly through the City-State Commission, developed the Capital District Master Plan in an effort to identify, encourage, and coordinate mutually beneficial development plans for the Capitol Complex, downtown Montpelier, and the Winooski River corridor. The plan presents recommendations and concepts for meeting the state's projected office space needs, establishing a greenway along the Winooski River, and considering numerous physical improvements to improve pedestrian and vehicular circulation and stimulate downtown redevelopment.

In 2005 the city released information on its Transportation Planning Project, with an eye toward reducing urban sprawl, encouraging alternative modes of transportation to the automobile, and making the city even more bicycle-friendly for both commuters and recreational bicyclists. Plans called for a new Winooski West Bike Path to meet with the existing Winooski East Bike Path at Stone Cutters Way, and in turn to connect with the Central Vermont Regional System that would eventually run all the way to East Barre. In 2002 voters approved $800,000 to be spent on turning the old Carr Lot train depot into a state-of-the-art transit center and public park.

Economic Development Information: Central Vermont Chamber of Commerce, PO Box 336, Barre, Vermont 05641; telephone (802)229-5711

Commercial Shipping

Montpelier is linked to major East Coast and Canadian cities by interstate highways and rail via the New England Railroad. The Burlington International Airport is located less than 40 miles away in Burlington, and corporate planes can fly to Montpelier via the Knapp State Airport in neighboring Berlin.

Labor Force and Employment Outlook

Vermont's labor force is described as productive and loyal with a low rate of absenteeism. Due to its position as the state capital and as a center for various service-oriented businesses, employment in Montpelier is dominated by professional and service-oriented jobs.

Montpelier's workforce is well educated, with nearly 17 percent of its adult residents holding an advanced degree, 50 percent holding a college degree, and 88.4 percent as high school graduates. Workers are well paid compared to regional and state averages. Average household incomes are the highest in Washington County and among the highest in Vermont.

With a preponderance of its jobs in state government, utilities, and education, the economic base for the greater Montpelier region is very stable. But the true advantage is the region's relatively high number of small businesses; there are nearly 2,300 employers in the central Vermont region, plus an estimated 2,500 self-employed workers. The average business in the region employers fewer than a dozen people, which is an advantage because small businesses tend to react to change much more rapidly than larger corporations. Analysts predict that most new jobs in the near future will be in non-manufacturing areas, especially services and trade. Finance, insurance, and real estate should remain stable.

The following is a summary of data regarding the Burlington and South Burlington, Vermont metropolitan area labor force, 2004 annual averages.

Size of nonagricultural labor force: 113,300

Number of workers employed in . . .
  construction and mining: 6,100
  manufacturing: 15,300
  trade, transportation and utilities: 22,000
  information: 3,200
  financial activities: 5,400
  professional and business services: 10,000
  educational and health services: 18,100
  leisure and hospitality: 10,700
  other services: 3,700
  government: 19,100

Average hourly earnings of production workers employed in manufacturing: $13.65 (statewide average)

Unemployment rate: 3.1% (Statewide average, 2005)

Largest employers
(Central Vermont region, 2003)	Number of employees
State of Vermont	9,250
Central Vermont Medical Center	1,178
National Life Insurance Co.	1,000
Sugarbush Ski Resort (in season)	980
Rock of Ages Quarries	854
Cabot Cooperative Creamery	575
Washington County Mental Health	560
Green Mountain Coffee Roasters	540
New England Culinary Institute	506

Cost of Living

The following is a summary of data regarding several key cost of living factors in the Montpelier area.

2004 ACCRA Average House Price: Not reported

2004 ACCRA Cost of Living Index: Not reported

State income tax rate: 24% of federal tax liability (2005)

State sales tax rate: 6.0%

Local income tax rate: None

Local sales tax rate: None

Property tax rate: $2.65 per $100 of assessed value (2005)

Economic Information: Vermont Department of Employment & Training, PO Box 488, Montpelier, VT 05601-0488; telephone (802)828-4000; fax (802)828-4022. Department of Planning & Development, City Hall, 39 Main Street,

Montpelier, VT 05602-2950; telephone (802)223-9506; fax (802)223-9524; email planning@montpelier-vt.org

Education and Research

Elementary and Secondary Schools

The management of the Montpelier public schools is vested in a Board of School Commissioners, which appoints a superintendent. According to the superintendent, test scores of public school students in Montpelier are above state and national norms, and 80 percent of high school graduates go on to college. Each school building is supplemented by an Educational Support Team that assists with academic remediation, behavioral support, and motor and language development. Preschool special education and at-home or daycare education is coordinated through the Essential Early Education System.

The following is a summary of data regarding the Montpelier public schools as of the 2004–2005 school year.

Total enrollment: 1,077

Number of facilities
  elementary schools: 1
  middle schools: 1
  high schools: 1

Student/teacher ratio: 18:1

Teacher salaries
  average: $38,636

Funding per pupil: $9,353

Public Schools Information: Superintendent of Schools, Montpelier School District, 58 Barre Street, Montpelier, VT 05602; telephone (802)223-9796

Colleges and Universities

Montpelier is home to Vermont College, which offers a full range of undergraduate majors, coeducational military lifestyle at the Northfield Campus, nationally renowned adult degree and creative writing programs, a nursing program, and the state's only school of architecture at its 35 acre Montpelier campus. In 2001 the 1,000-student Vermont College was acquired by Union Institute and University, which also maintains a campus in Brattleboro, Vermont. The Community College of Vermont is also located on the Vermont College campus and offers associate degrees and other educational services to approximately 900 students annually. Norwich University's adult degree program is also operated from Vermont College. The New England Culinary Institute, with 400 students, offers an Associate's degree in Occupational Studies and a Bachelor's degree in Service and Management. The school occupies a four-acre Main Street campus. In addition to the main campus, the school owns and operates the Chef's Table and the Main Street Bar & Grill restaurants and the La Brioche Bakery & Cafe downtown. In 2004 the New England Culinary Institute was named Best Cooking School by the International Association of Culinary Professionals. Woodbury College, which offers programs in mediation, paralegal studies, prevention and community development, and psychology is also located in Montpelier. More than half of the seventeen colleges in the Vermont Consortium of Colleges are within 90 minutes of the city.

Libraries and Research Centers

The Kellogg-Hubbard Library, privately endowed in 1894, houses a collection of more than 69,000 items in its Adult Library; its Children's Room offers a collection for ages up to 14.

The Vermont Historical Society Library in nearby Barre holds more than 50,000 volumes on Vermont history, Vermontiana, and New England history and genealogy, as well as photographs and maps. The library's manuscript collection offers letters, diaries, business records, and personal papers documenting the lives of ordinary Vermonters, including a special Civil War collection and documents tracing Vermont's history with the underground railroad. The Historical Society also maintains a museum in Montpelier.

The State of Vermont Department of Libraries has extensive microfiche and software as well as 220,000 volumes on current state and federal statutory law. The Nature Conservancy of Vermont conducts research on rare plants and animals.

Public Library Information: Kellogg-Hubbard Library, 135 Main St., Montpelier, VT 05602; telephone (802)223-3338; fax (802)223-3338; email kellogg_hubb@dol.state.vt.us

Health Care

The health care needs of Montpelier residents are attended to at the Central Vermont Medical Center, which is comprised of the 122-bed Central Vermont Hospital in nearby Berlin, Vermont (a 24-hour acute care facility), the 10-member Central Vermont Physician Practice Corporation, and the Woodbridge Nursing Home. The hospital is staffed by more than 150 physicians and nearly 1,000 full- and part-time nurses, technicians, and other support personnel.

Recreation

Sightseeing

The Montpelier skyline is dominated by the gold dome of the State House, standing out in elegant relief against the surrounding green hills. Dedicated in 1859, the State House is constructed in the Grecian style of granite quarried in Barre; a statue of Ceres, the Roman goddess of agriculture, surmounts the dome; a marble statue of Ethan Allen, a Revolutionary War hero from Vermont, stands at the front entrance. The interior decor is Victorian, with a number of interesting details. Visitors may observe legislative sessions from January to April. Across the street is the Supreme Court Building, an example of modern architecture. On a hill off State Street a few blocks west of the capitol, Green Mount Cemetery was founded in 1854 and has been a memorial for the area's talented sculptors and prominent citizens.

Hubbard Park, behind the State House, offers a good view of the Worcester Mountains and the Winooski River Valley; the park was created through a gift of 125 acres to the City of Montpelier by John E. Hubbard in 1899. Since then several other parcels have been added to the park which now consists of 185 acres and roughly 7 miles of hiking and skiing trails, numerous picnic areas, a soccer and baseball field, a small pond, a sledding hill, and a 54 foot observation tower. The observation tower offers spectacular views of from the highest point in the city.

World War II mementos from the USS *Montpelier* are on view at the second floor of Montpelier City Hall. Architecture buffs may enjoy a stroll through the Vermont College campus, where many fine examples of Victorian architecture are preserved. Montpelier has the largest historic district in Vermont, and walking tours are offered by the Montpelier Heritage Group, the local historical society and preservation organization.

Rock of Ages Quarry in Barre, producer of one-third of the country's memorial granite, offers visitors a surreal view of a working quarry. Nearby Waterbury is home to Ben & Jerry's Ice Cream Factory, which offers tours year-round. The world-famous Cabot cheddar cheese is produced in nearby Cabot, Vermont, where factory tours are available. Wanderers will discover several historic covered bridges throughout the region.

Arts and Culture

Thousands of tourists visit Central Vermont each year, allowing the development of cultural activities in Montpelier beyond what would be expected in an area its size. The Montpelier Theater Guild, a long-time local theater troupe that was recently resurrected after a several-year intermission, offers theater productions at Montpelier's Union Elementary School Auditorium. The Lost Nation Theater presents professional theatrical performances at the City Hall Arts Center. The Onion River Arts Council presents performances by touring companies in a variety of disciplines, including theater, dance, music, and readings at City Hall and at the elegant Barre Opera House. The finest in world cinema, past and present, is offered at the Savoy Theater, while contemporary films run at the Capitol Theater.

Music lovers enjoy the Vermont Philharmonic's season of concerts performed at the Barre Opera House. Band concerts are held on the State House lawn from June through August, and concerts from a variety of musical genres are presented on Sunday afternoons at Bethany Church. The Montpelier Chamber Orchestra Society has offered unique training and performing opportunities for talented string players in the Central Vermont area since the early 1990s.

The history of Vermont is interpreted through exhibits at the Vermont Historical Society Museum in Montpelier. The T. W. Wood Art Gallery, which celebrated its centennial year in 1997, and the Vermont College Art Center offer permanent exhibits by Thomas Waterman Wood, a Civil-War era artist, as well as changing exhibits by New England artists. The Artisans Hand gallery on Main Street features the handcrafted work of more than 125 local artisans.

Arts and Culture Information: Onion River Arts Council, 43 State Street, Montpelier, VT 05602; telephone (802)229-ARTS; toll-free (800)639-1383

Festivals and Holidays

The State House lawn is the scene of a variety of celebrations during the summer months, such as the Vermont Dairy Celebration in June, and Victorian Ice Cream Social. The Vermont Quilt Festival in nearby Northfield is one of the nation's oldest quilt events, featuring quilt displays, classes, and a merchant's mall. The Vermont Festival of the Arts in the nearby Mad River Valley goes on for three weeks in mid-summer with culinary events, art exhibitions, musical performances, and children's events. Each September brings the Granite Festival in Barre and the Celebrate the Winooski Parade and Festival in Montpelier. Winter brings the Kids' Fest in January and February, a series of six weekly live performances. Sugaring season, which usually begins in March, is celebrated at various locales in the area.

Sports for the Spectator

Burlington, Vermont, less than hour's drive from Montpelier, is home to the Vermont Grizzlies minor league baseball team, which plays at Red Oak Park. The Grand Prix Tennis Tournament is held in nearby Stowe in early August.

Sports for the Participant

One of the principal attractions to life in central Vermont is the easy accessibility to nearly limitless outdoor recreation. Because of this the region attracts outdoor enthusiasts and encourages active, healthy lifestyles among the people who live there. In 1997 Montpelier initiated the first major Central Vermont bicycle and pedestrian paths. The paths provide unrestricted access to the riverbanks and views of the river and both downtown and rural areas of the city. There is excellent mountain biking in the Green Mountains throughout the region. Swimming is available at the Recreation Field pool, at a beach in nearby Wrightsville, or at any of a number of smaller lakes in the area. Winter events include sledding, cross country skiing, and snowshoeing at Hubbard Park, and ice skating outdoors or at a local indoor rink. Montpelier is located within 25 miles of four major ski areas, including Sugarbush, Stowe, and Mad River Glen; there are also dozens of lakes and streams for fishing and canoeing, mountains, golf courses, tennis courts, bowling alleys, and other recreational attractions. The Green Mountain National Forest covers much of the area.

Shopping and Dining

Downtown Montpelier offers a variety of specialty shops, such as The Artisan's Hand, a cooperative craft shop featuring works by Vermont artists, and Bear Pond Books, stocking a good selection of New England titles. Salaam Boutique has trendy fashions from local designers. The Vermont Trading Co. has natural fiber clothing, and Onion River Sports features quality outdoor clothing and gear. Morse Farm, a few miles away, specializes in maple syrup, fresh produce, and cheese. Bragg Farm Sugarhouse and gift shop, in nearby East Montpelier, offers films and tours about maple sugarmaking, as well as tasty food specialties and unique gifts. The Hunger Mountain Co-Op at Stone Cutters Way features local and regional beers and wines.

The presence of New England Culinary Institute offers a unique advantage to the hospitality industry in Montpelier. The institute maintains three restaurants, including the celebrated Chef's Table restaurant, a bakery, and a catering service, offering nouvelle cuisine and other items prepared by students. The GoldenDomer Brewery offers tastes of the latest brews. Conoscenti and Giasole offer Italian and Mediterranean cuisine. J. Morgan's is a steakhouse right near the railroad tracks. McGillicuddy's is an Irish pub and Thrush Tavern claims the best burger in town. The area offers scores of other dining opportunities ranging from fast-food to elegant restaurants and charming country inns.

Visitor Information: Central Vermont Chamber of Commerce, PO Box 336, Barre, Vermont 05641; telephone (802)229-5711; email CVChamber@AOL.com. Vermont Department of Tourism and Marketing, toll-free (800)-Vermont

Convention Facilities

A principal meeting facility in Montpelier is the Capitol Plaza, which offers a total of 190 rooms and 14,000 square feet of conference space, plus accommodations for groups from 20 to 300 people. There is an Econo Lodge in Montpelier, and a number of bed and breakfast facilities have opened their doors for small groups. The Inn at Montpelier adds an elegant touch and boasts an authentically beautiful wraparound Victorian porch. Facilities at Vermont College are also available, and the Central Vermont region offers more than a dozen other hotels, motels, meeting sites, and many inns. Larger groups can be accommodated in Burlington, 40 minutes drive to the west.

Convention Information: Vermont Lodging and Restaurant Association, Three Main Street, Suite 106, Burlington VT 05401; telephone (802)660-9001

Transportation

Approaching the City

Montpelier is located 30 miles from Burlington International Airport and is within minutes of E. F. Knapp (Barre-Montpelier) Airport. Amtrak's *Vermonter* offers train service, with daily service between Washington, D.C., New York, and St. Albans; it makes nine stops along the length of Vermont. Bus service is available from New York and Boston with connections south and west. Interstate 89 in the Central Vermont region has won awards for its beauty. The state bans billboard advertising along its highways to emphasize the scenic beauty of its countryside.

Traveling in the City

Locals appreciate the bike paths and safe bike routes throughout Montpelier. Three principal streets, Main, State, and Elm, follow the Winooski River and its tributary, North Branch. In 1995 Montpelier's Towne Hill Road became the site of the United States' first modern roundabout, a circular intersection design able to slow traffic while lowering higher traffic volumes. Walking tour guides of the Montpelier Historic District are available at the Vermont Historical Society Museum. The city is serviced by the Green Mountain Transit Authority, which operates the Capital Shuttle in around downtown Montpelier. They also run the LINK Express bus service between Montpelier and Burlington.

Communications

Newspapers and Magazines

Newspaper readers in Montpelier are served by the *Times-Argus,* published weekdays in the evening and in the morning on weekends. *Seven Days Newspaper* is a weekly covering Vermont news, views, and culture. Magazines published in Montpelier include *Vermont Life,* self-described as the "most beautiful magazine in the world," *American Journal of Art Therapy,* and *Organic Farmer.*

Television and Radio

Television viewers in the Montpelier area may choose from three network affiliates and a public television station. Cable television is supplied by Adelphia Entertainment. One FM radio station broadcasts from Montpelier. A variety of radio formats emanate from surrounding communities, including Burlington, although signals can be unpredictable depending on location due to interference from the Green Mountains.

Media Information: Times-Argus, 540 N. Main St., PO Box 707, Barre, VT 05641; telephone (802)479-0191. *Vermont Life,* 6 Baldwin St., Montpelier, VT 05602; telephone (802)828-3241

Montpelier Online

Central Vermont Chamber of Commerce. Available www .central-vt.com

City of Montpelier Home Page. Available montpelier-vt.org

Kellogg-Hubbard Library. Available www.kellogghubbard .lib.vt.us

Montpelier Public Schools. Available fc.mpsvt.org/~mps

Seven Days Newspaper. Available www.sevendaysvt.com

State of Vermont Department of Economic Development. Available www.thinkvermont.com

Times-Argus. Available www.timesargus.com

Vermont Department of Tourism & Marketing. Available www.1-800-vermont.com

Vermont Life Magazine. Available www.state.vt.us/vtlife

Vermont Lodging and Restaurant Association. Available www.visitvt.com

Vermont Newspapers and Magazines. Available www .vtliving.com/newspapers

The World (Central Vermont's online newspaper). Available www.vt-world.com

Selected Bibliography

Beardsworth, Gary, *Recipes from the Moon: More Recipes from the Horn of the Moon Cafe* (Ten Speed Press, 1995)

Lager, Fred, *Ben & Jerry's: The Inside Scoop: How Two Real Guys Built a Business with a Social Conscience and a Sense of Humor* (Three Rivers Press, 1995)

Thompson, Daniel P., *History of the Town of Montpelier, From the Time It Was First Chartered in 1781 to the Year 1860. Together with Biographical Sketches of Its Most Noted Deceased Citizens* (Montpelier: E. P. Walton, printer, 1860)

Rutland

The City in Brief

Chartered: 1761 (incorporated, 1892)

Head Official: Mayor John P. Cassarino (since 1999)

City Population
  1980: 18,436
  1990: 18,230
  2000: 17,292
  2004 estimate: 17,103
  Percent change, 1990–2000: −5.1%
  U.S. rank in 1990: Not reported
  U.S. rank in 2000: 1,657th

Metropolitan Area Population (Rutland County)
  1980: 58,347
  1990: 62,142
  2000: 63,400
  Percent change, 1990–2000: 2.0%

U.S. rank in 1980: 690th
U.S. rank in 1990: 714th
U.S. rank in 2000: 764th

Area: 7.64 square miles (Rutland city, 2000)
Elevation: 560 feet above sea level
Average Annual Temperature: 42.8° F
Average Annual Precipitation: 23 inches of rain, 140 inches of snow (state-wide averages)

Major Economic Sectors: Agriculture, tourism, manufacturing
Unemployment Rate: 3.3% (April 2005)
Per Capita Income: $17,075 (1999)
2004 ACCRA Average House Price: Not reported
2004 ACCRA Cost of Living Index: Not reported
2002 Crime Index Total: Not reported

Major Colleges and Universities: College of St. Joseph

Daily Newspaper: *Rutland Daily Herald*

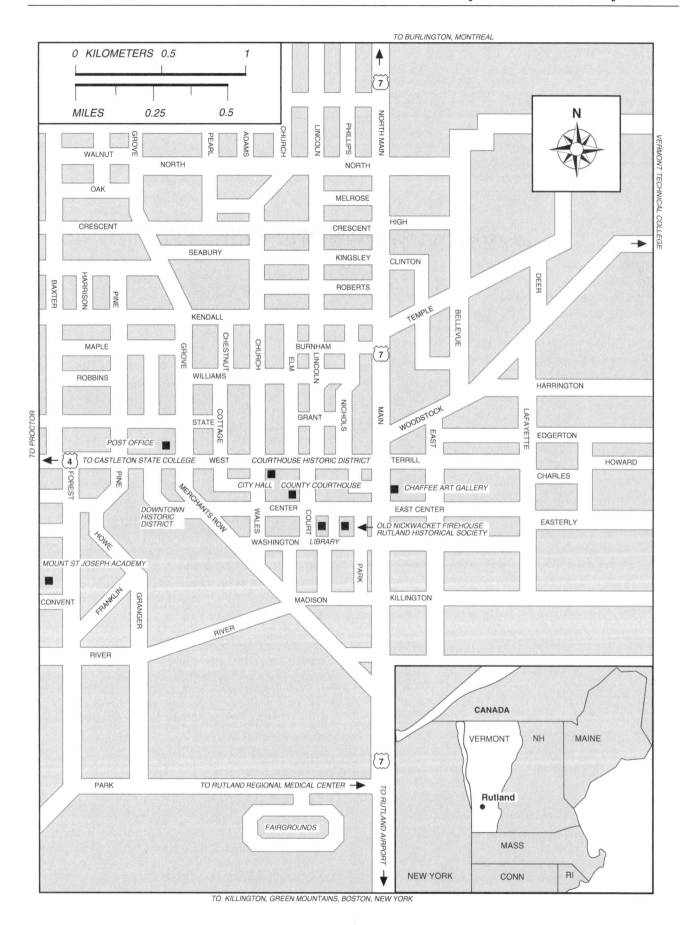

TO BURLINGTON, MONTREAL

0 KILOMETERS 0.5 1

MILES 0.25 0.5

N

VERMONT TECHNICAL COLLEGE

WALNUT
GROVE
PEARL
ADAMS
CHURCH
LINCOLN
PHILLIPS
NORTH MAIN
NORTH
OAK
NORTH
MELROSE
HIGH
CRESCENT
CRESCENT
SEABURY
KINGSLEY
CLINTON
ROBERTS
BAXTER
HARRISON
PINE
KENDALL
TEMPLE
BELLEVUE
DEER
MAPLE
GROVE
CHESTNUT
CHURCH
BURNHAM
ELM
LINCOLN
7
HARRINGTON
ROBBINS
WILLIAMS
GRANT
NICHOLS
MAIN
WOODSTOCK
EAST
LAFAYETTE
EDGERTON
STATE
COTTAGE
HOWARD
TO PROCTOR
4 TO CASTLETON STATE COLLEGE
POST OFFICE
WEST
COURTHOUSE HISTORIC DISTRICT
TERRILL
CHARLES
FOREST
PINE
CITY HALL COUNTY COURTHOUSE
CHAFFEE ART GALLERY
EAST CENTER
EASTERLY
MERCHANTS ROW
DOWNTOWN HISTORIC DISTRICT
WALES
CENTER
COURT
OLD NICKWACKET FIREHOUSE
RUTLAND HISTORICAL SOCIETY
HOWE
WASHINGTON
LIBRARY
MOUNT ST JOSEPH ACADEMY
PARK
FRANKLIN
GRANGER
KILLINGTON
CONVENT
MADISON
RIVER
RIVER
PARK
TO RUTLAND REGIONAL MEDICAL CENTER
7
TO RUTLAND AIRPORT
FAIRGROUNDS

CANADA
VERMONT NH MAINE
Rutland
MASS
NEW YORK CONN RI

TO KILLINGTON, GREEN MOUNTAINS, BOSTON, NEW YORK

Introduction

Rutland is the second largest city in Vermont and the center of one of the world's largest marble quarrying districts. Located near the famed ski areas of Killington and Pico, and the popular tourist destination of Woodstock, Rutland is a trading center for the surrounding towns and farms. The city's industrial, recreational, and cultural activities, and its beautiful natural setting make Rutland a highly livable small community.

Geography and Climate

Rutland is located in the fertile Otter Creek Valley in south central Vermont, approximately 30 miles north of Massachusetts and 20 miles east of New York. It is bounded by the Taconic and Green mountains. The city enjoys a four-seasons climate.

Area: 7.64 square miles (Rutland city, 2000)

Elevation: 560 feet above sea level

Average Temperatures: January, 19° F; August, 69° F; annual average, 42.8° F (state-wide averages)

Average Annual Precipitation: 23 inches of rain, 140 inches of snow (state-wide averages)

History

Various Native American tribes knew the Otter Creek Valley where Rutland now stands primarily as a place to fish and hunt beaver. The first description of the creek's falls was recorded in the journal of James Cross, a fur trader, in 1730. Otter Creek served as a junction on the military road connecting the Champlain forts to the north with the Connecticut Valley during the French and Indian War, and settlement was not attempted until that hostility ceased. The first grantee of a patent to settle the territory was John Murray of Rutland, Massachusetts, who was responsible for the name of the town. The first actual settler was John Mead, who brought his wife and ten children there in 1770. Mead built a gristmill and sawmill, and Rutland soon became an active frontier community. Fort Rutland was built in 1775, and in 1778 the city became the headquarters for state troops during the American Revolution.

Among the city's early notables was the Reverend Samuel Williams, brilliant scholar, author of the first history of Vermont, and founder in 1794 of the *Rutland Herald,* Vermont's oldest continuously published newspaper. Between 1800 and 1880 Rutland's population grew from 2,124 to 12,149 people, surpassing for the first and only time the population of Burlington, the largest community in the state. This explosive growth is attributed to the arrival in 1849 of the railroad and the resulting boom in the marble industry, which had been operating on a small scale since the early nineteenth century. Colonel Redfield Proctor is credited with transforming the marble business into one of the country's greatest industries, bringing prosperity to Rutland and power to Proctor. In 1886 Proctor succeeded in convincing the state legislature that two new townships should be created from the original town. The new townships of Proctor and West Rutland, largely owned or controlled by the Proctor family, contained some of the richest marble deposits in the world; thus did Rutland lose its title as Marble City (in 1993 a long chapter in the city's history sadly came to a close when the Vermont Marble company closed its quarry operations in Proctor).

The city continued to prosper, however, largely due to the Howe Scales company, which moved there in 1877. The opening up of the ski industry in the 1930s added considerably to Rutland's prosperity, as did the decision in the 1960s of General Electric Corporation to build two defense contract plants in the area. City leaders have been engaged since the 1960s in the renovation of the downtown core, and the modern city exists as a retail trading and industrial center as well as the gateway to two famous ski resorts. Rutland's tree-lined streets and Victorian mansions add to the charm of this vigorous small community.

A small, progressive community with the cultural and recreational attractions of a much larger city, Rutland is the kind of city many of today's younger professional and high-technology workers seem drawn to. For that reason the city's economic picture remains bright.

Historical Information: Rutland Historical Society, 96 Center Street, Rutland, VT 05701; telephone (802)775-2006

Population Profile

Metropolitan Area Residents
 1980: 58,347
 1990: 62,142
 2000: 63,400
 Percent change, 1990–2000: 2%
 U.S. rank in 1980: 690th

U.S. rank in 1990: 714th
U.S. rank in 2000: 764th

City Residents

1980: 18,436
1990: 18,230
2000: 17,292
2004 estimate: 17,103
Percent change, 1990–2000: −5.1%
U.S. rank in 1990: Not reported
U.S. rank in 2000: 1,657th

Density: 2,264 people per square mile (2000)

Racial and ethnic characteristics (2000)
  White: 16,912
  Black or African American: 76
  American Indian and Alaska Native: 42
  Native Hawaiian and Pacific Islander: 9
  Asian: 74
  Hispanic or Latino (may be of any race): 156
  Other: 22

Percent of residents born in state: 67.3% (2000)

Age characteristics (2000)
  Population under 5 years old: 996
  Population 5 to 9 years old: 1,076
  Population 10 to 14 years old: 1,214
  Population 15 to 19 years old: 1,027
  Population 20 to 24 years old: 982
  Population 25 to 34 years old: 2,194
  Population 35 to 44 years old: 2,783
  Population 45 to 54 years old: 2,377
  Population 55 to 59 years old: 876
  Population 60 to 64 years old: 623
  Population 65 to 74 years old: 1,376
  Population 75 to 84 years old: 1,230
  Population 85 years and older: 538
  Median age: 39.3 years

Births
  Total number: 599 (2002, Rutland County)

Deaths
  Total number: 588 (2002, Rutland County)

Money income (1999)
  Per capita income: $17,075
  Median household income: $30,478
  Total households: 7,436

Number of households with income of . . .
  less than $10,000: 1,018
  $10,000 to $14,999: 718
  $15,000 to $24,999: 1,318

  $25,000 to $34,999: 1,034
  $35,000 to $49,999: 1,337
  $50,000 to $74,999: 1,366
  $75,000 to $99,999: 363
  $100,000 to $149,999: 179
  $150,000 to 199,999: 50
  $200,000 or more: 53

Percent of families below poverty level: 10.3% (56.1% of which were female householder families with related children under 5 years)

2002 FBI Crime Index Total: Not reported

Municipal Government

Rutland voters elect an eleven-member board of aldermen and a mayor to two-year terms.

Head Official: Mayor John P. Cassarino (since 1999; current term expires 2006)

Total Number of City Employees: 181 (2005)

City Information: City Hall, PO Box 969, Rutland, VT 05702; telephone (802)773-1800

Economy

Major Industries and Commercial Activity

The thriving economy of the Rutland region is based on a balance of agriculture, tourist-related services, and small manufacturing businesses producing nontraditional durable goods. The region initially thrived on the basis of its high quality marble quarrying operations, and marble is still a key component to the local economy. In the early 2000s, however, local business leaders are seeking to further diversify the economic structure of Rutland by attracting firms in the high technology sector.

Rutland is the financial and commercial center of south central Vermont. General Electric Corporation maintains two plants in the region, and since the late 1960s a thriving electronics industry has developed.

Items and goods produced: food, wood, and marble products; scales; jet blades and vanes; stone-working machinery; home repair products

Incentive Programs—New and Existing Companies

Local programs—The Rutland Economic Development Corporation (REDC) offers a revolving loan fund to help new businesses relocating to the area or for the expansion of existing businesses. Loans of between $5,000 and $75,000 are available to qualifying firms. Housed at REDC, the Small Business Development Center (SBDC) provides free technical assistance to starting and growing small businesses. Operated through the Vermont State College System, SBDC links businesses with higher education, state and federal programs, as well as other businesses.

The Rutland Regional Chamber of Commerce informs business owners or prospective owners about tax incentives. They include payroll tax credits; credits for incremental payroll; Workforce Development Tax Credit for eligible employee training costs; Research and Development Tax Credit for eligible research and development costs; Investment Tax Credit for new capital equipment exceeding an annual threshold of $250,000; and an Export Sales Incentive.

State programs—The Vermont Economic Development Authority (VEDA) is a state-wide organization that provides low-interest loans, mortgage insurance, revenue bonds, and a loss reserve fund to encourage small business loans by participating banks. VEDA can make direct loans to manufacturing firms and other eligible loans under state statute for the acquisition of land, building and improvements, machinery and equipment, and working capital. VEDA also offers a training assistance program for new and existing businesses. These individually designed programs may include on-the-job, classroom, skill upgrade or other specialized training. The Vermont Manufacturing Extension Center (VMEC) provides assistance to Vermont's small and medium size manufacturers (under 500 employees).

Vermont's tax incentive program offers incentives based on quality jobs. These tax incentives are available based on whether or not the proposed economic development meets certain guidelines, and whether a cost/benefit model analysis points to a positive net fiscal effect on Vermont's tax revenue. The cost benefit model and other functions of the program are mainly coordinated by the Vermont Economic Progress Council. Vermont's Downtown Development Act is an incentive to help benefit Vermont's downtowns; incentives include assistance with rehabilitation of certified historic or older buildings, sprinkler system rebates, reallocation of sales tax on construction materials, downtown transportation, related capitol improvement fund, planning grant for qualifying for designation, and others.

Vermont's Act Relating to Education, Taxation, and Education Financing provides financial incentives to grow businesses that are the most comprehensive in the state's history.

Vermont's program incorporates a strategic framework that emphasizes quality jobs and symbolizes the state's core values with regard to meaningful employment opportunity. The statute creates an innovative approval process for awarding tax incentives to both businesses and municipalities for economic development activity, especially companies that already call Vermont home, with a special focus on small businesses. The state also offers sales tax exemptions on certain resources vital to industry, including electricity, building materials in excess of $1 million, industrial fuels, and heavy machinery and equipment.

Job training programs—The Community College of Vermont (with a branch in Rutland) and Green Mountain College (in nearby Poultney) offer two and four-year associates degrees in dozens of career-oriented concentrations. Stafford Technical Center, a public educational center primarily aimed at providing technical and career training to 11th and 12th graders from 10 regional high schools, also provides adult diploma programs and specialized training programs for business and industry. The Vermont Department of Employment and Training offers an apprenticeship training program to help employers upgrade the quality of their workforce. The department also offers on-the-job-training programs that reimburse the employer for a significant portion of employer-provided new hire training.

Development Projects

The Rutland Partnership, a public private partnership for the revitalization of downtown Rutland, has created a master plan for the commercial heart of the Rutland region. Continuing efforts include complete renovation of the downtown plaza, new streetscaping, increased office and commercial space, and a renewed emphasis on the nineteenth- century character of the main streets.

Efforts had begun as early as the early 1990s to restore the long-neglected Playhouse Theater of Rutland, built in 1912 and once considered among the finest smaller performing arts theaters in America. The successful restoration of the renamed Paramount Theatre was completed in February 2000 and an Opening Night Gala in March 2000 honored the artisans and contributors who made the historic project possible. The Paramount Theatre has again assumed its role as an arts, cultural, and educational leader, and as a significant and valuable community resource.

In 2003 large-scale development, and some attendant controversy, came to Rutland with the opening of a Home Depot store on the site of the old Rutland Mall, which was demolished due the popularity of the newer Diamond Run Mall. Fears were calmed, however, as initial studies of the economic impact of the large discount hardware chain showed negative effects on existing smaller and family-owned businesses of a similar nature were minimal.

In 2005 the Rutland Amateur Hockey Association was more than halfway to its goal of raising $3.3 million toward the construction of a new Rutland Regional Fieldhouse. Aside from hosting local youth and adult hockey leagues, the multi-use facility would be available for regional Vermont and New England hockey tournaments, bringing additional tourist dollars to the city. The proposed Fieldhouse will also attract additional meetings and exhibitions and other indoor sporting events.

Economic Development Information: Rutland Economic Development Corporation, 256 N. Main St., Rutland, VT 05701; telephone (802)773-9147. Rutland Region Chamber of Commerce, 256 North Main Street, Rutland, Vermont 05701; telephone (802)773-2747; fax (802)773-2772

Commercial Shipping

Strategically located between the markets of Boston, New York, and Montreal, Canada, Rutland County is on the shipping routes of major trucking firms, and more than 20 trucking firms are located in the area. The city is situated at the intersection of U.S. highways 4 and 7, providing east-west and north-south access and linking the region with interstates 89, 91 and 87. Railroad freight service is available throughout the area and a number of trucking companies offer services. The city is within easy reach of several major seaports and the Foreign Trade Zone at Burlington International Airport. All of the major national and international package delivery services operate in the city.

Labor Force and Employment Outlook

A small, progressive community with the cultural and recreational attractions of a much larger city, Rutland is the kind of city many of today's younger professional and high-technology workers seem drawn to. For that reason the city's economic picture remains bright. The Rutland region's workforce is viewed as among the most stable, mature, and educated in the Northeast. Once dominated by agriculture, today's working population is comprised of occupations from banker and lawyer to engineer and advertising agency and nearly everything in between. The local workforce is, in relative terms, middle-aged, most often married couples with children; own single family homes; have moderate to high incomes; are employed in professional, managerial or other white-collar occupations; with 79.4 percent as high school graduates (the national average is 75.2 percent). In a survey of Rutland area manufacturers, the high productivity and strong work ethic of employees was cited as the area's greatest business advantage. Stability and loyalty were also mentioned as characteristic of Rutland workers. It is projected that the 20- to 49-year-old age group will continue to grow.

The continued presence of General Electric Corporation is expected to provide the strength to maintain employment

growth in the area. Analysts predict that most new jobs will be in non-manufacturing sectors, especially services and trade (nearly 30 percent of the local workforce in 2005).

The following is a summary of data regarding the Burlington and South Burlington, Vermont metropolitan area labor force, 2004 annual averages.

Size of nonagricultural labor force: 113,300

Number of workers employed in . . .
   construction and mining: 6,100
   manufacturing: 15,300
   trade, transportation and utilities: 22,000
   information: 3,200
   financial activities: 5,400
   professional and business services: 10,000
   educational and health services: 18,100
   leisure and hospitality: 10,700
   other services: 3,700
   government: 19,100

Average hourly earnings of production workers employed in manufacturing: $13.65 (statewide average)

Unemployment rate: 3.3% (April 2005)

Largest employers (Rutland County, 2005)	*Number of employees*
Killington Ltd.	1,950
Casella Waste Systems	1,325
General Electric Corporation-Aircraft Engines	1,100
Rutland Region Medical Center	1,100
Carris Community of Companies	500-999
Central Vermont Public Service Corp.	542
Vermont Country Store	400

Cost of Living

The following is a summary of data regarding several key cost of living factors in the Rutland area.

2004 ACCRA Cost of Living Index: Not reported

2004 ACCRA Average House Price: Not reported

State income tax rate: 24% of federal tax liability (2005)

State sales tax rate: 6.0%

Local income tax rate: None

Local sales tax rate: None

Property tax rate: Averages $2.73 per $100 of assessed value (2005)

Economic Information: Director of Community Development, City of Rutland, PO Box 609, Rutland, VT 05702;

telephone (802)773-1800. Vermont Department of Employment and Training, PO Box 488, Montpelier, VT 05601-0488; telephone (802)828-4000

Education and Research

Elementary and Secondary Schools

The Rutland City Public School district is comprised of 3,000 students in six schools and three special programs, supported by a staff of about 500. In 2002 Rutland voters passed a $4.3 million school bond issue which, after an additional $2.3 million in state contributions, provided $6.6 million for improvements to school buildings, fields, and a community track facility. In addition to elementary, middle, and high schools, the district's Stafford Technical Center is a public educational center serving students in grades 11 and 12 from the 10 regional high schools in the Rutland area. It offers an evening adult education program and adult diploma programs.

The following is a summary of data regarding the Rutland public schools as of the 2004–2005 school year.

Total enrollment: 3,000

Number of facilities
  elementary schools: 3
  junior high/middle schools: 1
  senior high schools: 1
  other: 1 technical school

Student/teacher ratio: 13.3:1

Teacher salaries
  average: $40,812 (statewide Vermont)

Funding per pupil: $10,306

Several private and parochial schools also operate in the Rutland area.

Public Schools Information: Rutland City Public Schools, 6 Church Street, Rutland, VT 05701; telephone (802)773-1900

Colleges and Universities

Rutland is home to the College of St. Joseph, a small private business, liberal arts, and teachers' college with a 2005 enrollment of about 500 students. The Community College of Vermont, the second largest college in the state, has classrooms at Howe Center in Rutland and offers associate degrees in self-designated concentrations. Other colleges in the area are Castleton State College, Green Mountain College, Middlebury College, Vermont Law School, St. Michael's College, and Vermont Technical College. All area colleges serve as a resource for local industries and work with manufacturers to meet their training needs.

Libraries and Research Centers

The Rutland Free Library holds more than 87,000 volumes within its 24,000 square foot facility on Center Street. The library initiated humanities and reading/discussion programs in the state, creating a model that has been used by the American Library Association and others. Its Nella Grimm Fox Room hosts regular cultural events, and the Vermont Room contains genealogical items.

Rutland is also home to the Southeast Regional Library, which has 60,000 volumes. Central Vermont Public Service Corporation's library specializes in energy, business, management, and electrical engineering. Other libraries in the region include one at the Rutland Regional Medical Center, containing medical and health information. The Community College of Vermont houses a small collection, and libraries are available at the College of St. Joseph in Rutland and Castleton State College, approximately 13 miles from Rutland. Each of these institutions opens its doors to the public.

Public Library Information: Rutland Free Library, 10 Court Street, Rutland, VT 05701; telephone (802)773-1860; fax (802)773-1825; email rutland_free@dol.state.vt.us

Health Care

Rutland is served by the Rutland Regional Medical Center, which has been qualified as a Medicare-designated Rural Referral Center and is Vermont's second largest medical facility. The Medical Center, with 188 licensed beds, has a staff of more than 120 physicians in 35 specialty areas. The center offers a 24-hour emergency department, a cardiac unit, a community cancer center, an eating disorders clinic, an HIV/AIDS clinic, MRI imaging, renal dialysis, a diabetes center, a rehabilitation center, a sleep disorders center, and women's and children's services.

Recreation

Sightseeing

Newly opened in 2004 and designed with site-sensitive structures by world renowned architect Peter Bohlin, the Vermont Institute of Natural Science's Nature Center in nearby Quechee won a 2005 *Yankee Magazine* Editor's Choice award in its annual Travel Guide to New England.

Located next to one of New England's natural wonders, the Quechee Gorge, the Nature Center includes a state-of-the art Raptor Exhibit, displaying one of North America's finest collections of birds of prey, where visitors can come face to face with Snowy Owls, Peregrine Falcons, Red-tailed Hawks, Bald Eagles, and other birds of prey.

Rutland's restored Downtown Historic District contains many architecturally interesting buildings, some constructed of or embellished with local marble. Examples of these are the Opera House, the Gryphon Building, and Merchants Row. The Rutland Courthouse Historic District includes 85 residential, public, and religious buildings. Significant among these are the Italianate Revival-style County Courthouse, the U.S. Post Office, and the Queen Anne-style residences on South Main Street. Main Street Park, once the site of the courthouse jail, now teems with activity during the summer months. The Rutland Area Cultural Alliance offers guided tours of the historic downtown daily from July through mid-October.

The Vermont Marble Exhibit in Proctor attracts more than 100,000 visitors annually, who enjoy a view of the country's largest marble production center; also featured are a geological display, a sculptor-in-residence, a movie, and a gift shop. Near Proctor, Wilson Castle, a 32-room nineteenth century stone chateau on a 115-acre estate, is furnished with elaborate Oriental and European artifacts, stained glass, and wood paneling.

Rutland bills itself as ''Heart of the Maple World,'' and many sugar houses in the area are open to visitors. The New England Maple Museum in nearby Pittsford houses one of the largest collections of antique maple sugaring artifacts in the world. Hathaway Farm in Rutland is locally famous for its massive and extremely challenging Corn Maze.

Arts and Culture

Rutland's Crossroads Arts Council presents performances including classical music, opera, dance, jazz, theater, and family events at a variety of locales throughout the area.

The Rutland Historical Society Museum, housed in the Old Nickwacket Fire House, interprets the history of the area through its collection of tools, clothing, artifacts, and photographs. The Chaffee Center for the Visual Arts, formerly a private home and now listed on the National Register of Historic Places, displays traditional and contemporary paintings, sculptures, crafts, and photographs, and hosts two art festivals annually. Moon Brook Arts Union Gallery in the Opera House showcases the works of area artists. Contemporary art can also be found at the Night Owl and Farrow galleries. The Norman Rockwell Museum displays more than 2,500 pictures as well as Rockwell memorabilia, covering more than 60 years of the artist's career.

Arts and Culture Information: Crossroads Arts Council, 5 Court Street, Rutland, VT 05701; telephone (802)775-5413

Festivals and Holidays

The Killington Music Festival holds a variety of different musical events during the ski resort's off-season. There is a Fireworks Extravaganza each July 4th on the Vermont State Fairgrounds. Thousands of visitors are attracted to Rutland in early September for the Vermont State Fair, featuring a rodeo, races and other contests, and a midway. The second week in October is peak foliage season in the area and many communities hold festivals and country fairs. For 15 years the city has celebrated a New Year's Eve First Night Rutland party with music, arts, magic, family fun, and fireworks at midnight.

Sports for the Participant

Rutland is perhaps best known to visitors for its proximity to outstanding ski resorts. Pico Peak, one of the country's few major ski areas dating back to World War II, is 9 miles east of the city; the Killington ski area is located 15 miles east and is arguably the northeast's best ski area, with 212 trails, 6 high-speed quad lifts, a new heated 8-seat lift, and the brand new K1 Gondola. Okemo Mountain in Ludlow has 112 trails. More than 56,000 acres of national forest and many state parks in the area offer year-round recreational opportunities of all kinds, and an 18-hole golf course is available at the Rutland Country Club. Rutland is situated just 10 miles from the Green Mountains National Forest. Long Trail, the south-north hiking route from Massachusetts to Canada which is part of the Appalachian Trail System, passes near there.

Shopping and Dining

The Downtown Rutland Partnership, a public private partnership for the revitalization of downtown Rutland, has created a master plan for the commercial heart of the region. Efforts completed include a complete renovation of the downtown plaza, new streetscaping, restoration of the Paramount Theater, increased office and commercial space and a renewed emphasis on the 19th century character of the main streets. Clusters of specialty shops are located throughout downtown Rutland. North and South Main streets feature many interesting and unusual stores, such as Creative Hands, offering the work of Vermont craftspeople, and Charles E. Tuttle Company of Rutland and Tokyo's Antiquarian Books, stocking one of the largest collections of used and rare books in New England as well as books on Oriental art. Rutland's two market towns, Oakham and Uppingham, are the main shopping centers. Nearby Stamford is also very popular and warrants a visit. Other major shopping areas include the Diamond Run Mall, a 450,000-square-foot facility whose anchor stores include K-Mart, Sears and JC Penney. Downtown's Rutland Shopping Plaza has a Price Chopper Superstore, Movieplex 9, Wal-Mart, and other shops.

The Rutland region offers a wide variety of shopping experiences. Of unique interest are the Haunted Mansion Bookshop in Cuttingsville, located across from an unusual cemetery and now filled with antiquarian books; a genuine general store, herb farm and retail shop; and several arts, crafts, and antique shops.

Rutland has attracted distinguished chefs who prepare sophisticated fare with French, Austrian, and Belgian accents. For those seeking something less formal, several area restaurants serve traditional New England fare in informal settings. The Rutland region also supports many country inns whose restaurants are open to the public. Of note is the Fair Haven Inn in nearby Fair Haven.

Visitor Information: Rutland Region Chamber of Commerce, 256 N. Main St., Rutland, VT 05701; telephone (802)773-2747; toll-free (800)756-8880; fax (802)773-2772; email info@rutlandvermont.com

Convention Facilities

A principal meeting place in Rutland is the Holiday Inn Centre of Vermont complex, offering 8,000 square feet of meeting space accommodating groups up to 500 people. Located five miles from Rutland State Airport, this facility provides 151 renovated guest rooms. The Franklin Conference Center at the Howe Center can host meetings with from 25 to 300 participants. The recently renovated Best Western in Rutland has 56 guest rooms. Meeting space for groups from 30 to 800 people is available at six locations in the region, which is also home to many country inns for those in need of accommodations. Larger meeting rooms and halls are available within a reasonable distance in Burlington, Vermont (65 miles) and Albany, New York (110 miles). The Rutland Free Library's meeting rooms can accommodate up to 200 people for meetings or events.

Convention Information: Vermont Travel Division, 134 State Street, Montpelier, VT 05602; telephone (802)828-3236

Transportation

Approaching the City

The Rutland State Airport's new terminal building and expanded parking have made the facility both modern and convenient. Continental Connection, operated by Commutair, offers two daily flights Monday through Friday to Boston's Logan Airport. Flights to several large northeast-ern cities can be booked from Burlington, and there is an international airport in Albany. Amtrak provides passenger rail service in Vermont with both the Vermonter (Washington, D.C. to St. Albans, via White River Junction) and the Ethan Allen Express (New York City to Rutland, via Albany, New York). U.S. Routes 4 and 7 intersect in Rutland and link the region with interstates 89, 91, and 87.

Traveling in the City

The main thoroughfares in Rutland are Main Street, which runs north-south, and U.S. Route 4, running east-west; side streets head westward and downhill. Marble Valley Regional Transit District "The Bus" provides local transportation on set routes. The Bus links riders to all train routes heading in and out of Rutland, as well as the airport. A shuttle service operates between Killington Ski Resort, Diamond Run shopping mall, and downtown Rutland.

Communications

Newspapers

The *Rutland Herald,* the oldest newspaper in the state and frequent winner of journalism awards, is published every morning. *Rutland Business Journal,* a monthly, publishes a special section on new businesses, a calendar of events, and local business news.

Television and Radio

One television station broadcasts from Rutland; others are available from nearby communities. Three FM radio stations operate within town, while broadcasts from a variety of radio stations from neighboring towns and cities provide a broad spectrum of programming.

Media Information: Rutland Herald, 27 Wales Street, PO Box 668, Rutland, VT 05701; telephone (802)747-6121; fax (802)775-2423. *Rutland Business Journal,* 110 Merchants Row, Rutland, VT 05701; telephone (802)775-0650

Rutland Online

City of Rutland. Available www.rutlandcity.com

Rutland Business Journal. Available www.business vermont.com/rbj

Rutland Downtown Partnership. Available www.rutland downtown.com

Rutland Economic Development Council. Available www .rutlandeconomy.com

Rutland Free Library. Available www.rutlandfree.org

Rutland Herald Online. Available www.rutlandherald.com

Rutland Public Schools. Available at rutlandhs.k12.vt.us

Rutland Region Chamber of Commerce. Available www
.rutlandvermont.com

Vermont Department of Economic Development. Available
www.thinkvermont.com

Vermont Department of Tourism and Marketing. Available
www.travel-vermont.com

Vermont Historical Society. Available www.vermonthistory
.org

Vermont Life Magazine. Available www. vtlife.com

Vermont Small Business Development Center. Available
www.vtsbdc.org

Selected Bibliography

Moore, William, *The Story of a Young Man's Tramp Across Three
States; Cooking His Meals and Camping Along Three Hundred
Sixty Miles of Road in New Hampshire, Vermont, and New York*
(New York: Markey Press, 1911)

Shaughnessy, Jim, *The Rutland Road* (Syracuse, NY: Syracuse
University Press, 1997)

Smith, H.P., *History of Rutland County, Vermont, with Illustrations
and Biographical Sketches of Some of Its Prominent Men and
Pioneers* (Syracuse, N.Y.: D. Mason, 1886)

Cumulative Index

The one hundred eighty-nine cities featured in *Cities of the United States,* Volume 1: *The South,* Volume 2: *The West,* Volume 3: *The Midwest,* and Volume 4: *The Northeast,* along with names of individuals, organizations, historical events, etc., are designated in this Cumulative Index by name of the appropriate regional volume, or volumes, followed by the page number(s) on which the term appears in that volume.